"Finally, we have a comprehensive, evidence-b⎯⎯⎯⎯⎯⎯⎯⎯⎯⎯⎯⎯⎯⎯⎯⎯n
when counseling their patients about compleme⎯⎯⎯⎯⎯⎯⎯⎯⎯⎯⎯⎯⎯⎯⎯⎯ therapies.
In-depth reviews of the research are thoroughly digested into concise summary tables, placing key information at the reader's fingertips. This book is perfect for the busy healthcare professional who needs a practical and evidence-based guide to CAM practices. No doubt, it will be used time and time again in your daily clinical practice."

—*Brian Berman, MD*
*Professor and Founding Director for the Center for Integrative Medicine*
*University of Maryland School of Medicine*
*Coordinator, Complementary Medicine Field, Cochrane Collaboration*
*Founding Chair, Consortium of Academic Health Centers for Integrative Medicine*

"A practical, well researched summary that will help integrate unconventional healing approaches into the mainstream healthcare system."

—*Mehmet Oz, MD*
*Vice Chair and Professor of Surgery, NY Presbyterian Hospital, Columbia University*

"This edition provides a valuable and indeed essential compendium of a broad range of CAM therapies and evidence of their efficacy and safety, or lack thereof, for different clinical applications. It includes practical recommendations that the busy clinician can use in considering the responsible use of CAM therapies as part of a comprehensive approach toward patient care."

—*Ralph Snyderman, MD*
*Chancellor Emeritus, Duke University*

"This book is a must-read for healthcare professionals interested in using an evidence-based approach toward integrating alternative therapies into clinical practice. Drawing on exhaustive research reviews, the authors present their material in an easy-to-read format, including summary tables in each chapter with bottom-line recommendations organized by treatment and condition. I believe this book will be of great help to busy healthcare professionals who need scientifically sound guidance about CAM practices."

—*Andrew Weil, MD*
*Director, Arizona Center for Integrative Medicine, University of Arizona*

Visit www.acponline.org/acp_press/comp_alt_med
for more information on
**Complementary & Alternative Medicine**

The ACP Evidence-Based Guide to

# COMPLEMENTARY &
# ALTERNATIVE MEDICINE

The ACP Evidence-Based Guide to

# COMPLEMENTARY &
# ALTERNATIVE MEDICINE

Bradly P. Jacobs, MD, MPH
Katherine Gundling, MD

AMERICAN COLLEGE OF PHYSICIANS • PHILADELPHIA

*Associate Publisher and Manager, Books Publishing:* Tom Hartman
*Production Supervisor:* Allan S. Kleinberg
*Senior Production Editor:* Karen C. Nolan
*Publishing Coordinator:* Angela Gabella
*Cover Design:* Lisa Torrieri
*Index:* Kathleen Patterson

Printed in the United States of Americas
Printing/Binding by Versa
Composition by Scribe, Inc.

The authors have exerted reasonable efforts to ensure that the complementary and alternative medicine (CAM) therapy selection and the dietary supplement selection and dosage, in particular, as set forth in this volume are in accord with current recommendations and practice at the time of publication. In view of ongoing research, occasional changes in government regulations, and the constant flow of information relating to CAM therapies, including dietary supplement reactions and interactions, the reader is urged to check the FDA CFSAN Dietary Supplements Warnings and Safety Information website (http://www.cfsan.fda.gov/%7Edms/ds-warn.html), and the NIH National Center for Complementary and Alternative Medicine (NCCAM) Alerts and Advisories website (http://nccam.nih.gov/health/alerts/) for any added warnings and precautions, as well as check the NIH Office of Dietary Supplements Fact Sheets website (http://ods.od.nih.gov/ Health_Information/Information_About_Individual_Dietary_Supplements.aspx) and the International Bibliographic Information on Dietary Supplements (IBIDS) database (http://ods.od .nih.gov/Health_Information/IBIDS.aspx) for any change in indications and dosage. This care is particularly important given the nature of the subject matter in this volume in which the evidence base is frequently limited, the research is rapidly evolving, and new findings regarding interactions, precautions, optimal dosage, and new indications are in constant flow. The American College of Physicians, the volume editors, and chapter authors are not responsible for any accident or injury resulting from the use of this publication.

**Library of Congress Cataloging-in-Publication Data**

The ACP evidence-based guide to complementary and alternative medicine / [editors, Bradly Jacobs, Katherine Gundling].
    p. cm.
Includes bibliographical references.
ISBN 978-1-934465-04-2
1. Alternative medicine. 2. Evidence-based medicine. I. Jacobs, Bradly. II. Gundling, Katherine. III. American College of Physicians. IV. Title: American College of Physicians evidence-based guide to complementary and alternative medicine. V. Title: Evidence-based guide to complementary and alterna-tive medicine.
    [DNLM: 1. Complementary Therapies—methods. 2. Evidence-Based Medicine. WB 890 A185 2009]
    R733.A27 2009
    610—dc22                                                    2008038682

ISBN: 978-1-934465-04-2

09  10  11  12  13 / 10  9  8  7  6  5  4  3  2  1

# Contributors

**Aditya Bardia, MD, MPH**
Clinical Fellow
Department of Medical Oncology
Johns Hopkins University
Baltimore, Maryland

**Brent A. Bauer, MD, FACP**
Director
Complementary and Integrative
  Medicine Program
Mayo Clinic
Rochester, Minnesota

**LeAnne T. Bloedon, MS, RD**
Instructor
School of Nursing
University of Pennsylvania
Philadelphia, Pennsylvania

**Leo Galland, MD, FACP, FACN**
Director
Foundation for Integrated Medicine
New York, New York

**Christian Gluud, MD, Dr Med Sci**
Director
The Copenhagen Trial Unit
Center for Clinical Intervention
  Research
Rigshospitalet, Copenhagen
  University Hospital
Denmark

**Harley Goldberg, DO**
Director
Spine Care Program
Director
Complementary and Alternative
  Medicine
Kaiser Permanente Northern
  California Medical Care Program
Assistant Physician-In-Chief
Kaiser Permanente San Jose Medical
  Center
Oakland, California

**Katherine Gundling, MD, FACP**
Associate Clinical Professor of
  Allergy and Immunology
Department of Medicine
University of California-San
  Francisco
San Francisco, California

**Bradly Jacobs MD, MPH**
Founder and Director
Institute for Healthy Aging at
  Cavallo Point
Sausalito, California

**Ronald Koretz, MD**
Emeritus Professor of Clinical
  Medicine
David Geffen-UCLA School of
  Medicine
Los Angeles, California

**Esther L. Langmack, MD**
Assistant Professor of Medicine
Division of Pulmonary Medicine and
  Critical Care
National Jewish Health
University of Colorado Denver
  School of Medicine
Denver, Colorado

**Jianping Liu, MD, PhD**
Professor and Director
Center for Evidence-Based Chinese
  Medicine
Beijing University of Chinese
  Medicine
Beijing, China
National Research Centre in
  Complementary and Alternative
  Medicine (NAFKAM)
University of Tromso
Tromso, Norway

**Charles L. Loprinzi, MD**
Emeritus Chair
Medical Oncology
Professor of Oncology
Mayo Clinic
Rochester, Minnesota

**Wolf E. Mehling, MD**
Assistant Professor of Family
  Medicine
Department of Family and
  Community Medicine
Osher Center for Integrative
  Medicine
University of California-San
  Francisco
San Francisco, California

**Jacquelyn M. Paykel, MD**
Private Practice
Obstetrics & Gynecology
Portsmouth, Virginia

**Max H. Pittler, MD, PhD**
Senior Research Fellow,
  Complementary Medicine
Peninsula Medical School
Universities of Exeter and Plymouth
Exeter, United Kingdom
Head of Science (Directorate)
Institute for Quality and Efficiency
  in Health Care
Cologne, Germany

**Cristina Porch-Curren, MD**
Private Practice
Camarillo, California

**Sudha Prathikanti, MD**
Associate Professor of Psychiatry
Osher Center for Integrative
  Medicine
University of California-San
  Francisco
San Francisco, California

**Joseph E. Scherger, MD, MPH**
Professor
Department of Family and
  Preventive Medicine
University of California, San Diego
San Diego, California

**Pearl B. Scott, MD**
Department of Allergy/Clinical
  Immunology
Kaiser Permanente
Santa Clara, California

**Philippe O. Szapary, MD, MSCE**
Adjunct Assistant Professor of
  Medicine
Department of Medicine
University of Pennsylvania Health
  System
Philadelphia, Pennsylvania

**Suzanne S. Teuber, MD**
Division of Rheumatology, Allergy
    and Clinical Immunology
University of California–Davis
Davis, California

**Jason Tokumoto, MD**
Assistant Clinical Professor of
    Medicine
University of California at San
    Francisco
Associate Clinician
National HIV/AIDS Clinicians'
    Consultation Service
San Francisco, California

**Viviane Ugalde, MD**
Associate Professor
Department of Physical Medicine &
    Rehabilitation
University of California–Davis
Sacramento, California

**Barbara Wider, MA**
Research Fellow, Complementary
    Medicine
Senior Editor
FACT—Focus on Alternative and
    Complementary Therapies
Peninsula Medical School,
    Universities of Exeter and
    Plymouth
Exeter, United Kingdom

# Contents

FOREWORD    xiii
*Ralph Snyderman*

PREFACE    xv

INTRODUCTION    xix

PART I. FUNDAMENTALS OF COMPLEMENTARY AND ALTERNATIVE MEDICINE

1. **Complementary and Alternative Medicine:
   Definitions and Patterns of Use**    3
   *Bradly Jacobs and Katherine Gundling*

2. **The Clinical Encounter**    23
   *Katherine Gundling and Bradly Jacobs*

PART II. EVALUATION OF COMPLEMENTARY AND ALTERNATIVE MEDICINE
SYSTEMS AND THERAPIES

3. **Allergic Disorders**    43
   *Suzanne S. Teuber, Cristina Porch-Curren, and Katherine Gundling*

4. **Asthma**    59
   *Pearl B. Scott and Esther L. Langmack*

5. **Cancer**    77
   *Aditya Bardia, Brent A. Bauer, and Charles L. Loprinzi*

6. **General Medicine**    101
   *Bradly Jacobs and Katherine Gundling*

7. **Gastrointestinal Health**    133
   *Jianping Liu, Christian Gluud, and Ronald Koretz*

8. **Coronary Heart Disease**    161
   *LeAnne T. Bloedon and Philippe O. Szapary*

9. **Human Immunodeficiency Virus**    201
*Jason Tokumoto*

10. **Men's Health**    223
*Joseph E. Scherger*

11. **Women's Health**    241
*Jacquelyn M. Paykel*

12. **Musculoskeletal Disorders**    289
*Wolf E. Mehling, Viviane Ugalde, and Harley Goldberg*

13. **Obesity and Overweight: A Review of Dietary Supplements**    327
*Barbara Wider and Max H. Pittler*

14. **Depression**    353
*Sudha Prathikanti*

15. **Drug-Supplement Interactions:
The Good, The Bad and The Undetermined**    387
*Leo Galland*

APPENDIX 1: SYSTEMS OF PRACTICE    405
*Bradly Jacobs and Katherine Gundling*

APPENDIX 2: COMPLEMENTARY AND
ALTERNATIVE MEDICINE TERMS    421

INDEX    427

# Foreword

"It was the best of times, and it was the worst of times." The opening sentence of Charles Dickens' *A Tale of Two Cities* is an apt description of today's healthcare in the United States. Scientific advances, particularly over the last two decades, have created therapies that would have been considered miracles fifty years ago. The development of recombinant DNA technology, genomics, proteomics, metabolomics, digital imaging, minimally invasive medical devices, and other technologies have revolutionized the practice of medicine and offer a cascade of new advances. Nonetheless, the American healthcare system is expensive, inefficient, uncoordinated, reactive, and leaves even the insured with a dizzying array of confusing choices. The current system focuses on the treatment of acute episodes of chronic disease rather than on promoting wellness and avoiding disease. In addition, progress in the medical sciences has led to the creation of dozens of narrowly focused clinical specialties, resulting in the virtual disappearance of the intimate physician-patient relationship that was characteristic of past medical practice. Patients are often left to ponder confusing healthcare choices on their own, and it is not surprising that a large number have sought alternative approaches.

What has been termed complementary and alternative medicine (CAM) offers patients opportunities not found in conventional allopathic medical practice. The conventional healthcare system focuses on powerful therapies designed to specifically deal with established disease using approaches that frequently have significant side effects. CAM, on the other hand, offers choices that are designed to enhance or restore wellness and often involve hands-on and ongoing relationships with the caregiver. To many, this seems far more natural than the highly technical mono-therapies offered by allopaths.

The popularity of CAM with the American public is evidenced by their willingness to spend more of their own dollars on such therapies than they do for primary care. This is but one reason it is important that providers of conventional medicine better understand the CAM options that many of their patients are choosing, often without informing them. Conventional medicine has generally resisted CAM approaches because they are not based on reductionist science, and the underlying concepts evoked to explain CAM's therapeutic effectiveness often don't conform to scientific understanding of the pathophysiology of disease. Moreover, there is little scientific evidence for the efficacy of many CAM therapies. Nonetheless, if continued use and satisfaction is a measure of the benefit, CAM approaches merit careful consideration for adoption into conventional medical practice. Certainly, the disease-focused orientation of conventional medicine leaves broad areas of patients' needs unmet. Rather than avoiding CAM, it is reasonable for conventional practitioners to understand and encourage the adoption of those CAM therapies that do no harm and appear to benefit many. While the development of a scientific base to prove the efficacy of CAM therapies is important, it must be understood that the reductionist approach that works well for the evaluation of drugs and medical devices may not be directly applicable to the evaluation of CAM approaches, which are far more heterogeneous in content and often depend on the holistic way these therapies are delivered. In my view, conventional medicine should be open to adopting CAM therapies that have credible evidence of being non-toxic and that provide patients with feelings of benefit.

In the *ACP Evidence-Based Guide to Complementary and Alternative Medicine*, Bradly Jacobs and Katherine Gundling have assembled an impressive group of authors who have studiously and comprehensively analyzed the range and value of CAM approaches to important clinical areas. This volume provides a valuable and indeed essential compendium of a broad range of CAM therapies and evidence of their efficacy and safety, or lack thereof, for different clinical applications. To ensure that readers gain easy-access, bottom-line recommendations, every chapter includes at-a-glance tables that are concise and easy to read. You will find a state-of-the-art approach toward evaluating the quality of evidence based on the Grading of Recommendations Assessment, Development and Evaluation (GRADE) working group, a system now endorsed by the World Health Organization, the International Cochrane Collaboration, the U.K. National Institute for Clinical Excellence (NICE), the US Department of Health and Human Services Agency for Healthcare and Research Quality (AHRQ), the American College of Physicians, and others. Consistent with the cutting-edge nature of this book, Drs. Jacobs and Gundling incorporate this widely endorsed and increasingly accepted grading system for the evaluation of CAM therapies.

It is essential for conventional medicine to recognize the needs of patients who are crying out for more comprehensive and holistic approaches than are currently being provided to them by their physicians. Integrating the best of scientific medicine with CAM strategies is termed "integrative medicine" and is, in my view, a more effective as well as a compassionate approach to healthcare. This book provides practical recommendations that the busy clinician can use in clinical practice to facilitate a dialogue on the responsible use of CAM therapies as part of a comprehensive approach toward patient care. Certain CAM approaches may well provide valuable assets to the armamentarium needed to improve health and minimize disease. Fortunately, although slow to adopt, conventional medicine, including academic medicine, is increasingly embracing selective CAM therapies. The willingness of the American College of Physicians to publish this book is evidence of this growing trend. Integrative medicine recognizes the responsibility of physicians to mentor, teach, learn from, and care for their patients in the broadest sense of their needs. This book provides the busy clinician, other primary care providers, and the motivated consumer with in-depth and at-a-glance information and tools to help them incorporate a more holistic and evidence-based approach to managing health and illness.

*Ralph Snyderman, MD*
*Chancellor Emeritus*
*Duke University*

# Preface

In recent years a formidable "new" body of medical information has emerged. The busy physician, already challenged to see patients in a competent, caring, and efficient manner, has been presented with the field of complementary and alternative medicine (CAM), as well as "integrative medicine", which in our view signifies the responsible incorporation of CAM and conventional therapies within a larger context health and healing. With more than one-third of Americans using CAM therapies, including 40-50 million Americans taking dietary supplements, clinicians have been compelled to become conversant in this rapidly growing and evolving field.

Patients come to their doctors armed with literature from the Internet, talk shows, family members, and other sources, hoping for treatments or cures to improve their quality of life. For some doctors, it is a welcome change to have patients pursue CAM modalities, particularly for chronic, hard-to-treat illnesses. For others, the field seems vague and overwhelming, especially because so few physicians have received formal training in this area. Additionally, the lack of supportive scientific evidence for CAM treatments engenders (appropriate) skepticism.

What progress has been made to clarify this vast array of data? Fortunately, recent years have seen a growing understanding of which patients use CAM therapies and why. Evidence regarding the safety and efficacy of CAM, a previously ill-defined and somewhat chaotic database, is becoming more organized and approachable. Necessary attention is being paid to the more basic questions of how (and occasionally even whether) medical claims should be studied. All of this is good for doctors and patients, both of whom want accurate and timely information about all types of medical treatments.

At the institutional level, several organizations in the United States and abroad have worked tirelessly to analyze and critique both old and newer "alternative" therapies, and a host of basic research and clinical trials have added to our knowledge. As of April 2008, there were almost 10,000 clinical trials indexed in PubMed, of which 40% were published in the past 5 years alone. Recognizing that people now create their own treatment plans by accessing vast databases of information, the National Institutes of Health and academic medical centers (both independently and collectively as the Consortium of Academic Health Centers for Integrative Medicine) have devoted time and resources to the understanding of CAM therapies. Other organizations, such as the Academic Consortium for Complementary and Alternative Health Care, are working to enhance collaboration and knowledge among health care disciplines, with efforts such as the National Education Dialogue (http://ihpc.info/ned/ned.shtml).

Importantly, the vast majority of patients use CAM treatments in addition to, rather than instead of, their conventional medical regimen. They also tend to seek help from their physicians before starting one or more CAM therapies. This means that physicians have an opportunity to play a vital role in guiding patients toward the best medical care. Both physicians and patients will benefit from a timely, evidenced-based book that can provide information at the point of care.

With this in mind, we developed the *ACP Evidenced-Based Guide to Complementary and Alternative Medicine* to provide readers with a comprehensive review of CAM treatments organized according to medical condition. Within each chapter, you will find in-depth reviews of the research, as well as concise tables displaying bottom-line analyses based on our expert evaluation of the literature.

Chapter 1 addresses basic questions such as "What is CAM?", "Which patients are using CAM?", "What is the terminology that might be unfamiliar to doctors?", and "How does one evaluate evidence for CAM treatments?" Chapter 2 hones in on the practical implications of CAM in the office. How can physicians approach this topic with competence and caring? Even beyond direct patient interaction, there are legal, insurance, and regulatory issues that demand attention, and these are addressed in this chapter as well.

Chapters 3 to 15 cover the common conditions that characterize most patient/physician interactions. Although patients might ask about an entire system of practice ("Would Traditional Chinese medicine help?), or a specific treatment ("Does Echinacea help colds?"), most frequently these questions are asked in the context of a particular health concern ("What will help my osteoarthritis?). This problem-based approach focuses on the immediate concern of the patient and whether complementary therapies can be of benefit or cause harm.

Each physician's approach to the vast body of data called "CAM" is likely to be different, depending on location of practice, patient population, medical specialty, and a host of other factors. It is hoped that this text will be a handy and useful tool for doctors in practice, who are undoubtedly most interested in what works, regardless of labels such as "conventional" or "alternative." We salute the efforts of all those individuals who work so hard to serve their patients.

We would like to thank the authors who worked with diligence and persistence to write their respective chapters. We would also like to thank Alan Dumoff, JD, MSW, for taking the time to review our section on legal issues, as well as John Weeks, Pamela Pappas, MD, MD(h), Elizabeth A. Goldblatt, PhD, MPA/HA, Felicia Marie Tomasko, RN, David M. Sale, Michael Traub, ND, David O'Bryon, and Reed Phillips, DC, for providing their expertise in defining the Systems of Practice in Appendix 1. We each have been blessed with wonderful mentors who have provided us with the knowledge and perspective to accomplish tasks we might otherwise never have considered. With deep appreciation, we acknowledge Joseph Acquah, LAc, OMD, Andy Avins, MD, MPH, Brian Berman, MD, Steven Cummings, MD, FACP, Joseph DeBold, PhD, David Eisenberg, MD, Edzard Ernst, MD, PhD, FRCP, FRCPEd, Faith Fitzgerald, MD, Susan Folkman, PhD, Harley Goldberg, DO, Deborah Grady, MD, MPH, Ellen Hughes MD, PhD, Jeffrey Lee, LAc, Stephen McPhee, MD and Barry Rosen MD.

Finally, we feel deep gratitude to our families who supported us as we created this book.

*Bradly Jacobs, MD, MPH*
*Katherine Gundling, MD, FACP*

# Introduction

"Tools are needed to aid conventional practitioners' decision-making about offering or recommending CAM, where patients might be referred, and what organizational structures are most appropriate for the delivery of integrated care. The committee believes that the overarching rubric for guiding the development of these tools should be the goal of providing comprehensive care that is safe, effective, interdisciplinary, and collaborative; is based on the best scientific evidence available; recognizes the importance of compassion and caring; and encourages patients to share in the choices of therapeutic options."

—*Institute of Medicine Report on Complementary and
Alternative Medicine in the United States (2005)*

The primary purpose of this book is to provide the busy clinician with at-a-glance access to a comprehensive evidence-based analysis of complementary and alternative medicine (CAM) therapies. Recognizing that the busy clinician has limited time, we included tables in each of the condition-based chapters that allow the reader to identify bottom-line evidence-based summaries at a glance. Given that the field of CAM is composed of a diverse range of disciplines and therapies that may be as different from each other as they are from conventional medicine, we included additional chapters that provide an overview of fundamental concepts. The first chapter and both appendices define terminology and systems of practice and describe the epidemiology and unique challenges to conducting rigorous research in this field. For busy clinicians interested in engaging in thoughtful conversations with their patients regarding CAM, Chapter 2 will provide readers with practical recommendations and resources for the busy clinical practice. Chapters 3-15 provide exhaustive reviews of individual CAM therapies organized by condition.

The book provides the engaged reader with the opportunity to read details on the research findings supporting the indication-specific treatment recommendations. While evidence should serve as the bedrock of our treatment recommendations, understanding the patient's unique values, preferences, and beliefs is equally critical in helping patients make decisions appropriate to their unique circumstances. We included material in the first two chapters and both appendices to enable clinicians to participate in these conversations as they pertain to CAM treatments with ease and confidence.

## How to Read the Evidence Summary Tables

There are multiple systems for evaluating clinical evidence. We chose to incorporate a grading system developed by the GRADE working group (www.gradeworkinggroup.org) to determine 1) the confidence in the estimate of the effect size, and 2) the strength of the recommendation. This system has gained international acceptance as a universal standard. It is now endorsed and/or is being used by UpToDate, the World Health Organization, QUORUM, the Cochrane Collaboration, and the American College of Physicians, among others.

There are four major domains that comprise the core of our evidence-based evaluation methodology:

1. Confidence in the estimate of the effect size. This algorithm follows the GRADE working group approach. There are four possible levels: A (high); B (moderate); C (low); or D (very low).
2. Magnitude of the effect. We categorized this data element into four levels (none, small, moderate, and large).
3. Safety grade. We evaluate safety based on the frequency and severity of adverse events and interactions. We categorized safety into five levels (double thumbs up, single thumbs up, unclear, single thumbs down, double thumbs down).
4. Strength of the recommendation. This algorithm follows the GRADE working group approach. There are five possible levels (strong recommendation in favor, weak recommendation in favor, no recommendation, weak recommendation against, and strong recommendation against).

## 1. Confidence in the Estimate of the Effect Size

An evaluation of the confidence in the estimate of the effect size provides an opportunity to assess the reliability of statements on the effectiveness of a specific intervention. In other words, how much impact will future research have on the estimate of the effect? For example, it is highly unlikely that future research will impact the evidence-base, suggesting that aspirin is effective in improving survival during acute myocardial infarction. Therefore, there is a high level of confidence (Level A) in the role of aspirin for the treatment of acute myocardial infarction.

It is important to recognize that the confidence in the estimate does not consider directionality of the effect (i.e., whether it is or is not effective). For example, there are several randomized, controlled trials (RCTs) suggesting that acupuncture appears not to be effective for tobacco cessation. Consequently, there is a moderate level of confidence (Level B) to suggest this treatment is NOT effective for this health issue.

The GRADE criteria used to calculate a grade for the confidence in the estimate of effect is as follows:

*High (A):* Further research is very unlikely to change our confidence in the estimate of effect.

- Several high-quality RCTs with consistent results
- In special cases: one large, high-quality multi-center RCT

*Moderate (B):* Further research is likely to have an important impact on our confidence in the estimate of effect and may change the estimate.
- One high-quality RCT
- Several RCT with some limitations

*Low (C):* Further research is very likely to have an important impact on our confidence in the estimate of effect and is likely to change the estimate.
- One or more RCTs with severe limitations

*Very low (D):* Any estimate of effect is very uncertain.
- Expert opinion
- No direct research evidence
- One or more RCTs with very severe limitations

*Factors that may modify the grade include:*
1. Factors that would increase your confidence in the quality of the evidence:
   - Dose-response gradient
   - Large magnitude of effect
   - All plausible confounding would reduce a demonstrated effect

2. Factors that would decrease your confidence in the quality of the evidence:
   - Poor quality of RCT suggesting high likelihood of bias
   - Inconsistency of results
   - Indirectness of results
   - Sparse evidence
   - Reporting bias

## 2. Magnitude of the Effect

The magnitude of the effect is a straightforward estimate of effect size. If the evidence suggests that a treatment is not effective, the magnitude of effect would classified as "none." If the summary estimate suggests the odds ratio is 1.01–1.20, 1.2–2.0 or >2.0, the magnitude of effect would be classified as "small," "moderate," or "large," respectively.

## 3. Safety Grade

Formulating the safety grade is dependent on the frequency and severity of adverse events and interactions. The criteria we developed are as follows:

1. Double thumbs up: appears safe with infrequent adverse events and interactions.
2. Single thumbs up: appears relatively safe but with frequent but not serious adverse events and interactions.
3. Unclear: safety not well understood or conflicting
4. Single thumb down: appears to have safety concerns that include infrequent but serious adverse events and/or interactions.
5. Double thumbs down: has serious safety concerns that include frequent and serious adverse events and/or interactions.

## 4. Strength of the Recommendation

We adopted the GRADE working group criteria, which uses a five-level system: Strong recommendation in favor, Weak recommendation in favor, No Recommendation, Weak recommendation against, and Strong recommendation against. For example, a *strong recommendation against* a treatment for a specific indication suggests that the risks far outweigh the benefits (e.g., colloidal silver for rheumatoid arthritis). Aspirin for acute myocardial infarction would be an example where the benefits far outweigh the risks and therefore would receive *a strong recommendation in favor*. For weak recommendations, different patients may choose different treatments. Hormone replacement therapy for osteoporosis is a good example of a therapy that receives a *weak recommendation in favor* because a recommendation of this therapy requires that the provider determine the patient's risk for various diseases (cancer, heart disease, osteoporosis), as well as engage in a discussion with the patient about their risk tolerance, values, and preferences. In addition to the quality of the evidence, the authors considered a number of additional factors when calculating the strength of the recommendation and are listed below.

## Factors Influencing the Strength of the Recommendation

Note: Information in this section was adopted from *Gordon Guyatt et al. An Emerging Consensus on Grading Recommendations? ACP Journal Club. 2006; 144:A8-9 [editorial].*

1. Methodological quality of the evidence for effect, safety, cost, convenience:
   *Example:* RCTs have shown benefit of inhaled corticosteroids for asthma, while only case series have shown benefit of pleurodesis for pneumothorax.

2. Importance of the outcome:

   *Example:* Thrombolytic therapy preventing death due to pulmonary embolism versus treating post-phlebitic syndrome of deep vein thrombosis.

3. Magnitude of effect (e.g., relative risk 1.2 vs 5.5; NNT 5 vs 500; ARR 2% vs 80%):

   *Example:* Clopidogrel vs aspirin leads to a smaller risk reduction than anti-coagulation vs placebo for stroke prevention (RRR 8.7% vs 68%).

4. Precision of the estimate of treatment effect (wide/narrow confidence intervals):

   *Example:* Aspirin vs placebo for atrial fibrillation has a wider confidence interval than aspirin for stroke prevention after transient ischemic attack.

5. Risks associated with therapy:

   *Example:* Aspirin administered with clopidogrel is associated with a higher risk for bleed than aspirin alone in acute coronary syndrome.

6. Burden of therapy:

   *Example:* Taking warfarin requires frequent monitoring and consumption of stable doses of vitamin K intake, compared with use of clopidogrel or aspirin.

7. Cost:

   *Example:* Clopidogrel is associated with higher costs than aspirin.

8. Varying values:

   *Example:* Younger people put high value on prolonging life; older and infirm people may be less willing to endure suffering in order to prolong life.

## Consistency in Language and Use of Summary Tables

Each chapter contains tables that summarize the literature based on the GRADE working group criteria and uses consistent language to describe the evidence for effect and safety based on this system, as well. The summary evidence tables contain the following data elements: indication, CAM category, specific therapy, dose, main outcomes studied, confidence in estimate of effect, magnitude of effect, safety, strength of the recommendation, and comments. Based on the work of the Evidence-Based Medicine Guidelines (http://ebmg.wiley.com), we developed a glossary to ensure that consistent language is used throughout the book when describing the evidence-base for effectiveness (Table 1) and safety (Table 2) of individual treatments for specific indication. Both tables appear on the following page.

Table 1    Guide to Using Consistent Language to Describe the Quality of Evidence for the Effectiveness of Treatments

|  | Level A<br>High | Level B<br>Moderate | Level C<br>Low | Level D<br>Very Low |
|---|---|---|---|---|
| Effective | Is effective; are the most effective | Appears to be effective | May be effective | Seems effective; although there is no evidence from controlled trials |
| Some effect | Has some effect | Appears to have some effect; appears to have more effect than | May have limited effect | Seems to have limited effect; although there is no evidence from controlled trials |
| Similar effect | Are both effective | Both appear effective | May both be effective | Seems to have similar effect; although there is no evidence from controlled trials |
| No effect | Is not effective | Appears not to be effective | Is probably not effective; probably has no effect | Seems to have no effect; although there is no evidence from controlled trials |

Table 2    Guide to Using Consistent Language to Describe the Safety of Treatments

|  | Double thumbs up | Single thumb up | No recommendation | Single thumb down | Double thumbs down |
|---|---|---|---|---|---|
| Safety | Appears safe with infrequent adverse events and interactions | Appears relatively safe but with frequent, not serious adverse events and interactions | Safety profile not well understood; data on safety is conflicting | Appears to have safety concerns that include infrequent but serious adverse events and/or interactions | Has serious safety concerns that include frequent and serious adverse events and/or interactions |

# Complementary &
# Alternative Medicine

# PART I

# FUNDAMENTALS OF COMPLEMENTARY AND ALTERNATIVE MEDICINE

## Chapter 1

ℬℑ

# Complementary and Alternative Medicine: Definitions and Patterns of Use

BRADLY JACOBS, MD, MPH
KATHERINE GUNDLING, MD

Good health is core to the quality of human existence. How do we become healthy and stay that way? Our genetic make-up, environment, education, cultural values and traditions all play a role in how we define, strive for and achieve wellbeing. Modern western medicine has made remarkable strides in helping people to live longer, healthier and more prosperous lives. Simple good hygiene practices of safe water and food have helped to prevent disease, and vaccinations have almost wiped out illnesses that previously maimed and killed both children and adults. Our understanding of the human body, and our ability to study it, has allowed the development of new and targeted therapies.

With this optimistic view of modern medicine, why might patients look elsewhere for help? Perhaps, in part, because of recent human prosperity and longevity, the types of ailments and conditions that worry people have changed. Our ancestors were more likely to die at younger ages, and they suffered infections, starvation, trauma and acute illnesses that are now less common. Although some areas of the world still suffer in this way, the concerns of many people in industrialized countries today focus on chronic problems and diseases of aging for which there are no easy cures, and for which quality of life takes an increasingly important role. When problems persist it is easy to understand how people might look to other cultures and traditions of care. In addition, there has been a shift toward optimizing health and vitality and increased interest in the domain of "Healthy Aging" or "Aging Gracefully."

Certainly much more information is available via the Internet, and our patients are learning about and purchasing treatments that were previously inaccessible or non-existent. Time is an important factor, and busy physicians are often unable to spend a satisfying amount of time required to address a patient's problems, particularly the chronic ones. People often believe alternative treatments are safer, which may or may not be true. Why people use complementary and alternative modalities will be explored later, but, whatever the reason, we know that a large proportion of our patients use them.

Although a small subset of patients has philosophical differences with (and therefore avoids) anything perceived to be western medicine, most patients just want something that works, and don't care so much what label is attached to it.

Owing to the vast array of practices and treatments used by patients, which frequently are not familiar to physicians, a fledgling "Office of Alternative Medicine" was founded at the National Institutes of Health (in the United States) in 1992. In 1999, the office subsequently was elevated to center-level status and was renamed the National Center for Complementary and Alternative Medicine (NCCAM) with an annual budget of $121 million dollars for 2008. This organization's goal has been to explore complementary and alternative practices within the context of rigorous science. Other organizations, such as the University of Exeter in England and the Cochrane Collaboration, have also worked tirelessly to investigate alternative practices, and a growing list of international investigators has contributed to an expanding body of knowledge.

Recognition of patient use of alternative modalities has led to development of specific curricula in medical schools in the United States. The National Institutes of Health funded 5-year education projects at 14 health professional schools and at the American Medical Students Association from 2000 to 2003 (1). They were funded to develop curricular models for the education of conventional medical and nursing students, with a long-term vision of developing more unified, evidence-based curricula. About 24% of American medical schools have mandatory curricula in complementary and alternative medicine (2). An additional two-thirds of schools offer limited electives or incorporate information about CAM into existing curricula. Given the widespread use of these therapies, academic medicine has become increasingly interested in investigating and educating medical students and residents about the benefits and risks associated with these healing systems and therapies. Consequently, the "Consortium of Academic Health Centers in Integrative Medicine" was created in 2002 and currently includes at least 39 academic medical centers. In addition, dozens of integrative medicine clinical practices exist in both academic centers and communities throughout the United States. Many physicians have developed their own interests in complementary modalities by learning and incorporating them into their practices. Some insurance companies already offer coverage of CAM treatments, and certainly as health care resources become more restricted, we will need to expend them in areas where benefit is likely to result.

For all these reasons it is imperative that we learn whether any of these modalities benefit our patients beyond the healing that comes from the careful attention and touch of another individual. Armed with a better understanding of the strengths and weaknesses of these treatments, clinicians can provide patients with thoughtful, intelligent and comprehensive care.

## What Is Complementary and Alternative Medicine?

Although conventional medicine is clearly the dominant healthcare delivery system in the United States, it coexists with many other healing systems and practices. Many of these systems originated outside of the United States and Western Europe. Systems that have originated in the West and developed outside of conventional medical practice frequently remain outside of the standard curriculum taught in medical schools and are generally not available in hospitals or routinely reimbursed by medical insurance. There are a variety of terms used to describe these healing systems and practices.

"Complementary and Alternative Medicine (CAM)" is the name chosen by the National Institutes of Health. It is defined as encompassing a "broad range of healing philosophies (schools of thought), approaches, and therapies that mainstream Western (conventional) medicine does not commonly use, accept, study, understand, or make available" (3). CAM therapies may be used alone, as an alternative to conventional therapies, or in addition to conventional, mainstream medicine to treat conditions and promote well being. CAM encompasses a variety of new and old approaches to health care. Some of these approaches, such as traditional Chinese medicine (TCM), are well known and practiced widely in other parts of the world. Others, such as chiropractic, have more recent histories. They may come in the form of an entire system of practice, such as Ayurvedic medicine, with its multiple treatment modalities prescribed at once, or they can be single remedies, such as use of an herbal preparation for migraine headache.

For purposes of organizing CAM into useful categories, NCCAM (3) recognizes five different domains (Table 1-1):

- Whole Medical Systems
- Mind-Body Medicine
- Biologically Based Practices
- Manipulative and Body-Based Practices
- Energy Medicine

These categories are artificially constructed but nevertheless offer a way to categorize different interventions in the field of CAM. NCCAM points out that some strategies previously considered alternative, such as omega-3 fatty acids, patient-support groups and cognitive-behavioral therapy, are now considered a routine part of mainstream medicine.

Patients ask about CAM treatments in several ways. For example, the inquiry may pertain to whether a specific herb, such as *Ginkgo biloba*, will help improve memory function. Or the question may pertain to whether homeopathy or Ayurveda (systems of practice) offer benefit for chronic fatigue. Appendix 1 (Systems of Practice) describes these systems of practice in greater detail. Appendix 2 (Complementary and Alternative Medicine Terms) describes many individual treatments in detail; in addition, you will find treatment definitions in relevant chapters throughout the book. For the most part,

---

**Table 1-1    National Center for Complementary and Alternative Medicine
Categories of CAM Modalities**

---

*Whole Medical Systems*

Complete systems of theory and practice: traditional Chinese medicine, Ayurvedic
    medicine, homeopathy, chiropractic, and naturopathy.

*Mind-Body Medicine*

Practices that "enhance the mind's capacity to affect bodily function and systems and
    health outcomes": meditation, music therapy, prayer, and components of whole
    medical systems such as yoga.

*Biologically Based Practices*

Substances that are thought to occur in nature and often ingested by mouth, such as
    botanical agents, some foods, vitamins, and other supplements; and botanical
    products, dietary supplements such as glucosamine, chromium picolinate, and
    vitamins, and some foods.

*Manipulative and Body-Based Practices*

Human touch and/or manipulation of the body: chiropractic, massage and osteopathic
    treatments.

*Energy Medicine*

There are two categories: 1) Biofield therapy purports to manipulate energy fields
    around the body. The nature of these (as yet unproven) fields is reported to affect the
    health of the body. Biofield therapy also includes therapeutic touch and qi gong. 2)
    Bioelectromagnetic-based therapies "involve the unconventional use of
    electromagnetic fields, such as pulsed fields, magnetic fields, or alternating-current or
    direct-current fields."

---

however, patients come to their physicians with specific medical concerns, and
the patient-physician team takes a problem-based approach to improving the
patient's health. Consequently, this book is organized into chapters by problem
according to the area of clinical specialty such as heart disease, cancer, or
obesity.

## Terminology

It is worth taking a moment to explore and clarify the terminology one hears
in discussions of complementary therapies. The medical literature is not yet
consistent in its use or indexing of the different terms that characterize unconventional practices, products and therapies (4). Nevertheless there is a general
understanding of the definition of certain terms that are commonly used.

**Alternative** medicine by definition implies something different or outside
of conventional western medicine. Alternative therapies are used *instead of*
conventional western therapies. Survey research suggests that less than 5% of
people use these therapies to the exclusion of conventional medical care (5).

**Complementary** medicine includes therapeutic modalities that are used
alongside of conventional medicine. For example, music therapy given to

patients undergoing cancer treatment is an adjuvant treatment. Although the term "complementary" is sometimes used in the clinical setting, it is commonly used in research applications.

**Complementary and alternative medicine (CAM)**, according to NCCAM, is an inclusive term that represents a "group of diverse medical and health care systems, practices, and products that are not presently considered to be part of conventional medicine" (6). Whereas some of these practices have evidence to support them, most require more evidence to demonstrate safety and efficacy before they can be recommended on a widespread basis. NCCAM emphasizes that the pool of CAM therapies changes as scientific evidence defines the validity (or lack thereof) of therapies, and as new questions emerge. In this text, we will frequently use the designation "CAM" to reflect the broad scope of practices, techniques and therapies under discussion.

**Integrative Medicine** is commonly used to suggest an evidence-based approach toward combining the best of mainstream medical therapies and CAM treatments, and to address the inclusive biological, psychological, social and spiritual aspects of health and illness. It emphasizes respect for the human capacity for healing, the importance of the relationship between the practitioner and the patient, the importance of self-care in the management of chronic conditions (such as sleep hygiene, good nutrition and effective mind-body interventions), and a collaborative approach to patient care among practitioners. The term integrative medicine has also been incorporated into the marketing strategies of various health care practitioners, but not all of them are well versed with the challenges of the above-stated aims.

## Other Common Terms and Phrases

Patients sometimes use terminology that they have heard elsewhere, and these terms may be unfamiliar to physicians. "Cleansing" is a word often seen on products that claim to be of benefit to specific organs. "Liver cleansers" can be found in many health food stores and usually contain a combination of herbs in conjunction with a botanical agent known as milk thistle. The word "toxin" is often used generically, and products are claimed to "detoxify" or flush out toxins that cause illness. Such non-specific terminology can be attractive to patients (who wouldn't want to be cleansed and detoxified?) who adopt its use, but are baffling to western physicians when patients inquire about "detoxification" or "cleansing" regimens. Many such terms have their origins in other systems of practice. The concept of detoxification, for example, is important in Ayurvedic medicine. In current conventional practice, however, it is appropriate to identify the specific toxins these products are purported to "cleanse" in order to understand their mechanism of action and specific pathophysiologic effects, and to question their record of safety and efficacy.

Another term that has gained popularity with the public and even the medical community is "allopathic medicine." One who practices allopathic medicine is called an "allopath." At first glance this term would seem to be a convenient way to distinguish the practice of conventional western medicine from other types of practice and training, including naturopathy, osteopathy, etc. In fact, this term was coined by Samuel Hahnemann, the founder of homeopathy, who used it to describe the punishing treatments (emetics, purgatives, etc.) prevalent in the late 1700s. Hahnemann used the term "allopathy" to contrast the harsh conventional therapies of the day with "homeopathy," which used highly diluted substances that were therefore unlikely to cause any adverse effects. Historically, "allopathy" implied a negative and narrow perspective that does not characterize the practice of medicine in the 21st century. More information on the history of this term is available (7).

The term "phytomedicine" refers to the medicinal properties of plants. The word "nutraceutical" has had several meanings. Currently, the term refers to substances isolated from foods, and generally sold separate from foods. They are purported to have specific physiologic effects to promote health. Examples include lycopene, which is sold in supplement form, originates from tomatoes and has been thought to have anti-cancer properties, and red yeast rice, derivatives of which lower cholesterol. Previously, it has been used to mean any food or part of a food that is used specifically for health benefit. It has also been defined as any food to which vitamins, minerals or other supplements have been added to make them healthier. These food products are now frequently called "Functional Foods." "Functional medicine," as defined by the Institute of Functional Medicine (8), is grounded in the following principles: existence of biochemical individuality, patient-centered medicine, recognition of the multiple interconnections of physiologic factors, recognition of the dynamic balance between internal and external factors, recognition of health as a "positive vitality," and the promotion of 'organ reserve' to enhance longevity. It shares many attributes with naturopathic medicine such as a focus on primary prevention and underlying causes of symptoms for chronic disease.

Patients use other terms related to diagnostic modalities within the CAM community. For example, some practitioners use a modality called "applied kinesiology" to diagnose allergies and other ailments. "Iridology" has been used to diagnose systemic disease by examination of the iris. Both techniques have been invalidated, but they are still used in practice, and it is therefore important to be familiar with the terms, particularly because patients inquire about them.

## Dietary Supplements

The term, "dietary supplement" as used in the United States was formally defined by the Dietary Supplement Health and Education Act (DSHEA) of 1994 (9) as follows:

A dietary supplement:

- is a product (other than tobacco) that is intended to supplement the diet that bears or contains one or more of the following dietary ingredients: a vitamin, a mineral, an herb or other botanical, an amino acid, a dietary substance for use by man to supplement the diet by increasing the total daily intake, or a concentrate, metabolite, constituent, extract, or combinations of these ingredients.
- is intended for ingestion in pill, capsule, tablet, or liquid form.
- is not represented for use as a conventional food or as the sole item of a meal or diet.
- includes products such as an approved new drug, certified antibiotic, or licensed biologic that was marketed as a dietary supplement or food before approval, certification, or license (unless the Secretary of Health and Human Services waives this provision).
- is labeled as a "dietary supplement."

In other words "dietary supplements" consist of many types of substances that are packaged in different forms. The term, "herbal medicine" is often used mistakenly for non-herbal dietary supplements, such as glucosamine, which is derived from the skeleton of shellfish. Strictly speaking, herbs refer to plants whose stems whither away with the season.

The term "homeopathy" is also used mistakenly to mean herbal compounds, when the remedies may actually contain animal, mineral or vegetable constituents. Homeopathic remedies are considered drugs in accordance with the Food, Drug and Cosmetic Act of 1938, and there is a separate pharmacopoeia for them. Their status was not affected by the DSHEA.

## Effectiveness Claims

Claims about dietary supplements are not allowed to include statements about diagnosing, preventing, mitigating, treating or curing a specific disease. In contrast, claims are allowed that address how the product alters "structure" or "function" of the body. For example, supplements can be promoted to "support healthy cholesterol levels" but not to "treat cardiovascular disease." If claims are made, they must be accompanied by the phrase, "This statement has not been evaluated by the Food and Drug Administration. This product is not intended to diagnose, treat, cure, or prevent any disease."

## Quality Assurance

DSHEA as originally defined did not require manufacturers to ensure that good manufacturing guidelines were followed. However, in June 2007, the FDA issued the final rule establishing regulations to require current good manufacturing practices (cGMP) for dietary supplements effective June 2008 for large companies; June 2009 for companies with less than 500 employees; and June 2010 for companies with fewer than 20 employees (10). The primary non-profit and independent agencies conducting quality-assurance testing for cGMPs include the United States Pharmacopeia (11) and the NSF International (12) and the Natural Products Association. Products that have passed these agencies' testing will have a "seal of approval" demarcation on the bottle label.

## Standardization of Botanical Products

Many herbal medicines are "standardized," which means that the manufacturer has prepared the product in such a way as to contain a consistent amount of one or two active ingredients. For example, most St. John's wort products are standardized to 3% hypericin because that particular ingredient is thought to have the greatest activity against depression. If the more important constituent is hyperforin, as some people believe, the standardization does not necessarily imply a more effective product, just a more consistent one.

## Safety and Adverse Effects

Are dietary supplements safe? Most supplements are safe, but some are not. Safety regulations for dietary supplements in the United States differ from prescription medicines in that the usual rigorous standards applied to prescription medications do not apply to dietary supplements, as noted above. Dietary supplements are regulated in a manner similar to foods. It is the manufacturer's responsibility to ensure correct labeling and safety of the products. Removal of any product from the market is quite difficult because it requires proof that the product is a hazard to the population. The most recent final rule on good manufacturing practices issued by the FDA should improve the quality of products available to consumers; however, historically, the FDA has had inadequate resources to enforce their requirements within the dietary supplement industry.

Adverse effects from dietary supplements occur due to:

- Natural toxicity: The botanical agent itself may be toxic. For example, the amphetamine-like effects of ephedra are associated with cardiovascular events such as stroke, hypertension and myocardial infarction at sufficient doses.
- Contamination: Poisonous look-alike plants (mistaken identity) and heavy metals are examples of two kinds of contaminants found in some dietary supplements.
- Adulteration: Adverse effects also occur due to adulteration of supplements, such as the addition of nonsteroidal anti-inflammatory agents to Chinese herbal remedies (13).
- Drug interaction: Drug-drug or herb-drug interactions can occur due to pharmacokinetic or pharmacodyamic interactions. In general, prescription medications that have the highest known incidence of drug-drug

interaction will be most likely to interact with botanical agents as well. For example, warfarin, protease inhibitors and anti-cancer medications, compounds with a high incidence of drug interaction, are also those most commonly known to interact with plant compounds.

St. John's wort has become the "poster" example of botanical agents that interact with pharmaceutical agents. This plant is a potent inducer of CYP 3A4 and P-glycoprotein, and probably acts on a number of other enzymes, too (14,15). Perhaps the vigor of the drug clearance induced by St. John's wort lends weight to its traditional reputation as a "detoxifier." The topic of drug-supplement interactions is covered more extensively later in this book.

## Who Uses What and Why?

Most Americans report using CAM because they believe they will get better results using a combination of CAM and conventional medicine, as opposed to using conventional medicine alone (16). Furthermore, chronic disease accounts for more than 70% of total health expenditures each year, and conventional medicine is limited in its ability to improve the quality of life. Consequently, people are increasingly inquiring about and trying therapies offered outside their physician's office.

A recent large survey has shed significant light on the use of CAM therapies by the American population (17). The survey was conducted by the National Center for Health Statistics (NCHS) at the Centers for Disease Control and Prevention (CDC). Developmental assistance was provided by NCCAM, and the survey was conducted as part of the 2002 National Health Interview Survey (NHIS). Computer-assisted personal interviews were conducted of 31,044 adults over the age of eighteen.

The survey asked about the use of 27 types of CAM therapies commonly used in the United States, including 10 types of provider-based therapies, such as chiropractic and acupuncture. There were also many questions about the use of supplements that are obtainable without a prescription.

Table 1-2 summarizes the types of CAM therapies most commonly used. Prayer for purposes specifically related to illness was very common and lends weight to the current research interest in the impact of prayer on clinical outcomes. When this type of prayer was included in the analysis, 75 percent of adults reported use of CAM at sometime in the past, and 62% reported use within the past 12 months. When prayer specifically for health reasons was excluded, 36% of Americans reported using CAM therapies within the previous 12 months. The survey suggests that 40 to 50 million Americans are using dietary supplements, which underscores the urgency of defining the efficacy and safety of these agents.

Factors reflective of greater CAM use included female sex, higher education, urban living, hospitalization within the last year and a past history of smoking (as opposed to current smoking or never smoking). A U-shaped curve defined the relationship of age to use of any CAM therapy, with the youngest

Table 1-2    Most Common Types of CAM Therapies Used by
             Adults in the United States

| | |
|---|---|
| Prayer for own health | 43% |
| Prayer by others for the respondent's health | 23% |
| Natural products (herbs, other botanicals, and enzymes) | 19% |
| Deep breathing exercises | 12% |
| Participation in prayer group for own health | 10% |
| Meditation | 8% |
| Chiropractic care | 8% |
| Yoga | 5% |
| Massage | 5% |
| Diet-based therapies (such as Atkins, Pritikin, Ornish, and Zone diets) | 4% |

and oldest adults showing the least use. However, when prayer specific to health problems was included in the definition of CAM, use was associated with increased age.

One of the advantages of the large size of the survey is that novel information was obtained regarding minority use of complementary and alternative medicine. For example, it was discovered that blacks were more likely than whites or Asians to use megavitamin therapy and prayer. However, when megavitamins and prayer were excluded from the analysis, Asians were found to be greater overall users than whites or blacks. Whites were more likely than other groups to use manipulative and body-based therapies. Many other patterns were noted, and the strengths and limitations of the data are noted in the descriptive article.

Why did the survey participants choose to use CAM therapies? The authors summarize this data as follows:

- 55% of adults said they were most likely to use CAM because they believed that it would help them when combined with conventional medical treatments;
- 50% thought CAM would be interesting to try;
- 26% used CAM because a conventional medical professional suggested they try it; and
- 13% used CAM because they felt that conventional medicine was too expensive.

Previous surveys found evidence that users were not dissatisfied with conventional medicine, but most frequently used CAM in addition to it. This survey found that about 28% of adults used CAM because they believed conventional medical treatments alone would not help them with their health problem. The response to this question could be dependent upon a number of factors, including age and sex of the respondents and type and chronicity of illness.

One interesting finding is that only 12% of those questioned sought care from licensed CAM practitioners. A large proportion of respondents likely are using CAM treatments without the guidance of a health professional, i.e., use of over-the-counter dietary supplements. When patients do access a CAM-trained health professional, they may or may not be receiving care from a 'licensed' provider depending on the discipline. While some disciplines such as acupuncture, chiropractic and naturopathy have state and/or national licensing bodies and competency exams, many other disciplines have not developed such standards; examples include massage, therapeutic yoga, Ayurveda, homeopathy and herbalism, to name a few. Chiropractors are licensed in all 50 states; acupuncture is licensed in 42 states, and naturopathy in 14 states. It is important for providers and patients to ask the treating CAM practitioner about his or her training, experience and licensure status.

Box 1-1 lists the most common physical concerns that led people to use CAM therapies, according to the survey. Cherkin et al sought similar information by analyzing 20 consecutive patient visits in practices of randomly sampled licensed acupuncturists, chiropractors, massage therapists and naturopathic physicians practicing in Arizona, Connecticut, Massachusetts, and Washington (18). Visits to chiropractors and massage therapists were mostly for musculoskeletal problems, whereas visits to naturopathic physicians and acupuncturists were for a greater variety of reasons.

## Evidence-Based Medicine and CAM

Evidence-based medicine is a relatively new concept. In 1747, Surgeon James Lind was the first person to conduct a clinical trial when he gave sailors limes or vinegar to identify a potential treatment for scurvy. In 1835, the Surgeon of Nurmberg was the first to conduct a double-blind experiment to end the public debate on homeopathy. In the 1950s, the concepts of randomization and blinding were introduced to evaluate the merits of psychic healing and hypnosis. In the 1970s, the FDA determined that the randomized clinical trial should be considered the gold standard for conducting clinical research to determine the effectiveness of novel therapies. In 1992, the term "evidence-based medicine" made its official debut in a publication in the *Journal of the American Medical Association*.

Currently, the gold standard for evaluating the effectiveness of interventions remains the randomized controlled trial (RCT). Once there is

| Box 1-1 Most Common Problems Treated with CAM |
|---|
| Back pain or problems |
| Colds |
| Neck pain or problems |
| Joint pain or stiffness |
| Anxiety or depression |
| Sinusitis |
| Cholesterol |
| Asthma |
| Hypertension |
| Menopause |

a sufficient evidence-base of RCTs, systematic reviews and meta-analyses of these trials can be conducted to provide summary evidence statements on the safety and effectiveness of specific interventions for specific conditions. These summary statements provide the core evidence-base for health policy and evidence-based practice guidelines (19). Surprisingly, there are thousands of such RCTs evaluating CAM therapies. The Cochrane Central Register of Controlled Trials (CENTRAL) on The Cochrane Library identified 9707 controlled studies (2.3% of the total of 427,807 registered references) that used the terms "alternative" or "complementary" (20). In addition to RCTs, there are thousands of cohort studies, case-control studies, and case reports. However, these clinical designs provide less reliable information due to the potential for selection bias, confounding and other methodological concerns (20,21).

Even randomized, double-blind controlled trials are prone to methodological shortcomings. Admittedly, randomization can prevent many confounding variables from influencing the results of a study; however, they are vulnerable to other methodological challenges such as random (i.e., type I or type II errors) and systematic (i.e., bias) errors. Conducting large trials and limiting the number of outcomes in the analysis can limit the probability of random errors. Avoidance of systematic bias requires precision in design and implementation of the clinical trial. Examples include inappropriate randomization techniques (e.g. randomization based on even or odd date of hospital admission); inadequate allocation concealment such that the study participant themselves are more likely than not to know what treatment arm the study participant was assigned to; poor documentation of study participants who withdrew from the study or were lost to follow-up, and publication bias. RCTs with high methodological quality tend to document smaller treatment effects (19-24). Since CAM interventions usually focus on symptoms, the RCTs frequently measure subjective outcomes. Blinding is therefore an essential component of the study design. Furthermore, some CAM RCTs, like non-CAM RCTs, focus on surrogate outcome measures (e.g., laboratory tests). The RCTs may report beneficial effects, but these outcomes may not really be of importance for patients or healthcare providers (25). The methodological quality of many RCTs of CAM is low (26,27). Publication bias can also be an important issue (28,29). Historically, published studies from Asia or Eastern Europe are almost always positive and are frequently conducted with inadequate methods (30).

Appropriately, most scientists and clinicians believe that CAM should undergo a process of scientific inquiry at least as rigorous as conventional medical treatments. With the increased funding coming from the National Institutes of Health as well as other governmental agencies worldwide since the late 1990s, there is a rapidly growing evidence-base. Historically, there are four primary reasons why most CAM therapies had not been subject to scientific inquiry. First, most CAM therapies such as Ayurveda, traditional Chinese medicine and many herbal medicines were developed prior to the advent of clinical trials, and in more recent years they remained outside the mainstream health delivery system. Second, in contrast to therapeutic agents newly developed by medical device or pharmaceutical companies, it has been extremely difficult to patent the technology or intellectual property in most CAM therapies. Venture capital funding or in-house pharmaceutical and medical device support have therefore been comparatively lacking. Third, prior to the advent of the National Center for CAM at the National Institutes of Health, there were limited sources of funding from governmental agencies. Fourth, historically there were few scientists interested in investigating CAM therapies and a paucity of CAM practitioners trained in the scientific method.

CAM represents such a diverse cross section of cultures, belief systems and data sets that current methods of assessing evidence do not always apply well or equally to CAM techniques. Consequently, to understand the relative quality of CAM research, it is important to address the unique challenges to designing and evaluating research in this area.

In traditional novel therapeutic drug development, there is a step-by-step process for evaluating the safety and effectiveness of novel therapeutics. Often a novel therapy is first considered after identification (in the laboratory or clinical setting) of biologically active compounds with potentially beneficial properties. This results in a hypothesis that through animal or human study results in hypothesis refinement, and in vitro or ex vivo proof of concept analyses, which subsequently gives sufficient rationale to merit conducting a pilot study in humans. Assuming the pilot study shows promise, investigators then conduct Phase 1, Phase 2, Phase 3 and finally Phase 4 post-marketing surveillance studies, all the while determining whether there is a consistent evidence-base for effectiveness and tolerable risk.

This "from the ground up" approach implies a step-by-step process in which one proceeds no further if the evidence does not support moving to the next step. Contemporary treatments and medications developed in the modern scientific era must generally survive this arduous process. In contrast, many CAM therapies originated prior to or outside of the scientific method, and most of them did not undergo careful scrutiny until the 1990s. Since many of these therapies were (and are) already in widespread use, the initial scientific discovery process was bypassed, and investigation has started with Phase 1 or higher clinical trials.

## Unique Challenges to Conducting Research in the Field of CAM

There are several challenges unique to conducting research in CAM that deserve attention (Box 1-2).

*A proposed treatment was developed before current concepts of scientific analysis could influence its evolution.*

As described above, several whole medical systems, including traditional Chinese medicine and Ayuvedic medicine, have existed for millenia and evolved long before they could be influenced by the scientific principles that are applied today. Concepts of chiropractic care, a relatively new modality, were also formulated prior to a modern understanding of the central and

peripheral nervous systems and before the availability of newer imaging techniques. In addition, chiropractic is practiced outside of the mainstream health delivery system. Only recently has there been an adequate number of scientists (trained in and outside of chiropractic) interested and able to perform rigorous clinical trials. This is also true of other areas of CAM, where there have been few interested, well-trained scientists who possess adequate funding for research.

While this rationale provided reasonable justification for the paucity of research prior to the turn of the century, at this time there should no longer be a challenge to furthering high-quality research in this field within the limits of available funding. There are adequate opportunities for CAM practitioners and young scientists to gain the training necessary to conduct high-quality scientific inquiries.

## A fundamental concept of the treatment or desired outcome is difficult to measure, define, or manipulate.

Many principles of whole medical systems have no corollary in conventional medical theory or practice. For example, the concept of "Qi," is a central tenet of Chinese medical theory and practice. Qi is the "life force" that exists in all living beings and when properly regulated flows through the body evenly and with vitality. In traditional Chinese medical theory, poor health is associated with an imbalance in this flow of energy and might manifest for example as an excess or deficiency in one function or organ in the body. Qi has not yet been isolated, quantified or identified in a manner that permits valid and reliable measurement and therefore cannot be reliably studied as a research outcome. Concepts such as Qi were an outgrowth of the knowledge base as it existed at the time. One can only speculate how the concept of Qi would have evolved if the ancestral Chinese healers had understood, say, molecular biology or physical chemistry.

One method to cope with this dilemma is to focus on identifying valid and reliable health-related outcomes that are most relevant to a particular condition, and that are used to evaluate conventional medical interventions. While this does not prove that a specific core principle such as Qi is the mechanism by which the intervention renders its health benefits, it helps to provide an evidence-base necessary to evaluate the intervention's relative effectiveness. For example, acupuncture is one of the tools used by traditional Chinese medicine practitioners, who place needles in specific locations on the body (acupuncture points) to influence Qi and ultimately improve health. In conducting a clinical trial on the use of acupuncture for knee osteoarthritis, investigators may choose to evaluate health-related outcomes such as pain and function. One must then consider whether the absence of a logical underlying mechanism of action requires a higher level of proof at the clinical trial level (see below).

## A proposed mechanism of action does not correlate with currently accepted principles of science.

Perhaps because many CAM modalities were developed a long time ago, some of them are proposed to work by methods that do not correlate with currently accepted principles of science. For example, the fundamental claim of homeopathy that remedies become more potent with increasing dilutions, even beyond Avogadro's number (no molecules left in solution), has not been supported by reproducible experiments. How, then, can one believe any claims for efficacy? In such a case can we merely set a higher threshold for proof of efficacy? If so, who decides the level of the threshold?

Brien et al performed the largest, most strictly controlled "proving" trial for any homeopathic remedy using Belladona 30C (a very dilute solution) (31), which should theoretically induce symptoms in healthy people. "Proving" is a term in homeopathy that refers to the process that Samuel Hahnemann, the founder of homeopathy, used to test a variety of concentrations of different substances on healthy people to define the induction of symptoms. Homeopaths would expect subjects receiving the dilute Belladona to have symptoms not seen with the controls. This trial, however, failed to elicit symptoms different from placebo. In 1988, Davenas et al claimed that human basophil degranulation could be stimulated by very dilute (up to 1037) solutions of antibodies to immunoglobulin E (32). However, these observations could not be duplicated and the claim was dismissed.

Even though homeopathy seems to defy our current concepts of how therapies may work, clinical trial data have shown both positive and negative results. In 1991, a systematic review observed that positive results were seen in 15 of 22 relatively high-quality (including double blinded) RCTs. A subsequent meta-analysis pooling 89 RCTs found a statistically significant odds ratio of 2.45 (95% confidence interval [CI] 2.05 to 2.93) favoring homeopathy. While many of the trials were methodologically flawed, the methodological quality was similar to RCTs found in the standard medical literature. There was evidence of publication bias and, as the quality of the trial increased, the size of the effect decreased. Nonetheless, when only the highest quality trials were considered, a statistically significant effect was still present (odds ratio 1.66, 95% CI 1.33 to 2.08). It was concluded that the effects of homeopathy could not be entirely ascribed to a placebo effect. Two subsequent meta-analyses came to the same conclusion. The authors of one of these did note that the trials were often intended more to placate a hostile audience than to undertake a legitimate scientific inquiry. The individual nature of the usual treatments for homeopathy makes it even more daunting to test it in a controlled manner but, in general, high-quality individual clinical trials have had positive and negative results. The controversy continues (33-40).

While meta-analyses have found statistically significant effects when pooling trials across multiple conditions, there are frequently too few clinical trials for any specific condition except for perennial allergies, for example, but even in this circumstance, the trials were mostly conducted by a single investigator, and therefore there is a paucity of validation of results from independent investigators. The Cochrane library has concluded that there is insufficient clinical evidence to support or refute the use of homeopathy for dementia, induction of labor, or asthma. Other investigators have found insufficient evidence to evaluate the efficacy of homeopathy for migraines, osteoarthritis, or delayed-onset muscle soreness. It is hard to find sufficient evidence to adequately assess the efficacy of homeopathy for any specific treatment at this point in time. Because there is no known mechanism by which high dilutions of substances might exert powerful effect, many scientists feel that a very high threshold of proof is needed to claim that homeopathy works.

### The intervention is typically composed of multiple treatments.

An Ayurvedic medicine practitioner might prescribe a program of several treatments, such as a dietary supplement, yoga exercises and dietary changes. How can one then design a trial to answer the question, "Does Ayurvedic medicine work for this specific problem?" The optimal way to study the effect of a particular therapy is to evaluate an individual treatment while holding other variables constant. However, the community standard for clinical practice of many CAM whole medical systems is to bundle several treatments simultaneously. CAM co-investigators who contribute to the design of clinical trials often comment that isolating one treatment from a group is equivalent to "asking a surgeon to use only one hand or a subset of instruments when performing surgery." If the efficacy of a treatment is dependent upon several simultaneous interventions, creativity is required to design a methodologically sound research study.

### The challenge of creating standardized interventions makes it difficult to replicate clinical trial protocols and clinical practice.

Unlike a pharmaceutical drug that is usually composed of a single biologically active agent synthesized in a controlled environment, many CAM therapies, such as herbal and non-herbal dietary supplements, massage therapy and acupuncture, vary with each treatment rendered. For example, the potency of an herbal medicine such as *Ginkgo biloba*, even when produced by a single manufacturer, can vary from batch to batch depending on method and location of cultivation, method and timing of harvest and the method of manufacturing for commercial production. These factors influence the potency and expression of the various biologically active compounds in a given product. There is the potential for even greater product variation when comparing herbal medicines from different manufacturers. Consequently, most brands of botanical agents differ from one another enough that comparing the results of clinical trials can be challenging and potentially misleading For example, when combining all clinical trials of Echinacea, investigators have documented conflicting results. Greater consistency in outcomes is found when trials are categorized according to the species of Echinacea (*Echinacea augustifolia* or *Echinacea purpurea*, for example), the part of plant used, and the manufacturer. The potency and identification of active ingredients can also be helpful to stratify trials, but they are usually more difficult to obtain. Many of the trials are for proprietary products, and full disclosure of contents may not be provided. Botanical agents frequently have multiple (even many) active constituents, and it might be unclear which are most important.

All of these issues make it harder to summarize, compare or perform meta-analyses of the data. If one proprietary product has been shown in three high-quality, manufacturer-sponsored trials to have significant efficacy, can such results be generalized to other brands?

In another example of the difficulty of creating standardized clinical trials, Chinese acupuncture uses fewer and larger needles, whereas Japanese acupuncture uses more and smaller needles; some acupuncturists use electroacupuncture techniques, while others do not. Can the results of a clinical trial using one technique be generalized to others? We would suggest that combining results from diverse treatments can be misleading and inappropriate.

Reaching consensus on a single standardized intervention to use for all study subjects with a specific condition is particularly challenging among senior practitioners in yoga, tai chi, massage, chiropractics and others. For example, there are many different styles of yoga. It would be quite unusual for yoga teachers from different styles to reach consensus on a single intervention. Let's assume the investigator decides to select a single style such as Iyengar Yoga for a specific condition such as back pain. The investigator can use one provider to help design a yoga intervention or create an expert panel that will reach consensus on a single standardized intervention. Alternatively, some investigators choose to use a semi-standardized intervention that includes a core group of mandatory body positions (asanas), as well as optional sets of body positions that are prescribed to the individual based on unique health circumstances. Precise and clear documentation of the prescribed poses are required to enable future investigators to replicate the study protocol.

### Adequate placebo controls, including proper concealment of treatment assignment, are particularly difficult to design.

If the gold standard is a randomized, double-blind, placebo-controlled trial, how does one design such a trial for chiropractic manipulation, acupuncture, tai chi, yoga or massage? Creating a sham chiropractic, yoga or tai chi intervention to serve as a control can be quite challenging. The obvious limitation is that the practitioner would know the difference between real and sham and therefore possibly communicate this to the subject, even if in a subtle manner. If the patient has had previous experience with the intervention under study, he is more likely to know whether he has been randomized to the real or sham group. Researchers have achieved some success in creating sham acupuncture interventions that are indistinguishable from real acupuncture to the study subject. The newest sham acupuncture protocols use either a collapsible acupuncture needle, or (believe it or not) a toothpick. With these methods, study subjects have not been able to tell whether they received real or sham acupuncture treatments. Other sham acupuncture interventions include inserting real acupuncture needles in non-acupuncture points or piercing the skin over the real acupuncture site without deep stimulation. Some of these approaches, however, are thought to induce a diffuse noxious inhibitory response that influences the pain threshold. Consequently, investigators need to consider such interventions as an active control, and increase enrollment to ensure that there is adequate statistical power to detect a difference between groups (if indeed a difference does exist).

Rather than design a sham intervention, other investigators have chosen to compare the therapy of interest with other active or inactive interventions such as usual care, standard physical therapy, information booklets or attention-controls such as group support or physician counseling.

In summary, the methodological issues specific to CAM interventions create significant challenges for investigators motivated to create high-quality clinical research. At the same time, this field of medicine provides a unique opportunity to expand the current research methodological paradigm to create novel approaches that can be applied to clinical evaluation of potential therapies regardless of origin, route of administration or clinical specialty.

## REFERENCES

1. **Pearson NJ, Chesney MA.** The CAM Education Program of the National Center for Complementary and Alternative Medicine: an overview. Acad Med. 2007;87: 921-6.

2. **Brotherton SE, Rockey PH, Etzel SI.** US Graduate Medical Education, 2003-2004. JAMA. 2004;292:1032-7.

3. **National Center for Complementary and Alternative Medicine.** www.nccam.nih.gov/health

4. **Murphy LS, Reinsch S, Najm WI, et al.** Searching biomedical databases on complementary medicine: the use of controlled vocabulary among authors, indexers and investigators. BMC Complementary and Alternative Medicine 2003;3:3.

5. **Astin JA.** Why patients use alternative medicine: results of a national study. JAMA. 1998; 279:1548-53.

6. http://nccam.nci.nih.gov/health/whatiscam/index.htm.

7. **Gundling KE.** "When did I become an allopath?" Arch Intern Med. 1998;158:2185-6.

8. http://www.functionalmedicine.org/.

9. http://vm.cfsan.fda.gov/~dms/dietsupp.html

10. http://www.cfsan.fda.gov/~dms/dscgmps6.html#fr

11. http://www.usp.org/uspverified

12. http://www.nsf.org

13. **Ko RJ.** Adulterants in Asian patent medicines. N Engl J Med. 1998;339:847.

14. **Mills E, Montori VM, Wu P, et al.** Interaction of St. John's wort with conventional drugs: systematic review of clinical trials. BMJ. 2004;329:27-30.

15. **Zhou S, Chan E, Pan SQ, et al.** Pharmacokinetic interactions of drugs with St. John's wort. J Psychopharmacol. 2004;18:262-76.

16. **Eisenberg DM, Kessler RC, Van Rompay MI, et al.** Perceptions about complementary therapies relative to conventional therapies among adults who use both: results from a national survey. Ann Intern Med. 2001;135:344-51.

17. **Barnes PM, Powell-Griner E, McFann K.** Complementary and Alternative Medicine use among Adults: United States, 2002. www.cdc.gov/nchs/data/ad/ad343.pdf Advance Data from Vatl and Health Statistics No. 343. May 27, 2004.

18. **Cherkin DC, Deyo RA, Sherman KJ, et al.** Characteristics of visits to licensed acupuncturists, chiropractors, massage therapists, and naturopathic physicians. J Am Board Fam Pract. 2002; 15:463-72.

19. **Sackett DL, Haynes RB, Guyatt GH, Tugwell P.** Clinical Epidemiology: A Basic Science for Clinical Medicine. Second Edition. Boston; Little, Brown and Company, 1991.

20. **The Cochrane Central Register of Controlled Trials (CENTRAL).** The Cochrane Library, Issue 4, 2004. Chichester, UK: John Wiley & Sons, Ltd.

21. **Kunz R, Vist G, Oxman AD.** Randomisation to protect against selection bias in healthcare trials (Cochrane Methodology Review). In: The Cochrane Library, Issue 3, 2004. Chichester, UK: John Wiley & Sons, Ltd.

22. **Kjærgard LL, Villumsen J, Gluud C.** Reported methodological quality and discrepancies between large and small randomized trials in meta-analyses. Ann Intern Med. 2001;135:982-9.

23. **Als-Nielsen B, Chen W, Gluud LL, et al.** Are trial size and reported methodological quality associated with treatment effects? Observational study of 523 randomised trials. 12 Cochrane Colloquium. Ottawa, Ontario, Canada 2004:102-103.

24. **Als-Nielsen B, Gluud LL, Gluud C.** Methodological quality and treatment effects in randomised trials: a review of six empirical studies. 12th Cochrane Colloquium. Ottawa, Ontario, Canada 2004:88-89.

25. **Chan AW, Hrobjartsson A, Haahr MT, et al.** Empirical evidence for selective reporting of outcomes in randomized trials: comparison of protocols to published articles. JAMA. 2004; 291:2457-65.

26. **Tang J-L, Zhan S-Y, Ernst E.** Review of randomized controlled trials of traditional Chinese medicine. BMJ. 1999; 319:160-161.

27. **Linde K, Jonas WB, Melchart D, Willich S.** The methodological quality of randomized controlled trials of homeopathy, herbal medicines and acupuncture. Int J Epidemiol. 2001;30:526-31.

28. **Dickersin K, Rennie D.** Registering clinical trials. JAMA. 2003; 290:516-23.
29. **AW Krleza-Jeric K, Schmid I, Altman DG.** Outcome reporting bias in randomized trials funded by the Canadian Institutes of Health Research. CMAJ. 2004 Sep 28;171:735-40.
30. **Vickers A, Goval N, Harland R, Rees R.** Do certain countries produce only positive results? A systematic review of controlled trials. Control Clin Trials 1998;19:159-6.
31. **Brien S, Lewith G, Bryant T.** Ultramolecular homeopathy has no observable clinical effects. A randomized, double-blind, placebo-controlled proving trial of Belladonna 30C. Br J Clin Pharmozol. 2003; 56:562-8.
32. **Poitevin B, Davenas E, Benveniste J.** In vitro immunological degranulation of human basophils is modulated by Lung Histamine and Apis mellifica. Br J Clin Pharmacol. 1988; 25:439-44.
33. **Linde K, Clausius N, Ramirez G, et al.** Are the clinical effects of homeopathy placebo effects? A meta-analysis of placebo-controlled trials. Lancet. 1997; 350:834-43.
34. **Linde K, Scholz M, Ramirez G, et al.** Impact of study quality on outcome in placebo-controlled trials of homeopathy. J Clin Epidemiol. 1999;52:631-6.
35. **Cucherat M, Haugh MC, Gooch M, Boissel JP.** Evidence of clinical efficacy of homeopathy. A meta-analysis of clinical trials. HMRAG. Homeopathic Medicine Research Advisory Group. Eur J Clin Pharmacol. 2000;56:27-33.
36. **Kleijnen J, Knipschild P, ter Riet G.** Clinical trials of homeopathy. BMJ. 1991;302:316-23.
37. **Reilly D, Taylor MA, Beattie NG, et al.** Is evidence for homeopathy reproducible? Lancet 1994; 344:1601-6.
38. **Shang A, Huwiler-Muntener K, Nartey L, et al.** Are the clinical effects of homoeopathy placebo effects? Comparative study of placebo-controlled trials of homeopathy and allopathy. Lancet. 2005;366:726-32.
39. **Jonas WB, Anderson RL, Crawford CC, Lyons JS.** A systematic review of the quality of homeopathic clinical trials. BMC Complement Altern Med. 2001;1:12. EPub 2001 Dec 31.
40. **Jonas WB, Kaptchuk TJ, Linde K.** A critical overview of homeopathy. Ann Intern Med 2003; 138:393-399.

# Chapter 2

# The Clinical Encounter

KATHERINE GUNDLING, MD
BRADLY JACOBS, MD, MPH

Whether clinicians are supportive of complementary and alternative medicine (CAM) treatments or merely see them as an unavoidable nuisance, the reality is that many patients seek care from CAM practitioners and directly purchase treatments over-the-counter. From the moment the patient enters the office until the last administrative detail of the appointment is completed, the patient and clinician can both benefit if there is an organized and defined approach to questions about CAM. The information in this chapter is designed to provide a framework for addressing these issues in the individual clinician's practice.

## Why Health Professionals Need to Know About CAM

Sick patients are often more open-minded than their physicians about unconventional treatments. They have the clear goal of feeling better, and they have (generally) not read the scientific data about what works and what doesn't or what is "conventional" vs "alternative". They have the trusted resource of family and friends (not to mention the Internet) suggesting health cures, and they just want something that works. Moreover, being sick can alter a person's assessment of the risk/benefit ratio of any given treatment. Most patients thus enter any clinician's office with a strong desire to learn about things that can help and may not draw a distinction between what is conventional and what isn't.

Let's consider the patient encounter from the physician's perspective. Every appointment is important and should contribute to the patient's well-being. In order to provide good care, the physician has attended four years of medical school and usually 3-7 years of residency. He or she attends regular meetings and continuing education programs to master an immense and ever-increasing body of knowledge. In the office, time limitations due to low reimbursement, high overhead, "performance" mandates, and other requirements already restrict interactions with patients. Physicians might also be concerned about the legal responsibilities of involving themselves in a patient's

CAM treatments. No wonder this vast, new body of data is not always received by physicians with great enthusiasm.

One might therefore ask why the physician should care if his patient is using CAM treatments. Certainly many such treatments are benign or, at worst, do no harm. CAM practitioners often spend significant time with patients and, if nothing else, the human interaction and touch can have positive effects. If the treatments have benefit beyond the human interaction, so much the better.

However, while a "don't ask, don't tell" strategy is taken by many patients and physicians, it is not necessarily in the patient's best interest. There are multiple reasons for clinicians to maintain a working knowledge of CAM therapies and to be aware of patient interest in and use of these modalities.

## Many Patients Use CAM Treatments

As noted in Chapter 1, a national Centers for Disease Control (CDC) survey of over 30,000 Americans found that approximately two-thirds of them reported using CAM in the past 12 months. When excluding the use of prayer for health purposes, more than one-third of people surveyed reported using CAM therapies (1). Furthermore, there are an estimated 40-50 million Americans who consume dietary supplements (including vitamins and herbs) each year, increasing the potential for drug-herb and herb-herb interactions.

To the surprise of many clinicians, recent research suggests that people using CAM are more engaged in receiving conventional medical care than their peers (2). A recent analysis of this same CDC survey found that CAM users received more vaccinations and immunizations and sought more physician visits than their peers. These findings supplement previous work showing that dissatisfaction with conventional medical care was not associated with CAM use. (3)

Most Americans report using CAM because they believe they will get better results by using these therapies alongside conventional medicine rather than by using conventional medicine alone. Increasingly, patients are giving more credence to the importance of quality of life in making decisions regarding treatment options, and they understand the importance of health promotion and prevention. Research suggests that patients use CAM because such health disciplines reflect their beliefs and values toward health and healthcare (3).

## Patients Are Referred to Physicians for Information on CAM Treatments

Patients are frequently advised to consult their physicians about the use of CAM therapies. For example, a University of Maryland website outlines the role of essential fatty acid supplements in the treatment of allergic rhinitis. It concludes, "Work with your healthcare provider to first determine if it is safe for you to try GLA (gamma linoleic acid) and then follow your allergy symptoms closely for any sign of change". Another statement on the same page, "...you may want to talk to your doctor about whether it is safe for you to try nettle as a possible alternative treatment" (4).

The National Institutes of Health website (National Center for Complementary and Alternative Medicine) advises patients to do the following: "Talk to your health care practitioner(s). Tell them about the therapy you are considering and ask any questions you may have about safety, effectiveness, or interactions with medications (prescription or non-prescription)..." (5). Memorial Sloan Kettering's Integrative Medicine website requires the user to agree that physicians should be consulted prior to patient use of information about botanical products (6).

## Clinicians Will Enhance Their Relationship with Patients

Patients might fear that disclosing the use of CAM treatments will antagonize the doctor, particularly if the subject has not yet been raised. If the clinician is unusually hurried, the patient may choose not to ask additional questions, and the topic of CAM is left unaddressed. A lack of communication or understanding becomes even more important when a patient chooses to use an alternative therapy instead of a conventional treatment. A good working relationship, enhanced by the clinician's understanding of the patient's belief system, increases the likelihood that the clinician can monitor the patient for adverse effects and advise him or her if intervention is needed. A basic knowledge of the alternative treatment allows the clinician to weigh the risks and benefits of the patient's choice and explain them in a more thoughtful manner.

In some circumstances a clinician and patient might completely disagree about a CAM therapy in question. Moreover, patients who are particular adherents to CAM treatments might simply reject conventional therapies, even curative ones, because of their core values and belief systems regarding CAM therapies. Adams (7) argues that it is incumbent upon the clinician to accept these core values and how they change the nature of the patient-physician interaction (this may be most challenging for the clinician whose core belief system specifically excludes all things "alternative"). "Good" patient care, it is suggested, is based upon not only evidence-based practice but also upon how this information is best applied to the individual patient. This requires the clinician to explain his position yet remain supportive of the patient who chooses a different path, even to his detriment. Most clinicians will recognize that this issue is not unique to CAM therapies.

## Coordination of Care Is Critical to High-Quality Service, Particularly in the Primary Care Office

Clinicians willing to ask patients about their use of CAM will be better equipped to identify direct and indirect adverse effects, as well as positive effects.

Interactions between drugs and dietary supplements are one obvious area of concern. For example, as seen in Chapter 9, a clinician who is unaware that his patient is taking St. John's wort will fail to anticipate the drop in serum crix-ivan levels, leading to potentially severe clinical effects.

Dietary supplements, which include not only plant-based products but also a host of biological agents and other products, might also cause unexpected symptoms independent of other medications; a clinician who is unaware of patient use of these products will have a much harder time determining the origin of associated symptoms. Or symptoms might be falsely attributed to a different diagnosis or to a prescription medication. Supplements have been found to contain contaminants (such as heavy metals or pesticides) or adulterants (such as prescription medications), a problem likely intensified by the lack of regulatory oversight in the United States and other countries.

Dietary supplements and other over-the-counter purchases can be subject to recall or market withdrawal. Awareness of patient use of supplements allows clinicians to inform patients of recall information and safety advisories. Clinicians can also provide helpful resources for product recall advisories on a patient information handout (Box 2-1). Beyond supplements, manipulative treatments and other physical modalities can have adverse effects that will be unrecognized or unsuspected if the clinician is not informed of them. Indirect adverse effects could theoretically occur if there were a delay in diagnosis due to use of an ineffective alternative therapy. For example, colon cancer could be missed if colonoscopy were delayed in favor of an alternative treatment for rectal bleeding.

Just as awareness of the potential sources for adverse effects can enhance the quality of care, so can alertness to potential sources for benefits. Clinicians

---

**Box 2-1  Resources for Product Recall Advisories**

1. Background and Definition of Recalls by FDA
*http://www.fda.gov/oc/po/firmrecalls/recall_defin.html*
Description:  Provides information on different classes and types of recalls for medications or dietary supplements.

2. FDA Center for Food Safety and Applied Nutrition Dietary Supplement Warning and Safety Information Resource
*http://www.cfsan.fda.gov/~dms/ds-warn.html*
Description: Provides a listing of dietary supplements that were withdrawn from the market and supplements with safety concerns and links to other FDA alerts and additional safety information.

3. FDA Market Recalls, Market Withdrawals, and Safety Alerts
*http://www.fda.gov/opacom/7alerts.html*
Description: Provides listing of FDA recalls, market withdrawals, and safety alerts. This resource provides a much broader listing of products and medications.

can provide helpful resources to patients on the risks and benefits of CAM treatments (Box 2-2). Clinicians can also provide patients with summary tables explaining the general risks and benefits of specific complementary therapies, as addressed in the individual chapters of this book.

## Physicians Can Provide Consultation with CAM Providers Who Seek Collaboration with a Medical Doctor

Increasing numbers of CAM health professionals feel comfortable referring patients to conventionally trained health professionals for more severe illness or clarification of diagnosis. In addition to the clear benefit to patients who need such evaluation, this process expands the clinician's referral base. Patients are often grateful to find a clinician who is willing to help them consider treatment options from a range of healing disciplines.

In summary, good communication and a working knowledge of CAM therapies allows the clinician to provide better care. Drug-supplement interactions can be anticipated or avoided, and clinicians can help patients understand whether time-consuming and potentially costly treatments have any potential

---

**Box 2-2  Patient Resources for Risks and Benefits of Specific CAM Treatments**

National Institutes for Health National Center for Complementary and Alternative Medicine: http://nccam.nih.gov/health/

New York Online Access to Health Directory of Websites and Resources: http://www.noah-health.org/en/alternative/

McMaster University Health Care Information Resources: Alternative Medicine Directory of Websites: http://hsl.lib.mcmaster.ca/tomflem/altmed.html

Kids Health Website on Complementary and Alternative Medicine for Teens: http://www.kidshealth.org/teen/your_body/medical_care/alternative_medicine.html

American Association for Family Physicians: http://familydoctor.org/online/famdocen/home/otc-center/otc-medicines/860.html

American Society of Anesthesiologists: Information on Dietary Supplements When Preparing for Surgery: http://www.asahq.org/patientEducation/herbPatient.pdf

Alternative Medicine Foundation (A 501(C) non-profit organization formed to "respond to the public and to the professional need for responsible and reliable education, information, and dialogue about the integration of alternative and conventional medicne"), including an FAQ Sheet for Patients: http://www.amfoundation.org/faqs.htm

benefit. Where scientific claims are presented about alternative treatments, the clinician can help interpret their merit. Even if the patient rejects all conventional treatments, the clinician can still work to ensure the proper diagnosis, advise the patient of best evidence regarding conventional treatments, and discuss any known contraindications of the proposed CAM treatment. An open line of communication encourages the patient to return for advice and assistance if needed at a later date.

## Office Practice Basics

### How Can Clinicians Maximize Patient Care and Practice Efficiency?

Depending on the clinician's knowledge of CAM and the clinical circumstance, one or more of the following strategies might be helpful.

Prior to the appointment:

- Include a paragraph on your website, brochures, and introductory packet information about your practice's approach to CAM.
- Incorporate a list of questions into the new patient intake form so the patient can describe their current and previous use of dietary supplements, other CAM therapies, and experience with CAM practitioners. The clinician can then determine at a glance which items require discussion during the new patient or follow-up appointment. Figure 2-1 provides a list of CAM-specific questions to incorporate into your patient questionnaires and in-person history taking. For established patients, a notice can be placed in the waiting room advising patients of the CAM questionnaire (Box 2-3).
- Consider asking questions about health-related behaviors and lifestyle that might otherwise be missed and that will provide additional information on CAM use (e.g., use of functional foods, raw or macrobiotic diet, prayer, or meditation tapes etc.) (see Figure 2-1).

At the point of care:

- Maintain quick access to helpful information resources. Several websites, desk references and hand-held resources provide particularly high-quality and easily accessed information (Box 2-4, Box 2-5).

---

**Box 2-3  Sample Waiting Room Notice**

**To our patients:**
Are you using complementary and alternative medical diagnostic tests or treatments? If so, please help us to provide you with the best care by filling out our questionnaire.

Help us take better care of your health issues and needs.  We are very interested in better understanding what complementary and alternative therapies you use or lifestyle activities you enjoy doing to manage your health.  Please complete this questionnaire to help us provide you with the best care possible.

1. What are your goals and/or health concerns for this visit?

_____
_____
_____

## USE OF COMPLEMENTARY AND ALTERNATIVE MEDICINE

2.  What CAM practitioners are you currently receiving care from?

| Name | Contact Info | Reason | When started | Helpful? |
|------|--------------|--------|--------------|----------|
|      |              |        |              |          |
|      |              |        |              |          |
|      |              |        |              |          |
|      |              |        |              |          |
|      |              |        |              |          |

3. List the vitamins, minerals, herbs, and other supplements you are presently taking and indicate if they have been helpful or not?

| Name | Reason | When started | Dosage | Helpful? |
|------|--------|--------------|--------|----------|
| *Example:* | | | | |
| St John's wort | Feeling Down | 2 months ago | 3 caps/day | Not sure |
|      |        |              |        |          |
|      |        |              |        |          |
|      |        |              |        |          |
|      |        |              |        |          |
|      |        |              |        |          |

4. What PREVIOUS experiences have you had with Complementary and Alternative Medicine therapies such as herbal medicine, vitamins, massage, acupuncture etc.?

_____
_____
_____
_____
_____
_____
_____

*Continued on next page*

**Figure 2-1**  CAM Questionnaire.

## NUTRITION

5. Please describe your typical diet:

Breakfast _____

Lunch _____

Dinner _____

Snacks _____

6. Do you change your eating habits when you are upset, worried, or sad?   Yes    No

7. Do you eat when you are rushed?   Yes    No

8. Do you skip meals?        Yes        No

        Breakfast        Lunch            Dinner

9. How many glasses of fluids (water, juice) do you drink in a day?  _____

10. How many cups/cans of caffeinated drinks (soda, coffee, tea) do you drink a day? __

## EXERCISE

11.  Do you exercise?   Yes    No

If No, what type of exercise do you enjoy doing?

_____

_____

_____

If Yes, please describe the type of exercise you do and how often.

|  | Type | How often | How long |
|---|---|---|---|
| Weight-bearing exercise: | _____ | _____ | _____ |
| Strengthening: | _____ | _____ | _____ |
| Cardiovascular: | _____ | _____ | _____ |
| Stretching and flexibility: | _____ | _____ | _____ |

## STRESS MANAGEMENT

12. Please list the major stressors in your life.

_____

_____

_____

13. What do you do to relax?

_____

_____

_____

14. How well can you manage your stress on a scale of 1 to 10 (1= not well at all; 10 = no problem)? _____

*Continued on next page*

15. What interests/hobbies do you have?

_____

_____

_____

## SLEEP

16. Please describe your sleeping patterns.

Is it easy for you to get to sleep?        Yes        No

How many times do you wake-up?    _____

What causes you to wake-up?    _____

Do you awaken earlier than you would like?      Yes        No

If Yes, why?    _____

_____

_____

_____

## SUPPORT NETWORK

17. Describe your support network (family, friends, religion, spiritual or secular groups and community, pets).

_____

_____

_____

_____

_____

- Provide practical information sheets for commonly asked questions. For example, if your office has a self-care sheet for upper respiratory infections, add information about zinc, Echinacea, vitamins, etc., and your assessment of the evidence (or lack thereof). Information about specific dietary supplements can be kept on hand or downloaded by doctors or office staff at the time of discharge. The NIH NCCAM website contains an excellent list of FAQs for dietary supplements. (8)
- Provide a prepared list of recommended resources for self-education about CAM issues (see Box 2-1), which can be modified to suit the individual physician's practice. This is particularly helpful if a follow-up appointment is arranged for further counseling or discussion.
- Counsel patients according to the situation.

In some circumstances, the clinician might want to direct more time or energy to a CAM issue. Because these can be lengthy conversations, one option

**Box 2-4  National Library of Medicine and National Institutes of Health's PubMed Database on CAM**

The PubMed Database on CAM: The number of Medline citations in this field has increased dramatically over the past decade. The National Library of Medicine recently changed the MESH category for these modalities from "alternative medicine" to "complementary therapies." A PubMed database on CAM has been developed jointly by the National Library of Medicine and NCCAM and can be found by searching under the MESH term "complementary therapies". Over 120,000 citations are currently listed under this MESH term. Narrowing the search to "human" "clinical trials" provides a list of almost 10,000 citations.http://www.ncbi.nlm.nih.gov/sites/entrez?db=pubmed&Term= "Complementary%20Therapies"[Mesh]&itool=EntrezSystem2.PEntrez.Mesh.Mesh_ ResultsPanel.Mesh_RVFull&ordinalpos=1

PubMed definition of "complementary therapies": Therapeutic practices which are not currently considered an integral part of conventional allopathic medical practice. They may lack biomedical explanations but as they become better researched some (PHYSICAL THERAPY MODALITIES; DIET; ACUPUNCTURE) become widely accepted whereas others (humors, radium therapy) quietly fade away, yet are important historical footnotes. Therapies are termed as Complementary when used in addition to conventional treatments and as Alternative when used instead of conventional treatment. Year introduced: 2002(1986)

Listing of MESH terms for CAM: This listing will allow you to refine your search to a specific treatment or class of treatments of interest.

Therapeutics
  Complementary Therapies
    Acupuncture Therapy
      Acupressure
      Acupuncture Analgesia
      Acupuncture, Ear
      Electroacupuncture
      Meridians +
      Moxibustion
    Anthroposophy
    Holistic Health
    Homeopathy
    Medicine, Traditional
      Medicine, African Traditional
      Medicine, Arabic +
      Medicine, Ayurvedic
      Medicine, Kampo
      Medicine, Oriental Traditional +
      Shamanism
    Mind-Body and Relaxation Techniques
      Aromatherapy

Biofeedback (Psychology)
Breathing Exercises
Hypnosis +
Imagery (Psychotherapy)
Laughter Therapy
Meditation
Mental Healing
Mind-Body Relations
(Metaphysics)
Psychophysiology
Relaxation
Relaxation Techniques
Tai Ji
Therapeutic Touch
Yoga
Musculoskeletal Manipulations
Kinesiology, Applied
Manipulation, Chiropractic
Manipulation, Osteopathic
Manipulation, Spinal +
Massage +

*Continued on next page*

Box 2-4  National Library of Medicine and National Institutes of Health's
PubMed Database on CAM  (continued)

| | |
|---|---|
| Myofunctional Therapy | Music Therapy |
| Relaxation Techniques | Play Therapy |
| Naturopathy | Psychodrama + |
| Organotherapy | Spiritual Therapies |
|   Tissue Therapy |   Faith Healing |
| Phytotherapy |   Homeopathy |
|   Aromatherapy |   Magic |
|   Eclecticism, Historical |   Medicine, African Traditional |
| Reflexotherapy |   Meditation |
| Rejuvenation |   Mental Healing |
| Sensory Art Therapies |   Occultism |
|   Acoustic Stimulation |   Radiesthesia |
|   Aromatherapy |   Shamanism |
|   Art Therapy |   Therapeutic Touch |
|   Color Therapy |   Witchcraft |
|   Dance Therapy |   Yoga |

is to schedule a separate appointment. In preparation for the appointment the
clinician can provide the patient with suggested readings or references as noted
above. As part of counseling, the clinician can opt to explain what clinical
studies have shown about the proposed treatment or advise the patient of
known indications and contraindications to the treatment. The clinician can
coach the patient on what questions to ask an alternative medicine provider
and propose a plan for monitoring the patient. Suggested point-of-care counseling strategies are outlined in Box 2-6.

After the visit:

- Use applicable problem-based or counseling ICD-9 codes. Unfortunately,
  there are no special ICD-9 codes for CAM discussions and interventions
  other than "manipulation," "acupuncture treatment," etc., and the usual
  extended clinic visits, general counseling and lifestyle counseling.
  Patients may request additional time that is not covered by insurance or
  not easily reimbursed. Consider posting prices for in-depth individual
  counseling (specific to discussions regarding CAM treatments and/or
  referrals) that cannot easily occur within the confines of the routine
  office visit. In preparation for the next visit, consider using PubMed,
  which contains a CAM database with over 123,000 citations, including
  almost 10,000 clinical trials. Box 2-3 provides you with a quick and easy
  guide on specific CAM MESH terms to allow for quick and easy search
  using this robust database.

---

**Box 2-5  Complementary and Alternative Medicine Resources**

**Web Sites**
*NIH National Center for Complementary and Alternative Medicine (FREE)*
This site contains information on multiple aspects of CAM. Downloadable information sheets contain short summaries of the current state of research. There are also downloadable information sheets about herbal agents. Several medical problems are addressed, including arthritis, depression and menopause.
http://nccam.nih.gov

*Recalls.gov*
This is a one stop site for recall information from the Food and Drug Administration and the United States Department of Agriculture
www.recalls.gov

*FDA Center for Food Safety and Applied Nutrition Dietary Supplement Warning and Safety Information Resource*
http://www.cfsan.fda.gov/~dms/ds-warn.html
This site provides a listing of dietary supplements that have been withdrawn from the market, as well as those supplements for which there are safety concerns. It also provides links to other FDA alerts, as well as additional safety information.

*FDA Market Recalls, Market Withdrawals, and Safety Alerts*
http://www.fda.gov/opacom/7alerts.html
This site provides a listing of FDA recalls, market withdrawals, and safety alerts. It contains a much broader listing of products and medications.

*NNIH Office of Dietary Supplements  (FREE)*
http://dietary-supplements.info.nih.gov

*American Medical Student Association*
"It's our goal to provide you the latest links and updates to CAM research activities, electives, references and educational tools; everything you would need to pursue your interest in complementary medicine."
http://www.amsa.org/humed/CAM/resources.cfm

*Cochrane Collaboration*
The Collaboration is comprised of an international network of health professional volunteers who perform systematic reviews of randomized controlled trials on the full range of health topics.  Access to this database can be obtained through academic medical centers.  However, you can obtain free access to the summary guidelines at http://www.cochrane.org/reviews/index.htm

*Bandolier :Evidence Based Thinking About Healthcare": CAM section (FREE)*
http://www.jr2.ox.ac.uk/Bandolier/booth/booths/altmed.html
This is a print and Internet-based journal that provides recommendations about specific treatments or conditions for health professionals and consumers.  These recommendations are presented as abstracts in which they summarize systematic reviews and meta-analyses allowing for easy and quick understanding of the subject matter.

*Continued on next page*

---

**Box 2-5  Complementary and Alternative Medicine Resources (continued)**

*Tufts Evidence-Based Complementary and Alternative Medicine Site (EBCAM)*
"The website is intended to teach students and faculty how to gather and synthesize
information about complementary and alternative (CAM) modalities, which many
of their patients are using, and to serve as an interactive electronic resource center to
support the teaching of CAM using the evidence-based medicine (EBM) model."
http://www.tufts.edu/med/ebcam/index.html

*Memorial Sloan-Kettering Cancer Center- Integrative Medicine*
This site provides excellent summary information on herbs and other dietary
supplements.
http://www.mskcc.org/mskcc/html/11570.cfm

*U.S. Pharmacopoeia (FREE)*
The Pharmacopoeia offers information about dietary supplement companies that are
certified by the USP for quality assurance.
http://www.usp.org

*Rosenthal Center at Columbia University Center for CAM and University of Pittsburgh
Alternative Medicine Homepage (FREE)*
Each provides a comprehensive list of Directories of Databases in the field of
Complementary and Alternative Medicine.
http://www.rosenthal.hs.columbia.edu/Databases.html and
http://www.pitt.edu/~cbw/database.html

*ConsumerLab.com (fee for full access)*
An excellent source of information about dietary supplements. They charge $29.95
for access to product information and excellent reviews, and list products that failed
to contain the quantity or quality of claimed ingredients. They also provide general
information about the dietary supplement.  You can have limited access to the
website for free or pay an individual membership for access to the full website.
www.ConsumerLab.com

*Natural Standard, Natural Medicine Comprehensive Database and Micromedex's
AltMedDexTM System (all require a fee for access)*
Commercially available websites with outstanding, evidence-based reviews of herbs
and supplements, and other CAM therapies. They also provide an herb, drug, food
interaction checker. An individual membership to the website costs $92-99/year. A
few of these companies also provide PDA and Desktop book versions of their
database for a reduced price. These are good resources for clinicians or patients who
want clinically relevant, well-researched information in this rapidly growing field.
http://www.naturalstandard.com and http://www.naturaldatabase.com/ and
http://www.micromedex.com/products/altmeddex/

*Consortium of Academic Health Centers for Integrative Medicine*
This is a collection of more than 39 academic medical centers that have Centers for
Integrative Medicine, and which are focused on education, research, and/or direct
patient care.
www.imconsortium.org/

*Continued on next page*

---

**Box 2-5  Complementary and Alternative Medicine Resources (continued)**

**CAM Reference Books**
This is a partial list of the many books available on complementary and alternative medicine. Readers are cautioned that some of these books provide extensive information about the large variety of CAM treatments, but less information about supportive evidence.

The Desktop Guide to Complementary and Alternative Medicine: An Evidence-Based Approach by Edzard Ernst, Max H. Pittler, and Barbara Wider (Paperback - Aug 16, 2006)

Integrative Medicine: Text with BONUS Pocket Consult Handheld Software by David Rakel (Hardcover - Feb 7, 2007)

Fundamentals of Complementary and Integrative Medicine by Marc S. Micozzi (Hardcover - Nov 29, 2005)

Integrative Cardiology by John H.K. Vogel and Mitchell W. Krucoff (Hardcover - May 15, 2007)

Textbook of Integrative Mental Health Care by James Lake (Hardcover - Oct 31, 2006)

Alternative Medicine in Pain Management (Contemporary Pain Medicine) by Joseph F. Audette and Allison Bailey (Hardcover - Mar 15, 2008)

Complementary and Integrative Medicine in Pain Management by Michael I. Weintraub, Ravinder Mamtani, and Marc S. Micozzi (Hardcover - May 12, 2008)

Holistic Pediatrician, The by Kathi J. Kemper (Kindle Edition - Jun 1, 2007) - Kindle Book

PDR for Nonprescription Drugs, Dietary Supplements, and Herbs, 2008 (Physicians' Desk Reference (PDR) for Nonprescription Drugs and Dietary Supplements) by PDR Staff (Hardcover - Sep 1, 2007)

The Practice of Integrative Medicine: A Legal and Operational Guide by Michael H. Cohen, Mary Ruggie, and Marc S. Micozzi (Hardcover - Nov 30, 2006)

Clinicians and Educators Desk Reference on the Complementary and Alternative Healthcare Professions. ACCAHC publishing (www.accahc.org) September 2008.

**Newsletters and Review Journals**
Natural Medicine News (no charge)
Free weekly email newsletter on recently published articles on CAM created by Forrest Batz, Pharm.D.
Subscribe by emailing fbatz@sonic.net

Alternative Medicine Alert (subscription fee)
Published by American Health Consultants
3525 Piedmont Rd, NE, Building 6, Suite 400, Atlanta, GA 30305
(800) 688-2421
customerservice@ahcpub.com
http://www.ahcpub.com

*Continued on next page*

---

**Box 2-5  Complementary and Alternative Medicine Resources (continued)**

Focus on Alternative and Complementary Therapies (FACT)
Provides quarterly reviews of the most important research publications with associated commentary.
http://www.medicinescomplete.com/journals/fact/current/

---

- Use continuing medical education as an opportunity to develop and maintain an up-to-date working knowledge of CAM topics. Many specialty and subspecialty societies have published reviews of the scientific evidence for CAM treatments.

## Medical-Legal Aspects of CAM Therapy

### What the Clinician Needs to Know

The disarray of the medico-legal system with respect to CAM is a reflection of the heterogeneity of therapies, the complex licensure systems, variability of policies in different states, and a host of other confusing issues. For the individual clinician there are few good resources to provide guidance in this area. For example, what are the legal risks, if any, to the clinician who refers patients for massage therapy? Is the primary care clinician responsible for medical complications related to alternative therapies chosen by the patient? Is the clinician at legal risk if he does not advise patients of complementary therapies available for a given medical problem?

There are few cases and minimal legal precedent on which to base clear guidelines for clinicians. Several recent attempts have been made, however, to establish general policies and approaches, some of which are described here in greater detail.

In 2002 the Federation of State Medical Boards in the United States (FSMB) published model guidelines "for state medical boards to use in educating and regulating (9) physicians who use CAM in their practices, and/or (10) those who co-manage patients with licensed or otherwise state-regulated CAM providers". The guidelines are readily available to physicians and the public (11). Individual states are to determine whether the guidelines are appropriate for its physicians.

In developing these guidelines the FSMB noted that its goal was to provide guidelines that were "clinically responsible and ethically appropriate". It encouraged consistency in the evaluation of health care practices, whether labeled conventional or CAM, and it stressed that "…a licensed physician shall not be found guilty of unprofessional conduct for failure to practice medicine in an acceptable manner solely on the basis of utilizing CAM". The guidelines

---

**Box 2-6  Suggested Point of Care Counseling Strategies**

- Provide a patient information sheet with helpful resources to complement the discussion
- Offer to schedule a separate appointment to address the patient's interest in CAM
- Explain what clinical studies have shown about the proposed treatment
- Advise the patient of known indications and contraindications to the treatment
- Coach the patient on what questions to ask an alternative medicine provider
- Propose a plan for monitoring the patient

---

are recommended as a way to determine whether a physician's conduct was appropriate in any given encounter.

The FSMB additionally stresses the importance of physician education regarding the status of CAM therapies and discusses the advisability (or lack thereof) of physicians selling supplements and other health care products from the office (see below). There is also a small section directed to clinical investigators. In summary, the FSMB comments that "State medical boards should ensure a balance between the goal of medical practices being evidence-based while remaining compassionate and respectful of the dignity and autonomy of patients. This balance should also ensure informed consent and minimize the potential for harm".

In another (related) approach, Cohen outlines a medico-legal strategy to assist with clinical decision making and to reduce the risk of malpractice liability. With respect to CAM therapies the clinician should:

- Determine the clinical risk level
- Document the literature supporting the therapeutic choice
- Provide adequate informed consent
- Continue to monitor the patient conventionally
- For referrals, inquire about the competence of the complementary and alternative medicine provider.

CAM therapies should be viewed with respect to whether evidence in the medical and scientific literature supports (12,13):

- Safety and efficacy
- Safety but not efficacy
- Efficacy but not safety
- Either safety nor efficacy.

## Insurance Coverage

With few exceptions, most physicians accept payment for services from insurance plans. Over the years, insurance plans have adopted federally based ICD-9 codes (originally patented by the American Medical Association for use with Medicare billing), which can be nearly useless for unusual or poorly categorized services. This discourages clinicians from assisting patients with services related to complementary and alternative medicine. As noted elsewhere in this chapter, the ICD-9 codes that can be used by clinicians who assist patients with CAM issues are largely limited to extended duration of the clinical visit and individual counseling.

Most non-physician providers of complementary and alternative services require cash payments, which greatly reduces overhead and increases the percentage of reimbursement. Straight billing for time also clarifies up-front the cost of services. Given the varied product quality in the marketplace, many offices have elected to sell dietary supplements or other products which they believe have superior quality. The commercial sale of products also provides these clinicians with additional revenue sources (see Office Sale of Products).

There is no national standard that dictates what CAM therapies, if any, should be covered by insurance, whether the treatments are provided by doctors or alternative providers. Coverage varies significantly from state to state and from plan to plan. The state of Washington, for example, requires the inclusion of alternative practitioners in private, commercial insurance products.

A 2004 survey from the Kaiser Family Foundation and Health Research and Educational Trust defined trends in the industry within the United States. The survey included over 3000 insurance plans (public and private) that covered three or more employees. One conclusion was that employer coverage of acupuncture increased 14% from 2002 to 2004. 47% of all employers surveyed offered acupuncture as a covered health benefit, up from 33% in 2002. Large companies and point-of-service plans were most likely to offer this service.

Coverage of chiropractic care also increased. In 2004, 87% of surveyed companies provided chiropractic benefits compared to 79% in 2002. Limited information is available regarding coverage of other alternative/complementary therapies. A 2003 survey by Mercer Human Resource Consulting found that 7% of large firms covered homeopathy and biofeedback, and 13% covered massage therapy. Similar to the Kaiser foundation data, Mercer noted a 10% increase in coverage for acupuncture between 1998 and 2003.

Cherkin et al evaluated insurance status at the point of service (14). They studied patients who were visiting licensed acupuncturists, chiropractors, massage therapists and naturopathic physicians practicing in Arizona, Connecticut, Massachusetts and Washington (states where Naturopathic physicians are licensed to practice). They determined that most visits to naturopathic physicians and chiropractors were covered by insurance, whereas about one-third of visits to massage therapists and acupuncturists were covered. Interestingly, of over 1800 visits about two-thirds were based on self-referral and only about 10% on physician referral. Of note, naturopathic medical practice is particularly strong in several of these states owing to the presence of naturopathic medical schools.

In general, there are limited data regarding the expense of CAM insurance. The use of alternative providers by cancer patients in Washington was assessed by Lafferty et al (15). In 2002, 7.1% of cancer patients (all of whom were insured) had a medical insurance claim for naturopathy, acupuncture or massage services, and 11.6% of patients had a claim for chiropractic care. Musculoskeletal pain was the most common reason for these visits. Virtually all of the patients who visited CAM practitioners also claimed to be under the care of at least one conventional physician. The services of the alternative providers accounted for less than 2% of the overall medical costs.

There are many challenges to developing a standardized, effective policy regarding insurance coverage for CAM therapies. They include but are not limited to cost, credentialing issues, evidence for benefit, different patterns of acceptance among states, and the sheer variety of services offered. Some authors have suggested strategies for CAM provider credentialing, a major challenge in its own right (16).

## Office Sales of CAM Products

Professional medical societies have focused on whether it is ethical for physicians to sell supplements and other medical products to their patients. Although much of the controversy is centered on "dietary supplements" that may have limited scientific support for use, the topic transcends any CAM/conventional boundaries.

In its position paper from 1997, the American Medical Association concluded that, with rare exception, physicians should not sell products from the office. The paper stated that physicians are not simply business people with high standards; they have different and higher duties to serve as fiduciaries of their patients. This position was applauded by some and heavily criticized by others, who argued that the position was too narrow and did not reflect the scope of practice and realities of practice in current times.

The sale of supplements to patients, some argue, creates an inherent conflict of interest. The clinician's recommendations cannot remain unbiased if he or she stands to achieve financial gain. Additionally, patients may feel obligated to purchase products in order to please the clinician. Lastly, some think that it demeans the practice of medicine by undermining the trust between patient and clinician and equates the office setting with a supermarket or bazaar.

Proponents of product sales in the office often state that patients will buy and use supplements anyway, and it is better to know that they are using quality products. Ophthalmologists have sold eyewear for many years and cosmetic surgeons and dermatologists often sell products that complement the procedures for which patients are already paying out of pocket. Proponents believe that office sales can be accomplished in a professional manner and bolster income at a time of decreasing revenues and increased expenses.

The American Medical Association, in response to criticism from its members, eased its position somewhat. A position paper from the American College of Physicians was published in *Annals of Internal Medicine* in 1999 (17).

The authors suggested that each physician should decide whether to sell supplements based upon:

- Urgency of the patient's need
- The clinical relevance to the patient's condition
- The adequacy of evidence to support use of the product
- Geographic and time constraints for the patient in otherwise obtaining the product

For example, obtaining products from physicians makes particular sense when it would allow the patient to avoid driving long distances to obtain needed products elsewhere.

The authors of the statement advocate that clinicians who decide to sell supplements should make full disclosure about their financial interests in selling the product and inform patients about alternatives for purchasing the product. Furthermore, charges for products sold through the office should be limited to the reasonable costs incurred in making them available.

Clearly, many physicians do not adhere to the recommendations of these two professional organizations. A *New York Times* article in 2002 (8/26/02) quoted Nutritionbusiness.com that supplements sales by doctors increased tenfold from 1997 to 2001, to nearly $200 million in 2001 (18).

## REFERENCES

1. **Barnes PM, Powell-Griner E, McFann K, Nahin RL.** Complementary and alternative medicine use among adults: United States, 2002. Adv Data. 2004;:1-19
2. **Stokley S, Cullen KA, Kennedy A, Bardenheier BH.** Adult vaccination coverage levels among users of complementary/alternative medicine: results from the 2002 National Health Interview Survey (NHIS). BMC Complement Altern Med. 2008;8:6.
3. **Why patients use alternative medicine: results of a national study.** JAMA. 1998;279:1548-53.
4. www.umm.edu/altmed/articles/allergic-rhinitis-000003.htm.
5. nccam.nih.gov/health/decisions/index.htm.
6. Mskcc.org/mskcc/html/11570.cfm.
7. **Adams KE, Cohen MH, Eisenberg D, Jonsen AR.** Ethical considerations of complementary and alternative medical therapies in conventional medical settings. Ann Intern Med. 2003;137:660-4.
8. ods.od.nih.gov/Health_Information/ODS_Frequently_Asked_Questions.aspx.
9. **Murphy LS, Reinsch S, Najm WI, et al.** Searching biomedical databases on complementary medicine: the use of controlled vocabulary among authors, indexers and investigators. BMC Complement Altern Med. 2003;3:3.
10. Http://nccam.nci.nih.gov/health/whatiscam/index.htm.
11. www.fsmb.org.
12. **Cohen MH, Eisenberg DM.** Potential physician malpractice liability associated with complementary and integrative medical therapies. Ann Intern Med. 2002;136:596-603.
13. **Cohen MH.** Legal issues in complementary and integrative medicine. A guide for the clinician. Med Clin North Am. 2002;86:185-96.

14. **Cherkin DC, Deyo RA, Sherman KJ, et al.** Characteristics of visits to licensed acupuncturists, chiropractors, massage therapists, and naturopathic physicians. J Am Board Fam Pract. 2002;15:463-72.

15. **Lafferty WE, Bellas A, Corage Baden A, et al.** The use of complementary and alternative medical providers by insured cancer patients in Washington State. Cancer. 2004;100:1522-30.

16. **Eisenberg DM, Cohen MH, Hrbek A, et al.** Credentialing complementary and alternative medical providers. Ann Intern Med. 2002;137:965-73.

17. **Povar GJ, Snyder L.** Selling Products Out of the Office (Position Paper). Annals of Internal Medicine. 1999;131:863-4.

18. **New York Times article 8/26/02 quoting Nutritionbusiness.com.**

# PART II

# EVALUATION OF COMPLEMENTARY AND ALTERNATIVE MEDICINE SYSTEMS AND THERAPIES

## Chapter 3

ℒ∂

# Allergic Disorders

SUZANNE S. TEUBER, MD
CRISTINA PORCH-CURREN, MD
KATHERINE GUNDLING, MD

To medical doctors, the disorders that come under the heading of "Allergic" include those mediated in large part by IgE- and/or Th2-driven inflammation and reflect a complex array of inflammatory mediator synthesis, release and subsequent cellular response. Such conditions include allergic rhinitis or allergic rhinosinusitis, asthma with an atopic component (addressed separately in another chapter), allergic conjunctivitis, atopic dermatitis, IgE-mediated food allergy, and other acute IgE-mediated reactions to medications, insect stings or bites, or topical antigen exposures (natural rubber latex, for example).

Physicians might also use the term "allergy" more broadly to denote an abnormal immune response or hypersensitivity response that is not IgE-mediated, such as when describing the full range of "drug allergy" reactions (including maculopapular and morbilliform eruptions) or "food allergy" (e.g., gluten-sensitive enteropathy).

There are as many varied ways CAM is used in allergic disorders as there are combinations of CAM diagnostic tests and therapies. Some CAM practitioners (especially physicians) approach allergic disorders from a conventional framework but use herbal supplements and vitamins as first-line treatments or to complement standard therapy.

Alternative medicine practitioners may also include many medical conditions under the general heading of "allergy." They often emphasize the holistic treatment of underlying hypersensitivities (not recognized as such in western medicine) in order to abrogate the manifestation of a variety of bodily symptoms. Sometimes the underlying approach stems from a concept of energy imbalance as the cause of symptoms. Indeed, many practitioners may link symptoms and health conditions to a sensitivity ("allergy") to foods, chemicals and pollutants in the general environment. This type of diagnosis and management is no longer limited to practitioners who identify themselves as "environmental physicians" or "clinical ecologists" (1).

Headache is an example of a common symptom that an alternative practitioner might address with a comprehensive "allergy" evaluation and diagnosis of multiple sensitivities. Such sensitivities are subsequently treated with single or multiple modalities, including acupressure or acupuncture, homeopathy, a 4-day rotation diet, herbal supplements, and vitamin or mineral supplements, along with advice on reducing allergen exposure in the home, exercise and stress reduction.

## CAM Diagnostic Tests for Allergic Disorders

There are several diagnostic tests used within the alternative medicine community that are unfamiliar to medical doctors. Because these tests are used to diagnose and treat disease, this section defines what is known about them and how they differ from tests used by western medical doctors.

In conventional medicine, diagnostic tests are used to narrow the differential diagnosis that has already been shaped by a complete history and further refined by the physical exam. In the practice of an allergy and immunology physician, common diagnostic tests include skin testing with aeroallergens, venom or food extracts, skin testing in selected circumstances with medications, in vitro specific IgE assays as an alternative, pulmonary function testing, and food challenges, looking for objective responses such as immediate rash or lip swelling. Alternative practitioners will often look for sensitivities to substances or foods for which there is no clear clinical correlation in the patient's history (by conventional history taking). The type of testing used may sound scientific and the equipment might look sophisticated (as in electrodermal apparatii). However, sometimes the test itself may be a standard laboratory assay that is unproven for use in that clinical situation, a test that has been disproved for use, or be entirely without scientific rationale. Many of the following tests are used to detect hidden "food allergies" that are believed by CAM practitioners to contribute to asthma, allergic rhinitis, and atopic dermatitis and many other conditions.

### Specific IgG Assays

These tests are used by CAM practitioners to determine if food sensitivities are the cause of non-specific symptoms, or if they underlie the "total allergic burden" of a patient with true allergic disorders. Food specific IgG panels are advertised by several large commercial laboratories in the United States as IgG RASTs (radioallergosorbent tests) and vary in offering total IgG towards a food, or IgG4, with or without food immune complex assays. This testing is considered unproven for use in food intolerance or allergy. Its proponents state that such antibodies can identify food intolerances that cause or contribute to chronic fatigue, headache, "sinus," hyperactivity, irritable bowel syndrome, arthritis, difficulty concentrating, and almost any somatic or mental symptom.

It is normal to produce specific IgG and IgG4 and IgA (most of which is intra-luminal) to commonly eaten foods without manifesting symptoms of food allergy (2,3). In a recent study of children with peanut or cow's milk allergy and normal, age-matched controls, the specific IgG antibody values in milk-allergic patients were not different from the controls. In the controls, the presence of food-specific IgG was correlated with regular ingestion of that food, thus, if the food was avoided, levels could be expected to be lower (3). The same can be said for food immune complexes in relation to regular ingestion. For instance, in another recent report, 12 of 37 human breast milk samples contained ovo-mucoid in an immune complex with IgA (4). There are no studies that com-bine IgG levels with verified double-blind, placebo-controlled food challenges to investigate possible links with objective or subjective symptoms. Thus, at the current time, there is no evidence to support the diagnostic efficacy of food-spe-cific IgG in any particular disorder (see Box 3-1).

One disease reported to be related to extremely high levels of IgG to food antigens, visualized in a precipitin assay, is food-induced pulmonary hemo-siderosis. This has been reported rarely in small children with cow's milk hyper-sensitivity and in case reports with egg and pork (5,6). However, there are no Medline publications in the past decade that contain reference to a more con-temporary measurement of IgG by ELISA in these rare cases.

## Cytotoxicity Assays or Cell-Volume Change Assays

Another assay for hidden "food allergies," cytotoxic food testing, was popular in the 1970s and 1980s (7). The test hinged on the theory that the morphol-ogy of peripheral blood mononuclear cells was affected by contact with foods to which a patient is "allergic," reflecting activation of the cells. A dried film of food extract on a slide was the substrate to which a fresh drop of whole blood was added. Any morphologic change was considered positive. This test was shown to be non-reproducible (8). However, the core concept behind this test—that of leukocytes reacting to food antigen exposure in a way that predicts sensitivities or intolerances— drives at least two current assays available to patients over the internet. These tests use modern Coulter system machines in a modified way. Diluted blood in a cuvette containing a film of food extract is run on a Coulter system counter to assess cell volume compared to a sample of the patient's blood that has not been exposed to food antigen. Leukocytes or platelets can be assessed and any changes can be considered

> **Box 3-1  Unproven or disproved CAM diagnostic tests for allergic disorders**
>
> - Specific IgG assays for food allergy
> - "Cytotoxicity" assays for food allergy
> - "Provocation/neutralization" testing for sensitivities to foods or chemicals
> - Pulse test for food allergy
> - Muscle response testing ("applied kinesiology") for aeroallergen and food sensitivities
> - Electrodermal testing (developed to help refine homeopathic prescriptions)

significant. The use of this type of assay is not supported by the available literature (9).

## Provocation/Neutralization

Provocation/neutralization is a method to both diagnose and set up a treatment regimen for sensitivities to foods or chemicals (e.g., cigarette smoke, ethanol, formaldehyde, cologne) not detected by the standard (IgE mediated) prick skin testing used in conventional practices. Testing involves either sublingual or (more commonly) intradermal "provocation" by a test antigen, followed by an observation period of 10 minutes after each injection, at which time the wheal response is measured and any subjective symptoms are reported. Symptoms such as drowsiness, dry mouth, inability to concentrate or headache are considered a positive challenge, meaning that the person is "allergic" to the food. The patient is then given a different dose of the antigen as either a sublingual drop or another injection until the "reaction" is "neutralized." This "neutralization" dose would then be taken in a desensitization series or to neutralize a reaction (10-12). Adverse outcomes of such testing are extremely rare. There is a report of angioedema following application of sublingual drops when a patient had an IgE-mediated food hypersensitivity (13). Practitioners normally avoid this by not testing patients who have a history suggestive of an IgE-mediated reaction. A life-threatening reaction was described in a patient with systemic mastocytosis, including extensive skin involvement, who underwent provocation/neutralization and had a severe reaction due to massive mediator release after intradermal injections (14).

Two blinded, controlled studies have been published showing that the testing relies on a placebo response, the first in 1990 and the second in 1999 (15,16). Both studies were double-blind and placebo-controlled, but practitioners of the technique criticized the earlier study on methodological grounds. The Nova Scotia Environmental Health Centre sought to reinvestigate the issue, and the results clearly confirmed the first study. The group concluded that provocation of symptoms by intradermal testing should not be used to make diagnostic or therapeutic decisions (16). It should now be considered a disproved technique, rather than unproven.

## Pulse Test

The "pulse test" is often incorporated into provocation/neutralization sessions as an additional measure of a response, but sometimes it is used alone. A change in the pulse of 16 beats per minute from baseline is considered positive for an intolerance or allergy after a sublingual drop, intradermal injection, or open challenge. There are no blinded clinical trials to support or refute the use of this test, which could be due in part to the observation time of up to 2-3 hours that may be required to watch for a "delayed reaction," depending on how the test is utilized (17).

## Muscle-Response Testing

Muscle response testing, or applied kinesiology, is frequently used to diagnose inhalant, food or chemical sensitivities as well as nutritional imbalances. It is commonly practiced by chiropractors. Practitioners state they can detect both IgE- and non-IgE mediated allergy or intolerance based on positive or negative energy balances that manifest as muscle weakness. During this procedure the patient holds a vial with a specific item in one hand while the practitioner tests the muscle strength of the opposite arm by applying light pressure to the forearm. (If performed while the patient is supine, the arm is held erect approximately perpendicular to the body and the practitioner applies pressure with two fingers just proximal to the wrist.) If the practitioner can overcome the strength of the patient's arm, the individual is deemed "allergic" to the specific contents in the vial. A review of 20 studies favorable to applied kinesiology found that none of the studies fulfilled basic research criteria. Therefore no conclusions regarding the validity of the procedure could be drawn (18). A study in Germany published in 2001 concluded that there was no inter-tester reliability and no correlation with specific IgE, IgG or lactose breath hydrogen testing (19). Finally, also from Germany, investigators looked at individuals with a clinical history of insect venom allergy and positive allergy tests including skin tests (prick and intradermal) and specific IgE antibodies by ImmunoCAP assay (Pharmacia, Uppsala) (20). This study, which was blinded, using venom and placebo vials for the muscle testing, concluded that muscle response testing as a diagnostic tool is no better than random guessing. The weight of the evidence to date suggests that this diagnostic modality is not valid.

## Electrodermal Testing

Electrodermal testing was developed to help with refining homeopathic prescriptions. It involves placing the patient in a circuit with a machine that uses a galvanometer to measure skin conductance. The patient holds the negative electrode in one hand and the positive electrode is applied to certain acupuncture points. A sealed glass vial of the aeroallergen, food, chemical, medication, vitamin or heavy metal is put in contact with an aluminum plate within the circuit. If there is a drop in conductance, "allergy" is diagnosed based on the perturbation in the electromagnetic field. Two double-blind, placebo-controlled studies of this technique for diagnosing aeroallergen sensitivity were published, in 2001 and 2002. In the first, a popular electrodermal measurement device called the Vegatest (Vega Medizinische Gerate, Schiltach, Germany) was used to compare the diagnostic capability of electrodermal testing with skin prick testing to house dust mite and cat allergens. Over 1500 individual tests were performed in total on 15 atopic and 15 non-atopic volunteers. The testing could not distinguish the two groups (21). Similarly, the DBE204 (Tekav S.r.l., Rovigo, Italy) electrodermal device was also unable to distinguish between allergens and negative controls, and hence no differences between atopic and control patients were observed. A poor reproducibility of the method was noted in particular (22).

## CAM Therapies for Allergic Disorders

Some of the diagnostic tests described above lead directly into therapeutics. For instance, muscle response testing is linked to acupressure or acupuncture for the diagnosed allergies. Electrodermal testing is often used to prescribe homeopathic remedies. Provocation/neutralization testing leads to a series of sublingual drops or injections that the patient continues to use on a regular basis. IgG and cytotoxic assay testing lead to the recommendation of specific rotation diets. When patients list or describe their "allergies," clinicians should therefore ask what kinds of testing methods were used. This can guide understanding of the legitimacy (or lack thereof) of the diagnoses and prescribed treatment plan.

### Allergic Rhinitis

CAM use is now quite common, with up to half of all patients with rhinitis or atopic dermatitis reporting use. There are no surveys specific to allergic rhinitis, but there are two surveys in the U.S. that have looked at rhinosinusitis. Among 175 patients with nasal or sinus symptoms in Northern California recruited by random digit dialing, 43% reported use of CAM (ephedra products, Chinese herbs, caffeine, homeopathy, acupuncture and others) (23). In a Florida community-based otolaryngology practice, a survey of 120 patients with rhinosinusitis found that 29% had used herbal therapy, 19% acupuncture, and 35% had used chiropractic treatment (24). In Germany, 351 individuals with atopic disorders (allergic rhinitis, asthma, atopic dermatitis, and/or food allergy) participated in a survey. Of these, 26.5% reported using CAM, with most using it for allergic rhinitis (62% of positive respondents). However, this study did not include botanical agents or other dietary supplements, treatments that would be considered CAM in other surveys. Thus, the percentage of patients using CAM in Germany is certainly higher than reported in this study. Interestingly, the most common alternative treatments for rhinitis were homeopathy (38.6%), autologous blood injection (28.1%), acupuncture (17.5%) and bioresonance (7.0%) (25). Autologous blood injection and bioresonance are not commonly used in the United States.

#### Homeopathy

Clinical trials of "homeopathy" for allergic rhinitis have engendered controversy even within the homeopathic community. In classical homeopathy, as described by early practitioners, remedies were chosen based upon their ability to cause symptoms in healthy individuals (see Chapter 1 for a more complete discussion of this topic). Clinical trials of homeopathic treatments for allergic rhinitis, however, have often used "isopathic" solutions, which are diluted preparations of substances to which the patient is allergic. Such allergens, however, do not cause symptoms in healthy people, leading some to say they cannot be the source of true homeopathic remedies. Nevertheless, there has been publication of double-blind studies that claim an advantage to dilute isopathic solutions over placebo (26,27), but controversy has accompanied them (28-30).

In studies of conventional injection immunotherapy for inhalant allergy, which consists of increasing doses followed by maintenance doses of antigen for 3-5 years, defined higher doses of antigen are effective in a reproducible manner and lead to long-term reduction of symptoms and medication usage after treatment is discontinued. Low-dose allergen immunotherapy has been shown in clinical trials to be ineffective. Notably, the ineffective low doses in conventional trials are significantly higher than the concentrations used in homeopathic isopathy remedies (31). This means that the homeopathic remedies would have to work by a different mechanism of action than the known immunomodulatory effects of conventional antigen immunotherapy, yet a specific mechanism of homeopathy has not yet been demonstrated.

A meta-analysis of treatment with the homeopathic preparation *Galphimia glauca* was supportive of homeopathy for treatment of ocular symptoms. There was significant variability of quality among the trials included, and they appear to have been conducted by the same group in Germany (32). It would be desirable to see these results reproduced independently in high-quality trials.

A 2006 systematic review of CAM treatments for rhinitis (limited to Medline, Cochrane Library and in English) concluded that on the basis of both positive and negative clinical trials, some of which were apparently of high quality, it was currently not possible to provide evidence-based recommendations for homeopathy in the treatment of allergic rhinitis (33).

## Botanical/Herbal Medicine

Plants are rich in antioxidant polyphenolics and other phytochemicals. In vitro, many of these compounds have been shown to have immunomodulating effects, but there is much less evidence from human trials to support clinically relevant effects in allergic disorders.

In allergic rhinitis, two Chinese herbal mixtures have been studied in randomized, double-blind, placebo-controlled trials. Both studies were small. In one, a formulation called Bimminne (or bimin) was given to 26 patients in Sydney, Australia, with 32 receiving placebo capsules (33a). At the end of 12 weeks, there was significant improvement in some symptoms of allergic rhinitis and a trend towards significant improvement in others. Of note, total IgE decreased significantly at the end of the study in the group receiving Bimminne. A second study, from the RMIT Chinese Medicine Research Group in Bundoora, Australia, treated 28 patients with a mixture of 18 herbs in capsule formulation and 27 with placebo for 8 weeks. Both nasal and non-nasal symptoms were improved in the active group over placebo. Interestingly, 60.7% of the active group reported moderate to marked improvement compared to 29.6% in the placebo group (34). There is little information on other Asian herbal preparations from Japan (Kampo) or other regions in allergic rhinitis.

Grapeseed extract has been the subject of one randomized, double-blind, placebo-controlled trial in seasonal allergic rhinitis (ragweed) with 28 in the active arm and 26 in the placebo arm. At the end of 8 weeks, there was no difference between the two groups, thus no evidence for clinical efficacy (35).

Interesting trials have been performed with Butterbur (*Petasites hybridus*); however, all have been of very short duration: 2 weeks or 1 week. A 2007 systematic review analyzed herbal medications for allergic rhinitis and identified six randomized clinical trials on Butterbur extract. The report that Butterbur extract was "superior to placebo or similarly effective compared with non-sedating antihistamines for intermittent allergic rhinitis" and concluded that these findings provide "encouraging evidence suggesting that Butterbur may be an effective herbal treatment for seasonal allergic rhinitis" (35a). Butterbur in tablet formulation was studied in comparison to cetirizine in the treatment of allergic rhinoconjuncitivitis. The study was a randomized, double-blind parallel group trial involving 125 volunteers for 2 weeks. Butterbur treatment did not differ in efficacy from cetirizine on the SF-36 and clinical global impression scale instruments. However, no disease-specific measures were performed (36). In a more recent study, butterbur was compared to fexofenadine 180 mg daily and placebo, for 1 week. Nasal symptoms scores were equivalent between butterbur and fexofenadine and superior to placebo. Although the trial was of extremely short duration, it was strengthened by measuring peak nasal inspiratory flow after an adenosine monophosphate challenge. Attenuation of nasal congestion was equivalent between butterbur and fexofenadine and again superior to placebo (37). In 2004, Gray et al did not find improvement compared to placebo on multiple symptom scores or nasal inspiratory peak flow in a 2-week trial for intermittent rhinitis (38).

A prospective, randomized trial by Schapowal in 2005 for a proprietary butterbur product concluded that butterbur and fexofenadine were comparably efficacious relative to placebo for intermittent allergic rhinitis. The same study group found a dose-response effect of butterbur in a clinical trial of 186 patients in 2005 (39). Interestingly, the same proprietary product was found to have no effect on skin-test reactivity induced by different stimuli, but they looked at wheal and flare reactions with codeine, histamine, methacholine, and an inhalant allergen 90 minutes after a double dose of Ze 339 (proprietary butterbur), arivastine, or placebo. They concluded that the mechanism by which Ze 339 is effective in the treatment of seasonal allergic rhinitis still needs to be elucidated (40). In summary, the specific formulation of butterbur extract used in these clinical trials appears relatively safe in the short term and effective. Of note, three of the six clinical trials included in the 2007 review received funding from the manufacturer. Overall, there is sufficient evidence to support a weak recommendation of butterbur extract for the treatment of intermittent allergic rhinitis (see Evidence Summary table at end of chapter).

Spirulina, a filamentous cyanobacterium, sometimes called "blue-green algae," has a high natural content of nutrients. It demonstrates a number of biological activities in vitro but has limited in vivo investigation. Mao et al demonstrated in a randomized double-blind placebo controlled trial that a proprietary spirulina product at 2000 mg per day was associated with reduced production of Interleukin-4. IL-4 plays an important role in the differentiation of Th2 inflammatory products, which are key to allergic disease (41). Currently there is too little information from controlled clinical trials to recommend the use of blue-green algae for allergic rhinitis.

Stinging nettle, in freeze-dried form, is promoted as an effective therapy for allergic rhinitis without evidence of efficacy. In a Medline search there was one inadequate trial of 1 week duration that had a 30% drop-out rate (42).

Preliminary clinical trials indicate that bromelain, a protein derived supplement from pineapple, might be of benefit in rhinosinusitis (43). It has not been studied well enough in allergic rhinitis to make specific recommendations.

## Vitamins

Vitamin C in large doses is commonly recommended for allergic rhinitis in lay articles. However, there is no evidence to support this recommendation (44).

## Other Nutritional Supplements

Quercetin, a purified bioflavonoid found in many plant foods, is also promoted in popular texts as a natural supplement helpful for allergy based on in vitro reports. However, there are no published clinical trials.

Honey is sometimes used by patients with allergies in the belief that the pollen contained therein will render future immunity to pollens. Honey was studied for efficacy in allergic rhinitis in a small trial that included 36 patients in the active arm who ingested 1 tablespoon of honey daily starting in spring and going through ragweed season in August. There were no significant differences in symptoms compared with the placebo group (45). Honey ingestion has also been associated with allergic reactions, ranging from mild local itching in the mouth to severe anaphylaxis (46). Bee pollen is similarly used as a natural oral immunotherapy. Formal trials of bee pollen in allergic rhinitis were not located, but severe allergic reactions have been reported upon ingestion (47).

## Acupressure/Acupuncture

There are few high-quality clinical trials of acupuncture for allergic rhinitis, and trials use varied types of acupuncture regimens. Several studies combine acupuncture with other modalities. The general challenges of studying the efficacy of acupuncture were reviewed in Chapter 1. Most available trials of acupuncture for allergic rhinitis have small sample size. The few clinical trials have evaluated the effects of acupuncture on perennial allergic rhinitis in children, seasonal allergic rhinitis in adults, and perennial allergic rhinitis in adults. The limited available data show mixed results that are difficult to compare or summarize, and no specific recommendation can be given based upon the evidence (see Evidence Summary table at end of chapter) (48-53).

## Atopic Dermatitis

Atopic dermatitis can be a frustrating and difficult-to-control condition despite increasing availability of improved therapies. Similar to asthma, the prevalence has been rising in recent years (54). Several studies have found that CAM use increased in those with more extensive skin involvement and a failure of improvement with conventional therapy (55,56). In a survey of young adults with AD in Norway, 51% reported use of CAM (55). In the United Kingdom, of 100 pediatric patients, families reported that 46% were using or had used CAM, and an additional 17% of caregivers were planning to try CAM (56). The most common CAM approach used was Chinese herbal therapy, for which there have been favorable trials reported. Similarly, in the United States, a recent survey of 70 patients at Oregon Health & Sciences University found that 50.4% used CAM, with vitamin supplements and herbal cream remedies being most popular (see Evidence Summary table at end of chapter) (57).

### Botanical/Herbal Medicine

Traditional Chinese herbal medicine has become popular in Europe for atopic dermatitis after two successful double-blind trials in moderate-severe disease were published by the same United Kingdom group in the early 1990s (58,59). Reversible increases in aspartate aminotransferase were seen in two children, but otherwise the therapy was well-tolerated (60,61). The original enthusiasm has been tempered by the possibility of significant adverse reactions as herbal treatments are further scrutinized. Hepatitis and dilated cardiomyopathy have been reported in the treatment of atopic dermatitis with Chinese herbal medicine, but the formulations were not the same as those used in the published trials (62,63). More recently, countering the positive clinical benefits seen in the U.K. studies, a Hong Kong team used the same combination of herbs versus placebo in 40 patients with recalcitrant atopic dermatitis (64). The trial used a randomized cross-over design with 8 weeks of treatment followed by a 4-week washout period. Patients improved over the treatment period irrespective of which group they were in. Racial differences or dosage considerations (the Chinese patients were smaller and the dose was proportionally decreased) were raised as possible reasons for the negative study; however, no other group has replicated the early success of this particular Chinese herbal mixture. Results of these clinical trials were summarized in a Cochrane systematic review performed in 2004 and updated in 2005. The authors found four evaluable trials and concluded that the trials were small, poorly reported and of the same product, which is no longer available (65).

More recently, Hon et al studied 85 children with long-standing moderate to severe atopic dermatitis using placebo vs. a five-herbal concoction. The trial achieved a Jadad 5 score, indicating a higher quality clinical trial. Over 12 weeks improvements were noted in quality of life with the herbal concoction using validated atopic dermatitis scores, and the total amount of topical corticosteroid used was significantly reduced by one third compared to the placebo group. The herbal concoction was well tolerated. It is unclear whether this could be replicated in adults (66).

Evening primrose oil and borage oil, as sources of essential fatty acids rich in gamma linolenic acid, have been used as supplements for treatment of atopic dermatitis based on in vitro data showing anti-inflammatory activity and early clinical trial data. However, a well-controlled trial was recently performed that addressed criticisms of earlier studies using too low of a dose. Eighty-one patients took borage oil capsules for 12 weeks, and 52 took placebo. There was similar improvement in both the placebo and active group, suggesting that ingesting evening primrose or borage oil as sources of immunomodulating fatty acids is probably not effective (67,68).

## Acupuncture

Acupuncture is not actively recommended for atopic dermatitis (69). In the United States, there has been an adaptation of acupuncture in which it is combined with muscle-response testing for diagnosis and treatment of any allergy or intolerance, be it inhalant, food, chemical, or medication. After the diagnostic testing is completed, the patient is treated with acupuncture (or acupressure) on specific points to drain the energy blockages out of the body (70). After treatment, the patient is asked to remain in the office for several minutes. The patient is then retested by muscle-response testing with the substance to which they were "allergic." If upon retesting they are strong, the patient is then advised to avoid the allergen for the next day. After the avoidance period, the patient may then be re-exposed to the allergen. There are no controlled trials of this type of acupuncture therapy, but the previous critique of muscle response testing as a diagnostic method applies here as well when it is then used to assess effectiveness of acupuncture or acupressure therapy.

## Food Allergy or Intolerance

There is little information on CAM use in food allergy, but an abstract based on a survey distributed to 188 families attending a Food Allergy and Anaphylaxis Network conference was presented in 2003. The authors found that 16%

of patients had used alternative diagnostic practices (food specific IgG assays, muscle-response testing, provocation/neutralization, pulse test, and electrodermal testing) and 14% used CAM therapies (see Evidence Summary table at end of chapter) (71).

Because food allergy can be a fatal disorder, it is extremely important that clinical trials with food exposure be conducted only by individuals with significant knowledge and experience in recognizing and treating anaphylaxis. Two recent reviews highlight some of the emerging concepts in food allergy, and potential future treatments, one of which is a Chinese herbal remedy. Li et al have studied a combination herbal product in the laboratory to provide supportive data for ongoing early clinical trials. To date, however, there is insufficient evidence to recommend these treatments (72-74).

Descriptive narratives provide information about Ayurvedic approaches to food allergy and intolerance, but there is unfortunately little scientific data to guide specific treatments (75).

### Four-Day Rotation Diets

Rotary diets, or the 4-day rotation diet, are unproven diet therapies most commonly recommended for individuals with positive specific IgG or food immune complex assays, but in several other situations as well. The diet was first used in 1934 with the idea that it would help a patient avoid cumulative food reactions (76). This therapy has been used to treat individuals with chronic fatigue syndrome (77), "environmental hypersensitivity disorder" (78), food allergy and food intolerance, sometimes in combination with other lifestyle modalities, homeopathy or neutralization therapy (79). It is felt that rotation is necessary to prevent continued sensitization to specific foods (77,79), preserve tolerance acquired by prolonged elimination of the food (77), and as a prophylactic measure in allergic individuals (see Evidence Summary table at end of chapter) (76).

Foods are organized into biologic groups (citrus, fungi, mulberry etc.). The diet allows one to eat all members of a food group on a specified day. Each day allows for several different groups, and a specific quantity is not restricted (78). The cycle rotates every 4-7 days. Foods to which the individual is sensitive are eliminated. A literature search did not reveal any clinical trials evaluating the effectiveness of rotary diets. However, a study published in 1998 assessed adherence to rotary diets (79). The results revealed that the diets were very difficult to follow and individuals frequently consumed foods that were not allowed on a particular day. Adherence to this technique appears to be difficult. In addition, nutrition is of concern, given that one can only consume from specified groups. This method does not seem practical and it is without objective evidence to support its use.

# Conclusions

Allergic disorders are common and are chronic for many patients. Thus it is not surprising that CAM approaches to their management have also become common (see Evidence Summary table at end of chapter). Although the effectiveness of therapies such as herbals, vitamins, restricted diets, homeopathy, acupuncture and relaxation/spiritual techniques (not covered here) have yet to be clearly determined, most pose no harm to the patient, except in the pocketbook, and may effectively harness the placebo response for improved health, even if there is no real treatment effect. Exceptions include toxicities from herbals or vitamins. Another exception is if a patient with a life-threatening allergy to food, venom, natural rubber latex or medications believes he has been cured of his sensitivity by acupuncture or other modality, and encounters the antigen again only to suffer an anaphylactic reaction.

A unique aspect of CAM in regard to allergic disorders is the importance of perceived food allergies contributing to ill health in multiple body systems. In most cases, this means a diagnosis of "food allergy" when there is none. This is actually not surprising, considering that much of our daily life revolves around the procurement, preparation and ingestion of foodstuffs. True adverse reactions to foods may be immune-mediated, a true food "allergy," or non-immune mediated, a "food intolerance," which is far more common. In many cases, we can acknowledge to our patients that we truly do not know all the possible effects of various phytochemicals, lectins, lipids, proteins and fibers on humans, and that the possibility of various unexplained adverse reactions to specific foods is real. We can then offer blinded challenges to the suspected food(s). Such acknowledgement may keep patients from spending money on unproven diagnostics or treatments.

**Evidence Summary of CAM Treatments for Allergic Disorders**

| Clinical Indication | Category | Therapy | Dose | Specific Outcome | Effectiveness | Confidence of Magnitude of Effect* | Safety† | Clinical Recommendation‡ | Comments |
|---|---|---|---|---|---|---|---|---|---|
| Allergic rhinitis | System of practice | Homeopathy | Variable remedies | Variable | Grade B | Variable | Double thumbs up | No recommendation | Unclear mechanism. |
| Allergic rhinitis | Dietary supplements | Chinese herbal remedies | Varied | Nasal and non-nasal symptoms | Grade C | Moderate | No recommendation | No recommendation | Not enough data to recommend. |
| Allergic rhinitis | Dietary supplements | Butterbur extract | Varied | Nasal and/or non-nasal symptoms | Grade B | Small | Single thumbs up | Weak recommendation in favor | Trials of short duration and 3 of the larger studies funded by manufacturer. |
| Allergic rhinitis | System of practice | Acupuncture | Varied regimens | Nasal and/or non-nasal symptoms | Grade C | Variable | Double thumbs up | No recommendation | Not enough data to recommend. |
| Atopic dermatitis | Biologically based therapies | Chinese herbal remedies | Varied herbal combinations (one proprietary no longer available) | Quality of life, atopic dermatitis scores corticosteroid use | Grade C | Moderate | No recommendation | No recommendation | One good-quality trial in children deserving of further research. History of contamination/adulteration of other products. |

| | Biologically based therapies | Borage oil | Varied doses | Atopic dermatitis scores | Grade C | None | Single thumbs up | Weak recommendation against | The best trial shows no difference from placebo. |
|---|---|---|---|---|---|---|---|---|---|
| Atopic dermatitis | Biologically based therapies | Borage oil | Varied doses | Atopic dermatitis scores | Grade C | None | Single thumbs up | Weak recommendation against | The best trial shows no difference from placebo. |
| Food allergy | Biologically based therapies | 4-day rotation diets | N/A | None | NA | NA | No recommendation | No recommendation | No evidence available. Exclusion diets can be difficult, and isolating. |

* Small, moderate (OR>1.2-2) or large (OR>2)

† 5 categories: Double thumbs up, single thumb up, no recommendation, single thumb down, double thumb down

‡ 5 categories: Strong (in favor), weak (in favor), no recommendation, weak (against), strong (against)

## SELECTED REFERENCES*

2. **Morgan JE, Daul CR, Lehrer SR.** The relationship among shrimp-specific IgG subclass antibodies and immediate adverse reactions to shrimp challenge. J Allergy Clin Immunol. 1990;86:387-92.

14. **Teuber SS, Vogt PJ.** An unproven technique with potentially fatal outcome: provocation/neutralization in a patient with systemic mastocytosis. Ann Allergy Asthma Immunol. 1999;82:61-5.

15. **Jewett DL, Fein G, Greenberg MH.** A double-blind study of symptom provocation to determine food sensitivity. New Engl J Med. 1990;323:429-33.

16. **Fox RA, Sabo BMT, Williams TPW, Joffres MR.** Intradermal testing for food and chemical sensitivities: a double-blind controlled study. J Allergy Clin Immunol. 1999;103:907-11.

18. **Klinkoski B, Leboeuf C.** A review of the research papers published by the International College of Applied Kinesiology from 1981-1987. J Manipulative Physiol Ther. 1990;13:190-4.

22. **Semizzi M, Senna G, Crivellaro M, et al.** A double-blind, placebo-controlled study on the diagnostic accuracy of an electrodermal test in allergic subjects. Clin Exp Allergy. 2002;32:928-32

23. **Blanc PD, Trupin L, Earnest G, et al.** Alternative therapies among adults with a reported diagnosis of asthma or rhinosinusitis. Chest. 2001;120:1461-7.

25. **Schafer T, Riehle A, Wichmann H-E, Ring J.** Alternative medicine in allergies: prevalence, patterns of use, and costs. Allergy. 2002;57:694-700.

32. **Ludtke R, Wiesenaure M.** A meta-analysis of homeopathic treatment of pollinosis with Galphimia glauca. Wien Med Wochenschr. 1997;147:323-7.

33. **Passalacqua G, et al.** ARIA update: Systematic review of complementary and alternative medicine for rhinitis and asthma. J Allergy Clin Immunol. 2006;117:1054-62.

33a.**Hu G, Walls RS, Bass D, et al.** The Chinese herbal formulation bimminne in management of perennial allergic rhinitis: a randomized, double-blind, placebo-controlled, 12-week clinical trial. Ann Allergy Asthma Immunol. 2002;88:478-87.

36. **Schapowal A.** Randomized controlled trial of butterbur and cetirizine for treating seasonal allergic rhintitis. BMJ. 2002;324:144-6.

37. **Lee DK, Gray RD, Robb FM, et al.** A placebo-controlled evaluation of butterbur and fexofenadine on objective and subjective outcomes in perennial allergic rhinitis. Clin Exp Allergy. 2004;34:646-9.

38. **Gray RD, Haggart K, Lee DK, et al.** Effects of butterbur treatment in intermittent allergic rhinitis: a placebo-controlled Ann Allergy Asthma Immunol. 2004;93:56-60.

47. **Greenberger PA, Flais MJ.** Bee pollen-induced anaphylactic reaction in an unknowingly sensitized subject. Ann Allergy Asthma Immunol. 2001;86:239-42.

52. **Xue CC, AnX, Cheung TP, et al.** Acupuncture for persistent AR: a randomized, controlled trial. Med J Aust. 2007;187:337-41.

57. **Simpson EL, Basco M, Hanifin J.** A cross-sectional survey of complementary and alternative medicine use in patients with atopic dermatitis. Am J Contact Dermat. 2003;14:144-7.

64. **Fung AYP, Look PCN, Chong L-Y, et al.** A controlled trial of traditional Chinese herbal medicine in Chinese patients with recalcitrant atopic dermatitis. Int J Dermatol. 1999;38:387-92.

65. **Zhang W, Leonard T, Bath-Hextall F, et al.** Chinese herbal medicine for atopic eczema. Cochrane Database Syst Rev. 2005;2:CD002291.

67. **Takwale A, Tan E, Agarwal S, et al.** Efficacy and tolerability of borage oil in adults and children with atopic eczema: randomized, double-blind, placebo controlled parallel group trial. BMJ. 2003;327:1385-8.

71. **Lee JI, Li X, Furlong TJ, Sicherer SH.** Complementary and alternative medicine (CAM) in food allergy: a survey. J Allergy Clin Immunol. 2003;111:S254.

72. **Li XM.** Traditional Chinese herbal remedies for asthma and food allergy. J Allergy Clin Immunol. 2007;120:25-31.

79. **Taylor J, Krondl M, Csima A.** Assessing adherence to a rotary diversified diet, a treatment for 'environmental illness'. J Am Dietetic Assoc. 1998;98:1439-44.

---

\* The complete reference list is to be found on the book's Web site.

# Chapter 4

# Asthma

Pearl B. Scott, MD
Esther L. Langmack, MD

Asthma is a chronic disease that often requires the long-term use of medications. Preventive measures, such as avoidance of environmental triggers, can be useful. Allergen immunotherapy can prevent the development of asthma in atopic children and ameliorate symptoms in adults, but many patients continue to experience symptoms. Persistent asthma is treated with inhaled corticosteroids, which reduce airway inflammation and prevent asthma symptoms, and bronchodilators, which relieve acute bronchospasm. Administration of corticosteroids and bronchodilators in inhaled form minimizes, but does not eliminate, the risk of systemic side effects. Oral corticosteroids are sometimes required for severe asthma. Risks associated with high-dose oral steroids include weight gain, osteoporosis, cataracts, immune suppression, adrenal insufficiency, hyperglycemia, and diminished growth. Bronchodilator side effects may include nervousness, palpitations, and tremors.

As a result of these limitations to standard therapy, the use of complementary and alternative medicine (CAM) has become an attractive option for asthmatics who seek a more "natural" approach. Many CAM users are attracted to its perceived safety, compared to conventional asthma therapy, particularly in light of public awareness of steroid side effects.

From a clinician's perspective, the key questions about CAM therapies for asthma are "Do they work?" and "What are the risks?" This chapter addresses these questions about herbal remedies, homeopathy, acupuncture, chiropractic care, yoga, breathing techniques, and mind-body therapies for asthma.

## Prevalence of CAM Use

The prevalence of CAM use by asthmatics varies depending on the population studied and the survey methodology. Estimates are as high as 42% in a random population of adult asthmatics in California and 59% in the United Kingdom (1,2). The use of CAM for the treatment of asthma may be higher in children, with 89% of inner city children in New York reporting use of some form of

CAM within a given year (3,4). Surprisingly, 44% of survey respondents in the New York study used CAM as first-line treatment for their asthma attacks (3). Many perceived CAM to be as effective as conventional therapy and hence were more likely to use CAM again (3,4).

There are limited data about the factors that motivate asthmatics to use CAM. CAM use may be a marker for severe asthma or for poorly controlled asthma. In one survey, respondents who described their asthma as "severe" were 2-3 times more likely than those with "mild" asthma to have tried CAM for asthma (2). Some CAM users may be influenced by their friends or relatives, as 61% of CAM users in one study had family members who also used CAM (4). Concerns over medication side effects and the desire for more control over their illness may lead other patients to try CAM. Despite the perceived effectiveness of CAM, 70% of asthmatics continue to use medications prescribed by their clinician (1,4), but as many as 82% fail to inform their doctors of their CAM use (3).

## CAM Therapies

Asthmatics may turn to CAM to relieve symptoms, improve quality of life, and reduce the need for medications. A survey of 4741 adult patients in the United Kingdom described the most popular CAM therapies used in asthma. Overall, 30% used breathing techniques, 12% used homeopathy, 11% took herbal medications, 9% practiced yoga, 7% used acupuncture, 3% used osteopathy and 1% tried reflexology (2). A random population survey in California of 125 adults reported that 26% used caffeine, 21% used herbal products, 14% used reflexology, massage, or aromatherapy, 9% used homeopathy, and 5% used acupuncture (1). Chiropractic care and mind-body therapies, such as meditation, were used by 7.5% and 3.8% of respondents, respectively, in a survey of asthmatic children living in New York (5). Figure 4-1 summarizes the prevalence of different types of CAM use in asthma.

### Herbal Remedies

Herbalism involves the use of botanical products for medicinal use. Herbal remedies usually contain a mixture of herbs, plant material, and sometimes animal substances. Some conventional drugs used for asthma were derived from the pharmacologically active constituents of plants (e.g., theophylline, ephedrine, cromolyn).

Herbal therapies often complement the use of other healing modalities. For example, in traditional Chinese medicine (TCM), herbs are integrated into a comprehensive treatment program for asthma that includes acupuncture, diet, and behavioral modification. In the United States, herbal products are frequently

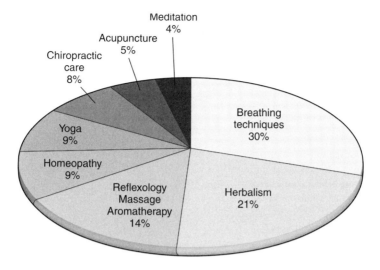

**Figure 4-1**

purchased commercially, without the direct involvement of an herbalist. Herbs may be used individually or in combination for their synergistic effects.

Many herbs used to relieve asthma symptoms contain pharmacologically active properties (Table 4-1). Several, such as coltsfoot, have anti-tussive and expectorant properties. Some act as a bronchodilator through their symptathomimetic or anticholinergic actions (i.e. *coleus forskholii*, *Datura stramonium*). Some herbal remedies are thought to have anti-bacterial or anti-inflammatory properties, but the scientific evidence for the mechanisms of action of these agents is extremely limited (6).

Among herbs used to treat asthma, *ephedra sinica*, also known as *ma huang* is perhaps the most widely used plant with bronchodilator activity. It is a central ingredient of many Asian herbal asthma preparations and is also found in Western dietary supplements and teas. L-ephedrine, the primary active ingredient in ephedra, is responsible for 80% of its pharmacologic properties. Other alkaloids found in ephedra include pseudoephedrine and norephedrine. Ephedrine is also present in other Asian herbal remedies for asthma, including *Pinellia* and the traditional Japanese preparations, *saibuko-to* and *sho-saiko-to* (6,7).

Other herbal remedies may potentially reduce chronic airway inflammation central to the pathogenesis of asthma. For example, the gingkolide compound BN 52021 from *Gingko biloba* has been shown in animal studies to antagonize platelet activating factor, a pro-inflammatory mediator (6). It is used to inhibit bronchial hyperreactivity and limit coughing. Licorice (*Glycyrrhiza glabra*) may have anti-tussive and anti-inflammatory effects. The active ingredient in licorice, glycyrrhetinic acid, inhibits 11-Beta-dehydroxysteroid dehydrogenase,

### Table 4-1   Selected Plants Used in Botanical Preparations for Asthma

**Anti-tussive agents**
*Glycyrrhiza glabra* (licorice)
*Zingiber officinale* (ginger)
*Pinellia ternata*
*Tussilago farfara*
*Prunus armeniaca* (apricot)

**Expectorants**
*Glycyrrhiza glabra* (licorice)
*Brassica nigra, Brassica alba* (mustard)
*Armoracia rusticana* (horseradish)
*Adhatoda vasica* (malabar nut)
*Zizyphi fructusia*
*Verbascum thapsus* (mullein)
*Panax ginseng* (ginger root)
*Schisandra chinensis*
*Tylophora asthmatica/indica*

**Anti-inflammatory agents**
*Schisandra chinensis*
*Scutellaria baicalensis*
*Bupleurum chinense*
*Cinnamomum species* (cinnamon)
*Zizyphi fructusia*
*Panax ginseng* (ginseng root)
*Cordyceps sinensis*
*Perilla frutescens*
*Glycyrrhiza glabra* (licorice)
*Gingko biloba*
*Boswellia serrata*
*Ledebouriella seseloides*
*Rehmannia glutinosa*
*Paeonia suffruticosa*
*Picrorrhiza kurroa*
*Allium cepa* (onion)

**Bronchodilator (sympathomimetic)**
*Ephedra sinica (ma huang)*
*Coleus forskohlii*

**Bronchodilator (anti-cholinergic)**
*Atropa belladonna* (deadly nightshade)
*Hyoscyamus niger*
*Datura stramonium* (jimsonweed)
*Ligusticum wallichii*

**Bronchodilator (unknown mechanism)**
*Tylophora indica*

Common names appear in parentheses. See references 6-8.

thereby increasing plasma levels of endogenous cortisol and medications such as prednisolone (6). Licorice is found in several Asian herbal products, including *saiboku-to* and *sho-saiko-to*, and may account for their corticosteroid-sparing effects and ability to suppress lipoxygenase and cyclooxygenase activity (7). By altering corticosteroid metabolism, licorice may reduce the amount of oral corticosteroid needed to control asthma, but the risks of corticosteroid and mineralocorticoid side effects still exists.

Some herbal remedies have been evaluated *in vitro* or in animal models of asthma, but very few have been evaluated in clinical trials of good quality (6). Huntley and Ernst reviewed 17 randomized controlled trials of botanical preparations for asthma, only half of which were double-blinded (8). A significant improvement in lung function and symptoms was reported in trials, but the studies had a Jadad score less than 3 (the Jadad scoring system awards a maximum of 5 points for a well-designed study featuring adequate randomization, double-blinding, and reporting of subject withdrawals). Due to significant methodological flaws, the reviewers concluded that current evidence does not support or refute the effectiveness of herbal products for asthma (8).

A more recent review concluded that *tylophora indica, ma-huang, saiboku-to,* and *boswellia serrata* appear to have some effect in improving lung function, symptom scores, and reducing bronchodilator use (9). Butterbur may have a limited effect on bronchial inflammation, but the use of *picrorrhiza kurroa* was not found to be effective (9). Eight of the 11 trials reviewed had a Jadad score of 2 or 3 (9).

Although herbal remedies may be derived from natural sources, their use is not necessarily risk free. There is currently little pre-market testing of botanical preparations for purity, safety, or efficacy in the United States, and adverse events are likely under-recognized. There are the risks of mistaken plant identification, incorrect preparation, and lack of standardization with herbal products. Extreme caution should be exercised when children or the elderly use herbal products. Botanicals are generally contraindicated in pregnant and nursing women and the during the period before and after surgery.

Specific precautions vary based on the herbal remedy used. Hyper-sensitivity reactions ranging from dermatitis to anaphylaxis may occur. For example, the gingkolic acid in *gingko biloba* can cause skin hypersensitivity, gastrointestinal upset, and headache. Some preparations have been shown to be adulterated with aspirin or ibuprofen, which poses a danger to aspirin-sensitive asthmatics. Other products may be contaminated with undeclared corticosteroids or heavy metals. Adverse effects may result from the pharmacologically active agents contained in the plant itself. Adverse events associated with ephedra include hypertension, heart palpitations, myocardial infarction, stroke, seizures, and even death, which has led the FDA to ban the sale of supplements containing ephedrine alkaloids (9a).

Drug interactions with herbal remedies have been reported. Ephedra can lead to arrhythmias by interacting with cardiac glycosides, halothane, guanethidine, and monoamine oxidase inhibitors (10). There are case reports that *Gingko biloba* use can result in increased bleeding and spontaneous hemorrhage in patients using aspirin, platelet inhibitors, nonsteroidal anti-inflammatory drugs, or anticoagulants, but solid evidence for a clear association is lacking. Knowledge of drug interactions with herbal products is still limited, and the use of any herbal remedy should be closely monitored. Hospital pharmacists, library reference books, and computerized databases are available to help clinicians understand the pharmacology and side effects of botanical agents.

Several herbs show promise for the treatment of asthma; these include *ma-huang*, TJ96 (*saiboku-to*), *boswellia serrata, tylophora indica*, dried ivy extract, *gingko biloba*, and butterbur (8,9). However, due to the poor quality and heterogeneity of randomized trials and potential safety concerns, there is insufficient evidence to support or refute the use of herbal therapy in the treatment of asthma (see Evidence Summary table at end of chapter). Since herbal products are popular and readily available, clinicians should be aware of their risks and benefits in order to have an educated conversation with patients who may be considering using these agents.

## Homeopathy

Homeopathy is a popular alternative treatment with many asthmatics because it is perceived as natural and risk-free. Classical homeopathy and homeopathic "immunotherapy" are the two main approaches used to treat asthma. In homeopathy the term "immunotherapy" is also referred to as "isopathy," in which dilute remedies are prepared using the exact substance thought to cause symptoms in allergic patients but not in healthy people (see the discussion of how this contradicts the principles of classical homeopathy in the Allergy chapter). In conventional medicine "allergen immunotherapy" uses *increasing* doses of specific antigens to retrain the immune system, resulting in clinical improvement through the induction of T regulatory cells.

Because therapy is highly individualized, classical homeopathy is difficult to study in scientific trials. In a randomized, double-blind, placebo-controlled trial involving 96 asthmatic children, treatment with classical homeopathy produced no significant improvement in active quality-of-life scores, peak expiratory flow rate, or medication use, compared to placebo (11). The evidence that homeopathic immunotherapy for asthma is beneficial for asthma is mixed, and many of the published studies have methodological flaws (12). Reilly reported that homeopathic immunotherapy reduced severity of asthma symptoms in a randomized, double-blind, placebo-controlled study of 28 patients with allergic asthma (13). There was a trend toward a greater increase in $FEV_1$ (forced expiratory volume in one second) for the homeopathy group compared to the placebo group, but the difference was not statistically significant. In a larger, double-blind, randomized, controlled study of 242 asthmatics who were skin-prick-test positive to the house dust mite, treatment with a homeopathic preparation of house dust mite resulted in no significant change in lung function or symptom severity compared to placebo (14). A review of six randomized controlled trials involving 556 patients concluded that the evidence is insufficient to determine the efficacy of homeopathic treatment for asthma (12).

Unlike botanical preparations, properly manufactured homeopathic remedies are extremely dilute and therefore likely to be safe to use, although there is a paucity of prospective phase IV surveillance studies to confirm this assumption (14a).

There is no FDA (Food and Drug Administration) regulation of homeopathic remedies in the United States. Side effects of homeopathic remedies may include allergic reactions or an "aggravation" of symptoms in some patients. Homeopathy is contra-indicated in pregnancy, lactation, and life-threatening conditions (15). The prevalence of drug interactions with homeopathy is unknown.

In summary, homeopathy appears to be relatively safe; however, there is insufficient evidence to support or refute the use of homeopathy in the treatment of asthma (12) (see Table 4.3 and Evidence Summary table at end of chapter).

## Acupuncture

Acupuncture is a therapeutic modality in which fine-gauge needles are inserted at specific points along the body surface to regulate the flow of energy (or *chi*) and restore health. Related techniques include the use of pressure (acupressure), laser (laser-acupuncture), and electricity (electro-acupuncture). Acupuncture has been used for centuries in China for the treatment of asthma, and its use in Western countries is increasing. Most patients in the United States receive care from a certified acupuncturist. The location and duration of needle insertion vary, depending upon the patient's exam and symptoms. Treatment is generally performed weekly for a total of 6-8 weeks, but more sessions may be recommended, depending on the response to therapy. The mechanism through which acupuncture may improve asthma is unknown, and the existence of *chi* has not been confirmed.

Evidence that acupuncture may have an effect in asthma comes from a limited number of studies describing acute improvements in pulmonary function. In a randomized, double-blind, crossover study of 12 asthmatics, Tashkin found that standardized acupuncture attenuated acute bronchospasm induced by methacholine compared to sham acupuncture, nebulized saline, or no intervention (16). However, acupuncture was considerably less effective than inhaled isoproterenol, a bronchodilator medication. Negative results have been reported in randomized, double-blind studies of acute asthma provoked by histamine (17), exercise, and cold air (18).

Studies of acupuncture for chronic asthma also present contradictory results. In a randomized, controlled, double-blind study of 17 adult asthmatics, Christensen reported statistically significant improvements in PEFR (peak expiratory flow rate), rescue bronchodilator use, and respiratory symptoms after standardized electro-acupuncture, compared to sham electro-acupuncture (19). However, even with real electro-acupuncture, subjects still exhibited poor asthma control, using an average of four puffs of albuterol per day. In a randomized, partially blinded study by Medici, a transient decrease in peak expiratory flow variability and blood eosinophils was observed with acupuncture (20). In contrast, Tashkin found that 4 weeks of standardized acupuncture had no significant effect on asthma symptoms, medication use, or pulmonary function in a randomized, controlled, double-blind trial of 25 children and adults (21). A similar study by Shapira reported no significant change in lung function, bronchial hyper-reactivity, or asthma symptoms in adult asthmatics who received acupuncture (22).

A systematic review of acupuncture for asthma has pointed out methodological shortcomings in many studies, including small sample size, lack of randomization, and inadequate blinding (23). Studies that employ standardized acupuncture (patients receive needles at the same points and length of time) may not reflect usual practice because acupuncture is typically individualized. The use of different acupuncture techniques, variable outcome measurements, and inconsistent results make assessment of the current evidence difficult.

Acupuncture is generally considered safe with the incidence of minor adverse events (such as tiredness, needle discomfort, or slight bleeding) occurring with moderate frequency, and serious adverse events (such as fainting, pneumothorax, infection) are extremely rare (23a). There is insufficient evidence to support or refute a recommendation about the use of acupuncture for asthma treatment at this time (see Table 4-3 and Evidence Summary table at end of chapter). Some studies show promising results in subjective symptoms and medication use, but additional well-designed trials are needed.

## Chiropractic Spinal Manipulation

Chiropractic spinal therapy involves the manipulation of the spine and other joints with the goal of improving general health and nervous system function. The use of chiropractic therapy in asthma is intended to reduce symptoms, medication use, and improve quality of life. Chiropractic treatment is widely available in the community from licensed chiropractors. Treatments vary, but sessions can last 3-6 months, starting at three times a week, reducing to twice a week, and then eventually reducing to once a week. Periodic sessions may be used for prophylaxis. Children are reported to have a faster clinical response than adults.

The mechanism through which chiropractic management might improve asthma has not been evaluated. It is hypothesized that vertebral joint dysfunction results in a complex autonomic reflex that affects chest wall function and airway hyper-responsiveness in asthma. Biomechanical stress in asthma results in perceived "chest tightness" independent of bronchial constriction (24).

Spinal manipulation could theoretically optimize chest movement, improve postural drainage, and correct nervous system function, thus reducing airway obstruction.

There are only a limited number of good-quality trials evaluating the efficacy of spinal manipulation in asthma. Most reported benefits from manual therapies are based on case studies, descriptive reports, or inadequately controlled studies. Two well-designed randomized, controlled studies of chiropractic manipulation for the treatment of asthma failed to demonstrate a benefit (25,26). Nielsen compared 4 weeks of active chiropractic spinal manipulation with sham spinal manipulation in a randomized, blinded, crossover trial of 31 adults with moderate asthma (25). Active spinal manipulation had no significant effect upon objective measures of lung function, asthma severity, and medication use compared to sham manipulation (25). Balon compared 4 months of chiropractic spinal manipulation with sham manipulation in a blinded, randomized controlled study of 80 children with mild-to-moderate asthma (26). No statistically significant differences were detected between the sham and active therapy groups for PEFR, asthma symptoms, or quality of life.

Contraindications to chiropractic care include fractures or spinal instability, advanced osteoporosis, bleeding abnormalities, and anticoagulation. Minor adverse effects include local discomfort. Rare serious adverse effects include stroke, arterial dissection, and cauda equina syndrome.

There is insufficient evidence to support or refute the use of chiropractic or other manual therapies for the treatment of asthma at this time (Table 4-2 and see Evidence Summary table at end of chapter).

## Mind-Body Therapies

Emotional stress can adversely affect asthma and result in hyperventilation, increased autonomic hyper-reactivity, and bronchoconstriction. Therapies that emphasize relaxation and alter breathing patterns have been advocated to reduce the sense of anxiety or panic in asthma. The mind-body techniques used to relieve asthma symptoms include yoga, breathing techniques, progressive muscle relaxation, hypnosis, biofeedback, and meditation. All of these therapies are readily available and can be learned by enrolling in classes or watching videos.

The mechanisms by which yoga and other mind-body therapies might improve asthma symptoms are unclear. They may reduce bronchospasm by improving posture, respiratory mechanics, and decreasing hyperventilation. In the Buteyko breathing technique the depth and frequency of breathing is reduced. It is theorized that decreasing hyperventilation will reduce tissue hypoxia and increase carbon dioxide, thus encouraging bronchodilation. Nagarathna hypothesizes that yoga and breathing exercises increase airway caliber and reduce airway inflammation by modifying vagal efferent activity (27). Mind-body therapies may also have an indirect psychological benefit. Because

**Table 4-2  Randomized Controlled Trials of Manual Therapies**

| Source, y | Main Treatment | Comparison Group(s) | Age Range, y | Condition | Outcomes | Results | Comments |
|---|---|---|---|---|---|---|---|
| Nielson et al, 1995 | Manipulation | Simulated manipulation | 18-44 | Chronic moderate asthma | Long function tests<br>Symptoms<br>Bronchodilator use | U<br>U<br>U | Both groups had 34% decrease in symptom severity and 36% decrease in bronchial hyperactivity. |
| Balon et al, 1998 | Manipulation | Simulated manipulation | 7-16 | Chronic, medically stable, mild-to-moderate asthma | PEFR<br>Lung function tests<br>Symptoms<br>Bronchodilator use<br>Quality-of-life score (PAQL) | U<br>U<br>U<br>U<br>U | No objective changes. Both groups showed improved symptoms and quality-of-life scores and decreased bronchodilator use. |
| Field et al, 1998 | Massage therapy | Relaxation therapy | 4-8 and 9-14 | Mild-to-severe asthma (based on self-reported symptoms only) | PEFR<br>Lung function tests<br>Anxiety<br>Salivary cortisol | P/U<br>P/U<br>P/U<br>P/U | No hands-on comparison group. Some lung function changes. Younger group did better on outcomes. |
| Bronfort et al, 2001 | Manipulation | Sham | 6-17 | Chronic, medically stable, mild-to-moderate asthma | Lung function tests<br>Symptoms<br>Bronchodilator use<br>Quality-of-life score (PAQL) | U<br>U<br>U<br>U | No objective changes. Quality-of-life scores increased 10%-28% and self-reported improvement increased 50%-75% for 1 year. |

| Brygge et al, 2001 | Reflexology | Simulated reflexology | 18-60 | Chronic, mild-to-moderate asthma | PEFR<br>Lung fuction tests<br>Symptoms and medication use<br>Quality-of-life score (SF-36) | U<br>U<br>U<br><br>U | No objective changes. Both groups experienced a decrease in symptoms. |
|---|---|---|---|---|---|---|---|
| Ali et al, 2002 | Chiropractic care at center | No treatment at center, No treatment at home control | All ages; trial ongoing | Chronic, mild-to-moderate asthma | Quality-of-life score<br>Salivary IgA<br>Salivary cortisol | P/U?<br>P?<br>U? | Clinically important increase in quality of life and IgA levels. Results to date preliminary and based on minimal information from proceedings abstract. |

Abbreviations: P, statistically significant difference between groups tested; PAQL, Pediatric Asthma Quality of Life Questionnaire; PEFR, peak expiratory flow rate; SF-36, 36-item Short-Form Health Survey; U, analysis revealed no statistically significant difference between groups tested.

From Balon JW, Mior, SA. Chiropractic care in asthma and allergy. Ann Allergy Asthma Immunol. 2004;93(Suppl 1):S55–S60; with permission.

these therapies focus on relaxation, the patient's response to asthma symptoms may be altered and the perceived need for medication reduced. Improved quality of life may also give the patient a better sense of asthma control.

In a handful of small, randomized, controlled trials, yoga practice has been reported to increase PEFR (27,28) and decrease asthma symptoms (27), bronchodilator use (27,29), and bronchial hyper-reactivity (30). The largest yoga study (n=106) by Nagarathna showed a 72 L/min increase in PEFR and a decrease of medication use in the yoga intervention group compared to matched controls (27). Other studies report no significant effect of yoga on lung function, asthma symptoms, medication use, or number of asthma exacerbations (29-31). There was a positive trend in reduction of medication use and improved symptom scores in a few studies but none were statistically significant (30,31), and any improvement in bronchial hyper-reactivity and symptom scores were not sustained after a 2-month follow-up (30).

A systematic review of breathing techniques for asthma concluded that yoga and breathing techniques might have some potential as an adjunctive therapy for asthma; however, their efficacy cannot be determined from the published literature (32). The evidence for the efficacy of yoga, breathing techniques, and mind-body therapies is limited to a handful of average-to-good quality, heterogeneous, randomized, controlled trials with small sample sizes. Most positive trials failed to show a sustained benefit at follow-up and reflect the challenges of long-term incorporation of yoga, breathing techniques, or a mind-body practice into the subjects' lifestyles.

Other mind-body therapies advocated for the use in asthma include muscular relaxation, hypnosis, biofeedback, and meditation. These therapies focus on the mind-body connection through relaxation and altering states of consciousness. A review of a small number of randomized, controlled trials (33) studying these techniques concluded that there was some evidence that Jacobsonian relaxation (a routine of tensing and relaxing certain muscle groups) improved PEFR (34) and $FEV_1$ (35). However, there was insufficient evidence to conclude that the other mind-body therapies were effective.

Yoga, breathing techniques, and mind-body therapies appear to be safe for most patients when used as an adjunct to conventional asthma therapy. Due to some of the extreme postures in yoga, overstretching and physical injury can occur, and some positions are contra-indicated with pregnancy. Caution should be used with meditation and relaxation therapies in patients with psychosis because of the theoretical risk of depersonalization. There are also concerns that mind-body modalities may alter patient symptom perception and delay treatment when it is needed.

Overall, there is no convincing evidence that mind-body therapies alter the underlying disease process or that there are sustained benefits in asthma. However, mind-body therapies may potentially be a useful adjunct for asthma treatment with respect to symptom control and quality of life (see Table 4-3 and Evidence Summary table at end of chapter).

## Recommendations and Conclusions

Although a small number of studies report positive effects on pulmonary function, subjective symptoms, and medication with some CAM therapies, there is insufficient scientific evidence to support or refute the role for CAM therapies in asthma treatment. In addition, information about the potential risks, mechanisms of action, and benefits of CAM therapies is very limited for many therapies. Among the better-quality studies, the magnitude of effects reported fails to demonstrate a sustained benefit and is rarely equivalent to that obtained with conventional medications. Although some botanicals appear to have anti-inflammatory effects, there is no convincing evidence yet that CAM therapies decrease airway inflammation in humans. All of these factors restrict application of findings to contemporary clinical practice.

Despite limited information, it seems likely that many asthmatics will continue to turn to CAM in an attempt to manage their disease. Some therapies, such as yoga, breathing techniques or relaxation, when used in addition to conventional treatment, likely pose little harm and may be of significant value in improving quality of life. Homeopathy is probably safe for most patients. Serious adverse events with acupuncture and chiropractic care are extremely rare but have been reported. Herbal remedies pose a potentially greater risk. Table 4-3 summarizes the efficacy and safety for the different complementary and alternative medicine therapies used in asthma. When CAM therapy is used, it should be done with clinician supervision, and conventional medications should be continued. Patients should be cautioned not to rely exclusively on CAM therapies in the event of an acute, serious exacerbation of asthma. A receptive, cooperative approach is useful in working with patients who wish to integrate CAM into their asthma treatment plan.

## Resources

- Medline Plus Herbal and Supplement Information: www.nlm.gov/medlineplus/druginformation.html
- FDA Poisonous Plant Database: www.cfsan.fda.gov/~djw/plantox.html
- Cochrane Library Evidence Based Reviews: www.thecochranelibrary.org
- Alternative Medicine Resources and Databases: www.pitt.edu/~cbw/database.html
- National Center for Complementary and Alternative Medicine (NCCAM): nccam.nih.gov

## Case Study 4-1

A 34-year-old woman complains of a dry cough and chest tightness provoked by exercise for several years at her visit. She awakens twice a

Table 4-3    Evidence of Efficacy and Safety for the Use of Complementary and Alternative Therapies in Asthma

| | Quality of Evidence | Efficacy | Potential Safety Concerns |
|---|---|---|---|
| Herbal Remedies | | | High |
| Tylophora indica | B | (+) Trend | |
| Butterbur | C | (+) Trend | |
| Ma-huang | B | (+) Trend | |
| Picrorrhiza kurro | C | Negative | |
| Saiboku-to (TJ96) | C | (+) Trend | |
| Boswellia serrata | C | (+) Trend | |
| Ivy | B | (+) Trend | |
| Gingko biloba | C | (+) Trend | |
| Homeopathy | B | (-) Trend | Unlikely |
| Acupuncture | B | Uncertain | Low Risk |
| Manual Therapies | | | |
| Chiropractic care | C | (-) Trend | Low Risk |
| Massage | D | (+) Trend | Unlikely |
| Reflexology | C | (-) Trend | Unlikely |
| Mind-Body Therapies | | | |
| Yoga | C | Uncertain | Low Risk |
| Breathing exercises | C | (+) Trend | Unlikely |
| Buteyko breathing | C | Positive | Unlikely |
| Relaxation | C | Uncertain | Unlikely |
| Hypnosis | C | (-) Trend | Low Risk |
| Biofeedback | C | (-) Trend | Low Risk |

Category of Evidence Quality:
High (A): Several high-quality studies with consistent results
Moderate (B): One high-quality study or several studies with severe limitations
Low (C): One or more studies with severe limitations
Very Low (D): No direct research evidence, one or more studies with severe limitations, or expert opinion

Adapted with permission from: Passalacqua G, Bousquet PJ, Carlsen K, Kemp J, et al. ARIA update: I-systematic review of complementary and alternative medicine for rhinitis and asthma. J Allergy Clin Immunol, 2006;117:1060.

week short of breath. Her symptoms have worsened since she adopted a stray cat last year, and skin-prick testing showed a significant reaction to cat dander. Three weeks ago, another physician prescribed a high-dose inhaled corticosteroid (fluticasone 440 mcg bid) for asthma. She wants to try any CAM therapy so that she can stop the inhaled corticosteroid. She wants to know what CAM therapy you would recommend.

You first acknowledge her concerns. "It sounds like you're worried about the corticosteroid inhaler and would like to try a CAM therapy. Please tell me why you want to stop the fluticasone." She relates a fear of developing osteoporosis and adrenal suppression. You acknowledge that these can be side effects of high-dose inhaled corticosteroids. After she finishes, you say, "I see that this is important to you. Let's work together to help you breathe better. Two things would help us achieve that goal. One is to confirm that you have asthma by doing some diagnostic tests, and the other is to identify any triggers for your asthma."

You continue, "Regarding CAM, there are very few good-quality research studies looking at CAM for asthma. So far, no CAM therapy has been shown conclusively to be effective for asthma. No CAM therapy has been shown to help reduce the need for corticosteroids, and there is no evidence that one CAM therapy is better than another. Let's talk more about corticosteroids next time. It may be possible to reduce or stop the corticosteroid inhaler eventually, but please continue it for now, since stopping it could make you worse."

The patient returns to see you after testing has been done. Her spirometry shows moderate airflow obstruction and a significant bronchodilator response, confirming the diagnosis of asthma. Based on her test results and symptoms, you conclude that she has moderate persistent asthma that is likely worsened by exposure to the cat. She is unwilling to get rid of the cat, but she agrees to keep the cat out of her bedroom and have it bathed regularly. You recommend a medium-dose inhaled corticosteroid (fluticasone 220 mcg one inhalation twice a day), with albuterol as needed for acute symptoms. You provide information about asthma, medications, and a written asthma action plan. In addition, you discuss the risks and benefits of the proposed medications and your plan to reduce the fluticasone dose further, if possible. Although she is not enthusiastic about continuing on an inhaled corticosteroid, she is pleased that the dose has at least been reduced. You ask her to monitor her peak flow rates, albuterol use, and asthma symptoms, so that you can assess the efficacy of these interventions.

Over the next 8 weeks, her symptoms and peak flow measurements improve significantly. She then decides to enroll in a yoga class. Although her peak flows and asthma symptoms do not change with the addition of yoga, she feels better, overall, and decides to continue with it. Over the next six months, because her asthma remains well controlled, you are able to gradually transition her to low-dose fluticasone (44 mcg one inhalation twice a day).

## Case Study 4-2

A 28-year-old man with severe persistent asthma has been under your care for 5 years. He tells you that he has decided to try acupuncture treatments for his asthma because he is tired of breathing poorly and needing oral corticosteroids several times a year for acute exacerbations. He wants to know what you think about acupuncture.

You take a moment to review his case. The diagnosis of severe persistent asthma was confirmed, and factors exacerbating his asthma have been reduced as much as possible. He has been educated in asthma self-management techniques. He is taking a high-dose inhaled corticosteroid, a long-acting $\beta_2$-agonist, albuterol, a leukotriene receptor antagonist, and theophylline for persistent asthma symptoms.

"I can see that you are frustrated about not being able to breathe better even with all of these medications, and why you'd be interested in trying acupuncture," you begin. "As with other alternative therapies for asthma, there is not yet solid evidence that acupuncture is effective for asthma or that it allows patients to reduce their prescription medications. Some studies suggest that acupuncture improves asthma control; others suggest that it does not. That's all I know about acupuncture for asthma, but I'm willing to help you learn more about it."

You recommend that he contact the board that licenses acupuncturists in your state and interview several providers. You suggest questions for him to ask each provider, including: "What will treatment entail? Will treatment be only acupuncture, or will herbs or supplements also be prescribed? How long will it take to see results? What are possible side effects? Can I stay on prescription medications? Would you be willing to communicate with my doctor?" You caution against selecting a provider who promises a cure for asthma or insists that prescription medications be stopped. You propose a plan to assess the efficacy of the acupuncture treatments, including tracking peak flow rates, symptoms, and medication use. You advise him to contact you before changing any prescription medications and document the discussion in his chart.

A few weeks later, he calls to tell you that he has selected a practitioner of Traditional Chinese Medicine who recommends a combination of acupuncture and Chinese herbs. He plans to start treatments next week and faxes you the list of herbs. You consult a pharmacist about the potential for herb-drug interactions, but you find that there is no information available for most of the herbs. To be on the safe side, you recommend checking a serum theophylline level while his acupuncture/herb regimen is being adjusted and advise him to visit you in 3 weeks to assess his progress.

**Evidence Summary of CAM Treatments for Asthma**

| Category | Specific Therapy | Outcome | Confidence Estimate on Effectiveness | Magnitude of Effect* | Safety† | Clinical Recommendation‡ | Comments |
|---|---|---|---|---|---|---|---|
| Herbal remedies | Regimens vary | Symptoms, lung function, medication use | Grade C | Small to moderate | Single thumbs down | No recommendation | Preliminary evidence holds promise for Ma-huang, boswellia serrata, tylophora, indica, saiboku-to, ginko, and butterbur. Conflicting evidence |
| Homeopathy | Regimens vary | Symptoms, lung function, medication use, quality of life | Grade B | Small | Single thumbs up | No recommendation | |
| Acupuncture | Regimens vary | Symptoms, lung function, medication use | Grade C | Small | Single thumbs up | No recommendation | |
| Chiropractic | Regimens vary | Symptoms, lung function, medication use | Grade C | No effect | Single thumbs up | No recommendation | |
| Mind-body therapies | Yoga, breathing techniques, relaxation | Symptoms, lung function, medication use, quality of life | Grade C | Small | Single thumbs up | Weak in favor | Best evidence for breathing exercises and Buteyko technique. |

* Small, moderate (OR>1.2-2) or large (OR>2)

† 5 categories: Double thumbs up, single thumb up, no recommendation, single thumb down, double thumb down

‡ 5 categories: Strong (in favor), weak (in favor), no recommendation, weak (against), strong (against)

## SELECTED REFERENCES*

1. **Blanc PD, Trupin L, Earnest G, et al.** Alternative therapies among adults with a reported diagnosis of asthma or rhinosinusitis: data from a population-based survey. Chest. 2001;120:1461-7.

2. **Ernst E.** Complementary therapies for asthma: what patients use. J Asthma. 1998;35:667-1.

3. **Braganza S, Ozuah PO, Sharif I.** The use of complementary therapies in inner-city asthmatic children. J Asthma. 2003;40:823-7.

4. **Reznik M, Ozuah PO, Franco K, et al.** Use of complementary therapy by adolescents with asthma. Arch Pediatr Adolesc Med. 2002;156:1042-4.

5. **Ang JY, Ray-Mazumder S, Nachman SA, et al.** Use of complementary and alternative medicine by parents of children with HIV infection and asthma and well children. Southern Medical Journal. 2005;98:869-75.

6. **Bielory L, Lupoli K.** Herbal interventions in asthma and allergy. J Asthma. 1999;36:1-65.

7. **Ziment I, Tashkin DP.** Alternative medicine for allergy and asthma. J Allergy Clin Immunol. 2000;106:603-14.

8. **Huntley A, Ernst E.** Herbal medicines for asthma: a systematic review. Thorax. 2000;55:925-9.

9. **Passalacqua G, Bousquet PJ, Carlsen K, et al.** ARIA update: I-systematic review of complementary and alternative medicine for rhinitis and asthma. J Allergy Clin Immunol. 2006;117:1054-62.

10. **Bielory L.** Complementary and alternative interventions in asthma, allergy, and immunology. Ann Allergy Asthma Immunol. 2004;93(Suppl 1):S45-S54.

11. **White A, Slade P, Hunt C, et al.** Individualized homeopathy as an adjunct in the treatment of childhood asthma: a randomized placebo controlled trial. Thorax. 2003;58:317-21.

12. **McCarney RW, Linde K, Lasserson TJ.** Homeopathy for chronic asthma. Cochrane Database of Systematic Reviews. 2004;1:CD000353.

13. **Reilly DT, Taylor MA, Beattie NG, et al.** Is evidence for homeopathy reproducible? Lancet. 1994;344:1601-6.

14. **Lewith GT, Watkins AD, Hyland MD, et al.** Use of ultramolecular potencies of allergen to treat asthmatic people allergic to house dust mite: double blind randomized controlled clinical trial. BMJ. 2002;324:520-4.

15. **Ernst E, Pittler M, Wider B.** The desktop guide to complementary and alternative medicine: an evidence-based approach. 2nd ed. St. Louis, Mosby, 2006.

16. **Tashkin DP, Bresler DE, Kroening RJ, et al.** Comparison of real and simulated acupuncture and isoproterenol in methacholine-induced asthma. Ann Allergy. 1977;39:379-87.

17. **Tandon MK, Soh PF, Wood AT.** Acupuncture for bronchial asthma? A double blind crossover study. Med J Aust. 1991;154:409-12.

23. **McCarney RW, Brinkhaus B, Lasserson TJ, Linde K.** Acupuncture for chronic asthma. Cochrane Database of Systematic Reviews. 2003;3:CD000008.

23a.**Ernst E.** Prospective studies of the safety of acupuncture: a systematic review. Am J Med. 2001;110:481-5.

24. **Balon JW, Mior SA.** Chiropractic care in asthma and allergy. Ann Allergy Asthma Immunol. 2004;93(Suppl 1):S55-S60.

32. **Holloway E, Ram FSF.** Breathing exercises for asthma. Cochrane Database of Systematic Reviews. 2004;1:CD001277.

33. **Huntley A, White AR, Ernst E.** Relaxation therapies for asthma: a systematic review. Thorax. 2002;57:127-31.

---

* The complete reference list is to be found on the book's Web site.

# Chapter 5

# Cancer

ADITYA BARDIA, MD, MPH
BRENT A. BAUER, MD
CHARLES L. LOPRINZI, MD

The use of complementary and alternative therapies (CAM) by cancer patients significantly exceeds that of the general population (1-3). This is not surprising when one considers the physical, emotional and spiritual burden that a diagnosis of cancer imposes upon individuals and their families. Patients primarily use these CAM therapies to enhance the body's healing ability, to fight cancer more directly, to manage treatment-related side effects, or to improve their overall quality of life, including general symptom management and potential complications. Unfortunately, many patients are reluctant to disclose this information to their provider (4-6). Given the pervasive utilization of these therapies, the patient's reluctance to speak openly about using these therapies with healthcare professionals due to fear of judgment, and the potential for biological activity of these therapies, it is critical for healthcare professionals to engage in open dialogue and provide a safe place for patients to learn the possible risks and benefits of incorporating such therapies into their conventional treatment regimen. This chapter will provide health professionals with a basic foundation of common CAM therapies organized by indication in order to enable such discussions as part of routine clinical practice.

## Prevalence of CAM Use

The results of numerous surveys suggest CAM therapies are used by 40%-85% of cancer patients (Table 5-1). There have been a number of more recent studies (published within the past 2 years) that suggest sustained interest and usage worldwide (7). People using CAM therapies are more likely to be women, have higher education and income, have a history of prior CAM use, and have more severe disease (6, 8-12).

Contrary to popular belief, surveys indicate that most patients do not use CAM therapies to cure their cancer. Most people use CAM therapies to enhance the body's healing response (such as "bolstering the immune system"), ameliorate side effects of conventional treatments, and improve their quality of

Table 5-1   Overview of CAM Use in Patients with Cancer

| Author | Location | Year | Subjects | Percent Usage |
|---|---|---|---|---|
| Eidinger | U.S. | 1984 | 190 | 7% |
| Richardson | Texas, U.S. | 2000 | 453 | 83% |
| Bernstein | Florida, U.S. | 2001 | 100 | 80% |
| Jordan | Midwest, U.S. | 2001 | 89 | 39.5% |
| Paltiel | Israel | 2001 | 1027 | 51.2% |
| Patterson | Washington, U.S. | 2002 | 356 | 70.2% |
| Madsen | Europe | 2003 | 622 | 53% |
| Kim | Korea | 2004 | 186 | 78.5% |
| Molassiotis | Europe | 2005 | 956 | 35.9% |
| Hyodo | Japan | 2005 | 6607 | 44.6% |
| Tovey | Brazil | 2006 | 89 | 62.9% |

life. A Finnish study revealed reasons such as "restoring hope in the future" (women 36% and men 36%) and "to do as much as they could" for themselves (women 46% and men 29%) (13). A multi-center study of men with prostate cancer showed that 90% of the respondents believed that the use of CAM therapy would help them live longer and improve their quality of life, and 47% also expected CAM to lead to a cure of the disease (14). Finally, use of CAM therapies may be higher among those with more advanced cancer or significant cancer therapy–related symptoms (12).

Breast cancer patients have been identified as the most common users of CAM therapies. Whether this is true or reflects a sampling bias (because breast cancer patients may be over-represented in clinical studies) is a matter of debate. Nonetheless, studies suggest 40%-85% of breast cancer patients are using CAM therapies (10,13,15). Of particular note, there is widespread use of CAM among pediatric cancer population: research suggests that one-third to three-quarters of children with cancer are using CAM therapies (16-18).

## Breast Cancer

Breast cancer patients are definitely interested in CAM therapies. Salmenpera reviewed a questionnaire from 216 Finnish women and 190 men who had breast and prostate cancer, respectively. 53% of the women used complementary therapies (13). Moschen studied 117 female outpatients with breast cancer in Austria (10), and 47% of these patients reported that they had used CAM therapies, in addition to conventional therapies.

## Prostate Cancer

Of 190 Finnish men with prostate cancer, 50% reported using CAM therapies. A multi-center survey of 1099 prostate cancer patients found 23% had previously used and 18% were currently using CAM therapies. An interesting study by Jones found 6 out of 84 patients reported using CAM therapies by standard history taking but upon directed questioning pertaining to CAM therapy, an additional 25 patients reported using CAM therapies, totaling 31 patients (37%) (5). Other studies have highlighted the need to specifically prompt patients (in a non-judgmental fashion) about their use of CAM therapies in order to obtain accurate usage information (6).

## Colon Cancer

A study from Alberta, Canada in 2002 used survey results from 871 colon cancer patients to determine that 49% of the respondents had used CAM therapies (2).

## Gynecological Cancer

Also in 2002, Swisher evaluated 113 women with gynecological cancer seen at an outpatient midwestern university practice (11). 50% had used CAM therapies since being diagnosed with cancer. Von Gruenigen et al went a step further and compared usage of CAM therapies between gynecology patients with and without cancer (19). A total of 529 patients were surveyed, and the authors found that 52% of gynecology patients without cancer and 66% of patients with cancer used CAM therapies.

## Pediatric Cancer

CAM use among children with cancer in Saskatchewan was evaluated between 1996 and 1997 via telephone interviews with parents (17). Of the 44 families who participated, 36% reported using CAM therapies for their child's cancer, and another 21% at least considered it. Neuhouser conducted telephone interviews with parents of 75 children with cancer and found that 73% of the patients used at least one alternative treatment or therapy (16). 21% of patients consulted an alternative provider (such as an acupuncturist or naturopathic physician). Recent studies have found similar results (18). Among the pediatric cancer population, one can assume one-third to three-quarters of children with cancer are using CAM therapies.

## Specific CAM Therapies

Perhaps one of the most prevalent therapies encountered are dietary supplements (5,10) with 65% utilization in one study (8). In another study Bernstein found that 81% took vitamins, 54% took herbal products, 30% of the patients used relaxation techniques (meditation and deep breathing), 20% received massages, and 10% used home remedies (20). Vitamins C and E were the most commonly used vitamins. The most common biologic and botanical remedies were green tea, echinacea, shark cartilage, grape seed extract, and milk thistle. Kumar looked exclusively at the use of alternative nutritional therapies in 820 patients diagnosed with cancer (21). 29% had used some form of alternative nutritional therapy not prescribed by their physicians. High-dose single vitamins were the most frequently reported agent (86.9%) followed by botanicals/biologics (43.8%) and mineral supplements (28.6%).

Cancer patients also frequently employ mind-body interventions. Many of these therapies have been shown to be safe and probably effective in improving quality of life among cancer patients. Psychotherapy, support groups, meditation, yoga, music therapy, and spiritual healing are some of the most commonly used mind-body therapies (2,5,22). While a conventional physician or other care provider cannot be expected to know about all of them, developing basic familiarity with some of the most common therapies will enable better communication with patients facing these choices.

The general topic of dietary supplements is covered in detail in Chapters 1 and 15. In regard to cancer, it is important to remember that a number of chemotherapeutics have been derived from plant sources (23). These include taxol, podophyllotoxin (with synthetic modification leading to the development of etoposide), camptothecin, vincristine, vinblastine, and colchicine. Thus, it is somewhat understandable that cancer patients continue to hope for new herbal products that have near-magical properties. However, what cancer patients can purchase on the Internet or in their corner grocery store are a far cry from the heavily researched and refined plant products just mentioned.

Employing herbs or other botanicals to aid quality of life is therefore fraught with difficulty, at least in the U.S. The Dietary Supplement Health and Education Act of 1994 (DSHEA) established that dietary supplements (including herbal supplements) must be regulated under an FDA category separate from both food and drugs. This shifted the onus for demonstrating product safety from manufacturers of dietary supplements to the FDA. Under DSHEA, before the FDA can remove a dietary supplement from the market it must first prove that it is unsafe. This has raised concerns about safety. Because product content, purity or qualities are not guaranteed, risks are high. Lack of standardization across brands (and often within the same brand across different lots) means that results from clinical trials can vary tremendously.

Dietary supplements can have various adverse effects. Firstly, like any pharmacological agent, these agents can cause direct toxicity. The literature is rife with reports of hepatotoxicity from a number of herbal therapies (e.g., chaparral, comfrey). Toxicity of supplements can also be caused by adulterants or contaminants, particularly heavy metals (24). Amato et al investigated the estrogenic effect of several commonly used herbs by looking at cell proliferation of MCF-stem cells (a human breast cancer cell) and found that Dong quai (*Angelica sinensis*) and ginseng (*Panax ginseng*) both significantly induced the growth of MCF stem cells (25). The clinical implication of these findings is uncertain.

Secondly, therapies can interfere or react with conventional agents. St. John's wort exemplifies the hidden risks of a seemingly innocuous agent.

Though it has been used for close to two centuries in Europe, the powerful effect of St. John's wort on the cytochrome P450 system has only recently been recognized (26). In vivo and in vitro studies have shown that St. John's wort alters the serum level of many substances. Thus, a patient who starts St. John's wort before a cycle of chemotherapy may experience a significant reduction in efficacy of that cycle due to drug interaction.

Thirdly, antioxidant substances can also interfere with cancer treatments. Most patients have become well versed in the potential side effects of chemotherapy and radiation. Many have "learned" that taking antioxidants at the time of treatment can ameliorate adverse effects of the therapy. Unfortunately, such substances might also reduce treatment efficacy. With radiation therapy, for example, the oxidative mechanism may be key to the therapeutic effect, and the consumption of high-dose antioxidants could offset this action.

Finally, the use of dietary supplements (and for that matter any alternative treatments) can cause adverse effects indirectly if the supplement delays correct diagnosis and efficacious conventional treatment. A recent study among 22 patients with breast cancer found that those using alternative therapies as primary treatment for breast cancer (instead of surgery) had an increased recurrence of the cancer and death due to cancer (27).

In addition to concerns about interactions, and other adverse effects, DSHEA does not require products do undergo quality assurance testing prior to sale and distribution; consequently, the quality of products being sold over the counter has historically not been reliable. A handful of companies has voluntarily opted to undergo third-party quality assurance testing through reputable organizations such as the United States Pharmacopeia (www.usp.org) or NSF International (www.nsf.org). Products that have undergone testing will have a USP or NSF label designating the product has passed independent quality-assurance testing. The majority of companies, however, do not submit their products to testing. These products are vulnerable to misidentification of plant materials, contamination, product adulteration, and other quality deficiencies. In June 2007, the FDA issued regulations requiring the dietary supplement industry to abide by good manufacturing practices beginning June 2008 for large companies, June 2009 for companies with fewer than 500 employees, and June 2010 for companies with fewer than 20 employees.

At this time, and unless the current market regulations improve, recommendation of dietary supplements for the treatment of cancer should be deferred until well-conducted clinical trials determine which supplements have benefits that outweigh their risks.

## CAM Practitioner Qualifications

Few people will deny the pleasant feelings associated with a massage. Massage recipients commonly describe feelings of relaxation and decreased muscle tension. That such a generally recognized beneficial intervention might have special application to cancer patients seems likely. However, proper use of massage therapy requires careful consideration by the care team and the patient. Gecsedi recommends screening massage therapists to verify that they have graduated from accredited programs, meet state licensure requirements, and have specialized training in massage for patients with cancer (28). Qualified therapists can potentially improve quality of life for some cancer patients, as some recent studies highlight.

Similar high standards should be considered for all CAM practitioners who provide care to cancer patients. There are an increasing number of postgraduate training programs in CAM disciplines focused on caring for the cancer patient.

Referring providers and patients should ask CAM practitioners if they received formal training in caring for people with cancer, what proportion of their practice is composed of people living with cancer, and how many years they have specialized in cancer care.

## Effectiveness and Safety of CAM Therapies

### CAM Therapies for Cancer Treatment

Do any complementary or alternative treatments cure cancer? The answer at this time is, unfortunately, "no." There are no scientifically sound, evidence-based studies that show that any CAM therapy has significantly and consistently improved survival for a cancer population. On the other hand, several trials investigating CAM therapies (such as shark cartilage) have been negative (29). While agents such as green tea and anti-oxidants have intriguing preliminary data, pending the results of ongoing (or yet to be conducted) trials, it is premature to recommend any CAM modality as a cancer treatment.

## CAM Therapies for Improving Quality of Life

In the past decade, the cancer community has recognized the importance of improving quality of life during and after treatment. The Institute of Medicine issued a report called From Cancer Patient to Cancer Survivor: Lost in Transition in November 2005, which focused on improving the quality of life for cancer survivors (find it at www.iom.edu/Object.File/Master/34/764/ recommendations. pdf). During treatment, it is becoming increasingly clear that asking "How does the patient feel?" may be as important as asking "Has the tumor decreased in size?" While therapeutic advances in the conventional treatment of cancer have been nothing short of phenomenal in the past 3 decades, the cost of these advances has sometimes been increased toxicity and pain for the patient undergoing treatment.

Are there any CAM treatments that improve quality of life for cancer patients? Here, the evidence is more optimistic. The fact that this question is being asked reflects a welcome complement to the usual scientific questions asked in cancer research. The American Cancer Society Guidelines for Using Complementary and Alternative Methods state that "some people find that certain complementary methods such as aromatherapy, biofeedback, massage therapy, meditation, tai chi or yoga are very helpful when used in conjunction with conventional treatment." CAM therapies for specific conditions affecting quality of life are discussed below.

## Nausea and Vomiting from Chemotherapy or Surgery

### Acupuncture

Acupuncture is one of the most frequently cited examples of CAM therapy that has evidence of efficacy for specific indications. The NIH Consensus statement (30) suggests that acupuncture is effective for adult post-operative and chemotherapy-induced nausea and vomiting. More recently, Shen et al found electroacupuncture to be effective in reducing chemotherapy-induced nausea and vomiting (31), and a recent systematic review found similar findings (32). Recent research also found similar results for acupuncture and surgery-related nausea/vomiting (33). There is good evidence to support a weak recommendation favoring acupuncture as effective in treating chemotherapy- and surgery-induced nausea and vomiting (see Evidence Summary table at end of chapter).

### Mind-Body Techniques

Molassiotis evaluated 71 chemotherapy-naïve breast cancer patients at the oncology unit of a Hong Kong university hospital (34). Thirty-eight subjects were randomized to the experimental group and 33 to the control group. The intervention group received progressive muscle relaxation training one hour before chemotherapy and daily thereafter for another five days. Each session lasted approximately 25 minutes and was followed by five minutes of imagery techniques. The intervention group showed a considerable decline in the duration of nausea and vomiting and also a trend toward a lower frequency of nausea and vomiting. The authors concluded that progressive muscle relaxation training is a "useful adjuvant technique to complement anti-emetics for chemotherapy-induced nausea and vomiting."

A second review of behavioral intervention literature (54 studies) found good evidence that behavioral intervention can effectively control anticipatory nausea and vomiting in adult and pediatric cancer patients undergoing chemotherapy (35). The efficacy for post-chemotherapy nausea and vomiting is less clear. While a variety of behavioral methods have been shown to reduce acute treatment-related pain, the authors state that "Hypnotic-like methods, involving relaxation, suggestion, and distracting imagery hold the greatest promise for pain management." Overall there is good evidence to support a strong recommendation of behavioral interventions to treat anticipatory chemotherapy-related nausea and vomiting and insufficient evidence to support or refute the use of these interventions in the post-chemotherapy setting (see Evidence Summary table at end of chapter).

A meta-analysis of the current literature on relaxation training in cancer patients showed significant positive effects for treatment-related symptoms (nausea, pain, blood pressure, pulse rate) (36). Relaxation training also had a significant effect on depression, anxiety, and hostility. The authors state "according to these results, relaxation training should be implemented into clinical routine for cancer patients in acute medical treatment." Overall, there is moderate evidence to support a weak recommendation in favor of using relaxation training to improve treatment-related symptoms (see Evidence Summary table at end of chapter).

## Hot Flashes

### Acupuncture

In one study, 15 breast cancer patients (all of whom were taking tamoxifen) were enrolled to assess the efficacy of acupuncture in treating menopause-related symptoms. Patients were evaluated before treatment and after 1, 3, and 6 months using the Greene Menopause Index. Anxiety, depression, somatic and vasomotor symptoms were all improved concurrent with the treatment administration, and libido was not affected (37). However, a recent large study did not find acupuncture to be more effective than placebo in reducing menopausal symptoms among those with cancer (38). At this time, there is insufficient evidence to support or refute the effect of acupuncture for the cancer treatment–induced menopausal-related symptoms (see Evidence Summary table at end of chapter).

Acupuncture (when performed by appropriately trained providers) is generally safe. Acupuncture should generally be avoided in patients with severe clotting disorder, neutropenia, or lymphedema (39). For those conventional providers who have access to qualified acupuncture providers, consideration of collaboration on some of the difficult problems faced by cancer patients may be rewarding.

## Fatigue

A recent review examining cancer-related fatigue found promising preliminary results for a range of CAM therapies including acupuncture, massage, levocarnitine, and the use of mistletoe. While these trials appear promising, more trials are needed. Currently, there is insufficient evidence to support or refute the effect of these therapies in the treatment of cancer-related fatigue.

## Mind-Body Techniques

Mind body therapies are one of the few therapies that have been shown to improve cancer-related fatigue (40-45). Overall, there is limited evidence to support a weak recommendation in favor of mind-body medicine to treat cancer-related fatigue (see Evidence Summary table at end of chapter).

## Cancer Pain

### Acupuncture

A recent systematic review on CAM therapies for cancer pain found that acupuncture might be efficacious in reducing cancer-related pain for a short duration (12). Mehling et al randomized 138 cancer patients undergoing surgery in a 2:1 fashion to receive either massage or acupuncture on postoperative days 1 and 2 in addition to usual care or usual care alone which included a pain management consult team. The active treatment arm reported reductions in pain and a decrease in depressive mood compared with controls over the 3-day study period (46). Wong et al randomized 25 people with non-small cell lung carcinoma who received thoracotomy to patients who received electroacupuncture or sham acupuncture in addition to usual oral analgesics and patient-controlled intravenous analgesia (PCA) postoperative pain control. They found a trend for lower pain scores that did not reach statistical significance. They did find a statistically significant reduction in PCA morphine given (7.5 mg versus 15.6 mg) on day 2 (47). Alimi et al randomized 90 cancer patients with inadequate pain management despite analgesic treatment for 1 month. At 2 months, there was a statistically significant reduction in pain between the active and sham placebo groups (pain intensity reduced by 36% versus 2%, p<0.05) (48). Overall, there is moderate evidence to support a weak recommendation favoring acupuncture for the treatment of cancer-related or cancer surgery–related pain (see Evidence Summary table at end of chapter).

### Massage

Several studies have found massage to be promising in reducing cancer-related pain (particularly short-term post-intervention), fatigue, and in improving quality of life (49-46). Overall, there is moderate evidence to support a weak recommendation in favor of massage for cancer-related pain, anxiety, and quality of life. The authors conclude that caregivers can benefit from massage therapy in the correct clinical setting.

Most adverse effects are generally associated with exotic types of manual massage or massage delivered by laymen, while massage therapists rarely caused adverse effects (55).

## Mental Health (Mood, Stress, Anxiety, Depression)

It is well recognized that cancer, and the treatments aimed at it, can cause a tremendous degree of stress for cancer patients. It is also being increasingly acknowledged that such stress can have a direct impact on health. Thus, non-toxic, inexpensive treatments that can reduce stress (for both patients and their caregivers) are greatly needed.

### *Mind-Body Techniques*

A meta-analysis of the current literature on relaxation training in cancer patients showed significant positive effects for treatment-related symptoms (nausea, pain, blood pressure, pulse rate) (36). Relaxation training also had a significant effect on depression, anxiety, and hostility. The authors state "according to these results, relaxation training should be implemented into clinical routine for cancer patients in acute medical treatment."

Baider evaluated 116 patients (49 men, 67 women) who were being treated at Hadassah University Hospital in Israel (56). Each of these patients had recently been diagnosed with a localized cancer. Progressive muscle relaxation with guided imagery was used as a behavioral intervention. In the actively treated group, reduced psychological distress was noted at a statistically significant level using the global severity index.

Wright provided patients with a 10-week autogenic training course, which emphasized techniques of deep relaxation and self-hypnosis (57). The results indicated a significant reduction in anxiety as well as an increase in "fighting spirit." Participants also noted an improved sense of coping and improved sleep.

Petersen looked at 53 patients with gynecological cancer who were randomized to a control group or to an intervention consisting of relaxation and counseling sessions (58). The relaxation training was associated with a significant reduction in total Hospital Anxiety and Depression Scale score (p=0.002), and the reduction was seen in both anxiety and moderate depression subscales (p=0.001 and p=0.02).

Carlson looked at the effects of a mindfulness meditation–based stress reduction program on mood and symptoms of stress in cancer outpatients in Canada (59). A total of 89 patients were enrolled and 54 completed the six-month follow-up. Patient scores decreased significantly on the chosen instruments (Profile of Mood States [POMS] and Symptoms of Stress Inventory [SOSI]), indicating less mood disturbance and fewer symptoms of stress. The authors concluded that this program "was effective in decreasing mood disturbance and stress symptoms for up to six months in both male and female patients with a wide variety of cancer diagnoses, stages of illness, and educational background, and with disparate ages."

Because stress and anxiety may persist beyond the treatment period, it would be particularly attractive to identify therapies that patients can learn and self-administer. Jacobsen looked at the efficacy and costs of two forms of stress management for cancer patients (60). 411 patients who were about to start chemotherapy were randomly assigned to usual psychosocial care, a professional-administered form of stress management training, or a patient self-administered form of stress management training. Compared with patients who received usual care only, patients receiving the self-administered intervention reported statistically significant improvements in physical functioning, greater vitality, fewer role limitations because of emotional problems, and better mental health. Costs of the self-administered intervention were about 67% lower than the average cost associated with the professionally administered psychosocial intervention. Overall, there is moderate evidence to support a weak recommendation in favor of mindfulness meditation, autogenic training, progressive muscle relaxation, relaxation training (in general), and stress management to support mental health and well-being among cancer patients (see Evidence Summary table at end of chapter).

## Massage Therapy

Smith evaluated 41 patients who were admitted to an oncology unit of a large urban medical center in the U.S. for chemotherapy or radiation therapy (61). Twenty participants received therapeutic massage and 21 received a control therapy (nurse visit). Mean scores for pain, sleep quality, symptom distress, and anxiety all improved from baseline for the subjects who received therapeutic massage. Only anxiety improved from baseline for participants in the comparison group. A recent systematic review found that massage appears to improve psychological well-being and physical symptoms among cancers (62). A 2007 American College of Chest Physicians guideline on "complementary therapies and integrative oncology in lung cancer" concluded that massage was likely beneficial for anxiety, mood, and pain for cancer patients (63). Overall, there is moderate evidence to support massage for short-term decreasing of anxiety and improvement of mood among cancer patients (see Evidence Summary table at end of chapter).

## Music Therapy

Bringing music therapy to the cancer patient's treatment regimen is not simply a matter of providing personal CD players to patients. In fact, at least one study showed that simply having patients choose music to listen to while undergoing radiation therapy did not decrease anxiety during therapy (61). In fact, true music therapy involves the skills of a music therapist, who has time to assess and work with the patient. Magill notes that music therapists perform comprehensive assessments that include reviews of social, cultural and medical history, current medical status, and the ways in which emotions are affecting pain or other symptoms (64). A variety of music therapy techniques can be used which include vocal, listening and instrumental techniques.

When the effects of music therapy on cancer patients have been evaluated, the results are generally positive. Burns undertook a pilot study of the therapeutic effects of music therapy at a cancer help center (65). Twenty-nine cancer patients were enrolled into a group music therapy intervention consisting of listening to recorded/live music in a relaxed state and improvisation. Both interventions were associated with increased well-being and relaxation, and the improvisation also was associated with increased energy. Participants in both interventions were found to have increased levels of salivary immunoglobulin A (IgA) and decreased levels of cortisol after the sessions. In a small study that looked at a combination of music and guided imagery intervention, Burns evaluated eight volunteers with a cancer history who were randomly assigned to either an experimental or wait-list control group (66). The active group did show better scores on both mood and quality-of-life scores post-test than those participating in the control group. Even after the sessions were complete, scores continued to improve in the experimental group. However, trials evaluating music therapy for alleviation of cancer-related pain have been largely negative (67,68).

Music therapy has also been beneficial to pediatric cancer patients. Barrera examined the use of music therapy in 65 children who were hospitalized with the diagnosis of cancer (69). This study showed a significant improvement in children's ratings of their feelings from pre- to post-music therapy, and the parents perceived an improved play performance after music therapy in preschoolers and adolescents (but not in school-aged children).

The recognition that music and music therapy can play a significant role in cancer patients' lives has led to the forming of a partnership between the Cleveland Clinic Foundation and the Cleveland Music School (70). As a result, music therapy has become a standard part of the care in the palliative medicine inpatient unit. Overall, there is moderate evidence to support a weak recommendation for music therapy to support mental health and well-being for cancer patients (see Evidence Summary table at end of chapter).

## Insomnia

### Mind-Body Techniques

Mind-body therapies have been generally found to be an efficacious therapy for insomnia (71,72). A recent randomized trial among 57 patients with breast cancer found that 56.5% of patients treated with cognitive behavioral therapy had a sleep efficiency of 85% or greater compared to only 20.7% in the control group (73). Another recent pre-post intervention study found that women who received cognitive behavioral therapy had a significant reduction in insomnia which led to significant improvements in fatigue, anxiety, depression and quality of life (74).

Another means of reducing costs and increasing efficiency is to deliver interventions in group settings. A sleep therapy program was developed for cancer patients with insomnia and studied with 12 participants (75). The group program included stimulus control therapy, relaxation training, and other strategies aimed at consolidating sleep and reducing cognitive emotional arousal. Total sleep time and fatigue were significantly improved at the end of the study. The program was associated with improved sleep, reduced fatigue, and an enhanced ability to perform activities in relatively well individuals attending the cancer center. There is moderate evidence to support a strong recommendation of mind-body medicine techniques for improving sleep among cancer patients, and it should be recommended (see Evidence Summary table at end of chapter).

Yoga has become increasingly popular in the United States, including among cancer patients. Lorenzo et al and other co-investigators at the MD Anderson Cancer Center randomized 39 lymphoma patients to a Tibetan form of yoga called Tsa Lung and Trul Khor, which incorporate gentle postures, visualizations, controlled breathing, and mindfulness techniques in a 7-week course. At the end of 3 months, participants reported improved sleep quality across multiple dimensions compared with wait-list controls (76). However, there is limited evidence suggesting that yoga is effective for improving sleep among cancer patients. At this time there is insufficient evidence to support or refute recommending yoga for sleep problems (see Evidence Summary table at end of chapter).

## Quality of Life and Symptom Management Outcomes

### Acupuncture

There are few randomized, controlled trials evaluating the effect of acupuncture on cancer treatment–related symptoms for outcomes other than pain and nausea/vomiting. Johnstone reviewed his experience treating 123 cancer patients with acupuncture between August 1999 and May 2000. The major reasons for referral included pain (53%), xerostomia (32%), hot flashes (6%), and nausea/loss of appetite (6%). He claimed that 60% of the patients showed at least a 30% improvement in their symptoms. Notably, there was no benefit perceived by one third of the patients. No untoward effects related to acupuncture were noted. Regardless of their response to therapy, 86% of the patients considered it "very important" that acupuncture continues to be offered. In a separate paper Johnstone reviewed results of acupuncture for treating resistant xerostomia. Response (defined as improvement of 10% or better over baseline Xerostomia Inventory measures) occurred in 35 of 50 patients. As mentioned previously, Mehling et al conducted a randomized clinical trial among hospitalized cancer surgery patients and found acupuncture and massage were associated with lower pain scores and less depressed mood. At this time, there is insufficient evidence to support or refute recommending acupuncture to improve quality of life or symptom management except for the management of pain and nausea/vomiting (see Evidence Summary table at end of chapter).

## Mind-Body Medicine

Targ examined 181 women with breast cancer who were randomized to either a 12-week standard group support or a 12-week CAM support intervention (77). The CAM intervention included meditation, affirmation, imagery, and ritual. The standard group received cognitive behavioral approaches along with group sharing and support. Both interventions were associated with improved quality of life, decreased depression, and increased "spiritual well-being." However, at the conclusion of the intervention, the CAM support group showed higher satisfaction and fewer dropouts compared to the standard group. There is limited evidence to support a weak recommendation in favor of mind-body medicine to improve quality of life among cancer patients (see Evidence Summary table at end of chapter).

## Homeopathy

Thompson looked at 100 consecutive patients who were attending a cancer clinic (78). They were seen for a consultation and prescription of a homeo-pathic medicine. Scores for fatigue and hot flashes improved over this study, but pain scores did not improve. The usefulness of this study is limited by the fact that only 52 patients completed this study. Nevertheless, satisfaction was high, with 75% of the 52 patients rating the approach as helpful or very helpful for their symptoms. However, whether homeopathy has any role to play in improv-ing quality of life in cancer patients is unclear, and a more satisfactory study is needed. There is insufficient evidence to support or refute the use of homeop-athy for quality-of-life issues among cancer patients (see Evidence Summary table at end of chapter).

## Aromatherapy

Dunwoody suggests that quantitative studies using questionnaire data have shown aromatherapy may reduce psychological distress and enhance symptom control in cancer patients (79). Wilkinson conducted a multi-center random-ized clinical trial involving 280 cancer patients and found that aromatherapy massage was associated with short-term improvements in anxiety compared with controls at 6 weeks post-intervention; however these benefits did not per-sist at 10 weeks (15). Two reviews have questioned the additional benefit of aromatherapy to a standard massage therapy intervention (62,63). Again, the relative paucity of well-conducted trials makes definitive statements regarding the role of aromatherapy premature. Many non-cancer patients anecdotally ascribe relaxation and enhanced sense of well being to its use. That some can-cer patients should also find similar results is not unlikely, and the risk of adverse events is very limited. There is insufficient evidence to support or refute the use of aromatherapy for quality-of-life issues among cancer patients (see Evidence Summary table at end of chapter).

## Reflexology

In a study performed in Scotland, 20 cancer patients reported that they were satisfied with reflexology and that their quality of life was improved through reduction of physical and emotional symptoms (80). Such small but intriguing reports do little to help establish a definitive assessment of a therapy. Pending results of larger and well-conducted studies, the best approach is to recognize that some patients feel reflexology has been helpful to them. With little inherent risk, it is probably best at this point to neither endorse nor condemn its use, as long as it is not being used in place of known conventional therapy. There is insufficient evidence to support or refute the use of reflexology for quality-of-life issues among cancer patients (see Evidence Summary table at end of chapter).

## Magnet Therapy

Fascination with magnet therapy seems to be increasing year by year. The majority of golfers on the Senior Tour are purported to be using magnets to help counter age-related degenerative musculoskeletal pains. Thus it is not surprising that some cancer patients have begun to look to magnets to treat symptoms. Carpenter evaluated the use of magnetic therapy for the treatment of hot flashes after breast cancer treatment (81). Eleven patients were studied, and results indicated that magnetic therapy was no more effective than placebo in decreasing hot flash severity. There is insufficient evidence to support or refute the use of magnet therapy for quality-of-life issues among cancer patients (see Evidence Summary table at end of chapter).

# Caregiver Quality of Life

An increasingly important aspect of comprehensive cancer care is the health of the caregiver of the cancer patient. Massage has been shown to have a role here as well. Thirty-six caregivers were placed into three groups, 13 in the control group, 13 in the massage therapy group, and 10 in the healing touch group. Treatment consisted of two 30-minute massages or healing touch treatments per week for 3 weeks. Caregivers in the control group received usual nursing care and a 10-minute supportive visit from one of the researchers. Results showed significant declines in anxiety scores, depression, general fatigue, motivation fatigue, and emotional fatigue for individuals in the massage therapy group only.

## Case Study 5-1

A 65-year-old man recently diagnosed with unresectable lung cancer complains of fatigue, weakness and pain. He has started working with a local chiropractor "to help me beat this cancer." The patient is undergoing regular acupuncture treatments, taking shark cartilage, mega-dose vitamin C and coffee enemas to help "detoxify my system."

His physician carefully reviewed the current literature on each of the modalities he was using. She pointed out that acupuncture has been found effective for some pain problems and chemotherapy- or surgery-induced nausea and vomiting, but that no studies suggested it would directly impact his cancer. Studies regarding shark cartilage and vitamin C were also reviewed and shown not to support their use for treating cancer. Finally, his physician was able to share some of the reports of toxicities (such as hyponatremia) that have occurred with the use of coffee enemas. The patient stated that he recognized these treatments were unlikely to be helpful but he felt the need to "do something." Together, the patient and physician agreed that he should discontinue the shark cartilage, vitamin C and coffee enemas. He decided to continue with the acupuncture because he felt that it provided some relief to his increasing difficulties with pain. They discussed the research supporting the effect of several different mind-body medicine therapies on improving mental health, quality of life, fatigue and pain, and the physician suggested several mind-body medicine practitioners in his local area, as well as an 8-week course, and reading references. At the same time, his physician started him on a pain management regimen and agreed to see him in 1 week to help refine his overall program.

### Discussion

A patient's decision to use a CAM treatment may sometimes indicate an unmet need. By carefully taking the time to learn why this patient was interested in using a variety of therapies, the physician was able to provide specific information about the pros and cons of each therapy and then direct the patient to conventional resources where needed, or endorse the evidence-based use of CAM therapies when indicated. Such a collaborative approach helps validate the patient's concerns and beliefs about their own healthcare while allowing for the provision of reliable information to help inform their decisions.

### General Recommendations

Patients who have been diagnosed with cancer are particularly vulnerable and face many life stressors. When they encounter information regarding

CAM therapies, many of which, on the surface, will sound attractive, they are naturally going to seek expert opinion. It is also important to be cognizant that barriers often exist for the ideal kind of communication being sought. Tasaki interviewed 143 cancer patients and used interview data from 93 CAM users to determine three themes that seem to inhibit communication between physicians and patients (82). The first was a perception of the physician's indifference or opposition to CAM therapy use. The second was the physician's emphasis on scientific evidence, and the third was the patient's anticipation of a negative response from the physician. The authors suggest that "given a difference in epistemiologic beliefs about cancer and its treatment, the challenge is to find a common ground for an open discussion in which physicians consider that scientific evidence is not all that counts in the life of an individual facing a serious disease." Being open to discussion does not require abandonment of scientific truth. Nor does discussion imply endorsement. Being willing to listen to a patient's questions and then addressing them in a compassionate and honest manner can, however, be the critical step that leads a patient to making informed choices, rather than decisions based on the latest Internet fad or the next-door neighbor's recommendations.

The evidence for many CAM therapies is currently preliminary and constantly evolving. A list of useful CAM-related websites is presented in Table 5-2 and Figure 2-1 and could be of value while counseling patients. A good first place to obtain background information is from the American Cancer Society (ACS). The ACS website maintains a section devoted to CAM under the title "Making Treatment Decisions." There are five main areas of focus: Mind, Body and Spirit; Manual Healing and Physical Touch; Herbs, Vitamins and Minerals; Diet and Nutrition; and Pharmacological and Biological Treatment. Each section is subdivided into topics that are easy to read, referenced and balanced.

Both the National Cancer Institute (NCI) and the National Center for Complementary and Alternative Medicine (NCCAM) maintain websites with helpful information. The NCI website contains a section devoted to CAM under the "Treatment" section. Approximately 12 common therapies are reviewed in detail, and general principles regarding evaluation of CAM modalities are highlighted. The NCCAM website covers CAM in a broad sense, (i.e., without a specific focus on cancer) and contains excellent background material on CAM therapies and links to many informative sites.

Finally, while there are many academic sites that stand out, two in particular deserve special attention. The first, the MD Anderson Cancer Center website contains a section called Complementary/Integrative Medicine Education Resources. Here one will find detailed

**Table 5-2    List of some reliable websites for information on CAM therapies**

| Source | Website link |
| --- | --- |
| National Center for Complementary and Alternative Medicine (NCCAM): Health Information | http://nccam.nih.gov/health/ |
| American Cancer Society (ACS): Complementary and Alternative therapies | http://www.cancer.org/docroot/ETO/ETO_5.asp?sitearea=ETO |
| National Cancer Institute (NCI): Complementary and Alternative Medicine | http://www.cancer.gov/cancertopics/treatment/cam |
| CAM on PubMed | http://www.nlm.nih.gov/nccam/camonpubmed.html |
| Natural Standard Database | http://www.naturalstandard.com |
| Natural Medicines Comprehensive Database | http://www.naturaldatabase.com |
| Herbmed Database | http://www.herbmed.org |
| MD Anderson: Complementary Integrative Medicine Education Resources (CIMER) | http://www.mdanderson.org/departments/cimer/dIndex.cfm?pn=5AC57A83-0F8D-4A3F-B743A0CDF23F193C |
| Memorial Sloan Kettering Cancer Center: Herbs | http://www.mskcc.org/mskcc/html/11571.cfm |
| Mayo Clinic: Complementary and Alternative Medicine | http://www.mayoclinic.com/health/alternative-medicine/CM99999 |
| American Botanical Council: Herbal Gram | http://www.herbalgram.org/ |
| Consumer Reports: Natural Products Encyclopedia | http://www.consumerlab.com/tnp.asp |
| Phytotherapies: Monographs | http://www.phytotherapies.org/ |
| UpToDate | http://www.uptodate.com/ |
| Micromedex | http://www.micromedex.com/ |

reviews of a variety of therapies that are frequently encountered by cancer patients. The reviews are presented both in a less detailed, patient-friendly format, as well as in a detailed scientific format, complete with references. There are numerous other features, including educational resources, links to other quality sites, etc. The second site that deserves special mention is the Memorial Sloan-Kettering Cancer Center website for herbal information. Here one can find easily searchable information on herbs, botanicals, vitamins and other supplements. Succinct, referenced monographs are available for most of the common dietary supplements. They contain excellent information that can be readily shared with patients.

**Evidence Summary of CAM Treatments for Cancer**

| Clinical Indication | Category | Specific Therapy | Dose | Outcome | Confidence of Estimate on Effectiveness | Magnitude of Effect* | Safety† | Clinical Recommendation‡ |
|---|---|---|---|---|---|---|---|---|
| Chemotherapy- and surgery-induced nausea and vomiting | Whole medical system | Acupuncture | Varying regimens | Nausea severity and frequency and vomiting episodes | Grade B | Moderate | Double thumbs up | Weak in favor |
| Anticipatory chemotherapy-related nausea and vomiting | Mind-body medicine | Behavioral interventions | Varying regimens | Nausea severity and frequency and vomiting episodes | Grade A | Moderate | Double thumbs up | Strong in favor |
| Chemotherapy-induced nausea and vomiting | Mind-body medicine | Behavioral interventions | Varying regimens | Nausea severity and frequency and vomiting episodes | Grade C | Small | Double thumbs up | No recommendation |
| Nausea and other treatment-related symptoms | Mind-body medicine | Relaxation training | Varying regimens | Treatment-associated nausea, pain, depression, anxiety, hostility, blood pressure, pulse rate | Grade B | Small | Double thumbs up | Weak recommendation in favor |
| Hot flashes | Whole medical system | Acupuncture | Varying regimens | Symptoms | Grade B (see Deng G et al, JCO 2007) | None | Double thumbs up | No recommendation |

| | | | | | | | | |
|---|---|---|---|---|---|---|---|---|
| Fatigue | Mind-body medicine | Mind-body therapies | Varying regimens | Fatigue | Grade C | Unknown | Double thumbs up | Weak recommendation in favor |
| Cancer pain | Whole medical system | Acupuncture | Varying regimens | Pain including post-thorocotomy pain | Grade B | Moderate | Double thumbs up | Weak recommendation in favor |
| Cancer pain | Manipulative and body-based practices | Massage | Varying regimens | Pain | Grade B | None (see Bardia A, JCO 2006) | Double thumbs up | No recommendation |
| Mental health | Mind-body medicine | Autogenic training, progressive muscle relaxation, mindfulness meditation | Varying regimens | Depression, anxiety, hostility | Grade B | Small | Double thumbs up | Weak recommendation in favor |
| Mental health | Manipulative and body-based practices | Massage | Varying regimens | Anxiety, mood, well-being | Grade B | Small | Double thumbs up | Weak recommendation in favor |
| Mental health | Mind-body medicine | Music therapy | Varying regimens | Reduced serum cortisol, well-being, relaxation, energy level, mood, QOL | Grade B | Small | Double thumbs up | Weak recommendation in favor |

*Continued on next page*

**Evidence Summary of CAM Treatments for Cancer (continued)**

| Clinical Indication | Category | Specific Therapy | Dose | Outcome | Confidence of Estimate on Effectiveness | Magnitude of Effect* | Safety† | Clinical Recommendation‡ |
|---|---|---|---|---|---|---|---|---|
| Insomnia | Mind-body medicine | Mind-body therapies | Varying regimens | Insomnia | Grade B | Moderate | Double thumbs up | Strong recommendation in favor |
| Insomnia | Mind-body medicine | Yoga | Varying regimens | Sleep quality, onset, duration, and use of sleep medications | Grade C | Small | Double thumbs up | No recommendation |
| Quality of life or symptom management | Whole medical system | Acupuncture | Varying regimens | Quality of life or symptom management | Grade C | Unknown | Double thumbs up | No recommendation |
| Quality of life or symptom management | Mind-body medicine | Meditation, imagery, ritual, and affirmation | Varying regimens | Quality of life, depression, spiritual well-being | Grade C | Small | Double thumbs up | Weak recommendation in favor |
| Quality of life or symptom management | Whole medical systems | Homeopathy | Varying regimens | Fatigue, hot flashes, pain | Grade D | Unknown | Double thumbs up | No recommendation |
| Quality of life or symptom management | Biologically based systems | Aromatherapy | Varying regimens | Mental health, symptom control | Grade D | Unknown | Double thumbs up | No recommendation |
| Quality of life or symptom management | Manipulative therapies and body-based practices | Massage | Varying regimens | Pain, anxiety, quality of life | Grade B | Small | Double thumbs up | Weak recommendation in favor |

| Quality of life or symptom management | Manipulative therapies and body-based practices | Reflexology | Varying regimens | Quality of life | Grade D | Unknown | Double thumbs up | No recommendation |
| --- | --- | --- | --- | --- | --- | --- | --- | --- |
| Quality of life or symptom management | Energy medicine | Magnet therapy | Varying regimens | Hot flashes | Grade D | Unknown | Double thumbs up | No recommendation |

* Small, moderate (OR>1.2-2) or large (OR>2)

† 5 categories: Double thumbs up, single thumb up, no recommendation, single thumb down, double thumb down

‡ 5 categories: Strong (in favor), weak (in favor), no recommendation, weak (against), strong (against)

## SELECTED REFERENCES*

1. **Richardson MA, Sanders T, Palmer JL, et al.** Complementary/alternative medicine use in a comprehensive cancer center and the implications for oncology. J Clin Oncol. 2000;18:2505-14.

3. **Eisenberg DM, Davis RB, Ettner SL, et al.** Trends in alternative medicine use in the United States, 1990-1997: results of a follow-up national survey. JAMA.1998;280:1569-75.

5. **Jones HA, Metz JM, Devine P, et al.** Rates of unconventional medical therapy use in patients with prostate cancer: standard history versus directed questions. Urology. 2002;59:272-6.

6. **Metz JM, Jones H, Devine P, et al.** Cancer patients use unconventional medical therapies far more frequently than standard history and physical examination suggest. Cancer Journal. 2001;7:149-54.

12. **Bardia A, Greeno ED, Bauer BA.** Dietary supplement usage by patients with cancer undergoing chemotherapy: does prognosis or cancer symptoms predict usage. J Support Oncol. 2007;5:195-8.

26. **Sparreboom A, Cox MC, Acharya MR, Figg WD.** Herbal remedies in the United States: potential adverse interactions with anticancer agents. J Clin Oncol. 2004;22:2489-503. Review.

27. **Chang EY, Glissmeyer M, Tonnes S, et al.** Outcomes of breast cancer in patients who use alternative therapies as primary treatment. Am J Surg. 2006;192:471-3.

29. **Loprinzi CL, Levitt R, Barton DL, et al.** Evaluation of shark cartilage in patients with advanced cancer: a North Central Cancer Treatment Group trial. Cancer. 2005;104:176-82.

30. **Acupuncture.** NIH Consensus Statement. 1997;15:1-34.

32. **Ezzo J, Vickers A, Richardson MA, et al.** Acupuncture-point stimulation for chemotherapy-induced nausea and vomiting. J Clin Oncol. 2005;23:7188-98.

36. **Luebbert K, Dahme B, Hasenbring M.** The effectiveness of relaxation training in reducing treatment-related symptoms and improving emotional adjustment in acute non-surgical cancer treatment: a meta-analytical review. Psycho-Oncology. 2001;10:490-502.

38. **Vincent A, Barton DL, Mandrekar JN, et al.** Acupuncture for hot flashes: a randomized, sham-controlled clinical study. Menopause. 2007;14:45-52.

42. **Jacobsen PB, Meade CD, Stein KD, et al.** Efficacy and costs of two forms of stress management training for cancer patients undergoing chemotherapy. J Clin Oncol. 2002;20:2851-62.

43. **Barsevick AM, Dudley W, Beck S, et al.** A randomized clinical trial of energy conservation for patients with cancer-related fatigue. Cancer. 2004;100:1302-10.

44. **Yates P, Aranda S, Hargraves M, et al.** Randomized controlled trial of an educational intervention for managing fatigue in women receiving adjuvant chemotherapy for early-stage breast cancer. J Clin Oncol. 2005;23:6027-36.

51. **Post-White J, Kinney ME, Savik K, et al.** Therapeutic massage and healing touch improve symptoms in cancer. Integr Cancer Ther. 2003;2:332-44.

68. **Beck SL.** The therapeutic use of music for cancer-related pain. Oncol Nurs Forum. 1991: 18:1327-37.

71. **Murtagh DR, Greenwood KM.** Identifying effective psychological treatments for insomnia: A meta-analysis. J Consult Clin Psychol. 1995;63:79-89.

72. **Morin CM, Culbert JP, Schwartz SM.** Nonpharmacological interventions for insomnia: A meta-analysis of treatment efficacy. Am J Psychiatry. 1994;151:1172-80.

82. **Tasaki K, Maskarinec G, Shumay DM, et al.** Communication between physicians and cancer patients about complementary and alternative medicine: exploring patients' perspectives. Psycho-Oncology. 2002;11:212-20.

---

\* The complete reference list is to be found on the book's Web site.

# Chapter 6

ℰ℈

# General Medicine

Bradly Jacobs, MD, MPH
Katherine Gundling, MD

## Anxiety

Approximately 4%-15% of Americans meet DSM-IV criteria for generalized anxiety disorder (GAD), with milder forms of anxiety being even more common. Many people with GAD also have other psychiatric conditions such as major depression, phobias, post-traumatic stress disorder, obsessive-compulsive disorder and/or panic disorder. The economic costs associated with anxiety approach $46 billion annually in the United States.

People presenting initially with GAD should be evaluated for coexisting psychiatric conditions and those underlying conditions should be treated aggressively. Mainstay treatment for GAD includes exercise, medications, and psychological counseling including cognitive behavioral therapy (1,2). Medications include anti-depressants (tricyclic anti-depressants, selective serotonin reuptake inhibitors, selective serotonin and norepinephrine reuptake inhibitors), buspirone, and benzodiazepines.

CAM therapies are used as monotherapy as well as combination therapy in the treatment of GAD (2). A 2004 review of these therapies found the best evidence for kava, exercise, and relaxation therapies. They report limited evidence for acupuncture, music, autogenic training, and meditation. The more widely used CAM therapies are described below.

## Dietary Supplements

### Kava

Kava is a member of the pepper family and grows as a shrub in the South Pacific. Kava is has been used for ceremonial purposes throughout the pacific islands for centuries. Traditionally the root is pulverized with a mortar and pestle and mixed with water or coconut milk. Kava is typically ingested as a drink in ceremonial bowls and is used socially as a mild intoxicant like alcohol. The active ingredients are called kavalactones including kavain, dihyrdomethysticin, and methysticin. Dietary supplement extracts can be standardized to specific kavalactone concentrations, with most clinical trials using 100 mg kavalactones three times daily.

More than a dozen randomized blinded trials have been conducted that suggest kava is effective in treating anxiety, although one large internet-based randomized blinded trial found kava no more effective than placebo (3). Multiple systematic reviews have reported favorable therapeutic benefits and found kava to be associated with mild and transient side effects (4-6).

In March 2002, however, the FDA issued a Consumer Advisory after Germany, Switzerland and the United States identified 11 patients who used kava-containing products and experienced fulminant liver failure requiring liver transplantation (7,8). Nonetheless, some reviews suggest the benefits of Kava when used in otherwise healthy individuals on a short-term basis outweigh the remote risk of liver toxicity (4). Until there is better understanding of the mechanisms, products, and populations at-risk for hepatotoxicty, we believe risks outweigh the benefits particularly given the myriad of pharmaceutical, psychological, and mind-body interventions available to manage this condition (see Evidence Summary table at end of chapter).

### Passionflower

Passionflower is commonly found in dietary supplement products purporting to relieve stress and anxiety. One randomized trial enrolled 36 people with GAD to passionflower extract 45 drops/day plus placebo tablet or oxazepam 30 mg/day plus placebo drops for 4 weeks. Both were effective in the treatment of anxiety, and no significant differences were observed between groups. Oxazepam was found to have a more rapid onset but also to be associated with impaired job performance (9). While this preliminary research is promising, there is currently insufficient evidence to refute or recommend passionflower for the treatment of anxiety (see Evidence Summary table at end of chapter).

### Hops (Humulus lupulus)

Hops is commonly found in stress and anxiety dietary supplement products; however, there is a paucity of clinical trial data available to evaluate its effectiveness. Consequently, at this time, there is insufficient evidence to refute or recommend Hops for the treatment of anxiety (see Evidence Summary table at end of chapter).

### Bach Flower Remedy

A systematic review identified four controlled clinical trials of Bach Flower remedy that met inclusion criteria for their review. Two of these trials reported positive benefits; however, after controlling methodological issues, Bach flower remedy was no better than placebo (10). Two of the more rigorous randomized trials found no benefit over placebo (11,12). At this time, the evidence suggests that Bach Flower remedy appears not to have therapeutic benefit over placebo for the treatment of anxiety (see Evidence Summary table at end of chapter).

## Acupuncture

As described in more depth in Appendix 1, acupuncture is frequently associated with neurophysiologic and biochemical changes such as increases in endomorphin-1, beta endorphin, encephalin, and serotonin levels. Many of these physiologic effects are associated with relaxation and analgesia. In clinical practice, most patients will describe feeling a sense of calm and well-being after acupuncture treatments. Two reviews have found limited evidence suggesting that acupuncture has increasing promise as an effective treatment for anxiety (13,14). Specifically, there are several randomized clinical trials reporting reductions in anxiety symptoms for procedure-related anxiety among those treated with acupuncture compared with controls, including subjects undergoing extracorpeal shock wave lithotripsy (15), colonoscopy (16), dental procedure–related anxiety (17), pre-operative anxiety (18), and pre-hospital transport (19). Other trials have examined anxiety symptoms among people living with chronic conditions such as chronic neck and shoulder pain (20) and fibromyalgia (21). One trial found acupuncture was not better than sham control for anxiety related to oocyte retrieval (22), and another found similar results for anxiety related to alcohol withdrawal symptoms (23).

There are only a few randomized trials evaluating the effects of acupuncture for people diagnosed with GAD or anxiety related to other psychiatric illness. One study randomized 43 patients with minor depression and 13 patients with GAD to 10 sessions of real versus sham acupuncture. Treatment was associated with statistically significant improvement on the Clinical Global Impression Scale (primary outcome) compared with controls. Multivariate analysis demonstrated a trend toward lower anxiety scores using the Hamilton Anxiety Rating scale compared with sham. Investigators concluded that acupuncture was associated with reductions in anxiety symptoms in people with minor depression and among people with GAD (24). A multi-center trial randomized 241 inpatients with depression to electroacupuncture + placebo, amitriptyline alone, or electroacupuncture + amytriptyline. Based on results from the Hamilton Rating Scale for Depression, and Clinical Global Impression scales, investigators report electroacupuncture was superior to amitriptyline for depressive disorders, including anxiety somatization and cognitive process disturbance with a reduced side effect profile (25). Finally, one study randomized 55 healthy volunteers to sham acupuncture, shenmen ear acupuncture point (the 'relaxation' ear acupuncture point) and found reduced anxiety among volunteers randomized to the 'relaxation' point compared with sham acupuncture at 30 minutes, 24 hours post-treatment (26).

In summary, there is moderate evidence that acupuncture may be effective for procedure-related anxiety, and limited evidence for anxiety symptoms related to selected medical conditions. There is insufficient evidence to support or refute recommending acupuncture for treating GAD (13) (see Evidence Summary table at end of chapter).

## Aromatherapy

Aromatherapy involves the use of fragrant essential oils for healing purposes. It frequently is applied on the skin or inhaled in dilute form through a vaporizer. A 2000 review identified 6 randomized trials evaluating the effect of aromatherapy on relaxation measures pertaining to a range of conditions and issues. Five of the six trials reported positive benefits; however, all were of poor methodological quality. Consequently, the authors concluded that aromatherapy likely provides transient and mild anxiolytic effects that are likely not strong enough to be beneficial for the treatment of anxiety. They did not identify evidence to suggest aromatherapy provides any long-term health benefits. (27). There are no randomized trials evaluating its effectiveness for people with GAD.

One randomized trial found aromatherapy no more effective than smelling a pleasant odor among people scheduled for a medical procedure (28). A large trial randomized 313 patients undergoing cancer radiation treatment and found no benefit of inhalation aromatherapy compared to controls (29). Another trial did not find benefit to adding aromatherapy to massage among 42 palliative care cancer patients who were randomized to receive four weekly massages with lavender essential oil or massage only or no intervention (30). A Cochrane review evaluated the effect of massage or aromatherapy massage for symptom relief in cancer patients (31). Anxiety measures were evaluated in four trials involving 207 patients with 19%-32% reduction in symptoms reported. There was conflicting evidence on the benefit of the addition of aromatherapy to massage on anxiety measures. Another trial found short-term benefits associated with aromatherapy massage among cancer patients diagnosed with clinical anxiety and/or depression. In this multi-center trial, they randomized 288 patients to aromatherapy massage or usual care and found improvements in self-reported anxiety at 10 weeks (OR 3.4), and in clinical anxiety scores at 6 weeks (OR 1.4) without sustained benefit at 10 weeks (32).

In summary, there is no evidence to suggest that aromatherapy is an effective treatment for anxiety disorders. Therefore, there is insufficient evidence to support or refute the use of aromatherapy for these conditions (see Evidence Summary table at end of chapter). However, there is moderate evidence to suggest that aromatherapy massage may confer short-term anxiolytic benefits among hospitalized patients; there is conflicting evidence on the additional benefit that aromatherapy itself has when provided in the context of a therapeutic massage.

## Meditation

Meditation enables people to consciously regulate their attention or "moment to moment" awareness. The two major types of meditation commonly practiced in the United States are concentration meditation and mindfulness mediation. The primary goal of concentration meditation is to focus attention on a single object such as a sound, image, or one's breath. The most popular practices include the Relaxation Response and Transcendental Meditation. When the natural tendency of the mind to wander occurs, the practitioner gently redirects attention back to the object of focus time and time again. Practitioners purport the mind gently settles into a relaxed and aware state of consciousness that is incompatible with high states of arousal such as anxiety or agitation. Mindfulness meditation focuses on cultivating a moment-to-moment awareness of thoughts and perceptions in the absence of self-ridicule or judgment. As the mind wanders, the practitioner gently brings attention back to the present moment including the corresponding thoughts and perceptions. Primary examples of this technique include Mindfulness-Based Cognitive Therapy and Mindfulness-Based Stress Reduction. Over time, practitioners are said to become much more accepting of themselves and also more aware of their psychological processes. Given the importance of directing attention in the psychotherapeutic encounter, one trial evaluated the effect of training psychotherapists in mindfulness meditation. Eighteen psychotherapists in training (treating 124 inpatients) were randomized to a 9-week Zen meditation course or usual care. The intervention group received significantly higher evaluations, and patients reported greater symptom improvement across multiple measures including the Global Severity Index and 8 scales of the Symptom Checklist (SCL-90-R) including Somatization, Insecurity in Social Contact, Obsessiveness, Anxiety, Anger/Hostility, Phobic Anxiety, Paranoid Thinking and Psychoticism (33).

The scientific literature in this area of study, however, is quite limited. A 2006 Cochrane review identified only two randomized clinical trials evaluating the effect of meditation on anxiety conditions and concluded there was insufficient evidence to render an opinion on the effectiveness of meditation therapy for anxiety disorders (34). Another review identified five randomized trials on the effect of meditation on GAD and high trait anxiety (2). Four of these trials found that meditation was no different than relaxation therapies and biofeedback and was superior to wait list control. In conclusion, there is limited evidence suggesting that meditation may be effective for reducing anxiety symptoms among people with GAD or high-trait anxiety; however, further research is needed before making a recommendation (see Evidence Summary table at end of chapter).

## Relaxation Therapies

Relaxation therapies include a range of therapies that promote a sense of calm and well-being. The two most common forms are progressive muscle relaxation and the "relaxation response" as defined by Herbert Benson. Relaxation techniques teach patients to recognize symptoms of anxiety, as well as triggers and cues. These techniques are said to induce a state of consciousness that is incompatible with elevated states of arousal such as anxiety and agitation (2). A 2007 review found muscle relaxation techniques effective for GAD (35). A 2007 meta-analysis found relaxation therapies superior to control and as effective as cognitive behavior therapy, meditation, autogenic training and biofeedback for GAD (36). In summary, there is strong evidence supporting the effectiveness of relaxation therapies for the treatment of GAD (see Evidence Summary table at end of chapter). This class of interventions is well-tolerated and generally safe.

# Common Cold

Upper respiratory infections are the leading reason for primary care visits in the United States. Unfortunately, antibiotics are still routinely prescribed for the treatment of this viral infection despite widespread education on the lack of efficacy and the safety concerns regarding the growing emergence of antibiotic resistance partly secondary to over-prescribing practices. There are no effective mainstay treatments to prevent or treat the common cold. There are numerous dietary supplements sold over-the-counter that purport to prevent or treat the common cold. We will review four of the more widely used products: zinc, Echinacea, vitamin C, and garlic.

## Dietary Supplements

### Zinc

Sufficient serum levels of zinc are required for an optimally functioning immune system. There are more than nine clinical trials demonstrating that adequate zinc levels are associated with fewer respiratory, gastrointestinal and other infections in children and in elderly nursing home residents (37-45). For the treatment of the common cold, however, it is the topical application of zinc onto mucosal surfaces such as the buccal or nasal mucosa that seems to provide benefit. Zinc lozenges or nasal gel when applied to the mucosa have been found to inhibit cold viruses, such as rhinovirus, from adhering to the mucosal epithelium, thereby limiting infection or preventing it all together.

There are multiple randomized blinded trials evaluating zinc for the treatment of the common cold, with the balance showing beneficial effects and a good safety profile (46). One trial randomized 100 people to 13.3 mg zinc gluconate or placebo at onset of cold symptoms and found statistically significant reduction in duration of cough, sore throat, and rhinorrhea (47). Zinc as a treatment for the common cold comes in nasal and oral preparations, multiple formulations, and flavorings. The greatest scientific evidence is for zinc gluconate and zinc acetate lozenges without flavorings (48). Nasal gel formulations should be avoided due to the risk of insomnia and pain with use. Overall, there is sufficient evidence to support a weak recommendation for zinc gluconate or zinc acetate lozenges for the treatment the common cold (see Evidence Summary table at end of chapter). For optimal effect, however, these products should be taken in the first 24 hours of cold symptoms. Frequent dosing requirements may limit its use. Patients should be informed that favorable results require lozenges to be taken every 2 hours. These products are generally well-tolerated.

## Echinacea

Echinacea comes in many species (*E. purpurea*, *E. pallida*, *E. angusifolia*), formulations, dosages, active ingredients, and routes of administration. Over the past several decades, studies have shown conflicting results, largely because investigators use different preparations. For example, a well-conducted trial by Turner et al randomized 437 healthy volunteers to receive prophylaxis *Echinacea angustifolia* root extract after experimental inoculation with rhinovirus type 39. They found no statistically significant benefits in preventing or shortening infection (49).

Overall, the best evidence for the therapeutic benefit of Echinacea is with the above-ground preparations of *Echinacea purpurea* (stems, flowers, and leaves). A Cochrane review identified 16 trials, including 22 comparisons using a variety of Echinacea preparations (50). Nineteen comparisons evaluated its effect for the treatment of the common cold, and three comparisons evaluated its efficacy for cold prevention. None of the prevention trials showed benefit over placebo. Among the treatment comparisons, nine reported statistically significant benefit over placebo, one reported a trend, and six showed no benefit. They concluded that Echinacea preparations differed greatly in therapeutic benefit and the most promising evidence was for above-ground preparations of the *Echinacea purpurea* for the early treatment of colds. The evidence is inconclusive for other Echinacea preparations (50). Other systematic reviews have suggested that Echinacea when taken immediately after exposure or at first onset of symptoms may abort infection by the common cold (51) and reduce the duration and severity of symptoms among people suffering from the common cold (52).

The most recent meta-analysis reviewed 14 trials including 1600 people and found that Echinacea reduced the odds of getting a cold by 58% and shortened the duration of symptoms by 1.4 days compared to placebo. Subgroup analysis limited to Echinaguard/Echinacin use or controlling for concomitant supplement use, method of cold exposure, Jadad scores less than 3, or use of a fixed-effects model did not effect the benefits seen (53).

There has been controversy over whether immune-compromised patients should be using Echinacea for the long-term due to theoretical immune-stimulating effects. Recent research suggests that short-term use of Echinacea may have immune-stimulating effects, but long-term use appears not to have these effects (54-56).

In summary, Echinacea comes in varied preparations with varying clinical benefits. The best evidence is for above-ground preparations of E. *purpurea*. Overall, there is sufficient evidence to make a weak recommendation in favor of using this specific species and plant part for the treatment of the common cold (see Evidence Summary table at end of chapter). People with allergies to ragweed, chrysanthemums, marigolds, and daisies should not take this herb because there is cross reactivity.

## Vitamin C

There has been significant controversy as to whether vitamin C is effective in the prevention or treatment of the common cold. A recent Cochrane systematic review evaluated the effect of vitamin C prophylaxis and treatment for the common cold. They identified 30 trials involving 11,350 subjects for vitamin C prophylaxis and found a 4% reduction in incident colds episodes which achieved borderline statistical significance (RR= 0.96, 95% CI 0.92 to 1.00) and questionable clinical significance. Among a subgroup of trials in which subjects were exposed to brief periods of severe physical or environmental stress (marathon runners, skiers, and solders on sub-artic exercises), they identified 50% reduction in incident cold infection when compared to placebo. Furthermore, vitamin C when taken prophylactically reduced cold symptom duration across all subgroups by 8% in adults and 13% in children when compared with placebo. Vitamin C when taken after the onset of symptoms, however, failed to shorten duration or severity of symptoms compared to placebo (57).

Overall, there is moderate evidence to suggest that vitamin C is not effective in reducing cold symptom severity or duration of symptoms when taken at onset of symptoms (see Evidence Summary table at end of chapter). There is moderate evidence to suggest that taking vitamin C prophylactically appears effective in reducing symptom duration (see Evidence Summary table at end of chapter). There is moderate evidence to suggest taking vitamin C prophylactically does not provide clinically meaningful benefits in preventing the common cold, except in subjects placed under severe stress, in which case it does appear to be quite effective (see Evidence Summary table at end of chapter).

## Garlic

Folklore has portrayed garlic as the wonder herb, conquering infections and evil spirits. The only randomized trial identified enrolled 146 people and reported fewer colds (24 vs 65, p<0.001), and shorter symptom duration (1.5 vs 5, p<0.001) compared with placebo (58). There is promising preliminary data on the possible therapeutic benefit of garlic for the prevention and treatment of the common cold; however, there is insufficient evidence to refute or recommend the use of garlic for this indication at this time (see Evidence Summary table at end of chapter).

# Diabetes

Type 2 diabetes mellitus affects many people worldwide. Although it has traditionally been considered a disease of adulthood, it is occurring with increasing incidence in young people, particularly as more and more youngsters develop obesity. The estimated number of new cases of diagnosed diabetes in people aged 20 years or older in 2005 in the United States was 1.5 million, with a total prevalence of 20.8 million people. Total costs (direct and indirect) for diabetes care in 2002 were approximately $132 billion (59).

Although some type 2 diabetics are able to improve their conditions with physical activity, dietary changes and weight loss, many patients have difficulty with these lifestyle changes, and they look for solutions both within and outside of the conventional medical setting (60). A regional analysis of 2474 adult patients with diabetes at Medical University of South Carolina revealed that 48% of adults with diabetes used some form of CAM (in a broad definition) (61). Use of CAM was independently associated with receipt of pneumonia vaccination (but not influenza vaccination), visits to the emergency department, and six or more visits to a primary care office. Whereas previous studies suggested that diabetic patients might use CAM independent of the conventional medical system, this study suggested that most diabetics use CAM in addition to conventional medicine.

Use of CAM and conventional treatments simultaneously was also found in a broader demographic in a national survey study discussed in Chapter 1, in which the vast majority of diabetic patients who used CAM were also under the care of a medical doctor (62). This means that medical doctors have an excellent opportunity to determine what remedies their patients are using, to offer guidance, and to follow their patients' progress.

CAM therapies have been tried for a number of manifestations of diabetes, including glycemic control, peripheral neuropathy, quality of life, lipid parameters, leg ulceration, and others.

## Dietary Supplements

### Cinnamon

Cinnamon is a delightful and exotic spice that became a popular supplement for diabetes after the publication of a clinical study performed in Pakistan (63). This study reported that cinnamon powder (*Cinnamomum cassia*), taken over a 40-day period, reduced mean fasting serum glucose, LDL cholesterol, and total cholesterol. Three doses were studied, and all reported to be effective. There are no validated studies of western populations at that time.

By 2006 Dugoua and colleagues performed a systematic review of the effects of cinnamon for type 2 diabetes, surveying nine databases along with the Complete German Commission E Monographs, Natural Database and Natural Standard (64). They also hand searched relevant review papers and reference lists of original research publications. They found three randomized clinical trials of aqueous cassia extract.

The first used 3 gm vs placebo for 4 months in 79 people. They found a significantly greater reduction in fasting glucose in the cinnamon group, but no difference was seen in hemoglobin A1c (HbA1c) or cholesterol levels. In the second study 60 participants were given 1 gm, 3 gm or 6 gm vs placebo for 40 days. The authors found significant improvement in blood glucose control and reductions in cardiovascular risk factor biomarkers. They did not follow HbA1c levels. Fasting baseline glucose levels were noted to be quite high. The third study used 1.5 gm daily vs placebo for 6 weeks in 25 postmenopausal patients. No improvements were seen in fasting glucose, plasma insulin, or lipid parameters.

In 2006 a clinical trial of 60 patients randomized to 1.5 gm cassia powder or placebo for 12 weeks showed HbA1c to be similarly decreased in both groups. There were no significant differences in lipid profiles. The mean start fasting plasma glucose was 154 +/- 24 mg/dL (65).

More recently, Solomon looked at the effects of short-term cinnamon ingestion on in vivo glucose tolerance in seven lean, healthy male volunteers in their mid 20's. They underwent three oral glucose tolerance tests, supplemented with 5 gms of placebo, 5 gms of cinnamon, or 5 gms of cinnamon taken 12 hours before a randomized cross-over design. Use of cinnamon was associated with improvement in total plasma glucose responses and insulin sensitivity by the Matsuda model, with sustained effects seen after 12 hours (66).

A 2008 meta-analysis of randomized controlled trials of cinnamon supplementation evaluated five prospective, randomized controlled trials with 282 patients and did not find a difference in A1c, fasting blood glucose or lipid parameters. Subgroup and sensitivity analyses also showed no significant changes (67).

Blevins et al, evaluated 60 patients with 1 gm cinnamon daily versus placebo for 3 months. Forty-three patients completed the study, dropouts were accounted for appropriately and adherence was high. The participants were of mixed ethnicity. 77% of the cinnamon group also used diabetes medications, whereas 91% of the placebo group used medication. There were no significant differences between the cinnamon and placebo groups in the change in any measure (fasting glucose, lipid A1C or insulin levels) from baseline to 1, 2, or 3 months (68).

In summary, although there is an increasing number of well-designed clinical trials, there is currently insufficient evidence to recommend use of cinnamon for treatment of diabetes, particularly not as an alternative to medications with well-established hypoglycemic effects (see Evidence Summary table at end of chapter). Both common and cassia cinnamon have been studied and, as with all dietary supplements, the exact composition of cinnamon might have varied significantly in the different trials.

## Omega-3 Fatty Acids

Omega-3 fatty acids are found in a number of foods, such as fish, walnuts, certain seeds, wheat germ and several vegetable oils. They are commonly purchased as dietary supplements in the form of fish oil capsules.

In the original Cochrane evaluation in 2001 of 18 randomized, double-blind, placebo-controlled trials, patients with type 2 diabetes who consumed fish oils lowered triglyceride and slightly raised LDL cholesterol, but had no significant effect on fasting blood glucose, HbA1c, total cholesterol, or HDL cholesterol (69). In the last substantive update in 2008, Hartweg et al concluded that supplementation lowered triglycerides and VLDL cholesterol, had no effect on blood glucose or fasting insulin levels, and might slightly raise LDL cholesterol (although these findings did not achieve statistical significance). There were no adverse effects (70).

The Agency for Healthcare Research and Quality published an independent analysis in 2004 of 18 studies on omega-3 fatty acids for a number of measurable outcomes in type 2 diabetes. The authors concurred with the Cochrane authors' findings, except for finding no significant effect on LDL cholesterol (71). See the Evidence Summary table at the end of the chapter.

While consumers should be aware of the theoretical risk of poorly manufactured supplements that contain mercury, two studies conducted random testing of omega-3 dietary supplements and found no evidence of high levels of mercury in the brand names tested (72). Nonetheless, we recommend that consumers identify companies that abide by the FDA final rule for current Good Manufacturing Practices to ensure supplements are free of toxic levels of mercury. Even better, consumers can look for the NSF, USP seal of approval of good manufacturing practices or go to consumerlab.com to identify products that have passed their quality-control testing.

## Chromium

Chromium has been studied more extensively than other complementary treatments for type 2 diabetes with mixed results. It is abundant in the earth's crust and found in numerous foods, such as vegetables, beef, potatoes with skin, brewer's yeast, cheese and others. Chromium is required for normal glucose metabolism. It may play a role in helping insulin bind to insulin receptors, theoretically augmenting carbohydrate and lipid metabolism. The recommended daily allowance for healthy adults is 50-200 mcg (73). Supplemental chromium does not cause hypoglycemia in healthy people. It may be that chromium is helpful for some patients who are deficient in it, or for certain other populations. Kleefstra et al found no benefit to adding chromium 400 mcg (in the form of chromium yeast) for 6 months beyond usual care, including oral hypoglycemic agents, to Western patients with type 2 diabetes (74).

This is in contrast to the study performed by Anderson et al in China, which found that patients treated with 1000 mcg of chromium picolinate dropped their HbA1C levels more than patients who took placebo, in a study of 180 patients over 4 months (75).

In 2002 Althuis et al looked at 20 clinical trials, including 15 randomized trials with enough data for evaluation. Trials used chromium chloride, chromium nicotinate, chromium niacin, chromium "rich" yeast, Brewer's yeast and chromium picolinate. The dose ranged form 10.8 to 1000 mcg. There were several different controls. Glucose and insulin concentration were assessed after fasting and at 120 minutes after an oral glucose tolerance test. The effects of chromium were studied in diabetic patients (193 patients with type 2 diabetes) and non-diabetic patients (425 patients). The reviewers concluded that there is no evidence that chromium has any effects on glucose or insulin levels in non-diabetic patients, and there was insufficient evidence to determine the effect of chromium on diabetic patients. This analysis looked at only two databases, and patient populations may have differed considerably between studies. The authors recommend further safety testing (76). See the Evidence Summary table at the end of the chapter for a summary of the evidence.

## Chinese Herbs

A Cochrane review of Chinese herbs for diabetes identified 66 trials involving 8302 participants that met their criteria for inclusion. Methodologic quality was generally low. Sixty-nine different herbal medications were evaluated compared to placebo, hypoglycemic drugs or herbal medications plus hypoglycemic drugs. Compared with placebo, holy basil leaves, Xianzhen Pian, Qidan Tongmai, traditional Chinese formulae Huoxue Jiangtang Pingzhi, and Inolter showed a significant hypoglycemic response. No high-quality trials were identified.

In conclusion, some Chinese herbal medications show hypoglycemic effects in type 2 diabetes. However, these findings should be carefully interpreted because of the low methodological quality of these trials. The authors felt that in light of some positive findings, some herbal medicines deserve further examination (77). The safety of these herbs also needs further evaluation. Given that Chinese herbal treatments (albeit unrelated to the ones studied for diabetes) have been associated with liver and kidney adverse effects (78-81), the safety issues should be more fully evaluated as part of any clinical program evaluating the efficacy of these treatments. If patients intend to take Chinese herbs, they should limit themselves to products that have been independently certified for good manufacturing practices by the NPA, USP, or NSF. Alternatively, they can go to consumerlab.com and verify which specific brand names passed their quality-assurance testing.

## Other Agents

Other agents, such as aloe vera and ginseng, have been used for diabetes without strong evidence based upon clinical investigation (82,83).

## 2003 Summary of Dietary Supplements for Diabetes

Yeh et al summarized available clinical data for dietary supplement treatments of diabetes in 2003, which is now somewhat dated. The systematic review of multiple databases selected studies that looked at glycemic control. The authors concluded that there was insufficient evidence to draw definitive conclusions about the efficacy of individual herbs and supplements, but that several supplements, including *Coccinia indica* and American ginseng, deserve further study. Other supplements judged to have "positive preliminary results" include *Cymnema sylvestre*, Aloe vera, vanadium, *Momordica charantia* and nopal (84).

## Acupuncture for Diabetic Neuropathy

Peripheral neuropathy is a painful complication experienced by some diabetic patients. Safe, effective alternative therapies would be a welcome addition to the physician's armamentarium of treatments. Although much has been written about use of acupuncture for diabetic neuropathy, high-quality clinical trials are lacking. One pilot study treated 46 diabetic patients with diabetic peripheral neuropathy with acupuncture and found 77% reporting significant improvement and 67% reduced their related medications (85). Currently there is insufficient evidence to recommend or refute the use of acupuncture for treatment of diabetic peripheral neuropathy (see Evidence Summary table at end of chapter).

## Ayurvedic Interventions for Diabetes Mellitus

As noted in the Appendix, Ayurvedic medicine is a medical system that uses single or multiple modalities simultaneously in the treatment of disease. With respect to the treatment of patients with diabetes, a summative analysis has been published by the Agency for Healthcare Research and Quality. The reviewers identified 54 articles containing 62 clinical trials of Ayurvedic therapy for diabetes that met their inclusion criteria. Meta-analysis was not possible owing to the heterogeneity of the trials.

Clinical trials were limited almost exclusively to herbal preparations, and no other modalities could be assessed. Unfortunately, there were no studies that tested multiple simultaneous Ayurvedic interventions, or Ayurveda as a whole system. Several clinical trials from India (published in English) could not be located, and several trials in India written in other languages were not reviewed.

Based on the current evidence, the reviewers note that the single herbs *Coccinia indica*, holy basil, fenugreek and *Gymnema sylvestra*, and the herbal formulas Ayush-82 and D-400 show preliminary evidence of glucose-lowering effect and should be studied further. There are currently too few randomized controlled trials of sufficient quality to make firm conclusions, and therefore there is insufficient evidence to recommend or refute the effect of these treatments for active treatment of diabetes (see Evidence Summary table at end of chapter). The authors recommend field studies to determine how Ayurvedic medicine is used in real-life clinical practice, and they encourage investigation of the interaction between botanicals and other Ayurvedic modalities, such as yoga (86).

NCCAM is currently sponsoring research into the effects of chromium, yoga, ginkgo, vitamin C, and the safety of glucosamine on diabetes.

# Herpes Infection

Genital herpes infection is a sexually transmitted disease caused by both herpes simplex virus 1 (HSV-1) and herpes simplex virus 2 (HSV-2) viruses. HSV-1 predominately causes mouth sores and HSV-2 infection can cause both genital and mouth sores. Approximately 20% of the US population is infected with genital herpes infection with a greater predominance among women. More than 371,000 initial visits to physician offices occurred in 2006 related to herpes infection. Approximately 200,000 to 500,000 new cases of herpes infection occur annually. Transmission occurs through release of the virus during a "herpes outbreak" (when blisters are present) but can also occur when no skin lesions are identified. Herpes infection can facilitate transmission of HIV virus, particularly when skin lesions are present.

There is no cure for herpes infection and therefore people carry the virus throughout the duration of their life. Mainstay therapy includes anti-viral medications such as valcycolvir and acyclovir. These medications can prevent and shorten the duration of outbreaks. When taken regularly as a daily prophylactic, these medications can reduce the frequency of symptomatic herpes for individuals prone to recurrent outbreaks, as well as reduce transmission rates to uninfected partners.

## Dietary Supplements

### L-Lysine

L-lysine is an amino acid widely used by consumers for the prevention and treatment of herpes infection. A review of several randomized blinded clinical trials using 1.25 to 3 grams daily dose reported reductions in recurrent episodes (87). One trial randomized 52 people with genital herpes to 3 grams daily or placebo for 6 months and found a statistically significant reduction of 2.4 fewer recurrences than the control group (88). An earlier multi-center study by the same author also found benefit (89). McCune conducted a randomized blinded cross-over trial of 42 patients taking 1.25 grams of lysine and found reduced recurrence rates. Of note, they found no benefit using the lower dose of 624 mg daily. They also noted lysine did not appear to heal lesions more quickly than placebo (90). DiGiovanna randomized 21 people to 400 mg three times daily of lysine hydrochloride compared to placebo and found no benefit (91). Milman randomized 65 people with recurrent herpes simplex labialis infections to 12 weeks of 1000 mg lysine daily in a randomized, blinded, crossover study. Investigators found no effect on the recurrence rates; however, significantly more people were recurrence-free during the lysine intervention period than during the placebo treatment period. They found no effect of lysine on healing of skin lesions (92). Overall, there is limited evidence to suggest that 3 grams daily of L-lysine monohydrochloride may reduce recurrence rates of symptomatic herpes infection among at-risk populations (93). Overall, there is sufficient evidence make a weak recommendation in favor of L-lysine for this indication (see Evidence Summary table at end of chapter).

There is significant discussion among consumers and in media regarding the benefits of a high-lysine and low-arginine diet to prevent recurrent symptomatic herpes outbreaks. Foods containing more arginine than lysine include whole wheat, oats, chocolate, peanuts, walnuts, orange juice, and blueberries, for example. Foods containing more lysine than arginine include meats and dairy products.

There are no clinical trials or large cohort studies evaluating these claims. There are in vitro studies, however, suggesting that arginine-rich environments are critical for herpes virus function and growth (94,95). At this time there is insufficient evidence to support or refute using this modified diet as effective treatment for herpes.

### Lemon Balm (*Melissa officinalis*)

Topical lemon balm is sold in Europe as a topical cream for the treatment of oral and genital herpes. In one study, 116 people with oral or genital herpes were randomized to lemon balm or placebo cream for 10 days, and the treatment group experienced a more rapid recovery than controls (96). Another trial evaluated 66 people with oral herpes and reported similar findings on day 2 (97). At this time, there is insufficient evidence to support or refute the use of lemon balm for the treatment of genital herpes (see Evidence Summary table at end of chapter).

## Migraine Headaches

Migraine headaches can be unilateral or bilateral and may or may not involve prodromal symptoms. The cause remains unclear but is thought to be mediated by neurotransmitters such as serotonin and dopamine, which are thought to initiate an inflammatory cascade leading to vasodilation and secondary perivascular changes. The International Headache Society recently redefined migraines such that "classic migraine" is now defined as a migraine with aura and "common migraine" is now defined as a migraine without aura. The latter accounts for 80% of all migraine episodes.

Approximately 17% of women and 6% of men in the United States have suffered from migraine headaches. Migraines are the second most common headache following tension headaches. Surprisingly, less than half of migraine sufferers are diagnosed by their doctors. Overall, this condition remains largely undertreated and underdiagnosed. Symptoms include intense pain, as well as nausea, visual disturbances, and, in cases of complicated migraines, neurological deficits. Some people experience early warning signs such as changes in energy or mood, fatigue, food cravings, or visual disturbances such as flashing lights, colors, and transient loss of peripheral vision.

Many people benefit from keeping a journal in order to identify factors that may trigger their migraines. Examples of triggers include lack of sleep, skipping meals, birth control pills or hormonal changes including menstrual cycle, smoking tobacco, intense physical activity or emotional reactivity. Specific foods that trigger migraines in certain people include aspartame, monosodium glutamate, cured or processed meats, alcohol (particularly red wine), caffeine, chocolate, nuts and peanuts, preserved or pickled foods, and soy sauce, among others.

Treatments for migraine headaches fall into two categories: prevention and acute treatment. If migraines are interfering with daily functioning or occur more than twice monthly, daily medication to prevent recurrent migraines is recommended. Medications for prevention of migraines include beta-blockers, tricyclic anti-depressants, ergot derivatives, antihistamines, and anti-convulsants. Management of acute migraines includes a range of effective medications including simple analgesics (acetaminophen, aspirin, codeine), non-steroidal anti-inflammatory drugs, 5-HT1 serotonin receptor agonists (sumatriptans, zolmitriptan, and Rizatriptan), ergot alkaloids and their derivatives (ergotamines, dihydroergotamines), and combination drugs (isometheptene/dichloralphenazone/acetaminophen, and acetaminophen/butalbital/caffeine). In addition, people benefit from stress management therapies such relaxation techniques, breathing practices, lying down in a quiet and dark room, and self-massage to the scalp.

## Dietary Supplements

### Butterbur (Petasites hybridus)

Butterbur (Petasites hybridus) can be found in southwest Asia, North Africa, and Western Europe. The unprocessed herb contains pyrrolizidine alkaloids (PAs), which can cause hepatotoxicity. Consequently, a special Butterbur root extract that is free of PAs has been used for clinical trials. The most widely evaluated compound is called Petadolex, which is manufactured by high-pressure carbon dioxide extraction. This special extract has been evaluated in three randomized double-blind clinical trials. A systematic review analyzed two of the larger studies in which the proprietary product, Petadolex, was evaluated. They concluded that there is moderate evidence for effectiveness (98). One trial randomized 245 patients meeting the International Headache Society criteria for migraine to 4 months of twice daily specialized Patasites extract at 75 mg, 50 mg, or placebo. Over the course of the study, per-protocol analysis found the 75 mg dosage reduced migraine frequency by 48% (p=0.001 vs placebo), compared with 36% for the 50 mg dosage (p=0.13 vs placebo), and 26% for the placebo group. In addition, 68% of the high-dose group, compared with 49% of the placebo group, had a 50% or greater reduction in migraine frequency (p< 0.05) at 4 months (99). An earlier trial randomized 60 people to 3 months of 50 mg twice daily Butterbur PA-free extract or placebo and found a statistically significant reduction in migraine frequency compared with placebo. 75% of patients reported improvement compared with 25% taking placebo (100). Another trial, not included in the systematic review, randomized 33 people to 50 mg butterbur twice daily or placebo and found reductions in monthly migraine frequency from 3.4 at baseline to 1.8 after 3 months compared to a reduction from 2.9 to 2.6 reported for the control group. In addition, 45% of the verum group compared with 15% of the placebo group had a 50% or greater reduction in migraine frequency (101).

In summary, there is moderate evidence suggesting pyrrolizidine alkaloid (PA)–free butterbur extracts such as Petadolex appear effective and safe for the prevention of migraine headaches at 75 mg and 50 mg twice daily dosing. Animal and human research suggest the PA-free product is generally well-tolerated (102). There is sufficient evidence to support a strong recommendation for this treatment (see Evidence Summary table at end of chapter).

## Feverfew

A recent Cochrane systematic review identified five randomized clinical trials (including 343 people) and reported inconsistent evidence on the beneficial effect of feverfew for migraine prevention. Only transient and mild adverse effects were reported (103). Overall, the best evidence can be found among the trials evaluating a liquid carbon-dioxide extraction.

One trial randomized 170 people who met criteria according to the International Headache Society criteria for migraines to a liquid carbon-dioxide extraction of 6.25 mg three times daily of feverfew or placebo in a multi-center, parallel-group, double-blind, placebo-controlled trial. At the end of 4 months, migraine frequency was reduced by 1.9 attacks per month in the feverfew group compared with 1.3 attacks per month in the placebo group (p= 0.046). There were no differences in adverse events between groups (104). An earlier trial using the same formulation found benefit limited to a sub-group with more frequent attacks (105).

Two other randomized trials, both published in the 1980s, used whole feverfew leaf and found feverfew to be safe and effective (106,107); however, a trial evaluating feverfew in combination with riboflavin and magnesium compared to low-dose riboflavin found no benefit (108).

Overall, there is conflicting evidence regarding the effectiveness of feverfew for the prevention of migraines. In general, feverfew appears generally safe with mild and transient side effect profile. There is insufficient evidence to refute or support feverfew for the prevention of migraine headaches at this time (see Evidence Summary table at end of chapter).

## Magnesium

One study enrolling 60 people with migraines found intravenous magnesium sulphate was an effective treatment for acute migraines with aura for treating pain and for associated symptoms in subjects compared to placebo (109). Cete et al enrolled 120 people presenting to an emergency department who met International Headache Society criteria and randomized them to 10 mg intravenous metoclopramide, 2 grams intravenous magnesium, or normal saline and found neither treatment more effective than placebo (110). Another trial randomized 44 people to intravenous 20 mg metoclopramide with or without 1 gram intravenous magnesium sulfate and found magnesium was associated with worsened symptoms (111).

Two multi-center trials examined the use of oral magnesium for migraine prophylaxis. In one multi-center trial, investigators randomized 81 people who met International Headache Society criteria for migraine to 600 mg oral trimagnesium dicitrate daily or placebo for 12 weeks and found a marked reduction in headache frequency of 42% compared with 16% in the placebo group; however, these differences did not achieve statistical significance. Duration and intensity of migraine episode also decreased compared with placebo but also did not achieve statistical significance (112). A second multi-center trial randomized 118 children and adolescents with moderate to severe migraines to 3 mg/kg of magnesium oxide three times daily or placebo. Magnesium was associated with a reduced number of headache days and severity compared with placebo (113).

Overall, there is conflicting evidence regarding the effect of intravenous magnesium sulfate for the acute treatment of migraine headaches; consequently there is insufficient evidence to refute or support its use (see Evidence Summary table at end of chapter). There is limited evidence suggesting that oral magnesium oxide may prevent migraines; however, the evidence is too limited to render a recommendation at this time (see Evidence Summary table at end of chapter).

## Coenzyme Q10

One trial randomized 42 people with migraines to receive 100 mg three times daily of coenzyme Q10 or placebo and found 48% experienced at least a 50% reduction in attack frequency in the treatment group compared with 14% in the placebo group. Based on these findings, only three people would need to be treated to prevent one migraine (NNT= 3) (114). Coenzyme Q10 was well tolerated. These findings are very promising and suggest larger clinical trials are warranted. At this time, however, there is insufficient evidence to refute or support Co-Q10 for the treatment of migraines at this time (see Evidence Summary table at end of chapter).

## Acupuncture

A 2001 Cochrane review identified 26 randomized or quasi-randomized trials involving 1151 patients evaluating the effect of acupuncture for the treatment of idiopathic (primary) headaches. Sixteen of these trials were conducted among migraine sufferers, six among patients with tension-type headaches, and four among patients with miscellaneous headache-types. Among the eight trials comparing real to sham acupuncture, real acupuncture was superior; in four trials there was a trend favoring real acupuncture; and in two studies real acupuncture provided no additional benefit over sham. They concluded that the evidence suggests a clinical benefit of acupuncture for idiopathic headache, including migraine headaches, but called for more studies to confirm these findings under real-life circumstances and for cost-effectiveness studies to affirm its utility (115).

Several large clinical trials were subsequently published. One trial randomized over 400 primary care patients with predominantly migraine headaches to 12 weekly sessions of acupuncture or usual care (116). Compared with controls, patients randomized to acupuncture had 22 fewer headache days per year, scored better on the SF-36, used 15% less medication, made 25% fewer visits to general practitioners and took 15% fewer days of sick leave. Overall, acupuncture was more expensive than usual care; however, there was a 0.021 QALY gain in that group associated with a cost of GBP9180 per QALY gained. The investigators concluded that acupuncture is associated with clinically relevant and persistent benefits for primary care patients that are cost-effective compared with other interventions provided by conventional care. A 2008 clinical trial randomized 3182 headache patients to acupuncture or usual care and also found costs were higher in the acupuncture group compared with usual care (117). Investigators performed a cost-effectiveness analysis and determined that acupuncture was associated with a cost of 11,657 Euro per 1 Quality-Adjusted Life Year (QALY) gained. The authors report that according international cost-effectiveness threshold values is a cost-effective treatment for this population.

A 2007 review concluded that the evidence-base now suggests a 6-week course of acupuncture is not inferior to a 6-month course of prophylactic drug treatment (118). The review also noted the evidence suggests that specific acupuncture point location, stimulation, and needle depth are not as important as previously thought. They concluded the evidence is sufficient such that acupuncture should be added to evidence-based practice guidelines for the prevention of migraine headache.

Overall, there is sufficient evidence to support a strong recommendation favoring the use of acupuncture for the prevention of migraine headaches (see Evidence Summary table at end of chapter).

## Manipulative and Body-Based Practices

A 2005 review found physical therapy to be more effective than massage or acupuncture for tension-type headache and for people with frequent attacks. PT was most effective for migraine when used in combination with other therapies such as exercise, relaxation training, and biofeedback (119). They found no convincing evidence on the benefits of chiropractic or spinal manipulation for the treatment of migraine headaches and this has been confirmed in other reviews (120). These findings contradict a 2004 Cochrane review reporting evidence suggesting that spinal manipulation may be effective for short-term treatment for migraine headache with similar effect to amitriptyline (121).

Overall, the methodological quality of the evidence limits the ability to generalize these findings to everyday clinical practice. Consequently, physical treatments should be considered only within the context of a multi-disciplinary treatment plan at this time (119) (see Evidence Summary table at end of chapter).

## Mind-Body and Behavioral Therapies

There is strong evidence to support mind-body and behavioral interventions such as biofeedback, cognitive behavioral therapy, stress management and relaxation training for the prevention and treatment of migraine headaches (122-125) (see Evidence Summary table at end of chapter). The literature suggests that these interventions are consistently superior to control conditions, providing patients with 35%-55% improvement in symptoms. Consequently, many professional organizations now recommend using these mind-body and behavioral interventions as primary therapeutic options for the management of headache, including migraine headaches.

# Recurrent Urinary Tract Infections

Recurrent urinary tract infections (UTI) are common among young healthy women with normal urinary tract anatomy and function, with approximately one-quarter of college women having a recurrent infection within 6 months of their first UTI (126). Some women have genetic factors that make them prone to recurrent infection such as a cellular defect of the uroepithelial cells or being an ABH blood group antigen nonsecretor, both of which encourage adherence of uropathogenic organisms. Behavioral factors also play a large role in predicting recurrence. Frequent sexual intercourse, use of spermicides, and recent antibiotic use are each independent risk factors. Among post-menopausal women, urinary incontinence, ABH blood group antigen nonsecretor status, and history of UTI are the strongest risk factors for recurrent UTI.

A range of treatments available to women include self-treatment with antimicrobials, post-coital prophylactic use of antimicrobials or continuous antimicrobial prophylaxis. The decision between these regimens depends on patient preference, identifiable risk factors such as sexual activity, and/or the frequency and severity of episodes. For post-menopausal women, one randomized blinded trial involving 93 women with recurrent UTI reported a 90% risk reduction (5.9 to 0.5 episodes) over 8 months using an intravaginal estriol cream (127). Treated women also demonstrated a marked reduction in E. coli and an increase in lactobacilli vaginal colonization when compared with placebo.The most popular supplement for prevention of recurrent UTI is cranberry.

## Dietary Supplements

### Cranberry (*Vaccinium macrocarpon*) Juice and Supplements

Cranberry has been used for the prevention of recurrent urinary tract infections by Native Americans for centuries. Because cranberry can acidify the urine and E. coli does not proliferate in acidic environments, this was thought to be the mechanism of action for its therapeutic benefits. More recent research indicates that the mechanism of action is likely the decreased adherence of uropathic E. coli strains to uroepithelial bladder cells (128).

A recent Cochrane review identified 10 randomized clinical trials including over 1000 people, and reports that cranberry juice (including cranberry-lignonberry juice) and supplements are associated with a 35% reduction in the frequency of urinary tract infections when compared with placebo (129). The greatest effect was seen in women with recurrent UTI. One of the more well-conducted clinical trials randomized 150 women with recurrent E. coli–related UTI to 50 cc cranberry-lingonberry juice concentrate daily for 6 months or 100 cc lactobacillus drink 5 days weekly for 1 year or no intervention. At 6 months follow-up, 16% of women assigned to the cranberry group, 39% assigned to lactobacillus and 36% assigned to placebo experienced one or more recurrent UTI. Overall, there was a 20% absolute risk reduction in the cranberry group compared with the control group, which is equivalent to a number needed to treat of 5 (130). Another study evaluated the cost-effectiveness of cranberry products and randomized women with recurrent UTI to cranberry tablets + placebo juice, placebo tablets + cranberry juice, or placebo tablets + placebo juice. Tablets were taken twice daily and 250 mL of juice were taken three times daily. Overall, they found 18% and 20% of patients experienced at least one symptomatic UTI/year for cranberry tablets and cranberry juice, respectively, compared to 32% of patients randomized to the control group. Prophylaxis cost $624 and $1400 for cranberry tablets and juice, respectively, for 1 year. Antibiotic use was less annually in both treatment groups compared with placebo. Cranberry tablets provided the most cost-effective therapeutic option in this trial for preventing UTIs (131). In general, cranberry products are well-tolerated and are relatively safe. Overall, there is sufficient evidence to support a strong recommendation in favor of cranberry products for the prevention of recurrent UTIs (see Evidence Summary table at end of chapter). Evidence indicates the appropriate dose is 400 mg capsule twice daily of cranberry concentrated extract (standardized to contain 11% to 12% quinic acid) or 8 ounces of unsweetened cranberry juice from concentrate taken three times daily. Be sure patients avoid cranberry cocktail, which contains minimal cranberry juice.

**Evidence Summary of CAM Treatments in General Medicine**

| Clinical Indication | Category | Specific Therapy | Dose | Outcome | Confidence of Estimate on Effectiveness | Magnitude of Effect* | Safety† | Clinical Recommendation‡ | Comments |
|---|---|---|---|---|---|---|---|---|---|
| Anxiety: generalized anxiety disorder | Biologically based practices | Kava | 100 mg kava-lactones three times daily | Anxiety | Grade B | Moderate | Single thumbs down* | Weak against | *11 case reports of fulminant liver failure requiring transplantation |
| Anxiety: generalized anxiety disorder | Biologically based practices | Passionflower | Variable | Anxiety | Grade C | Unclear | No recommendation | No recommendation | 1 small equivalency trial suggesting no different than oxazepam |
| Anxiety: nonspecific | Biologically based practices | Hops | Variable | Anxiety | Grade D | Unclear | No recommendation | No recommendation | — |
| Anxiety: nonspecific | Biologically based practices | Bach Flower Remedy | Variable | Anxiety | Grade B | None | No effect | Weak against | — |
| Anxiety: procedure-related | Whole medical system | Acupuncture | Variable | Anxiety | Grade B | Small | Single thumbs up | Weak in favor | — |
| Anxiety: generalized anxiety disorder | Whole medical system | Acupuncture | Variable | Anxiety | Grade D | Unclear | Single thumbs up | No recommendation | — |
| Anxiety: symptoms related to underlying medical conditions | Whole medical system | Acupuncture | Variable | Anxiety | Grade C | Moderate | Single thumbs up | Weak in favor | — |

(continued)

**Evidence Summary of CAM Treatments in General Medicine (continued)**

| Clinical Indication | Category | Specific Therapy | Dose | Outcome | Confidence of Estimate on Effectiveness | Magnitude of Effect* | Safety† | Clinical Recommendation‡ | Comments |
|---|---|---|---|---|---|---|---|---|---|
| Anxiety: generalized anxiety disorder | Manipulative and body-based | Aromatherapy | Variable | Anxiety | Grade D | Unclear | Double thumbs up | Weak against | Clinical trials for milder conditions suggest lack of effect |
| Anxiety: among palliative care | Manipulative and body-based | Aromatherapy Massage | Variable | Anxiety | Grade B | Small | Double thumbs up | No recommendation | Evidence suggests that benefits are mild, and transient (several weeks) and aromatherapy may not provide additional benefit over massage alone. |
| Anxiety: generalized anxiety disorder and high trait | Mind-body medicine | Meditation | Variable | Anxiety | Grade C | Small | Double thumbs up | Weak in favor | — |
| Anxiety: generalized anxiety disorder | Mind-body medicine | Relaxation training | Variable | Anxiety | Grade A | Moderate | Double thumbs up | Strong in favor | — |
| Common cold | Biologically based practices | Zinc gluconate lozenges | 13.3 mg | Symptom duration | Grade B | Small | Double thumbs up | Weak in favor | Requires every 2 hour dosing, which may limit its use. |

| Common cold | Biologically based practices | Extract from above-ground preparations of *Echinacea purpurea* | 300 mg three times daily | Prevention of incident common cold episodes; symptom duration | Grade B | Moderate | Double thumbs up | Weak in favor | People with allergies to ragweed, daisies marigolds, and chrysanthemums should avoid this herb. |
|---|---|---|---|---|---|---|---|---|---|
| Common cold | Biologically based practices | Vitamin C prophylaxis | Variable | Symptom duration | Grade B | Small | Double thumbs up | Weak in favor | — |
| Common cold | Biologically based practices | Vitamin prophylaxis | Variable | Prevention of the common cold | Grade B | No effect | Double thumbs up | No recommendation | Vitamin C appears quite effective among people under severe physical or environmental stress. |
| Common cold | Biologically based practices | Vitamin C treatment at onset of symptoms | Variable | Symptom duration and severity | Grade B | No effect | Double thumbs up | Weak against | — |
| Common cold | Biologically based practices | Garlic | Variable | Prevention of the common cold, and symptom duration | Grade C | Small | Double thumbs up | No recommendation | — |

*(continued)*

**Evidence Summary of CAM Treatments in General Medicine (continued)**

| Clinical Indication | Category | Specific Therapy | Dose | Outcome | Confidence of Estimate on Effectiveness | Magnitude of Effect* | Safety† | Clinical Recommendation‡ | Comments |
|---|---|---|---|---|---|---|---|---|---|
| Type 2 diabetes | Biologically based practices | Cinnamon | 1.5 gm to 5 gm, 1 day to 4 months | HbA1C, fasting glucose, glucose tolerance test | Grade B | Conflicting | Double thumbs up | No recommendation | Different kinds of cinnamon; different outcomes tested; healthy and diabetics tested; conflicting results. |
| Type 2 diabetes | Biologically based practices | Omega 3 fatty acids | Varied | 1. Blood glucose, 2. Triglycerides | 1. Grade A 2. Grade A | 1. None 2. Small 3. Unclear | No recommendation | 1. Strong against 2. Strong in favor | No hypoglycemic effect. No clinically meaningful effect on LDL levels. |
| Type 2 diabetes | Biologically based practices | Chromium | Different chromium preparations at different doses | Fasting glucose, HbA1c | Grade C | Unclear | No recommendation | No recommendation | May have different effects in different populations. |
| Type 2 diabetes | Biologically based practices | Chinese herbs | Many herbs, some formulas, varied doses | Mortality, quality of life, long-term diabetic complications, glycemic control, weight or | Grade C | Varied | No recommendation | No recommendation | Some herbs may be beneficial but interpretation of trials limited by poor quality. Evaluation of safety profile is needed. |

| Condition | Domain | Intervention | Dose/technique | Outcome | Grade | Effect | Rating | Recommendation | Comments |
|---|---|---|---|---|---|---|---|---|---|
| Diabetic neuropathy | Whole medical systems | Acupuncture | Different techniques | body mass index, fasting insulin levels Pain | Grade D | Unclear | Single thumbs up | No recommendation | — |
| Type 2 diabetes | Whole medical systems | Ayurvedic herbal medicines: Coccinia indica, Holy basil, fenugreek and Gymnema sylvestra; Ayush-82, D-400 (29) | Varied doses | Glucose lowering effect and other measurements | Grade C | Small | Side-ways thumb | No recommendation | Agency for Healthcare Research and Quality recommends further study of Coccinia indica, holy basil, fenugreek, Gymnema sylvestra, Ayush-82, D-400. |
| Genital herpes | Biologically based practices | L-Lysine monohydrochloride | 3 grams daily | 1. Prevention of recurrent episodes 2. Duration of symptoms | 1. Grade C 2. Grade C | 1. Moderate 2. No effect | Double thumbs up | 1. Weak in favor 2. Weak against | — |
| Genital herpes | Biologically based practices | Lemon balm topical cream | Variable | Duration of symptoms | Grade C | Small | Double thumbs up | No recommendation | — |

*(continued)*

**Evidence Summary of CAM Treatments [f]in General Medicine (continued)**

| Clinical Indication | Category | Specific Therapy | Dose | Outcome | Confidence of Estimate on Effectiveness | Magnitude of Effect* | Safety† | Clinical Recommendation‡ | Comments |
|---|---|---|---|---|---|---|---|---|---|
| Migraine headaches prophylaxis | Biologically based practices | Buterbur extract, liquid-carbon-dioxide PA-free | 50-75 mg twice daily | Migraine recurrence | Grade B | Moderate | Double thumbs up | Weak in favor | — |
| Mgraine headaches prophylaxis | Biologically based practices | Feverfew | Variable | Migraine recurrence | Grade B | Conflicting | Single thumbs up | No recommendation | — |
| Migraine headaches prophylaxis | Biologically based practices | Trimagnesium dicitrate | 600 mg oral daily dose | Migraine recurrence | Grade B | Small | Double thumbs up | No recommendation | — |
| Migraine headaches treatment | Biologically based practices | Magnesium sulfate | 1-2 grams IV | Migraine symptom management | Grade C | Conflicting | Unclear | No recommendation | One trial reported symptom worsening |
| Migraine headaches prophylaxis | Biologically based practices | Co-enzyme Q10 | 100 mg three times daily | Migraine recurrence | Grade C | Large | Double thumbs up | No recommendation | One trial which reported NNT=3 |
| Migraine headaches prophylaxis | Whole medical system | Acupuncture | Variable | Migraine recurrence | Grade A | Moderate | Single thumbs up | Strong recommendation | Identified as cost-effective treatment. 6-week acupuncture not inferior to 6-month prophylactic regimen. |

| Condition | Category | Intervention | Dosage | Outcome | Grade | Magnitude | Thumbs | Recommendation | Safety |
|---|---|---|---|---|---|---|---|---|---|
| Migraine headaches prophylaxis | Manipulative and body-based practices | Physical therapy, massage, chiropractic and spinal manipulation | Variable | Migraine recurrence | Grade C | Conflicting | Single thumbs up | No recommendation | Generally safe excluding precautions with cervical manipulation (See Muscular-Skeletal chapter). |
| Migraine headaches prophylaxis | Mind-body medicine and behavioral therapies | Biofeedback, cognitive behavioral therapy, stress management and relaxation training | Variable | Migraine recurrence | Grade B | Moderate | Double thumbs up | Strong in favor | — |
| Urinary tract infection | Biologically based practices | Cranberry, supplements and juice | 400 mg bid (11% quinic acid) or 8 03 unsweetened juice tid | Fewer recurrent episodes, cost-effectiveness | Grade A | Large NNT=5 | Double thumbs up | Strong in favor | Avoid juice cocktails that contain minimal quantity of fruit. |

* Small, moderate (OR>1.2-2) or large (OR>2)

‡5 categories: Double thumbs up, single thumb up, no recommendation, single thumb down, double thumb down

‡5 categories: Strong (in favor), weak (in favor), no recommendation, weak (against), strong (against)

## SELECTED REFERENCES*

2. **Jorm AF, Christensen H, Griffiths KM, et al.** Effectiveness of complementary and self-help treatments for anxiety disorders. Med J Aust. 2004;181(7 Suppl):S29-46.

3. **Jacobs BP, Bent S, Tice JA, et al.** An internet-based randomized, placebo-controlled trial of kava and valerian for anxiety and insomnia. Medicine (Baltimore). 2005;84:197-207.

5. **Pittler MH, Ernst E.** Kava extract for treating anxiety. Cochrane Database Syst Rev. 2003;(1):CD003383. Review

7. **MMWR.** 2002;51:1065-7.

13. **van der Watt G, Laugharne J, Janca A.** Complementary and alternative medicine in the treatment of anxiety and depression. Curr Opin Psychiatry. 2008;21:37-42.

25. **Luo H, Meng F, Jia Y, Zhao X.** Clinical research on the therapeutic effect of the electro-acupuncture treatment in patients with depression. Psychiatry Clin Neurosci. 1998; 52(Suppl):S338-40.

31. **Fellowes D, Barnes K, Wilkinson S.** Aromatherapy and massage for symptom relief in patients with cancer. Cochrane Database Syst Rev. 2004;(2):CD002287.

34. **Krisanaprakornkit T, Krisanaprakornkit W, Piyavhatkul N, Laopaiboon M.** Meditation therapy for anxiety disorders. Cochrane Database Syst Rev. 2006 Jan 25;(1):CD004998.

36. **Siev J, Chambless DL.** Specificity of treatment effects: cognitive therapy and relaxation for generalized anxiety and panic disorders. J Consult Clin Psychol. 2007;75:513-22.

46. **Marshall S.** Zinc gluconate and the common cold: review of randomized controlled trials. Can Fam Physician. 1998;44:1037-42.

47. **Mossad SB, Macknin ML, Medendorp SV, et al.** Zinc gluconate lozenges for treating the common cold: a randomized, double-blind, placebo-controlled study. Ann Intern Med. 1996;125:81-8.

50. **Linde K, Barrett B, Wolkart K, et al.** Echinacea for preventing and treating the common cold. Cochrane Database Syst Rev. 2006;CD000530.

53. **Sachin A, Sander S, White, M.** Evaluation of echinacea for the prevention and treatment of the common cold: a meta-analysis. Lancet Infectious Diseases. 2007;7:473-80.

57. **Douglas RM, Hemilä H, Chalker E, Treacy B.** Vitamin C for preventing and treating the common cold. Cochrane Database Syst Rev. 2007 Jul 18;(3):CD000980.

64. **Dugoua JJ, Seely D, Perri D, et al.** From type 2 diabetes to antioxidant activity: a systematic review of the safety and efficacy of common and cassia cinnamon bark. Can J Physiol Pharmcol 2007; 85:837-47.

77. **Liu JP, Zhang M, Wang WY, Grimsgaard S.** Chinese herbal medicines for type 2 diabetes mellitus. Cochrane Database of Systematic Reviews 2004, Issue 3. Art. No.:CD003642. DOI: 10.1002/14651858.CD003642.pub2 Last substantive update: May 2002.

93. **Perfect MM, Bourne N, Ebel C, Rosenthal SL.** Use of complementary and alternative medicine for the treatment of genital herpes. Herpes. 2005;12:38-41.

98. **Agosti R, Duke RK, Chrubasik JE, Chrubasik S.** Effectiveness of Petasites hybridus preparations in the prophylaxis of migraine: a systematic review. Phytomedicine. 2006;13:743-6.

103. **Ernst E, Pittler MH.** Feverfew for preventing migraine. Cochrane Database Syst Rev. 2004;(1):CD002286.

113. **Wang F, Van Den Eeden SK, Ackerson LM, et al.** Oral magnesium oxide prophylaxis of frequent migrainous headache in children: a randomized, double-blind, placebo-controlled trial. Headache. 2003;43:601-10.

114. **Sándor PS, Di Clemente L, Coppola G, et al.** Efficacy of coenzyme Q10 in migraine prophylaxis: a randomized controlled trial. Neurology. 2005;64:713-5.

117. **Witt CM, Reinhold T, Jena S, et al.** Cost-effectiveness of acupuncture treatment in patients with headache. Cephalalgia. 2008;28:334-45.

---

* The complete reference list is to be found on the book's Web site.

124. **Rains JC, Penzien DB, McCrory DC, Gray RN.** Behavioral headache treatment: history, review of the empirical literature, and methodological critique. Headache. 2005;45(Suppl 2):S92-109.

129. **Jepson R, Craig J.** Cranberries for preventing urinary tract infections. Cochrane Database Syst Rev. 2008;CD001321.

131. **Stothers L.** A randomized trial to evaluate effectiveness and cost effectiveness of naturopathic cranberry products as prophylaxis against urinary tract infection in women. Can J Urol. 2002;9:1558-62.

# Chapter 7

୫ଚ

# Gastrointestinal Health

Jianping Liu, MD, PhD
Christian Gluud, MD, Dr Med Sci
Ronald Koretz, MD

Allopathic medical practitioners believe that their advice and interventions are based on sound laboratory and clinical science. As such, they tend to dismiss complementary and alternative medicine (CAM) practitioners as charlatans because there is inadequate scientific evidence backing the interventions they use. However, CAM practices are becoming more widely employed. Gastrointestinal disorders were among the ten most frequently reported medical conditions for using CAM in the US (1). The reasons may be due to the recurrent characteristics of the diseases and dissatisfaction with conventional treatments, especially for functional conditions such as irritable bowel syndrome (IBS) and non-ulcer dyspepsia.

## Prevalence of CAM use

According to a survey by Smart and colleagues of 96 patients with IBS, 143 patients with organic upper gastrointestinal tract disorders and 222 patients with Crohn's disease (2), patients with IBS were more likely to consult a complementary practitioner (16%), consider trying a CAM remedy (41%), or be currently using CAM remedies (11%) than either of the other two conditions. The prevalence of CAM use is growing for gastrointestinal disorders (3). Herbal medicine and homeopathy were the most frequently employed complementary remedies. An inadequate response to orthodox treatment was at least one reason why these patients were more likely to use CAM.

A similar conclusion was reached by Verhoef and her colleagues in a survey of 395 patients who attended a gastroenterological clinic (4). Nine percent of these patients had consulted a CAM practitioner for the gastrointestinal problem, and a further 18% had sought CAM treatment for some other reasons. Nearly half of the CAM users had consulted more than one practitioner. Verhoef et al also found that patients with a functional disorder were more likely to seek CAM treatment than those with an organic disorder. The main reason for seeking such therapy was dissatisfaction with the allopathic treatment; users of complementary medicine were becoming significantly more skeptical of orthodox medicine (49% versus 13%). A recent survey indicated that the incidence of CAM use was 49.5% for inflammatory bowel disease, 50.9% for IBS, 20% for general gastrointestinal diseases, and 27% for conventional therapy (5), while data from an internet survey showed 46% of IBD patients have used complementary therapies during the previous 2 years, and 34% were current users (6).

## CAM Therapies

Our discussion in this chapter will be limited to RCTs that assessed herbal and other natural products, acupuncture, hypnotherapy, or homeopathy (examples of typical CAM modalities) for patients with gastroenterological conditions. We have chosen to disregard evidence from cohort studies, case-control studies, or other sources due to the fact that evidence from such studies regarding intervention effects are much weaker than evidence from RCTs (7,8). The RCTs and systematic reviews discussed below were identified by several strategies. The trials regarding the treatment of irritable bowel disease (IBD) and liver disease came from literature searches in conjunction with preparations of systematic reviews for The Cochrane Library (9-11). The other RCTs employing herbal interventions came from a search of the medical literature.

Gastrointestinal symptoms are potential adverse effects of any orally ingested herb or natural product. From a teleological perspective, such effects may be part of a plant's defensive system to prevent animals from eating it. In practice these adverse effects appear to be infrequent and may even be incorrectly attributed to these agents. For example, a conclusion that berberine-containing goldenseal (*Hydrastis canadensis*) causes gastrointestinal distress may have been inappropriately extrapolated from toxicologic studies of berberine in animals and/or from 19th-century homeopathic literature (12). Similarly, while gastrointestinal distress has been attributed to saw palmetto (*Serenoa repens*) used in the treatment of benign prostatic hypertrophy, such adverse effects occur equally frequently in placebo recipients (9). Some gastrointestinal toxicity can be due to overdose, adulteration, misidentification, or inappropriate marketing of a toxic plant product.

## Peptic Ulcer Disease/Dyspepsia

### Herbal and Other Natural Products

Peppermint and caraway oils have been used as spasmolytics for a variety of digestive symptoms. In a systematic review, peppermint oil (usually combined with caraway oil) was effective compared to placebo in patients with non-ulcer dyspepsia in three RCTs, and one RCT found no difference between peppermint oil and cisapride (11). Two European commercial combination preparations (both including peppermint and caraway, albeit as herbs, not as oils) of nine herbs (STW5), or just six of them (STW5-II), appeared to be effective compared to placebo and both STW5 and cisapride appear effective (9,13). A multicenter trial showed that the combination preparation consisting of peppermint oil and caraway oil appeared to be effective for treatment of non-ulcer dyspepsia compared with cisapride (14). There is moderate evidence to suggest the combination of peppermint and caraway oils appears effective for non-ulcer dyspepsia and appears relatively safe (see Evidence Summary table at end of chapter).

Licorice (liquorice), or a pharmaceutical product made from its active ingredient (glycyrrhizinic acid) heals ulcers (15). However, it is not used because of its mineralocorticoid adverse effects and the availability of other effective medications. Moderate evidence from early double-blind, placebo-controlled trials showed that using glycyrrhizinic acid–reduced or deglycyrrhizinised licorice seems to have no beneficial effect for gastric ulcer or duodenal ulcer (16,17). There is moderate evidence to suggest that licorice is not effective and may cause harm. There is sufficient evidence to recommend that people not use this supplement (see Evidence Summary table at end of chapter).

While chili pepper (and its pungent ingredient capsaicin) elicits dyspepsia in sensitive individuals in the short term, it does seem to relieve non-ulcer dyspepsia (18). It has been speculated that, with chronic use, capsaicin desensitizes selective visceral nociceptive C-fibers. Moderate evidence shows that capsaicin in low-concentration range appears to protect against gastric injuries induced by ethanol or indomethacin in healthy human subjects, which is attributed to stimulation of the sensory nerve endings (19). There is moderate evidence to suggest red chili pepper appears to have no effect on non-ulcer dyspepsia; however, it may help ethanol-induced gastic injury (see Evidence Summary table at end of chapter).

Turmeric (Curcuma plant) is used in Ayurvedic medicine (a type of herbal medicine practiced in India) for biliary problems and dyspepsia and to improve appetite. Dyspeptic symptoms did improve with this agent (20), but peptic ulcer healing did not. There is limited evidence to suggest that tumeric may be beneficial; however, the evidence base is insufficient to recommend it (see Evidence Summary table at end of chapter).

An herbal preparation STW 5-II containing extracts from bitter candy tuft, matricaria flower, peppermint leaves, caraway, licorice root and lemon balm appears to improve dyspeptic symptoms in patients with non-ulcer dyspepsia compared with placebo (21). There is moderate evidence to suggest that it is effective and appears relatively safe. Overall, the evidence base is sufficient to recommend this formulation as an effective treatment of non-ulcer dyspepsia (see Evidence Summary table at end of chapter).

Based on moderate evidence, artichoke leaf extract (ALE) appeared to alleviate symptoms and improve the disease-specific quality of life in patients with non-ulcer dyspepsia (22) (see Evidence Summary table at end of chapter). Other herbs (or herbal combinations) found to be effective for non-ulcer dyspepsia in single RCTs include amalaki, banana powder, greater celandine, Liu-Jun-Zi-Tang, lomatol, mastic, Shenxiahewining, Xin wei decoction and TJ-43 (23,24). However, many of these studies had significant methodological problems, thereby weakening the strength of the evidence.

Probiotics are live, non-pathogenic bacteria (e.g., *Lactobacillus spp., Bifidobacterium spp., Streptococcus thermophilus*) or yeast (e.g., *Saccharomyces boulardii*) that can be ingested in capsule or tablet form or as a yogurt-type drink. A recent systematic review of 14 RCTs assessing concomitant probiotic usage in the treatment of *Helicobacter pylori* indicated that such an intervention increased the eradication rate and reduced side effects, particularly antibiotic-related diarrhea (25). The benefit may simply be due to better compliance because of fewer side effects, but recent evidence from both in vitro and in vivo studies as well as meta-analysis shows that probiotics can inhibit *Helicobacter pylori* growth and improve eradication rate (25,26). There is strong evidence suggesting that these strains of probiotics are relatively safe and are effective as adjunctive treatment for *Helicobacter pylori* eradication and improving adherence to standard treatment. There is strong evidence to recommend probiotics for these indications (see Evidence Summary table at end of chapter).

## Hypnotherapy

Two RCTs have claimed that hypnotherapy is effective in patients with non-cardiac chest pain (27) and non-ulcer dyspepsia (28). Because the outcomes were subjective and the trials were not blinded, these claims should be interpreted with skepticism. Given the limited evidence base, no recommendation can be made at this time (see Evidence Summary table at end of chapter).

## Acupuncture and Homeopathy

A randomised pilot study using acupuncture and homeopathy showed no trend or significant clinical effect in patients with dyspepsia compared with normal GP care. However, the finding was not conclusive due to under power of the study (29). Acupuncture appeared to be of therapeutic benefit in patients with mild to moderately active Crohn's disease, despite a remarkable placebo effect (30). Given the limited evidence base for both medical systems for this indication, no recommendation can be made at this time (see Evidence Summary table at end of chapter).

# Irritable Bowel Syndrome/Colic

## Herbs and Other Natural Products

Fiber, which may be considered a crude herbal medicine, is frequently recommended for IBS. However, the data from RCTs suggest that psyllium is no better than placebo for symptoms of abdominal pain or bloating, although it may help constipation (31). Therefore, psyllium should not be recommended as treatment for abdominal pain or bloating related to IBS; however, there is limited evidence to suggest that it may be beneficial for constipation related to IBS (see Evidence Summary table at end of chapter).

As already noted, peppermint oil is a smooth muscle relaxant. In Europe, it is combined with caraway oil and used for IBS. This therapy was found to be beneficial in a meta-analysis of five RCTs and two subsequent RCTs (32-34). Intraluminal peppermint oil decreased spasm during barium enemas, colonoscopies, and gastroscopies. Peppermint oil is strongly recommended for IBS-related pain (see Evidence Summary table at end of chapter).

A Cochrane systematic review identified 75 RCTs using herbal medicines in 7957 participants with IBS (9). Among RCTs compared with placebo, several different preparations were associated with global symptom improvement (Table 7-1), including: a standard Chinese herbal formula (20 herbs mainly composed of Codonopsis pilosulae, Agastaches seu pogostemi, Ledebouriellae sesloidis, Coicis lachryma-jobi, Bupleurum chinense, Artemesiae capillaris, et al), individualized Chinese herbal medicine (constituents not described), STW5 and STW5-II, Tibetan herbal medicine Padma-Lax, traditional Chinese formula Tongxie Yaofang, and an Ayurvedic preparation (Marmelos correa [Bilva] plus Monniere Linn) (9). Fifty-one other herbal preparations were compared with conventional therapy in 65 individual RCTs in this review (9), and 22 herbal medicines (see Evidence Summary table at end of chapter) demonstrated significant improvement of symptoms, while other 29 herbs were not significantly different from conventional therapy. However, the majority of the 65 RCTs suffered from methodological weakness, thereby limiting the strength of the evidence. A multi-herb tea (containing German chamomile) improved infantile colic (35). There is moderate evidence suggesting that a multi-herb tea (containing German chamomile) appears effective for infantile colic (35) (see Evidence Summary table at end of chapter). Neither Fumaria officinalis (fumitory) nor Curcuma xanthorrhiza (Japanese turmeric) extracts were more effective than placebo (36).

The effect of probiotics in IBS has been tested in over 20 RCTs (37-52). A variety of clinical outcomes in terms of symptoms were assessed. Some studies have shown improvements in pain and flatulence in response to probiotic administration, whilst others have shown no symptomatic improvement. No consistent effects of the probiotic preparations were demonstrated. Interpretation of the inconsistent effects may be attributed to variations of participants (with different characteristics and IBS undefined or mixed with diarrhea or

Table 7-1   Herbal Medicines Superior to Conventional Therapy for Global Symptom Improvement in Randomized Trials

| Herbal Medicines | Control Drugs | Relative Benefit (RR [99% confidence interval]) |
|---|---|---|
| Tongxie Yaofang | Cisapride | 1.51 [1.06 to 2.15] |
| Acanthopanacis senticosi | Lactobacillus agent plus oryzanol | 3.93 [2.15 to 7.17] |
| Baile Ercha (extracts of two herbs) | SMZ-TMPco, propantheline, oryzanol, and chlordiazepoxide | 1.23 [1.03 to 1.46] |
| Buzhong Yiqi Tang | Oryzanol plus sodium cromoglycate | 1.41 [1.22 to 1.63] |
| Buzhong Yiqi Tang | Oryzanol plus bifidobacteria agent | 1.37 [1.05 to 1.78] |
| Chaicang Yuxiang Tang | Oryzanol | 1.85 [1.05 to 3.24] |
| Chaihu Shugan Yin | Cisapride | 1.62 [1.11 to 2.38] |
| Ganpi Lunzhi | Licheiformobiogen | 1.74 [1.25 to 2.43] |
| Individualised herbal treatment | Pinaverium bromide | 1.60 [1.04 to 2.47] |
| Jiechang Kang | Oryzanol | 3.17 [1.54 to 6.51] |
| Lichang Tang | Licheiformobiogen plus lacidophilir | 1.52 [1.22 to 1.90] |
| Pingheng Zhixie Jianpi | Nifedipine plus bifidobiogen | 1.27 [1.04 to 1.56] |
| Pingyi Zhixie or Pingyi Tongbian Tang | Symptomatic treatment | 1.31 [1.05 to 1.65] |
| Sanbai San | Oryzanol plus berberine | 1.67 [1.06 to 2.64] |
| Senna leaf | Cisapride | 1.47 [1.12 to 1.93] |
| Shugan Jianpi Tang | Oryzanol plus berberine | 1.50 [1.09 to 2.07] |
| Tiaogan Yichang Tang | Gentamycin plus berberine | 1.62 [1.07 to 2.46] |
| Xiaoyao San | Oryzanol plus loperamide | 1.37 [1.07 to 1.74] |
| Xuefu Zhuyu Tang | Oryzanol plus nifedipine | 1.57 [1.20 to 2.04] |
| Yichang San | Oryzanol plus berberine | 1.59 [1.06 to 2.40] |
| Yigan Fupi Huatan Quyu | Oryzanol plus nifedipine | 1.52 [1.08 to 2.13] |
| Yiji Tiaochang Tang | Doxepin plus nifedipine | 1.30 [1.11 to 1.53] |

constipation prominent in one study), different preparations tested and outcomes used. At this time, there is conflicting evidence on the effectiveness of probiotics for IBS and the role of probiotics in IBS has not been clearly defined (see Evidence Summary table at end of chapter).

## Acupuncture

A Cochrane systematic review identified six RCTs using acupuncture in people with IBS (53). Most of the trials included in this review were of poor quality and were heterogeneous in terms of interventions, controls, and outcomes measured. Meta-analysis showed an insignificant difference between acupuncture and sham acupuncture (relative risk 1.28; 95% confidence interval 0.83 to 1.98; n=109) when either a global symptom score or a patient-determined treatment success rate was employed as the endpoint. The review concluded that there was insufficient evidence regarding whether acupuncture is more effective than sham acupuncture or other interventions for treating IBS (see Evidence Summary table at end of chapter).

## Hypnotherapy

Four of five RCTs indicated that hypnotherapy was beneficial in the treatment of IBS in terms of symptom reduction and reduced medication usage (54-58). The proposed mechanism may in part be due to changes in visceral sensitivity and reducing the sensory and motor component of the gastrocolonic response in patients with IBS (57,59). Like many psychodynamic therapies, it is often not possible to effectively blind the subject to the intervention. The lack of blinding may have influenced the perceived results. Hypnotherapy appears safe and there is moderate evidence suggesting that hypnotherapy appears effective in the treatment for IBS (see Evidence Summary table at end of chapter).

# Diarrhea

## Herbal and Other Natural Products

Various herbal substances (carob bean juice, apple pectin-chamomile extract combination, or tormentil root extract) were tested in three RCTs of children with diarrhea; all were effective (60-62) (see Evidence Summary table at end of chapter). A randomized, double-blinded trial showed that an extract of guava leaf reduced the degree of pain but not the frequency of bowel movements, in adults with acute diarrhea (63).

Systematic reviews and meta-analyses have suggested that probiotics are safe and effective in reducing severity, duration among adults or children with diarrhea, and reduce infant mortality among affected children (64,65). A meta-analysis of 34 RCTs indicated that probiotics may be effective in reducing the risk of diarrhea in individuals who are at risk, although the data were limited by not representing trials in the community or in third-world countries (66). Probiotics should be routinely recommended in treating infant or adult diarrhea (see Evidence Summary table at end of chapter).

In addition to the above-noted systematic reviews, several other meta-analyses have indicated that probiotics are effective in preventing antibiotic-associated diarrhea (67-71) and may be considered when prescribing antibiotics for patients at-risk for antibiotic-associated diarrhea (see Evidence Summary table at end of chapter).

## Homeopathy

Meta-analysis of three randomized trials shows that homeopathy shortened the duration of symptoms (3.3 versus 4.1 days) in children in third world countries with diarrhea (72). The reviewed RCTs—carried out by one group of researchers—were all reasonably well conducted, including being double-blinded. However, a subsequent double-blind, randomized trial did not confirm the benefit of a homeopathic combination therapy in children with acute diarrhea (73). Recent systematic review of double-blind, placebo-controlled trials on homeopathic therapy found conflicting results for acute diarrhea in children (74). Therefore, current evidence is not sufficient to recommend homeopathy in children with diarrhea. Further randomized trials by independent researchers are warranted (see Evidence Summary table at end of chapter).

Homeopathy probably has no intrinsic adverse side effects. If it is ineffective, the penalty paid by the patient is time and money spent and the risk of delaying a more effective therapy.

# Nausea and Vomiting

## Ginger

Ginger is marketed for nausea or motion sickness. There is an experimental model for motion sickness that alters head orientation as a rotating chair turns. Ginger was no more effective than placebo in preventing such experimental motion sickness (75-77). However, ginger did ameliorate the vertiginous effect of caloric stimulation of the vestibular apparatus (78).

In addition to this work with experimental nausea and vomiting, ginger has been tested in several disease states. It was effective in car or boat motion-sickness (79-82) and pregnancy-associated morning sickness (75,83). A meta-analysis of five RCTs has found that ginger at a fixed dose of at least 1 g can significantly reduce the incidence of 24-hour postoperative nausea and vomiting and postoperative vomiting in patients undergoing gynecological and lower-extremity surgery (84). There is moderate to strong evidence to suggest that ginger is effective for several types of nausea and vomiting (see Evidence Summary table at end of chapter).

## Acupuncture

One particular acupoint (the Neiguan or Pericardium 6 [P6] point), located about five cm above the proximal flexor palmar crease, is commonly used to control nausea and vomiting. A systematic review assessed 33 studies (of which 12 were RCTs) of P6 acupuncture in surgery, pregnancy, or cancer chemotherapy (85). Acupuncture was significantly better than the control intervention in 27 of these studies (including 11 of the 12 RCTs) (85). (See Evidence Summary table at end of chapter.)

### Postoperative Nausea/Vomiting

A Cochrane systematic review of 26 RCTs found that stimulation of P6 acupoint significantly reduced the risk of nausea/vomiting and the need for rescue antiemetics compared with sham acupuncture (86) (see Evidence Summary table at end of chapter). At least 18 additional RCTs that evaluated some form of acupuncture in postoperative patients were not included in that review (usually because they were published at a later date) (87-104). Statistically significant benefits were seen in 19 of them (including 14 out of 22 RCTs that provided sham acupuncture to the controls). There is strong evidence to recommend acupuncture for the treatment of post-operative nausea and vomiting (see Evidence Summary table at end of chapter).

### Pregnancy-Related Nausea/Vomiting

Two systematic reviews assessed acupuncture for nausea and vomiting in pregnancy (105,106). Although both reviews described positive effects, methodological issues (absent/inadequate blinding, large dropout rates, and the use of concomitant antiemetic agents [possibly masking an effect]) were often an issue. At least six other RCTs have been published (107-112), and a beneficial effect was seen in four of them; however, the magnitude of the effect was small. There is moderate evidence to recommend acupuncture for the treatment of pregnancy-induced nausea and vomiting (see Evidence Summary table at end of chapter).

### Chemotherapy-Induced Nausea/Vomiting

A Cochrane systematic review of 11 trials demonstrated that needle or electronic acupuncture appeared to help patients undergoing cancer chemotherapy, especially for reducing the incidence of acute vomiting (113). There is moderate evidence to recommend acupuncture for the treatment of chemotherapy-induced nausea and vomiting (see Evidence Summary table at end of chapter).

### Motion Sickness

Acupressure is used for motion sickness. There is even a commercial product containing a protrusion that presses on the P6 acupoint. At least three RCTs have assessed the utility of this product in the experimental model described above (the rotating chair) (114-116). Only one of these trials showed a benefit (111). There is insufficient evidence to recommend acupuncture for motion sickness (see Evidence Summary table at end of chapter).

## Hypnotherapy

One of two RCTs have described a modest effect of hypnotherapy in alleviating the nausea and vomiting associated with cancer chemotherapy (117,118). A third trial suggested that hypnotherapy could reduce the amount of antiemetic medication that was used (119). It must be remembered that these trials were not blinded. There is insufficient evidence to recommend hypnotherapy for chemotherapy-induced nausea and vomiting (see Evidence Summary table at end of chapter).

# Inflammatory Bowel Disease

## Herbs and Other Natural Products

Fish oil is a rich source of omega-3 polyunsaturated fatty acids (e.g., eicosapentanoic and docosahexenoic acid), agents that inhibit the formation of proinflammatory cytokines. Several RCTs have evaluated their use in IBD.

Six RCTs compared fish oil to placebo in patients with active ulcerative colitis. Benefits with regard to remission rates were demonstrated in three trials, and trends in the same direction were seen in two others. One trial did not show any effect (see Evidence Summary table at end of chapter) (UC acute, Grade B, single thumbs up, weak recommendation). However, fish oil (Omega-3 fatty acids) was not shown to be able to maintain remissions in ulcerative colitis in a systematic review (120) (UC maintenance: Grade B, double thumbs up, weak recommendation against). This agent did not show clinical benefits in individual trials in active Crohn's disease (121,122) (Grade B, single thumbs up, weak recommendation against). It may, or may not, maintain remissions in Crohn's disease (123).

Potential problems with the study designs of these trials should be appreciated. First, the distinctive taste of the fish oil complicates the blinding. Second, the placebos usually consisted of vegetable oils, and these agents are presumably precursors of more inflammatory cytokines. A summary of the evidence on omega-3 polyunsaturated fatty acids during the acute and maintenance phases of these two conditions is summarized in the Evidence Summary table at the end of the chapter.

A series of RCTs have assessed the utility of probiotics in IBD. There was no consistent effect of these agents in producing a remission of active ulcerative colitis (124-126). Probiotics may be useful in maintaining remissions, and possibly have a preventive effect on the relapse of ulcerative colitis (127,128). They were as useful as mesalamine in this regard (129-131). With regard to Crohn's disease, preliminary data have not shown any effect in treating active disease (132). A systematic review failed to identify any benefit from probiotics in patients with Crohn's disease (133), nor in two subsequent RCTs in patients who had undergone surgery (134,135). However, design flaws make it difficult to interpret much of the data. A summary of the evidence on probiotics during the acute and maintenance phases of these two conditions is summarized in the Evidence Summary table at the end of the chapter. It did appear that VSL#3 was effective in preventing the onset, or the recurrence, of pouchitis in three RCTs (136-138) (see Evidence Summary table at end of chapter).

In single RCTs, wheat grass juice, bovine colostrum enemas, aloe vera gel, and curcumin (139) all appeared to be more effective than placebo in improving symptoms and endoscopic appearances in patients with ulcerative colitis (140-142).

# Pain

## Acupuncture

Several systematic reviews assessed the use of acupuncture in chronic pain, in general (usually musculoskeletal or headache). While an effect was often found, its magnitude was inversely proportional to trial quality, particularly with the effort taken to ensure blinding.

Individual RCTs have assessed acupuncture for pain relief in specific gastroenterology-related conditions. The results have been mixed for postoperative pain (143-151) (see Evidence Summary table at end of chapter). For example, no significant differences were seen with regard to either the effect of acupuncture on inducing sedation or the effect of acupuncture on pain associated with sedation during endoscopy between acupuncture and standard premedication (152-156); however two studies have found that acupuncture may reduce the frequency of post-procedural dizziness (147,148). For management of biliary colic pain, one study has found that acupuncture was better than standard medical therapy (157). However, one study has found that acupuncture relieved pain related to chronic pancreatitis but no better than sham acupuncture (which is considered an active placebo intervention) (158). In general, there is conflicting evidence on the effect of acupuncture for the management of pain caused by gastroenterology-related conditions. Similar to the acupuncture literature as it pertains to pain management across health conditions, there is greater evidence for effect on acute pain condition such as biliary colic but less convincing or conflicting evidence for chronic conditions such as chronic pancreatitis (see Evidence Summary table at end of chapter).

## Hypnotherapy

Three RCTs suggested that hypnotherapy reduced the pain associated with invasive procedures (159-161) (although the specific procedures were not gastroenterologic). Again, these observations must be tempered by the fact that the trials were not blinded (see Evidence Summary table at end of chapter).

# Perioperative Care

## Acupuncture

Ear acupuncture seems to modestly reduce preoperative anxiety (162). A double-blinded randomized trial showed that preoperative insertion of intradermal needles reduced postoperative pain, the analgesic requirement, and opioid-related side effects after both upper and lower abdominal surgery (163). Two non-blinded trials found an association between the use of acupuncture, and an earlier extubation (164) and return of peristalsis (165). Acupuncture appears to be an effective treatment for both preoperative anxiety and postoperative pain (see Evidence Summary table at end of chapter).

## Homeopathy

Homeopathy seemed to reduce the duration of postoperative ileus by about 7 hours. However, most of the trials were not double-blinded (166). There is insufficient evidence to recommend using homeopathy (see Evidence Summary table at end of chapter).

# Alcohol Abuse

## Acupuncture

Six RCTs tested the utility of acupuncture in long-term alcohol rehabilitation (167-172). Acupuncture was effective in some of these trials (168,171), but not in the others (167,169,170,172). Neither laser nor needle acupuncture had any benefit in patients in active alcohol withdrawal (173) (see Evidence Summary table at end of chapter).

# Liver Diseases

## Herbs and Other Natural Products

In the last few years, the use of herbs or other natural substances in treating liver disease has received much attention. The agents of particular interest are milk thistle (*Silybum marianum*), S-adenosyl-L-methionine (SAMe), and traditional Chinese (and other Asian) herbs.

Two systematic reviews have included RCTs (of which majority RCTs were blinded) assessing milk thistle in various liver diseases (alcoholic liver disease, viral hepatitis B or C, drug-induced disease, and various etiologies) (174,175). Although the duration of treatment did vary widely, it was usually for at least several months. No clear-cut efficacy of milk thistle was established. While half of the studies found benefits in at least one outcome measurement (usually liver enzyme activities), the others did not. Survival and other clinical outcomes were less well evaluated, and the results were again mixed. The published evidence is also clouded by poor design and reporting.

One other RCT (patients with alcoholic cirrhosis) was subsequently published (176). No improvements in routine laboratory tests were seen. Clinical outcomes were not evaluated. A systematic Cochrane Hepato-Biliary Group Review identified a total of 13 RCTs assessing milk thistle in 915 patients with alcoholic and/or hepatitis B or C virus liver diseases (177). The methodological quality of these trials was low: only 23% of the trials reported adequate allocation concealment and only 46% were considered adequately double-blinded. Milk thistle versus placebo or no intervention had no significant effect on overall mortality, complications of liver disease, or liver histology. Liver-related mortality was significantly reduced by milk thistle in all trials (an estimated relative risk reduction of 50%), but this effect was not significant when only high-quality trials were considered. Milk thistle was not associated with a significantly increased risk of adverse events. More trials are needed before this agent can be recommended (see Evidence Summary table at end of chapter).

A systematic review of SAMe for alcoholic liver disease (178) identified eight RCTs; only one was deemed high quality. While no statistically significant clinical benefits were identified in that trial, there was a trend for a lower combined 2-year mortality/liver transplantation rate (16% versus 30%). Multiple controlled (mostly randomized) trials have claimed that SAMe reduces pruritus and/or bilirubin levels in cholestasis from pregnancy or other causes (179). However, most of these studies (especially in pregnancy) were small and of low methodological quality. SAMe relieved the pruritus at least as well as ursodeoxycholic acid in two trials, but was less effective in normalizing bilirubin or other markers of liver function (180) (see Evidence Summary table at end of chapter).

Chinese herbal formulations are widely used to treat liver disease in Asia, where there is a heavy burden of chronic viral hepatitis. Several systematic reviews have evaluated most of these RCTs, which were largely published in Chinese language journals.

One systematic review (including nine RCTs) evaluated single or compound Chinese medicinal herbs for chronic hepatitis B (10). Compared to nonspecific treatment or placebo, several herbs or herbal formulas (Fuzheng Jiedu Tang, Polyporus umbellatus extract, or Phyllanthus amarus) showed significant effects on clearance of hepatitis B virus (HBV) markers. Phyllanthus compound and kurorinone were comparable to interferon. Three other examined herbs (a licorice root formulation, Kangdu Wan formulation, and a combination extract of Anisodus tangutica plus Salvia miltiorrhizae) had no significant effects on viral markers. Improvements in patients' signs or symptoms were observed in the studies of Polyporus umbellatus extract and Kangdu Wan (10) (see Evidence Summary table at end of chapter).

Another systematic Cochrane Review (including three RCTs) assessed the effect of herbs on asymptomatic carriers of hepatitis B virus (i.e., normal liver enzyme activities) (181). One herbal compound (Jianpi Wenshen recipe) appeared to be better than interferon with regard to the clearance of viral markers. *Phyllanthus amarus* and *Astragalus membranaceus* could not be shown to be better than placebo as an antiviral (see Evidence Summary table at end of chapter).

A meta-analysis assessed 27 RCTs that compared various Chinese herbal medicines to alpha-interferon treatment for chronic hepatitis B (182). Patients using the herbal medicine alone were significantly more likely to clear hepatitis B surface antigen, but not hepatitis B e antigen or HBV-DNA. Seromarkers of active hepatitis B infection were more likely to disappear if herbs were combined with interferon than if interferon alone was given.

Two particular herbs, *Sophorae flavescentis* and *Phyllanthus spp*, were separately assessed as antiviral interventions in two separate systematic reviews (including 22 RCTs each) (183,184). Both agents were effective in clearing HBV markers and reducing aminotransferase and bilirubin elevations. In a few individual RCTs, their effects were comparable to interferon.

It should be appreciated that 77 of the 83 RCTs considered in these systematic reviews of Chinese herbs were rated as having low methodological quality. Most were not double-blinded.

What about hepatitis C? A systematic Cochrane review identified ten RCTs (four adequate quality, six low quality) that assessed herbal therapy (185). The former four indicated that glycyrrhizin, CH-100, and "Complete Thymic Formula" did not improve viral clearance or enzyme activities. In the six lower-quality trials, beneficial effects were reported with some preparations.

While a number of RCTs have suggested that some traditional Chinese herbal formulations may be effective for chronic viral hepatitis (at least on viral activity and liver biochemistry), the low methodological quality of most of the RCTs detracts from the claims of benefit. The evidence is far from convincing.

Liv-52, an Ayurvedic medicine containing eight different herbs, reduced clinical symptoms and bilirubin levels faster than placebo in acute viral hepatitis. In two RCTs including patients with alcoholic liver disease, this agent was either ineffective or even had a detrimental effect on survival (186,187) (see Evidence Summary table at end of chapter).

Hepatotoxicity as a more serious consequence of many natural products has been well reviewed. While reports are frequently published, the natural product may not always be the culprit. As just noted, "idiosyncratic hepatotoxicity" may actually be due to botanical misidentification, product contamination, or adulteration (with drugs, toxic herbs, heavy metals, or pesticides), or co-administration with other potentially toxic substances. On the other hand, causality is not always obvious because hepatotoxicity usually has a delayed onset.

Nonetheless, several herbal hepatotoxins have been well characterized. The subsequent liver pathology ranges over a wide spectrum (acute [and even fulminant] hepatitis, cholestasis, steatosis, veno-occlusion, chronic hepatitis, and cirrhosis). The liver histological appearances are typically non-specific and can resemble other liver diseases. The more common, well-characterized, and important herbal medicines and other supplements that are associated with hepatotoxicity include those listed in Table 7-2 (188,189).

## Prevention of Gastrointestinal Cancers

### Antioxidant Supplements

Oxidative stress may cause gastrointestinal cancers. The evidence on whether antioxidant supplements are effective in preventing gastrointestinal cancers has been contradictory. In a systematic Cochrane review, Bjelakovic et al identified 14 RCTs (525 participants) (170), assessing beta-carotene (nine trials), vitamin A (four trials), vitamin C (four trials), vitamin E (five trials), and selenium (six trials) (190). Trial quality was generally high. Supplementation with most of the reviewed antioxidants did not have any effect on the incidences of gastrointestinal cancers. However, in four trials (three with unclear/inadequate methodology), selenium showed significant beneficial effect on gastrointestinal cancer incidences. Due to the low quality of these trials, more evidence is needed before preventive measures can be recommended.

When seven high-quality trials assessing antioxidant supplements for prevention of gastroenterologic cancers were subjected to meta-analysis, the fixed-effect model suggested that such supplementation increased mortality (190). This observation is supported by a recent review of all preventive trials, demonstrating increased overall mortality following antioxidant supplements (191) (see Evidence Summary table at end of chapter).

## Recommendations and Conclusions

Data from RCTs have indicated that there may be some therapeutic efficacy attributable to some forms of CAM. However, these conclusions are in many instances hindered by methodological defects in the trials supporting the CAM. Low-quality trials should be suspect. In 2000, Bloom and coworkers undertook a quality assessment of 258 RCTs of CAM, employing a 100-point scale (192). The average score was low, 45. However, using the same scale, RCTs from the standard medical literature were of comparable low quality (average score 45) (192). We should consider all therapeutic intervention equally and ask for the evidence. We then need to examine the methodological quality of the trials supporting the intervention. As is true in allopathic medicine, data from RCTs have also indicated that CAM may be hazardous.

Conventional allopaths are usually skeptical of CAM practices, deeming them to be "non-scientific." It is fully appropriate to be skeptical. We should demand significant beneficial evidence from valid, high-quality RCTs—preferably

Table 7-2    Herbs and Supplements Associated with Hepatotoxicity

| Herb | Adverse Events | Cause (idiosyncratic, direct toxin, unknown, etc) | Frequency (if known) | Level of Association (unclear, possible, probable, definite) |
|---|---|---|---|---|
| Chaparral | Cholestasis, hepatitis | Unknown | Case reports | Probable |
| Germander | Hepatitis | Enzyme metabolism | Case reports | Possible |
| Greater celandine | Acute hepatitis | Unknown | Case reports | Probable |
| Kava | Severe hepatitis | Unknown | Case reports | Probable |
| Lipokinetix | Severe hepatitis | Unknown | Case series | Possible |
| Pennyroyal | Severe hepatitis | Toxin | Case reports | Possible |
| Pyrrolizidine alkaloids | Veno-occlusive disease | Unknown | Rare | Possible |
| Jin-bu-huan | Acute and chronic hepatitis | Adulteration | Case reports | Probable |
| Sho-saiko-to | Acute and chronic liver damage | Unknown | Case reports | Possible |
| Herbal weight loss products: chaso, onshido, sennomoto-kouno | Hepatitis | Adulteration with fenfluramine | Case reports | Probable |
| Ephedra (Ma Huang) | Hepatitis | Idiosyncratic | Case reports | Probable |
| Prostata (saw palmetto plus other herbs) | Hepatitis | Idiosyncratic | Case reports | Possible |
| Scullcap | Liver damage | Idiosyncratic | Case report | Probable |
| Mistletoe | Hepatitis | Idiosyncratic | Case report | Probable |

(continued)

Table 7-2    Herbs and Supplements Associated with Hepatotoxicity (*continued*)

| Herb | Adverse Events | Cause (idiosyncratic, direct toxin, unknown, etc) | Frequency (if known) | Level of Association (unclear, possible, probable, definite) |
|------|----------------|---------------------------------------------------|----------------------|-------------------------------------------------------------|
| Black cohosh | Acute hepatitis, liver failure | Idiosyncratic | Case reports | Probable |
| Valerian | Hepatitis | Idiosyncratic | Case report | Probable |
| Kombucha | Liver damage | Idiosyncratic | Rare | Possible |
| Copaltra | Liver damage | Idiosyncratic | Rare | Possible |
| Herbal laxatives (cascara, senna, psyllium) | Acute or chronic hepatitis | Unknown | Rare | Possible |

systematic reviews with meta-analyses of all valid, high-quality randomised trials—before adopting any new therapy. The conclusions of the RCTs of CAM should be viewed cautiously because of the methodological problems. However, CAM is a diverse field and we should consider the effects of specific interventions for individual conditions.

There seems to be enough "good" evidence supporting some CAM interventions to encourage practicing clinicians to develop a familiarity with CAM literature and even to consider trying some of the therapies for which the data seem more compelling. Most of these interventions are safe and compare favorably with conventional therapies regarding risk/benefit ratios and cost. The ones that could be so considered include peppermint for dyspepsia, for IBD, or for reducing intestinal spasm; ginger for nausea associated with motion sickness or pregnancy; acupuncture for postoperative nausea; probiotics for pediatric or antibiotic-associated diarrhea (VSL#3 in particular for the prevention of pouchitis) or in the treatment of *Helicobacter pylori*. The data for homeopathy in third-world children with diarrhea are certainly provocative, even if the mechanisms are totally obscure. These data need to be confirmed by independent research groups.

National and international assessment of CAM must undergo stringent evaluation in adequately sized and adequately conducted RCTs. As evidenced by some of the experiences in evidence-based CAM, there may be good arguments for reevaluating the contents of the U.S. Dietary Supplement Health and Education Act of 1994 as well as similar laws in other nations. Good evidence showing beneficial effects should be available before products are approved and marketed. Likewise, products that cause harm should be withdrawn from the market (or, if they also have therapeutic benefit, only be provided by prescription, considering the balance between benefit and harm). Any claim for benefit or therapeutic effects needs to be based on clinical evidence, especially randomized clinical trials.

Angell and Kassirer best summarized our attitude towards CAM. They said: "There cannot be two kinds of medicine—conventional and alternative. There is only medicine that has been adequately tested and medicine that has not, medicine that works and medicine that may or may not work. Once a treatment has been tested rigorously it no longer matters whether it was considered alternative at the outset" (193).

Evidence Summary of CAM Treatments of Gastrointestinal Disorders

| Clinical Indication | Category | Specific Therapy | Dose | Outcome | Confidence of Estimate on Effectiveness | Magnitude of Effect* | Safety† | Clinical Recommendation‡ | Comments |
|---|---|---|---|---|---|---|---|---|---|
| Non-ulcer dyspepsia | Biologically based therapies | Peppermint oil combined with caraway oil | Variable | Symptoms thumbs up | Grade B | Moderate | Double | Strong in favor | — |
| Dyspepsia | Biologically based therapies | STW5-I, STW5-II | Multiple compinents | Symptoms | Grade B | Moderate | Double thumbs up | STWS-I: weak in favor STWS-II: strong in favor | — |
| Gastric/duodenal ulcer | Biologically based therapies | Licorice | Variable | Ulceration healing | Grade B | No effect | Single thumb down | Weak against | — |
| Dyspepsia | Biologically based therapies | Red chili pepper | 2.5 g/day | Symptoms | Grade B | No effect | Single thumb up | Weak against | May help alcohol- or NSAID-induced gastric injury |
| Dyspepsia | Biologically based therapies | Turmeric (Curcuma) | 2 g/day | Symptoms | Grade C | Small | Single thumb up | No recommendation | — |
| Dyspepsia | Biologically based therapies | Artichoke leaf extract | 2 x 320 mg t.d.s. | Symptoms, quality of life | Grade B | Moderate | Double thumbs up | Weak in favor | — |
| Adjuvant therapy for H. Pylori eradication | Biologically based therapies | Probiotics | Varied from 0.2-1 g/day | H. Pylori eradication, reduced side effects such as antibiotic-related diarrhea | Grade A | Large | Double thumbs up | Strong in favor | — |

(continued)

**Evidence Summary of CAM Treatments of Gastrointestinal Disorders (Continued)**

| Clinical Indication | Category | Specific Therapy | Dose | Outcome | Confidence of Estimate on Effectiveness | Magnitude of Effect* | Safety† | Clinical Recommendation‡ | Comments |
|---|---|---|---|---|---|---|---|---|---|
| Dyspepsia | Mind-body and lifestyle therapies | Hypnotherapy | Variable | Symptoms | Grade C | Small | Double thumbs up | No recommendation | — |
| Dyspepsia | Whole medical system | Acupuncture | Variable | Symptoms | Grade C | Small | Double thumbs up | No recommendation | — |
| Dyspepsia | Whole medical system | Homeopathy | Variable | Symptoms | Grade C | Small | Double thumbs up | No recommendation | — |
| Crohn's disease (active) | Whole medical system | Acupuncture | Variable | Symptoms | Grade C | Small | Double thumbs up | No recommendation | — |
| IBS pain | Biologically based therapies | Fiber | 25 g/d | Symptom | Grade A | No effect | Double thumbs up | Weak against | — |
| IBS constipation | Biologically based therapies | Fiber | 25 g/d | Symptom | Grade C | Moderate | Double thumbs up | Weak in favor | — |
| IBS pain | Biologically based therapies | Peppermint extract, Peppermint combined with caraway | 1-2 capsules, TID | Symptoms | Grade A | Moderate | Single thumb up | Strong in favor | Used as enteric coated oil |
| IBS | Biologically based therapies | Tongxie Yaofang Chinese Herbal Medicine | 1 dosage/ day | Symptoms | Grade B | Moderate | Double thumbs up | Weak in favor | — |

| Condition | Category | Intervention | Dosage | Outcome | Grade | | | | Notes |
|---|---|---|---|---|---|---|---|---|---|
| IBS constipation | Biologically based therapies | Padma-Lax Tibetan formulation | 1-2 capsules/day | Symptoms | Grade B | Moderate | Double thumbs up | Weak in favor | — |
| IBS pain | Biologically based therapies | STW5, STW5-II | — | Symptoms | Grade B | Moderate | Double thumbs up | Weak in favor | — |
| Infantile colic | Biologically based therapies | Herbal tea containing German chamomile | | Symptoms | Grade B | Moderate | Double thumbs up | Weak in favor | — |
| IBS | Biologically based therapies | Probiotics | — | Symptoms | Grade B | Conflicting findings | Double thumbs up | No recommendation | — |
| IBS | Whole medical system | Acupuncture | — | Symptoms | Grade C | Conflicting findings | Double thumbs up | No recommendation | — |
| IBS | Mind-body and lifestyle therapies | Hypnotherapy | — | Symptoms | Grade B | Moderate | Double thumbs up | Weak in favor | — |
| Diarrhea in children | Biologically based therapies | Carob bean juice | — | Duration of diarrhea and stool output | Grade B | Moderate | Double thumbs up | Weak in favor | Adjunct to oral dehydration solution |
| Diarrhea in children | Biologically based therapies | Apple pectin-chamomile extract | — | Diarrhea symptoms | Grade B | Moderate | Double thumbs up | Weak in favor | Adjuvant to dehydration solution |
| Rotavirus diarrhea in children | Biologically based therapies | Tormentil root extract | 3 drops, TID | Duration of diarrhea and requirement of dehydration solutions | Grade B | Moderate | Double thumbs up | Weak in favor | — |

(continued)

**Evidence Summary of CAM Treatments of Gastrointestinal Disorders (Continued)**

| Clinical Indication | Category | Specific Therapy | Dose | Outcome | Confidence of Estimate on Effectiveness | Magnitude of Effect* | Safety† | Clinical Recommendation‡ | Comments |
|---|---|---|---|---|---|---|---|---|---|
| Adult/child diarrhea | Biologically based therapies | Probiotics | — | Duration/severity/infant mortality | Grade A | Moderate | Double thumbs up | Strong in favor | Use alone or in combination with oral dehydration solution |
| Antibiotic-associated diarrhea | Biologically based therapies | Probiotics | Single strain or combined strains | Duration/severity | Grade A | Moderate | Double thumbs up | Weak in favor | — |
| Acute diarrhea in children | Whole medical system | Homeopathy | — | Duration and symptoms | Grade B | Conflicting findings | Double thumbs up | No recommendation | — |
| Nausea/vomiting: motion sickness | Biologically based therapies | Ginger | — | Symptom | Grade A | Moderate | Double thumbs up | Weak in favor | Under power of trials |
| Pregnancy-induced nausea/vomiting | Biologically based therapies | Ginger | — | Symptom | Grade B | Moderate | Double thumbs up | Weak in favor | More studies needed to confirm |
| Postoperative nausea/vomiting | Biologically based therapies | Ginger | 0.3 to 1 g/day | Symptom | Grade A | Moderate | Double thumbs up | Strong in favor | Preventive efficacy from 5 RCTs |
| Postoperative nausea/vomiting | Whole medical system | Acupuncture stimulation to P6 acupoint | — | Symptom | Grade A | Moderate | Double thumbs up | Strong in favor | — |

| | | | | | Grade A/B | Small | Double thumbs up | Weak in favor | Systematic reviews and RCTs |
|---|---|---|---|---|---|---|---|---|---|
| Pregnancy-induced nausea/vomiting | Whole medical system | Acupuncture | — | Symptom | Grade A/B | Small | Double thumbs up | Weak in favor | — |
| Chemotherapy induced nausea/vomiting | Whole medical system | Stimulation on acupoint | — | Incidence of nausea | Grade B | Small | Double thumbs up | Weak in favor | — |
| Motion sickness | Whole medical system | Acupressure on P6 | — | Symptom | Grade C | Conflicting findings | Double thumbs up | No recommendation | — |
| Chemotherapy induced nausea/vomiting | Mind-body and lifestyle therapies | Hypnotherapy | — | Symptoms | Grade C | Small | Double thumbs up | No recommendation | — |
| Ulcerative colitis acute | Biologically based therapies | Fish oil | — | Symptoms | Grade B | Moderate | Single thumb up | Weak in favor | — |
| Ulcerative colitis maintenance | Biologically based therapies | Omega 3 fatty acids (fish oil) | — | Symptoms | Grade B | No effect | Double thumbs up | Weak against | — |
| Active Crohn's disease | Biologically based therapies | Fish oil | — | Symptoms | Grade B | No effect | Single thumb up | Weak against | — |
| Crohn's disease maintenance therapies | Biologically based | Omega 3 fatty acids (fish oil) | — | Symptoms | Grade C | Small | Double thumbs up | No recommendation | Maybe effective for enteric coated capsules |

*(continued)*

**Evidence Summary of CAM Treatments of Gastrointestinal Disorders (Continued)**

| Clinical Indication | Category | Specific Therapy | Dose | Outcome | Confidence of Estimate on Effectiveness | Magnitude of Effect* | Safety† | Clinical Recommendation‡ | Comments |
|---|---|---|---|---|---|---|---|---|---|
| Ulcerative colitis acute | Biologically based therapies | Probiotics | — | Symptom and remission | Grade C | Conflicting findings | Double thumbs up | No recommendation | — |
| Ulcerative colitis maintenance therapies | Biologically based therapies | Probiotics | — | Remission maintenance | Grade B | Moderate | Double thumbs up | Weak in favor | — |
| Crohn's disease acute, inducing and maintenance of remission | Biologically based therapies | Probiotics | — | Symptoms, inducing and maintenance of remission | Grade B | No effect | Double thumbs up | Weak against | — |
| Pouchitis | Biologically based therapies | Probiotics | — | Prevention of onset and recurrence | Grade B | Moderate | Double thumbs up | Weak in favor | — |
| Acute GI pain | Whole medical system | Acupuncture | — | Pain relief | Grade B | Moderate | Double thumbs up | Weak in favor | Including postoperative pain |
| Chronic pain | Whole medical system | Acupuncture | — | Pain relief | Grade C | Small | Double thumbs up | No recommendation | — |
| Invasive procedure-induced pain | Mind-body and lifestyle therapies | Hypnotherapy | — | Pain relief | Grade C | Small | Double thumbs up | No recommendation | — |

| Condition | Domain | Therapy | Dose | Outcome | Grade | Effect | Recommendation | | Notes |
|---|---|---|---|---|---|---|---|---|---|
| Pre-operative anxiety | Whole medical system | Ear acupuncture | — | Anxiety | Grade C | Small | Double thumbs up | Weak in favor | — |
| Post-operative pain | Whole medical system | Acupuncture | — | Pain relief | Grade B | Moderate | Double thumbs up | Weak in favor | — |
| Postoperative ileus | Mind-body and lifestyle therapies | Homeopathy | — | Duration | Grade C | Small | Double thumbs up | No recommendation | — |
| Alcohol abstinence | Whole medical system | Acupuncture | — | Craving and rehabilitation | Grade C | No effect | Double thumbs up | No recommendation | — |
| Alcohol withdrawal | Whole medical system | Acupuncture | — | Withdrawal | Grade C | No effect | Double thumbs up | Weak against | — |
| Liver diseases (mixed) | Biologically based therapies | Milk thistle | 200 mg tid | Liver protection | Grade B | No consistent effect | Double thumbs up | No recommendation | — |
| Alcohol liver disease | Biologically based therapies | SAMe | 200-800mg BID | Liver protection | Grade C | No effect | Double thumbs up | No recommendation | — |
| Chronic hepatitis B | Biologically based therapies | Chinese herbs (10) | — | HBV clearance | Grade C | Moderate | Single thumb up | No recommendation | Promising herbs: Phyllanthus, Sophorae |
| Asymptomatic carriers of HBV | Biologically based therapies | Chinese herbs | — | HBV clearance | Grade C | Small | Single thumb up | No recommendation | Promising herbs: Jianpi Wenshen recipe |
| Hepatitis C | Biologically based therapies | Chinese herbal therapies | — | Viral markers | Grade C | No effect | Single thumb up | No recommendation | — |

*(continued)*

**Evidence Summary of CAM Treatments of Gastrointestinal Disorders (Continued)**

| Clinical Indication | Category | Specific Therapy | Dose | Outcome | Confidence of Estimate on Effectiveness | Magnitude of Effect* | Safety† | Clinical Recommendation‡ | Comments |
|---|---|---|---|---|---|---|---|---|---|
| Alcohol liver disease | Biologically based therapies | Liv-52 Ayurvedic formulation | — | Liver function | Grade B | No effect | Single thumb down | Weak against | — |
| GI cancers | Biologically based therapies | Antioxidants (beta-carotene, Vit A, Vit C, Vit E) (189, 190) | — | Incidence of GI cancers | Grade B | No effect | Double thumbs down | Weak against | Worsened mortality |
| GI cancers | Biologically based therapies | Selenium (190) | — | Incidence of GI cancers | Grade C | No effect | Single thumb down | No recommendation | Potential risk of mortality |

* Small, moderate (OR>1.2-2) or large (OR>2)

† 5 categories: Double thumbs up, single thumb up, no recommendation, single thumb down, double thumb down

‡ 5 categories: Strong (in favor), weak (in favor), no recommendation, weak (against), strong (against)

SELECTED REFERENCES

3. **Tillisch K.** Complementary and alternative medicine for functional gastrointestinal disorders. Gut. 2006;55:593-6.

9. **Liu JP, Yang M, Liu YX, et al.** Herbal medicines for treatment of irritable bowel syndrome. Cochrane Database of Systematic Reviews. 2006;1:CD004116.

10. **Liu JP, McIntosh H, Lin H.** Chinese medicinal herbs for chronic hepatitis B. Cochrane Database of Systematic Reviews. 2000;4:CD001940.

11. **Thompson Coon J, Ernst E.** Systematic review: herbal medicinal products for non-ulcer dyspepsia. Aliment Pharmacol Ther. 2002;16:1689-99.

13. **Rosch W, Liebregts T, Gundermann K-J, et al.** Phytotherapy for functional dyspepsia: a review of the clinical evidence for the herbal preparation STW 5. Phytomedicine. 2006;13(Suppl5):114-21.

21. **Madisch A, Holtmann G, Mayr G, et al.** Treatment of functional dyspepsia with a herbal preparation. A double-blind, randomized, placebo-controlled, multicenter trial. Digestion 2004;69:45-52.

28. **Calvert EL, Houghton LA, Cooper P, et al.** Long-term improvement in functional dyspepsia using hypnotherapy. Gastroenterology. 2002;123:1778-85.

30. **Joos S, Brinkhaus B, Maluche C, et al.** Acupuncture and moxibustion in the treatment of active Crohn's disease: a randomized controlled study. Digestion. 2004;69:131-9.

32. **Pittler MH, Ernst E.** Peppermint oil for irritable bowel syndrome: a critical review and meta-analysis. Am J Gastroenterol. 1998;93:1131-5.

53. **Lim B, Manheimer E, Lao L, et al.** Acupuncture for treatment of irritable bowel syndrome. Cochrane Database Syst Rev. 2006;18:CD005111.

64. **Allen SJ, Okoko B, Martinez E, et al.** Probiotics for treating infectious diarrhoea. Cochrane Database of Systematic Reviews 2003;4:CD003048.

66. **Suzawol S, Hiremath G, Dhingra U, et al.** Efficacy of probiotics in prevention of acute diarrhea: a meta-analysis of masked, randomised, placebo-controlled trials. Lancet Infection. 2006;6:374-82.

83. **Borrelli F, Capasso R, Aviello G, et al.** Effectiveness and safety of ginger in the treatment of pregnancy-induced nausea and vomiting. Obstet Gynecol. 2005;105:849-56.

84. **Chaiyakunapruk N, Kitikannakorn N, Nathisuwan S, et al.** The efficacy of ginger for the prevention of postoperative nausea and vomiting: a meta-analysis. Am J Obstet Gynecol. 2006;194:95-9.

86. **Lee A, Done ML.** Stimulation of the wrist acupuncture point P6 for preventing postoperative nausea and vomiting. Cochrane Database of Systematic Reviews. 2004;3:CD003281.

113. **Ezzo JM, Richardson MA, Vickers A, et al.** Acupuncture-point stimulation for chemotherapy-induced nausea or vomiting. Cochrane Database of Systematic Reviews. 2006;2:CD002285.

120. **Turner D, Steinhart AH, Griffiths AM.** Omega 3 fatty acids (fish oil) for maintenance of remission in ulcerative colitis. Cochrane Database of Systematic Reviews. 2007;3:CD006443.

141. **Langmead L, Feakins RM, Goldthorpe S, et al.** Randomized, double-blind, placebo-controlled trial of oral aloe vera gel for active ulcerative colitis. Aliment Pharmacol Ther 2004;19:739-47.

163. **Kotani N, Hashimoto H, Sato Y, et al.** Preoperative intradermal acupuncture reduces postoperative pain, nausea and vomiting, analgesic requirement, and sympathoadrenal responses. Anesthesiology. 2001;95:349-56.

177. **Rambaldi A, Jacobs BP, Iaquinto G, Gluud C.** Milk thistle for alcoholic and/or hepatitis B or C liver diseases—a systematic cochrane hepato-biliary group review with meta-analyses of randomized clinical trials. Am J Gastroenterol. 2005;100:2583-91.

178. **Rambaldi A, Gluud C.** S-adenosyl-L-methionine for alcoholic liver diseases. Cochrane Database Syst Rev. 2006;2:CD002235.

* The complete reference list is to be found on the book's Web site.

183. **Liu J, Lin H, McIntosh H.** Genus Phyllanthus for chronic hepatitis B virus infection: a systematic review. J Viral Hep. 2001;8:358-66.

184. **Liu J, Zhu M, Shi R, Yang M.** Radix Sophorae flavescentis for chronic hepatitis B: A systematic review of randomized trials. Am J Chinese Med. 2003;31:337-54.

185. **Liu JP, Manheimer E, Tsutani K, Gluud C.** Medicinal herbs for hepatitis C virus infection. Cochrane Database of Systematic Reviews. 2001;4:CD003183.

188. **Pittler MH, Ernst E.** Systematic review: hepatotoxic events associated with herbal medicinal products. Aliment Pharmacol Ther. 2003;18:451-71.

191. **Bjelakovic G, Nikolova D, Gluud LL, et al.** Mortality in randomized trials of antioxidant supplements for primary and secondary prevention: systematic review and meta-analysis. JAMA. 2007;297:842-57.

# Chapter 8

℘ↄ

# Coronary Heart Disease

LeAnne T. Bloedon, MS, RD
Philippe O. Szapary, MD, MSCE

Cardiovascular disease (CVD) is still the leading cause of morbidity and mortality in the U.S. (1). It is a chronic disease often requiring multiple, conventional pharmacologic and invasive interventions that make CAM a concomitant therapy attractive to patients. CAM therapies are utilized more by adults with chronic diseases compared to adults with no chronic disease (2), and use among patients with CVD mirrors this finding (3). Data from the National Health Interview Survey (NHIS) of 2002 included 10,572 patients with CVD (34% of the population surveyed) and revealed that the most common reason (59%) patients with CVD utilized CAM therapies was the belief that "CAM combined with conventional medical treatments would help" (3). The second most common reason reported was "it would be interesting to try (50%)." Patients with CVD used CAM primarily for non-cardiac conditions such as those affecting the musculoskeletal system, and most patients who used CAM did so in combination with conventional therapy. This suggests that CVD *per se* is not the factor promoting CAM use in these patients. Less than half of the CVD patients surveyed reported disclosing CAM use to their health care provider.

## Prevalence of CAM Use Among Patients with Cardiovascular Disease

Data from the 2002 NHIS reveal that 36% of patients with CVD used some form of CAM therapy in the previous 12 months, which was comparable to 35% of survey responders who did not have CVD but used CAM (3). In addition to the usual factors associated with CAM use, such as being female, having a higher education, and having a higher income, CAM use among patients with CVD is also more common in younger adults, the Asian race, and those with worse health status (3).

## CAM Therapies in Cardiovascular Disease

Based on available data, biologically based therapies (BBT) are the single most popular CAM therapy, followed by mind-body therapies (MBT) (3). Among participants reporting any form of CAM therapy in the 2002 NHIS, 61% reported using some form of BBT, primarily herbal therapies. In a cross-sectional study of 198 patients with CVD in a university hospital in New York City to assess the use of BBT, 42% reported using some form of BBT within the previous 12 months, and 32% reported using at least one form of BBT all of the time (4). The only significant predictor of BBT use was higher level of education (p=0.003). The most common products were vitamin E (44%), vitamin C (32%), multivitamins (25.5%), calcium (20.2%), vitamin B complex (18.1%), fish oil (12.8%), coenzyme Q10 (11.7%), glucosamine (10.6%), magnesium (8.5%), and vitamin D (6.4%). Sixty percent of the respondents reported disclosing use of BBT to their physician, and approximately 1/3 of the participants said they were ever asked about BBT use during a history or physician exam by a health care provider. Users of BBT believed BBT to be safer and more effective than prescription drugs than did non-users (p<0.001). Krasuki and colleagues reported 53.8% participants of a cohort of 210 patients with CVD being treated in a cardiovascular clinic in Texas currently using CAM, with vitamins E and C being the most commonly used (5). More than half of the patients reported disclosing CAM use to their physician. Almost half felt CAM was safer than traditional medications, but only 15% thought it was more efficacious.

Table 8-1 catalogues CAM therapies used specifically for secondary prevention of CAD. Given the multiple pharmacological therapies used in treating CVD, the lack of discussing CAM therapy use with health care providers and the risks associated with use of some dietary supplements alone and in combination with prescription medications common in CVD, patients with CVD who use BBT may be at a greater risk for developing adverse events. In this chapter, we review the best available efficacy and safety data on selected BBT and MBT used most commonly in secondary prevention of CVD. When data are unavailable in secondary prevention, available data in primary prevention of CVD will be reviewed.

## Biologically Based Therapies

### Case Study 8-1

A 61-year-old woman with a history of non-Q wave myocardial infarct 3 months prior presents to her internist for follow-up. She feels well and is without symptoms. She says she is "turning over a new leaf" and wants your help in advising her on how to prevent any more heart

Table 8-1    CAM Therapies Studied in Secondary Prevention of Cardiovascular Disease

| Biologically Based Therapies | Mind-Body Therapies | Alternative Medical Systems |
|---|---|---|
| *Dietary Supplements*<br>  Antioxidants:<br>    Vitamins E, C,<br>    beta carotene,<br>    coenzyme Q10<br>  Herbals: ginkgo biloba,<br>    horse chestnut,<br>    guggulipid, garlic,<br>    red yeast rice,<br>    Hawthorn,<br>    Danshen, policosanol<br>  B Vitamins (folate,<br>    B6, B12)<br>  Magnesium<br>  L-Arginine<br>  L-Carnititine<br><br>*Special Diets:*<br>*Macronutrient-Focused*<br>  Very-low-fat (Ornish,<br>    Pritikin)<br>  Low carbohydrate<br>    (Atkins)<br><br>*Special Diets: Special Foods*<br>  Mediterranean<br>  Fish/fish oil<br>  Plant sterols/stanols<br>  Soluble fiber<br>  Soy<br>  Alcohol<br><br>*EDTA Chelation Therapy* | Cognitive Behavioral<br>Meditation<br>  (Mindfulness,<br>  Transcendental)<br>Yoga<br>  (Iyengar, Integral)<br>Qi Gong<br>Tai Chi | Traditional Chinese medicine<br>  (TCM), including<br>  acupuncture<br>Ayurvedic medicine,<br>  including complex botanical<br>  mixtures |

attacks. She has started a walking program and has started taking several dietary supplements based on advice from friends and the Internet.

She is a non-smoker; does not have diabetes; has a family history of pre-mature coronary heart disease in her mother. Her current medications are: metoprolol 50 mg PO BID, simvastatin 20 mg PO QHS, ramipril 10 mg PO QD, enteric-coated aspirin 325 mg PO QD, vitamin E 400 IU PO QD. On further questioning, she hesitantly reveals that she has received three chelation treatments but is not sure if she should continue them. She asks you for advice on her medical regimen and her alternative therapies.

## Dietary Supplements

Dietary supplements are defined and regulated under The Dietary Supplement Health and Education Act (DSHEA) of 1994 by the Food and Drug Administration (FDA) (www.cfsan.fda.gov/~dms/dietsupp.html). A dietary supplement is defined as a product taken by mouth that contains a dietary ingredient (vitamin, mineral, herb or other botanical, amino acid, and substance such as enzymes, organ tissues, glandulars, metabolites, extracts or concentrates) that is intended to supplement the diet. Dietary supplements are not regulated under the umbrella of "drugs". Information on the label must clearly define the product as a dietary supplement and must not represent the product as a conventional food or a sole item of a meal or a diet. While the product must include a statement that the FDA has not reviewed or approved any claims made on this product, DSHEA does not give the FDA pre-marketing regulatory authority to reject most dietary supplements prior to reaching the market and the consumer, but rather puts responsibility on the manufacturer to produce safe products. The FDA has the authority to pull a dietary supplement off the market if it is proven to be unsafe. Without well-designed clinical trials or phase IV surveillance studies (which unfortunately aren't as prevalent as drug trials because you cannot patent compounds found in nature), it is difficult to prove that a product is unsafe from available case reports or other anecdotal information. The FDA announced in November 2004 three major regulatory initiatives as part of DSHEA designed to improve the safety and labeling of dietary supplements, which should give consumers greater confidence in purchasing products in the future.

### *Antioxidant Vitamins*

Theoretically, antioxidants are an attractive means of secondary prevention of CVD by protecting LDL against oxidation. Additional benefit may include reducing the proliferation of smooth muscle cells, platelet adhesion and aggregation, expression and function of adhesion molecules and synthesis of leukotrienes; improving endothelial function; reducing ischemia; and stabilizing atherosclerotic plaques (6).

#### Vitamin E (Tocopherol)

Tocopherols represent a broad class of lipid-soluble antioxidant vitamins commonly used in the treatment and prevention of chronic disease ranging from CVD to dementia. The most commonly studied vitamin E analogue is $\alpha$-tocopherol, but data are emerging that other isomers such as $\gamma$-tocopherol and tocotrienols may also have a role in human therapeutics. Vitamin E is the most frequently used dietary supplement by patients interested in preventing CVD (4). Multiple large observational studies have suggested a benefit of vitamin E in preventing CVD events (7,8). Only two randomized controlled trials (RCTs) have shown some type of benefit with vitamin E supplementation in secondary coronary heart disease (CHD) prevention. In the Cambridge Heart Antioxidant Study (CHAOS), vitamin E reduced the risk of nonfatal myocardial infarction (MI) but not fatal MI in patients with established CHD (9). This study investigated two doses of vitamin E (800 IU and then 400 IU) over 1.4 years and found a 47% relative risk reduction in a composite endpoint of cardiovascular death and non-fatal MI (p=0.005). This study has been criticized because the two groups did not appear equal at randomization and because of a questionable increase in non-CVD mortality in subsequent analysis. The second and more recent positive study found that 800 IU reduced the incidence of a composite cardiovascular endpoint (MI, ischemic stroke, peripheral vascular disease and unstable angina) by 54% in 196 patients with CVD with end-stage renal disease (ESRD) receiving chronic hemodialysis (10). However, larger and longer trials using 300-400 IU of vitamin E have failed to substantiate a benefit in secondary prevention (11,12) or in heterogeneous populations of patients at high risk for CVD events (12,13).

In the Heart Outcomes Prevention Evaluation-The Ongoing Outcomes (HOPE-TOO) trial, supplementation with 400 IU of vitamin E for a median duration of 7 years had no effect on major cardiovascular events in primary or secondary prevention and may increase risk of heart failure (14). Of the 738 subjects enrolled in the HOPE-TOO trial, subjects randomized to vitamin E had a higher risk of heart failure (RR, 1.13; 95% CI, 1.01-1.26; p=0.03) and hospitalization for heart failure (RR, 1.21; 95% CI, 1.00-1.47; p=0.045) compared to subjects randomized to placebo. A meta-analysis of seven RCTs including 81,788 subjects with vitamin E doses of 50-800 IU found no benefit on mortality, cardiovascular death or cerebrovascular accident (15), while a larger meta-analysis looking at a dose effect suggested an increased risk of mortality with vitamin E doses of at least 400 IU per day. However, it is unclear whether combination with other dietary supplements such as beta carotene could explain the increase in mortality (16).

This issue of whether antioxidant "cocktails" that include vitamin E are protective against CVD risk has been the subject of recent investigation. Three RCTs of antioxidant combination therapy involving vitamin E in high-risk patients have not shown any beneficial effects, and one has suggested possible harm (17-19). In the Heart Protection Study involving 20,536 subjects at high risk for CHD, combination antioxidant therapy including vitamin E (600 mg), vitamin C (250 mg), and beta carotene (20 mg) for 5 1/2 years had no benefit. In an angiographic study of combination simvastatin + niacin, the addition of daily vitamin E (800 IU), vitamin C (1000 mg), beta-carotene (25 mg), and selenium (100 mcg) blunted the HDL-raising effect of the lipid-lowering drugs (18). There is significant evidence to suggest that vitamin E at doses exceeding 400 IU either alone or in combination with other antioxidants is not effective in primary and secondary prevention of CVD and may possibly do harm (see Evidence Summary table at end of chapter).

## Beta-Carotene

RCTs involving beta-carotene have either demonstrated no clinical benefit on CVD or potential harm. A recent meta-analysis suggests beta-carotene may increase mortality (20). In the 6-year post-trial follow-up in the alpha-tocopherol and beta-carotene cancer prevention (ATBC) study, daily use of 20 mg beta-carotene in smokers was associated with an increased risk of non-fatal MI (RR, 1.11; 95% CI, 0.99-1.25) and fatal CHD (RR, 1.11; 95% CI, 0.99-1.25) (21,22). Furthermore, earlier results from this study revealed male smokers randomized to 20 mg beta-carotene had a higher incidence of lung cancer compared to participants who did not receive beta-carotene (23). Thus, supplementation with beta-carotene should be discouraged (see Evidence Summary table at end of chapter).

## Coenzyme Q10 (Ubiquinone)

Co-enzyme Q10 (CoQ10) or ubiquinone is the lipid-soluble co-enzyme part of the inner mitochondrial enzyme complex involved in oxidative phosphorylation (ATP production). It also acts as a free radical scavenger and regenerates reduced (active) forms of alpha-tocopherol. HMG-Co A reductase is involved in the regulation of the biosynthesis of CoQ10 and therefore statins, which may inhibit this enzyme. Both animal and human studies have shown that inhibition of HMG-CoA reductase through use of statins reduces CoQ10 serum levels (24-27). This has been shown in both normal and hypercholesterolemic patients with lovastatin, pravastatin, atorvastatin and simvastatin. It has also been shown that concomitant supplementation of a statin with 100 mg of CoQ10 blunts this reduction in serum CoQ10 (28,27).

A recent study found that 100 mg CoQ10 did not improve statin tolerance or myalgia in patients who had previously experienced statin-related myalgia and were then randomized to simvastatin 10 mg and titrated up to 40 mg with or without CoQ10 (29). Cardiac failure and aging decrease myocardial CoQ10 content (30-32). 121 patients preparing to undergo elective cardiac surgery were randomized to CoQ10 (300 mg/d) or placebo for 2 weeks preoperatively. CoQ10 levels in serum, atrial trabeculae and isolated mitochondria were significantly increased compared to levels in placebo-treated patients ($p<0.001$ for all variables) (33). Mitochondrial respiration was more efficient ($p=0.012$), and mitochondrial malondialdehyde content was lower ($p=0.002$) with CoQ10 compared to placebo. Pectinate trabeculae exposed to 30 minutes of hypoxia in vitro from subjects receiving CoQ10 demonstrated a greater recovery of developed force compared with tissue taken from patients receiving placebo ($p=0.001$). Singh et al found that daily intake of 120 mg initiated within 48 hours of an MI and taken for 1 year in 140 patients significantly reduced the risk of cardiac events compared to placebo both within 4 weeks (15.0 vs. 30.9%, $p<0.02$) of follow-up (34) and at one year (35). All subjects were instructed to take aspirin and 49.3% and 43.6% of subjects in the CoQ10 and placebo groups, respectively, received lovastatin.

Total cardiac events, including cardiac deaths and non-fatal infarction were significantly lower in the CoQ10-treated group compared to placebo (24.6 vs. 45.0, p<0.02). There were 13.7 reports of non-fatal myocardial infarction in the CoQ10 group compared to 25.3 events in the placebo-treated group (p<0.05). In addition, CoQ10 significantly increased plasma levels of vitamin E and HDL and decreased measures of oxidative stress including TBARS, malondialdehyde, and diene conjugates as compared to the placebo group (p<0.05). Nausea (30.1 vs. 9.8%) and vomiting (13.7 vs. 11.2%) were more commonly reported in the CoQ10 group compared to placebo, whereas fatigue (6.8 vs. 40.8%) was more common in the placebo group.

In a different study, these same authors found that 120 mg of CoQ10 reduced Lp(a) levels by 23% over 1 month in 50 patients immediately post-MI (36). There are case reports of CoQ10 reducing the efficacy of warfarin, a drug commonly used in the CVD population (37,38); however, results from a RCT cross-over trial showed that concomitant use of CoQ10 and warfarin did not affect INR levels (39).

In summary, it is not known whether decreased serum CoQ10 levels, seen with co-administration of statin drugs, is detrimental. It is therefore premature to recommend routine co-administration of CoQ10 with a statin. There is preliminary evidence to suggest that preoperative administration of CoQ10 for 2 weeks might have some effect on cardiac function among patients undergoing elective cardiac surgery and that administration of CoQ10 for 1 year given within 48 hours of an acute MI might reduce cardiac mortality and subsequent non-fatal MI. When evaluating the effectiveness of any therapy, one must also consider the monetary cost, which, for the 100 mg dose, is on average between $20 and $50 per month, adding considerably to the expense of statin therapy, an already expensive (but proven) treatment. Overall, there is insufficient evidence to support or refute the use of CoQ10 for CHD at this time (see Evidence Summary table at end of chapter).

## B-Vitamins

Serum homocysteine concentrations are regarded as an independent risk factor for coronary artery disease. Meta-analyses of epidemiologic studies consistently show a significant positive association between homocysteine concentrations and cardiovascular events and stroke (40-42). These studies suggest that a reduction in serum homocysteine by 3 μmol/L lowers the risk of MI by 15% and stroke by 24%. Prospective studies have shown that supplementation with folic acid, vitamin B6 (pyroxidine) and vitamin B12 (cobalamin) reduce serum homocysteine levels by 5-25% (40). The question is whether pharmacologic intervention to reduce homocysteine concentrations results in reduced morbidity and/or mortality associated with CVD. Several of these trials are in progress and some have been reported. The Vitamin Intervention for Stroke Prevention (VISP) was the first trial reported. It investigated whether high-dose (2.5 mg folic acid, 25 mg B6, 0.4 mg of B12) or low-dose (20 μg folic acid,

200µg B6, and 6µg B12) vitamin formulation affected the risk of recurrent stroke over 2 years in 3680 adults with nondisabling cerebral infarction (43). While the high-dose vitamin formulation reduced serum homocysteine levels by 2.0, 2.2, and 2.3 µmol/L greater than the low-dose vitamin formulation group at 1 month, 1 year and 2 years, respectively, there was no difference in risk of ischemic stroke within 2 years comparing the high-dose (9.2%) with the low-dose (8.8%) group (p=0.80). In a subgroup analysis, the authors reported that among people who achieved a 3 µmol/L reduction in homocysteine level with supplementation, there was a 10% lower risk of stroke (p=0.05), a 26% lower risk of CHD events (p<0.001), and a 16% lower risk of death (p=0.001) in the low-dose group. However, in the high-dose group, this level was associated with a non-significant reduction in corresponding risk of 2%, 7%, and 7%. Additional studies will need to explore effects based on baseline homocysteine levels associated with dose.

More recent trials exploring the role of vitamin B therapy in prevention of cardiovascular events in high-risk patients have also found no effect (44,45), and two have reported possible harm (46,47). In the Heart Outcomes Prevention Evaluation (HOPE) 2 study, 5522 volunteers with vascular disease or diabetes were randomized to receive daily treatment of 2.5 mg folic acid, 50 mg B6, and 1 mg of B12 or placebo for a mean of 5 years. While mean plasma homocysteine levels decreased by 2.4 µmol/L in the active group and increased by 0.8 µmol/L in the control group, there was no significant difference in the primary endpoint, which was composite of death from cardiovascular causes, myocardial infarction and stroke (relative risk, 0.95; 95 CI, 0.84-1.07, p=0.41). There were no significant differences when each of these was analyzed separately. More subjects in the active group were hospitalized for unstable angina (9.7%) compared to the control group (7.9%; relative risk, 1.24; 95% CI, 1.04-1.49; p=0.02). Fewer patients in the active group had a stroke (4.0%) compared to those in the placebo group (5.3%) (relative risk 0.75; 95% CI, 0.59-0.97; p=0.03), however, the number of stroke events was small, and the data are not adjusted for the multiplicity of outcomes compared.

In patients suffering from an acute MI, vitamin B therapy may be harmful. Bonaa et al investigated the effects of 0.8 mg folic acid, 0.4 mg B12, or 40 mg B6 as combination therapy or monotherapy compared to placebo on recurrent MI, stroke, and sudden death associated with CAD over a mean of 36 months. While homocysteine levels decreased by 27% in subjects receiving folic acid with B12, combination therapy (with or without B6) did not affect the risk of recurrent cardiovascular events or death after an acute MI. In the group receiving all three vitamins, there was a trend toward an increased risk (relative risk, 1.22; 95% CI, 1.00-01.50; P=0.05). The data relating to combination vitamin B therapy on restenosis are inconsistent. Data suggest that combination B therapy may decrease the rate of restenosis in patients undergoing coronary balloon angioplasty (48) but may increase the rate after coronary stenting (47).

Limited studies suggest that high-dose folic acid therapy may improve endothelial function, independent of homocysteine concentrations, in patients with CVD as measured by flow-mediated vasodilation (FMD). Moens and colleagues performed a cross-over RCT where 40 subjects with acute MI who underwent rescue percutaneous coronary intervention were randomized to either group A (10 mg folic acid) or group B (matched placebo) each for 6 weeks duration (49). After 6 weeks, subjects completed a 2-week wash-out period and then switched to the other group. Endothelial function, measured by FMD and blood analyses, were performed at baseline, 6 weeks, and the end of the study. Folic acid increased FMD by 61.8% at 6 weeks and persisted when followed by placebo. There were no changes in FMD after 6 weeks on placebo in Group B, but FMD increased by 45.4% after 6 weeks of folic acid. The authors report there was no correlation between improvement in FMD and changes in homocysteine levels. Similarily, Doshi et al reported that 5 mg folic acid significantly improved FMD in patients with stable CAD, before a reduction in homocysteine levels were detected (50).

Based on the available data to date, B vitamin therapy after acute MI or in high-risk patients appears to have no effect on cardiovascular events and limited data suggest it may cause harm. It is unclear whether B vitamin therapy has any effect on rates of coronary artery restenosis. In summary, there is currently insufficient evidence to support or refute vitamin B therapy for primary or secondary prevention of CVD (see Evidence Summary table at end of chapter).

### Omega-3 Fatty Acids

Increasing evidence suggests that omega-3 fatty acids (n-3 PUFA) play an important role in secondary prevention of CVD. N-3 PUFA include both marine-derived (eicosapentaenoic acid, C20:5n-3 [EPA] and docosahexaenoic acid, C22:6n-3 [DHA]) and plant-derived (alpha-linolenic acid, C18:3n-3 [ALA]) sources.

#### Marine Sources

Long-chain n-3 PUFA such as EPA and DHA are found in high concentrations in fish oil. They can be consumed in small quantities in foods (primarily in fatty, cold water fish such as salmon, mackerel, sardines, herring or trout) or in larger quantities via dietary supplements. Farm-raised and wild fish do not significantly differ in their EPA and DHA content, but farm-raised fish contain on average higher levels of saturated and polyunsaturated fat (51). N-3 PUFA from fish oil appear to have multiple cardioprotective mechanisms of action including reducing triglycerides, inflammation, and platelet adhesion, inhibiting plaque formation, decreasing blood pressure, improving lipid profiles, decreasing ventricular arrythymias, and cardiac mortality, particularly sudden death (52).

Secondary prevention trials have primarily included male subjects and have found positive effects of EPA and DHA from both diet and dietary supplements.

The Diet and Reinfarction Trial (DART) found that 2033 male MI survivors who received advice to consume fish twice weekly (e.g., 200-400 g, which provides 500 to 800 mg/d of n-3 PUFA) had a significant reduction in total mortality of 29% after 2 years compared to "usual care" (53). The largest prospective RCT testing effects of supplemental EPA and DHA on secondary prevention of CVD is the GISSI Prevention Study (11). In this study, 11,324 patients (85% male) who suffered a recent MI (< 3 months) were randomized to receive one of the following treatments for 3.5 years: 850 mg of purified and concentrated EPA and DHA as ethyl esters, vitamin E 300 mg, both or neither. After 3.5 years, the group that received n-3 PUFA alone experienced a 15% reduction in nonfatal MI and stroke (P < 0.02). Compared with the control group, there was a 20% RRR in total mortality and a 45% reduction in sudden death (P<0.001). There were no reports of significant bleeding and only 3.8% of fish oil–treated patients stopped therapy because of side-effects (primarily dyspepsia) compared to 2.1% of patients on vitamin E. The more recent Japan EPA Lipid Intervention study (JELIS) investigated the effects of low-dose statin (10 mg pravastatin or 5 mg simvastatin/day) with or without 1800 mg highly purified EPA over 5 years in 18,645 subjects with hypercholesterolemia or major cardiovascular events. In subjects with CVD, the risk of major coronary events was 19% lower in the EPA group compared to the statin-only group (p=0.048) (54).

A study conducted in Norway by Nilsen et al, however, did not find a protective effect of supplemental DHA +EPA at 3.5 g/day on cardiac events in post-MI patients after 1.5 years of treatment (55). Several differences in this study compared to the GISSI-Prevention Study may explain negative findings, including: smaller sample size (n=300), a higher dose of EPA and DHA (3.5 g vs. 850 mg), and the possibility that background diet in Scandinavian populations is higher in fatty marine fish than the Italian diet, obscuring any differences in outcomes in the Norwegian study.

A meta-analysis of randomized clinical trials assessing the effects of n-3 PUFA on secondary prevention showed a cardioprotective benefit of EPA and DHA from both dietary intake and supplements on fatal MI, sudden cardiac death, and all-cause mortality (56). Many national, international and professional organizations have made recommendations for consuming fish as well as EPA and DHA.

The Dietary Guidelines for Americans 2005 report states, "Evidence suggests consuming approximately 2 servings of fish per week (approximately 8 ounces) may reduce the risk of mortality from CHD and that consuming EPA and DHA may reduce the risk of mortality from CVD in people who have already experienced a cardiac event" (www.health.gov/dietaryguidelines/dga2005/report). For secondary prevention, the American Heart Association recommends consuming approximately 1 g EPA + DHA per day, which equals about two to three 3-oz servings of fish per day (57). Patients should avoid commercially prepared fish (e.g., fish sticks) due to low n-3 PUFA content and high concentration of trans-MUFAs. In meeting recommendations, patients need to consider safety concerns such as methylmercury and polychlorinated biphenyls (PCBs). Mercury levels are high in large fish that have lived a long period of time such as shark, swordfish, king mackerel and tilefish, whereas PCBs were found to be higher in farm-raised salmon compared to wild salmon (51). Therefore, it may be best to choose fish high in n-3 PUFA that are low in mercury while choosing a variety of wild and farm-raised fish within these species.

It should be noted that most patients with CHD will not be able to eat enough fish every day to meet the requirements for secondary prevention, making fish oil supplements a possible option. Most fish oil supplements contain approximately 180 mg EPA and 120 mg DHA per 1000 mg capsule. Therefore, patients with CHD need approximately 3 capsules per day to meet the requirement. While fish oil supplements at this level are safe, they can cause nausea, dyspepsia, modest increases in low-density lipoprotein cholesterol and a fishy after taste. Anecdotally, the fishy after taste can be reduced by freezing the supplements and ingesting them with meals. EPA and DHA may affect platelet aggregation and/or vitamin K-dependent coagulation factors. There are limited data regarding the safety of fish oil taken concomitantly with antiplatelet and/or anticoagulant medications. One study reported a trend toward increased bleeding in patients receiving fish oil and aspirin or warfarin (58), whereas results from a RCT suggested that supplemental fish oil between 3 and 6 grams per day has no effect on anticoagulation status of patients receiving chronic warfarin therapy (59). There have been several case reports suggesting fish oil can provide additive anticoagulant effects when given with warfarin and antiplatelet effects when given with warfarin and aspirin in combination (60). Patients undergoing anticoagulation and/or antiplatelet therapy where fish oil supplementation is being considered should be educated about and monitored for possible drug-herb interactions. A prescription form of fish oil called Omacor and later renamed Lovaza (Reliant Pharmaceuticals) is now approved by the FDA. Each capsule contains 840 mg EPA/DHA. There is strong evidence to suggest that marine sources of omega-3 fatty acids ingested as food or as dietary supplements (e.g., fish oil) appears relatively safe and is effective for primary and secondary prevention of cardiovascular disease events such as nonfatal MI and stroke and cardiac-related mortality (see Evidence Summary table at end of chapter).

### Plant-Derived Sources

ALA, an essential fatty acid, is the short chain n-3 PUFA found in various plant sources. ALA is the plant-derived n-3 PUFA. Major sources of ALA are limited to flaxseeds (and flaxseed oil), walnuts (and walnut oil), soybeans (and soybean oil), and rapeseed (and canola oil). Research suggests that ALA may protect against cardiovascular disease by interfering with production of pro-inflammatory eicosanoids prostaglandin $E_2$ ($PGE_2$), thromboxane $A_2$ ($TXA_2$) and leukotriene $B_4$ ($LTB_4$), produced from the "n-6" pathway that converts linoleic acid (LA) to arachidonic acid (AA). These pro-inflammatory eicosanoids are involved with promoting platelet aggregation, vasoconstriction, and thrombosis (61). However, the eicosanoids produced from the conversion of ALA to EPA (n-3 series) have less inflammatory effects.

Epidemiological evidence suggests a strong correlation between ALA intake and risk of CHD in both men and women. In the Nurses' Healthy Study, Hu et al found a dose-response relationship between ALA intake and risk of ischemic heart disease, with a 45% reduction in risk of those consuming the highest levels of ALA (62). Similar results were reported in the 30-year follow-up of the Chicago Western Electric Company consuming fish (not plant-derived ALA) (63). Men who consumed at least 35 g of fish daily had a relative risk of death from CHD of 0.62 and a relative risk of non-sudden death from MI of 0.33 compared to men who did not consume fish daily. While several dietary trials have claimed to investigate the role of ALA in secondary prevention of CVD, these involved multifactorial dietary interventions in which it is impossible to single out ALA as the beneficial nutrient. Several of these trials are discussed under Special Diets/ Mediterranean Diet, below. The only published study to date investigating the effects of supplemental ALA on cardiovascular events in patients with CVD is the Indian Experiment of Infarct Survival trial in which patients admitted to the hospital with suspected acute MIs were randomized to fish oil capsules (1.8g/d of EPA + DHA), mustard oil (20 g/d providing 2.9 g ALA) or placebo every day for 1 year (64). At the end of one year, total cardiac events were 25%, 28%, and 35% in the fish oil, mustard oil, and placebo groups, respectively (P<0.01). Non-fatal infarctions were also significantly less in the fish oil and mustard oil groups compared with the placebo group (13.0%, 15.0%, and 25.4%, P< 0.05).

Currently, there are no specific recommendations for patients with CVD, although the AHA suggests intakes of 1.5-3.0 g per day (equivalent to 1-2 tablespoons of ground flaxseed or 1-2 ounces of English walnuts) seem to be beneficial (65). In cancer epidemiologic studies, higher intakes of ALA are associated with an increased risk of prostate cancer (66). This association has not been confirmed in clinical trials, but recommendations to increase ALA beyond current levels cannot be made at this time. Patients should be encouraged to replace low ALA oils (corn oil and safflower oil) with canola, soybean and/or flaxseed oil. For additional sources of ALA, patients can consider incorporating ground flaxseed and/or walnuts into their diets; however, patients should be made aware that these foods are high in calories, a concern for patients who need to lose or maintain weight. There is limited evidence to suggest that plant-derived sources of omega-3 fatty acids provided as dietary supplements appear safe and might be effective in primary and secondary prevention of CVD (see Evidence Summary table at end of chapter).

### Herbals: Garlic (*Allium sativum*)

Garlic may positively affect lipids, fibrinolytic activity, platelet aggregation, blood pressure and blood glucose (67). There are many formulations and preparations of garlic leading to difficulty in comparing findings across studies. Currently, published data investigating the effects of garlic in the secondary prevention of CVD are limited. There are animal, in vitro and in vivo data suggesting that aged garlic extract (AGE) improves endothelial function, decreases LDL oxidation and inflammatory properties, and retards the development of experiential atherosclerosis (68). AGE contains antioxidants that may inhibit the oxidation of LDL in vitro (69). One week of treatment with AGE decreased the susceptibility of isolated LDL to copper ion oxidation in healthy volunteers (70) and in vivo lipid oxidation (71). AGE has been shown to enhance nitric oxide (NO) production and NO-dependent vascular relaxation in animals (72,73). In a short-term cross over RCT in 15 men with CHD, 2.4 g AGE/day for 2 weeks significantly increased FMD and was correlated with low baseline values and body weight. There was no change in biological markers of endothelial function (plasma VCAM-1), oxidative stress or inflammation (68).

There have been several meta-analyses of placebo-controlled human studies on hypocholesterolemic effects of garlic suggesting a modest lipid-lowering effect (74,75). Since the meta analyses were done, two RCTs have been published, both finding a negative result (76,77). If these latest trials were to be figured into the analysis, the benefit of garlic powder on serum lipids would likely vanish. There is moderate evidence to suggest that there is conflicting evidence on whether garlic is effective at lowering cholesterol; however, if subsequent evidence suggests benefit, the magnitude of the effect will likely be relatively modest.

Multiple human studies have documented antiplatelet, anti-thrombotic, and antioxidant effects of garlic products (78). However the antihypertensive and hypoglycemic effect of garlic preparation is mixed, and the data are inconclusive to date (78,79). Although there are no data on garlic with hard endpoints, one study did evaluate the effect of long-term consumption of garlic powder on carotid and femoral atherosclerosis as measured by ultrasound (80). In this study, 280 adults with established CVD were randomized to garlic powder 900 mg/day vs. placebo and treated for up to 4 years. Only 152 completed the full protocol and had carotid or femoral ultrasounds that could be evaluated. Despite very incomplete follow-up and a lack of standardized technique, subjects in the garlic group had evidence of plaque stabilization and some regression compared to placebo (80). One reason for the inconsistency in data with garlic may be due to drastic differences in the composition and quantity of components of different garlic preparations used in the studies. There are many different types of garlic supplements, including dehydrated powder, garlic oil, garlic oil macerate and aged garlic extract. Additionally, the purported major bioactive constituent, allicin, is volatile and unstable. Thus, product standardization, processing and delivery are especially important when considering garlic preparations.

Garlic is well known to cause malodorous breath and dyspepsia. Another concern is the theoretical risk of bleeding from the antiplatelet effects. Bleeding has been seen in case reports but has not been reported in clinical trials of garlic supplements (81). Another issue is the possibility of drug-supplement interaction. Notably, garlic powder has been shown to reduce saquinavir levels (82). This clinically relevant interaction is important to know about because patients with HIV-associated dyslipidemia frequently treat themselves with garlic supplements and thus may be reducing the efficacy of their antiretroviral regimens.

In conclusion, while garlic has been extensively studied for its cholesterol-lowering effects, the evidence is conflicting as to whether it lowers blood pressure or cholesterol and therefore it is premature to make a recommendation. If it does have an effect, the effect is likely to be small. Garlic may, however, be more useful for its non-lipid effects, especially its antiplatelet and antioxidant properties, but data are currently lacking. Thus a role in secondary prevention is yet to be determined, so there is insufficient evidence to support or refute the use of garlic for CHD at this time (see Evidence Summary table at end of chapter).

## Phytoestrogens

Phytoestrogens are biologically active compounds found in plants that have a chemical structure similar to endogenous estrogen or estradiol. Due to this structural similarity, phytoestrogens are able to bind to estrogen receptors of various cells and elicit proestrogenic responses or inhibit estrogenic effects. There are three classes of phytoestrogens: isoflavones, lignans and coumestans, with isoflavones and lignans being the most common and best studied. The primary sources of isoflavones are soybeans and soy-based products. Lignans, however, are found in a variety of plants, including seeds, whole grains, legumes and vegetables. Phytoestrogens found in soy protein and flax have gained a lot of attention over the previous few decades due to various mechanisms of action that may prevent or retard CVD, including improving blood lipid levels and arterial compliance, as well as reducing LDL oxidation. There are no studies published to date that have investigated soy protein, flax or their individual phytoestogens in secondary prevention of CVD. There are, however, extensive human, animal and in vitro data in relation to primary CVD prevention.

### Soy Isoflavones

Isoflavones are phenolic compounds whose carbohydrate conjugate is removed by intestinal bacteria to form the bioactive isoflavones, genistein, daidzein, and glycitein. The major bioactive, and most studied, soy isoflavones are genistein and daidzein. All isoflavones are found in the protein portion of the soybean. Isoflavone content of soybeans and soy products vary based on type of soybean, conditions surrounding cultivation, and processing methods.

Epidemiological studies suggest soy protein plays a role in the striking difference between the higher mortality rates of CHD in the US compared to Japan (83). Most of the experimental research surrounding soy protein has focused on its ability to lower LDL cholesterol levels and provide other cardiovascular benefits in primary prevention. The first meta-analysis reported that dietary soy protein improved LDL cholesterol (approximately -13%), fasting triglycerides (approximately -10%) and HDL cholesterol (approximately +2%) in patients with hypercholesterolemia (84). The degree of LDL cholesterol reduction was found to be inversely associated with LDL cholesterol level (i.e., higher baseline levels were associated with greater reductions, whereas lower baseline levels were associated with less reduction in LDL cholesterol). There were several limitations with this meta-analysis, which prompted additional investigation. The AHA Nutrition Committee recently reviewed the cumulative data on soy protein and soy isoflavones (with or without soy protein) on LDL cholesterol and other risk factors for CVD (85). The group concluded that consuming a large amount of soy protein (approximately 50 g/day, which is equivalent to approximately 6 cups of cooked soybeans) in substitution for animal or dairy protein may slightly reduce LDL-C (mean reduction of approximately 3%) with no effects on HDL-C or triglycerides (TG). Because of the statement from AHA, Clerici and colleagues reported in a cross-over trial that a novel soy-based pasta containing 33 mg of isoflavones/80 g serving as part of a low-saturated-fat (< 7% total calories) and low-cholesterol (< 200 mg) diet significantly reduced LDL cholesterol and improved arterial stiffness and hs-CRP concentrations at 4 weeks in patients with newly diagnosed hypercholesterolemia compared to when the participants consumed the same diet with conventional pasta (86). Although there are no RCT data on the effects of soy or its components on secondary prevention of CVD, limited data suggest potential benefit. Isolated isoflavones from soy have been shown to significantly improve systemic arterial compliance (87,88) but not endothelial function (87,89). Soy protein has also been shown to significantly reduce lipid peroxidation in vivo and increase the resistance of LDL to oxidation (90,91).

There is no substantial evidence to suggest isolated soy isoflavones affect LDL cholesterol or CVD risk. Although incorporating soy protein may not significantly affect cholesterol, soy beans and products made from soy, such as soy milk, tofu, miso, soy nuts, and soy butter, may help reduce the risk of CVD in other ways and are beneficial to overall health in that they are high in protein but low in saturated fat and contain PUFAs, calcium, potassium, and vitamin K. Based on available research, CVD patients should be encouraged to replace animal protein in the diet with soy protein via various soy-based products in conjunction with a prudent diet. Practically, this means replacing main protein-containing foods (meats, dairy foods, eggs) with low-fat soy products (e.g., low-fat soy milk, tofu-based products, texturized vegetable protein-based products). The long-term safety of isoflavone supplementation is not known. Because isoflavones are able to act as partial estrogen agonists, some worry about adverse effects at levels greater than typically consumed by Asian populations (e.g., more than 200 mg total isoflavones/day). There is insufficient evidence on the effectiveness and safety to refute or support the use of isolated isoflavone dietary supplements for CVD prevention at this time (see Evidence

Summary table at end of chapter). However, there is ample safety and efficacy evidence to recommend the consumption of plant-based protein, specifically soybean or soy-based products, instead of animal protein.

## Lignans

Flaxseed (linseed) is the richest known source of the main mammalian lignan precursor, secoisolariciresinol (SDG). Aside from flax, plant lignans are found in significantly lesser amounts in a variety of legumes (soybeans), cereal brans, whole grain cereals, vegetables (carrots, broccoli and spinach) and fruit (strawberries, cucumbers, and apples) (92). The levels of SDG in flaxseed vary between 0.6 to 1.8 g/100 g (93) which is 245x greater than amounts in strawberries and almost 900x greater than levels in broccoli (94). SDG is metabolized by enteric bacteria to the bioactive mammalian lignan, enterodiol, which then can be oxidized to enterolactone. Human consumption of flaxseed increases urinary levels of enterodiol, enterolactone and total lignans in a linear, dose-response manner (95). Evidence suggests that SDG may reduce oxidative stress (96), directly lower serum cholesterol (93) and decrease platelet aggregation through blocking the pro-inflammatory actions of platelet activating factor (97). Evidence of these mechanisms in humans, however, is lacking.

While there are no intervention studies addressing the effects of flax or its lignans in patients with CVD, there are two case-control studies assessing the association between enterolactone concentrations and risk of CVD. The first is a case-control study by Vanharanta et al, who found that higher serum levels of enterolactone were associated with lower risk of acute coronary events, raising the possibility that the lignan component of flax may have cardioprotective effects (98). A follow-up study by the same group revealed that after controlling for potential dietary and other confounders, low serum enterolactone concentrations were associated with enhanced in vivo lipid peroxidation (measured by plasma F2-isoprostanes) in a sample of mildly hypercholesterolemic men (99). The second, more recent case-control study randomly selected a cohort of male smokers from the ATBC study who were randomized to placebo (100). A total of 350 cases and 420 controls comprised the study population. After adjusting for classic CVD risk factors for all CHD events there was a trend toward an association based on increasing quintiles of enterolactone (0.85, 95% CI, 0.51-1.43; 0.59, 95% CI, 0.35-1.0; 0.69, 95% CI, 0.4-1.16; and 0.63, 95% CI, 0.33-1.11; P trend was 0.07). Evidence also suggests that SDG may directly lower serum cholesterol (93) through modulation of the enzymes 7alpha-hydroxylase and acyl CoA cholesterol transferase, both involved in cholesterol metabolism (101). While there are no human studies investigating the effects of extracted flax lignans on lipids, Kuroda et al evaluated the lipid effects of a series of synthetic lignans (arylnaphthalene lignans) and reported that they significantly lower TC, LDL cholesterol, while raising high-density lipoprotein (HDL) cholesterol (102).

It is not known whether the beneficial effects of flaxseed are due to the lignans, soluble fiber or its high ALA content. There are no published human studies addressing the effects of isolated SDG supplements on markers of CVD. Therefore, isolated lignans are not recommended at this time; however, based on the potential benefits of several constituents in flaxseed, there is limited evidence to suggest that daily consumption of 25-50 grams (3-6 tbsp) of flaxseed meal (which would also meet AHA's recommendation for ALA) appears safe and might be effective in reducing CVD events.

## Amino Acids

### L-Arginine

L-Arg is a non-essential amino acid that is readily available in the diet. There has been an increased interest in using L-Arg to treat CVD over the past decade primarily due to effects on NO production. L-Arg serves as the main substrate for the synthesis of NO, the endothelium-derived relaxing factor required for regulating vascular tone. Vascular NO bioavailability is reduced in patients with CVD, leading to vasoconstriction and increased adhesion molecule expression, LDL uptake by macrophages and smooth muscle cell proliferation, thus contributing to endothelial dysfunction and atherosclerosis. Endothelial dysfunction begins early in the pathogenesis of atherosclerosis, and improving endothelial function may reduce future coronary events. Therefore, researchers have investigated the possibility of improving endothelium function through increasing NO production via exogenous L-Arg administration. L-Arg may be given intravenously but is primarily used orally. In relatively short-term studies, L-Arg been shown to improve endothelial function in healthy elderly subjects (103) and in patients with vascular disease (104,105), yet others have reported no effects on endothelial function (106).

The Vascular Interaction with Age in Myocardial Infarction (VINTAGE MI) study is the largest prospective RCT in patients with CVD designed to investigate whether adding 9 g L-Arg or placebo to standard postinfarction therapy reduces vascular stiffness as well as improves ejection fraction and clinical events over 6 months in 153 patients following acute MI (107). The mean age of participants was 60±13.6 years. There were no significant changes in vascular stiffness measures (arterial elastance, arterial compliance, pulse pressure or pulse wave velocity) or left ventricular ejection fraction in either group; however, the study was interrupted early when 6 subjects (8.6%), all over the age of 60 years, died from the L-Arg group compared to 0 subjects in the placebo group (p=0.01). While limited data on endothelial function seem promising, based on data from the VINTAGE MI study, L-Arg should not be recommended following an acute MI and the risk/benefit ratio should be carefully considered before recommending L-Arg to CVD patients over 60 years old. Limited evidence suggests that L-Arginine is ineffective in reducing CVD events and actually might cause harm in the acute post-MI period, particularly among men aged 60 years and older (see Evidence Summary table at end of chapter).

### L-Carnitine

L-Car is a naturally occurring amino acid that plays a crucial role in energy metabolism. L-Car is involved with the metabolism of fatty acids, a basic substrate for oxidative energy metabolism in muscle. Thus, it may improve muscle metabolism of ischemic tissues. L-Car and its derivative, propionyl-L-carnitine (PLC), are being studied in treating various disorders, including angina, MI, heart failure, peripheral vascular disease and metabolic abnormalities of dialysis. L-Car is synthesized in the liver, kidney and brain from the amino acids lysine and methionine. It may also be obtained through the diet, primarily from red meats and dairy products, but also in some vegetables such as beans and avocado. Levels of L-Car are depleted during several metabolic abnormalities including cardiac ischemia, heart failure and in dialysis patients. Therefore, there is an interest in investigating whether supplemental L-Car can enhance the metabolism of long-chain fatty acids to energy in these ischemic tissues. In patients with chronic stable angina, data reveal a mild positive effect on physiologic parameters, which may or may not be clinically significant. In an Indian study, 47 patients with chronic stable angina were randomized to 2 g L-Car/d or placebo for 3 months. The L-Car treated group had an increase in exercise duration (p=0.006) and a reduction in the time needed for the ST changes to revert to baseline (p=0.019) (108). Similar results were found in a smaller, Italian crossover RCT, in which 18 patients with chronic stable angina were randomized to 500 mg TID of PLC or placebo for 75 days (109).

L-Car has shown mixed effects after acute MI. In the multicenter CEDIM trial, Iliceto et al randomized 472 patients with a first acute MI to either L-Car or placebo within 24 hours of onset of diagnosis (110). Patients assigned to L-Car received 9 g/day IV for the first 5 days followed by oral administration of 6 g/d x 12 months. In the L-Car group, a significant attenuation of left ventricular dilation was observed at 1 year compared with those receiving placebo, but there were no differences in outcomes. This same group in the CEDIM 2 multicenter trial studied the effects of L-Car on clinical benefit and survival in patients with acute MI (111). A total of 2,330 patients with acute anterior ST segment elevation MI were randomized to receive 9 g/day of IV L-Car x t days followed by oral administration of 4g/day x 6 months added to standard therapeutic therapy adopted at each clinical site. At 6 months, 75 subjects in the placebo group had died from death and/or heart failure (primary end point) compared to 67 subjects in the L-Car group with a cumulative 6-month mortality rate of 6.5 and 5.7%, respectively, producing a non-significant 12% reduction in mortality (p=0.48). As part of a secondary endpoint, there was a reduced mortality seen in the L-Car group on day 5 (HR=0.61, 95% CI, 0.37-0.98; p=0.041) compared to the placebo group. The trial aimed at enrolling a total of 4000 subjects but was stopped early due to a lower than expected enrollment rate; therefore, it is possible that the primary endpoint was underpowered to detect an effect.

Oral L-Car preparations have been shown to cause heart burn and dyspepsia but are not associated with any serious side effects. There is limited evidence to suggest that L-Carnitine might be effective in improving exercise tolerance and ECG ST changes post-exertion among patients with stable angina. There is insufficient evidence to assess whether L-Carnitine is beneficial for post-acute MI patients (see Evidence Summary table at end of chapter).

## Special Diets

### Case Study 8-2

A 54-year-old male accountant with a recent history of MI presents to your office for a follow-up visit. His MI was uncomplicated and was treated in part with a stent. He informs you that he has already quit smoking and is "eating right." Some of his colleagues from his firm have taken up the Atkins diet with some success and he wants to know if this type of diet is right for him. His current medications include an aspirin 325 mg per day, atorvastatin 10 mg per day, lisinopril 10 mg per day, metoprolol 25 mg twice daily, and 1 gram of fish oil supplements daily. On physical exam, his blood pressure is 135/82, pulse of 74, weight of 220 lbs and height of 5'11" (BMI = 30.7 kg/m²). His lipids on his current regimen are: total cholesterol = 176 mg/dl, triglycerides= 200 mg/dl, HDL = 38 mg/dl, LDL = 98 mg/dl. What advice can you give him about popular diets?

Diet plays a major role in cardiovascular health. The AHA Guidelines for Primary Prevention of Cardiovascular Disease and Stroke: 2002 Update state "Data from the Nurses Health Study suggest that in women, maintaining a desirable body weight, eating a healthy diet, exercising regularly, not smoking, and consuming a moderate amount of alcohol could account for an 84% reduction in risk.... Clearly, the majority of the causes of cardiovascular disease are known and modifiable". Nutrition and dietary factors can affect body weight, lipoproteins, blood pressure, blood glucose, inflammation, endothelial function, and coagulation. Therefore, diet should be an important part of both primary and secondary prevention of CVD. Several popular diet books have emerged in the last decade promising weight loss and improved health. In general, diets can be classified as those focusing on altering macronutrient (fat, carbohydrates and protein) intake or the inclusion or exclusion of particular foods or food groups. Table 8-2 reviews several of the distinguishing features of commonly used diets. Here we focus on the cardiovascular implications of three diet types that differ by macronutrient content.

Table 8-2  Overview of Popular Diets

| Diet Systems | Total Fat | Carbohydrate | Protein | Other |
|---|---|---|---|---|
| Atkins (112) | High | Very low | High | Very low in carbs. Induction/ketotic phase. High in saturated fat. Low in fiber, calcium. Encourages supplements. |
| Carbohydrate Addicts (113) | High | Very low | High | Claims that some are true carb addicts and that carbs trigger excess insulin. Allows a daily "reward" meal with limited carbs. |
| Jenny Craig (114) | Low | High | Moderate | Emphasizes portion control & exercise. Uses concept of exchanges. Part of international chain of support groups. |
| Mediterranean (115) | Moderate | Moderate | Moderate | High in mono (nuts, olive oil) and polyunsaturated (fish) fats. Suggests modest alcohol use. |
| Ornish (116) | Very low | Very high | Moderate | Mostly vegetarian diet. No added fats. Part of multidisciplinary approach including stress management, exercise, and group support. |
| Pritikin (117) | Low | Very high | Moderate | Low-fat, calorie-restricted. Focuses on calorie density (volumetrics). |
| Protein Power (118) | High | Very low | High | Similar to Atkins. Focuses on carb restriction. No limit on fat. |
| Schwarzbein Diet (119) | High | Low | High | Focuses on cutting carbs, esp refined. Geared to diabetics and women. No alcohol or caffeine. |
| Sugar Busters (120) | High | Moderate | High | Focuses on restricting refined carbs (white flour, sugar). |
| Suzanne Somers (121) | High | Low | Moderate | Focuses on restricting refined carbs. Eliminates caffeine, alcohol. Emphasizes restrictive food combinations. |

(continued)

Table 8-2    Overview of Popular Diets (continued)

| Diet Systems | Total Fat | Carbohydrate | Protein | Other |
| --- | --- | --- | --- | --- |
| Therapeutic Lifestyle Changes | Low to moderate | High | Moderate | NCEP diet aimed at lowering LDL cholesterol. Adds plant stanol esters. Emphasizes soluble fiber. |
| Weight Watchers (122) | Low | High | Moderate | Uses point budget based on calories, fat and fiber. Part of international chain of support groups. |
| Andrew Weil (123) | Moderate | High | Moderate | Focuses on calorie restriction, food variety, and unprocessed foods. Suggests dietary supplements. |
| Zone (124) | Moderate | Moderate | Very high | Focuses on ratio of carbs to protein to fat (40:30:30). |

Fats: Very low (<15% total energy), low (15-30%), moderate (31-40%), high (>40%)
Carbohydrates: Very low (<10%), low (10-30%), moderate (31-55%), high (>55%)
Protein: Low (<10%), Moderate (10-20%), High (21-30%), Very high (>30%).

## Very-Low-Fat Diets

By most standards, VLFD are diets in which patients consume <15% of their total calories (kcal) from fat. Thus for a typical 2,000 kcal diet, less than 300 kcal should come from all fat sources, realistically meaning this diet is primarily vegetarian and very high in carbohydrates (>60% of total kcal). VLFD have been associated in epidemiologic studies with longevity and low rates of CVD. In this country, VLFD were popularized by Dr. Dean Ornish, a cardiologist from the San Francisco Bay area, who promoted and later tested a comprehensive, multi-disciplinary program for motivated patients with known CAD (116). The general idea is that patients adopt a VLFD supplying 10% of kcal from fat, 15% kcal from protein and 75% kcal from carbohydrates in combination with moderate aerobic exercise, stress management training, smoking cessation and group psychological support. Using this model, Dr. Ornish has shown that this program modestly mitigates the course of CAD as measured by PET scanning and coronary angiography at 1 and 5 years. The first paper published in 1995 showed that in an RCT of 35 patients with documented CAD, Ornish's program reduced PET-measured perfusion abnormalities when compared to "usual care" at 5 years time (125). A follow-up study (The Lifestyle Heart Trial [LHT]) published in 1998 using conventional coronary angiography found a 4.5% relative improvement after 1 year in the experimental group compared to a 5.4% worsening of stenosis in the control group (126). The results were more impressive at 5 years favoring the intervention group. More importantly, there were fewer CVD events in the experimental group at 5 years compared to placebo (25 vs. 45 events, P<.001). The experimental group patients lost more weight and had less episodes of angina but had equal LDL lowering (37% reduction) compared to control patients, most of whom were taking statins. In the Multicenter Lifestyle Demonstration Project (MLDP), the Ornish program was implemented at eight hospitals in 440 patients (347 men and 93 women) with CAD for 12 months (127). As was seen in the LHT, subjects significantly reduced body weight and blood pressure but also reduced total and LDL cholesterol. These effects were seen in both genders when analyzed separately.

Despite concerns that VLFD can raise TG and lower HDL-C (128), there were no differences in these lipoproteins between the intervention and control groups in the LHT study and no differences at 12 months in the MLDP compared to baseline. Critics of the Ornish approach have raised the theoretical concern of adverse effects on the TG-HDL axis, as well as nutrient deficiency over the long term, especially in elderly; however, there are a paucity of data to support these claims. Other issues include non-adherence to the diet and costs of the program. A recent report of 3-month findings from the ongoing Multisite Cardiac Lifestyle Intervention Program, which adopts the Ornish program and is administered by insurance companies, suggests that dietary, exercise and stress management components of this program are individually, additively, and interactively related to improvements in multiple coronary risk factors in 869 non-smoking CHD patients (129). Eighteen women and 22 men (4.5% of the population) did not complete the 3-month follow up. A VLFD was associated with greater weight loss and improvements in total and LDL cholesterol, as well as lower perceived stress in the presence of increased exercise. While exercise was not associated with weight loss after adjusting for dietary fat intake and stress management, it was associated with a reduction in total cholesterol in women. Stress management via yoga and meditation was associated with reduced hostile attitudes (a known risk factor for subsequent CVD events), reduction in triglycerides, and weight loss after adjusting for dietary fat intake and exercise. In men, increased stress management was associated with lower total cholesterol/HDL-C ratio and, in patients with diabetes, it was associated with improved glycemic control. In 2006, Medicare agreed to cover a limited number of sessions for patients enrolled in Ornish's program. Overall there is strong evidence to support the Ornish Diet in secondary prevention of CVD and very limited evidence to support its use for primary prevention (see Evidence Summary table at end of chapter).

## The Mediterranean Diet

There is a low incidence of CVD in Mediterranean countries, which in part has been attributed to their unique diet (130-132). A Mediterranean-type diet characterized by low consumption of meat and meat products; moderate consumption of fish, milk and dairy products; moderate intake of alcohol; and high consumption of nuts, olive oil, fruits, vegetables, legumes and cereals is now recommended for secondary prevention of CHD (133). In contrast to the

VLFD, the Mediterranean diet is higher in total fat (up to 35% of kcal), but the fat primarily comes from monounsaturated (olives, nuts) and n-3 PUFA (ALA from plants and EPA and DHA from fish) sources, while keeping saturated fat low (<10%).

Two clinical trials with clinical endpoints have investigated the effects of the Mediterranean diet in secondary prevention of CVD (134,135). Most notably, the Lyon Heart Trial investigated the effects of a "European" Mediterranean diet enriched with ALA (from a provided canola-based margarine) compared to a standard low fat diet on reoccurrence of cardiac events in 605 post MI (< 6 months) patients (134). After a mean of 27 months, coronary events were lowered by 73% and total mortality was reduced by 70% in the treatment group. More specifically, there were 20 cardiac deaths in the control group vs. 3 in the experimental group (P=0.02). The ALA intakes between the active vs. control group were 0.5 and 1.5 g/d, respectively. A follow-up study of this cohort found that the mortality benefit was maintained at 4 years of follow-up in patients who adhered to the Mediterranean diet (136). The follow-up also confirmed that elevated serum cholesterol and blood pressure were independent predictors of recurrent events and implied that the benefit of this diet went beyond improving these traditional risk factors. There are, however, several limitations with study design that raise questions regarding the impact of the intervention diet (and specifically ALA) on the results, including: the baseline diet of the control group was not analyzed, the authors did not assess compliance with dietary changes in the control group, and other nutrient differences existed between the two groups including vitamins E and C and dietary cholesterol. In addition, some have postulated that it is the higher bioflavonoid content (quercetin, myricetin, kaempferol) of the Mediterranean diet that mediates the protective effect (137).

Singh et al conducted a study investigating the effects of an "Indian" Mediterranean diet on 1000 South Asian patients with clinical CAD or with established CVD-risk factors (135). All patients were instructed to follow a local diet conducive to the Step 1 National Cholesterol Education Program (NCEP) diet. In addition, subjects assigned to the intervention group were advised to consume at least 400-500 g of combined fruits vegetables and nuts per day (i.e., 2-3 servings of fruit, 1-2 servings of vegetables and 1-2 ounces of nuts). This group was also encouraged to eat 400-500 g of combined whole grains, legumes, rice, maize, and wheat daily (i.e., 4-6 servings) and mustard seed or soy bean oil (rich in ALA) in three to four servings per day. The mean intake of ALA was twice as high in the active group (1.8 g ± 0.4) vs. the control group (0.8 ± 0.2) (P<0.001). More than half the patients in each group had CAD at baseline. Total cardiac end points were significantly less in the treatment group (n=39) vs. the controls (n=76) (P<0.001). Sudden cardiac deaths (6 vs. 16, p=0.015) as well as non-fatal MIs (21 vs. 43, p<0.001) were also reduced in the intervention group. The authors conclude from their data that "a diet rich in fruit, vegetables, legumes with a high ALA content is associated with a decrease in cardiovascular events."

More recently, Estruch and colleagues investigated the events of a Mediterranean diet on CVD risk factors in high-risk CVD patients (138). 772 subjects with diabetes or 3 or more CHD risk factors were randomized to one of the following 3 diets for 3 months: a standard low-fat diet, a Mediterranean diet with mixed nuts or a Mediterranean diet with virgin olive oil. Subjects receiving the Mediterranean diets had decreased systolic and diastolic blood pressure, blood glucose levels, total cholesterol/HDL cholesterol ratio, and higher HDL-C concentrations compared to the low-fat group. CRP concentrations significantly decreased in the Mediterranean plus olive oil group; however, IL-6, ICAM-1 and VCAM-1 decreased significantly in both Mediterranean diet groups and increased in the low-fat group. Not all studies investigating the effects of the Mediterranean diet on secondary prevention of CVD have been positive. In a study of 101 patients with established and treated CAD (80% receiving statins), following the Mediterranean diet for 1 year had no effect on inflammatory markers, homocysteine, insulin, or serum lipids compared to the control group (139). A major distinguishing feature of this study compared to those discussed above is that the majority of subjects were medically treated for CAD, and baseline CRP levels were relatively low, which may have masked any potential effect of the diet. In contract to these findings, others have reported in non-CVD patients that a Mediterranean diet (140) and a diet high in n-3 PUFA (141) improves CRP and other inflammatory markers.

The Mediterranean diet has always suggested moderate alcohol intake (1-2 drinks per day). However, the role of alcohol in CVD prevention is always controversial. Population studies indicate that the association between alcohol intake and mortality is represented by a J-shaped curve, meaning that moderate alcohol intake may be beneficial, whereas excess intake may be detrimental (142). Most of the benefit of moderate alcohol is related to reduced risk of CVD, and excessive intake is related to cirrhosis, pancreatitis, neurological disorders, certain cancers, and addiction, as well as motor vehicle accidents related to impaired decision making. Moderate alcohol intake is defined as $\leq 2$ drinks per day for men and $\leq 1$ drink per day for women (one drink is equivalent to 5 oz of wine, 1.5 oz 80 proof liquor or 12 oz beer). Ethanol in all alcoholic beverages and polyphenols found in red wine are believed to be involved in the proposed protective effects on CVD risk. Alcoholic beverages may decrease coagulation, platelet aggregation, thrombosis, and inflammation while increasing HDL cholesterol. Phenolic compounds (flavonoids and non-flavonoids) found in red wine may have additional benefit by improving endothelial function, decreasing LDL oxidation and proliferation of smooth muscle cells (143). There are no available RCT data on the impact of alcohol, specifically red wine, on CVD risk, so it is important to recognize that the available data suggest an association but not a cause and effect. It is reasonable to recommend to current drinkers no more than 1 alcoholic beverage/day in women and no more than 2 in men to reduce CVD risk. However, it is important to recognize that the narrow therapeutic window of alcohol and therefore the risk:benefit ratio suggests we should not recommend drinking alcoholic beverages to non-drinkers to decrease risk. In addition, history or risk of alcohol abuse should be carefully assessed prior to recommending even moderate alcohol intake.

Based on the efficacy data available and known safety data with food typically consumed in the Mediterranean diet, patients with CVD should be encouraged to consume 3-5 combined servings of fruit and vegetables and 3-6 combined servings of whole grains, legumes and tree nuts daily, as well as several servings of fish per week. There is strong evidence to support the Mediterranean diet for secondary prevention of CHD and moderate evidence for primary prevention (see Evidence Summary table at end of chapter).

## Low Carbohydrate Diets

In 1869, William Banting published *Letter on Corpulence*, which many believe to be the first low carbohydrate diet book. Since then, a multitude of popular books have exalted the virtues of limiting carbohydrates in attempts to lose weight, improve glycemic control and reduce cholesterol (144). By far the most popular of these diets is the Atkins Diet, which was first published in 1972 and revitalized in several books published in the 1990s (112). The principle of Dr. Atkins Diets is to severely limit carbohydrates (20g/day) initially in an "induction phase," which induces ketosis. This ketosis causes a diuresis and a rapid loss of water weight. During the "maintenance phase," carbohydrate intake may be increased to as much as 60g/day (20% of calories). This diet contains relatively minimal amounts of dietary fiber due to the low intake of fruits and vegetables because these foods are primarily carbohydrates. Low dietary fiber may lead to constipation. In addition, fiber has many beneficial effects that may be important to the CVD patient, including improving glucose homeostasis and lowering LDL cholesterol. Additionally, the Atkins diet recommends a large consumption of meat, which, while it appeals to Western tastes, is very high in both fat and protein. This could theoretically raise cholesterol and uric acid and increase the risk of CVD, gout and renal stones (145). Only one study has examined the effects of the Atkins diet in patients with CVD (146). Twenty-six subjects with CHD self-selected either a VLFD (n=16) or a low carbohydrate, high-protein (n=10) diet and were followed for 1 year. Myocardial perfusion improved on the VLFD, but worsened on the Atkins diet. Fibrinogen, Lp(a), and CRP increased by 14%, 106%, and 61%, respectively.

There have been six RCTs investigating the effects of low carbohydrate diets on CVD risk for at least 6 months (147-153). The maximum follow-up of these trials was 12 months using surrogate markers of CVD risk. Therefore, caution needs to be used when assessing this data for use in patients with CVD. A meta-analysis was published in 2006 that included five of these six trials (154). All trials compared the effects of a low-carbohydrate diet supplying a maximum of 60 g per day without energy restriction to a low-fat diet supplying a maximum of 30% energy from dietary fat. Most subjects studied were younger adults with severe overweight or obesity. Therefore, findings from this report cannot be generalized to older individuals, individuals with moderate obesity or individuals with CVD. At 6 months, the low-carbohydrate diets produced greater weight loss than the low-fat diets (weighted mean difference, -3.3 kg; 95% CI, -5.3 to -1.4 kg; p=0.02), but there was no significant difference by 12 months. In addition, there was no significant difference in attrition rate at 12 months between the diets. Total cholesterol and LDL-C levels changed more favorably in the subjects assigned to the low-fat diet, whereas HDL-C and TG were more favorable in the low-carbohydrate diet group. Drop out rates in all studies were substantial in both the low-fat diet group (37-50%) and the low-carbohydrate diet group (31-48%).

In the one RCT published after the meta-analysis, 311 overweight/obese premenopausal women were randomized to follow one of the following 4 diets for 12 months: Atkins, Zone, LEARN (macronutrient content comparable to conventional low-fat diet), or Ornish, which represented a broad spectrum of dietary carbohydrate and fat intake. At the end of 12 months, approximately 80% of the participants completed the trial. At 1 year, mean weight change was -4.7 kg (95% CI, -6.3 to -3.1 kg) for Atkins; -1.6 kg (95% CI, -2.8 to 0.4 kg) for Zone; -2.2 kg (95% CI, -3.6 to -0.8 kg) for LEARN; and -2.6 kg (95% CI, -3.8 to -1.3 kg) for Ornish. The overall diet group x time interaction was significant (P<0.001), and there was a significant difference for Atkins vs. Zone (P<0.05). Through one year, HDL-C levels significantly increased by 4.99.1 mg/dL, 2.2±6.1 mg/dL, 2.8±7.7 mg/dL in the Atkins, Zone and LEARN groups, respectively, with no change in the Ornish group. At 2 and 6 months, there were significant decreases in LDL-C in the LEARN and Ornish groups compared to the Atkins and Zone diets, but when comparing the change in LDL-C at 12 months to baseline, there were no significant differences between groups (Mean LDL-C change: 0.8±22.6 mg/dL, Atkins; 0.0±17.6 mg/dL, Zone; 0.6±17.0 mg/dL, LEARN, and -3.8±19.0 mg/dL, Ornish). At 12 months, mean blood pressure levels were greatest in the Atkins group and systolic blood pressure was significantly greater for Atkins vs. any of the other 3 diet groups.

RCTs investigating the efficacy of low carbohydrate diets on weight loss and CVD risk suggest in non-CVD patients, following a low carbohydrate diet for up to 1 year is safe, and are as effective at reducing weight as the conventional low fat or the VLFD. While the lipid effects of this diet are unlikely to be of immediate concern in this population, it is not known what effects would occur in a population with CVD and what effects would be expected beyond one year in any population. Further, it is unknown what the long-term consequences of this diet are on renal function, bone formation and exercise tolerance (144,145). In addition, low carbohydrate diets provide less than the recommended intakes of many water soluble B-vitamins, antioxidant vitamins, and calcium, often requiring additional supplementation. This supplementation only increases the cost of a diet that is already quite expensive due to the high intake of animal protein. These and many other questions will need to be addressed in RCTs before this diet can be recommended to patients with CVD.

There is limited evidence to suggest that low carbohydrate diets are effective, and they may be harmful for secondary prevention of CVD (see Evidence Summary table at end of chapter).

### Conclusions on Special Diets

The issue of which diet is optimal for patients with CVD is yet to be firmly established. Certainly there are ample data supporting low-fat, VLFD, and the Mediterranean diet (see Evidence Summary table at end of chapter). The AHA has not endorsed the Ornish program for the general population due to adherence concerns, but rather suggested this program be reserved for motivated, high-risk patients who have documented CHD and high levels of LDL-C. Recent data suggest the Ornish program can be followed successfully by a general CVD population for up to 3 months. The choice of which of these diets to follow or prescribe needs to be based on individual preferences. Until data from RCTs on the risks and benefits of low carbohydrate diets in patients with CVD become available, these popular diets should not be followed by patients with CVD.

## Chelation Therapy

Chelation therapy is one of the most controversial topics in CAM today. It involves an intravenous infusion of the synthetic amino acid, ethylenediamine tetraacetic acid (EDTA) given concomitantly with oral vitamins and minerals. While there is no universally recognized standard protocol, most EDTA chelation therapy protocols include peripheral intravenous (IV) administered solutions of 3 grams of EDTA with concomitant administration of magnesium, B vitamins, vitamin C, and sometimes low-dose heparin administered in 500 mL to 1000 mL normal saline over 1.5 to 3 hours and repeated weekly or biweekly. After the initial period, a maintenance program is usually recommended of less frequency providing a total cycle of between 30 and 40 infusions.

Use of EDTA chelation therapy is FDA-approved in treating heavy metal toxicity such as from lead or iron; its use in treatment of CVD is controversial among clinicians but popular among patients. It is estimated that US patients with CVD spend between $400 million and $3 billion per year out of pocket for this procedure (155,156). Proposed mechanisms of action in treatment of CVD include calcium chelation resulting in dissolution of plaques, antioxidant effects that may improve endothelial function and binding of heavy metals such as iron, which reduce total body load (156-158). Calcium chelation has been criticized because EDTA is a water soluble compound, which may be unable to effectively bind with calcium in plaque (159).

There have been four systematic reviews of clinical trials conducted investigating the effects of EDTA chelation in patients with CVD (158,160-162), which have all concluded that the evidence to date does not support a clinical benefit for treatment of CVD. The most recent review included seven RCTs, with two earlier studies finding a beneficial effect and three larger, more recent studies finding no effect (158). Several of these trials had one or more of the following major limitations: high attrition rates, inadequate blinding, and/or no description of sample size determination or randomization. The only RCT not included in these reviews explores the effects of EDTA chelation therapy on FMD in patients with CAD (157). Forty-seven patients with CAD were randomized to 33 EDTA chelation treatments or placebo over 6 months. There was no change in the brachial artery studies after the end of the first treatment or at the end of 6 months between treatments. The majority of the literature supporting EDTA chelation therapy is based on anecdotal reports, uncontrolled case-series and even "meta-analyses" of these reports (163,164). To answer whether EDTA chelation therapy is efficacious in patients with CVD, the NIH is funding a 5-year multicenter RCT in patients with CAD, which is expected to be completed in 2009.

EDTA chelation therapy has been associated with various potential side effects including gastrointestinal and musculoskeletal complaints, diaphoresis, fever, leucopenia, thrombocytopenia, kidney damage, mineral depletion and hypocalcemia (165-168). Additionally, each chelation session costs approximately $100, which can total approximately $3,000/cycle, little if any of which is reimbursed by conventional medical insurance. There is moderate evidence to suggest that chelation therapy is not effective and may be harmful in secondary prevention of CHD (see Evidence Summary table at end of chapter).

## Conclusions on Biologically Based Therapies

Clinicians should ask their patients with CVD about CAM use and specifically inquire about BBTs commonly used. Based on data suggesting that patients do not openly disclose CAM therapy use to health care providers or understand potential safety risks, physicians should initiate discussions about the available efficacy and safety data on commonly used CAM therapies discussed in this review. Data available to date suggest the Mediterranean diet, low-fat and VLFD, as well as omega-3 fatty acids from fish or dietary supplements and plant sources may benefit the patient with CVD. Therefore, the physician or other health care provider needs to carefully assess the patient's medical history, resources/capabilities and motivation to determine individual recommendations to ensure long-term adherence. Until more data are available, dietary supplements beyond a standard multi-vitamin and mineral supplement supplying 100% of the recommended dietary allowance, fish oil, and possibly coQ10 for patients with stable angina should not be recommended for the primary or secondary prevention of CHD. Furthermore, EDTA chelation for secondary prevention should not be recommended.

# Mind-Body Therapies

## Case Study 8-3

A 72-year-old woman with a history of angina, hypertension and generalized osteoarthritis presents to your office for follow-up. Her angina is stable and begins after a 1/2 mile brisk walk. She has never had an MI or a coronary intervention and is being medically managed on an aspirin, pravastatin 40 mg per day, metoprolol 100 mg per day, hydrochlorothiazide 25 mg per day, isosorbide mononitrate 60 mg once daily and 1g marine-derived omega-3 fatty acids three times weekly. She has been told to walk to reduce her cardiovascular risk, but her knee arthritis is limiting. She asks you about your advice on other modalities that might reduce her cardiovascular risk.

Psychological stress has been reported to influence the development and progression of CVD (169,170). Specific negative emotions of interest include depression, anxiety, anger, hostility, cynicism and denial. Negative emotions can have direct effects on activation of platelets, the sympathetic-adrenal-medullary system (SAM), the hypothalamic pituitary axis (HPA), and cardiac electrical stability. Whether the effect of these negative emotions results in cardiac events may also depend on social/behavioral factors such as healthy behaviors, coping resources and social support. Two earlier meta-analyses of MBTs in coronary artery disease suggests that adding a variety of psychosocial or psychoeducation interventions improves cardiac and all-cause mortality and cardiac events (171,172). Additionally, there are limited data that prayer might improve clinical outcomes in post-MI patients. Here we focus on meditation and movement therapies.

## Meditative Therapies

Meditative therapies are used to describe sedentary mental techniques aimed at reducing perceived stress. Although there are several forms of meditation ranging from Western-based approaches (mindfulness, visualization, progressive muscle relaxation) to traditional Eastern forms (Buddhist, Transcendental) (Table 8-3), only transcendental meditation (TM) has been specifically studied in patients with established CVD or in patients with multiple risk factors for CVD.

### Transcendental Meditation

TM is one component of Maharishi Vedic Medicine (MVM), a multimodal system of medicine developed in India. TM is the stress management component of MVM and involves a mental technique that allows the normal thinking process to become quiescent and induces a state of "restful alertness." TM was

Table 8-3   Commonly Used Mind-Body Therapies by Type

| Behavorial Therapies | Meditative Therapies | Movement Therapies |
|---|---|---|
| Social support | Guided imagery | Yoga |
| Cognitive- behavioral therapy (CBT) | Mindfulness meditation | Tai Chi |
| | Transcendental meditation | Qi Gong |
| | Hypnosis | Art therapy |
| | Music therapy | Dance therapy |
| | Progressive muscle relaxation | |

found to significantly improve several features of metabolic syndrome in patients with stable CHD (173). In this RCT, 103 subjects (82% completed the study) were randomized to 16 weeks of TM or active control (same number, size and frequency of TM group meetings but with focus on lectures and discussions surrounding CHD risk factors, impact of stress, diet and exercise on CHD). Adjusted systolic blood pressure (-3.4±2.0 vs. 2.8±2.1 mm Hg; P=0.04) and insulin resistance as measured by HOMA (-0.75±2.04 vs. 0.52±2.84; P=0.01) significantly improved in the TM group vs. the control with a trend in improvement in heart rate variability (0.10±0.17 vs -0.5±0.17; P=0.07). TM has been studied alone or as part of an MVM program to show that it reduces carotid intimal medial thickness (IMT) in hypertensive African-American patients (174-176). Specifically, one study found that 60 hypertensive adults randomized to TM had a mean reduction of 0.098 mm in carotid IMT compared to a 0.054 mm increase in IMT in a health education control group (175). This change in IMT was independent of effects on blood pressure, lipids, weight loss and physical activity or other known cardiovascular risk factors. This same TM program practiced by patients twice daily for 20 minutes reduced SBP by 11 mm Hg and DBP by 6 mm Hg, statistically more so than a progressive muscle relaxation program (174). Although these results are encouraging, a systematic review has concluded that, based on methodological weaknesses and potential conflicts of interest biases, there is insufficient evidence to indicate that TM decreases blood pressure (177). This review is limited to six RCTs and thus additional high-quality research in other, larger populations is needed. The TM technique is intensive, requiring 40 minutes per day and may not appeal to larger unselected populations and thus may not be generalizable. In summary, TM has a good safety profile, and there is moderate evidence to suggest its effectiveness; consequently, the evidence supports a weak recommendation in favor of TM for reducing systolic blood pressure and atherosclerosis (see Evidence Summary table at end of chapter).

## Movement Therapies

This group of therapies integrates light exercise and stretching and has received increasing acceptance in mainstream US society. However, there is currently little scientific evidence that movement therapies are useful specifically for patients with CVD. However, there is a developing literature that specific movement therapies such as Yoga and Tai Chi improve blood pressure, which might translate to improved outcomes in the future. Additionally, because these types of therapies are less likely to result in physical injury to patients, they might be especially useful in elderly populations and those affected by arthritis who might not be able to engage in moderate aerobic physical activity. Below, we review data from the peer-reviewed literature on both Yoga and Tai Chi.

## Yoga

Yoga involves stretching, breathing and posture exercises that originated in India. There are several types of yoga, including Iyengar, Hatha, Bikram and Ashtanga, which, although somewhat different, all emphasize the importance of breath control, postures and stretching, all of which are thought to favorably affect well-being and health. Innes conducted a systematic review of the effects of yoga on physiologic indices as well as clinical endpoints of CVD (178). Seventy studies (22 RCTs, 21 non-randomized controlled trials, 26 uncontrolled studies and 1 observational study) were included. The majority of studies were conducted in India (70%) and were small in size (>40% included under 25 subjects). Other common limitations included lack of randomization, low power, lack of adequate comparison groups, uncontrolled potential confounders, unknown or high attrition rates, unclear statistical analyses, possible selection bias, and multiple or poorly defined interventions. With these limitations in mind, the available evidence suggests that yoga may have beneficial effects on glucose metabolism, lipid profiles, anthropometric indices, blood pressure, oxidative stress, coagulation measures, and cardiovagal function, and may improve several clinical endpoints. Overall, there is limited evidence to suggest that yoga may be effective in CHD, and the evidence base supports a weak recommendation favoring its use (see Evidence Summary table at end of chapter).

## Tai Chi/Qi Gong

Tai Chi/Qi Gong emphasize slow rhythmic motions, breathing and mental attention. Although related to and part of traditional Chinese medicine, Tai Chi and Qi Gong have some distinct differences that are outside the scope of this review. Although there are no RCT data on these Chinese movement therapies in patients with established CVD, there are data to suggest that Qi Gong may have a favorable impact on blood pressure (179,180). There are more studies of Tai Chi with some data supporting benefit on blood pressure (181,182), whereas other studies did not find an effect (183,184). One RCT in subjects with prehypertension or stage I hypertension found that 12 weeks of Tai Chi practiced 3 times per week significantly reduced both SBP and DBP while reducing serum cholesterol and increasing HDL-C

(182). There is limited evidence to suggest that Qi Gong might lower blood pressure and conflicting evidence on the effect of Tai Chi. In summary, the evidence-base is insufficient to refute or support the use of Tai Chi or Qi Gong for the treatment of CHD (see Evidence Summary table at end of chapter).

## Conclusions on Mind-Body Therapies

Accumulating evidence suggests that there appears to be measurable physiologic changes in response to stress and that stress has negative health consequences. Furthermore, early research using intervention trials suggest that mind-body therapies might be able to mitigate the physiologic and pathologic consequences of chronic stress. If found safe and effective, mind-body therpies have the potential to be very useful in CVD because of their lack of interactions with prescription drugs, their generally low cost, and their emphasis on self-healing. Thus clinicians can recommend all forms of mind-body therpies to patients with CVD, especially to patients who cannot engage in regular physical activity. As with diets, specific recommendations must be individualized based on patient preferences, resources, and capabilities.

# Final Thoughts

CAM therapies continue to be popular among patients with CVD. Clinicians need to ask patients about their use of CAM, including dietary supplements, especially in light of possible drug-supplement interactions. In addition, clinicians should also be knowledgeable about the CAM therapies, the available evidence and potential risks. For patients with CVD interested in further reducing their risk of a cardiac event, the clinician needs to carefully assess the patient's medical history, resources/capabilities and motivation to determine individual recommendations to ensure long-term adherence.

**Evidence Summary of CAM Treatments of Cardiovascular Disorders**

| Clinical Indication | Category | Specific Therapy | Dose | Outcome | Confidence of Estimate on Effectiveness | Magnitude of Effect* | Safety† | Clinical Recommendation‡ | Comments |
|---|---|---|---|---|---|---|---|---|---|
| Primary and secondary prevention of CHD | Biologically based therapies | Vitamin E α-tocopherol | 400 IU | CHD event | Grade A | No effect | Single thumb down | Weak against | Doses >400 IU have been associated with harm. |
| Primary and secondary prevention of CHD | Biologically based therapies | Beta-carotene | 20 mg | Fatal and non-fatal MI | Grade A | No effect | Double thumbs down | Strong against | Dose of 20 mg associated with harm. |
| Statin-associated CoQ10 deficiency | Biologically based therapies | CoQ10 | 100 mg | CHD event | Grade B | Conflicting | Single thumbs up | No recommendation | $20-$50/month |
| Cardiac surgery | Biologically based therapies | CoQ10 | 300 mg | Cardiac function | Grade C | Moderate | No recommendation | No recommendation | $80/month |
| Acute MI | Biologically based therapies | CoQ10 | 100-120 mg | Non-fatal MI and cardiac mortality | Grade C | Moderate | Single thumbs up | No recommendation | $50/month |

(continued)

**Evidence Summary of CAM Treatments of Cardiovascular Disorders (Continued)**

| Clinical Indication | Category | Specific Therapy | Dose | Outcome | Confidence of Estimate on Effectiveness | Magnitude of Effect* | Safety† | Clinical Recommendation‡ | Comments |
|---|---|---|---|---|---|---|---|---|---|
| High-risk or known CAD | Biologically based therapies | B vitamins | Regimens vary | CVD events | Grade B | No effect | Single thumbs down | Weak against | Only supplementation of folic acid, B6 and B12 in setting of significant hyperhomocystenemia. |
| Post-acute MI | Biologically based therapies | B vitamins | Regimens vary | CVD event | Grade C | No effect | Single down | Weak against | Potential for harm. |
| Coronary artery restenosis | Biologically based therapies | B vitamins | Regimens vary | CVD events | Grade B | Conflicting | Single down | No recommendation | — |
| Primary and secondary CVD | Biologically based therapies | Marine Sources of Omega-3 Fatty Acids | 1 g daily for secondary prevention; 1 g twice weekly for primary prevention | CVD events including cardiac mortality | Grade A | Large | Single thumbs up | Strong in favor | Potential for additive anticoagulant effects when given with warfarin and antiplatelet effects when given with warfarin and aspirin. |

| Primary and secondary CVD | Biologically based therapies | Plant-derived sources of omega-3 fatty acids | 1.5-3 g | CVD events | Grade B | Moderate | Double thumbs up | Weak in favor | — |
|---|---|---|---|---|---|---|---|---|---|
| High cholesterol | Biologically based therapies | Garlic | 900 mg/day | LDL cholesterol | Grade B | Conflicting findings | Single thumbs up | No recommendation | Has been shown to reduce saquinavir levels among HIV positive individuals. |
| High Blood pressure | Biologically based therapies | Garlic | 900 mg/day | Blood pressure | Grade B | Conflicting findings | Single thumbs up | No recommendation | Has been shown to reduce saquinavir levels among HIV positive individuals. |
| CVD | Biologically based therapies | Soy Protein | 50 g | 1. LDL levels and oxidation, 2. Blood pressure, 3. CVD events | 1. Grade A 2. Grade B 3. Grade C | 1. Small 2. Moderate 3. Small | Double thumbs up | Weak in favor | — |

(continued)

**Evidence Summary of CAM Treatments of Cardiovascular Disorders (Continued)**

| Clinical Indication | Category | Specific Therapy | Dose | Outcome | Confidence of Estimate on Effectiveness | Magnitude of Effect* | Safety† | Clinical Recommendation‡ | Comments |
|---|---|---|---|---|---|---|---|---|---|
| CVD | Biologically based therapies | Isolated soy isoflavones | Unclear but definitely <200 mg isolated isoflavones | CVD events | Grade A | Contradictory effects | Single thumbs up | No recommendation | Theoretical concern of promoting estrogen-responsive cancers in doses >200 mg/day. |
| CVD | Biologically based therapies | Lignans (flaxseed) | 25-50 g | CVD events | Grade C | Moderate | Double thumbs up | Weak in favor | — |
| CVD | Biologically based therapies | L-arginine | Unclear | CVD events | Grade C | No effect | Single thumbs down | Weak against | Increased mortality among >60 years old post-acute MI (99). |
| Stable angina | Biologically based therapies | L-carnitine | 2 g daily | Exercise duration, post-exercise ECG ST segment changes | Grade C | Small | Double thumbs up | Weak in favor | — |
| Post-acute MI | Biologically based therapies | L-carnitine | 9 g/d IV then 4 g/d | CHD mortality | Grade C | Unclear | Double thumbs up | No recommendation | — |

| | | | | | | | | | |
|---|---|---|---|---|---|---|---|---|---|
| Secondary prevention | Biologically based therapies | Ornish Diet | NA | CHD events | Grade A | Large | Double thumbs up | Strong in favor | — |
| Primary prevention | Biologically based therapies | Ornish Diet | NA | CHD events | Grade D | Unclear | Double thumbs up | Weak in favor | — |
| Secondary prevention | Biologically based therapies | Mediterranean | NA | CHD events | Grade A | Large | Double thumbs up | Strong in favor | — |
| Primary prevention | Biologically based therapies | Mediterranean | NA | CHD events | Grade B | Large | Double thumbs up | Strong in favor | — |
| Secondary prevention | Biologically based therapies | Low carbohydrate diet | NA | CHD events | Grade C | No effect | Single thumbs down | Weak against | Certain individuals prone to significant elevations in LDL-C. Suggest monitoring. |
| Primary prevention | Biologically based therapies | Low carbohydrate diet | NA | CHD events | Grade D | No effect | No recommendation | No recommendation | — |
| Secondary prevention | Biologically based therapies | Chelation | NA | CHD events | Grade B | No effect | Single thumbs down | Weak against | — |
| Secondary and primary prevention | Mind-body therapies | Transcendental meditation | Regimens vary | Blood pressure and atherosclerosis | Grade B | Moderate | Double thumbs up | Weak in favor | — |

(continued)

**Evidence Summary of CAM Treatments of Gastrointestinal Disorders (Continued)**

| Clinical Indication | Category | Specific Therapy | Dose | Outcome | Confidence of Estimate on Effectiveness | Magnitude of Effect* | Safety† | Clinical Recommendation‡ | Comments |
|---|---|---|---|---|---|---|---|---|---|
| Secondary and primary prevention | Mind-body therapies | Yoga | Regimens vary | CV surrogate markers | Grade C | Moderate | Double thumbs up | Weak in favor | — |
| Secondary and primary prevention | Mind-body therapies | Tai Chi | Regimens vary | Blood pressure | Grade C | Conflicting evidence | Double thumbs up | No recommendation | — |
| Secondary and primary prevention | Mind-body therapies | Qi Gong | Regimens vary | Blood pressure | Grade C | Moderate | Double thumbs up | No recommendation | — |

* Small, moderate (OR>1.2-2) or large (OR>2)

† 5 categories: Double thumbs up, single thumb up, no recommendation, single thumb down, double thumb down

‡ 5 categories: Strong (in favor), weak (in favor), no recommendation, weak (against), strong (against)

## SELECTED REFERENCES*

3. **Yeh GY, Davis RB, Phillips RS.** Use of complementary therapies in patients with cardio-vascular disease. Am J Cardiol. 2006;98:673-80.

11. **Anonymous.** Dietary supplementation with n-3 polyunsaturated fatty acids and vitamin E after myocardial infarction: results of the GISSI-Prevenzione trial. Gruppo Italiano per lo Studio della Sopravvivenza nell'Infarto miocardico. Lancet. 1999;354:447-55.

15. **Vivekananthan DP, Penn MS, Sapp SK, et al.** Use of antioxidant vitamins for the prevention of cardiovascular disease: meta-analysis of randomised trials.[see comment][erratum appears in Lancet. 2004;363:662]. Lancet. 2003;361:2017-23.

16. **Miller ER III.** Meta-analysis: high-dosage vitamin E supplementation may increase all-cause mortality. Pastor-Barriuso R, Dalal D, Riemersma RA, Appel LJ, Guallar E, editors. Ann Intern Med. 2005;142:37-46.

20. **Bjelakovic G.** Mortality in randomized trials of antioxidant supplements for primary and secondary prevention: systematic review and meta-analysis. JAMA. 2007;297:842-57.

27. **Mabuchi H, Nohara A, Kobayashi J, et al.** Effects of CoQ10 supplementation on plasma lipoprotein lipid, CoQ10 and liver and muscle enzyme levels in hypercholesterolemic patients treated with atorvastatin: a randomized double-blind study. Atherosclerosis. 2007;195:e182-e189.

35. **Singh RB, Neki NS, Kartikey K, et al.** Effect of coenzyme Q10 on risk of atherosclerosis in patients with recent myocardial infarction. Mol Cell Biochem. 2003;246:75-82.

43. **Toole J.** Lowering homocysteine in patients with ischemic stroke to prevent recurrent stroke, myocardial infarction, and death. JAMA. 2004;291:565-75.

46. **Bonaa KH, Njolstad I, Ueland PM, et al.** Homocysteine lowering and cardiovascular events after acute myocardial infarction.[see comment]. N Engl J Med. 2006;354:1578-88.

49. **Moens A, Claeys M, Wuyts F et al.** Effect of folic acid on endothelial function following actue myocardial infarction. Am J Cardiol. 2007;99:476-81.

53. **Burr M, Fehily A, Gilbert J.** Effects of changes in fat, fish and fibre intakes on death and myocardial reinfarction: Diet and Reinfarction Trial. Lancet. 1989;2:757-61.

56. **Bucher H, Hengstler P, Schindler C, Meier G.** N-3 polyunsaturated fatty acids in coronary heart disease: a meta-analysis of randomized controlled trials. Am J Med. 2002;112:298-304.

64. **Singh RB, Niaz MA, Sharma JP, et al.** Randomized, double-blind, placebo-controlled trial of fish oil and mustard oil in patients with suspected acute myocardial infarction: the Indian experiment of infarct survival—4. Cardiovascular Drug Ther. 1997;11:485-91.

75. **Stevinson C, Pittler MH, Ernst E.** Garlic for treating hypercholesterolemia. A meta-analysis of randomized clinical trials. Ann Intern Med. 2000;133:420-9.

77. Plasma lipid levels in moderately hypercholesterolemic adults. Atherosclerosis. 2001;154:213-20.

85. **Sacks FM, Lichtenstein A, Van HL, et al.** Soy protein, isoflavones, and cardiovascular health: an American Heart Association Science Advisory for professionals from the Nutrition Committee. Circulation. 2006;113:1034-44.

107. **Schulman SP, Becker LC, Kass DA, et al.** L-arginine therapy in acute myocardial infarction: the Vascular Interaction With Age in Myocardial Infarction (VINTAGE MI) randomized clinical trial.[see comment]. JAMA. 2006;295:58-64.

110. **Iliceto S, Scrutinio D, Bruzzi P, et al.** Effects of L-carnitine administration on left ventricular remodeling after acute anterior myocardial infarction: the L-Carnitine Ecocardiografia Digitalizzata Infarto Miocardico (CEDIM) Trial. J Am Coll Cardiol. 1995;26:380-7.

126. **Ornish D, Scherwitz LW, Billings JH, et al.** Intensive lifestyle changes for reversal of coronary heart disease [published erratum appears in JAMA. 1999;281:1380] [see comments]. JAMA. 1998;280:2001-7.

---

* The complete reference list is to be found on the book's Web site.

134. **de Lorgeril M, Renaud S, Mamelle N, et al.** Mediterranean alpha-linolenic acid-rich diet in secondary prevention of coronary heart disease. Lancet. 1994;343:1454-9.

135. **Singh RB, Dubnov G, Niaz MA, et al.** Effect of an Indo-Mediterranean diet on progression of coronary artery disease in high risk patients (Indo-Mediterranean Diet Heart Study): a randomised single-blind trial. [see comment]. Lancet. 2002;360:1455-61.

154. **Nordmann A, Nordmann A, Briel M, et al.** Effects of low-carbohydrate vs low-fat diets on weight loss and cardiovascular risk factors. Arch Intern Med. 2006;166:285-293.

158. **Seely DM, Wu P, Mills EJ.** EDTA chelation therapy for cardiovascular disease: a systematic review. BMC Cardiovascular Dis. 2005;5:32.

170. **Ketterer M, Fitzgerald F, Thayer, B et al.** Psychosocial and traditional risk factors in early ischaemic heart disease: cross-sectional correlates. J Cardiovascular Risk. 2000;7:409-13.

177. **Canter PH, Ernst E.** Insufficient evidence to conclude whether or not Transcendental Meditation decreases blood pressure: results of a systematic review of randomized clinical trials. [see comment]. [Review]. J Hypertens. 2004;22:2049-54.

# Chapter 9

# Human Immunodeficiency Virus

Jason Tokumoto, MD

From the beginning of the HIV epidemic to the present time, many HIV-positive individuals have incorporated CAM into their medical care (1-4). Prior to the introduction of highly active antiretroviral therapy, the main reasons for using CAM was to treat HIV and improve the immune system. Today, the reasons for using CAM are to treat symptoms due to HIV, decrease side effects from antiretroviral therapy and increase one's sense of well-being. The majority of HIV-positive individuals who use CAM do not replace allopathic medicine with CAM but instead supplement allopathic medicine with CAM (5-7). The minority of HIV patients who do use CAM in place of allopathic medicine often view allopathic medicine as a "last resort."

Clinicians do not often know that their HIV patients are using CAM. For example, in one study, 33% of clinicians were not aware that their patients were using CAM; in this same study, 25% of patients were using a CAM that had a potential for an adverse event (2). One of the most important reasons why clinicians must be aware of CAM use in this population is that some of the most commonly used herbs can decrease blood levels of antiretroviral agents, which can result in resistance to these agents and subsequent virological failure (8-11). The following case illustrates how a commonly used herb can affect the virological response to antiretroviral therapy:

## Case Study 9-1

A 42 year-old heterosexual female was diagnosed with the human immunodeficiency virus type 1 (HIV-1) 2 years ago. At that time, her CD4 cell count was 250 cells/mm$^3$ and HIV viral load by PCR was 120,000 copies/mL. The patient did not want to take any antiretroviral therapy. One year later, the CD4 cell count was 200 cells/mm$^3$ and the HIV viral load was 300,000 copies/mL, so combivirand indinavir was started. Four months after starting antiretroviral therapy, the CD4 cell count was 280 cells/mm$^3$ and the HIV viral load 100 copies/mL.

However, 4 months later a repeat HIV viral load was 80,000 copies/mL without a change in the CD4 cell count. After ruling out nonadherence, acute infection, occult malignancy, and recent vaccination as causes for the increased viral load, an indinavir blood level was done. The indinavir blood level was subtherapeutic. After further investigation, the patient reported taking St. John's wort for mild depression. St. John's wort is known to decrease indinavir (and other protease inhibitors) blood levels by over 50%. Fortunately, genotypic resistance testing showed no resistance and after stopping the St. John's wort, the HIV viral load decreased significantly.

For HIV patients who are on antiretroviral therapy and are using CAM, another important concern is whether these patients are less adherent in taking their antiretroviral medications. While a few studies have shown a weak association between CAM use and nonadherence, most studies have shown no difference between CAM users and non-CAM users on adherence to their HIV medications (3,12).

## Prevalence of CAM Use

At any given time, approximately 60% of HIV patients may be using some type of CAM (2,3). In the Alternative Medicine Care Outcomes in AIDS (AMCOA) study, which enrolled 1675 HIV patients between 1995 and 1997, 63% reported the use of 1600 different types of CAM (1). In several recent smaller studies in which 50% of HIV patients were on antiretroviral therapy, 36% to 88% reported using CAM (3,13). A telephone survey involving 180 patients found that for HIV patients who saw a CAM practitioner, the patient visited the CAM practitioner 12 times a year while visiting the primary provider 7 times a year (14).

HIV-positive individuals who use CAM are more likely to be involved in the medical decision-making process, have HIV for a longer period of time, have a negative attitude towards antiretroviral therapy, and have progression of their HIV disease (2,13,15).

In the AMCOA study, the most common therapies were prayer (58.3%), garlic (53%), massage therapy (48.8%), meditation (45.9%), and acupuncture (45.5%) (1). In recent studies, common therapies have included vitamins, herbs, and prayer (3,13). CAM therapies used by HIV patients will be discussed under the following 3 major domains: biologically based therapies (herbs and dietary supplements), whole medical systems (acupuncture), mind-body medicine (spirituality, mental healing), and manipulative and body-based practice (massage).

# Biologically Based Practices

## Herbs and Dietary Supplements Used for Antiretroviral and/or Immunostimulatory Activity

Prevalence of herbal and dietary supplement usage among HIV patients ranges from 21% to 81% (1,4,15,16). In one study, the most common herbs used by HIV patients were garlic, ginseng, echinacea, and aloe (1). In another study, 81% of HIV patients surveyed took vitamins and minerals (4). The main reasons for using herbs and dietary supplements is to treat HIV, comorbidities, and to help alleviate symptoms due to HIV and/or medications.

Several herbs have been investigated for their antiretroviral activity. In a randomized, double-blind, placebo-controlled 24-week study carried out in Thailand involving 60 HIV patients, 40 patients received zidouvidine and zalcitabine plus a mixture of herbs and 20 patients received the same antiretroviral agents plus placebo. The main outcome measures were CD4 cell count and HIV viral load. While both groups experienced a significant decline in HIV viral load (p < 0.001), the group that took the herbs had a greater decline in HIV viral load than the group who took the placebo. No adverse events were reported (17).

In another study looking at a mixture of 35 Chinese herbs, some of which demonstrated anti-HIV activity in-vitro, 68 HIV patients with a CD4 cell count of <500 cells/mm$^3$, a median HIV viral load of <100,000 copies/mL, and on stable antiretroviral therapy for at least 3 months or no antiretroviral therapy, were prospectively randomized to receive seven pills of a standard preparation of these 35 Chinese herbs or placebo for 6 months. Outcome measures included symptoms, HIV disease progression, CD4 cell count, HIV viral load, and quality-of-life scores. At the end of 6 months, there were no difference in these measurements (18).

One of the more promising plants that has been studied for its antiretroviral effect is calanolide A. Calanolide A is derived from the tropical tree, *Calophyllum lanigerum*, which grows in the Malaysian rain forest. In vitro, calanolide A in combination with other antiretroviral agents have shown significant anti-HIV activity. Calanolide A inhibits reverse transcriptase, which is a key enzyme that HIV requires for production of new virus. Calanolide A functions like a non-nucleoside (examples of FDA-approved agents in this class are efavirenz and nevirapine). In one study, 43 HIV patients were enrolled in a Phase IB randomized, double-blind, placebo-controlled study to assess the antiretroviral effects of calanolide A. Patients were randomized to receive 14 days of oral calanolide A at 200 mg or 400 mg or 600 mg twice a day. At 600 mg twice a day, there was a mean HIV viral load reduction of 0.81 log 10 from baseline. This reduction was significantly greater when compared to the placebo group (p=0.027) (19).

Based on current available data, there is only preliminary evidence in a handful of studies suggesting that certain herbs may be clinically useful in lowering

HIV viral load. More definitive research is required before recommending herbal therapies for suppressing HIV (see Evidence Summary table at end of chapter). Therefore, any patient who is taking an herb for its anti-HIV activity should be appropriately counseled.

## Vitamins and Minerals Used for Antiretroviral and/or Immunostimulatory Activity

Prior to the availability of highly active antiretroviral therapy, numerous studies showed that serum levels of vitamin A, B6, B12, E, B-carotene, selenium, and zinc were lower in HIV-positive individuals compared to HIV-negative individuals (20). Observational studies also demonstrated that low blood levels of vitamins A, E, B12, selenium, and zinc were associated with a more rapid progression and death (20). In longitudinal studies, higher intake of vitamins B, C, and multivitamins was associated with improved CD4 cell counts, less disease progression, and decreased mortality (20).

Since the availability of highly active antiretroviral therapy, one study assessed zinc, vitamin E, selenium, and vitamin A blood levels in 288 HIV patients on antiretroviral therapy, with about 60% having an undetectable HIV viral load. Except for zinc, vitamin E, selenium, and vitamin A deficiency was much less common in patients taking antiretroviral therapy (21).

Despite previous studies that suggest low levels of minerals and vitamins in HIV-positive patients, there are few randomized, double-blind, placebo-controlled trials examining the benefit of supplemental vitamins and minerals in HIV patients. In a prospective, double-blind, placebo-controlled study, 40 HIV patients (CD4 >200 cells/mm$^3$, viral load <400 copies/mL) on antiretroviral therapy were randomized to receive either micronutrients or placebo twice a day for 12 weeks. Micronutrients included vitamins A, B, C, D, and E, N-acetyl cysteine, acetyl L-carnitine, various minerals, folic acid, choline, and biotin. At the end of the study, the group that took micronutrients had a CD4 cell increase of 64 cells compared to a decrease of 6 cells in the placebo group (P = 0.029) (22). While this study suggests that this treatment might have some effect on HIV progression, more definitive research is required before recommending this therapy to HIV patients (see Evidence Summary table at end of chapter).

In another double-blind, randomized, placebo-controlled trial, 262 HIV-positive men and women were randomized to either 200 microgram selenium or placebo once a day. At the end of 9 months of treatment, CD4 cell count and viral loads were assessed. The group who took selenium and had a serum selenium increase to >26.1 ug/L had no change in their HIV viral load (- log 0.04) and had an increase in their CD4 cell counts (+27.9 cells/mm$^3$) while both groups who took selenium but did not have a serum selenium level to >26.1 ug/L and the placebo group had worse outcomes as indicated by an increase in their HIV viral load (at least +log 0.25) and a decrease in the CD4 cell count (at least -25 cells/mm$^3$). There were no adverse events related to the supplemental selenium (23). More definitive research is needed before recommending selenium to HIV patients.

In a study done in Africa, 1078 pregnant HIV-positive women were enrolled in a randomized, double-blind, placebo-controlled study to examine the effect of daily vitamins on disease progression, CD4 cell count, and viral load. The participants were randomized to one of four regimens: vitamin A only, multivitamins excluding vitamin A, multivitamins and vitamin A, or placebo. All of the women received antenatal iron and folic acid. Baseline CD4 cell count ranged from 204 to 653 cells/mm$^3$ and viral load ranged from log 4.56 +/-0.78 to 4.66 +/-0.77. Median follow-up was 5.91 years. The women who received multivitamins were significantly less likely to progress to AIDS or death (24.7% multivitamins only, 26.1% multivitamins + vitamin A, 29% vitamin A only, 31% placebo; p = 0.04). The women who took multivitamins had a significant reduction in upper respiratory infections, oral and gastrointestinal symptoms, rashes, and fatigue compared to placebo. In addition, the women who took multivitamins had a mean CD4 cell count that was higher by 48 cells/mm$^3$ compared to placebo (p=0.01) and a viral load that was lower by log 0.18 compared to placebo (p=0.02). Vitamin A alone did not differ significantly from placebo in terms of benefit (24). There is moderate evidence to suggest that a multi-vitamin and mineral combination dietary supplement may influence HIV progression and associated co-morbidities in this population (see Evidence Summary table at end of chapter).

How vitamins and minerals increase CD4 cell count and how they affect HIV viral replication is unknown. Vitamins C, E, and several of the B vitamins have been shown to help cellular immunity (22). Selenium's effect on HIV viral load may be due to its antioxidant properties (23).

In conclusion, limited research among HIV patients on HAART suggest that while zinc levels may continue to be low, vitamin A, E, and selenium may no longer be deficient. There is limited research to suggest that a combination of vitamins A, B, C, D, E, acetyl cysteine, acetyl L-carnitine, various minerals, folic acid, choline, and biotin may result in an increased CD4 cell count. There is also limited evidence to suggest that 200 mcg of selenium may stabilize HIV viral load and increase CD4 cell count. In addition, there is moderate evidence to suggest that among HIV-positive pregnant women living in Africa, multivitamins may improve survival, decrease the progression to AIDS, increase CD4 cell count, lower HIV viral load, and reduce upper respiratory infections, gastrointestinal symptoms, rashes, and fatigue (see Evidence Summary table at end of chapter).

## Herbs/Dietary Supplements Used for Treating HIV-Related Co-Morbidities

### High Cholesterol

Hypercholesterolemia is a major side effect associated with antiretroviral therapy. HIV patients may take garlic for its purportedly anticholesterol activity. As an anticholesterol agent, garlic may be effective in decreasing cholesterol levels (25), but a more important concern about the use of garlic in HIV patients is the interaction between garlic and protease inhibitors. In ten healthy individuals, garlic decreased saquinavir (a protease inhibitor) blood levels by 50%. Even after a 10-day wash-out period, saquinavir blood levels did not return to baseline values (10). Based on the results of this study, the January 2008 Department of Health and Human Service's (DHHS) Guidelines for the Use of Antiretroviral Agents in HIV-1–Infected Adults and Adolescents does not recommend the use of garlic and saquinavir (see Evidence Summary table at end of chapter). Another dietary supplement HIV patients may take for hypercholesterolemia is cholestin, which comprises natural statins produced by red yeast fermented on rice. Cholestin contains 9 monacolins (statins) and in 2 placebo-controlled trials involving 390 HIV-negative individuals, there was a 20%-30% decrease in LDL cholesterol and triglycerides in the group that received cholestin (26). However, like other statins, cholestin can cause myopathy and there have been 3 cases of myopathy due to red rice yeast (27). Although there is moderate evidence suggesting this treatment can substantially reduce elevated LDL cholesterol, this product is a HMG-coreductase inhibitor and therefore shares similar risks and toxicities. Given the paucity of standards for quality assurance in dietary supplements, the availability of alternative effective treatment approaches including similar compounds from pharmaceutical drug manufacturers who undergo vetted quality-assurance programs, there is sufficient evidence to recommend against using cholestin to treat hyperlipidemia (see Evidence Summary table at end of chapter).

Another naturally occurring statin is found in oyster mushrooms (*Pleurotus ostreatus*), and there is an on-going NIH-sponsored study assessing its lipid-lowering effect in HIV patients who have antiretroviral therapy–associated hyperlipidemia (28).

Hypertriglyceridemia is another side effect of antiretroviral agents. The American Heart Association recommends using fish oil as an effective treatment for hypertriglyceridemia (29). There are two studies that demonstrated that fish oil (omega-3-fatty acid) decreases triglyceride levels in HIV patients.

In a randomized, double-blind, prospective study, 122 HIV patients on antiretroviral therapy with a triglyceride level of >200mg/dL were randomized to either 2 grams of fish oil three times a day or placebo 3 times a day for 8 weeks. At the end of the study, triglyceride levels decreased by 25.5% in the treatment group compared to a 1% increase in the placebo group (p =.0033). There were no differences in adverse events between the groups (30).

In an open-label, randomized, 16-week study, 52 HIV patients on highly active antiretroviral therapy who had fasting triglyceride levels >200 mg/dL received either dietary and exercise counseling plus fish oil (1750 mg of eicosapentaenoic and 1150 mg of docosahexaenoic acid) or dietary and exercise counseling without fish oil. At the end of 4 weeks, the group that took fish oil had a 25% reduction in triglyceride levels, and the group that did not take fish oil had a 2.8% reduction (p = .007). At the end of 16 weeks, the fish oil group had a 19.5% decrease in triglyceride levels compared to a 5.7% decrease in the group that did not take fish oil. While clinically significant, this difference was not statistically significant (p = .12). These findings suggest that adequately powered studies are warranted. The fish oil was well tolerated in this study (31).

The 2003 Guidelines for the Evaluation and Management of Dyslipidemia in Human Immunodeficiency Virus (HIV)–Infected Adults Receiving Anti-retroviral Therapy: Recommendations of the HIV Medicine Association of the Infectious Disease Society of America and the Adult AIDS Clinical Trials Group recommends fish oils as an alternative therapy to fibrates. In summary, garlic seems to have limited effect in decreasing cholesterol levels, but, more importantly, it should not be used in any patient taking saquinavir because it can decrease blood levels. The data on cholestin and fish oil indicate that these agents appear to be effective in reducing cholesterol and triglyceride levels and appear to be generally safe; however, given that cholestin is a HMG-CoA reductase inhibitor, we recommend that patients obtain these products through pharmaceutical companies with superior quality assurance (see Evidence Summary table at end of chapter).

### Hepatitis

Hepatitis is common in HIV patients. Abnormal liver function tests can be due to chronic hepatitis C, hepatitis B, or hepatotoxicity from antiretroviral agents. Milk thistle may be attractive to HIV patients for its hepatoprotective or hepa-torestorative properties. Like other herbs, milk thistle can potentially interact with protease inhibitors. In 10 healthy individuals who took milk thistle and indinavir (a protease inhibitor), milk thistle decreased mean indinavir trough blood levels by 25%, but there was only a 9% decrease in the indinavir AUC after 3 weeks of dosing milk thistle.

Pharmacokinetically, therefore, milk thistle does not significantly affect indinavir blood levels (11). However, based on studies assessing the benefit of milk thistle in hepatitis in HIV-negative individuals, this herb probably has limited benefit for treating various hepatitis (32), and more prospective, ran-domized, double-blinded, placebo-controlled studies are needed in the HIV-positive population before any specific recommendations can be made (see Evidence Summary table at end of chapter).

### Depression

Depression is the most common mental health disorder in HIV-positive indi-viduals. It is estimated that up to 60% of HIV patients have depression some-time during the course of their illness (33). It is important to diagnose depression in HIV-positive individuals because depression has been associated with increased mortality (34). St. John's wort is a popular herb often used for depression. Studies indicate that St. John's wort may be an effective treatment for mild depression (35), but the major concern about using St. John's wort in

HIV patients is that it decreases indinavir (a protease inhibitor) blood concentrations by over 50%. This decrease was demonstrated in a study involving 8 healthy individuals who received both indinavir and St. John's wort (standardized to 0.3% hypericin). Indinavir area under the curve (AUC) blood levels decreased by 57%, and indinavir trough levels decreased by 81% (8).

This decrease in blood level is probably due to St. John's wort inducing the cytochrome P450 system. In another study, St. John's wort decreased nevirapine (a nonnucleoside analogue) blood concentrations by 20% (9). This decrease in blood levels of both protease inhibitors and nonnucleoside analogues can potentially lead to drug resistance and virological failure. Based on these pharmacokinetic studies, the DHHS's January 2008 Guidelines for the Use of Antiretroviral Agents in the HIV-1-Infected Adults and Adolescents does not recommend using St. John's wort with any of the FDA-approved protease inhibitors and nonnucleoside analogues (see Evidence Summary table at end of chapter).

S-adenosylmethionine (SAM-e) is a common dietary supplement used in Europe to treat depression. In an 8-week open-label study, 20 HIV patients diagnosed with Major Depressive Disorder (DSM-1V) received 200 mg of SAM-e twice daily. The dose of SAM-e was titrated up to 800 mg twice a day on an individual basis. At the end of 8 weeks, using two accepted depression ratings scales, there was a decrease in depression symptoms over the 8-week study. The SAM-e was well tolerated (36). There is moderate evidence to suggest that SAMe appears relatively safe and effective in treating depression (see Evidence Summary table at end of chapter).

Dehydroepiandrosterone (DHEA) a precursor of androgenic and estrogenic steroid is often advertised as a supplement that can improve one's overall sense of well being, energy, and libido. In a randomized, double-blind, placebo-controlled study involving 145 HIV patients, DHEA was shown to be effective in treating dysthymia after 8 weeks of treatment. Using accepted depression rating scales, the group that took DHEA had a 56% response rate, whereas the placebo group had a 31% response rate. The DHEA was generally well tolerated in this study, and there was no deleterious effect on the CD4 cell count and HIV viral load (37) (see Evidence Summary table at end of chapter).

In conclusion, St. John's wort may be effective for mild depression, but it lowers serum levels of protease inhibitor and non-nucleoside analogue drugs and therefore should not be used in patients taking these types of medications. SAM-e has moderate evidence to support its use; however, it is quite expensive. DHEA may have limited effect on depression and dysthymia, but more prospective, randomized, double-blind, placebo-controlled studies are needed to make any definitive recommendations (see Evidence Summary table at end of chapter).

### Weight Loss

Delta-9-tetrahydrocannibol (dronabinol) produced synthetically is approved by the FDA for anorexia-associated weight loss in HIV-positive individuals.

Despite the availability of dronabinol by prescription, 14%-43% of HIV patients continue to use marijuana for either medical or recreational use (38). The medical reasons for using marijuana are to increase appetite, gain weight, relieve pain, and decrease nausea associated with antiretroviral therapy. Because marijuana is a politically sensitive issue, it has been difficult to perform medical studies looking at its safety and efficacy. In a randomized, placebo-controlled study assessing the safety of marijuana, 67 non-wasting HIV patients received either a 3.95%-tetrahydrocannibol marijuana cigarette, a 2.5 mg dronabinol capsule, or a placebo capsule 3 times a day for 21 days. At the end of the study, marijuana did not have any negative effect on CD4 cell count, HIV viral load, and protease inhibitor blood levels. The patients who received the marijuana cigarette or dronabinol capsule had significant weight gain, but the weight gained was primarily adipose tissue rather than lean body mass (39). While there is limited evidence to suggest that marijuana/dronabinol may be effective for HIV-related cachexia, more research is needed before recommending it for this purpose (see Evidence Summary table at end of chapter).

Decreased testosterone levels have been implicated in loss of lean body mass in HIV patients. Some HIV patients have turned to dehydroepiandrosterone (DHEA) for its potential testosterone-like benefit. In a randomized, double-blind, placebo-controlled, 24-week study, 40 HIV-positive individuals with undetectable HIV viral loads on a stable antiretroviral regimen were randomized to daily oral DHEA (for males, 100 mg twice a day; for females, 50 mg twice a day) or placebo for 12 weeks and then an additional 12 weeks of open-label DHEA. The objective of the study was to observe the effect of DHEA on HIV viral load, immune markers, and other nonimmune factors such as body weight and composition. At the end of the study, there was no effect on the HIV viral load and immune markers. Although the group that took DHEA experienced an overall improvement in their quality of life, there was no effect on weight gain, especially not lean muscle mass (40).

In another study, 29 HIV-positive women on antiretroviral therapy were randomized to either 50 mg of DHEA or placebo daily for 6 months. At the end of 6 months, the women who took DHEA had gained a mean of 1.4 kg compared to the women in the placebo group, who lost 1.2 kg. In addition, the DHEA group had an increase of 107 cells/mm$^3$ in their CD4 cell count compared to the placebo group, which had a decrease in CD4 cell count by 11 cells/mm$^3$ (41).

Creatine in doses of 25 gm/day increases muscle mass by increasing muscle phospho-creatine. In a randomized, placebo-controlled study, 40 HIV-positive men received supervised resistance exercise for 14 weeks. Two weeks prior to starting the exercise program, the patients were randomized to receive either creatine or placebo. The dose of creatine was 20 grams a day for the first 5 days and then 4.8 grams for the remainder of the study, 6 weeks. The creatine group experienced a gain of 2.3 kilograms in lean body mass compared to the placebo group. Although this difference was statistically significant, most of the increase was due to fluid retention in the muscle (42).

In addition, the long-term toxicity of high-dose creatine is renal insufficiency. Flutamine in large doses can help protect and heal intestinal mucosa that is disrupted in diarrheal states, which can cause weight loss. In a randomized, placebo-controlled study involving 21 HIV patients with clinical wasting, patients who took 40 grams of glutamine + antioxidants had significant improvement in weight and muscle compared to the placebo group (43).

In conclusion, marijuana may be effective in increasing the weight of HIV-positive individuals, but this weight gain is primarily due to adipose tissue. DHEA does not appear to be effective in increasing the weight in HIV-positive men but may be effective in HIV-positive women. Marijuana and DHEA do not appear to have a deleterious effect on CD4 cell count and HIV viral load. Marijuana, DNEA in women, creatine, and glucosamine appear relatively safe for short-term use and may be effective for weight gain in HIV patients, but more studies are needed.

### Neuropathy

It is estimated that about 35% of HIV-positive individuals will have HIV-related neuropathy (44). In addition, about 20%-30% of patients on didanosine or stavudine experience neuropathy although the use of these agents have declined during the last several years. Neuropathy is often difficult to treat and often requires polypharmacy. In the case of antiretroviral therapy–induced neuropathy, the mechanism is due to neuronal mitochondrial toxicity. Acetyl-L-carnitine (ALCAR) is vital for mitochondrial function and also enhances nerve growth factor and promotes peripheral nerve regeneration. Furthermore, serum ALCAR levels are reduced in antiretroviral therapy–related neuropathy. To assess the benefit of supplemental ALCAR, 21 HIV patients with antiretroviral toxic neuropathy received ALCAR 1500 mg twice a day for up to 33 months. Prior to starting ALCAR and at 6-12 months, leg skin biopsies were done to assess for epidermal, dermal and sweat gland innervation. An equivalent skin biopsy was also performed on HIV-negative patients who had no neuropathy. At the end of 6 months of ALCAR treatment, there was a significant increase in nerve regeneration compared to baseline ( p= <0.0001) in the HIV patients. Innervation continued to improve after 24 months of treatment. In addition, neuropathic pain scores improved in 76% of patients. This study enrolled only a small number of patients and had no placebo group (45).

In conclusion, ALCAR may improve drug-induced neuropathy, but further research is needed before any specific recommendations can be made (see Evidence Summary table at end of chapter).

## Whole Medical Systems

### Acupuncture

Up to 46% of HIV-positive individuals have included acupuncture in the course of their illness (1), yet there is limited research evaluating its effectiveness in the

HIV population. There are many reasons why HIV patients get acupuncture, but one of the most common reasons is for pain relief from either HIV- or drug-related peripheral neuropathy. In the late 1990s, the Community Programs for Clinical Research on AIDS (CPCRA) recognized that a high number of HIV patients were incorporating acupuncture for painful neuropathy refractory to allopathic treatment modalities and designed one of the few trials to assess the efficacy of acupuncture and amitriptyline (75 mg once a day) for relieving neuropathic pain. In a 14-week randomized, placebo-controlled trial, 250 HIV patients entered one of the following three options (all double-blinded): 1) a standardized acupuncture regimen (SAR) + amitriptyline or control points + amitriptyline or SAR+ placebo amitriptyline or control points + placebo amitriptyline; 2) SAR or control points; and 3) amitriptyline or placebo amitriptyline The SAR was chosen by acupuncturists. Although there was some reduction in mean pain scores at 6 and 14 weeks in all groups, there was basically no difference in the level of pain reduction among these groups. Thus, acupuncture or amitriptyline was no better than the placebo in reducing neuropathic pain (46).

In a non-placebo, controlled study, 21 HIV patients with pain due to neuropathy received acupuncture twice a week for 5 weeks. Based on pretreatment and post-treatment results using the Pain Rating Scale and the Subjective Peripheral Neuropathy Screen, there was a significant reduction in pain during the treatment period (47).

In a recent 12-week, two-arm, double-blind, randomized controlled study, 119 HIV patients were enrolled in a study to assess the effect of relaxation and acupuncture in improving the quality of life of these patients. Patients were required to have at least one of the following symptoms: sinus problem, headache, nausea, diarrhea, vomiting, myalgias, arthralgia, neuropathy, weakness, dental pain or bleeding gums, depression, anxiety, or insomnia. The intervention group listened to audiotapes (instructions to elicit the relaxation response followed by soft music) while receiving acupuncture. At the end of the study, based on three quality-of-life scales, the intervention group showed significant improvements in mental and physical health (p=0.0003), emotional health (p=0.0002), and spiritual peace (p=0.02). The control group only experienced significant improvements in emotional health (p<0.01) (48).

In summary, acupuncture may be effective in treating HIV-related neuropathy and in improving the quality of life of HIV patients, but more prospective randomized, double-blind, placebo-controlled studies are needed to make any definitive recommendations. See the Evidence Summary table at the end of the chapter.

## Mind-Body Medicine

### Spirituality

In surveys inquiring about CAM, up to 60% of HIV patients reported being involved in a spiritual activity during the course of their disease (2,14). In a study of HIV-negative individuals, most wanted their spiritual needs addressed and welcomed inquiry into their spiritual needs, but < 20% of physicians routinely took a spiritual history (49).

It is therefore important that a clinician respect a patient who expresses an interest in discussing spirituality. If the clinician is uncomfortable in addressing the spiritual needs of the patient, an appropriate referral should be made. The majority of studies on spirituality have been either descriptive or exploratory. In a study involving 901 HIV patients, the goal was to see if there was an association between psychotherapy and spiritual therapy and a reduced risk of death. The patients completed three questionnaires on usage of psychotherapy and spiritual therapy between 1995 and 1998. Death was subsequently ascertained from the National Death Index. Psychotherapy for 1 year was associated with a reduced risk of death (HR: 0.5, 95% CI 0.3-0.9). Spiritual activity was associated with a reduced risk of death (HR: 0.4, 95% CI 0.2-0.9) but only in those patients not on antiretroviral therapy (50).

In another study, the investigators sought to look at sources that influenced a patient's decision to take antiretroviral therapy. Among the 202 HIV patients in this study, prayer was the second most important source (the first being physicians) (51). In another study with 90 HIV-positive individuals, the role of spirituality in making end-of-life decisions was assessed. In this study, resuscitation discussions were less likely in HIV patients who perceived HIV as punishment and more likely in HIV patients who believed in a forgiving God. Fear of death was more likely in HIV patients who saw HIV as punishment and less likely in HIV patients who read the Bible or attended church on a regular basis (52).

In summary, HIV patients not on antiretroviral therapy but who participate in spiritual activity may be at a reduced risk of death, but more well-controlled studies are needed to make any specific recommendations. In addition, spiritual practices may play a key role in a patient's decision to take antiretroviral therapy and on resuscitation decisions (53). The following case illustrates the important role spirituality played in an HIV-positive individual's adherence to antiretroviral therapy:

## Case Study 9-2

A 32-year-old Asian male tested HIV positive. His baseline CD4 cell count was 185 cells/ mm$^3$ and HIV viral load was 185,000 copies/mL. A repeat CD4 and HIV viral load was unchanged. Based on the latest DHHS guidelines, the patient was a candidate for antiretroviral therapy. However, the patient was reluctant in taking antiretroviral medications because he had heard they were "poisons" and was afraid of experiencing side effects he had heard and read about. After several months, it was discovered that he was a very "spiritual" individual and that in his culture "medications" prescribed by the healer were considered sacred, and these medications would be placed on an altar and prayed to for a month before taking them. The individual was encouraged to look at antiretroviral medications similar to medications prescribed by a healer. The patient decided to do this and placed his first month's supply of antiretroviral agents on the altar and prayed to them for a month. He started taking them and had no side effects. He continued to place his monthly supply on the altar for a month before taking them and since then has had no side effects, his CD4 cell count has increased to 500, and his HIV viral load is undetectable.

## Distant Healing

Distant healing (DH) can be defined as a "conscious dedicated act of mentation attempting to benefit another person's physical or emotional well-being at a distance" (53). In a randomized double-blind study carried out in the United States, 40 patients with late-stage AIDS (CD4 cell count <100 cells/mm3) received either 10 weeks of assigned DH or no DH while receiving standard medical care from their clinician. Patients were paired matched for age, CD4 cell count, and number of AIDS-defining diagnoses. DH was performed by a self-identified healer (different healing and spiritual practitioners were used). The patient and healer never met. At the end of 6 months, the DH group compared to the group that did not receive DH had significantly fewer new AIDS diagnoses (p = 0.04), less illness severity (p = 0.03), fewer physician visits (p = 0.01), and fewer hospital visits (p = 0.04). There was no change in the CD4 cell counts; viral loads were not assessed (53).

Based on the above results, a larger federally funded study was carried out to assess the benefit of DH. In this study, 150 HIV patients receiving antiretroviral therapy were randomized to receive DH by a healer, DH by a nurse trained in DH, or no DH. At the end of the study there was no improvement in various clinical outcomes in the patients who received DH (54). Based on the latter study, there is limited evidence suggesting that DH does not affect clinical outcome related to HIV status. See the Evidence Summary table at the end of the chapter.

## Manipulative and Body-Based Practices

### Massage

In the AMCOA study, massage was the third most common CAM used by HIV patients. Although massage is commonly used by HIV patients, there are only a few controlled studies that have assessed the benefits of massage.

In a study involving 42 HIV patients, the goal was to assess the effect of massage only or massage with either exercise or stress management counseling on immune function and quality of life. The patients were randomized into four groups: 1) massage only, 2) massage and exercise, 3) massage and stress management counseling, and 4) the control group. At the end of the 12-week study, only the control group had an increase in their CD4 cell count, whereas the massage/exercise and massage/stress management counseling had a drop in their CD4 cell count. There were no differences among the groups on any quality-of-life measures (55).

In conclusion, while relatively safe, this small study suggests that massage may not be helpful in improving immune function and quality of life. As this is true, there is insufficient evidence to support or refute use of massage to improve quality of life or immune function. See the Evidence Summary table at the end of the chapter.

## Integrating CAM into Clinical Practice

The care of HIV patients should encompass caring for the whole person. Care of the person involves addressing the physical, emotional, psychological, intellectual, and spiritual self. This requires a multi-dimensional approach incorporating the following into the care of an individual: 1) western medicine, 2) diet, 3) exercise, 4) CAM, and 5) emotional, psychological, and spiritual support. Because many HIV patients use CAM, it is of the utmost importance that clinicians ask their patients if they are using any of these therapies. Taking a CAM history can be a part of the medication history.

Access to CAM may be limited by cost and availability. Most health insurances do not cover CAM, so patients often need to pay out-of-pocket. In one study involving HIV patients, the average yearly out-of-pocket cost for CAM was $938.00 (14). Community-based organizations, non-profit organizations, and local schools (e.g., acupuncture, massage, Chinese medicine) often provide CAM for HIV patients on a sliding scale. It is important that the clinician be supportive, nonjudgmental, and willing to learn more about CAM in order thave an open discussion with patients. The clinician can be an important source of accurate and unbiased information on CAM.

**Summary of Evidence of CAM Treatments for Human Immunodeficiency Virus**

| Clinical Indication | Category | Specific Therapy | Dose/Duration | Primary Outcome | Confidence of Estimate on Effectiveness | Magnitude of Effect* | Safety† | Clinical Recommendation‡ | Comments |
|---|---|---|---|---|---|---|---|---|---|
| HIV disease progression | Biologically based therapy | Calanolide A | 600 mg BID | HIV Viral Load | Grade C | Small | Unclear | No recommendation | — |
| HIV disease progression | Biologically based therapy | Vitamins A, B, C, D, E, acetyl cysteine, acetyl L-carnitine, various minerals, folic acid, choline, and biotin. | — | CD4 count | Grade C | Small | Double thumbs up | No recommendation | — |
| HIV disease progression | Biologically based therapy | Multi-vitamin and multi-mineral | — | CD4 count, AIDS or death, co-infections | Grade B | Moderate | Double thumbs up | Weak in favor for this population | Large RBT among pregnant women in Africa. |
| HIV disease progression | Biologically based therapy | Selenium | 200 mcg | Viral Load and CD4 count | Grade C | Small | Single thumbs up | No recommendation | Response limited to subjects with >26.1 ug/L increase in serum selenium level. |

(continued)

## Summary of Evidence of CAM Treatments for Human Immunodeficiency Virus (continued)

| Clinical Indication | Category | Specific Therapy | Dose/ Duration | Primary Outcome | Confidence of Estimate on Effectiveness | Magnitude of Effect* | Safety† | Clinical Recommendation‡ | Comments |
|---|---|---|---|---|---|---|---|---|---|
| High cholesterol | Biologically based therapies | Garlic | 1 clove, 2 grams of fresh garlic or 650 mg/day of garlic powder containing 6 mg of allicin | LDL | Grade B | Small | Single thumbs down (10) | No recommendation | Safety concern among people taking protease inhibitors in which can reduce serum levels. |
| High cholesterol | Biologically based therapies | Cholestin (HMG-coA reductase inhibitor) | 1200 mg bid | LDL and triglycerides | Grade B | Large | Single thumbs down (27) | Weak against | Advise use of pharmaceutical statin due to superior quality assurance |
| High triglycerides | Dietary supplements | Omega-3 Fatty Acids | 3 grams omega-3 fatty acids | Triglycerides | Grade A | Large | Single thumbs up | Strong in favor | — |

| Hepatitis | Biologically based therapies | Milk Thistle | 200 mg tid (80% silymarin) | — | Grade C (32) | Small | Single thumbs down | No recommendation | Safety concern limited to interaction with protease inhibitors showing a 9% decrease in AUC of serum levels (11). |
| Depression | Biologically based therapies | St John's Wort | 300-900 mg/day containing 0.3% hypericin | Major depression | Grade B | Conflicting results | Single thumbs down | No recommendation | — |
| Depression | Biologically based therapies | St John's Wort | — | Mild-moderate depression | Grade B | Moderate | Single thumbs down | Weak against | Herb lowers levels of protease inhibitors, non-nucleotide analogues, and other therapies metabolized by cytochrome P450 system. |

(continued)

**Summary of Evidence of CAM Treatments for Human Immunodeficiency Virus (continued)**

| Clinical Indication | Category | Specific Therapy | Dose/Duration | Primary Outcome | Confidence of Estimate on Effectiveness | Magnitude of Effect* | Safety† | Clinical Recommendation‡ | Comments |
|---|---|---|---|---|---|---|---|---|---|
| Depression | Biologically based therapies | S-adenosyl-methionine (SAMe) | 200-800 mg twice daily | — | Grade A (see mental health chapter) | Moderate | Single thumbs up | Weak in favor | — |
| HIV-related depression | Biologically based therapies | Dehydroepiandrosterone (DHEA) | 100 mg/day (micronized) increasing up to 400 mg/day (37) | Mild depression | Grade C | Moderate | Unclear | No recommendation | Availability of alternative treatment options and theoretical concern of increased risk for estrogen-dependent cancer limit clinical utility. |
| HIV-related cachexia | Biologically based therapies | Marijuana | Variable | Weight gain | Grade C | Small | Single thumbs up | No recommendation | Weight gain primarily adipose tissue |

| HIV-related cachexia | Biologically based therapies | Dehydroepi-androsterone (DHEA) | 50-100 mg twice daily | Weight gain | Grade C | Small (in women) | Single thumbs down | No recommendation | — |
|---|---|---|---|---|---|---|---|---|---|
| HIV-related cachexia | Biologically based therapies | Creatine | 5-25 grams/day | Weight gain | Grade C | Small | Single thumbs up | No recommendation | Weight gain primarily fluid retention |
| HIV-related cachexia | Biologically based therapies | Glutamine | 40 grams | Weight gain, muscle mass | Grade C | Small | Single thumbs up | No recommendation | — |
| HIV-related neuropathy | Biologically based therapies | Acetyl-L-carnitine | 1500 mg twice daily | Nerve regeneration | Grade D | Large | Double thumbs up | No recommendation | Case series showed large benefit |
| HIV-related neuropathy | Whole medical system | Acupuncture | Varying regimens | Subjective peripheral neuropathy screen | Grade C | Conflicting results | Double thumbs up | No recommendation | — |
| HIV disease progression | Energy medicine | Distant Healing | — | CD4, Viral Load | Grade C | No effect | Double thumbs up | Weak against | — |
| HIV disease progression | Manipulative and body-based therapies | Massage | — | CD4, QOL# | Grade C | No effect | Double thumbs up | No recommendation | — |

* Small, moderate (OR>1.2-2) or large (OR>2)

† 5 categories: Double thumbs up, single thumb up, no recommendation, single thumb down, double thumb down

‡ 5 categories: Strong (in favor), weak (in favor), no recommendation, weak (against), strong (against)

# QOL: Quality of Life

## SELECTED REFERENCES*

1. **Greene KB, Berger J, Reeves C, et al.** Most frequently used alternative and complementary therapies and activities by participants in the AMCOA study. J Assoc Nurses AIDS Care. 1999;10:60-73.

2. **Hsiao AF, Wong MD, Kanouse DE, et al.** Complementary and alternative medicine use and substitution for conventional therapy by HIV-infected patients. J Acquir Immune Defic Syndr. 2003; 33:157-65.

3. **Bica I, Tang AM, Skinner S, et al.** Use of complementary and alternativetherapies by patients with human immunodeficiency virus disease in the era of        highly active anti-retroviral therapy. J Altern Complment Med. 2003;9:65-76.

4. **Dhalla S, Chan KJ, Montaner JSG, Hogg RS.** Complementary and alternative medicine use in British Columbia—a survey of HIV positive people on anti-retroviral therapy. Complement Ther Clin Pract. 2006;12: 242-8.

5. **Anderson W, O'Connor B, MacGregor R, et al.** Patient use and assessment ofconventional and alternative therapies for HIV infection and AIDS. AIDS. 1993;7:561-6.

6. **Langewitz W, Ruttimann S, Laifer G, et al.** The integration of alternative treatment modalities in HIV infection: the patient's perspective. J. Psychosom Res. 1994;38:687-93.

7. **Foote-Ardah, CE.** Sociocultural barriers to the use of complementary and alternative medicine for HIV. Qualitative Health Research. 2004;14:59

8. **Piscitelli SC, Burstein AH, Chaitt D, et al.** Indinavir concentrations and St. John's wort. Lancet. 2000;355:547-8.

9. **De Maat MMR, Hoetelmans RMW, van Gorp ECM, et al.** A potential inter-action between St. John's wort and nevirapine? First International Workshopon Clinical Pharmacology of HIV Therapy. Abstract 2.8, 2000; Netherlands.

10. **Piscitelli SC, Burstein AH, Welden N, et al.** The effect of garlic supplements on the pharmacokinetics of saquinavir. Clin Infect Dis. 2002;34:234-8.

11. **Piscitelli SC, Formentini E, Burstein AH, et al.** Effect of milk thistle on the pharmacokinetics of indinavir in healthy volunteers. Pharmacotherapy. 2002;22:551-6.

12. **Jernewall N, Zea MC, Reisen CA, Popper PJ.** Complementary and alternativemedicine and adherence to care among HIV-positive Latino gay and bisexual men. AIDS Care. 2005; 17:601-9.

13. **Risa KJ, Nepon L, Justis JC, et al.** Alternative therapy use in HIV-infected patientsreceiving highly active antiretroviral therapy. Int J STD AIDS. 2002;13:706-13.

14. **Fairfield KM, Eisenberg DM, Davis RB, et al.** Patterns of use, expenditures, and perceived efficacy of complementary and alternative therapies in HIV-infected  patients. Arch Intern Med. 1998;158:2257-64.

15. **de Visser R, Ezzy D, Bartos M.** Alternative or complementary? Allopathic therapies for HIV/AIDS. Altern Ther Health Med. 2000;6:44-52.

16. **Kassler WJ, Blanc P, Greenblatt R.** The use of medicinal herbs by human immunodeficiency virus-infected patients. Arch Intern Med. 1991;151:2281-7.

17. **Sangkitporn S, Shide L, Klinbuayaem V, et al.** Efficacy and safety of zidovudineand zalcitabine combined with a combination of herbs in the treatment of HIV-infected Thai patients. Southeast Asian J Trop Med Public Health. 2005;36:704-708.

18. **Weber R, Christen L, Loy M, et al.** Randomized, placebo-controlled trial of Chinese herb therapy for HIV-1 infected individuals. J Acquir Immune Defic Syndr. 1999; 22:56-64.

19. **Sherer R, Dutta B, Anderson R, et al.** A phase IB study of (+)-calanolide A in HIV-1-infected, antiretroviral therapy naïve patients. 7th Conference on Retrovirus and Opportunistic Infections, 2000, San Francisco.

20. **Fawzi W.** Micronutrients and human immunodeficiency virus type 1 disease progression among adults and children. Clin Infect Dis. 2003;37(suppl 2): S112-S116.

---

* The complete reference list is to be found on the book's Web site.

21. **Jones CY, Tang AM, Forrester JE, et al.** Micronutrient levels and HIV disease status in HIV-infected patients on highly active antiretroviral therapy in the nutrition for healthy living cohort. J Acquir Immune Defic Syndr. 2006;43:475-82.

22. **Kaiser JD, Campa AM, Ondercin JP, et al.** Micronutrient supplementation increases CD4 count in HIV-infected individuals on highly active antiretroviral therapy: a prospective, double-blinded, placebo-controlled trial. J Acquir Immune Defic Syndr. 2006;42:523-8.

23. **Hurwitz BE, Klaus JR, Llabre MM, et al.** Suppression of human immuno-deficiency virus type 1 viral load with selenium supplementation. Arch Intern Med. 2007;167:148-54.

24. **Fawzi WW, Msmanga GI, Spiegelman D, et al.** A randomized trial of multi-vitamin supplements and HIV disease progression and mortality. N Eng J Med. 2004;351:23-32.

25. **Ackermann RT, Mulrow CD, Ramirez G, et al.** Garlic shows promise for improving some cardiovascular risk factor. Arch Intern Med. 2001;161:813-24.

26. **Patrick L, Uzick M.** Cardiovascular: c-reactive protein and the inflammatory disease paradigm: HMG-CoA reductive inhibitors, alpha-tocopherol, red yeast rice, and olive oil polyphenols. A review of the literature. Altern Med Rev. 2001;6:248-71.

27. **Mueller PS.** Symptomatic myopathy due to red yeast rice. Ann Intern Med, 2006;145:474-5.

28. **Abrams DI, Couey P, Shade SB, et al.** Antihyperlipidemic effect of Pleurotus ostreatus (Jacq.: Fr.) P. Kumm in HIV: Results of a pilot proof-of-principle clinical trial. International Journal of Medicinal Mushrooms. 2005;7:339-40.

29. **Kris-Etherton PM, Harris WS, Appel LJ et al.** Omega-3 fatty acids and cardiovascular disease: new recommendations from the American Heart Association. Arterioscler Thromb Vasc Biol. 2003;23:151-2.

31. **Wohl DA, Tien HC, Busby M, et al.** Randomized study of the safety and efficacy of fish oil (omega-3 fatty acid) supplementation with dietary and exercise counseling for the treatment of antiretroviral therapy–associated hypertrigly-ceridemia. Clin Infect Dis. 2005;41:1498-504.

32. **Rambaldi A, Jacobs B, Gluud C.** Milk thistle for alcoholic and/or hepatitis B or C virus liver diseases. Cochrane Database Syst Rev, 2007.

34. **Mayne TJ, Vittinghoff E, Chesney MA, et al.** Depressive affect and survival among gay and bisexual men infected with HIV. 1996;156:2233-8.

35. **Linde K, Mulrow CD, Berner M, Egger M.** St. John's wort for depression. Cochrane Database Syst Rev, 2005.

36. **Shippy RA, Mendez D, Jones K, et al.** S-adenosylmethionine (SAM-e) for the treatment of depression in people living with HIV/AIDS. BMC Psychiatry. 2004;4:38.

39. **Abrams DI, Hilton JF, Leiser RJ, et al.** Short-term effects of cannabinoids in patients with HIV-1 infection. A randomized, placebo-controlled clinical trial. Ann Intern Med. 2003;139:258-66.

46. **Shlay JC, Chaloner K, Max MB et al.** Acupuncture and amitriptyline for pain due to HIV-related neuropathy: a randomized controlled trial. JAMA, 1998;280: 1590-1585.

48. **Chang B-H, Boehmer U, Zhao Y, Sommers E.** The combined effect of relaxation response and acupuncture on quality of life in patients with HIV: a pilot study. J Altern Complment Med. 2007;13:807-15.

49. **Ellis MR, Vinson DC, Ewigman B.** Addressing spiritual concerns of patients, family physicians' attitudes, and practices. J Fam Prac. 1999;48:105-9.

51. **Meredith KL, Jeffe DB, Mundy LM, Fraser VJ.** Sources of influencing patients in their HIV medication decisions. Health Education Behav. 2001;28:40-50.

54. **Astin JA, Stone J, Abrams DI, et al.** The efficacy of distant healing for HIV: results of a randomized trial. Altern Ther Health Med. 2006;12:36-41.

# Chapter 10

⅋

# Men's Health

Joseph E. Scherger, MD, MPH

This chapter focuses on CAM therapies that may be used for prevention and treatment of medical conditions unique to men. Topics include: men's health, male hormones, androgen deficiency, fitness and muscle bulk, sexual performance and dysfunction, prostate disorders, male pattern baldness and aging in men.

How often do men use CAM therapies? In general, men are not frequent users of health care of any kind. The principle marketing and use of CAM by men is in the areas of muscle buildup, strength and endurance, and sexual performance. These are addressed, although this chapter will not cover the illicit use of anabolic steroids.

## Male Health and Hormones

Preventive medicine for men under age 50 is simpler than for women. However, men tend to neglect prevention as a lifestyle, contributing to poorer health and a shorter lifespan than for women. Over age 50, preventive guidelines for men and women are very similar, focusing on avoidance of cardiovascular disease and the early detection of cancer. The best source for evidence-based preventive guidelines for men is the U.S. Preventive Services Task Force recommendations (1). None of these recommendations include CAM services.

There are no evidence-based CAM therapies for men for routine prevention. While supplement suppliers will market heavily to men, there are no supplements that men should take to be healthier or to avoid disease. Men will be as healthy as their genetics allow by avoiding tobacco and excessive alcohol, by eating healthy and staying physically active, and by sleeping well, managing stress, and engaging in meaningful relationships. Maintaining a positive attitude and being happily married also enhances health in men. Finally, because men tend to be risk takers and engage in athletic activities, practicing safety is important to avoid injury and premature death.

## Male Hormones and Androgen Deficiency

Male hormones are called androgens, and the only one of significance is testosterone. The Leydig cells in testicles produce testosterone with regulation by the pituitary gland through FSH and LH communicating from the pituitary to the testicle. Men also have some estrogen production, regulated by these same pituitary hormones. Male estrogen comes mainly from the adrenal gland, similar to testosterone in women. Male estrogen is derived by the adrenal hormone, DHEA, which declines with age. Ingesting DHEA, however, does not increase any male hormone, including estrogen. There will be more on DHEA later in this chapter.

Some senescence of testosterone production occurs in men similar to the senescence of the ovarian production of estrogen in women, both happening gradually after age 40 and being manifest in the 50s. The hormone senescence in men is sometimes referred to as andropause, and a noticeable change in sexual function usually occurs (to be discussed later).

Some men suffer from an excessive decline in testosterone, which is known as androgen deficiency. Such men have a decline of libido, some loss of sexual function and constitutional symptoms such as fatigue and loss of muscle mass. The current literature does not support a recommendation favoring any specific CAM therapy for androgen deficiency. Nonetheless, a number of therapies are in common use. The research and safety profiles of these therapies are presented in the subsequent sections of the chapter to enable clinicians to engage in an educated conversation with their patients.

The only effective therapy for androgen deficiency is hormone replacement with testosterone. The Endocrine Society has done a systematic review of testosterone replacement for male androgen deficiency and has provided evidence-based clinical guidelines (2). There is strong evidence to support a strong recommendation that testosterone replacement is effective for male androgen deficiency (see Evidence Summary table at end of chapter). Testosterone therapy in recommended dosages is relatively safe with frequent non-serious side effects.

There is no effective oral preparation for testosterone, so it is currently given by injection or topical preparations. A number of testosterone analogs are in development that should result in oral preparations being available in the near future (3).

## Fitness and Muscle Bulk

Chemical precursors of testosterone are commonly used as dietary supplements to improve fitness and muscle bulk. These include androstenediol, androstenedione, androstenetrione and creatine. All of these are used in an attempt to increase androgen function in men.

Androstenediol is also known as androdiol and is a weak steroid hormone and a direct precursor of testosterone. A systematic review indicates there is very limited evidence to suggest that androstenediol might be effective for increasing muscle bulk or improving athletic conditioning (4). As with any testosterone-related product, androstenediol appears to have safety concerns in men who are not androgen deficient, which include infrequent but serious adverse events such as aggressive behavior and an adverse effect on lipids (see Evidence Summary table at end of chapter). Given the very limited evidence on efficacy and the questionable safety profile, it is premature to render a recommendation for this compound (see Evidence Summary table at end of chapter).

Androstenedione is also known as "Andro" and was made famous because the baseball player, Mark Maguire, claimed he used it while breaking the home run record. Androstenedione is available "legally" and most think that Maguire actually used anabolic steroids instead to bulk up his muscles and add strength. A systematic review indicates that there is very limited evidence to suggest that androstenedione might be effective for increasing muscle bulk or improving athletic conditioning (4). A randomized controlled trial showed that androstenedione does not significantly increase muscle strength, muscle size or lean body mass (5). Even though testosterone blood levels are not increased with its use (5), there are similar safety concerns as with androstenediol (4) (see Evidence Summary table at end of chapter). Given the very limited evidence on efficacy and the questionable safety profile, it is premature to render a recommendation for this compound (see Evidence Summary table at end of chapter).

Androstenetrione is also known as 6-Oxo and ADT. Rather than being a precursor to testosterone (prohormone), it is an aromatase inhibitor and blocks the conversion of testosterone to estrogen. Despite anecdotal claims that it increases testosterone levels, a systematic review indicates there is very limited evidence to suggest that androstenetrione might be effective only for increasing muscle bulk or improving athletic conditioning (4). There are similar safety concerns as with androstenediol (see Evidence Summary table at end of chapter). Given the very limited evidence on efficacy and the questionable safety profile, it is premature to render a recommendation for this compound (see Evidence Summary table at end of chapter).

Creatine is not a steroid hormone. It is a natural food product found in vegetables and appears relatively safe with infrequent, not serious adverse events. Creatine is also naturally synthesized by the human body from amino acids, primary in the kidney and the liver. Creatine is a component of skeletal muscle and supplies energy (ATP). Creatine is excreted by the kidney in the form of creatinine.

A systematic review shows that creatine has moderate evidence suggesting it appears effective in increasing athletic performance during repeated bouts of brief, high-intensity exercise (4). Two small double blind studies have been reported showing effectiveness for short bursts of exercise in swimming and cycling. The effectiveness wore off quickly, and, interestingly, the effectiveness was shown for men but not for women (7,8). There is moderate evidence to support a weak recommendation of creatine for increasing muscle strength in men (see Evidence Summary table at end of chapter).

There is also limited evidence to suggest that creatine might be effective in the treatment of selective cardiac conditions, McArdle's disease, and in types of muscular dystrophy (6).

Some adolescents and adults have ingested large amounts of creatine, more than what is recommended by the FDA. Doses up to 25 grams a day have been studied. Side effects vary and include asthmatic symptoms and GI intolerance. Early concerns about kidney damage from high doses of creatine have been rested through experience, but reports of interstitial nephritis with its use have occurred. People with kidney and liver disease should avoid creatine (6).

## Sexual Performance and Dysfunction

Men, it seems, will do about anything to improve sexual performance. Sexual performance and dysfunction is a combination of biology and psychology, or body and mind. There are few CAM therapies that have an evidence base for potentially improving sexual function or treating a specific sexual dysfunction. However, therapies that improve overall well-being may in turn improve sexual function or treat a dysfunction.

Biologically, sexual function requires a combination of adequate male hormone, testosterone, and adequate circulation to achieve and maintain an erection. Testosterone naturally declines with age. Sexual function changes with age. A man's ability to have multiple orgasms in one day naturally declines with age. The time between orgasms is referred to as the refractory period, and that increases with age.

Some people, like Suzanne Somers, recommend that women and men take hormones to reverse the declines that occur with aging (9). They argue, why should we let our bodies get old? Using hormones to maintain younger levels will keep people functioning at a younger biologic age than their chronologic age. A review of the controlled trials of testosterone supplementation in healthy men shows a slight improvement only when testosterone levels are low and no improvement in men with normal levels (10).

Such tampering with normal biologic processes carries risk. Using testosterone above physiologic levels for age causes dyslipidemia and increased cardiovascular disease risk, abnormal muscle bulk and strength, increased growth of prostate cancer, depression and aggressive behavior. In more extreme cases, increased testosterone can cause paranoia and acts of violence. Consequently, for people who are testosterone deficient, there is moderate evidence to suggest testosterone replacement therapy appears to have some effect and is relatively safe; however, for men with normal testosterone levels, there is moderate evidence to suggest testosterone replacement appears not effective and has serious safety concerns that include frequent and serious adverse events and/or interactions (see Evidence Summary table at end of chapter).

Adequate circulation means the avoidance of atherosclerosis and the avoidance of drugs, which might impair vasodilatation such as some anti-hypertensive medications. There is no evidence that increasing circulation using erectile dysfunction drugs has any benefit.

Premature ejaculation (PE) is the most common sexual dysfunction of men. It is defined as either ejaculation before orgasm or a lack of voluntary control over ejaculation. Almost all men experience PE, especially early in their sexual lives. Control over ejaculation is a learned skill, a behavioral development. Traditional sexual therapy has used behavioral techniques for treatment. The Squeeze Technique has been used successfully for over 30 years, and there is strong evidence to support a strong recommendation for the Squeeze Technique as safe and effective therapy for PE (11) (see Evidence Summary table at end of chapter).

There are no FDA-approved treatments for PE; however, there are several "off-label" medications and topical applications that have been tried. These include the SSRI medications used for depression and other psychological disorders, beta-blockers, and topical anesthetic agents. One randomized controlled trial of venlafaxine (Effexor) showed that it was no better than placebo for PE (12). A meta-analysis of the SSRI agents showed that some ejaculation delay was found with daily use, but not on demand use, and that paroxetine showed the strongest effect (13). Dapoxetine is a new SSRI targeted for PE, and a comparison-controlled study showed it was no more effective than paroxetine (14). There is limited evidence to suggest that topical anesthetic treatments might be effective for PE (15).

There is no shortage of alternative therapies available for PE, but none have an evidence base. No research of any quality could be found. A review of current and future pharmacotherapies for PE is available (16). The most promising treatments for the control of ejaculation are behavioral techniques including the Squeeze Technique because this is a skill that can be learned.

Erectile dysfunction (ED) is common, but actual prevalence has skyrocketed with the availability of the Phosphodiesterase-5 (PDE-5) inhibitors, Sildenafil (Viagra), Vardenafil (Levitra) and Tedalafil (Cialas). Prescription ED drugs increase circulation through the nitrous oxide mechanism, a discovery that was worthy of a Nobel Prize. ED drugs are "blockbusters" for the pharmaceutical industry with multi-billion dollars in sales. There is strong evidence to support a strong recommendation for these treatments as effective treatments of ED when decreased circulation is the underlying cause.

Alternative treatment options related to biologically based therapies include Carnitine, Ginseng and L-Arginine. Carnitine is an amino acid used to turn fat into energy. Carnitine is not a necessary amino acid because it is made in the body. Supplemental carnitine is thought to increase energy in certain tissues, such as muscle and the heart. There is moderate evidence from three double-blind controlled trials to support a weak recommendation for carnitine in the treatment of ED, alone or taken with a PDE-5 (17-19). Carnitine is generally safe, but some evidence suggests that it might decrease thyroid hormone function (20) (see Evidence Summary table at end of chapter).

Asian or Korean Ginseng has been shown to help ED in two double-blind placebo controlled trials (21,22). There are insufficient data as of yet to make a clinical recommendation on the effect of Korean Ginseng in the treatment of ED (see Evidence Summary table at end of chapter). Ginseng is considered generally safe. Historically there has been concern about an estrogen effect in women (breast tenderness), but concerns have been discredited by better research (23) and there is no evidence of any concern with men.

L-Arginine is an amino acid found in many foods, including dairy products, meat, poultry, and fish. The body uses arginine to make nitric oxide, which relates it to the same function as the PDE-5 medications. L-arginine has been marketed as the "natural Viagra" but there is very limited evidence suggesting that it works. Just one small double-blind clinical trial of 50 men showed some modest improvement in ED compared with placebo (24). L-arginine is safe in moderate doses (2-3 grams per day); however, larger doses may be harmful. One study using 9 grams daily among patients in the immediate post-acute MI period found was terminated when 6 subjects died in the intervention group compared to 0 subjects in the placebo group (see CHD chapter). Higher doses also increase gastrin production in the stomach and may cause GI upset and aggravation of GERD or peptic ulcers (25,26). At this time, there is insufficient data to make a clinical recommendation on L-arginine for the treatment of ED (see Evidence Summary table at end of chapter).

One of the most commonly used and oldest CAM supplements for sexual function is Yohimbe, which is derived from West African tree bark. It is a traditional aphrodisiac. A few studies suggest that Yohimbe may have some effect on ED, helping less than half the men with moderate erectile dysfunction (27). A double-blind controlled trial suggested that Yohimbe combined with L-Arginine, both taken at 6 grams daily, was effective for ED (28). As discussed earlier, higher doses of L-arginine among men >60 years in the post-MI period may confer increased mortality risk.

Yohimbe itself has safety concerns. Some experts recommend against using Yohimbe because of risks of known side effects such as dizziness, anxiety, nausea, hypotension, abdominal pain, fatigue and hallucinations. However, in usual recommended doses, Yohimbe is usually well tolerated and appears to have safety concerns that include infrequent but serious adverse events and/or interactions. Given the very limited evidence for effectiveness in the setting of potential safety concerns, it is premature to recommend Yohimbe for ED (see Evidence Summary table at end of chapter).

# Prostate Disorders

Benign prostatic hypertrophy (BPH) is a common condition of middle aged and older men. Saw palmetto is widely used in Europe as a standard of care, and less so in the United States, although it is the most widely used herbal supplement in men. The use of saw palmetto dates back to the Mayan civilization and was also used by the Seminoles as a tonic and antiseptic (6). Research shows that saw palmetto does cause a small but definite shrinkage of the prostate gland, which means that it is not just treating symptoms but may be used to both prevent and alleviate BPH (29-31). The prescription drug finasteride (Proscar) works similarly, and one large randomized trial showed there was no difference in efficacy between these two treatments (32).

Over 10 RCTs have shown that the herb reduces nighttime urination, improves urinary flow and quality of life in men with BPH compared with placebo (33-42). There have been negative clinical trials, however, including a recent carefully designed study of 225 men that failed to show saw palmetto superior to placebo (43). Saw palmetto showed little or no toxicity in these controlled trials and is considered as safe as a food substance with infrequent, not serious adverse events and interactions. There is moderate evidence to support a weak recommendation for saw palmetto in the treatment of BPH (see Evidence Summary table at end of chapter).

Other herbs that are recommended for BPH include nettle root, pumpkin seed extract, and pygeum. Nettle root is a popular treatment in Europe for BPH. It is not as well studied as saw palmetto; there is moderate evidence to support a weak recommendation of nettle root for the treatment of BPH. In a randomized controlled trial in Iran, 558 men were given nettle root or placebo for 6 months. Nettle root was more effective than placebo on all major measures of BPH severity (44). Benefits were seen in three other double-blind studies as well, enrolling a total of more than 150 men (45,46). Another randomized blinded trial that involving 257 men with BPH found statistically and clinically significant improvements among men taking two capsules once daily of Prostagutt forte (a combination product containing 120 mg nettle root WS 1031 and 160 mg sabal palmetto WS 1473 per capsule) compared with placebo (47). A subsequent multi-center randomized equivalence trial involving 140 men found non-inferiority between Prostagutt forte with 0.4 mg daily of tamsulosin, a widely used prescription alpha1-adrenoceptor antagonist (48). Overall, there is moderate evidence to suggest that nettle root appears more effective, particularly when combined with other herbs, such as pygeum, sabal palmetto or saw palmetto (48,49) (see Evidence Summary table at end of chapter). Nettle root has been used in foods for many years and appears safe with infrequent, not serious adverse events and interactions.

Pumpkin seed extract or oil is also a popular treatment for BPH in Europe and is on Germany's Commission E. Randomized placebo-controlled studies have been limited to evaluating this therapy in combination with saw palmetto

(50,51). There is limited evidence to support a weak recommendation for using pumpkin seed in combination with saw palmetto to treat BPH. There is insufficient data to make a recommendation when it is used as monotherapy. There are no known safety risks with pumpkin seeds and they appear relatively safe with infrequent, not serious adverse events and interactions (see Evidence Summary table at end of chapter).

Pygeum is a tree native to central and southern Africa. Its bark has been used since ancient times to treat urinary problems. Today, pygeum is used to treat BPH. Many poorly designed placebo-controlled clinical trials have suggested an efficacy similar to saw palmetto. The best study was conducted at 8 sites in Europe and included 263 men between 50 and 85 years of age. Compared with placebo, the results showed moderate improvements in residual urine volume, voided volume, urinary flow rate, nighttime urination, and daytime frequency (52). There is limited evidence to support a weak recommendation for pygeum in combination with saw palmetto for the treatment of BPH. It appears safe for both short- and long-term use, and there are infrequent, not serious adverse events or interactions (see Evidence Summary table at end of chapter).

Prostate cancer is the most common cancer in men. Recent evidence suggests that virtually all men will get prostate cancer if they live long enough. There are two types of prostate cancer: an aggressive type, which occurs in younger men and has the risk of metastases and death, and an indolent type, which occurs in old age and usually does not cause death.

The National Center for Complementary and Alternative Medicine (NCCAM) has worked with the National Cancer Institute to investigate CAM therapies for cancer prevention and treatment. A number of dietary interventions are being studied to prevent prostate cancer. These include selenium, vitamins D and E, lycopene, phytoestrogens, flavonoids, and green tea polyphenols (53). PC-SPES is a formulation of eight natural products (seven herbs and one mushroom) and was released in 1996 as a treatment for prostate cancer. While long-term controlled trials of CAM therapies to prevent or treat prostate cancer are lacking, there are observational studies that indicate lower rates among patients taking some of these supplements.

Although the overall safety of vitamin E is being questioned, there is some data to suggest that vitamin E may help prevent prostate cancer. An epidemiological case-controlled study at Johns Hopkins showed decreased mortality from prostate cancer for both vitamin E and selenium, but only when gamma-tocopherol was included (54). This emphasizes the importance of recommending mixed tocopherols as the preferred form of vitamin E and not just alpha-tocopherol. A large NIH study of vitamin E for the prevention of prostate cancer showed negative overall results but a positive effect for gamma-tocopherol in reducing prostate disease (55). In summary, there is very limited evidence to suggest vitamin E in a mixed tocopherol form, including the possibility that gamma-tocopherol might prevent or improve the outcome of prostate cancer. Because ingestion of supplemental vitamin E has been associated with an increase in overall mortality at doses of 400 IU or higher, its safety is in question (56,57). Given the lack of RCT data to support its efficacy and the potential safety concerns, it is premature to make a recommendation for vitamin E (see Evidence Summary table at end of chapter). Of note, patients with Type 2 diabetes should not take supplemental vitamin E in doses of 400 IU or higher due to increased risks (58-60).

Lycopene is a carotenoid like beta-carotene that is found in high levels in tomatoes and pink grapefruit. Lycopene appears to exhibit about twice the antioxidant activity of beta-carotene and may be more helpful for preventing cancer. In one observational study, ingesting a diet high in tomato products reduced cancer incidence by 50% in men and women, with fewer GI cancers along with reduction in prostate cancer (61). A 4-year observational study of 47,894 men showed that a diet rich in lycopene greatly reduced prostate cancer incidence (62). Lycopene appears in reasonably high levels in the human prostate (63), and there is evidence that lycopene might slow DNA synthesis in prostate cells (64), which could lower risk of prostate cancer. There is very limited evidence to support a weak recommendation for lycopene for the prevention of prostate cancer. Dietary and supplemental lycopene is considered relatively safe with infrequent, not serious adverse events or interactions (see Evidence Summary table at end of chapter).

PC-SPES got its name from the abbreviation for prostate cancer and the Latin word *spes* meaning hope. Pilot research suggested that PC-SPES may decrease PSA levels in prostate cancer patients; however, subsequent chemical analysis of batches sold over the counter showed that this product was adulterated with diethylstilbestrol (DES) as well as indomethacin and warfarin (65). Other trials showed that PC-SPES reduced PSA levels, but it may be that the effect was due to the DES and not the natural products (66-68). Although these studies revealed promising results, there are significant safety concerns due to adulteration of the product, so this product should not be recommended (see Evidence Summary table at end of chapter).

## Male Pattern Baldness

Male pattern baldness is genetic and has probably been a concern among men forever. In the past, wigs have been used, but more recently hair transplantation and the use of medications such as minoxidil and finasteride (Propecia) are the most common treatments. Before these therapies became available, commercial entities were selling products for treating men's hair loss that had no evidence basis. While CAM therapies have been used with some effectiveness for alopecia areata (69-74), there is insufficient evidence evaluating CAM therapies for male pattern baldness.

# Aging and Men

Anti-aging is a popular topic among men, and has been so for a long time. Besides our genetic lifespan, lifestyle problems contribute heavily to early aging. Smoking, poor nutrition, a sedentary lifestyle and chronic stress all contribute to premature aging. Conversely, not smoking, healthy nutrition, regular physical activity, restful sleep, regular relaxation and stress management all contribute to a long and healthy life.

The most compelling evidence for enhancing longevity is the research on calorie restriction and keeping a lean body mass with low body fat. Originally, research in mice by Roy Walford and his student Richard Weindruch led to a popular book in 1988, *The Retardation of Aging and Disease by Dietary Restriction* (75). Since then, numerous studies of humans have been done confirming the benefits of calorie restriction. These benefits require that the person ingest sufficient quantities of vitamins, minerals and other important nutrients such as the essential fatty acids and amino acids. If a person is athletic, adequate nutrition must be consumed to support the physical activity.

More recent research suggests that the reduced calorie intake is not the factor that influences longevity: the factor is, rather, maintaining a lean body mass with low body fat (76,77). This can be obtained by ingesting a normal amount of calories and being physically active. Hence, exercise is just as important a contributor to longevity as nutrition. Healthy nutrition, regular exercise and maintaining lean body mass has a strong evidence base suggesting it can avoid premature aging and is considered safe.

DHEA, or dehydroepiandrosterone, is popular because of its anti-aging claims. DHEA is produced by the adrenal glands, liver and testes. It is converted to androstenedione, which is then converted to testosterone. DHEA is also the precursor to estrogen. DHEA levels do decline with aging, which has lead some people to believe that using it as a supplement will retard or reverse aging. DHEA is available without a prescription and is used throughout the world. It is a hormone synthesized for purchase and is not a natural product. DHEA is used and has been studied for a variety of conditions, including lupus, osteoporosis, depression, HIV, chronic fatigue and menopause. No randomized controlled trials have evaluated its effectiveness in improving longevity.

Because DHEA naturally decreases with age, this hormone has been widely hyped as a kind of fountain of youth. However, nine studies have found that DHEA supplementation does not improve mood, mental function, or general well being in older people (78-86). Three studies found that use of DHEA does not increase muscle mass in seniors (87,89). There is one study suggesting it might improve signs of aging skin (90).

DHEA appears to be safe if taken at usual recommended doses, 25-50 mg a day for short-term use. The effect of long-term use is not known. Because DHEA is a hormone, there are concerns about its long-term effects, including theoretically increasing risk of promoting hormone-dependent tumors. It does not increase testosterone levels in men. Most of the safety concerns have been found in women with DHEA interfering with estrogen-related functions. A 15-year observational study found no association between DHEA levels and breast cancer (91); however, another study found DHEA was associated with increased rates of ovarian cancer (92). At this time, there is insufficient evidence to recommend DHEA to improve longevity, and long-term safety is unknown (see Evidence Summary table at end of chapter).

**Evidence Summary of CAM Usage in Men's Health**

| Clinical Indication | Category | Specific Therapy | Dose | Outcome | Confidence of Estimate on Effectiveness | Magnitude of Effect* | Safety† | Clinical Recommendation‡ | Comments |
|---|---|---|---|---|---|---|---|---|---|
| Androgen deficiency | Medication | Testosterone | 50-400 mg IM or 5-10 gm topical-50-100 mg testosterone | Correct the deficiency, normal masculine functions | Grade A | Large | Single thumb up | Strong in favor | — |
| Athletic fitness | Biologically based therapies | Androstenediol | 100-600 mg daily | Increase muscle bulk and strength | Grade D | Small | Single thumbs down | No recommendation | Weak steroid precursor to testosterone. |
| Athletic fitness | Biologically based therapies | Androstenedione | 100 mg twice daily | Increase muscle bulk and strength | Grade D | Small | Single thumbs down | No recommendation | Also called Andro. |
| Athletic fitness | Biologically based therapies | Androstenetrione | 100-600 mg daily | Increase muscle bulk and strength | Grade D | Small | Single thumbs down | No recommendation | Known as 6-Oxo and ADT. |
| Athletic fitness | Biologically based therapies | Creatine | 2-5 gm daily | Increase muscle strength | Grade C | Moderate | Double thumb up | Weak in favor | Benefit is for short bursts of activity. |

| Sexual performance | Medication | Testosterone | 50-400 mg IM or 5-10 gm topically otherwise. 50-100 mg testosterone | Improved Sexual performance | Grade B | 1. Small if testosterone deficient; 2. No effect if normal levels. | 1. One thumb up if deficient; 2. Two thumbs down in men with normal levels. | 1. Weak in favor for testosterone deficient; 2. Weak against otherwise. | Replacement requires clinical judgment and should not be corrected above normal levels. |
|---|---|---|---|---|---|---|---|---|---|
| Premature ejaculation | Mind-body and lifestyle therapies | Squeeze technique | N/A | Increase time of erection before ejaculation | Grade A | Large | Two thumbs up | Strong in favor | Time-honored effective treatment |
| Erectile dysfunction | Biologically based therapies | Carnitine | 500-1000 mg three times daily | Improved erection | Grade B | Small | Single thumb up | Weak in favor | May be taken with a PDE-5 drug. |
| Erectile dysfunction | Biologically based therapies | Korean ginseng | 900 mg three times daily | Improved erection | Grade C | Small | Two thumbs up | No recommendation | Dosage varies widely. |
| Erectile dysfunction | Biologically based therapies | L-Arginine | 2-3 gm daily | Improved erection | Grade C | Small | Single thumb up | No recommendation | Known as the "natural Viagra." Avoid high doses due to increased mortality with 9 grams daily among post-MI patients. |

(continued)

**Evidence Summary of CAM Usage in Men's Health (continued)**

| Clinical Indication | Category | Specific Therapy | Dose | Outcome | Confidence of Estimate on Effectiveness | Magnitude of Effect* | Safety† | Clinical Recommendation‡ | Comments |
|---|---|---|---|---|---|---|---|---|---|
| Sexual performance | Biologically based therapies | Yohimbe | 200-800 mg twice daily | Aphrodisiac and general sexual performance | Grade C | Small | Single thumb down | No recommendation | Risk may exceed benefit. |
| Benign Prostatic Hypertrophy (BPH) | Biologically based therapies | Saw Palmetto | 160 mg twice daily | Reduce obstruction and night-time urination | Grade B | Moderate | Two thumbs up | Weak in favor | Good studies but more recent data is conflicting when compared with placebo. Albeit, a RCT showed it was no less effective than Finasteride. |
| BPH | Biologically based therapies | Nettle root | Varying | Reduce obstruction and night-time urination | Grade B | Moderate | Two thumbs up | Weak in favor as stand alone therapy and in combination with pygeum and saw palmetto | May be more effective combined with other BPH herbs. |

| Condition | Category | Supplement | Dose | Use | Grade | Size | Rating | Recommendation | Comments |
|---|---|---|---|---|---|---|---|---|---|
| BPH | Biologically based therapies | Pumpkin seed | 160 mg three times daily | Reduce obstruction and night-time urination | Grade C | Small | Two thumbs up | No recommendation as stand alone therapy. Weak in favor in combination with saw palmetto | — |
| BPH | Biologically based therapies | Pygeum | 50 mg twice daily | Reduce obstruction and night-time urination | Grade C | Moderate | Two thumbs up | Weak in favor in combination with saw palmetto | — |
| Prostate cancer | Biologically based therapies | Vitamin E mixed tocopherols | 50-400 mg | Prevent prostate cancer | Grade D | Small | No recommendation | No recommendation | Beware of using Vitamin E in diabetics. |
| Prostate cancer | Biologically based therapies | Lycopene | 4-8 mg daily | Prevent or treat prostate cancer | Grade D | Small | Two thumbs up | Weak in favor | Limited to observation studies only; dietary Lycopene may be more effective. |
| Prostate Cancer | Biologically based therapies | PC-SPES | 6-9 320 mg capsules daily | Treat prostate cancer | Grade C | Small | Two thumbs down | Strong against | Commercial formulation found to be contaminated with estrogen, and warfarin. |

(continued)

**Evidence Summary of CAM Usage in Men's Health (continued)**

| Clinical Indication | Category | Specific Therapy | Dose | Outcome | Confidence of Estimate on Effectiveness | Magnitude of Effect* | Safety† | Clinical Recommendation‡ | Comments |
|---|---|---|---|---|---|---|---|---|---|
| Aging and longevity | Mind-body and lifestyle therapies | Calorie restriction | Daily low calories or intermittent fasting | Increase healthy lifespan | Grade B | Moderate | Two thumbs up | Strong in favor | Exercise may increase the benefit. |
| Aging | Biologically based therapies | DHEA | 25-50 mg daily | 1. Longevity 2. QOL#, muscle mass and cognitive function in seniors | 1. Grade D 2. Grade B | 1. Unknown 2. None | 1. One thumb up 2. One thumb up | 1. No recommendation 2. Weak against | Long-term effects of taking this adrenal hormone are not known and include a theoretical risk of promoting estrogen-dependent cancers. |

* Small, moderate (OR>1.2-2) or large (OR>2)

† 5 categories: Double thumbs up, single thumb up, no recommendation, single thumb down, double thumb down

‡ 5 categories: Strong (in favor), weak (in favor), no recommendation, weak (against), strong (against)

# QOL: Quality of life

## SELECTED REFERENCES

1. **U.S. Preventive Services Task Force.** Recommended Preventive Services, 2007. http://www .ahrq.gov/clinic/pocketgd07/gcp1.htm.

2. **Bhasin S, Cunningham GR, Hayes FJ, et al.** Testosterone therapy in adult men with androgen deficiency syndromes: an endocrine society clinical practice guideline. J Clin Endocrinol Metab. 2006;91:1995-2010.

3. **Edelstein D, Sivanandy M, Shahani S, Basaria S.** The latest options and future agents for treating male hypogonadism. Expert Opin Pharmacother. 2007;8:2991-3008.

4. **Editors of the Prescriber's Letter and the Pharmacist's Letter.** Natural Medicines Comprehensive Database. Stockton, CA: Therapeutic Research Faculty. 2006.

5. **King DS, Sharp RL, Vukovich MD, et al.** Effect of oral androstenedione on serum testosterone and adaptations to resistance training in young men: a randomized controlled trial. JAMA. 1999;281:2020-8.

6. **National Library of Medicine.** Medline Plus. Drugs and Supplements. http://www.nlm .nih.gov/medlineplus/druginfo/natural/patient-creatine.html Accessed Nov. 27, 2007.

7. **Branch JD.** Effect of creatine supplementation on body composition and performance: a meta-analysis. Int J Sport Nutr Exerc Metab. 2003;13:198-226.

8. **Leenders N, Sherman WM, Lamb DR, et al.** Creatine supplementation and swimming performance. Int J Sport Nutr. 1999;9:251-62.

9. **Somers S.** The Sexy Years. New York: Random House. 2004.

10. **Isidori AM, Giannetta E, Gianfrilli D, et al.** Effects of testosterone on sexual function in men: results of a meta-analysis. Clin Endocrinol (Oxf). 2005;63:381-94.

11. **Mayo Clinic.** Premature Ejaculation. http://www.mayoclinic.com/health/premature-ejaculation/ DS00578/DSECTION=8 Accessed December 4, 2007.

12. **Safarinejad MR.** Safety and efficacy of venlafaxine in the treatment of premature ejaculation: a double-blind, placebo-controlled, fixed-dose, randomised study. Andrologia. 2008;40:49-55.

13. **Waldinger MD.** Premature ejaculation: state of the art. Urol Clin North Am. 2007;34:591-9.

14. **Safarinejad MR.** Comparison of dapoxetine versus paroxetine in patients with premature ejaculation: a double-blind, placebo-controlled, fixed-dose, randomized study. Clin Neuropharmacol. 2006;29:243-52.

15. **Morales A, Barada J, Wyllie MG.** A review of the current status of topical treatments for premature ejaculation. BJU Int. 2007;100:493-501.

16. **Hellstrom WJ.** Current and future pharmacotherapies of premature ejaculation. J Sex Med. 2006;3 Suppl 4:332-41.

17. **Cavallini G, Caracciolo S, Vitali G, et al.** Carnitine versus androgen administration in the treatment of sexual dysfunction, depressed mood, and fatigue associated with male aging. Urology. 2004;63:641-46.

18. **Gentile V, Vicini P, Prigiotti G, et al.** Preliminary observations on the use of propionyl-L-carnitine in combination with sildenafil in patients with erectile dysfunction and diabetes. Curr Med Res Opin. 2004;20:1377-84.

19. **Cavallini G, Modenini F, Vitali G, et al.** Acetyl-L-carnitine plus propionyl-L-carnitine improve efficacy of sildenafil in treatment of erectile dysfunction after bilateral nerve-sparing radical retropubic prostatectomy. Urology. 2005;66:1080-5.

20. **Benvenga S, Lakshmanan M, Trimarchi F.** Carnitine is a naturally occurring inhibitor of thyroid hormone nuclear uptake. Thyroid. 2000;10:1043-50.

21. **Choi HK, et al.** Clinical efficacy of Korean red ginseng for erectile dysfunction. Int J Impotence Res. 1995;7:181-6.

22. **Hong B, Ji YH, Hong JH, et al.** A double-blind crossover study evaluating the efficacy of Korean red ginseng in patients with erectile dysfunction: a preliminary report. J Urol. 2002;168:2070-3.

---

\* The complete reference list is to be found on the book's Web site.

23. **Wiklund IK, Mattsson LA, Lindgren R, et al.** Effects of a standardized ginseng extract on quality of life and physiological parameters in symptomatic postmenopausal women: a double-blind, placebo-controlled trial. Int J Clin Pharmacol Res. 1999;19:89-99.

24. **Chen J, Wollman Y, Chernichovsky T, et al.** Effect of oral administration of high-dose nitric oxide donor L-arginine in men with organic erectile dysfunction: results of a double-blind, randomized placebo-controlled study. BJU Int. 1999;83:269-73.

25. **AHFS Drug Information.** Bethesda, MD: American Society of Hospital Pharmacists. 2000: 2306-7.

26. **Luiking YC, Weusten BL, Portincasa P, et al.** Effects of long-term oral L-arginine on esophageal motility and gallbladder dynamics in healthy humans. Am J Physiol. 1998;274(6 pt 1):G984-G991.

27. **Riley AJ.** Yohimbine in the treatment of erectile disorder. Br J Clin Pract. 1994;48:133-6.

33. **Shi R, Xie Q, Gang X, et al.** Effect of saw palmetto soft gel capsule on lower urinary tract symptoms associated with benign prostatic hyperplasia: a randomized trial in Shanghai,China. J Urol. 2008;179:610-5.

41. **Gerber GS, Kuznetsov D, Johnson BC, et al.** Randomized, double-blind, placebo-controlled trial of saw palmetto in men with lower urinary tract symptoms. Urology. 2001;58:960-4.

43. **Bent S, Kane C, Shinohara K, et al.** Saw Palmetto for Benign Prostatic Hyperplasia. N Engl J Med. 2006;354:557-66.

48. **Engelmann U, Walther C, Bondarenko B, et al.** Efficacy and safety of a combination of sabal and urtica extract in lower urinary tract symptoms. A randomized, double-blind study versus tamsulosin. Arzneimittelforschung. 2006;56:222-9.

49. **Krzeski T, Kazon M, Borkowski A, et al.** Combined extracts of Urtica dioica and Pygeum africanum in the treatment of benign prostatic hyperplasia: double-blind comparison of two doses. Clin Ther. 1993;15:1011-20.

51. **Carbin BE, Larsson B, Lindahl O.** Treatment of benign prostatic hyperplasia with phytos-terols. Br J Urol. 1990;66:639-41.

53. **Syed DN, Khan N, Afaq F, Mukhtar H.** Chemoprevention of Prostate Cancer through Dietary Agents: Progress and Promise. Cancer Epidemiol Biomarkers Prev 2007;16:2193-204.

55. **Wright ME, Weinstein SJ, Lawson KA, et al.** Supplemental and dietary vitamin E intakes and risk of prostate cancer in a large prospective study. Cancer Epidemiol Biomarkers Prev. 2007;16:1128-35.

56. **Bjelakovic G, Nikolova D, Gluud LL, et al.** Mortality in randomized trials of antioxidant supplements for primary and secondary prevention: systematic review and meta-analysis. JAMA. 2007;297:842-57.

64. **Barber NJ, Zhang X, Zhu G, et al.** Lycopene inhibits DNA synthesis in primary prostate epithelial cells in vitro and its administration is associated with a reduced prostate-specific antigen velocity in a phase II clinical study. Prostate Cancer Prostatic Dis. 2006;9:407-13.

65. **Oh WK, Kantoff PW, Weinberg V, et al.** Prospective, multicenter, randomized phase II trial of the herbal supplement, PC-SPES, and diethylstilbestrol in patients with androgen-independent prostate cancer. J Clin Oncol. 2004;22:3705-12.

91. **Barrett-Connor E, Friedlander NJ, Khaw K-T.** Dehydroepiandrosterone sulfate and breast cancer risk. Cancer Res. 1990;50:6571-4.

92. **Helzlsouer KJ, Alberg AJ, Gordon GB, et al.** Serum gonadotropins and steroid hormones and the development of ovarian cancer. JAMA. 1995;274:1926-30.

# Chapter 11

# Women's Health

Jacquelyn M. Paykel, MD

Surveys have shown that women are more likely than men to pursue an integrative approach to their healthcare. The biggest sex differential is seen in the use of mind-body therapies (1).

Complementary medicine consists of those treatment modalities that are used in conjunction with conventional therapies. The National Center for Complementary and Alternative Medicine (NCCAM) categorizes complementary medicine into five categories. The most likely reasons for an individual to engage an integrative medicine provider are chronic pain and anxiety (2). This chapter provides a review of a number of female health conditions that may result in symptoms and the CAM methods currently employed and under investigation. When presenting the CAM evidence we will review biologically based practices (i.e., botanicals), mind-body medicine and lifestyle therapies (including behavioral therapy, hypnosis, smoking cessation, weight loss, dietary changes, exercise, supplements, etc.), manipulative and body-based practices (e.g., massage therapy, physical therapy), energy medicine (e.g., reflexology) and whole medical systems (e.g., traditional Chinese medicine and homeopathy), when applicable.

## Menopausal Symptoms: Hot Flashes

The average age of natural menopause in the United States is 51.4 years. Cigarette smokers undergo menopause on average two years earlier than non-smokers (3). Iatrogenic menopause may occur earlier if a woman undergoes surgical removal of both ovaries (i.e., bilateral oophorectomy) or experiences ovarian failure in response to chemotherapy or radiation. Within the next 10 years, over 36 million women will enter menopause in the United States (4).

As women complete the transition through menopause approximately 85% will experience at least one symptom (5). Approximately 40% of women in the menopause transition or menopause seek assistance from their physician for alleviation from symptoms such as hot flashes, vaginal dryness with resultant dyspareunia, mood disorders and dysfunctional sleep (6). Hot flashes are the most frequent symptoms of menopause and the most common reason why climacteric women seek medical advice (7). A hot flush is a sudden feeling of warmth that lasts an average of four minutes and is most intense over the face, neck and chest. It is often accompanied by sweating followed by a chill. Up to 65% of women experience hot flashes during the menopausal transition (3). The mainstay of conventional therapy, hormone therapy (HT), is not satisfactory for many. Thirty percent to 40% of women initiating HT will discontinue use within the first year due to bleeding disorders (8). In addition, the results of the Women's Health Initiative (WHI) study of hormone therapy in postmenopausal women have prompted many women and physicians to reconsider HT to alleviate menopausal symptoms (9).

As a part of a large study of menopause and hormone therapy Newton et al surveyed 886 women 45 to 65 years of age (10). Overall 76% of women reported using at least one CAM therapy, 22% for menopausal symptoms. The most commonly used modalities were stress management or relaxation techniques (43%); herbal, homeopathic, or natural remedies (37%); chiropractic therapy (32%); massage therapy (30%); dietary soy (23%) and acupuncture (10%). Up to 75% of the participants commented that the CAM therapies were very helpful.

## Biologically Based Therapies

Phytoestrogens constitute a group of over-the-counter therapies popular in the management of menopausal symptoms. Common categories of isoflavones include soy (dietary, supplements and extracts), red clover, black cohosh and others.

### Soy Isoflavones

A good-quality study randomized 111 breast cancer survivors to 90 mg per day of a soy drink compared to placebo. Both groups improved, and soy was no better than placebo (11). A review analyzed 18 RCTs of dietary and supplement-based soy. Only 4 out of 15 of the better-quality trials found soy superior to placebo (12). A subsequent review published similar findings (12,13). The long-term effect of exposure to soy isoflavones is unknown. However in one study there was no endometrial thickening in response to soy (14). Overall, there is moderate evidence to suggest that dietary and supplemental soy may not be effective in reducing hot flashes; therefore, at this time, the evidence-base supports a weak recommendation against its use (see Evidence Summary table at end of chapter).

## Red Clover

Red clover isoflavones do not appear to be more effective than placebo in reducing hot flashes, based on limited data. A Cochrane review of 5 randomized studies including perimenopausal or postmenopausal participants without a history of breast cancer who were experiencing vasomotor symptoms found red clover extract was no better than placebo for reducing the frequency of hot flashes. It is worth noting that like most trials evaluating hot flashes, participants randomized to the control group experienced a significant placebo response (up to 59%) (15). Several RCTs have found no benefit of red clover over placebo (16-18). There was no evidence of harm with use up to 2 years regardless the dose of red clover phytoestrogen used (15). Overall, there is moderate evidence supporting a weak recommendation against the use of red clover for hot flashes (see Evidence Summary table at end of chapter).

## Black Cohosh

Several studies have demonstrated that black cohosh is effective against hot flashes. A German double-blind, placebo-controlled trial published in 1987 established efficacy of black cohosh (19). Since then, research results have varied. However, the most recent and best studies do support the findings of the initial study (20). No studies have been published on long-term safety in humans. Some investigators believe these compounds have estrogenic properties. Until this issue is clarified, it is advisable for women with estrogen-receptor positive breast cancer, uterine cancer, or endometriosis, as well as pregnant and lactating women, to avoid using black cohosh (21). Case reports of idiosyncratic fulminant hepatic failure have been reported from products containing black cohosh; however, the strength of association has been questioned (22). Nonetheless, it is advised that people with liver conditions consult a healthcare professional when considering this therapy. It may interact with a number of medications, including antihypertensives, antibiotics, oral contraceptives, sedatives and hypnotics (21). Black cohosh is the most commonly prescribed remedy for menopausal symptoms in Germany. Until long-term safety studies are done, the recommended use is limited to 6 months. There is limited evidence supporting a weak recommendation in favor of black cohosh for hot flashes at this time.

## Other Agents

Other phytoestrogens have been used for treatment of menopausal symptoms including dong quai, evening primrose oil, ginseng, and wild yam, but inadequate data is available to make a recommendation on their effectiveness (23).

## Lifestyle and Mind-Body Medicine Therapies

### Exercise

A Cochrane review evaluating the effect of exercise for vasomotor menopausal symptoms identified only 1 trial comparing exercise to HT. This study found HT recipients experienced significantly fewer hot flashes than the exercise group (24). The authors found no RCTs on whether exercise is an effective treatment relative to other interventions or no intervention in reducing hot flashes and/or night sweats in symptomatic women. Observational studies showed that women who regularly exercised are less likely to experience hot flashes than their sedentary counterparts (25,26). At this time, there is insufficient evidence to support or refute exercise for hot flashes (see Evidence Summary table at end of chapter).

### Breath

Freedman compared paced respiration with progressive muscle relaxation or non-therapeutic alpha-wave electroencephalographic (EEG) biofeedback (control) in 33 postmenopausal women. Paced respiration therapy significantly decreased the frequency of hot flashes by 39% (p<0.02) (27). In a more recent trial by the same authors, 24 postmenopausal women with at least 5 hot flashes per day were randomized to receive 8 1-hour sessions of training in paced respirations or alpha-EEG biofeedback (placebo). Hot flash frequency declined significantly (p<0.001) for the treatment group (9.5 +/- 1.4/day pre-treatment vs. 5.5 +/- 1.5/day post-treatment) but not for placebo (28). There is limited evidence supporting a weak recommendation for breath therapy for hot flashes (see Evidence Summary table at end of chapter).

### Yoga

There is insufficient evidence to refute or support yoga for the treatment of hot flashes at this time (3).

### Other Modalities

Randomized clinical trials in mind-body and lifestyle therapies other than exercise include progressive muscle relaxation, low-frequency sound wave, counseling support, stress relief education and menopause education. The majority of these studies are viewed as poor in quality (12). Although these modalities proved beneficial for overall quality of life, they had little effect on menopausal symptoms (29).

## Manipulative and Body-Based Therapies

Limited research in this area has been performed. One fair-quality placebo-controlled study published in 1994 by Cleary and Fox comparing low-force osteopathic manipulation of the pelvis, spine and cranium with sham low-force touch in similar areas showed improvements in hot flashes, night sweats, urinary frequency, depression and insomnia in the treatment group vs. placebo (30). Less rigorous studies show similar results for massage therapy and yoga. At this time, there is insufficient evidence to support or refute manipulative body-based therapies for the treatment of hot flashes (see Evidence Summary table at end of chapter).

## Energy Therapies

Reflexology and magnetic devices have been evaluated for treatment of menopausal conditions. Neither has been found to be effective (31,32). There is insufficient evidence to refute or support these energy medicine therapies for the treatment of hot flashes at this time (see Evidence Summary table at end of chapter).

## Whole Medical Systems

### Acupuncture

Four studies have compared acupuncture with sham acupuncture using superficial needle insertion. None of the studies showed a benefit of genuine acupuncture for the treatment of hot flashes (33-36). It is worth noting that typically, acupuncture would not be used alone in traditional Chinese medicine (TCM) but would be used in conjunction with herbal therapies for the treatment of menopause. However, there are no studies published in the English language combining acupuncture and TCM. At this time, there is insufficient evidence to support or refute the use of acupuncture for hot flashes (see Evidence Summary table at end of chapter).

### Traditional Chinese Medicine Herbs

Oriental herbs are also gaining popularity as menopausal therapies. No trial has yet proved herbs have superior benefit over placebo for the management of hot flashes (29). Standardized ginseng compared with placebo in 384 women showed effectiveness for mood depression, overall well-being and health scores but no between-group differences in hot flashes (37). At this time, there is insufficient evidence to support or refute the use of TCM herbs for hot flashes (see Evidence Summary table at end of chapter).

## Premenstrual Syndrome

Premenstrual syndrome (PMS) is a complex psychoneuroendocrine disorder that is known to affect women's emotional and physical well-being (38). Broadly defined, PMS is a constellation of behavioral, psychological and physical symptoms that affect a woman during the luteal phase, 7 to 14 days before the onset of the menstrual flow. Over 200 symptoms have been associated with PMS. See Box 11-1 on p. 274 for a list of the most common symptoms of PMS.

It is estimated that up to 85% of women between 25 and 35 years old are affected by PMS symptoms. 20% to 40% suffer from PMS, defined as "the cyclic occurrence of symptoms that are of sufficient severity to interfere with some aspects of life and that appear with consistent and predictable relationship to the menses" (43). Two percent to 10% suffer from premenstrual dysphoric disorder (PMDD), which results in serious impairment of some aspect of their social, family, or work life.

PMS and PMDD are diagnoses of exclusion; other physical and psychiatric disorders must be ruled out before either diagnosis can be made. Disorders such as anemia, diabetes, thyroid disease, endometriosis, other endocrine abnormalities and breast disease need to be excluded as possible etiologic factors. Major depression, dysthymia, and anxiety disorders are among the key psychiatric disorders that also need to be ruled out (44).

The etiology of PMS remains unknown. Proposed etiologies include: hormonal dysregulation, fluid and electrolyte imbalances, neurotransmitter (serotonin) deficiency, prostaglandin excess or deficiency, vitamin and mineral deficiencies, genetic risk, psychological factors and social factors (45).

## Biologically Based Therapies

### Chaste Tree Berry (*Vitex agnus-castus*)

This dried ripe fruit of the chaste tree has been proven in vitro and in vivo to have central dopaminergic effects (46-48). Numerous double-blind RCTs have evaluated different preparations containing chasteberry for treating PMS. In 2001 Schellenberg published a well-conducted study using a standardized extract of chasteberry reporting significant improvement in self-reported symptoms associated with PMS and in physician-assessed clinical global impression scores (P=.001). The study specifically addressed breast fullness, not mastalgia. More than 50% of participants experienced a reduction in symptoms. Side effects were mild and rare (49). Another similar study compared the efficacy of tablet versus liquid form of chasteberry compared to placebo. The women in the treatment showed improvement of cyclical breast discomfort (50). Several other studies of lesser quality have showed improvement of various PMS symptoms (51-54). Two studies of lesser quality showed no improvement (55,56). Possible side effects include mild headache, diarrhea, abdominal cramps, anorexia, rash and itching. Possible drug interactions occur with antipsychotics, dopamine agonists and estrogen-containing compounds (57). Overall, there is limited evidence to support a weak recommendation in favor of chaste tree berry for PMS (see Evidence Summary table at end of chapter).

## Black Cohosh (*Cimicifuga racemosa*)

Compounds in black cohosh bind to 5-HT7 serotonin receptors, which may explain its positive effect on depressive and anxiety symptoms in PMS. The most recent study was published by Dittmar in 1992 and demonstrated a reduction of the symptoms of PMS including anxiety, tension and depression (58). The majority of studies looking at black cohosh have been for the treatment of menopausal symptoms. A number of studies do show a benefit for various menopausal symptoms, such as hot flashes, profuse sweating, sleep disturbance and depressed moods. Because these symptoms often exist in those suffering from PMS, many clinicians have recommended the use of black cohosh in this population (59). Black cohosh is approved by the German Commission E for use in women with PMS (60). Black Cohosh is generally safe and well tolerated when used for 6 months, but it has not been well-studied beyond 6 months duration. Please refer to the section on menopausal symptoms. At this time, there is insufficient evidence to support or refute the use of black cohosh for PMS.

## Ginkgo (*Ginkgo biloba*)

Ginkgo is commonly used to sharpen mental focus and improve circulation. A double-blind placebo-controlled trial has shown that standardized ginkgo extract, when taken daily from day 16 of one menstrual cycle to day 5 of the next menstrual cycle, alleviates psychological and congestive symptoms of PMS better than placebo (61). Further study is needed to determine if there is a significant role for ginkgo in treating PMS (59). Ginkgo is generally well tolerated and considered safe with similar side effect rates as placebo in several reviews. Ginkgo is thought to have anti-coagulation. Possible drug interactions can occur (62). At this time, there is insufficient evidence to support or refute the use of Ginkgo for PMS.

## Evening Primrose Oil (*Oenothera biennis*)

A systematic review of the literature published in 1996 revealed seven placebo-controlled trials conducted using evening primrose oil in the treatment of PMS, five of which were clearly randomized trials. None of these trials found a beneficial effect of EPO for PMS. However, it was noted that the sample sizes were not adequate in all studies to detect a modest but significant difference (63). Two well-designed RCTs failed to show efficacy (64-66). Potential side effects include headache, seizures among people with seizure disorder or taking anesthetics, nausea, vomiting, anorexia, diarrhea, hypersensitivity reactions, rash, inflammation and immunosuppression with long-term use. Physicians should counsel against using this herb among patients with seizure disorder and should discontinue use 2 weeks prior to undergoing surgery requiring anesthesia. Possible drug interactions include anticoagulants and phenothiazines (67).

There is moderate evidence to support a weak recommendation against the use of EPO at this time (see Evidence Summary table at end of chapter).

## Other Biologically Based Therapies

St. John's Wort (*Hypericum perforatum*) is primarily used to alleviate depressive symptoms. Kava (*Piper methysticum*) has been proven effective for treating anxiety, though has a questionable safety profile. Valerian (*Valeriana officinalis*) is a common over-the-counter ingredient for sleep preparations and relaxants. None have been adequately studied for the treatment of PMS.

## Lifestyle, Supplement and Mind-Body Therapies

### Exercise

Prior JC et al found in a prospective, controlled 6-month trial in 1987 that women who jogged on average 12 miles per week for 6 months experienced a reduction in breast tenderness, fluid retention, depression and stress (68). At this time, there is insufficient evidence to support or refute the use of exercise for PMS.

### Light Therapy

Full-spectrum bright-light therapy given in the evening has been shown to markedly reduce symptoms of PMS and PMDD. Lam conducted a 6-menstrual-cycle, randomized, double-blind, counter-balanced, crossover study of bright light therapy versus placebo fluorescent light (placebo) in 14 women with PMDD. The women completed 2 months of baseline symptom monitoring followed by 2 months of each treatment for 30 minutes every evening. The bright light therapy significantly reduced depression and premenstrual tension of the luteal phase, whereas the placebo did not (69). Another study lasting 3 menstrual cycles provided bright-light therapy vs. placebo only on the evenings of the luteal phase and showed a significant reduction of depressive symptoms (70). There is moderate evidence to support a weak recommendation in favor of light therapy for PMS (see Evidence Summary table at end of chapter).

### Diet

High estrogen levels are believed to correlate with PMS in some women. Estrogen is conjugated in the liver and deconjugated by intestinal flora for reabsorption into the system. Therefore, it is theorized that fiber-rich, low-fat diets that decrease the flora's ability to deconjugate estrogen would decrease systemic estrogen levels, as well. Several studies have shown that consuming a high-fiber, low-fat diet may reduce symptoms of PMS (71,72). In a study of Chinese women, increasing tea consumption was associated with increasing prevalence of PMS (73). Multiple studies have shown a correlation to caffeine consumption and increased frequency and severity of PMS symptoms (74,75). Diets high in tryptophan, a precursor to serotonin, may also benefit those with PMS (76). Diet modification is clearly safe and has beneficial effects for other health-related outcomes. At this time however, there is insufficient evidence to support or refute the role of diet specifically to treat PMS (see Evidence Summary table at end of chapter).

## Calcium

A multi-center randomized blinded trial found 3 months of 1200 mg daily calcium carbonate reduced PMS symptoms including depression, fatigue, insomnia, pain, water retention and food cravings when compared with the control group (77). A subsequent review of studies focusing on calcium for the treatment of PMS published in 1999 arrived at similar conclusions and suggested that 1200 to 1600 mg of calcium supplementation should be included as standard medical therapy for women with PMS, unless otherwise contraindicated (78). Calcium may impair absorption of tetracycline, iron, thyroid hormones and corticosteroids when calcium is taken with these compounds. Overall, there is moderate evidence to support a weak recommendation favoring the use of calcium to treat PMS (see Evidence Summary table at end of chapter).

## Vitamin B6

Many studies have studied pyridoxine in the treatment of PMS. A systematic review of 28 published trials found a statistically significant reduction in PMS symptoms with vitamin B6 supplementation (OR 1.57 [95%, 1.40-1.77]) (79). In general vitamin B6 is safe and well-tolerated. Peripheral sensory neuropathy has been reported, however, at doses greater than 100 mg/day. Overall, there is moderate evidence to support a weak recommendation favoring the use of vitamin B6 supplementation to treat PMS (see Evidence Summary table at end of chapter).

## Magnesium

Women with PMS have been reported to have lower serum magnesium levels (80,81). Several small, randomized, double-blind trials have evaluated the effect of magnesium supplementation on various premenstrual symptoms. One trial showed a significant reduction of fluid retention, weight gain, swelling, breast tenderness and bloating after only 2 months of treatment with 200 mg per day (82). A Cochrane review of the literature found three trials comparing magnesium supplementation to placebo for treatment of pain during the luteal phase (83). It is unclear if magnesium supplementation is helpful for women with PMS without pain. At this time, there is insufficient evidence to support or refute the use of magnesium for PMS.

Other supplements with preliminary research suggesting the potential for benefit include potassium (via food or supplementation since supplementation is usually inadequate for biological effects unless given as medical therapy), L-tryptophan, soy protein, vitamin E and krill oil (84-89).

## Manipulative and Body-Based Practices

### Massage Therapy

24 women meeting DSM-IV criteria for PDD were randomly assigned to massage therapy versus relaxation therapy. The massage group showed decreases in anxiety, depressed mood and pain immediately after the first and last massage sessions. Overall, the authors suggest that massage therapy may be an effective adjunct therapy for treating severe premenstrual symptoms (90). At this time, there is insufficient evidence to support or refute the use of massage for PMS.

## Energy Medicine

### Reflexology

Thirty-five women with PMS were randomly assigned ear, hand and foot reflexology or placebo reflexology. All subjects completed a daily symptom diary, which monitored 38 premenstrual symptoms. Over a 2-month period there was a significantly greater decrease in premenstrual symptoms for the women given true reflexology than placebo reflexology treatment (91). At this time, there is insufficient evidence to support or refute the use of reflexology for PMS.

## Whole Medical Systems

### Acupuncture

A meta analysis of seven controlled studies involving 807 women found acupuncture to be superior to active control interventions including conventional western medicine or Chinese herbal medicines. The authors concluded that acupuncture can effectively treat PMS and suggested that additional randomized controlled trials are needed to confirm these findings (92). At this time, there is moderate evidence to support a weak recommendation in favor of acupuncture for PMS (see Evidence Summary table at end of chapter).

### Homeopathy

A small well-designed RCT of individualized homeopathic prescription for PMS found individualized homeopathic prescription improved PMS symptoms better than placebo (93). At this time, there is insufficient evidence to support or refute the use of homeopathy for PMS.

# Dysmenorrhea and Endometriosis

Dysmenorrhea is defined as painful menstruation. It is characterized by painful cramping sensations in the lower abdomen often accompanied by other symptoms such as sweating, tachycardia, headaches, nausea, vomiting, diarrhea and tremulousness (94).

Primary dysmenorrhea typically occurs during adolescence beginning shortly after menarche. It is the most common gynecologic complaint in the adolescent population. An epidemiologic study of young women with primary dysmenorrhea found that up to 15% have grade-three dysmenorrhea, severe pain that inhibits daily activities (95). There is no specific pelvic pathology but is most likely a response of the myometrium to progesterone withdrawal and subsequent conversion of arachidonic acid (AA) to prostaglandins (PGF2$\alpha$ and PGE2) and leukotrienes. Prostaglandins (PG) and leukotrienes (LT) cause myometrial contractions, vasoconstriction and resultant uterine ischemia. They can also contribute to systemic smooth muscle contractions causing nausea, vomiting and diarrhea. Therefore, treatment modalities focus on decreasing AA stores and inhibition of PG and LT production (96).

Secondary dysmenorrhea generally begins after the age of 20 and is associated with other pelvic conditions such as endometriosis. Treatment for secondary dysmenorrhea generally includes PG and LT inhibition in addition to strategies based upon the specific underlying pathology. Endometriosis is a common cause of secondary dysmenorrhea. It is defined as the presence of endometrial cells outside of the uterus (usually found in the pelvis). Symptoms can range from nonexistent to severe and include dysmenorrhea, dyspareunia (painful intercourse) and infertility. It is a significant cause of morbidity in women 15 to 44 years of age with an estimated prevalence of 10%. Between 1990 and 1998 it was the third most common gynecologic diagnosis upon hospital discharge in this age group (97). Risk factors include family history, early menarche, shorter menstrual cycles and longer bleeding. The most widely accepted theory of pathogenesis is that of retrograde reflux of menstrual tissue through the fallopian tubes during menstruation that settles on and invades pelvic structures. Other theories include hereditary factors and impaired immune function. Endometriosis is a histologic diagnosis; biopsies are generally obtained via laparoscopy. Conventional treatment modalities are limited to prostaglandin inhibition, oral contraceptive pills, hormonal interruption of the menstrual cycle and surgery. Laparoscopic ablation of lesions, uterine nerve ablation and presacral neurectomy may decrease pain. Hysterectomy and bilateral oophorectomy are considered definitive treatments for endometriosis though there are no RCTs to support it.

## Biologically Based Practices

### Cramp Bark (*Viburnum opulus*) and Black Haw (*Viburnum prunifolium*)

Cramp bark and black haw have traditionally been used to relieve uterine cramping. Very little human research has been performed to verify its efficacy. Cramp bark contains oxalates and salicylates; therefore, it should be avoided by women with a history of kidney stones or aspirin allergy. Potential side effects include gastrointestinal upset and irritation. Possible drug interactions include anticoagulants, calcium, iron and zinc (98). At this time, there is insufficient evidence to support or refute the use of cramp bark for dysmenorrhea or endometriosis (see Evidence Summary table at end of chapter).

### Pine Bark (*Pinus maritime*)

Pine bark, an extract antioxidant, was found effective in reducing symptoms of endometriosis in a controlled clinical trial comparing a gonadotropin-releasing hormone agonist (GnRHa) with pine bark. Fifty-eight women who continued to suffer from dysmenorrhea after surgical intervention for endometriosis were assigned to one of the two treatment arms. The pine bark extract recipients experienced a within-group statistically significant reduction in symptoms of endometriosis by 33%. The GnRHa was more efficient, but the difference in the two treatment arms was not statistically significant by the study end. Another study by the same investigator showed a statistically significant (p<0.05) decrease in endometriosis-related symptoms after 2 months of treatment when compared to pretreatment values. Adverse effects with pine bark extract were mild and transient (99,100). At this time, there is insufficient evidence to support or refute the use of pine bark for dysmenorrhea or endometriosis (see Evidence Summary table at end of chapter).

## Lifestyle, Supplement and Mind-Body Therapies

### Diet

The goal in dietary changes is to decrease the production of arachidonic acid. This has been shown to be effective in adolescents (101). A cross-over design trial of 33 women showed that a low-fat, vegetarian diet increased serum sex-hormone-binding globulin concentration and reduced body weight, dysmenorrhea duration and intensity, and premenstrual symptom duration, and increase serum sex-hormone-binding globulin concentrations, suggesting this diet may affect estrogen activity (102). At this time, there is insufficient evidence to support or refute the use of diet for dysmenorrhea or endometriosis (see Evidence Summary table at end of chapter).

## Omega-3 Fatty Acids

In a Danish RCT, 78 women were randomized to 2.5 grams per day of fish oil or 2.5 grams per day of fish oil plus 7.5 micrograms per day of vitamin B12, or placebo. After 3 months, both fish oil plus vitamin B12 (p=0.01) and fish oil alone (p = 0.1) proved more effective than placebo. The benefits continued for up to 3 months after discontinuation of the combination therapy and up to 2 months for fish oil alone (103). A randomized crossover trial of 42 adolescents who received fish oil and vitamin had a significant reduction in dysmenorrhea (p<0.0004) (101). An observational study of 181 Danish women demonstrated that women who consumed low amounts of fish containing omega-3 fatty acids when compared to diets high in animal fats containing omega-6 fatty acids (n-3/n-6 ratio) correlated with more menstrual pain (p<0.001) (104). Overall, there is limited evidence to support a weak recommendation in favor of omega-2 fatty acids for the treatment of dysmenorrhea or endometriosis (see Evidence Summary table at end of chapter).

## Vitamin E

Two RCTs by the same investigator have shown that ingestion of as little as 400 international units of vitamin E beginning 2 days before the onset of menses has been shown to reduce dysmenorrhea (105,106). At this time, there is insufficient evidence to support or refute the use of vitamin E for dysmenorrhea or endometriosis (see Evidence Summary table at end of chapter).

## Vitamin B1 (Thiamine)

A Cochrane review cited one large RCT involving 500 women that showed vitamin B1 to be more effective than placebo in reducing pain (107). There is moderate evidence to support a weak recommendation in favor of the use of vitamin B1 for the treatment of dysmenorrhea or endometriosis (see Evidence Summary table at end of chapter).

## Vitamin B6

One small trial showed vitamin B6 was more effective than placebo or in combination with magnesium in controlling symptoms of dysmenorrhea (107). At this time, there is insufficient evidence to support or refute the use of vitamin B6 for the treatment of PMS (see Evidence Summary table at end of chapter).

## Magnesium

Three small trials comparing magnesium and placebo revealed that magnesium was more effective than placebo for pain relief and the need for additional medication was less (107). A Cochrane review of the literature found three trials comparing magnesium supplementation to placebo for treatment of PMS. The authors noted the trials were small "with poor measurement and reporting outcomes." They concluded that magnesium was more effective than placebo for pain associated with PMS (108). At this time, there is insufficient evidence to support or refute the use of magnesium for the treatment of PMS (see Evidence Summary table at end of chapter).

## Manipulative and Body-Based Therapies

High-frequency transcutaneous nerve stimulation (TENS) was found to be effective for treatment of primary dysmenorrhea in a Cochrane collaboration systematic review based on 8 RCTs (108). There is strong evidence to support a strong recommendation in favor of TENS for the treatment of dysmenorrhea (see Evidence Summary table at end of chapter).

### Osteopathic and Chiropractic Manipulation

There is insufficient evidence to support or refute the use of spinal manipulation as an effective treatment for dysmenorrhea (109) (see Evidence Summary table at end of chapter).

## Energy Systems

No studies available for review.

## Whole Medical Systems

### Chinese Herbal Medicine

Thirty-nine RCTs involving a total of 3475 women were included in a Cochrane review of Chinese herbal medicine (CHM) for primary dysmenorrhea. The review found evidence supporting the use of CHM for primary dysmenorrhea compared to conventional medicine such as NSAIDs, the oral contraceptive pill, acupuncture and heat compression; however, results were limited by the poor methodological quality of the included trials (110). Flower et al are currently underway with a review of CHM in relieving symptoms and improving fertility in endometriosis and comparing the effectiveness and the side effect profile of CHM with conventional bio-medicine in patients with endometriosis (111). Overall, there is moderate evidence to suggest that CHM may be effective for the treatment of dysmenorrhea, but results are compromised by poor study quality. Therefore, at this time there is insufficient evidence to support or refute the use of CHM for dysmenorrhea (see Evidence Summary table at end of chapter).

### Japanese Herbal Medicine

Toki-shakuyaku-san, a Japanese mixture of 6 herbs, when compared to placebo in a RCT of 50 women, was found to be more effective than placebo in treating primary dysmenorrhea after 6 months of therapy. Treatment also reduced the need for additional pain medication (112). At this time there is insufficient evidence to support or refute the use of this herbal medicine for dysmenorrhea (see Evidence Summary table at end of chapter).

### Acupuncture

Acupuncture increases production of endorphins, enkephalins and dynorphins. Numerous case series and at least one RCT showed acupuncture effective for dysmenorrhea (113-116). A Cochrane review of these studies cited insufficient evidence but offered that the RCT was methodologically sound and suggests benefits (117). There is limited evidence to suggest benefit, but the overall evidence base is insufficient to support or refute the use of acupuncture for dysmenorrhea at this time (see Evidence Summary table at end of chapter).

## Uterine Fibroids

Leiomyomas (fibroids) are smooth muscle cell tumors of the uterus. They are most likely of unicellular origin. Fibroids are the most common tumors of the female reproductive tract and the most likely reason for a woman to have a hysterectomy, accounting for more than 30% of these procedures. Women with enlarging fibroids generally present with bleeding irregularities and pain.

Depending upon the method of diagnosis used and the population studied, the prevalence of fibroids ranges from 5.4% to 77% (118,119). Day Baird et al performed ultrasonography on 1364 women chosen randomly from members of an urban health plan. All women were between 35 and 49 years of age. The estimated cumulative incidence of tumors by age 50 was > 80% for black women and nearly 70% for white women (120). Risk factors for developing fibroids include 40 years of age or older, African-American, family history of uterine fibroids, obesity and nulliparity (121).

It is important to understand the theorized etiology of fibroids when considering complementary treatment modalities: 1) familial chromosomal abnormalities (122); 2) systemic estrogen dominance (123); 3) systemic inflammation including a bacterial imbalance in the intestine resulting in gut-associated inflammatory mediators (124).

### Biologically Based Therapies

Herbs such as chaste tree berry, saw palmetto, lady's mantle, and yarrow flowers are theoretically considered for their anti-estrogenic properties. Other herbs such as milk thistle may be used to detoxify the liver thereby enhancing estrogen metabolism and elimination. Boswellia, turmeric and ginger are anti-inflammatory herbs. To date, none has been formerly studied for efficacy in prevention of fibroids or reduction of fibroid size (125).

## Lifestyle, Supplement and Mind-Body Therapies

### Diet

High-fiber diets decrease the de-conjugation of estrogen by gut flora therefore decreasing estrogen re-absorption and systemic estrogen levels. Anti-inflammatory dietary changes may help prevent or reduce fibroid size based upon the theory of fibroid development in response to systemic inflammation.

### Supplements

A number of supplements with immune-enhancing or antioxidant effect are considered. These may include coenzyme Q10, maitake mushrooms, zinc, selenium, beta-carotene, vitamins C and E and B complex (126). No formal studies have been published assessing independent supplement effect on uterine fibroids.

### Stress Reduction

Heightened cortisol levels increase dehydroepiandrosterone (DHEA) levels and contribute to a hyper-estrogenic state. Many mind-body therapies and lifestyle interventions reduce stress (e.g., regular exercise, meditation and journaling). Guided visualization has also been advocated. No formal studies have been published (125).

## Manipulative and Body-Based Therapies

Massage therapy and myofascial release may improve lymphatic drainage and blood flow to the pelvis, reducing pelvic stagnation as theorized by TCM (127). Massage therapy may also decrease stress levels. No studies are available for review as independent modalities. Please refer to "combination therapy" below.

## Energy Therapies

Energy therapies that decrease systemic inflammatory processes or enhance hepatic estrogen metabolism may theoretically be of help. No studies are currently available to support these modalities.

## Whole Medical Systems

### Traditional Chinese Medicine

An herbal Chinese medicine, Ban Zhi Lian (*Scutellaria barbata*), significantly reduced human myometrial and leiomyomal smooth muscle cell numbers in culture, arrested cell proliferation and induced apoptosis (128). In another study 120 women with uterine fibroids were treated with Kangfu Xiaozheng or

Guizhi Fuling. Patients in both treatment arms experienced an ultrasound-verified reduction in fibroid size and symptoms (129) (see Evidence Summary table at end of chapter).

## Combination Therapy

In 2002 Mehl-Madrona published a RCT pilot study of complementary medicine treatment for uterine fibroids. Seventy-four menstruating women aged 24-45 years with uterine fibroids received either experimental treatment or conventional treatment for up to 6 months. Experimental treatment consisted of weekly traditional Chinese medicine (acupuncture, herbal therapy and nutritional therapy), somatic therapy (myofascial release and deep-tissue massage), self-hypnosis and visualization training. Patients were evaluated on fibroid size, changes in symptoms and treatment satisfaction. Fibroids stopped growing or shrank in 22 patients of the treatment group compared with three in the control group (p<0.01). Cost of treatment (average $3800 USD) and patient satisfaction were significantly higher in the treatment group (127).

# Infertility

Infertility is defined as the inability of a couple to conceive after 12 months of regular, unprotected intercourse. It is a common condition affecting one of six couples during their reproductive lifetime (130). The etiology of infertility is frequently multifactorial. Body weight, physical activity levels and dietary factors such as certain fatty acids and dairy products may modulate ovulation thereby potentially influencing fertility (131,132). Infertility is also associated with endometriosis, luteal phase defects, elevated prolactin levels and oxidative stress, which have a negative impact on oocyte maturation, fertilization, embryo development and pregnancy. This has led to the use of antioxidants as a possible treatment for infertility. It has been well-documented that infertility causes stress (133-136) and that reduction of stress may improve fertility (137,138).

## Biologically Based Therapies
### Chasteberry

Chasteberry increases dopamine levels and therefore theoretically could enhance the fertility rates in those with elevated prolactin levels (139). One small study exists involving 96 women with secondary amenorrhea, luteal insufficiency or idiopathic infertility. Twice as many conceptions occurred in women with amenorrhea and luteal insufficiency who received an herbal mix primarily containing chasteberry compared to placebo (140). There is preliminary evidence suggesting that chasteberry might improve fertility among these women; however, it is premature to routinely recommend chasteberry (see Evidence Summary table at end of chapter). Overall, chasteberry is considered relatively safe and is well-tolerated.

### Fertility Blend

Fertility blend is a proprietary blend of chasteberry, green tea extracts, L-arginine, vitamins E, B6 and B12, folate, iron, magnesium, zinc and selenium. A pilot study randomly assigned 30 women ages 24-46 who were unsuccessful conceiving after 6 to 36 months of unprotected intercourse to receive three capsules per day of fertility blend versus placebo for three cycles. At 5 months 33% of the treatment arm had conceived versus 0% in the placebo arm (p<.01) (141). There is preliminary evidence suggesting this multi-nutrient and herbal formula may improve fertility; however, it is premature to routinely recommend this supplement formula for this indication (see Evidence Summary table at end of chapter). Overall, these nutrients and herbs at these doses appear relatively safe and are well-tolerated.

## Lifestyle, Supplement and Mind-Body Therapies

### Vitamin C

One large RCT studied 150 women with luteal phase defects on 750 mg/day of vitamin C versus placebo. After 6 months of treatment the fertility rate in the vitamin C group was significantly higher than in the placebo group (25% versus 11%; p=0.045). Serum progesterone levels were also increased in the treatment group, perhaps indicating improved oocyte maturation and fertilization (142). It is premature to routinely recommend vitamin C to infertile women (see Evidence Summary table at end of chapter).

### Other Supplements

There are too few trials involving vitamin E, vitamin A, vitamin B complex, selenium, magnesium, zinc, and manganese in infertility to warrant a recommendation.

### Behavioral Therapy

A study published in 1990 demonstrated that behavioral treatment approach might be efficacious in the treatment of the emotional aspects of infertility and may lead to increased conception rates. In this case series, the first 54 women completed a behavioral treatment program that included a relaxation response training. Investigators reported statistically significant reductions in anxiety, depression, and fatigue, as well as increases in energy levels. Thirty-four percent of these women became pregnant within 6 months of completing the program (143). These findings suggested a role for stress reduction in the long-term treatment of infertility. They further suggested that behavioral treatment should be considered for couples with infertility before or in conjunction with reproductive technologies, such as intrauterine insemination and gamete intra-fallopian transfer (144). Multiple mind-body techniques are used to decrease anxiety. Most techniques have not yet been adequately investigated for this indication. There is strong evidence suggesting that behavioral therapy can reduce anxiety and depression, which is quite high among couples with infertility. Research suggests that mind-body interventions may improve ovulation and uterine relaxation during in-vitro fertilization through improving mental health and well-being including anxiety, and stress. However, very limited research to date has rigorously evaluated these therapies and the precise mechanisms of action. Overall, given the safety of these treatments and the positive influence treatments have on psychological well-being for this population and the safety, we believe there is sufficient evidence to confer a weak clinical recommendation for these mind-body therapies.

## Hypnosis

Information in the scientific literature in reference to the role of hypnosis in the treatment of functional infertility is limited. However, case reports suggest that hypnotherapy may provide a beneficial effect through modification of attitude optimism, anxiety and mind-body interaction (145,146). The evidence is too limited to routinely recommend this treatment for this indication.

## Diet

In 2007 Chavarro et al published a large prospective study of 17,544 women without a history of infertility followed for 8 years as they tried to become pregnant or became pregnant. A dietary score based on factors previously related to lower ovulatory disorder infertility and other lifestyle information was prospectively related to the incidence of infertility. Those who consumed a "fertility diet" pattern (higher in monounsaturated rather than trans-fats, vegetable rather than animal protein, low glycemic carbohydrates, multivitamins and iron from plants and supplements) were at lower risk of ovulatory disorder infertility. The authors suggest that the majority of infertility cases due to ovulation disorders might be preventable through modifications of diet and lifestyle (147). There is insufficient evidence to routinely recommend this treatment for infertility; however, there is substantial evidence indicating this diet is beneficial for cardiovascular health and the prevention of many cancers.

## Manipulative and Body-Based Therapies

### Physical Therapy

The purpose of a study published by Wurn et al in 2004 assessed the effectiveness of site-specific manual soft-tissue therapy in treating infertility in women with a history indicating probable abdomino-pelvic adhesions. One case series evaluated 53 infertile, premenopausal patients who received a 10- to 20-hour series of site-specific manual physical therapy treatments. Seventeen patients hoped to achieve a natural pregnancy; 36 planned to undergo IVF within 15 months. Treatments were specifically designed to address biomechanical dysfunction of the pelvis, sacrum and coccyx and restricted soft tissue and visceral mobility due to adhesions affecting the pelvic organs and adjacent structures (148). Ten of 14 patients in the natural pregnancy group became pregnant within 1 year of therapy. Of the 25 IVF recipients clinical pregnancies were recorded in 22 of 33 embryo transfers. It is premature to routinely recommend this therapy to infertile women.

## Whole Medical Systems

### *Acupuncture*

Because acupuncture treatment affects beta-endorphin levels, which in turn affect GnRH secretion and the menstrual cycle, it is hypothesized that acupuncture may influence ovulation and fertility. Other potential mechanisms of action include acupuncture's effect on stress-modulating factors such as endorphins and cortisol, as well as its potential to increase blood flow to the uterus (149-151). A meta-analysis published in 2008 by Manheimer identified seven high-quality RCTs including 1366 women undergoing in vitro fertilization who received acupuncture within one day of undergoing embryo transfer (ET) vs control. Trials with "sham acupuncture" and "no treatment" control groups were included. The author concluded that acupuncture when administered within one day of ET statistically improved the following reproductive outcomes: clinical pregnancy (OR 1.65, 95% confidence interval 1.27-2.14; number needed to treat [NNT] was 10), ongoing pregnancy (OR 1.87, 1.40-2.49; NNT= 9) and live birth (OR 1.91, 1.39-2.64; NNT=9) (152). Of the most recent RCTs published, three were published in a single issue of *Fertility and Sterility* in 2006. Smith randomized 228 subjects all of whom received treatment on day 9 of stimulating injections, just prior to ET and following ET. Pregnancy rates were 31% in the acupuncture group compared with 23% in the sham acupuncture control group; ongoing pregnancies at 18 weeks were 28% and 18%, respectively. Although there was a clinically significant 50% increase in pregnancy rates related to acupuncture compared to active control, the differences between groups were not statistically significant. The authors concluded that smaller treatment effect could not be excluded (153).

To the contrary, Dieterle found luteal-phase acupuncture significantly more effective in reproductive outcomes than placebo acupuncture when measured in a RCT of 225 women receiving IVF/ICSI (154), as did Westergaard in a prospective RCT involving 186 women receiving IVF/ICSI in whom pregnancy rates were significantly higher when acupuncture was performed on day of ET vs. no acupuncture. Additionally, acupuncture performed 2 days following embryo transfer in conjuction with acupuncture on day of ET showed no additional benefit to reproductive outcomes (155). Paulus (156) randomized

160 women undergoing IVF or ICSI to acupuncture or usual care. Acupuncture was performed in 80 patients 25 minutes before and after embryo transfer. Only women with good-quality embryos were included in the study. After controlling confounding variables, clinical pregnancy rate for the acupuncture group was significantly higher than the control group (42.5% versus 26.3%). The authors concluded that further research is needed to demonstrate precisely how acupuncture causes physiologic changes in the uterus and reproductive system.

Overall, there is strong evidence to suggest acupuncture may improve pregnancy rates when performed just prior to and on the day of embryo transfer. There is conflicting evidence on whether performing acupuncture in the luteal and follicular phase improves pregnancy rates. The evidence base supports a weak recommendation in favor of acupuncture for improving the chances of having a live birth in the setting of in-vitro fertilization (see Evidence Summary table at end of chapter). Acupuncture is well-tolerated and appears relatively safe.

## Osteoporosis

Osteoporosis is defined as "a skeletal disease characterized by compromised bone strength predisposing a person to an increased risk of fracture" (157). The gold standard for diagnosis of osteoporosis is the bone mineral density (BMD) obtained by dual-energy x-ray absorptiometry (DEXA) of the lumbar spine or hip. The World Health Organization (WHO) proposed the following cutoffs in 1994 (158), which have since been validated by several prospective epidemiologic studies in osteoporosis: T score less than -2.5 (i.e., osteoporosis) is associated with an unacceptable risk of fractures; osteopenia (T score of -1.0 to -2.5) is associated with a moderately increased risk of fracture (159). Although the BMD is very useful in defining osteoporosis and fracture risk as a function of bone density, bone fragility is also a function of bone structure. Research, as such, generally looks at improvement of the BMD and/or change in fracture risk.

Forty-four million Americans suffer from osteoporosis or low bone mass (160). Fifty percent of women and 12% of men over the age of 49 will suffer an osteoporosis-related fracture in their lifetime (161). One and a half million osteoporotic fractures occur in the United States per year. Two thirds of these fractures are of the spine or hip (162). Such fractures can cause chronic pain, deformity, depression, disability and loss of independence. Fifty percent of those with hip fractures will never walk again without assistance, 25% will require long-term care and 24% will die in the year following a hip fracture (161). Fragility fractures result in direct cost of $18 billion annually (162). The purpose of addressing osteoporosis is to prevent such fractures.

A recent meta-analysis of 11 prospective observational studies with 2000 patients showed that BMD alone cannot identify those at risk for fracture; the combination of BMD and patient risk factors predicts osteoporotic fracture risk better than BMD or risk factor profile alone (163). The most important risk factor is a personal history of a prior fracture. Other important risk factors include advancing age, low body mass index (BMI), long-term steroid therapy, cigarette smoking, family history, excess alcohol intake and high levels of bone turnover markers. Fractures most often occur from falls that may stem from loss of balance, impaired vision, loss of sensation, loss of strength and mobility, use of excessive alcohol, certain medications or vitamin D deficiency (164). Therefore, the optimal integrative approach to reduce or prevent fractures includes measurement of BMD, eliciting risk factors, optimizing nutritional status and improving stability.

## Biologically Based Practices; Diet

### Soy Isoflavones

A recent case-series of 66 postmenopausal women received a daily standardized dose of soy isoflavones for 6 months. The study results noted a 2.2% increase in bone density of the lumbar spine but did not result in improved bone density of the hip (165). Xianglan et al reported a prospective cohort study of soy food consumption and risk of bone fracture among 24,403 Chinese postmenopausal women. During a mean follow-up of 4 1/2 years, 1770 new fractures of the wrist (17.6%), arm (15.1%), vertebrae (14.9%), ankle (13.1%), rib (7%) and hip (3.3%) were identified. After adjustment for total caloric intake and age, higher soy protein intake was significantly associated with lower risk of any type of fracture (p<0.001); the difference was more pronounced among women in early menopause. This inverse association was independent of major risk factors, including intake of calcium, fruits, vegetables and non-soy protein. Similar associations were found for intake of soy isoflavones (p<0.001) (166). There is very limited evidence to suggest that soy isoflavones may possibly reduce fractures. It is premature to routinely recommend soy isoflavones as a dietary supplement to prevent osteoporosis or fractures; however, there is substantial evidence to recommend substituting soy-based protein for meat-based protein to improve cardiovascular health (see Evidence Summary table at end of chapter).

## Mind-Body Therapies and Other Biologically Based Practices

### Exercise

The scientific literature supports a positive relationship between physical activity, physical fitness, muscle strength and BMD at the lumbar spine and femoral neck (167). A Cochrane Collaboration report reviewed 18 RCTs. Aerobics, weight bearing and resistance exercises were all effective on the BMD of the spine of postmenopausal women. There is insufficient evidence to determine if exercise prevents or treats osteoporosis; there is moderate evidence to support weight-bearing and strengthening exercises to prevent falls and limited evidence that it increases BMD.

## Tai Chi

Tai Chi chuan and its efficacy on treatment or prevention of osteoporosis have met with mixed results. Two meta-analyses of RCTs published in 2001 and 2004 were inconclusive (168,169). A more recent RCT published in 2007 by Woo et al evaluated 90 men and 90 women aged 65-74 randomized to Tai Chi or resistance exercise three times a week for 12 months. Women in both treatment groups had less BMD loss compared to controls (normal activity). No difference was seen in the male participants. Unlike prior studies, the treatment groups observed no difference in balance, flexibility or number of falls (170). Another prospective RCT reported by Chan cited a diminished rate of distal tibia, proximal femur and lumbar spine BMD of 67 women who participated in Tai Chi exercise (45 minutes per day, 5 days per week) for 12 months vs 65 sedentary controls (p<0.01) (171). A recent systematic review of the scientific evidence for Tai Chi as an intervention to reduce rate of bone loss in postmenopausal women was published in 2007 (172). The author reviewed 2 RCTs, 2 cohort studies and 2 cross-sectional studies and found reductions in BMD decline among post-menopausal women and higher BMD than age-matched sedentary controls. There is moderate evidence to suggest that Tai Chi may be an effective, safe and practical intervention for maintaining BMD in postmenopausal women. These findings are supported by additional evidence suggesting that Tai Chi improves fracture risk factors including fall frequency, and musculoskeletal strength. A subsequent review identified 5 RCTS and 2 controlled trials, in which 1 RCT found Tai Chi was associated with less BMD decline and 2 others showed no difference in BMD status when comparing Tai Chi to active controls (calcium supplementation or exercise) (173). Tai Chi is a safe therapy that is often practiced in a group setting and in natural environments, making it a particularly suitable therapy for the elderly.

Overall, given the moderate evidence that suggests Tai Chi may be effective in maintaining BMD in postmenopausal women, combined with the moderate evidence supporting its social, mental health, and physical benefits including fall frequency reduction and musculoskeletal strength improvement (174,175), there is sufficient evidence to support a weak recommendation of Tai Chi for people with or at risk for osteoporosis (see Evidence Summary table at end of chapter).

## Acid-Base Balanced Diet

A link between higher protein consumption and fracture risk has been demonstrated (176). It is well known that increasing dietary protein results in elevated urinary calcium excretion (177). The source of the serum calcium is yet to be deciphered; whether it results from increased intestinal calcium absorption or increased bone resorption and consequent mobilization and renal excretion of calcium. It has been shown that increased dietary protein, especially of animal sources, increases endogenous acid production (178,179). Elevated acidity has been shown to inhibit osteoblasts and stimulate osteoclasts Thus, bone acts as a buffer to decreased pH acting as an alkali reservoir with consequent mobilization of calcium (180,181). Common dietary sources that contribute to the endogenous acid load are those that contain sulfur amino acids including animal proteins, cheese, peanuts, nuts, legumes and grains (182-184). Reductions in animal protein consumption and increases in vegetable protein may decrease bone resorption, improve bone structure and favorably affect calcium balance (185-187). Similarly, the Dietary Approaches to Stopping Hypertension (DASH) intervention trial demonstrated a secondary finding that diets rich in fruits and vegetables significantly reduce bone turnover regardless of sodium intake. In one trial, 459 subjects were randomized to 3 weeks of a control diet, a diet rich in fruits and vegetables, or a diet with fruits, vegetables and low-fat dairy. An increase in fruits and vegetables from 3.6 to 9.5 servings daily resulted in a decrease of urinary calcium excretion from 157 mg/day to 110 mg/day (179). The Study of Osteoporotic Fractures (187) found that women with a higher ratio of animal-to-vegetable protein intake had increased bone loss at the femoral neck and a 4-fold increase in hip fracture. These data suggest that clinical trials evaluating the effect of diets rich in vegetable-based proteins and alkali-forming precursors on the risk of fracture are warranted. At this time, there is insufficient evidence to support or refute the role of acid-base balance diet on bone health (see Evidence Summary table at end of chapter) (188).

## Magnesium

Magnesium suppresses parathyroid hormone and therefore decreases calcium resorption from bone. Animal studies suggest the magnesium deficiency may result in decreased bone mineral density (189). Observational studies of elderly suggest that those whose diets have higher amounts of magnesium have higher bone mineral densities (190); however, there are no RCTs in humans. While magnesium supplementation is relatively safe and inexpensive, there is insufficient evidence to recommend routine magnesium supplementation for the prevention of osteoporosis at this time.

## Calcium

Calcium is the principal mineral of bone and decreased bone mineralization is due to net loss of calcium from bone. A review of 47 clinical, longitudinal, retrospective and cross-sectional studies documented that neither increased consumption of dairy products nor total dietary calcium consumption by children and young adults has shown increase in BMD or reduced fracture rate in childhood or later in life (191,192). Additionally, the scientific literature remains undecided regarding the benefits of calcium supplementation to prevent or treat postmenopausal osteoporosis. The Cochrane Collaborative reviewed fifteen trials including 1806 postmenopausal women randomized to calcium supplementation or usual calcium intake in the diet. They did not report serum vitamin D levels nor did they report calcium plus vitamin D supplementation.

This is an important caveat because vitamin D facilitates absorption of calcium. Calcium supplementation alone suggested a "small positive effect on bone density. The data show a trend toward reduction in vertebral fractures, but it is unclear if calcium reduces the incidence of non-vertebral fractures" (193). Tang recently published a systematic review of 29 RCTs including 63,897 subjects 50 years or older assessing calcium or calcium plus vitamin D supplementation and their effects on osteoporotic fracture risk. Analysis of the 23 trials reporting BMD as an outcome found improvement in hip BMD by 0.54% (0.35-0.73; p<0.0001) and lumbar spine BMD by 1.19% (0.76-1.61%; p<0.0001) with treatment. Seventeen trials reported fracture outcome where treatment was associated with a 12% risk reduction in osteoporotic fractures at all sites (OR 0.88, 95% CI 0.83-0.95; p=0.0004). Treatment results were better if calcium supplementation was at least 1200 mg/day and vitamin D at least 800 IU/day (194). Calcium is relatively safe with infrequent side-effects such as dyspepsia and constipation. Overall, there is moderate evidence to support a strong recommendation for using 1200 mg calcium daily, particularly in combination with 800 IU daily vitamin D, to reduce loss of BMD and fracture risk (see Evidence Summary table at end of chapter).

## Vitamin D

Vitamin D is essential for the growth and maintenance of bone growth throughout life; it regulates calcium absorption in the gut and renal tubular calcium reabsorption and up-regulates osteoblast production of osteocalcin. Vitamin D is absorbed through the diet or synthesized in the skin from 7-dihydrocholesterol in response to ultraviolet B light (164). Vitamin D deficiency is prevalent throughout the world. More than 50% of postmenopausal women receiving treatment for osteoporosis are vitamin D deficient (195). The Cochrane Collaboration reported that vitamin D alone showed no statistically significant effect on hip fracture, vertebral fracture or any new fracture. Vitamin D with calcium marginally reduced hip fractures and other non-vertebral fractures. There was no evidence of effect of vitamin D with calcium on vertebral fractures. The effect appeared to be restricted to those living in institutional care (196). Since this review was published, a meta-analysis of five clinical trials for hip fracture and seven clinical trials for non-vertebral fractures comparing vitamin D supplementation to calcium supplementation or placebo. The authors reported that 700 to 800 IU/day of vitamin D reduced hip fractures by 26% (OR 0.74; 95% CI, 0.61-0.88) and non-vertebral fractures by 23% (OR 0.77; 95% CI, 0.68-0.87) (197). Vitamin D supplementation also appears to improve muscular strength and decrease fall rates and resultant hip fractures in the elderly (198). Side-effects of vitamin D are rare but include hypercalciuria, hypercalcemia and kidney stone formation. Overall, vitamin D is relatively safe and there is moderate evidence to support a weak recommendation in favor of using vitamin D 800 IU daily to reduce risk for hip and non-vertebral fractures (see Evidence Summary table at end of chapter).

## Vitamin C

Vitamin C plays an essential role in collagen synthesis. Vitamin C deficiency can lead to bone deformation such as that seen with scurvy. In the Postmenopausal Estrogen/Progestin Interventions (PEPI) cohort study, there was a positive association of vitamin C with BMD in postmenopausal women with dietary calcium intakes of at least 500 mg (199). There is very limited evidence to suggest a possible association between vitamin C and BMD; however, there is insufficient evidence to routinely recommend vitamin C for the prevention of osteoporosis (see Evidence Summary table at end of chapter).

## Vitamin K

Vitamin K1 (phylloquinone, phytonadione, primarily found in green vegetables, soy and canola oil) and Vitamin K2 (menaquinone, found in meat and fermented products such as cheese) intake and bone status have been studied in multiple epidemiologic and intervention studies. The studies suggest that vitamin K deficiency results in undercarboxylation of osteocalcin, resulting in decreased BMD and increased fracture risk (200). In the Nurses' Health Study cohort of 72,327 women, vitamin K intake, as assessed by food-frequency questionnaires, was inversely related to hip fracture risk. The adjusted relative risk (RR = 0.70; 95%, CI 0.53-0.93) of hip fractures was 30% less in women who consumed >109 micrograms of vitamin K compared to those who consumed less (201). Numerous studies have shown a relationship between undercarboxylation of osteocalcin and decreased BMD and increased hip fracture. In a randomized, open-label study of 241 Japanese postmenopausal osteoporotic women the treatment group received 45 mg of menaquinone (vitamin K2) daily for 2 years. The treatment group had a significantly lower undercarboxylated osteocalcin serum level (p<0.0001). In addition, the fracture occurrence of the treatment group was significantly less than in the control group (p = 0.0273) (202). Another study conducted in the Netherlands, randomized 325 postmenopausal women to 3 years of 45 mg of menaquinone (vitamin K2) or placebo. Investigators report no differences in bone mineral density; however, statistically significant increases in femoral neck width and bone mineral content were noted. Furthermore, bone strength decreased significantly in the placebo arm and remained unchanged in the active intervention group at 3 years. Investigators concluded that Vitamin K2 may improve femoral neck bone strength through its effects on femoral neck width and bone mineral content, and likely has little effect on bone mineral density (203).

Of note, vitamin K may disrupt warfarin anticoagulation. There is limited evidence to support a weak recommendation favoring getting adequate vitamin K through foods or potentially as a dietary supplement as an effective means to reducing risk of hip fracture (see Evidence Summary table at end of chapter).

## Ipriflavone

Ipriflavone is a synthetic isoflavone derived from soy. In a large, multi-center RCT published in 2001, 473 patients were randomly assigned to 3 years of 200 mg 3 times per day and calcium 500 mg daily (n=234) or placebo and calcium 500 mg daily (n=240). The authors found ipriflavone supplementation did not prevent bone loss, and 13% of women in the intervention group developed sub-clinical lymphocytopenia (204). There is moderate evidence to suggest that ipriflavone is not an effective treatment for osteoporosis and may cause harm. Based on the lack of benefit and the existence of potential risk, we recommend against using this treatment for this indication (see Evidence Summary table at end of chapter).

## DHEA

Serum levels of DHEA and DHEAs correlate positively with BMD. Suboptimal levels of DHEAs are associated with decreased BMD (205). In a double-blinded RCT, 70 women and 70 men aged 60-88 years with low serum DHEAs levels were randomized to either 50 mg per day of DHEA versus placebo for 12 months. The authors concluded that DHEA replacement therapy for 1 year improved hip BMD in older adults and spine BMD in older women (206). Excessive levels of DHEA can have an androgenic effect such as acne, hirsutism and voice changes. There is limited evidence to suggest that DHEA may possibly be effective for osteoporosis; however, long-term treatment is accompanied by the theoretical risk of promoting hormone-dependent cancers (207,208). At this time, given there is only limited evidence available to suggest benefit and there is the theoretical potential of promoting prostate or breast cancer among select populations, it is premature to recommend DHEA for the prevention of osteoporosis at this time (see Evidence Summary table at end of chapter).

## Omega-3 Fatty Acids

Imbalanced consumption of omega-6 to omega-3 fatty acids is associated with lower bone mineral density at the hip in men and women (209). No RCTs or observational studies have been published; data are insufficient to support or refute its use (210).

## Manipulative and Body-Based Therapies

### Physical Therapy

Data are limited regarding physical therapy and prevention or treatment of osteoporosis. However, the literature does support physical therapy intervention for the elderly with lower-extremity impairments and balance problems to decrease fall risk (211). There is limited evidence to support physical therapy to decrease fall risk among the elderly with lower-extremity impairment and gait instability; however, there is insufficient evidence to support or refute its use for the treatment of osteoporosis specifically (see Evidence Summary table at end of chapter).

## Energy Systems

No studies found.

## Whole Medical Systems

### Acupuncture

An abstract printed in English of an article published in Chinese by Xu et al compared 96 patients randomized to acupuncture plus acupoint sticking of Migudan with a control group treated with Gaitianli (TCM). Acupuncture plus acupoint relieved the cumulative score of bone pain in patients with osteoporosis (p<0.01, 95% CI [4.05-4.31]); this combination also increased BMD of the lumbar spine compared with the control group (p<0.05, 95% CI [0.029-0.073 g/cm$^2$]) and the femoral neck BMD (p<0.05, 95% CI [0.013-0.047 g/cm$^2$]) (212). There is very limited evidence to suggest that acupuncture might possibly improve BMD; however, data are insufficient to support or refute acupuncture for osteoporosis at this time (see Evidence Summary table at end of chapter).

# Incontinence

The International Continence Society defines urinary incontinence (UI) as the involuntary loss of urine, which is objectively demonstrable, with such a degree of severity that it is a social or hygienic problem (213). Stress urinary incontinence (SUI) is the involuntary loss of urine in response to an increase of intra-abdominal pressure generally due to urethral hypermobility and/or intrinsic urethral sphincter deficiency. Urge incontinence is defined as involuntary loss of urine preceded by a strong urge to void, whether or not the bladder is full. It is a symptom of overactive bladder and is frequently referred to as detrusor instability or detrusor hyperreflexia. To avoid confusion, urge incontinence is referred to here as detrusor instability (DI).

UI is an under-diagnosed and underreported condition with significant economic and psychosocial effects on society. The 2007 National Institutes of Health State-of-the-Science Conference Statement reports that an estimated 20 million women in the United States currently have or have a history of UI. The prevalence of UI in women living in nursing homes ranges from 60%-78%. The prevalence of UI in community-dwelling women ranges from 19% at less than 45 years of age to 29% in ages over 80 (214). Despite the high prevalence, fewer than half of community-dwelling persons with UI consult physicians about the problem (215,216). The direct costs associated with treating UI of women in the United States approached $12.43 billion in 2001 (217).

Risk factors are important to understand because alteration of lifestyle may have a significant impact on the presence or severity of UI. Risk factors related to lifestyle include obesity, limited physical activity, depression, stroke, diabetes mellitus, constipation and smoking. Other risk factors include female sex, parity, advancing age, caucasian race, family history of incontinence, other neurologic disorders and history of gynecologic surgery (214).

## Biologically Based Practices

### Cranberry (*Vaccinium macrocarpon*) Juice

Cranberry has been used for the treatment of urinary tract infection (UTI), which is a frequent comorbidity among women with UI. Furthermore, women with UTIs may experience transient UI while they have a UTI (218). A Cochrane Review of ten studies (five cross-over, five parallel groups) involving 1049 people cites evidence that cranberry-containing products may decrease the number of UTIs over a 12-month period when compared with placebo (RR 0.65, 95% CI 0.46-0.90), particularly for women with recurrent UTIs (219). In general, cranberry is well-tolerated and is relatively safe. Side effects are infrequent and include diarrhea and hypersensitivity. Drug interaction reports are conflicting, with a hypothetical concern for interaction with cytochrome P450 2C9 substrates, and warfarin (220). In one small, double-blind, crossover, RCT of 7 patients on a stable dose of warfarin who consumed 250 mL of cranberry juice for 1 week and placebo for 1 week with a washout period of 7 days, the prothrombin time/INR did not significantly change with treatment (221). Overall, there is no research to make a recommendation on the utility of cranberry for the prevention or improvement of UI; however, there is moderate evidence to support a weak recommendation of cranberry for the prevention of UTIs among people with recurrent UTIs, which includes this population.

### Saw Palmetto (*Serenoa repens*)

Lay literature suggests that saw palmetto may be effective in men and women for urinary conditions. According to a Cochrane Review, saw palmetto is effective for benign prostatic hypertrophy in men (222), but no research has been published on female incontinence and therefore there is insufficient evidence to support or refute using saw palmetto for urinary incontinence (223).

## Mind-Body Medicine and Lifestyle Therapies

### Dietary Changes

Conventional practice suggests that women with UI may benefit from avoiding the following foods, which are considered bladder irritants: citrus fruits, tomatoes, spiced foods, caffeine, chocolate and aspartame (224,225). Such dietary changes are of particular benefit in patients with an underlying UI etiology of interstitial cystitis (IC) (221). While this treatment approach is without risk or harm, there are no RCTs or observational studies to support its recommendation for UI without IC at this time (see Evidence Summary table at end of chapter).

### Smoking Cessation

Two case-controlled studies found cigarette smoking as a risk factor for UI (226,227). UI caused by smoking may be due to the dynamic effects of a chronic cough or interference with collagen synthesis in the bladder (228). Furthermore, it is believed chronic and frequent coughing may lead to damage of urethral and vaginal supports and cause perineal nerve damage (229,230). There is very limited data to suggest that smoking cessation may improve UI. At this time, there is insufficient evidence to support or refute its use for this indication (see Evidence Summary table at end of chapter).

### Weight Loss

In the Heart and Estrogen/Progestin Replacement Study (HERS) large cohort study, Brown et al found BMI to be a risk factor for SUI, and in patients BMI with combined DI and SUI (231). In the National Overactive Bladder Evaluation (NOBLE) study, DI was 2.2 times more prevalent in women with a BMI of 30 or more than in those with a BMI under 24 (232). However, the effect of weight loss on UI has not been adequately studied (214). There are limited data to suggest obesity is associated with increased risk for UI; while there is strong evidence for the effectiveness of weight loss for improving survival across numerous health parameters among people with obesity, at this time data are insufficient to support or refute recommending weight loss for UI (see Evidence Summary table at end of chapter).

### Behavioral Training

In a systematic review including 15 RCTs evaluating conservative therapies (such as bladder retraining, pelvic floor muscle exercises, with or without biofeedback and/or electrical stimulation) for DI, there was weak evidence to suggest that bladder (re)training is more effective than no treatment and that bladder (re)training is better than drug therapy. Given the wide array of retraining techniques available, further research is required to determine which treatments are most effective. A 2000 Cochrane Review identified eight trials totaling 858 participants comparing bladder training to no training (3 trials, n=172), in conjunction with other treatments (2 trials [n=331, bladder training + anticholinergic medication vs. anticholinergic alone] and 1 trial [n=125, pelvic floor muscle training + biofeedback + bladder training vs. pelvic floor muscle training + biofeedback alone]) or bladder training compared to other treatments (3 trials, [n=159 bladder training vs. prescription drug] and 2 trials [n=164 bladder training vs. pelvic floor muscle therapy + biofeedback]). They concluded there was limited evidence to suggest that bladder training may be helpful for the treatment of UI. However, there was insufficient evidence to evaluate its effectiveness compared with other treatments (233). The same conclusion was reached of a Cochrane Review of habit retraining for the management of UI in adults (234). Overall, there is moderate evidence to support a weak recommendation for bladder retraining for the treatment of UI in adults (see Evidence Summary table at end of chapter).

## Biofeedback

In 1999 a meta-analysis of three RCTs (n=215) of pelvic floor muscle exercises with or without biofeedback was done. Although not statistically significant, there was a trend in favor of pelvic floor muscle exercises with biofeedback as more effective than pelvic floor muscle exercises alone. The authors concluded that the lack of statistical significance may be attributable to insufficient number of participants in the trials as well as the variability of SUI "cure" and suggested that larger trials are warranted (235). In 2002 Burgio, et al randomized 222 community-dwelling women with DI to behavioral training with biofeedback, behavioral training without biofeedback or a control group who received written instructions only. Though the treatment group participants were subjectively more satisfied with their progress than the control group, the active treatments were no better than the control intervention (236). The National Institutes of Health State-of-the-Science Conference Statement cites insufficient research exists on the sustained long-term benefits of biofeedback on preventing fecal or urinary incontinence (214). There is insufficient evidence on the effectiveness of biofeedback for UI and therefore it is premature to make a recommendation at this time (see Evidence Summary table at end of chapter).

## Hypnotherapy

In 1982 Freeman published a non-randomized cross-over study of 63 women with DI. After a month control period, 50 subjects received 12 sessions of hypnosis. Twenty-nine patients reported being symptom free, 14 considered themselves "improved" and seven patients showed no change in symptoms. Cystometry was completed at three and six months after completion of treatment in 44 participants (others declined). Cystometric results suggested an improvement in bladder capacity, volume to first contraction and a decrease in bladder contractile strength (237). At this time, there is insufficient evidence to support or refute the effect of hypnotherapy for UI (see Evidence Summary table at end of chapter).

Prompted voiding is a behavioral therapy used mainly in North American nursing homes; its aim is to use verbal prompts and positive reinforcement to improve continence in the elderly. A Cochrane Review identified nine trials (n=674) most of whom were elderly women. The authors cite limited evidence that suggested prompted voiding may decrease the number of incontinent episodes and improve self-initiated voiding in elderly with UI in the short term. No conclusions could be reached about the long term effects (238).

## Pessary

A Cochrane Review identified six trials (n=286) in the use of mechanical devices (including pesarries) to manage UI in females. Two trials compared mechanical device to no intervention; findings were inconclusive. Five trials compared one mechanical device to another. The heterogeneity of the studies prohibited quantitative synthesis of the data (239). Consequently, there is insufficient evidence to support or refute the effect of pessaries for UI (see Evidence Summary table at end of chapter).

## Manipulative and Body-Based Therapies

### Pelvic Floor Muscle Training

In 1948 Kegel reported a cure rate of 84% after training of the pelvic floor muscles for women with various types of incontinence (240). In 1999 Bo et al published a single blind, RCT of pelvic floor exercises, electrical stimulation, vaginal cones and no treatment in management of SUI in 122 women. Improvement was seen after all forms of treatment; however, only in the pelvic floor exercise group was the improvement significant when compared to the control group (p<0.01) (241). A 2006 Cochrane Review identified 13 trials involving 714 women and concluded that PFMT should be included as first-line therapy for women with SUI and DI. The treatment effect might be greater in younger women (in their 40's and 50's) with SUI, who participate in supervised PFMT for at least three months (242). There is strong evidence to support PFMT as effective therapy for SUI and DI (see Evidence Summary table at end of chapter).

### Pelvic Floor Electrical Stimulation

This technique involves stimulation of the pudendal nerve with electrodes placed in the vagina or anus. In a 1995 prospective, multicenter, randomized, double blind, placebo controlled trial involving 52 women lasting 15 weeks reported significant improvements in urinary leakage compared with controls (who used sham devices). Significant improvement was seen in vaginal muscle strength (p=0.02), decrease of incontinent episodes (weekly [p=0.009] and daily [p=0.04]) and pad testing (p=0.005) in the treatment group. Subjective criteria was significantly improved, as well, in the treatment group (243). In 1999 Yasuda published a critical evaluation of electro-stimulation for management of female UI. The author concluded that electro-stimulation has been verified in a RCT; however, its superiority over other conservative treatments, such as pelvic floor exercise, has not been confirmed (244). In 2003 Goode et al published a RCT stating that PFES did not increase effectiveness of a comprehensive behavioral program for women with SUI (245). In summary, there is moderate evidence to suggest that PFES appears effective when compared to sham treatment. There is limited evidence to suggest that PFES does not provide additional benefit when compared to a comprehensive behavioral SUI program. In summary, there is evidence to support a weak recommendation for PFES but it is premature to determine whether PFES provides additional benefit from gains made in a comprehensive behavioral program.

## Weighted Vaginal Cones

In 2005 a Cochrane Review that identified 16 RCTs involving 1246 women. Five hundred sixty-six subjects received weighted vaginal cones for treatment. Investigators reported evidence suggesting WVC was superior to no treatment for SUI (RR for failure to cure incontinence 0.74, 95% CI, 0.59-.93), and may be of similar effectiveness to pelvic floor muscle training (RR 1.09, 95% CI 0.86-1.38) and electro-stimulation (RR 1, 95% CI 0.89-1.13). However, due to the poor methodological quality of these trials. Larger and higher quality studies are needed (246).

## Energy Medicine

No studies available.

## Whole Medical Systems

### Acupuncture

A pilot case series conducted in Sweden by Bergstrom investigated manual acupuncture and its influence on DI or DI plus SUI among 15 elderly women who failed standard conventional therapy. Subjective and objective results were significantly improved and continued 3 months thereafter in 12 of 15 participants (247). In 2005 Emmons randomized 85 women with DI to acupuncture treatment for overactive bladder or to a placebo acupuncture designed for relaxation. The women who received acupuncture for overactive bladder reported fewer incontinence and urinary urgency episodes, improved voiding frequency, and bladder capacity. However, acupuncture for overactive bladder was no different than sham acupuncture in improving incontinent episodes (59% vs. 40%). The authors suggest that larger clinical trials that properly powered to detect differences in incontinent episodes are warranted (248). A 2005 Cochrane Review identified three small RCT trials among patients with UI secondary to a cerebral vascular accident and found statistically significant improvements in UI (RR 0.44; 95 CI 0.23-0.86); however, the quality of these studies was poor (249). A Cochrane Review protocol is currently underway evaluating acupuncture among adults with UI and without neurological diseases (250). Overall, there is limited evidence to support a weak recommendation for acupuncture for people suffering UI secondary to a CVA. There is insufficient evidence to make a recommendation regarding acupuncture for people with UI and without neurological disease (see Evidence Summary table at end of chapter).

---

**Box 11-1  Common Premenstrual Symptoms***

**Behavioral:** fatigue, insomnia, dizziness, changes in sexual interest, food cravings, overeating, social isolation

**Psychological:** irritability, anger, depressed mood, crying, tearfulness, anxiety, tension, mood swings, lack of concentration, confusion, forgetfulness, restlessness, loneliness, decreased self-esteem, tension, forgetfulness, restlessness, loneliness, decreased self-esteem, tension

**Physical:** headaches, breast tenderness, back pain, abdominal pain, bloating, weight gain, swelling of extremities, water retention, nausea and joint pain, acne, constipation, diarrhea, carbohydrate cravings

*See References 39-4

---

Evidence Summary of CAM Treatments in Women's Health

| Clinical Indication | Category | Specific Therapy | Dose | Outcome | Confidence of Estimate on Effectiveness | Magnitude of Effect* | Safety† | Clinical Recommendation‡ | Comments |
|---|---|---|---|---|---|---|---|---|---|
| Hot flashes | Biologically based therapies | Soy isoflavones | — | Hot flashes | Grade B | None | Single thumb up | Weak against | — |
| Hot flashes | Biologically based therapies | Red clover | — | Hot flashes | Grade B | No effect | Double thumbs up | Weak against | — |
| Hot flashes | Biologically based therapies | Black cohosh | — | Hot flashes | Grade C | Small effect | Single thumbs up | Weak in favor | Case reports idiopathic fulminant liver failure |
| Hot flashes | Lifestyle therapy | Exercise | — | Hot flashes | Grade C | Unclear | Double thumbs up | No recommendation | — |
| Hot flashes | Mind-Body | Paced Breath work | — | Hot flashes | Grade B | Moderate | Double thumbs up | Weak in favor | — |
| Hot flashes | Manipulative based therapies | Osteopathic manipulation | — | Hot flashes | Grade C | No effect | Double thumbs up | No recommendation | — |
| Hot flashes | Energy therapies | Reflexology | — | Hot flashes | Grade C | No effect | Double thumbs up | No recommendations | — |
| Hot flashes | Energy therapies | Magnetic devices | — | Hot flashes | Grade C | No effect | Double thumbs up | No recommendations | — |
| Hot flashes | Whole medical systems | Acupuncture | 6 to 14 sessions over 8 to 12 weeks | Hot flashes | Grade C | No effect | Double thumbs up | No recommendation | — |

(continued)

**Evidence Summary of CAM Treatments in Women's Health (continued)**

| Clinical Indication | Category | Specific Therapy | Dose | Outcome | Confidence of Estimate on Effectiveness | Magnitude of Effect* | Safety† | Clinical Recommendation‡ | Comments |
|---|---|---|---|---|---|---|---|---|---|
| Hot flashes | Whole medical systems | Traditional Chinese medicine herbs | — | Decreases hot flashes | Grade C | Unclear | Single thumbs up | No recommendation | — |
| PMS | Biologically based therapies | Chaste tree berry (Vitex agnus castus) | 175-225 mg/d (dry powder) 0.5% agnuside content | Decrease PMS symptoms | Grade C | Small | Single thumb up | Weak in favor | — |
| PMS | Biologically based therapies | Evening primrose oil | Varying | Symptoms | Grade B | None | No recommendation | Weak against | — |
| PMS | Energy medicine | Full spectrum light therapy | — | Symptoms | Grade B | Small | Double thumbs up | Weak in favor | — |
| PMS | Lifestyle | High fiber, low fat | — | Symptoms | Grade D | Moderate | Double thumbs up | Weak in favor | — |
| PMS | Biologically based therapies | Calcium | 1200 mg daily | Symptoms | Grade B | Moderate | Single thumbs up | Weak in favor | — |
| PMS | Biologically based therapies | Vitamin B6 | 50 mg | Symptoms | Grade B | Moderate | Single thumbs up | Weak in favor | — |
| PMS | Whole medical system | Acupuncture | Varying | Symptoms | Grade C | Small | Single thubms up | Weak in favor | — |

| Condition | Therapy category | Treatment | Dose | Indication | Grade | | | | |
|---|---|---|---|---|---|---|---|---|---|
| Dysmenorrhea | Biologically based therapies | Cramp bark (Viburnum opulus) | Unclear | Pain | Grade D | Unclear | No recommendation | No recommendation | — |
| Dysmenorrhea/endometriosis | Biologically based therapies | Pine bark (Pinus maritime) | Unclear | — | Grade D | Unclear | Double thumbs up | No recommendation | — |
| Dysmenorrhea | Lifestyle therapy | Low-fat, vegetarian diet | NA | Dysmenorrheal duration and intensity, PMS duration and serum sex-hormone binding globulin | Grade C | Small | Double thumbs up | No recommendation | — |
| Dysmenorrhea | Biologically based therapies | Omega-3 fatty acids | 2.5 grams fish oil per day | Dysmenorrhea | Grade C | Small | Double thumbs up | Weak in favor | — |
| Dysmenorrhea | Biologically based therapies | Vitamin E | 400 IU beginning 2 days the onset of menses | Dysmenorrhea | Grade C | Small | Double thumbs up | No recommendation | — |
| Dysmenorrhea | Biologically based therapies | Vitamin B1 | 100 mg | Dysmenorrhea | Grade B | Small | Double thumbs up | Weak in favor | — |

*(continued)*

**Evidence Summary of CAM Treatments in Women's Health (continued)**

| Clinical Indication | Category | Specific Therapy | Dose | Outcome | Confidence of Estimate on Effectiveness | Magnitude of Effect* | Safety† | Clinical Recommendation‡ | Comments |
|---|---|---|---|---|---|---|---|---|---|
| Dys-menorrhea | Biologically based therapies | Vitamin B6 | 25 mg bid | Dys-menorrhea | Grade D | Small | Single thumb up | No recommendation | — |
| Dys-menorrhea | Body-based therapy | Transcutaneous nerve stimulation | Varying regimens | Dys-menorrhea | Grade A | Moderate | Single thumb up | Strong recommendation | — |
| Dys-menorrhea | Manipulative therapy | Osteopathic and chiropractic manipulation | Varying regimens | Dys-menorrhea | Grade D | Unclear | Single thumb up | No recommendation | — |
| Dys-menorrhea | Whole medical systems | Chinese herbal medicine | Varying formulas | Dys-menorrhea | Grade C | Moderate | Unclear | No recommendation | Dozens of RCTs have been conducted showing moderate to large effects; however, study quality is poor. |
| Dys-menorrhea | Whole medical systems | Tokishaku-yakusan (6 herb combination) | Formula | Primary dysmenorrhea | Grade C | Small | Single thumb up | No recommendation | — |

| | | | | | | | | |
|---|---|---|---|---|---|---|---|---|
| Dys-menorrhea | Whole medical systems | Acupuncture | Varying regimens | Decreased dysmenorrhea | Grade C | Moderate | Single thumb up | No recommendation |
| Fibroids | Biologically based therapies | "Anti-estrogenic" herbs: Chaste tree berry, saw palmetto, lady's mantle, yarrow flowers | Varying doses | Decrease fibroid size | Grade D | Unclear | Single thumb up | No recommendation |
| Fibroids | Biologically based therapies | "Anti-inflammatory" herbs: Boswellia, turmeric, ginger | Varying doses | Decrease fibroid size | Grade D | Unclear | Single thumb up | No recommendation |
| Fibroids | Lifestyle therapy | High-fiber diet, anti-inflammatory diet | Varying doses | Decrease fibroid size | Grade D | Unclear | Double thumbs up | No recommendation |
| Fibroids | Biologically based therapies | Immune-enhancing/anti-oxidant: coenzyme Q10, maitake mushrooms, zinc, selenium, beta-carotene, vitamins C, E, B complex | Varying doses | Decrease fibroid size | Grade D | Unclear | Single thumb up | No recommendation |

(continued)

Evidence Summary of CAM Treatments in Women's Health (continued)

| Clinical Indication | Category | Specific Therapy | Dose | Outcome | Confidence of Estimate on Effectiveness | Magnitude of Effect* | Safety† | Clinical Recommendation‡ | Comments |
|---|---|---|---|---|---|---|---|---|---|
| Fibroids | Lifestyle | Stress reduction | Varying regimens | Decrease fibroid size | Grade D | Unclear | Double thumbs up | No recommendation | — |
| Fibroids | Manipulative and body-based therapies | Massage therapy | Varying regimens | Decrease fibroid size | Grade D | Unclear | Single thumb up | No recommendation | — |
| Fibroids | Manipulative and body-based therapies | Myofascial release | Varying regimens | Decrease fibroid size | Grade D | Unclear | Single thumb up | No recommendation | — |
| Fibroids | Biologically based therapies | Ban Zhi Lian (Scutellaria barbata) | Unclear | Decrease fibroid size | Grade D | Unclear | No recommendation | No recommendation | — |
| Fibroids | Biologically based therapies | Kangfu Xiaozheng, Guizhi Fuling | Unclear | Decrease fibroid size | Grade C | Small | No recommendation | No recommendation | — |
| Infertility | Biologically based therapies | Chasteberry | Unclear | Conception | Grade C | Moderate | Single thumbs up | No recommendation | — |
| Infertility | Biologically based therapies | Fertility blend | Doses vary | Conception | Grade C | Small | Single thumbs up | No recommendation | Formula containing multiple herbs and nutrients |
| Infertility | Biologically based therapies | Vitamin C | 750mg daily | Conception | Grade C | Small | Double thumbs up | No recommendation | — |

| Condition | Therapy category | Therapy | Regimen | Outcome | Grade | Magnitude | Recommendation | Safety | Comments |
|---|---|---|---|---|---|---|---|---|---|
| Infertility | Mind-body and lifestyle therapies | Behavioral therapy | Varying regimens | Ovulation and uterine relaxation | Grade D | Small | Weak in favor | None | Strongest evidence is is for benefit in well-being. |
| Infertility | Mind-body and lifestyle therapies | Hypnosis | Varying regimens | Conception | Grade D | Unclear | Double thumbs up | None | — |
| Infertility | Manipulative and body-based therapies | Site-specific manual soft-tissue therapy by physical therapists | Varying regimens | Clinical pregnancies | Grade D | Unclear | Double thumbs up | None | — |
| Infertility | Whole medical system | Acupuncture | Just prior and on day of embryo transfer | Pregnancy, ongoing pregnancy, and live births | Grade A | Moderate | Single thumbs up | Weak in favor | — |
| Prevent or treat osteoporosis | Biologically based therapies | Soy isoflavones | 50 mg | Increase bone density of lumbar spine but not hip, decreased fracture rate at all sites | Grade D | Unclear | Double thumbs up | No recommendations | Evidence suggests soy-based protein to meat-based protein for cardio-vascular health. |

(continued)

**Evidence Summary of CAM Treatments in Women's Health (continued)**

| Clinical Indication | Category | Specific Therapy | Dose | Outcome | Confidence of Estimate on Effectiveness | Magnitude of Effect* | Safety† | Clinical Recommendation‡ | Comments |
|---|---|---|---|---|---|---|---|---|---|
| Prevent or treat osteoporosis | Biologically based therapies | Magnesium | Decrease BMD loss | — | Grade D | Unclear | Single thumb up | No recommendation | — |
| Prevent or treat osteoporosis | Biologically based therapies | Calcium | 1200 mg/day | BMD, fracture risk | Grade B | Moderate | Double thumbs up | Strong in favor | Preferable to combine calcium 1200 mg/d with vitamin D 800IU |
| Prevent or treat osteoporosis | Biologically based therapies | Vitamin D | 800 IU/d | Fracture | Grade B | Moderate | Double thumbs up | Weak in favor | — |
| Prevent or treat osteoporosis | Biologically based therapies | Vitamin C | 500 mg/d | BMD | Grade D | Unclear | Double thumbs up | No recommendation | — |
| Prevent or treat osteoporosis | Biologically based therapies | Vitamin K2 | 45 mg/d | BMD | Grade C | Small | Single thumb up | Weak in favor | May disrupt warfarin anti-coagulation |
| Prevent or treat osteoporosis | Biologically based therapies | Ipriflavone | 200 mg tid | Osteoporosis | Grade B | None | Double thumbs down | Strong against | May cause subclinical lympho-cytopenia. |

| Goal | Category | Treatment | Dose | Outcome | Grade | | Rating | Recommendation | Comments |
|---|---|---|---|---|---|---|---|---|---|
| Prevent or treat osteoporosis | Biologically based therapies | DHEA | 50 mg/d | Hip and spine BMD in women | Grade C | Unclear | No recommendation | No recommendation | Theoretical concern for promotion of sex hormone-dependent tumors. |
| Prevent or treat osteoporosis | Biologically based therapies | Omega-3 fatty acids | 1.5 grams/day | Improve or stabilize BMD | Grade D | Unclear | Two thumbs up | No recommendation | — |
| Prevent or treat osteoporosis | Lifestyle | Weight bearing, muscle strengthening exercise | Unclear | BMD of the spine | Grade D | Unclear | Double thumbs up | No recommendation | Prevents falls and may increase BMD |
| Prevent or treat osteoporosis | Mind Body therapies | Tai Chi | 5 times per week | BMD loss, fracture, risk factors such as falls | Grade B | Moderate | Double thumbs up | Weak recommendation | — |
| Prevent or treat osteoporosis | Lifestyle | Acid-based balanced diet | — | BMD loss, fracture risk | Grade D | Unclear | Double thumbs up | No recommendation | — |
| Prevent or treat osteoporosis | Manipulative and body based therapy | Physical therapy | Unclear | Prevent or treat osteoporosis, decrease fall risk | Grade D | Unclear | Single thumb up | No recommendation | — |
| Prevent or treat osteoporosis | Whole medical system | Acupuncture | Unclear | Spine and hip BMD | Grade C | Unclear | Single thumb up | No recommendation | — |

*(continued)*

**Evidence Summary of CAM Treatments in Women's Health (continued)**

| Clinical Indication | Category | Specific Therapy | Dose | Outcome | Confidence of Estimate on Effectiveness | Magnitude of Effect* | Safety† | Clinical Recommendation‡ | Comments |
|---|---|---|---|---|---|---|---|---|---|
| Recurrent urinary tract infection | Biologically based therapy | Cranberry (Vaccinium macrocarpon) | — | UTI incidence | Grade C | Small | Double thumbs up | Weak in favor | — |
| UI# | Lifestyle therapy | Avoid bladder irritants: citrus fruits, tomatoes, spiced foods, caffeine, chocolate and aspartame. | NA | — | Grade D | Unclear | Double thumbs up | No recommendation | Most beneficial in patients with interstitial cystitis |
| UI# | Lifestyle therapy | Smoking cessation | None | — | Grade D | Unclear | Double thumbs up | No recommendation | — |
| UI# | Lifestyle therapy | Weight loss | NA | — | Grade D | Unclear | Double thumbs up | No recommendation | — |
| UI# | Mind-body therapy | Behavioral training | Regimens vary | Treat UI | Grade B | Moderate | Double thumbs up | Weak in favor | — |
| SUI## | Mind-body therapy | Biofeedback | Regimens vary | Treat SUI | Grade D | Conflicting | Double thumbs up | No recommendation | — |
| UI# | Mind-body therapy | Hypnotherapy | Regimens vary | Treat DI | Grade D | Unclear | Double thumbs up | No recommendation | — |
| UI# | Mind-body therapy | Prompted voiding | Regimens vary | Treat UI | Grade D | Unclear | Double thumbs up | No recommendation | — |

| SUI## | Manipulative and body based therapy | Pessary | Regimens vary | Treat SUI — | Grade C | Unclear | Single thumb up | No recommendation | — |
|---|---|---|---|---|---|---|---|---|---|
| UI# | Manipulative and body based therapy | Pelvic floor muscle training | Regimens vary | — | Grade A | Moderate | Double thumbs up | Strong in favor | — |
| UI# | Manipulative and body based therapy | Pelvic floor electrical stimulation | Regimens vary | — | Grade B | Small | Double thumbs up | Weak in favor | — |
| SUI## | Manipulative therapy | Weighted vaginal cones | Regimens vary | — | Grade D | Unclear | Double thumbs up | No recommendation | — |
| UI# | Whole medical systems | Acupuncture | Regimens vary | UI post CVA | Grade B | Small | Single thumb up | 1. Weak recommendation 2. No recommendation for UI without neurological disease | — |

* Small, moderate (OR>1.2-2) or large (OR>2)

† 5 categories: Double thumbs up, single thumb up, no recommendation, single thumb down, double thumb down

‡ 5 categories: Strong (in favor), weak (in favor), no recommendation, weak (against), strong (against)

# UI: Urinary incontinence

## SUI: Stress Urinary Incontinence

## SELECTED REFERENCES*

1. **CDC.** 2004. Complementary & Alternative Medicine Use Among Adults: United States, 2002. Advance Data. Issue 343.

7. **Haimov-Kochman R; Hochner-Celnikier D.** Hot flashes revisited: pharmacological and herbal options for hot flashes management. What does the evidence tell us? Acta Obstet Gynecolo Scand. 2005;84:972-9.

10. **Newton KM, et al.** Use of alternative therapies for menopause symptoms: results of a population-based survey. Obstet Gynecol. 2002;100:18-25.

12. **Nedrow A, et al.** Complementary and alternatives therapies for the management of menopause-related symptoms. A systematic evidence review. Arch Intern Med. 2006;166:1453-65.

15. **Lethaby AE, Brown J, Marjoribanks J, et al.** Phytoestrogens for vasomotor menopausal symptoms. Cochrane Database of Systematic Reviews 2007, issue 4. Art. No.: CD001395. DOI: 10.1002/14651858.CD001395.pub3.

29. **Rakel D.** Menopause. Integrative Medicine – Second Edition. Philadelphia, PA, Saunders Elsevier, 2007;54:589-600.

59. **Girman A, Lee R, Kligler B.** An integrative medicine approach to premenstrual syndrome. Clin J Women's Health. 2002;2:116-27.

60. **Blumenthal M, et al.** The Complete German commission E Monographs: Therapeutic Guide to Herbal Medicines. Austin: American botanical council and Boston: Integrative Medicine communications, 1998: 90.

66. **Hardy ML.** Women's Health Series: Herbs of Special Interest to Women. J Am Pharm Assoc. 2000;40):23-42.

72. **Low Dog T.** Integrative treatment for premenstrual syndrome. J Alt Therap Health Healing. 2001;7:32-9.

98. **Skidmore-Roth L.** Mosby's Handbook of Herbs and Natural Supplements – third Edition. St. Louis, MO, Elsevier Mosby, 2006:142-4.

110. **Zhu X et al.** Chinese herbal medicine for primary dysmenorrheal. Cochrane Database of Systematic Reviews 2007, Issue 4. Art. No.: CD005288.DOI:10.1002/14651858.CD005288.pub2.

117. **Proctor ML, et al.** Transcutaneous electrical nerve stimulation and acupuncture for primary dysmenorrhea. Cochrane Database of Systematic Reviews 2002, Issue 1.Art No.: CD002123. DOI: 10.1002/14651858.CD002123.

126. **Ostrezenski A.** Benign uterine disorders. Gynecology Integrating Conventional, Complementary and Natural Alternative Therapy. Philadelphia, PA. Lippincott Williams & Wilkins, 2002;19:255-64.

127. **Mehl-Madrona L.** Complementary medicine treatment of uterine fibroids: a pilot study. Alternative Therapies in Health and Medicine. 2002;8:34-6,38-40,42,44-6.

132. **Chavarro Je, et al.** Dietary fatty acid intakes and the risk of ovulatory infertility Am J Clin Nutr. 2007;85:231-7.

137. **Domar AD, Seibel MM, Benson H.** The mind/body program for infertility: a new behavioral treatment approach for women with infertility. Fertil Steril. 1990;53:246-9.

152. **Manheimer E, et al.** Effects of acupuncture on rates of pregnancy and live birth among women undergoing in vitro fertilization: systematic review and meta-analysis. BMJ 2008;DOI:1136/bmj.39471.430451.BE.

172. **Wayne PM.** The effects of Tai Chi on bone mineral density in postmenopausal women: a systematic review. Arch Phys Med Rehabil. 2007;88:673-80.

186. **Weikert C, et al.** The relation between dietary protein, calcium and bone health in women: results from the EPIC-Potsdam Cohort. Ann Nutr Metab. 2005;49:312-8.

---

* The complete reference list is to be found on the book's Web site.

193. **Shea B, et al.** Calcium supplementation on bone loss in postmenopausal women. Cochrane Database of Systematic Reviews 2003, issue 4. Art. No.: CD004526. DOI: 10.1002/14651858 .CD004526.pub3.

194. **Tang BM, et al.** Use of calcium or calcium in combination with vitamin D supplementation to prevent fractures and bone loss in people aged 50 years and older: a meta-analysis. Lancet. 2007;370:657-66.

211. **Tinetti ME, et al.** A multifactorial intervention to reduce the risk of falling among elderly people living in the community. N Engl J Med. 1994;331:821-7.

218. **ACOG.** Urinary Incontinence in Women. ACOG Practice Bulletin 2005, Number 63.

242. **Hay-Smith EJC, Dumoulin C.** Pelvic floor muscle training versus no treatment, or inactive control treatments, for urinary incontinence in women. Cochrane Database of Systematic Reviews 2006, Issue 1. Art. No.: CD005654. DOI: 10.1002/14651858.CD005654.

250. **Sung LM, Jiaqi W.** Acupuncture for urinary incontinence in adults without neurological disease. (Protocol) Cochrane Database of Systematic Reviews 2006, Issue r. Art. No.: CD006235. DOI: 10:1002/14651858.CD006235.

# Chapter 12

# Musculoskeletal Disorders

WOLF E. MEHLING, MD
VIVIANE UGALDE, MD
HARLEY GOLDBERG, DO

Complementary and alternative medicine (CAM) is an amorphous grouping of diagnostic and treatment philosophies and practices that are joined only by the fact that they lie outside the domain of generally accepted biomedical practice. Patients choose CAM either because they are pushed to it by persistent suffering or because they are pulled to it by philosophical congruence (1). The most common causes of persistent suffering are chronic pain and mental stress. These are the two most common groups of conditions for which people seek CAM (2). The most common cause of chronic pain is musculoskeletal pain, particularly back pain.

Most often people seek CAM with only a general hope that the treatment may help. Too often claims and recommendations for CAM are not grounded in any evidence of effectiveness, natural history or epidemiology, risk-benefit discussions, or with appropriate dosage recommendations or treatment goals. We expect this context in conventional medicine. Often the difficulty for conventional clinicians in accepting CAM therapies is that they do not come with enough scientific evaluation about indications, contraindications, and adverse effects to allow risk-benefit consent or clear treatment goals. However, as evaluation of CAM methods increases, the evidence base is building, showing evidence both for and against the effectiveness, safety, and cost-effectiveness of these therapies. In this chapter we review some of the most common CAM treatments and conditions for which they are used and review the evidence base that is developing.

## Acute Low Back Pain

In the US, back and neck pain are the domain of complementary and alternative therapies. In 1997 a nationally representative telephone survey among 2055 adults (3) with back or neck pain (acute and chronic) found that 54% had used complementary therapies compared with 37% who had seen a conventional provider, and 25% had used both. Twenty percent of adults received chiropractic treatments, 14% massage and 12% learned relaxation techniques. In a regional survey of adults with back pain in Washington state, where certain CAM therapies are routinely covered by insurance (4), 45% had seen a chiropractor and 24% had received massages. Whereas 27% of patients found conventional care "very helpful" for their back and neck pain, the majority of patients found their CAM therapies "very helpful" (61% of patients seeing a chiropractor, 65% of massage recipients and 43% of relaxation techniques) (3). There are few evidence-based options in conventional care, such as NSAIDs, physical therapy and exercises, and none of them show strong benefits (5,6). CAM providers fill a gap in the medical care for non-specific, mechanical back pain. Because acute low back pain generally is short-term and carries a good prognosis regardless of treatment, at least regarding return to work, it is not easy to demonstrate benefits from specific conventional or CAM therapies. The best data are available for spinal manipulation.

## Acupuncture

Most studies of acupuncture for low back pain are in patients with *chronic* pain. A review by the Cochrane Collaboration identified three trials that met inclusion criteria for patients with *acute* low back pain, and they reported that data were insufficient to draw firm conclusions (7). One high-quality study using a bilateral single-point single-session intervention compared with sham (8) and another high-quality study comparing a 2-week course of acupuncture to naproxen 500 mg BID showed good recovery in both arms with no differences in pain or function (9).

Acupuncture as practiced in the US and Europe is of negligible risk (10). The Cochrane review added reported complications from 14 trials and found 5% minor complications, such as tiredness, drowsiness, aggravation of pre-existing symptoms, itching at the needle site, dizziness, headache or chest pain. None of these required hospitalization (7). The relative effectiveness of acupuncture delivered by physicians or non-physician acupuncturists has not been studied (11). Acupuncture appears to be safe.

There is sufficient evidence to provide a weak recommendation in favor of acupuncture compared to no treatment for acute back pain; however, we do not know if it is superior to other treatments such as NSAIDs or non-specific point location needling (see Evidence Summary table at end of chapter).

## Massage

There are no studies on massage on patients with acute low back pain.

## Spinal Manipulation

Spinal manipulation is a form of manual therapy and is one of the most commonly used complementary and alternative methods (see Appendix 1, p. 410-411, for more details).

Spinal manipulation for uncomplicated low back pain is very safe if medical causes of back pain such as trauma, infection, inflammatory or malignant disorders and progressive neurologic deficits (radiculopathy or sciatica) are ruled out by the absence of so-called "red flags" (12) during the history and physical exam. Laboratory tests (i.e., erythrocyte sedimentation rate) and imaging may be appropriate when there are red flags, such as in the elderly or in high-risk populations. A review of 31 trials of spinal manipulation for low back pain included over 5000 participants without any complications (13). A systematic compilation of complications from spinal manipulation to the lumbar spine primarily from case reports estimated the risk for cauda equine syndrome at less than 1 in a million spinal manipulations (14).

There are as many systematic reviews for spinal manipulation (more than 50) as there are clinical trials. In a 2004 Cochrane review (15) of 39 trials with over 5400 participants, spinal manipulation was more effective than sham manipulation or ineffective therapies, and it was equally effective as other conventional therapies. The largest study as of today was conducted within the British National Health Service on 1334 participants, the BEAM trial: pragmatic spinal manipulation was shown to be effective at 2 and 12 months for pain, function, and costs above best primary care according to guidelines (16). However mean improvements were small.

International guidelines use inconsistent grading of the evidence (17) and are summarized as "likely to be beneficial" in acute low back pain, but the evidence is still inconsistent (18). These summary statements are based on studies that include generally all eligible patients regardless of clinical or other patient characteristics.

However, *some* patients experience a rather dramatic improvement from spinal manipulation, while others do not. The question "who benefits most from spinal manipulation?" has been asked and addressed only recently in clinical research. A subgroup of low back pain patients likely to benefit from spinal manipulation was defined by the following clinical prediction rule: 1) current episode less than 16 days; 2) no sciatica; 3) a low score (<19) on a Fear-Avoidance Beliefs scale; 4) at least one hypomobile segment in the L-spine; and 5) at least one well-functioning hip joint (>35° internal rotation) (19). When this clinical prediction rule was applied in a randomized controlled trial comparing spinal manipulation and physical therapy exercises with physical therapy exercises alone, the number needed to treat (NNT) with spinal manipulation for a successful outcome at 1 week were 1.3, and at 4 weeks 1.9, with a highly significant odds ratio of 60.8 (95% confidence interval: 5.2-704.7; p=0.001), a benefit maintained over 6 months (20). Results were confirmed in subsequent studies in different populations (21,22). The Clinical Efficacy Assessment Subcommittee of the American College of Physicians and of the American Pain Society Low Back Pain Guidelines Panel recommends: "For patients who do not improve with self-care options, clinicians should consider the addition of nonpharmacologic therapy with proven benefits for acute low back pain: spinal manipulation" (23).

Doctors of Chiropractic (DC) are trained in 16 chiropractic colleges (since 1897) in 4200 hours over 4 years, have no MD-equivalent training, and learn 555 hours of manual techniques (ACA website). Doctors of Osteopathy (DO) are trained in 23 osteopathic schools (since 1892), equivalent to medical school training, with additional mandatory 210 hours of Osteopathic Manipulative Therapy course training. Seventy-five percent of physical therapy schools expose their students to some manual therapy, only 22% offer any elective training in joint manipulation (24,25). After graduation, mechanisms of quality control for practitioners are non-existent. The National Institute of Health supports research in manual therapies for which, generally, the mechanisms of action are unclear (26).

Spinal manipulation is most effective in patients with acute uncomplicated low back pain of 2 weeks duration or less, without sciatica, without major hip joint pathology and without a strong belief that they should avoid any movement. Unfortunately, only a manually trained provider (chiropractor, osteopath or physical therapist) can determine, whether patients have a segmental hypomobility, but two to three sessions would suffice to determine whether spinal manipulation is helpful or not. The risk from spinal manipulation applied to the lower back for non-specific, mechanical back pain is negligible. Overall, there is moderate evidence for some effect on pain and function when compared with sham manipulation or ineffective therapies and for similar effect to conventional therapies. There is strong evidence that spinal manipulation is effective in a well-defined subgroup of patients screened by a manually trained provider. In summary, the evidence base supports a weak recommendation for spinal manipulation for acute low back pain (see Evidence Summary table at end of chapter).

## Summary Recommendations for Acute Low Back Pain

For acute uncomplicated low back pain with its relatively benign short-term prognosis, research data are very limited on all complementary methods other than spinal manipulation. Spinal manipulation appears to be most helpful in patients with recent onset (<16 days) low back pain not radiating below the knee, who do not have bilateral hip joint degeneration and do not believe that they have to avoid all activities for fear of worsening. The evidence base is insufficient for massage to support or refute a recommendation at this time, but it is sufficient to support a weak recommendation for spinal manipulation and for acupuncture-only compared with no treatment (see Evidence Summary table at end of chapter).

# Chronic Low Back Pain

A significant proportion of patients with acute low back pain have a poor functional outcome at 1 year (14%-29%) (27,28), continue to have high-intensity pain (7%-17%) (27-29), fail to return to work (6%) (30), and require a disproportional part of health care resources: total US expenses are approaching $26 billion annually (31). Chronic non-specific low back pain is not simply prolonged acute pain but rather a complex psychosomatic problem in the industrialized world strongly related to emotional suffering (32), with rather limited treatment options (5,33). Psychological factors play a major role in its course and prognosis (34,35), and patient preferences and expectations strongly influence treatment outcomes (36,37). Clinical recommendations can be based on data from research of acupuncture, massage, spinal manipulation, bodywork approaches, movement therapies (yoga, tai chi), mind-body therapies, and dietary supplements.

## Acupuncture

A review by the Cochrane Collaboration from 35 randomized controlled trials concluded that there is evidence of small short-term pain relief and functional improvement compared with no treatment or sham (7). Pooled data from four higher-quality studies showed that the addition of acupuncture to conventional therapies (including exercises, NSAIDs, heat, mud packs, ergonomics, and behavioral modification) was more effective than these conventional therapies alone (7), leading to a summary statement of acupuncture "likely to be beneficial" (5). This is echoed in a second meta-analysis that concludes that acupuncture effectively relieves chronic low back pain compared with inactive controls, but no evidence suggests it is superior to other active therapies (38). Since then (2005), several large pragmatic multi-center trials from England and Germany have been published. In England, 10 acupuncture sessions by acupuncturists led to slightly improved mean pain ratings ("a modest health benefit") than usual care only at 12 and 24 months follow-up for minor extra cost to the national health service: "cost effective in the longer term" (39,40). In Germany, a 11,630-patient, 3-arm unblinded study of up to 15 acupuncture sessions compared with usual care and a non-randomized observational study arm showed clinically significant improvements in pain and function and was considered cost-effective (41). In a third randomized controlled trial (partially blinded, 3-arm, 1162 German patients) of 10 acupuncture sessions versus sham needling at non-acupuncture points or usual care alone (drugs, physical therapy, exercises) showed similar improvement in *both* acupuncture groups compared with usual care alone (42). When the pooled data of four independent German randomized controlled trials of acupuncture for various pain-related diagnoses, including chronic low back pain, were examined, a significant association was shown between better improvements and higher patient expectations (37).

Acupuncture as practiced in the US and Europe is of negligible risk (10). The relative effectiveness of acupuncture delivered by physicians or non-physician acupuncturists has not been studied (11).

There is moderate evidence to support a weak recommendation for acupuncture or needling at non-acupuncture points in the treatment of chronic low back pain when added to conventional therapies (exercise, NSAIDs, behavior modification) or compared with inactive controls (see Evidence Summary table at end of chapter). According to two large British and German multi-center studies, acupuncture appears to be a cost-effective treatment option for chronic back pain.

## Massage Therapy

The use of massage for chronic low back pain has a long tradition and is a commonly used complementary medicine approach for this condition (43). It is safe if applied appropriately in patients without contra-indications (43). Possible contra-indications include skin lesions, deep vein thrombosis, fractures and osteoporosis.

A systematic review within the framework of the Cochrane Collaboration through 2001 included eight randomized trials, five of high methodological quality (44). Massage was inferior to manipulation and trans-cutaneous electrical nerve stimulation, equal to corsets and exercises and superior to inert treatment (sham laser), relaxation therapy, acupuncture, and self-care education, especially if given in combination with exercises and education. The beneficial effects of massage in patients with chronic low back pain lasted at least 1 year after the end of the treatment. The review concluded that massage might be beneficial for patients with chronic nonspecific low back pain, especially when combined with exercises and education. Another more recent systematic review of massage for non-malignant chronic pain conditions (45) found "fairly robust support" for the analgesic effects of massage for non-specific low back pain, but only modest to moderate support for other musculoskeletal pain conditions. In a randomized controlled trial comparing two 30-minute massages to relaxation therapy sessions per week for 5 weeks (46), massage recipients were found to have short-term improvements in pain, depression, anxiety, sleep and trunk and pain flexion performance, as well as higher serotonin and dopamine levels. One study comparing two different techniques of massage concluded in favor of acupuncture massage over classic (Swedish) massage. Benefits from massage are clearly stronger when patients have concordant expectations (47).

As mentioned above, chronic low back pain is a psychosomatic condition, with psychological factors exerting a major influence on its course. A systematic review of 37 randomized controlled multi-dose massage therapy studies found the largest standardized effect sizes among nine dependent variables for massage for the reduction of trait anxiety and depression; the magnitude was the same as for psychotherapy, which commonly is a component of multidisciplinary pain management. It is possible that the effect on chronic pain is at least in part mediated by benefits in the patient's psychology.

The evidence base is strong enough to recommend massage therapy for chronic low back pain, particularly in patients who have concordant expectations. Furthermore, massage appears to be cost-effective (10). Massage therapy should be delivered in combination with an exercise or educational component to support a longer-lasting effect. Because of the major variance in quality of massage eductation programs and because regulatory statutes vary by country, state, and city, massage therapists should be certified by a responsible organization such as the American Massage Therapy Association. In summary, there is moderate or stronger evidence to support a weak recommendation for massage for chronic low back pain (see Evidence Summary table at end of chapter).

## Spinal Manipulation

Meta-analyses on the efficacy or effectiveness of spinal manipulation for chronic low back pain show results comparable with acute low back pain: if studies include every patient with non-specific chronic low back pain, statistically significant benefits from spinal manipulation are only found when compared with sham or ineffective interventions, but not when compared with other recommended therapies (primary care, physiotherapy/physical therapy, exercises) (43). Benefits were stronger when spinal manipulation was combined with mobilization. Subgroup analyses comparable to the studies in patients with acute low back pain are not available. For additional safety information on spinal manipulation, please refer to Appendix 1, pp. 410-411.

There is moderate evidence for some effect on pain and function when compared with sham manipulation or ineffective therapies and for a similar effect to conventional therapies. There is strong evidence for a small additional benefit above when given as an adjunct to conventional care according to current guidelines (NSAIDs, acetaminophen, physical therapy, exercises). Overall, the evidence base supports a weak recommendation for spinal manipulation in the treatment of chronic low back pain (see Evidence Summary table at end of chapter).

## Feldenkrais Method, Alexander Technique, Body Awareness Therapy, and Breath Therapy

These approaches were developed in the early 20th century in Europe and gained increasing popularity among patients with chronic pain in the 1980s. They share a focus on inner body sensations but do not share the conventional avoidance of attention to the pain sensations. They entail the training and differentiation of body awareness, have a strong educational component and require substantial personal engagement from the patient. Few rigorous studies have been conducted in this field. The best data exist from two unpublished studies, one of moderate quality (48) and one of high-quality (49) for Alexander Technique (AT), which is popular in Great Britain. In the latter study (n=579), AT was compared with massage, aerobic exercises, or conventional care by a general practitioner: patients had a cost-effective and clinically meaningful reduction in pain after six sessions of AT and subsequent directed aerobic exercises. At this time, there is insufficient evidence to accept or refute AT for the treatment of chronic back pain (see Evidence Summary table at end of chapter).

One randomized controlled pilot study showed a lasting benefit from Breath Therapy, which is popular in Germany, equal to highly specialized physical exercise therapy (50,51). Studies of Body Awareness Therapy, which is popular in Sweden and delivered by specially qualified physical therapists, showed benefits for chronic musculoskeletal pain conditions including low back pain (52-54).

These therapies require significant motivation by the patients and thus future randomized controlled trials that include poorly motivated chronic pain patients might fail to show benefits from these approaches. In summary, these therapies appear to be promising and might have some effect in strongly motivated patients. However, at this time, there is insufficient evidence to accept or refute Breath Therapy or Body Awareness Therapy for the treatment of chronic back pain (see Evidence Summary table at end of chapter).

## Yoga Therapy

Evidence from several randomized controlled studies suggests benefit from yoga for chronic low back pain, when compared with waitlist or inactive controls (55-57). These studies are promising and suggest that yoga is effective compared with no intervention or a self-care book. In one of these studies, investigators randomized patients to yoga to an active control group. Sherman et al randomized patients to yoga, education pamphlet, or educational aerobic, strength and relaxation exercise class. They found statistically and clinically meaningful differences between yoga and the education control group and a statistical trend (of no clinical significance) towards better outcomes compared with an educational aerobic, strength and relaxation exercise class. Interestingly, several studies have reported marked reductions in serum cortisol levels, bothersomeness and improvements in sleep, and function with only modest (at best) improvements in pain. Researchers theorize that yoga may provide a controlled environment that enables patients to reduce fear-avoidance behavior and improve body awareness (58). NIH-funded research evaluating the underlying mechanism of action is underway. In the US, yoga is increasingly available as a low-cost option for self-care. The evidence supports a weak recommendation for yoga in the treatment of chronic low back pain (see Evidence Summary table at end of chapter).

## Meditation and Mindfulness-Based Stress Reduction

Meditation and the highly successful and popular mindfulness-based stress reduction (MBSR) program seem to influence the affective component of chronic pain (its bothersomeness) primarily through psychological means that reduce suffering and disrupt the chronic pain feedback loop resulting in a potentially long-lasting effect that reduces suffering and has been shown to disrupt the chronic pain feedback loop (59-61). MBSR contains an element of non-judgmental attention focusing on physical sensations from emotions, postures (yoga), movement (walking) and the inner experience of breath. A single, low-powered 3-arm randomized controlled trial (59) showed improvements in mental health but not in pain compared with standard primary care (see a doctor every 3 months, pain medications). The mental health improvement was similar to massage at the end of the intervention. But four weeks after the intervention for pain and mental health, benefits in the massage group were lost, whereas the mental health improvements in the MBSR group were maintained. While these findings are promising, there is insufficient evidence to accept or refute meditation and MBSR for the treatment of chronic back pain (see Evidence Summary table at end of chapter). As it is a safe, low-cost group self-care activiy with additional health benefits, we recommend it as adjunct therapy.

## Herbs and Supplements

The use of non-psychotropic herbs for pain conditions is more common among patients in Europe. A Cochrane review found strong evidence from two studies by the same author (n=325) for short-term effects of *harpagophytum procumbens* (Devil's Claw; 50 mg harpagoside extract/dose) on acute exacerbations of chronic low back pain compared with placebo and moderate evidence for a longer effect from one study using 100 mg (62). Preliminary experimental research suggests that commercially available extract from tart cherries might have an effect on pain similar to other, pharmacological cox-inhibitors (63,64). Adverse events of either herb or supplement were not reported. While these findings are promising, we are not yet able to make a clear recommendation for these regimens in low back pain (see Evidence Summary table at end of chapter).

Although is has not been studied in chronic low back pain, cannabis might aid in chronic neuropathic pain conditions (65) and can be smokeless if ingested through a vaporizer system (66). Derived from the poppy plants cultivated for several thousand years in Europe and the Orient, opiates have been shown to be beneficial in chronic low back pain and have become part of the armamentarium of conventional medicine.

## Summary Recommendations for Chronic Low Back Pain

Acupuncture, massage, spinal manipulation, yoga, Alexander technique and Body Awareness Therapy may have some effect when added to conventional treatment and applied in accordance with patient expectations and preferences. The recommendations of the Clinical Efficacy Assessment Subcommittee of the American College of Physicians and of the American Pain Society Low Back Pain Guidelines Panel are as follows: "For patients who do not improve with self-care options, clinicians should consider the addition of nonpharmacologic therapy with proven benefits...acupuncture, massage therapy, spinal manipulation, yoga" (23). Some researchers theorize that these therapies may exert some of their benefits by psychological means. As with most treatment recommendations, patient expectation and preferences should be considered when formulating treatment recommendations for patients with chronic low back pain (67).

# Acute and Chronic Neck Pain

As with low back pain, neck pain is common and is a common reason people seek CAM. In the United States, the economic loss from chronic neck pain in missed work, medical interventions and disability is $150-$215 billion per year (68).

## Acupuncture

In a recent systematic review of acupuncture and neck pain, Trinh et al reviewed 10 trials. They were of moderate quality, small sample size, and had short-term follow-up. Based on this review they found moderate evidence that acupuncture was better than sham for pain relief immediately post-treatment and at short-term follow-up. There was also moderate evidence that chronic neck pain with radicular findings improved (69). In summary, the evidence base supports a weak recommendation for acupuncture in the treatment of acute and chronic neck pain (see Evidence Summary table at end of chapter). For information on safety, see the section above on acute low back pain and see Appendix 1, pp. 410-411 for more detailed information.

## Massage

Limited evidence has been found that traditional Chinese massage helps patients with chronic neck pain (70). A non-blinded randomized controlled trial of acupressure massage with lavender oil for sub-acute non-specific neck pain found benefits in pain reduction and improved range of motion. However, the study was limited by short-term follow-up and the non-blinded study design (71). At this time, there is insufficient evidence to accept or refute massage for the treatment of neck pain (see Evidence Summary table at end of chapter).

## Spinal Manipulation

For acute, subacute and chronic mechanical neck disorders, strong evidence was found for long-term benefits from the combination of manipulation with mobilization and exercise in pain reduction, improved function and global effects compared with waitlisted controls (68). However, there is moderate evidence to suggest that there is no benefit when this combination is compared with exercises alone or when manipulation alone is compared with waitlist, placebo, ineffective or effective controls (68). It is unclear whether exercise was the active ingredient because patients were more satisfied with the combination than with any single element alone (68). The evidence base supports a weak recommendation in favor of spinal manipulation with mobilization and exercise and a weak recommendation against spinal manipulation alone in the treatment of neck pain (see Evidence Summary table at end of chapter).

There are no studies about sub-groups of patients who might benefit from spinal manipulation. Safety studies have identified vertebral artery dissection and stroke as extremely rare but life-threatening adverse events related to spinal manipulation of the neck (72). To limit risk, spinal manipulation of the neck should be performed without rotation of C1-C2.

## Electrotherapy

Strong evidence supports short- and long-term improvements in pain and function for low-level laser therapy in neck osteoarthritis compared with placebo (70). Variations in wavelength, intensity and application points may explain the conflicting results for other types of neck pain (73). A short course of treatment with low-frequency pulse electromagnetic field for acute neck pain associated with whiplash injuries, acute and chronic mechanical neck pain led to short-term reduction in pain (70). This therapy may assist in pain control for patients who have limited pharmacological options due to various comorbidities or due to adverse effects. Overall, the evidence base supports a weak recommendation in favor of electrotherapy for neck pain (see Evidence Summary table at end of chapter). No adverse effects were reported in 14 randomized controlled trials (74).

## Yoga, Tai Chi and Body Movement Therapies

No randomized controlled trials were found using these interventions.

## Herbs and Supplements

No specific randomized controlled trials for neck pain were found.

## Integrated recommendations

There is still much work to be done in researching the efficacy of various complementary therapies in neck pain. This assertion is also true of conventional treatments. Studies are still hampered by difficulties with blinding, co-interventions and compliance (68). One should not discount the value of education, not considered a traditional CAM therapy, but one which is increasingly lost in the pressures of today's traditional medicine. A study looking at cognitive-behavioral interventions in neck and back pain found a 5x decrease in disability compared with the traditional care group at 1 year follow-up (34). Regarding CAM therapies, the evidence supports a weak recommendation for acupuncture and electrotherapy for short-term and long-term (limited to electrotherapy) benefits. Additionally, the evidence supports a weak recommendation for spinal manipulation in combination with mobilization and exercises, and when performed by a practitioner who can ensure that C1-C2 rotation is avoided.

# Osteoarthritis of the Knee

Osteoarthritis of the knee is a common cause of pain and disability. With the recent concerns of adverse effects of NSAIDs, alternative treatments are increasingly sought out (75). Accepted outcome measures include the pain visual analog scale (VAS) and the Western Ontario and McMaster Universities Osteoarthritis Index (WOMAC), which has subsections of pain and function. Other outcomes include time or distance walking tests.

## Acupuncture

Three systematic reviews of acupuncture in knee osteoarthritis have been published recently. Two performed meta-analysis with varying results. Combining five studies, White et al found that acupuncture was superior to sham acupuncture in both pain and function on the WOMAC subscales (76). These effects were seen in both short- and long-term follow-up and of a similar degree to improvements seen with NSAIDs (76). However, the analysis by Mannheimer et al of nine pooled studies found clinically irrelevant short-term benefits when compared with sham controls. There were significant benefits when compared with waitlist controls (77). A third review looked at optimal acupuncture technique. The authors felt that climate factors (hotter), the use of at least four needles, at least 10 treatments, electroacupuncture, electrical stimulation to the muscles, ethnicity and patient expectations may all influence therapy and outcomes (78). Variability of acupuncture technique likely leads to heterogeneous results. A study of preoperative knee joint replacement patients found improvements in the acupuncture and the physical therapy 6-week treatment groups compared with a home exercise control group (79). Overall, the evidence supports a weak recommendation in favor of acupuncture for the treatment of knee osteoarthritis (see Evidence Summary table at end of chapter).

## Laser Acupuncture

In a small double-blinded randomized controlled trial with laser acupuncture, significant improvements were found in periarticular swelling compared with placebo laser. Ten treatments occurred over a 2-week period. No significant differences were found in pain or function (80) At this time, there is insufficient evidence to accept or refute laser acupuncture for the treatment of chronic back pain (see Evidence Summary table at end of chapter).

## Massage

In a randomized controlled trial of massage therapy for osteoarthritis of the knee, 68 adults with radiographically confirmed osteoarthritis of the knee were assigned either to treatment (twice-weekly sessions of standard Swedish massage in weeks 1-4 and once-weekly sessions in weeks 5-8) or to waitlist control (81). Primary outcomes were changes in the WOMAC pain and functional scores and the visual analog scale of pain assessment. The group receiving massage therapy demonstrated significant improvements in mean WOMAC global scores, pain, stiffness, and physical function domains and in the VAS of pain assessment, range of motion in degrees, and time to walk 50 ft (15 minutes) in seconds. The results are promising, but there is insufficient evidence to accept or refute massage for the treatment of chronic back pain (see Evidence Summary table at end of chapter).

## Herbs and Supplements

### Glucosamine/Chondroitin

Glucosamine is an important building block for components of articular surfaces, synovial fluid, tendons and ligaments. It is 90% absorbed in the small intestine, with 8%-12% retained in human tissues. Animal studies demonstrate a special affinity of glucosamine and chondroitin for joint tissues and synovial fluid (82-85). Glucosamine sulfate is the most studied, but contains less bioactive glucosamine when compared with glucosamine hydrochloride (82). Chondroitin sulfate is a glycosaminoglycan that contributes to the proteoglycan portion of the matrix of joint cartilage.

Quality control of products is poor, ranging from variable to none in some products, and bioavailability of glucosamine varies depending on the sulfate versus the hydrochloride form (82,86). Persons with underlying poorer insulin sensitivity might be at risk for worsening insulin resistance with the use of glucosamine (87). Glucosamine is made from shells of shrimp, crab and other shellfish, and rare hypersensitivity reactions including throat swelling and, potentially, asthma exacerbation have been reported. Theoretically it may increase the risk of bleeding.

The FDA does not regulate supplements to the degree of prescription medications. Studies have shown some products without any of the labeled supplement present. For formulations with amounts equivalent to their labeling, Consumer Reports published a list of products and their cost in their June 2006 issue; physicians and patients can also refer to www.consumerlab.com.

There is evidence for anti-inflammatory effects in animal models that are likely prostaglandin-independent and may come from stabilization of cell membranes. Glucosamine reverses the proinflammatory and joint-degenerating effects of interleukin-1 by inhibiting the cytokine intracellular pathway (88). A combination therapy demonstrated a reduction in scintigraphic synovitis and lameness (89). Studies looking at combination therapy of glucosamine with NSAIDs demonstrated an almost 3-fold reduction in the amount of NSAID needed to block carrageenan-induced inflammation (82).

There is evidence for disease alteration from animal model. In a rabbit model of cartilage degeneration from an instability model of osteoarthrosis, animals treated with a combination of glucosamine, chondroitin and manganese showed no severe lesions by histology, less linear lesion involvement and reduction in total grade of lesions. Solo treatment demonstrated improvements compared with controls, but less than the combined treatment. It also demonstrated in vitro synergistic stimulation of glycosaminoglycan synthesis (90).

A 2003 meta-analysis (91) of both glucosamine and chondroitin demonstrated a highly significant efficacy of glucosamine on all outcomes, including joint space narrowing and WOMAC score. Chondroitin was found to be effective on Lequesne Index, VAS pain, mobility, and responding status. Safety was excellent for both compounds. The authors noted study limitations, primarily industry bias, which were addressed in a "definitive" NIH-sponsored 24-week 5-arm trial (92): 1500 mg glucosamine hydrochloride and 1200 mg chondroitin overall was not significantly better than placebo (n=1583). However, in the subgroup of patients with moderate-to-severe pain (n=354), the combination succeeded in a significantly higher response rate for pain and function compared with 200 mg/d celecoxib or placebo (pain: 79% vs. 69% vs. 54%, p=0.06; 0.002). Results from a study in 222 European patients with hip osteoarthritis first presented in June 2007 did not show any difference between 2 years of glucosamine sulfate and placebo for pain and function (WOMAC), joint space narrowing, quality of life, and medication consumption (93,94).

In summary, glucosamine and chondroitin are bioavailable, have low toxicity and cause few side effects. Earlier research demonstrated evidence of anti-inflammatory and chondroprotection, with randomized controlled trials demonstrating improved function and pain, while more recent research suggests efficacy may be limited to people with moderate to severe osteoarthritis. Given the paucity of effective treatment options, and this compound's good safety profile, it is reasonable to consider a trial of 500 mg TID glucosamine (as hydrochloride or sulfate) and 400 mg TID chondroitin for patients with osteoarthritis of the knee, no allergy to shellfish and low bleeding risk. The evidence base supports a weak recommendation for glucosamine and chondroitin for people with moderate to severe knee osteoarthritis. For all other subgroups, at this time, there is insufficient evidence to accept or refute glucosamine and chondroitin for the treatment of chronic back pain (see Evidence Summary table at end of chapter).

## SAMe

S-adenosylmethionine (SAMe) is a compound naturally synthesized from L-methionine and adenosine triphosphate. Compared with placebo for osteoarthritis, one large randomized clinical trial showed a small to moderate effect in favor of SAMe. Compared with NSAIDs such as celecoxib, treatment with SAMe was not associated with a statistically significant difference in outcomes (95). A meta-analysis of 11 studies found improvements in function, but not pain reduction (96). Unfortunately, the cost may be prohibitive at $60-$95/month (97). SAMe also has the same difficulties in quality as does glucosamine and chondroitin. Because it is considered a supplement, it is not regulated by the FDA. Testing by an independent lab of SAMe available in the US found that 6/13 had less than 50% of the amount of SAMe stated on the label (www.consumerlab.com). Patients should look for a quality-assurance seal of approval from a third-party agency such as the USP or NSF. Overall, the evidence supports a weak recommendation in favor of SAMe for the treatment of knee osteoarthritis (see Evidence Summary table at end of chapter).

### Avocado Soybean Unsaponifiables

Four randomized controlled trials of high quality found improvement in pain with avocado soybean unsaponifiables (ASU) 300 mg daily. There was typically a 2-month delay to effect, with continuation of effect 2 months post-discontinuation. In vitro, ASU demonstrate anabolic, anticatabolic and anti-inflammatory effects of chondrocytes (98). Again, the cost may be prohibitive at $20-$30/month (97). Overall, the evidence supports a weak recommendation in favor of ASU for the treatment of knee osteoarthritis (see Evidence Summary table at end of chapter).

### Other Nutraceuticals and Functional Foods

There is also limited evidence from two small studies to support the use of methylsulfonylmenthane (MSM) for pain reduction in knee osteoarthritis (98). Studies were hampered by short duration and lack of comparison between groups. This compound is found in low amounts in fruits, corn, tomatoes, tea, coffee and milk. It is cheaper than ASU or SAMe, with its cost per month similar to glucosamine/chondroitin at $5.50 to $12 per month (97).

SKI306X is found in a concoction from the dried roots of *Clematius mandshurica* and *Trichosantes kirilowii* and in the dried flowers and stems of *Prunella vulgaris*. In two studies by the same author, SKI306X has shown significant pain-relieving characteristics when compared with placebo similar to Diclofenac (98). No functional outcome measures were reported.

There is limited evidence for pain reduction with Duhuo Jisheng Wan, an extract from 15 plants; cetyl myristoleate from sperm whale oil; lipids from New Zealand green-lipped mussels; and an extract from the South African plant, Devil's Claw or *Harpagophytum procumbens* (98). Overall, there is insufficient evidence on efficacy and safety to refute or support using MSM, SKI306X, or Duhuo Jisheng Wan in the treatment of knee osteoarthritis (see Evidence Summary table at end of chapter).

## Integrated Recommendations

It may be reasonable to consider a 4-month trial of glucosamine and chondroitin for patients with moderate to severe osteoarthritis. Keep in mind that clinical trials show clinical improvement beginning after 8 weeks of therapy. SAMe and ASU are also options, but the cost will likely be prohibitive for many patients. Acupuncture is also a reasonable consideration, and more insurance companies opt to cover this intervention. Without insurance coverage, however, the cost of acupuncture may prohibit its use. Although the data on massage appears promising, the evidence is too limited at this time to support a routine referral. Other plant and food extracts are promising but require further study.

# Lateral Epicondyle Pain

Lateral epicondylitis is seen commonly in sports and industrial injuries. A recent critical review found a relative lack of high-quality studies to support many conventional treatment options and recommended watchful waiting (rest from aggravating activity and oral acetaminophen or NSAIDs) as a reasonable option (99). However, watchful waiting may not be an option in industrial cases and NSAIDs are now less of an option for patients, considering that symptoms of lateral epicondylitis can persist for an average of 6-24 months (99).

## Acupuncture

There have been multiple systematic reviews and a meta-analysis of acupuncture as a treatment for lateral epicondylitis. The meta-analysis included four studies with acceptable quality ratings and suggested a short-term effect of 3 days to 2 months, but insufficient evidence of long-term benefit (100). In view of very limited data from randomized controlled trials, no recommendations can be made at this time (see Evidence Summary table at end of chapter).

## Massage

The use of deep tissue friction massage has long been used in physical therapy treatment approaches in tendinopathies. Unfortunately, studies to support a specific conclusion regarding this treatment are lacking (101). In view of very limited data from randomized controlled trials, no recommendations can be made at this time (see Evidence Summary table at end of chapter).

## Manipulation

A meta-analysis concluded there were no long-term studies of good design on manipulation in lateral epicondylitis. However, there are some studies of elbow and cervical manipulation of adequate quality indicating an immediate effect on improving pain free grip strength and pressure pain threshold (100). Spinal manipulation of the neck should be performed without rotation of C1-C2 to avoid the rare but life-threatening event of vertebral artery dissection. In view of very limited data from randomized controlled trials, no recommendations can be made at this time (see Evidence Summary table at end of chapter).

## Yoga, Tai Chi, Herbs and Supplements

No studies were found.

## Integrated Recommendations

Much work needs to be done to help understand appropriate CAM treatments for lateral epicondylitis. Short-term and immediate relief might be gained from acupuncture, but long-term effects are uncertain. Overall, in view of the limited data from randomized controlled trials, no recommendations can be made at this time regarding the role for CAM therapies in the treatment of lateral epicondylitis (see Evidence Summary table at end of chapter).

# Carpal Tunnel Syndrome

Carpal tunnel syndrome (CTS) with electrodiagnostic findings has a prevalence of 4.9% (102). Although surgery remains the definitive treatment for persistent, disabling CTS, alternatives are needed for those with chronic intermittent

CTS, those who are not surgical candidates, and those who do not desire surgical intervention. We are discussing conservative methods other than steroid injections, oral steroids or splinting.

## Acupuncture

No randomized controlled trials were found as an intervention for CTS.

## Massage

No randomized controlled trials were found.

## Yoga

One randomized controlled trial with a high bias rating found a significant reduction in pain and an improvement in grip when compared with a group using splints at 8 weeks. However, no significant change was seen in motor or sensory conduction in either group, and no long-term data were reported (102). In view of very limited data from randomized controlled trials, no recommendations can be made at this time (see Evidence Summary table at end of chapter).

## Herbs and Supplements

There is moderate evidence to suggest that vitamin B6 is not effective in the treatment of CTS, and therefore the evidence base supports a weak recommendation against its use (102) (see Evidence Summary table at end of chapter).

## Manipulation

A systematic review found no significant benefit with manipulation in the treatment of CTS. One trial of mobilization of the carpal bones after 3 weeks did lead to improvement of symptoms compared with no treatment (103). At this time, there is insufficient evidence to accept or refute manipulation for the treatment of carpal tunnel syndrome (see Evidence Summary table at end of chapter).

## Low-Level Laser Treatment

Two high-quality studies provide conflicting results regarding the use of low level laser therapy (LLLT). The study with positive results combined the laser treatment with TENS (102). In view of very limited data from randomized controlled trials, there is insufficient evidence to support or refute LLLT for CTS at this time (see Evidence Summary table at end of chapter).

## Integrated Recommendations

There is very limited evidence based information regarding CAM treatments for CTS. Yoga appears to help with pain relief at least in the short term. Vitamin B6 does not appear to be helpful in symptom management. Further study is needed before more definitive recommendations can be made (see Evidence Summary table at end of chapter).

# Fibromyalgia

Fibromyalgia is a common clinical, multi-facetted syndrome with chronic, widespread pain defined in 1990 by criteria from the American College of Rheumatology. Patients may also exhibit a range of other symptoms, including sleep disturbance, fatigue, irritable bowel syndrome, headache, and mood disorders. Although the etiology of fibromyalgia is not well understood, the syndrome is generally thought to arise from influencing factors such as stress, medical illness, and a variety of pain conditions in some, but not all patients, in conjunction with neurotransmitter and neuroendocrine disturbances (104), stress hormone disturbance (105) and cortical degeneration (106). Fibromyalgia remains relatively refractory to usual treatments (medication, exercise). In a recent study within a setting with insurance coverage for complementary medicine providers, the use of CAM by patients with fibromyalgia was 2.5 times higher than in a comparison group without fibromyalgia (56% versus 21%) (107). At the Mayo Clinic in Rochester, NY, 98% of patients enrolled in a fibromyalgia treatment program had used some type of CAM therapy during the previous 6 months, including exercise, prayers, massage therapy, chiropractic treatments, vitamins/supplements, and green tea (108).

## Acupuncture

In one review of five randomized controlled trials of mixed quality using acupuncture as an adjunct to conventional treatments, three randomized controlled trials suggested positive, mostly short-lived and primary psychological effects, and two yielded negative results regarding pain. All positive randomized controlled trials used electro-acupuncture (109). The reviewers concluded that acupuncture is not supported by the results from rigorous clinical trials as a treatment option for fibromyalgia. A second review summarizing three recent studies confirmed these conflicting results and stated that needling showed benefits independent of placement location in individuals. The authors remarked that patients with fibromyalgia had strong placebo responses in other blinded intervention trials (110). In view of the conflicting data from randomized controlled trials, there is insufficient evidence to accept or refute acupuncture for the treatment of fibromyalgia at this time (see Evidence Summary table at end of chapter).

## Massage

A well-designed randomized controlled trial compared the effects of 30-minute massage therapy twice weekly for 5 weeks with relaxation therapy on sleep, substance P, and pain. Both groups showed a decrease in anxiety and depressed mood immediately after the first and last therapy sessions. Compared with active control (Progressive Relaxation), the massage therapy group reported a short-term increase in the number of sleep hours, a decrease in their sleep movements, substance P levels, lower disease and pain ratings, and fewer tender points (111). The 24-hour urinary concentration of the corticotropin-releasing factor-like immunoreactivity (CRF-LI) in fibromyalgia patients was found to be related to depression, mood and the inability to take initiative. After massage and guided relaxation, the urinary CRF-LI concentrations, pain levels and emotional reactions were all decreased (112). The evidence supports a weak recommendation of massage for short-term benefits in the treatment of fibromyalgia (see Evidence Summary table at end of chapter).

## Spinal Manipulation

One pilot study showed improvements compared with waitlist controls (113), but considering the absence of well-designed randomized controlled trials, there is insufficient evidence to accept or refute spinal manipulation for the treatment of fibromyalgia at this time (see Evidence Summary table at end of chapter).

## Yoga and Tai Chi

No controlled trials were found on yoga and tai chi in the treatment of fibromyalgia.

## Mindfulness-Based Stress Reduction

A non-randomized controlled study in 58 women showed substantial improvements in pain, quality of life, coping with pain, anxiety, depression and somatic complaints sustained over 3 years (114). Mindfulness meditation with added Qigong movements was not superior to an equal-attention education-support group (115) but was superior to waitlist control in depression and somatic symptoms (116). There is insufficient evidence to accept or refute mindfulness-based stress reduction for the treatment of fibromyalgia at this time (see Evidence Summary table at end of chapter).

## Biofeedback

Although pre-post comparisons showed improvements through biofeedback, there are no controlled trials. There is insufficient evidence to accept or refute biofeedback for the treatment of fibromyalgia at this time (see Evidence Summary table at end of chapter).

## Herbs and Supplements

### SAMe

A Danish placebo-controlled study did not find significant benefits from SAMe for fibromyalgia (117).

### Magnesium

No RCTs were identified on the use of magnesium for fibromyalgia.

### Green Tea

No RCTs were identified on the use of green tea for fibromyalgia.

## Integrated Recommendations

Overall, there is very limited data from randomized controlled trials on the efficacy of herbs and supplements for fibromyalgia; therefore, there is insufficient evidence to accept or refute this category of therapies for the treatment of fibromyalgia at this time (see Evidence Summary table at end of chapter).

The multifaceted nature of fibromyalgia suggests that multimodal individualized treatment programs may be necessary to achieve optimal outcomes in patients with this syndrome (104). The quality of several CAM studies in fibromyalgia patients compares well with that of conventional therapies. Added to usual treatment (anti-depressants, exercise), acupuncture, massage and mind-body therapies have shown benefits in some studies, but generally not in high-quality comparison studies with other active interventions or placebo. Preliminary evidence suggests that acupuncture may provide short-term benefits for pain; however, data are too limited to support routine recommendation. The evidence base supports a weak recommendation for massage for short-term benefits. Massage is worth trying if in concordance with patient expectations but not as a stand-alone therapeutic intervention.

**Evidence Summary of CAM Treatments of Musculoskeletal Disorders**

| Clinical Indication | Category | Specific Therapy | Dose | Outcome | Confidence of Estimate on Effectiveness | Magnitude of Effect* | Safety† | Clinical Recommendation‡ | Comments |
|---|---|---|---|---|---|---|---|---|---|
| Acute low back pain | Whole medical systems | Acupuncture | Single treatment to multiple treatments over 2 weeks | Pain, function | B | 1. Small 2. Equivalency | Double thumbs up | 1. Weak in favor compared to no treatment. 2. No recommendation compared to NSAIDs or needling at non-acupuncture points. | Appears to be of similar effect on pain and function compared with sham acupuncture or usual therapy (NSAID). |
| Acute low back pain | Manipulative and body-based practices | Massage | Unclear | No studies | D | Unclear | Double thumbs up | No recommendation | — |
| Acute low back pain | Manipulative and body-based practices | Spinal manipulation | Doses vary (mostly treatment by doctor of chiropractic); spinal manipulation(s) in two physical therapy sessions | Pain, function | 1. B 2. A 3. A | 1. Small 2. N/A 3. Moderate | Double thumbs up (non-cervical) | Weak in favor | See clinical prediction rule on p. 291. 1. Has some effect on pain and function compared to sham manipulation or ineffective therapies (NNT=1.3 if |

| Chronic low back pain | Whole medical systems | Acupuncture | 10-15 acupuncture sessions | Pain, function, cost-effectiveness | a-c. B | 1. Moderate 2. Small 3. N/A | Double thumbs up | Weak in favor | meets clinical prediction rule). 2. Has similar effect to conventional therapies. Appears to be cost effective (Britain, Germany). 1. Adding point non-specific acupuncture to conventional therapies alone; 2. Some effect for pain and function compared to inactive controls; 3. Similar effect compared to other active therapies and non-acupoint acupuncture (dry needling). |

(continued)

**Evidence Summary of CAM Treatments of Musculoskeletal Disorders (continued)**

| Clinical Indication | Category | Specific Therapy | Dose | Outcome | Confidence of Estimate on Effectiveness | Magnitude of Effect* | Safety† | Clinical Recommendation‡ | Comments |
|---|---|---|---|---|---|---|---|---|---|
| Chronic low back pain | Manipulative and body-based practices | Massage | 10 weekly sessions | Pain, function, anxiety, depression | 1. A<br>2. B<br>3. B | a. Small<br>b. N/A<br>c. Small | Double thumbs up | Weak in favor | 1. Some effect for pain, anxiety and depression compared with inactive interventions; 2. Similar effect for pain, anxiety and depression compared with exercise; 3. Appears to have some effect for pain compared with acupuncture, relaxation therapy or educational booklet. |
| Chronic low back pain | Manipulative and body-based practices | Spinal manipulation | Doses vary | Pain, function | a. B<br>b. B<br>c. A | a. Small<br>b. N/A<br>c. Small | Double thumbs up (non-cervical) | Weak in favor | a. Some small effect on pain and compared |

| Condition | Domain | Therapy | Sessions | Outcomes | Grade | Effect | Symbol | Recommendation | Comments |
|---|---|---|---|---|---|---|---|---|---|
| | | | | | | | | No recommendation | to sham manipulation or ineffective therapies; b. Similar effect to conventional therapies; c. Minimal added benefit above care according to guidelines. |
| Chronic low back pain | Manipulative and body-based practices | Alexander Technique | 6-24 individual sessions over 4-20 weeks | Pain, function | C | Small | Double thumbs up | No recommendation | Appears to have some effect compared with massage, aerobic exercises or usual care. |
| Chronic low back pain | Manipulative and body-based practices | Body awareness therapy | 20 group sessions over 4 months | Pain, function | C | Small | Double thumbs up | No recommendation | Appears to have some effect on quality of life compared with usual care. |

(continued)

**Evidence Summary of CAM Treatments of Musculoskeletal Disorders (continued)**

| Clinical Indication | Category | Specific Therapy | Dose | Outcome | Confidence of Estimate on Effectiveness | Magnitude of Effect* | Safety† | Clinical Recommendation‡ | Comments |
|---|---|---|---|---|---|---|---|---|---|
| Chronic low back pain | Mind-body medicine | Breath therapy | 8 weekly individual sessions | Pain, function | C | Small | Double thumbs up | No recommendation | May have similar effect compared with physical therapy. |
| Chronic low back pain | Mind-body medicine | Yoga | 12-week Yoga class | Pain, function | B | Moderate | Double thumbs up | Weak in favor | Advise back-care specific classes by yoga-experienced instructor. |
| Chronic low back pain | Mind-body medicine | Meditation/MBSR | 8-week class, 2 2-hour sessions/week | Pain, function | C | Small | Double thumbs up | No recommendation | May have some effect on affective component of pain compared with massage. |
| Chronic low back pain | Biologically based practices | Tart cherries | Unclear | No RCT | D | Unclear | Double thumbs up | No recommendation | — |
| Chronic low back pain | Biologically based practices | Devil's Claw | 50-100 mg per day | Pain, function | C | Moderate | Double thumbs up | No recommendation | Appears to be effective compared with placebo. |
| Acute and chronic neck pain | Whole medical systems | Acupuncture | Doses vary | Pain, function | B | Small | Double thumbs up | Weak in favor | Appears to have some effect for pain compared to |

| Acute and chronic neck pain | Manipulative and body-based practices | Massage | Does vary | Pain, function | C | Small | Double thumbs up | No recommendation | sham in short term. Some effect in chronic NP with radicular findings. — |
| Acute and chronic neck pain | Manipulative and body-based practices | Spinal manipulation | Doses vary — | 1. A 2. B | | 1. Moderate 2. No effect | Single thumb up | 1. Weak in favor 2. Weak against. | If rotation at C1-C2 must be strictly avoided; if this is not guaranteed: safety grade converted to "one thumb down." 1. Some long-term benefit when combined with mobilization and exercise. 2. No benefit for manipulation alone. |

(continued)

Evidence Summary of CAM Treatments of Musculoskeletal Disorders (continued)

| Clinical Indication | Category | Specific Therapy | Dose | Outcome | Confidence of Estimate on Effectiveness | Magnitude of Effect* | Safety† | Clinical Recommendation‡ | Comments |
|---|---|---|---|---|---|---|---|---|---|
| Acute and chronic neck pain | Energy medicine | Electro-therapy (low level laser therapy) | Doses vary | Pain, function | A | Moderate | Double thumbs up | Weak in favor | Effective for weak osteo-arthritis |
| Acute and chronic neck pain | Mind-body medicine | Yoga, Tai Chi | Unclear | N/A | D | Unclear | Single thumb up | No recommendation | — |
| Acute and chronic neck pain | Biologically based practices | Herbs, supplements | Unclear | N/A | D | Unclear | No recommend-ation | No recommendation | — |
| Osteoarthritis of the knee | Whole medical systems | Acupuncture | 6-20 sessions over 2-20 weeks | Pain, function | a. B<br>b. B<br>c. B | 1. Small<br>2. Moderate<br>3. Moderate | Double thumbs up | Weak in favor | 1. Appears to have some effect compared to sham acupuncture;<br>2. Appears to be effective compared to waitlist;<br>3. Appears to have similar effect compared to NSAIDs. |

| | | | | | | | | | |
|---|---|---|---|---|---|---|---|---|---|
| Osteoarthritis of the knee | Whole medical systems | Electrotherapy (laser acupunture) | 10 treatments over 2 weeks | Pain, function, swelling | C | Small | Double thumbs up | No recommendation | Appears to have some effect in improving periarticular swelling but no effect in pain and function. |
| Osteoarthritis of the knee | Manipulative and body-based practices | Massage | 12 sessions over 8 weeks | | C | Small | Double thumbs up | No recommendation | — |
| Osteoarthritis of the knee | Biologically based practices | Glucosamine/ Chondroitin | 500 mg/ 400 mg TID | Pain, function | 1. B 2. B | 1. No effect 2. Moderate | Double thumbs up | 1. No recommendation overall. 2. Weak in favor for people with moderate-severe disease. | Controversy regarding whether glucosamine sulfate preparation (Rotta Pharmaceuticals) is superior to other preparations including glucosamine hydrochoride preparations. |

(continued)

**Evidence Summary of CAM Treatments of Musculoskeletal Disorders (continued)**

| Clinical Indication | Category | Specific Therapy | Dose | Outcome | Confidence of Estimate on Effectiveness | Magnitude of Effect* | Safety† | Clinical Recommendation‡ | Comments |
|---|---|---|---|---|---|---|---|---|---|
| Osteoarthritis of the knee | Biologically based practices | S-adenosyl-methionine (SAMe) then 400 mg daily | 800 mg daily x 2 weeks, | Pain, function | 1. B<br>2. B | 1. Small<br>2. N/A | Weak in favor | Weak in favor | 1. Appears to have some effect in function;<br>2. Appears to have similar effect compared with celecoxib; 58% less likely to report side effects compared to NSAID |
| Osteoarthritis of the knee | Biologically based practices | Avocado soybean unsaponifiables | 300 mg daily | Pain, function | B | Small | Double thumbs up | Weak in favor | — |
| Osteoarthritis of the knee | Biologically based practices | Methylsulf-onylmeth-ane (MSM) | 6 gm daily | May have some effect for pain compared with placebo. | C | Small | Unclear | No recommendation | — |

| Lateral epicondyle pain | Whole medical systems | Acupuncture | 1-10 sessions over 1-8 weeks | Pain, function | C | Small | Double thumbs up | No recommendation | Might have short-term effect (3d to 2 mos) compared to sham acupuncture, not significant compared to ultrasound. |
|---|---|---|---|---|---|---|---|---|---|
| Lateral epicondyle pain | Manipulative and body-based practices | Massage | Unclear | — | D | Unclear | Double thumbs up | No recommendation | — |
| Lateral epicondyle pain | Manipulative and body-based practices | Manipulation | 1 cervical and up to 9 wrist manipulations | Pain, function | D | Unclear | Single thumbs up | No recommendation | May have an immediate effect. |
| Lateral epicondyle pain | Mind-body medicine | Yoga, Tai Chi | Unclear | — | D | Unclear | Single thumb up | No recommendation | — |
| Lateral epicondyle pain | Biologically based practices | Herbs/ Supplements | Unclear | — | D | Unclear | Unclear | No recommendation | — |
| Carpal tunnel syndrome | Whole medical systems | Acupuncture | Unclear | — | D | Unclear | Double thumbs up | No recommendation | — |

(continued)

**Evidence Summary of CAM Treatments of Musculoskeletal Disorders (continued)**

| Clinical Indication | Category | Specific Therapy | Dose | Outcome | Confidence of Estimate on Effectiveness | Magnitude of Effect* | Safety† | Clinical Recommendation‡ | Comments |
|---|---|---|---|---|---|---|---|---|---|
| Carpal tunnel syndrome | Mind-body medicine | Yoga | 8 weekly classes | Pain, strength, nerve conduction | C | Small | Double thumbs up | No recommendation | May have some effect on grip strength and pain compared with splinting. |
| Carpal tunnel syndrome | Biologically based practices | Vitamin B6 | 50 mg | — | B | No effect | Double thumbs up | Weak against | — |
| Carpal tunnel syndrome | Manipulative and body-based practices | Wrist joint manipulation | 3 weeks | — | 1. B 2. C | 1. No effect 2. Small | Unclear | No recommendation | 1. Appears not to be effective above usual care (NSAIDs, splint); 2. May have limited effect compared with no treatment. |
| Carpal tunnel syndrome | Energy medicine | Low level laser therapy at acupuncture sites | 9-12 treatments over 3-5 weeks | Pain, function | C | Conflicting | Double thumbs up | No recommendation | Might not be effective |

| Condition | Category | Therapy | Regimen | Outcomes | | Effect size | | Recommendation | Notes |
|---|---|---|---|---|---|---|---|---|---|
| Fibromyalgia | Whole medical systems | Acupuncture | 6-40 sessions | Psychological and physical symptoms | B | Small | Double thumbs up | No recommendation | Electro-acupuncture may have limited short-term effect for pain when added to medical treatment and similar effect to sham acupuncture. Short-term benefits. |
| Fibromyalgia | Manipulative and body-based practices | Massage | 10 massages over 5 weeks | Sleep, pain tender points, anxiety, depression, substance P. | B | Small | Double thumbs up | Weak in favor | |
| Fibromyalgia | Manipulative and body-based practices | Spinal manipulation | 4 weeks by chiropractor | Symptoms | C | Small | Single thumb up | No recommendation | May have some effect compared with waitlist. |

*(continued)*

**Evidence Summary of CAM Treatments of Musculoskeletal Disorders (continued)**

| Clinical Indication | Category | Specific Therapy | Confidence of Dose | Confidence of Outcome | Estimate on Effectiveness | Magnitude of Effect* | Safety† | Clinical Recommendation‡ | Comments |
|---|---|---|---|---|---|---|---|---|---|
| Fibromyalgia | Mind-body medicine | Yoga, Tai Chi | Unclear | — | D | Unclear | Double thumbs up | No recommendation | — |
| Fibromyalgia | Mind-body medicine | MBSR | 8-week class twice a week | Symptoms | C | Small | Double thumbs up | No recommendation | May have some effect for pain, depression and anxiety compared with wait list or education. |
| Fibromyalgia | Mind-body medicine | Biofeedback | Unclear | — | D | Small | Double thumbs up | No recommendation | Case series suggests benefit |
| Fibromyalgia | Biologically based practices | SAMe | 600 mg IV daily for 10 days | Symptoms | B | No effect | Double thumbs up | Weak against | May have no effect compared to placebo. |
| Fibromyalgia | Biologically based practices | Magnesium | Unclear | — | D | Unclear | Double thumbs up | No recommendation | — |

| Fibromyalgia | Biologically based practices | Green tea | Unclear | — | D | Unclear | Double thumbs up | No recommendation | — |

* Small, moderate (OR>1.2-2) or large (OR>2)

† 5 categories: Double thumbs up, single thumb up, no recommendation, single thumb down, double thumb down

‡ 5 categories: Strong (in favor), weak (in favor), no recommendation, weak (against), strong (against)

## SELECTED REFERENCES*

15. **Assendelft W, Morton S, Yu EI, et al.** Spinal manipulative therapy for low back pain. Cochrane Database Syst Rev. 2004;1:CD000447.

20. **Childs JD, Fritz JM, Flynn TW, et al.** A clinical prediction rule to identify patients with low back pain most likely to benefit from spinal manipulation: a validation study. Ann Intern Med. 2004;141:920-8.

23. **Chou R, Huffman LH.** Nonpharmacologic therapies for acute and chronic low back pain: a review of the evidence for an American Pain Society/American College of Physicians clinical practice guideline. Ann Intern Med. 2007;147:492-504.

38. **Manheimer E, White A, Berman B, et al.** Meta-analysis: acupuncture for low back pain. Ann Intern Med. 2005;142:651-63.

42. **Haake M, Muller HH, Schade-Brittinger C, et al.** German Acupuncture Trials (GERAC) for chronic low back pain: randomized, multicenter, blinded, parallel-group trial with 3 groups. Arch Intern Med. 2007;167:1892-8.

43. **Cherkin DC, Sherman KJ, Deyo RA, Shekelle PG.** A review of the evidence for the effectiveness, safety, and cost of acupuncture, massage therapy, and spinal manipulation for back pain. Ann Intern Med. 2003;138:898-906.

44. **Furlan AD, Brosseau L, Imamura M, Irvin E.** Massage for low-back pain: a systematic review within the framework of the Cochrane Collaboration Back Review Group. Spine. Sep 1 2002;27(17):1896-1910.

51. **Mehling WE, Hamel KA, Acree M, et al.** Randomized, controlled trial of breath therapy for patients with chronic low-back pain. Altern Ther Health Med. 2005;11:44-52.

57. **Sherman KJ, Cherkin DC, Erro J, et al.** Comparing yoga, exercise, and a self-care book for chronic low back pain: a randomized, controlled trial. Ann Intern Med. 2005;143:849-56.

60. **Kabat-Zinn J, Lipworth L, Burney R.** The clinical use of mindfulness meditation for the self-regulation of chronic pain. J Behav Med. 1985;8:163-90.

62. **Gagnier JJ, van Tulder MW, Berman B, Bombardier C.** Herbal medicine for low back pain: a Cochrane review. Spine. 2007;32:82-92.

67. **NCCAM.** Low Back Pain: NCCAM Symposium (Sept. 2007). CAM at the NIH. Focus on Complementary and Alternative Medicine. 2007;14(4):website: nccam.nih.gov/news/newsletter/2007_fall/lowbackpain.htm; accesses 2001/2003/2008.

68. **Gross AR, Hoving JL, Haines TA, et al.** A Cochrane review of manipulation and mobilization for mechanical neck disorders. Spine. 2004;29:1541-8.

70. **Gross AR, Goldsmith C, Hoving JL, et al.** Conservative management of mechanical neck disorders: a systematic review. J Rheumatol. 2007;34:1083-1102.

72. **Ernst E.** Chiropractic spinal manipulation for neck pain: a systematic review. J Pain. 2003;4:417-21.

77. **Manheimer E, Linde K, Lao L, et al.** Meta-analysis: acupuncture for osteoarthritis of the knee. Ann Intern Med. 2007;146:868-77.

81. **Perlman AI, Sabina A, Williams AL, et al.** Massage therapy for osteoarthritis of the knee: a randomized controlled trial. Arch Intern Med. 2006;166:2533-8.

92. **Clegg DO, Reda DJ, Harris CL, et al.** Glucosamine, chondroitin sulfate, and the two in combination for painful knee osteoarthritis. N Engl J Med. 2006;354:795-808.

94. **Rozendaal RM, Koes BW, Weinans H, et al.** The effect of glucosamine sulphate on osteoarthritis: design of a long-term randomised clinical trial [ISrandomized controlled trialN54513166]. BMC Musculoskelet Disord. 2005;6:20.

98. **Ameye LG, Chee WS.** Osteoarthritis and nutrition. From nutraceuticals to functional foods: a systematic review of the scientific evidence. Arthritis Res Ther. 2006;8:R127.

---

* The complete reference list is to be found on the book's Web site.

100. **Bisset L, Paungmali A, Vicenzino B, Beller E.** A systematic review and meta-analysis of clinical trials on physical interventions for lateral epicondylalgia. Br J Sports Med. 2005;39:411-422; discussion 411-22.

102. **Piazzini DB, Aprile I, Ferrara PE, et al.** A systematic review of conservative treatment of carpal tunnel syndrome. Clin Rehabil. 2007;21:299-314.

109. **Mayhew E, Ernst E.** Acupuncture for fibromyalgia: a systematic review of randomized clinical trials. Rheumatology (Oxford). 2007;46:801-4.

110. **Rooks DS.** Fibromyalgia treatment update. Curr Opin Rheumatol. 2007;19:111-17.

111. **Field T, Diego M, Cullen C, et al.** Fibromyalgia pain and substance P decrease and sleep improves after massage therapy. J Clin Rheumatol. 2002;8:72-76.

# Chapter 13

ℱᚑ

# Obesity and Overweight:
# A Review of Dietary Supplements

BARBARA WIDER, MA
MAX H. PITTLER, MD, PHD

An increasing number of individuals, particularly in developed countries, are in excess of their ideal body weight. Data from the National Center for Health Statistics (NCHS) indicate that 65.2% of adults in the US are overweight, i.e. have a body mass index (BMI, weight in kg divided by the square height in m) over 25, and that 31.1% thereof are obese with a BMI over 30. In addition, 15.8% of children aged 6 to 11 years and 16.1% of adolescents aged 12 to 19 are overweight (1,2).

Overweight and obesity come at a substantial medical, public health and social cost and have been shown to predispose to cardiovascular disease, hypertension, diabetes, dyslipidemia, metabolic syndrome, osteoarthritis, and certain forms of cancer (3-5); conditions that are among the most expensive health care problems (6). Overweight and obesity are also linked to an increased risk for morbidity and mortality (7). Standard weight management programs are usually based on decreasing the energy intake through modification of the diet and increasing the energy expenditure through physical activity. Compliance with these two measures is notoriously poor. Many healthcare practitioners and overweight/obese individuals therefore turn to pharmacotherapeutics and dietary supplements for weight management. The popularity of complementary and alternative medicine has created a ready market for non-prescription weight loss products, which are also increasingly sold over the Internet. This chapter will examine the efficacy and safety of herbal and other dietary supplements in the management of body weight.

## Prevalence of CAM Use Among
## Overweight and Obese Individuals

The market for weight loss products is one of the fastest growing and most important sectors in the dietary supplement market in the US and Europe (8).

The global marketing and advertising of weight loss supplements has been facilitated particularly through the Internet (9). Despite regulatory attempts to prohibit such health claims, consumers may be mislead by vendors' promotional literature. A nationwide cross-sectional telephone survey in the US found that an estimated 15.2% of adults (20.6% of women and 9.7% of men) had ever used a weight-loss supplement and 8.7% had used them in the past year (10). Another US survey of a random population sample of 14,679 adults reported the use of dietary supplements for weight loss to be particularly high among young obese women, of whom 28% report using such products (11). Interestingly, 8% of women with no excess body weight were also reported to use such products.

Among past year users of the first survey only 30.2% discussed their use of weight-loss supplements with their doctor. Almost three-fourths (73.8%) used products classified as stimulants, and 55% took a product containing ephedra, and 27.4% took products containing chromium (10).

Among complementary and alternative medicine users, the most frequently used complementary therapies other than dietary supplements are yoga, meditation, acupuncture and massage (12).

## Dietary Supplements

A wide range of dietary supplements is available for weight loss. Over 50 individual and well over 100 commercial combination products are available in the US (13). For many of the dietary supplements there is no scientific evidence available to support their claims for weight loss. A large number of the most common individual weight loss supplements have not been tested in RCTs in humans. These include arginine (L-arginine), bromelain, Coenzyme Q10, evening primrose oil (*Oenothera biennis*), garlic (*Allium sativum*), goldenseal (*Hydrastis canadensis*), guggul (*Commifora mukul*), kava (*Piper methysticum*), licorice (*Glycyrrhiza glabra*), red clover (*Trifolium pratense*), red yeast rice (*Monascus purpureus*), and seaweed/kelp (*Fucus vesiculosus*) (14).

Herbal and other dietary supplements for which evidence from randomized clinical trials (RCTs) is available are discussed below. The results of the respective RCTs are summarized in Table 13-1, those of the systematic reviews and meta-analyses in Table 13-2. References of studies included are also provided in the tables.

## Ayurvedic Preparations

One placebo-controlled double-blind RCT compared three Ayurvedic herbal preparations against placebo; all groups also received 750 mg triphala per day. After three months weight loss ranged between 5.5 kg and 5.8 kg (=1.8-1.9 kg/month)

**Table 13-1 Randomized, Double-Blind Trials of Dietary Supplements for Body Weight Reduction**

| First Author, Source | Design; Quality Score | Intervention and Daily Dose | Control | Duration | Randomized/ Analyzed | Result | Adverse Events in Intervention Group (Cases) | Control of Lifestyle Factors |
|---|---|---|---|---|---|---|---|---|
| Paranjpe P, J Ethnopharmacol 1990;29:1-11 | Parallel; 3 | 1. Gokshuradi guggul (750 mg) 2. Sinhanad guggul (300 mg) 3. Chandraprabha vati (750 mg) | Placebo | 3 months | 70 / 48 | Intergroup differences for all intervention groups (p<0.05) | Diarrhea and nausea (8) | Participants received advice on diet and exercise. Dietary intake was not controlled. |
| Greenway F, J Med Food 2006;9:572-8 | Parallel; 2 | Bitter orange (Citrus aurantium) 150 mg combination product with pantothenic acid 40 mg, green tea leaf extract 200 mg, guarana 550 mg, white willow bark 50 mg, ginger root 10 mg, thermoblend 375 mg | Placebo | 8 weeks | 8 / 8 | Intergroup difference, greater weight gain in intervention group (+1.04, p<0.04) | Hypertension (1), musculoskeletal AE (1), neurological (2), headache/migraine (2), anxiety (1), other (5) | Calorie-restricted diet; participants were instructed to increase their exercise to 30 min per day. |

*(continued)*

**Table 13-1   Randomized, Double-Blind Trials of Dietary Supplements for Body Weight Reduction (continued)**

| First Author, Source | Design; Quality Score | Intervention and Daily Dose | Control | Duration | Randomized/ Analyzed | Result | Adverse Events in Intervention Group (Cases) | Control of Lifestyle Factors |
|---|---|---|---|---|---|---|---|---|
| Kaats GR, J Am Coll Nutr 2006; 25:389-94 | Parallel; 4 | Chitosan 3 g, combination product with beta-glucan 6 mg, snowhite oat fiber 6 mg, betaine HCL 6 mg, aloe saponins 6 mg | 1) Placebo 2) Minimum intervention control following any program of their own choosing | 60 days | 150 / 134 | Intergroup difference (-2.6 lbs over placebo, p<0.04) | None reported | Behavior-modification program. |
| Lukaski HC, Nutrition 2007;23:187-95 | Parallel; 4 | Chromium picolinate 187 µg | 1) Picolinic acid 1730 µg 2) Placebo | 12 weeks plus run-in of 2 weeks diet only | n. r. / 83 | Similar weight decrease in all three groups, 0.2 over placebo | No adverse effects on iron status, others not reported | All participants followed a basal chromium diet. |
| Støa Birketvedt G, Curr Top Nutraceutical Res 2005;3: 137-42 | Parallel; 4 | Common bean (Phaseolus vulgaris) 150 mg combination product with Ceratonia siliqua 25 mg | Placebo | 3 months | 62 / 52 | Intergroup difference | Flatulence (4), soft stool (1), constipation (1) | Participants were advised not to change their eating or exercise habits. |

| Reference | Design | Treatment | Control | Duration | N | Result | Adverse events | Notes |
|---|---|---|---|---|---|---|---|---|
| Celleno L, Int J Med Sci 2007; 4:45-52 | Parallel; 4 | Common bean (Phaseolus vulgaris) extract 445 mg, combination product with "small amounts of various other ingredients" | Placebo | 30 days | 82/60 | Intergroup difference (p<0.001) | No significant adverse events recorded | Participants followed a carbohydrate-rich, 2000 to 2200 calorie diet. |
| Thom L, J Int Med Res 2000; 28:229-33 | Parallel; 5 | Common bean (Phaseolus vulgaris) 1.2 g combination product with inulin 1.2 g, Garcinia cambogia 0.3 g | Placebo | 12 weeks | 40/40 | Change compared with baseline (p=0.001) | None reported | Participants were advised to follow a 5000 kJ per day diet. |
| Hioki C, Clin Exp Pharmacol Physiol 2004; 31:614-9 | Parallel; 4 | Ephedrine 24 mg, 280 mg caffeine combination product with 17 other ingredients (Bofu-tshusho-san) | Placebo | 24 weeks | 85/81 | Intergroup difference | No adverse events reported | Participants received instructions for exercise and diet. |

*(continued)*

**Table 13-1  Randomized, Double-Blind Trials of Dietary Supplements for Body Weight Reduction (continued)**

| First Author, Source | Design; Quality Score | Intervention and Daily Dose | Control | Duration | Randomized/ Analyzed | Result | Adverse Events in Intervention Group (Cases) | Control of Lifestyle Factors |
|---|---|---|---|---|---|---|---|---|
| Coffey CS, Int J Obes 2004; 28: 1411-9 | Parallel; 3 | Ephedra 10 mg, combination product with kola nut 250 mg and white willow bark id rathrk 100 mg; amount per protocol but tests revealed only half that amount in tested substance | Placebo | 12 weeks | 102 / 86 | Intergroup difference (p=0.002) | Compression fracture at L1 (1), elevated blood pressure (1), other AEs equally in both groups | Participants received a leaflet describing modifications for a healthier lifestyle. |
| Hackman RM, Int J Obes 2006;30: 1545-56 | Parallel; 4 | Eephedra 500 mg, guarana 550 mg, Garcinia cambogia 2000 mg, green/oolong tea 220 mg, multi-nutrient supplement with a further 43 ingredients | Vitamin and mineral supplement | 9 months | 61 / 41 | Intergroup difference (4.93kg over placebo, p=0.0022) | Decreased appetite (22), increased energy (19), headache (16), dry mouth (14), nervousness (13), palpitations (13), insomnia (7), nausea (7), dizziness (5) | None. |

| Reference | Design | Treatment | Control | Duration | N | Result | Adverse effects | Comments |
|---|---|---|---|---|---|---|---|---|
| Heymsfield SB, JAMA 1998; 280:1596-1600 | Parallel; 5 | Garcinia cambogia 3 g | Placebo | 12 weeks | 135 / 135 | No intergroup difference (p=0.14) | Headache (9), upper respiratory tract symptoms (16), gastrointestinal symptoms (13) | Participants were provided with a high-fiber 5000 kJ per day diet plan and asked not to change exercise habits. |
| Ramos (unpublished, cited in Heymsfield SB, JAMA 1998;280: 1596-1600 | Parallel; n.a. | Garcinia cambogia 1.5 g | Placebo | 8 weeks | 40 | Intergroup difference (p<0.05) | Not reported | Participants were provided with a low-fat 4200-6300 kJ per day diet. |
| Mattes RD, Physiology & Behavior 2000; 71:87-94 | Parallel; 4 | Garcinia cambogia 2.4 g | Placebo | 12 weeks | 167 / 89 | Intergroup difference (p=0.03) | Not reported | Participants were advised to follow a 5000 kJ per day diet. |
| Thom E, Int J Obes 1996; 20(Suppl4):75 | Parallel; 3 | Hydroxycitric acid from Garcinia cambogia 1.32 g | Placebo | 8 weeks | 60 / n. r. | Intergroup difference (p<0.001) | Stomach pain (1) | Participants were on a low-fat 5000 kJ per day diet and instructed to exercise 3 times per week. |
| Rothacker DO, Int J Obes 1997; 21(suppl2):53 | Parallel; 3 | Garcinia cambogia 2.4 g, caffeine 150 mg, chromium polynicotinate 120 μg | Placebo | 6 weeks | 50 / 48 | No intergroup difference (p=0.30) | None reported | Participants were advised to follow a 5000 kJ per day diet. |

(continued)

**Table 13-1  Randomized, Double-Blind Trials of Dietary Supplements for Body Weight Reduction (continued)**

| First Author, Source | Design; Quality Score | Intervention and Daily Dose | Control | Duration | Randomized/ Analyzed | Result | Adverse Events in Intervention Group (Cases) | Control of Lifestyle Factors |
|---|---|---|---|---|---|---|---|---|
| Kaats (unpublished, cited in Heymsfield SBJAMA 1998; 280:1596-1600 | Parallel; n.a. | Garcinia cambogia 1.5 g, chromium picolinate 600 µg, L-carnitine 1.2 g | Placebo | 4 weeks | 200 ÷ | Intergroup difference for fat mass loss (p<0.01) | Not reported | Participants were provided with a low-fat, high-fiber diet. |
| Antonio J, Curr Ther Res 1999; 60:220-7 | Parallel; 4 | Garcinia cambogia 750 mg, calcium phosphate 750 mg, guggul extract 750 mg, L-tyrosine 750 mg | Placebo / no treatment | 6 weeks | 20 / 18 | No intergroup differences (p>0.05) | None reported | All participants were provided with a low-fat 7500 kJ per day diet plan and exercised 3 times per week. |
| Walsh DE, Int J Obes 1983;8: 289-93 | Parallel; 3 | Glucomannan fiber 3g | Placebo | 8 weeks | 20 / n. r. | Intergroup difference (p<0.005) | None reported | Participants were advised not to change their eating or exercise habits. |
| Woodgate DE, Curr Ther Res 2003;64:248-62 | Parallel; 5 | Glucomannan, chitosan, fenugreek, G sylvestre, vitamin C 1395 mg | Placebo | 6 weeks | 24 / 22 | Intergroup difference (p<0.01) | Constipation (1), headache (1), indigestion (1) | Participants were advised not to change their eating or exercise habits. |

| Reference | Design | Intervention | Comparison | Duration | N | Result | Adverse events | Diet/exercise |
|---|---|---|---|---|---|---|---|---|
| Dellalibera O, Phytotherapie 2006;4:194-7 | Parallel; 3 | Green coffee extract 400 mg | Placebo | 60 days | 50 | Intergroup difference (p<0.001) | Not reported | Low-calorie diet. |
| Nagao T, Obesity (Silver Spring) 2007;15:1473-83 | Parallel; 3 | Green tea high in catechins (583 mg) | Green tea low in catechins (96 mg) | 12 weeks plus 2 weeks diet run-in | 270 / 240 | Intergroup difference (p<0.05) | None recorded | Patients were advised not to change their eating or exercise habits. |
| Pan Ling L, Chin J Clin Rehab 2005; 9:231-3 | Parallel; 5 | Green tea combination product with Lotus rhizome, and Panax notoginseng, 9 g | Placebo | 7 weeks | 82 / 78 | Intergroup difference (p<0.01) | Nausea (2), irritability (1) | Participants were advised not to change their eating or exercise habits. |
| Pilaczyńska-Szcześniak L, Arch Med Sci 2006;2: 171-8 | Parallel; 3 | Green tea 600 mg combination product with asparagus 1 g, bean pod 200 mg | Placebo | 56 days | 51 / 42 | No intergroup difference | Not reported | Not mentioned. |
| Opala T, Eur J Med Res 2006; 11:343-50 | Parallel; 4 | Combination product of asparagus, green/ black tea, guarana, mate, kidney bean combination product, and kidney bean pod, Garcinia cambogia, chromium yeast | Placebo | 12 weeks | 105 / 98 | No intergroup difference | Gastrointestinal complaints (8) | Participants followed an exercise program. |

(continued)

**Table 13-1 Randomized, Double-Blind Trials of Dietary Supplements for Body Weight Reduction (continued)**

| First Author, Source | Design; Quality Score | Intervention and Daily Dose | Control | Duration | Randomized/ Analyzed | Result | Adverse Events in Intervention Group (Cases) | Control of Lifestyle Factors |
|---|---|---|---|---|---|---|---|---|
| Rodríguez-Morán M, J Diabetes Comp 1998;12:273-8 | Parallel; 4 | Plantago psyllium 15 g | Placebo | 6 weeks | 125 / 123 | No intergroup difference (p>0.05) | None reported | Participants were advised to adhere to a 105 kJ/kg per day diet. |
| Kalman D, Nutrition 1999; 15:337-40 | Parallel; 4 | Pyruvate 6 g | Placebo | 6 weeks | 26 / 26 | Within group change compared with baseline (p<0.001) | Not reported | Subjects exercised 3 days per week and were instructed to follow a 8400 kJ per day diet. |
| Kalman D, Curr Ther Res 1998;59:793-802 | Parallel; 3 | Pyruvate 6g | Placebo / no treatment | 6 weeks | 53 / 51 | Within group change compared with baseline for fat mass loss (p<0.001) | None | Subjects exercised 3 days per week and were instructed to follow a 8400 kJ per day diet. |
| Greenway FL, Int J Obes 2006;30: 1737-41 | Parallel; 3 | Rhubarb (Rheum), combination product with astragalus (Astragalus), red sage (Salvia miltiorrhiza), | Placebo | 12 weeks | 24 / 21 | Lower weight loss/greater weight gain in intervention groups | Diarrhea (24), musculoskeletal (11), other gastrointestinal (5), oral (4), dermatologic (1), vaginal | None. |

| | | turmeric (Curcuma longa) and ginger (Zingiber officinale): escalating doses up to 6 g bed dried NT, 6 g freeze dried NT, 12 g freeze dried NT | | | | irritation (1), headache/migraine (1), upper respiratory symptoms (1) | |
| Roberts AT, J Med Food 2007;10: 184-8 | Parallel; 3 | Rhubarb (Rheum), combination product with astragulus (Astragalus), red sage (Salvia miltiorrhiza), turmeric (Curcuma longa) and ginger (Zingiber officinale) with herbal gallic acid (GA): 1) 300 mg NT and 1.2 g GA 2) 600 mg NT and 2.4 g GA | Placebo | 24 weeks but terminated after 8 weeks | 105 / 64 (completing 24 weeks) | Interim analysis at week 8 showed no evidence of efficacy, remaining subjects continuing the study showed no difference between groups | Not reported | Participants were instructed in a diet 700 kcal per day below weight maintenance requirements. |

(continued)

Table 13-1 Randomized, Double-Blind Trials of Dietary Supplements for Body Weight Reduction (continued)

| First Author, Source | Design; Quality Score | Intervention and Daily Dose | Control | Duration | Randomized/ Analyzed | Result | Adverse Events in Intervention Group (Cases) | Control of Lifestyle Factors |
|---|---|---|---|---|---|---|---|---|
| Andersen T. J Hum Nutr Dietet 2001; 14:243-50 | Parallel; 3 | Yerbe maté 1.0 g, guarana 0.9 g, damiana 0.3 g | Placebo | 45 days | 47 / 47 | Not reported | Not reported | Participants were instructed not to change their eating habits. |
| Kucio C, Isr J Med Sci 1991; 27:550-6 | Parallel; 2 | Yohimbine 20 mg | Placebo | 3 weeks | 20 / 20 | Intergroup difference (p<0.005) | None | Participants were advised to follow a 4200 kJ per day diet. |
| Sax L, Int J Obes 1991;15:561-5 | Parallel; 4 | Yohimbine 16 to 43 mg | Placebo | 6 months | 47 / 33 | No intergroup difference (p>0.05) | Impaired sleep (3), nervousness (1), headache (1), arthralgia (1) | Participants were advised to follow a 7500 kJ per day diet and exercise three times per week. |
| Berlin I, J Pharmacol (Paris) 1986; 17:343-7 | Parallel; 2 | Yohimbine 18 mg | Placebo | 8 weeks | 19 / 19 | No intergroup difference (p>0.05) | Not reported | Participants were advised to follow a 4200 kJ per day diet. |

**Table 13-2   Systematic Reviews and Meta-Analyses of Dietary Supplements for Body Weight Reduction**

| First Author, Source | Design | Intervention and Daily Dose | Duration | Randomized/ Analyzed | Mean Difference (kg, 95% confidence interval*) | Adverse Events (cases) | Control of Lifestyle Factors |
|---|---|---|---|---|---|---|---|
| Bent S, Am J Cardiol 2004; 94:1359-61 | Systematic review of 1 placebo-controlled RCT | Bitter orange (Citrus aurantium, combination product 975 mg, St John's wort 900 mg, caffeine 528 mg | 6 weeks | 23/20 | -1.4 | Not reported | All followed a 3 day/week exercise program and received dietary counseling. |
| Ni Murchu, Cochrane Database Syst Rev 2005;3: CD003892 | Systematic review of 14 RCTs | Chitosan 3.8 g (1.0 to 15 g) | 4 -24 weeks | 1071 | -1.7 (-2.1 to -1.3) | No clear differences in frequency between groups | Half the studies continued their normal diet, the other half had restricted calorie diets. |
| Pittler MH, Am J Clin Nutr 2004;79:529-36 | Meta-analysis of double-blind, placebo-controlled RCTs | Chromium picolinate 200 to 924 µg | 9 to 14 weeks | 601 / 489 | -1.1 (-1.8 to -0.4) | None | In most trials patients were instructed not to change their eating habits and exercise regularly. |
| Haugen M, Tdsskr Nor Laegeforen 2004;124:3051-4 | Systematic review of 13 placebo-controlled RCTs | Conjugated linoleic acid 0.7-6.8 g | 4 weeks to 1 year | 616 | Not reported | Results indicate potential negative impact on carbohydrate and lipid metabolism | Not reported. |

*(continued)*

**Table 13-2   Systematic Reviews and Meta-Analyses of Dietary Supplements for Body Weight Reduction**

| First Author, Source | Design | Intervention and Daily Dose | Duration | Randomized/ Analyzed | Mean Difference (kg, 95% confidence interval*) | Adverse Events (cases) | Control of Lifestyle Factors |
|---|---|---|---|---|---|---|---|
| Shekelle PG, JAMA 2003; 289:1537-45 | Meta-analysis of 20 controlled trials | Ephedra/ephedrine n.r./20-150 mg | 8 to 24 weeks | 1514 | -0.9kg/ month | Safety data from 50 trials yielded estimates of 2.2 to 3.6-fold increases in odds of psychiatric, autonomic, or gastrointestinal symptoms, and heart palpitations | Not reported. |
| Pittler MH, Am J Med 2001;110: 724-30 | Meta-analysis of 20 double-blind, placebo-controlled RCTs | Guar gum 9 to 30 g | 4 to 24 weeks | 203 / 192 | -0.04 (-2.22 to 2.14) | Diarrhea, flatulence (28), gastrointestinal complaints (8) | In most trials patients were instructed not to change their eating habits. |

* Where available.

in the intervention group compared to the placebo group (15). Systematic safety data for these Ayurvedic herbal preparations are not available. Overall, there is limited evidence to suggest that ayurvedic preparations may possibly be effective for weight loss; however there is insufficient evidence to make a recommendation regarding these products at this time (see Evidence Summary table at end of chapter).

## Bitter Orange (*Citrus aurantium*)

In response to the 2004 Food and Drug Administration (FDA) ban of products containing ephedrine alkaloids due to safety concerns, many manufacturers started producing "ephedra-free" products by substituting ephedra with bitter orange (*Citrus aurantium*). Bitter orange extracts contains m-synephrine, a sympathetic alpha-2 adrenergic agonist similar to phenylephrine. A systematic review (16) of one RCT and a subsequent small pilot RCT (17) found that two bitter orange combination products appear not to be effective for weight loss. Safety information of bitter orange is extremely limited, and consumption may lead to increases in blood pressure and pulse and cardiovascular events. There is limited evidence to suggest that bitter orange may not be effective for weight loss and may cause harm; therefore, at this time, the evidence base supports a weak recommendation against the use of bitter orange for weight loss (see Evidence Summary table at end of chapter).

## Chitosan

Chitosan is a cationic polysaccharide produced from chitin, a substance derived from the exoskeleton of crustaceans such as crabs and lobster. It is promoted as a remedy to reduce fat absorption. A Cochrane systematic review of 14 RCTs including 1071 participants found that chitosan was associated with a statistically significant reduction in weight of 1.7 kg, and in systolic and diastolic blood pressure (5.9 mmHg and 3.4 mmHg, respectively) when compared with placebo. There were no differences in adverse rate frequency nor fecal fat excretion between groups. Trials of higher methodological quality were associated with a lower effect size that was of statistical significance but of questionable clinical significance (18). A subsequently published RCT randomized 150 overweight adults to 3 grams chitosan daily and use of a pedometer, active control (weight loss program of choice), or placebo (including pedometer). The intervention group lost more weight (-2.8 lbs vs. +0.8 lbs) and fat mass (-2.6 lbs vs. +0.1 lbs, p = 0.006) than the active control group, and had statistically significant reductions of similar magnitude when compared with the placebo group (18). Some adverse events such as gastrointestinal symptoms have been reported, but no systematic safety data are available. Overall there is moderate evidence to support a weak recommendation in favor of using chitosan for weight loss; however, the size of the effect that may be achievable seems negligible (see Evidence Summary table at end of chapter).

## Chromium Picolinate

Chromium picolinate is an organic compound of trivalent chromium, an essential trace mineral and cofactor to insulin, and picolinic acid, a naturally occurring derivative of tryptophan. It enhances insulin activity and has been the subject of a number of studies assessing its effects in carbohydrate, protein and lipid metabolism. A meta-analysis of 10 double-blind RCTs (19) indicated a weight loss of 1.1 to 1.2 kg compared with placebo during an intervention period of 10 to 13 weeks (~0.1 kg/week). A subsequent RCT found no significant weight loss over and above that with placebo (20). It thus seems that the effect observed with chromium picolinate is, although statistically significant, too small to be clinically meaningful. Few serious adverse events have been reported, but there is no systematic safety data available. Overall, it appears that chromium picolinate is relatively safe but there is moderate evidence to suggest that chromium picolinate has such a negligible effect on weight loss such that no recommendation can be made at this time (see Evidence Summary table at end of chapter).

## Common Bean (*Phaseolus vulgaris*)

The common bean (*Phaseolus vulgaris*) is a so-called "starch-blocker"; its mechanism of action is assumed to be linked to the alpha-amylase–inhibiting effect of the bean. The lipase activity purportedly inhibits the triglyceride hydrolysis. A double-blind RCT using white kidney bean (*P. vulgaris*) and locust bean gum (*Ceratonia siliqua*) found a significant reduction in body weight of 3 kg over that in the placebo group after 3 months (= 1 kg/month) and further weight loss during a 9-month open-label follow-up (21). One double-blind RCT of white kidney bean (*P. vulgaris*) extract in combination with several other compounds found a weight loss in the bean group of 2.58 kg above that of placebo after 30 days (= 2.58 kg/month) (22). A weight loss of 2.3 kg in 12 weeks (= 0.8 kg/month) over that with placebo is reported in an RCT of a combination product containing common bean (*P. vulgaris*) extract, inulin and *Garcinia cambogia* extract (23). Adverse events reported in these trials were usually few and minor. It appears relatively safe based on limited safety data. Overall, there is moderate evidence to support a weak recommendation for the common bean for weight loss (see Evidence Summary table at end of chapter).

## Conjugated Linoleic Acid

Conjugated linoleic acid (CLA) refers to a family of trans-fatty acids that have been found to reduce fat deposition in obese mice, possibly through increased fat oxidation and decreased triglyceride uptake in adipose tissue. A systematic review of 13 placebo-controlled RCTs found no weight or fat mass reduction with CLA products in humans (24). Studies in animals and humans have shown a negative impact on carbohydrate and lipid metabolism by inducing insulin resistance and hyperlipidaemia. Concerns about its safety during pregnancy and lactation have also been raised (24). Overall, there is moderate evidence to suggest that CLA appears to have no effect on weight loss and may cause harm. Consequently, the evidence base currently supports a weak recommendation against the use of CLA for weight loss (see Evidence Summary table at end of chapter).

## Ephedra/Ephedrine

The Chinese botanical ephedra (*Ephedra sinica*), or ma huang, is a natural source of the alkaloids ephedrine and pseudoephedrine. Ephedrine is a sympathomimetic agent that enhances the release of norepinephrine from sympathetic neurons and stimulates alpha and beta receptors. It may function as an anorectic by acting on the satiety centre in the hypothalamus. In 2004, after the publication of several studies highlighting the potential risks of ephedra, the FDA banned the sale of dietary supplements containing ephedrine alkaloids because they present an "unreasonable risk of illness or injury."

Ephedrine has been studied alone and in combination with caffeine. A meta-analysis of 20 controlled trials found that the short-term use of ephedrine at high doses (n=5, weight loss 0.6 kg/month above placebo), of ephedrine and caffeine (n=12, weight loss 1 kg/month above placebo), herbal ephedra (n=1, weight loss 0.8 kg/month above placebo), and herbal ephedra with other herbs containing caffeine (n=4, weight loss 1 kg/month above placebo) reduces weight (25). Caffeine added additional efficacy to ephedrine (weight loss 0.4 kg/month above ephedrine alone); the effects of ephedrine and caffeine, and ephedra with or without herbs containing caffeine, are approximately equivalent. The weight loss is, however, only modest, about 0.9 kg per month more than with placebo. Long-term effects have not been assessed.

Subsequently published studies have reported weight loss of 3.9 kg over 6 months (= 0.6 kg per month) over that with placebo for ephedrine and caffeine (26), 1.5 kg over 3 months (= 0.5 kg/month) for a combination product of ephedrine, kola nut, willow bark, and other herbal components (27), and 4.93 kg (=0.5kg/month) for ephedra and caffeine (28).

Ephedra and ephedrine have been associated with serious adverse events. The above meta-analysis also assessed safety based on RCTs and case reports.

The safety data from 50 RCTs yielded estimates of 2.2- to 3.6-fold increases in odds of psychiatric symptoms, autonomic hyperactivity, upper gastrointestinal symptoms, and heart palpitations. Case reports of serious adverse events include deaths, myocardial infarctions, cerebrovascular accidents, seizures and psychiatric cases as sentinel events with prior ephedra and ephedrine consumption, many of them occurring in persons aged 30 years or younger (25). There is strong evidence to suggest that ephedra- and ephedrine-containing products have some effect on weight loss and equally strong evidence to suggest that these products can be harmful. The evidence base supports a strong recommendation against the use of ephedra- and ephedrine-containing products for weight loss because of serious safety concerns (see Evidence Summary table at end of chapter).

## Garcinia cambogia

Hydroxycitric acid obtained from extracts of *Garcinia cambogia*, has been shown to inhibit citrate cleavage enzyme, suppress *de novo* fatty acid synthesis and food intake, and decrease body weight gain. Data from a double-blind RCT of G. *cambogia* extract suggest no beneficial effects for weight loss compared with placebo (29). Two smaller placebo-controlled, double-blind RCTs, however, report significant differential effects in patients treated with G. *cambogia* (29a, 29b), while a trial testing hydroxycitric acid also found positive effects (30). Other double-blind RCTs investigated the effects of G. *cambogia* extract or hydroxycitric acid containing combination preparations with or without dietary alterations (31-33) and report conflicting results. No systematic safety data are available. Overall, there is conflicting evidence on the effect of G. *cambogia* extract and hydroxycitric acid for weight loss and therefore no recommendation can be made at this time (see Evidence Summary table at end of chapter).

## Glucomannan

Glucomannan is a component of konjac root, derived from *Amorphophallus konjac*. Its chemical structure is similar to that of galactomannan from guar gum and is composed of a polysaccharide chain of glucose and mannose. One double-blind RCT suggests beneficial effects compared with placebo (34). A stimulant-free combination product of glucomannan, chitosan, fenugreek, *Gymnema sylvestre*, and vitamin C was assessed in a small double-blind, placebo-controlled RCT (35) and showed a weight reduction of 2.3 kg over 6 weeks (= 1.5 kg/month) above that in the placebo group. No systematic safety data are available but esophageal or gastrointestinal obstruction has been reported with the administration in tablet form. Further study of this supplement is required for firm statements regarding its safety and effectiveness. There is limited data suggesting that glucomannan might have some effect in weight loss. Given the limited evidence base and the rare risk of esophageal and intestinal obstruction based on case reports, there is insufficient evidence to make a recommendation about this dietary supplement at this time (see Evidence Summary table at end of chapter).

## Green Coffee Extract

A decaffeinated green coffee extract, which is rich in chlorogenic acids and has a specific ratio between 5-caffeoylquinic acid and other caffeoylquinic acid isomers, is claimed to be a fat burner. Its proposed mechanisms of action include the inhibition of glucose absorption in the small intestine, the limitation of the release of glucose from glycogen into the general circulation and insulinemia by inhibiting the activity of glucose-6-phosphatase. One RCT reported weight loss in the green coffee extract group of 2.52 kg after 60 days (= 1.13 kg/month) over that of the placebo group (36). Systematic safety data are not available. There is limited evidence to suggest that this product might have some effect on weight loss; however, overall, the evidence base is insufficient to make a recommendation at this time (see Evidence Summary table at end of chapter).

## Green Tea (*Camellia sinensis*)

A green tea (*Camellia sinensis*) extract high in catechins was found to be associated with greater weight loss than tea low in catechins over 12 weeks (37). A double-blind RCT of a combination of green tea, lotus rhizome and *Panax notoginseng* produced a weight loss of 0.9 kg over that of placebo (38). A combination product of green tea extract, bean peel and asparagus extract was not associated with a difference in weight loss compared to placebo in a double-blind RCT (39). No significant differences in body weight after 12 weeks were found in a double-blind, placebo-controlled RCT of the botanical extract-based formula Nutrifen containing asparagus, green/black tea, guarana, mate, kidney bean, a kidney bean pod and *Garcinia cambogia*, as well as a chromium yeast combination product (40). Only limited safety data are available, but mild adverse effects such as gastrointestinal complaints and insomnia have been reported. Overall, green tea appears safe but there are conflicting results on the effect of green tea for weight loss. Consequently, there is insufficient evidence at this time to make a recommendation regarding green tea for weight management (see Evidence Summary table at end of chapter).

## Guar Gum

Guar gum is a dietary fiber derived from the Indian cluster bean (*Cyamopsis tetragonolobus*). This fiber prevents the absorption of fat by binding it in the gut. Its beneficial effects for lowering body weight were assessed in a meta-analysis (41). Twenty double-blind, placebo-controlled RCTs were included and the data of 11 trials were pooled. The results of the meta-analysis suggested that guar gum is not effective for reducing body weight. The agreement between the analyzed RCTs, suggesting the absence of a differential effect, confirms the overall result of the meta-analysis. Mainly gastrointestinal adverse events have been reported with guar gum consumption, but no systematic safety data are available. There is moderate evidence to suggest that Guar gum is not effective for weight loss, and therefore the evidence base supports a weak recommendation against it for this indication (see Evidence Summary table at end of chapter).

## Psyllium (*Plantago ovata*)

Psyllium derived from the husks of ripe seeds from *Plantago ovata* (*P. isphagula* Roxburgh) is a water-soluble fiber postulated to increase satiety. Whether this results in weight loss was tested in a double-blind RCT (42). After 6 weeks of treatment there were no significant changes in body weight in either the treatment or placebo group. In general psyllium is widely consumed by the general population to regulate bowel movements and is well-tolerated. However, no systematic safety data are available but serious allergic reactions including anaphylactic shock and obstruction of the gastrointestinal tract have been reported. There is limited evidence to suggest that psyllium is not effective for weight loss. At this time, the evidence base is insufficient to make a recommendation (see Evidence Summary table at end of chapter).

## Pyruvate

Pyruvate is generated in the body via glycolysis and seems to enhance exercise performance and improve measures of body composition when supplemented externally. Two double-blind RCTs assessing the effects of pyruvate supplementation did not report significant differential effects for weight reduction (43,44). No systematic safety data are available. There is limited evidence to suggest that pyruvate is not effective for weight loss. At this time, there is insufficient evidence to make a recommendation (see Evidence Summary table at end of chapter).

# Rhubarb (Rheum)

An herbal supplement made from 40% rhubarb (*Rheum*) root and stem, astragulus (*Astragalus*), red sage (*Salvia miltiorrhiza*), turmeric (*Curcuma longa*) and ginger (*Zingiber officinale*) is postulated to reduce food intake. One RCT found it to be associated with less weight loss than placebo, or even with slight weight gain after 11 weeks (45). Due to the dose-limiting gastrointestinal toxicity it appears not to be useful as a weight loss product. Also, when administered in combination with gallic acid in an RCT, there was no dose-related weight loss or reduction in food intake after 8 weeks (46). It can therefore not be recommended as a slimming aid. There is limited evidence to suggest that Rhubarb is not effective for weight loss and that it is associated with gastrointestinal toxicity. Therefore, the evidence base supports a weak recommendation against using this compound as a weight loss aid (see Evidence Summary table at end of chapter).

# Yerbe Maté (*Ilex paraguayensis*)

Yerbe maté (*Ilex paraguayensis*) is an evergreen tree native to South America. In a combination preparation also containing guarana (*Paullinia cupana*) and damiana (*Turnera diffusa*) it was tested in overweight or obese patients. *Ilex paraguayensis* and in particular *Paullinia cupana* contain relatively large amounts of caffeine. These herbs, which exhibit effects on the central nervous system, have also been shown to prolong gastric emptying time using ultrasound scanning (47). The descriptive results of this study suggest that this combination preparation has potentially beneficial effects for lowering body weight, but there are not enough data available to make any recommendations. Systematic safety data for yerbe maté are not available. Therefore, there is insufficient evidence to make a recommendation at this time (see Evidence Summary table at end of chapter).

# Yohimbe (*Pausinystalia yohimbe*)

Yohimbine is the main active constituent of the ground bark of yohimbe (*Pausinystalia yohimbe*) and is also present in other plants such as the Indian snakeroot (*Rauwolfia serpentina*). Most clinical studies concentrate on the effects of this isolated constituent, which is an alpha-2 receptor antagonist. Three double-blind RCTs of yohimbine for weight loss report conflicting results (48-50). No systematic safety data are available but adverse events such as rapid heart rate, high blood pressure, skin flushing, painful urination, genital pain, agitation, headache and insomnia have been reported. Overall, the evidence for efficacy is conflicting in a compound that has been associated with adverse events; therefore, the evidence base supports a weak recommendation against using yohimbe for weight loss at this time (see Evidence Summary table at end of chapter).

## Conclusions and Recommendations

There is a wealth of dietary supplements for weight loss available but only a relatively small number have been tested in controlled trials. For many of the tested dietary supplements no recommendation can be given. These are: Ayurvedic preparations, chromium piccolinate, *Garcinia cambogia*, glucomannan, green coffee extract, green tea (*Camellia sinensis*), *Plantago psyllium*, pyruvate, and yerbe mate. Weak recommendations in favor could be given for chitosan and common bean (*Phaseolus vulgaris*). Weak recommendations against use could be given for bitter orange (*Citrus aurantium*), conjugated linoleic acid, guar gum, rhubarb (*Rheum* spp) and yohimbe (*Pausinystalia yohimbe*),and there are strong recommendations against the use of ephedra (*Ephedra sinica*) and ephedrine-ontaining supplements.

In conclusion, a large number of herbal and other dietary supplements for body weight reduction are on offer. However, based on the evidence of safety and effectiveness available to date, none of them can be considered of clinical relevance.

**Evidence Summary of Dietary Supplements for Body Weight Reduction**

| Clinical Indication | Category | Specific Therapy | Dose | Outcome | Confidence of Estimate on Effectiveness | Magnitude of Effect* | Safety† | Clinical Recommendation‡ | Comments |
|---|---|---|---|---|---|---|---|---|---|
| Weight loss | Biologically based practices | Ayurvedic preparations | Variable | Weight loss | C | Moderate | Unclear | No Recommendation | — |
| Weight loss | Biologically based practices | Bitter orange (Citrus aurantium) | Variable | Weight loss | C | No effect | Single thumbs down | Weak against | — |
| Weight loss | Biologically based practices | Chitosan | 3.8 g | Weight loss, lean body mass, % body fat, blood pressure | B | Small (<1lb/month) | Double thumbs up | Weak in favor | — |
| Weight loss | Biologically based practices | Chromium picolinate | 200 mcg-934 mcg daily | Weight loss | B | Small (<.5 lbs/month) | Double thumbs up | No recommendation | — |
| Weight loss | Biologically based practices | Common bean (Phaseolus vulgaris) | Variable | Weight loss | B | Small (2lbs/month) | Double thumbs up | Weak in favor | Often studied as part of a combination product |
| Weight loss | Biologically based practices | Conjugated linoleic acid | Variable | Weight loss | B | No effect | Single thumbs down | Weak against | Potential harm on carbohydrate and lipid metabolism |

(continued)

## Evidence Summary of Dietary Supplements for Body Weight Reduction (continued)

| Clinical Indication | Category | Specific Therapy | Dose | Outcome | Confidence of Estimate on Effectiveness | Magnitude of Effect* | Safety† | Clinical Recommendation‡ | Comments |
|---|---|---|---|---|---|---|---|---|---|
| Weight loss | Biologically based practices | Ephedra/ephedrhine | Variable | Weight loss | A | Small | Double thumbs down | Strong against | Banned by FDA in 2004 |
| Weight loss | Biologically based practices | Garcinia cambogia | Variable | Weight loss | C | Conflicting results | Unclear | No recommendation | — |
| Weight loss | Biologically based practices | Glucomannan | Variable | Weight loss | C | Small | Single thumbs down | No recommendation | Case reports of esophageal and intestinal obstruction. |
| Weight loss | Biologically based practices | Green coffee extract | Variable | Weight loss | C | Small | Unclear | No recommendation | — |
| Weight loss | Biologically based practices | Green tea (Camellia sinensis) | Variable | Weight loss | C | Conflicting results | Double thumbs up | No recommendation | — |
| Weight loss | Biologically based practices | Guar gum | Variable | Weight loss | B | No effect | Unclear | Weak against | — |
| Weight loss | Biologically based practices | Psyllium (Plantago ovata) | Variable | Weight loss | C | No effect | Single thumbs up | No recommendation | — |

| | | | | | | | | |
|---|---|---|---|---|---|---|---|---|
| Weight loss | Biologically based practices | Pyruvate | Variable | Weight loss C | No effect | Unclear | No recommendation | — |
| Weight loss | Biologically based practices | Rhubarb (Rheum) | Variable | Weight loss C | No effect | Single thumbs down | Weak against | — |
| Weight loss | Biologically based practices | Yerbe maté (Ilex paraguayensis) | Variable | Weight loss D | Unclear | Unclear | No recommendation | — |
| Weight loss | Biologically based practices | Yohimbe (Pausinystalia yohimbe) | Variable | Weight loss B | Conflicting results | Single thumbs down | Weak against | — |

* Small, moderate (OR>1.2–2) or large (OR>2)

† 5 categories: Double thumbs up, single thumb up, no recommendation, single thumb down, double thumb down

‡ 5 categories: Strong (in favor), weak (in favor), no recommendation, weak (against), strong (against)

## REFERENCES

1. **National Center for Health Statistics.** Health, United States, 2004 with Chartbook on Trends in the Health of Americans. Hyattsville, MD: Department of Health and Human Services, 2004.
2. **Wyatt SB, Winters KP, Dubbert PM.** Overweight and obesity: prevalence, consequences, and causes of a growing public health problem. Am J Med Sci. 2006;331:166-74.
3. **Klein S, Burke LE, Bray GA, et al.** Clinical implications of obesity with specific focus on cardiovascular disease: a statement for professionals from the American Heart Association Council on Nutrition, Physical Activity, and Metabolism: endorsed by the American College of Cardiology Foundation. Circulation. 2004;110:2952-67.s
4. **Field AE, Coakley EH, Must A, et al.** Impact of overweight on the risk of developing common chronic diseases during a 10-year period. Arch Intern Med. 2001;161:1581-6.
5. **Key TJ, Allen NE, Spencer EA, Travis RC.** The effect of diet on risk of cancer. Lancet 2002;360:861-8.
6. **Friedman N, Fanning EL.** Overweight and obesity: an overview of prevalence, clinical impact, and economic impact. Dis Manag. 2004;7(Suppl 1): S1-6.
7. **Allison DB, Fontaine KR, Manson JE, et al.** Annual deaths attributable to obesity in the United States. JAMA. 1999;282:1530-8.
8. **Madley R.** Big and getting bigger. Nutraceuticals World. 2002;October:48-64.
9. **Morris CA, Avorn J.** Internet marketing of herbal products. JAMA. 2003;290:1505-9
10. **Blanck HM, Serdula MK, Gillespie C et al.** Use of nonprescription dietary supplements for weight loss is common among Americans. J Am Diet Assoc. 2007;107:441-7.
11. **Blanck HM, Khan LK, Serdula MK.** Use of nonprescription weight loss products. JAMA. 2001;286:930-5.
12. **Sharpe PA, Blanck HM, Williams JE, et al.** Use of complementary and alternative medicine for weight control in the United States. J Altern Complement Med. 2007;13:217-22.
13. Natural Medicines Database, www.naturaldatabase.com, accessed August 2007.
14. Natural Standard, www.naturalstandards.com, accessed August 2007.
15. **Paranjpe P.** J Ethnopharmacol 1990;29:1-11.
16. **Bent S.** Am J Cardiol 2004; 94:1359-61.
17. **Greenway F.** J Med Food 2006;9:572-8.
18. **Ni Murchu.** Cochrane Database Syst Rev 2005;3:CD003892.
19. **Pittler MH.** Am J Clin Nutr 2004;79:529-36.
20. **Lukaski HC.** Nutrition 2007;23:187-95.
21. **Støa Birketvedt G.** Curr Top Nutraceutical Res 2005;3:137-42.
22. **Celleno L.** Int J Med Sci 2007;4:45-52.
23. **Thom L.** J Int Med Res 2000;28:229-33.
24. **Haugen M.** Tidsskr Nor Laegeforen 2004;124:3051-4.
25. **Shekelle PG.** JAMA 2003;289:1537-45.
26. **Hioki C.** Clin Exp Pharmacol Physiol 2004;31:614-9.
27. **Coffey CS.** Int J Obes 2004;28:1411-9.
28. **Hackman RM.** Int J Obes 2006;30:1545-56.
29. **Heymsfield SB.** JAMA 1998;280:1596-1600.
29a. **Ramos.** (unpublished, cited in Heymsfield SB, JAMA 1998;280:1596-1600.
29b. **Mattes RD.** Physiology & Behavior 2000;71:87-94.
30. **Thom E.** Int J Obes 1996;20(Suppl4):75.
31. **Rothacker DO.** Int J Obes 1997;21(suppl2):53.
32. **Kaats.** (unpublished, cited in Heymsfield SBJAMA 1998;280:1596-1600.
33. **Antonio J.** Curr Ther Res 1999;60:220-7.
34. **Walsh DE.** Int J Obes 1983;8:289-93.
35. **Woodgate DE.** Curr Ther Res 2003;64:248-62.
36. **Dellalibera O.** phytotherapie 2006;4:194-7.
37. **Nagao T.** Obesity (Silver Spring) 2007;15:1473-83.

# Chapter 14

# Depression

Sudha Prathikanti, MD

> Canst thou not minister to a mind diseased, pluck from the memory a rooted sorrow, raze out the written troubles of the brain, and with some sweet oblivious antidote cleanse the fraught bosom of that perilous stuff which weighs upon the heart?
>
> *from* William Shakespeare, *Macbeth*

In the United States, the experience of depression or other psychological distress appears to predict greater use of complementary and alternative medicine (CAM). For example, in a national survey of U.S. households (1), respondents meeting criteria for one or more mental disorders were significantly more likely to use CAM therapies than their counterparts without a mental disorder. In another large survey of U.S. residents (2), self-report of mental conditions increased the likelihood of having visited a CAM practitioner. In a third large community sample of U.S adults (3), respondents with self-reported anxiety or depression sought CAM therapies to treat their symptoms more often than did respondents with any other medical condition except neck or back problems. Of note, individuals with emotional distress who use CAM remedies are likely to do so in conjunction with conventional mental health treatments, rather than to replace such treatments (1,4).

These epidemiological studies invite one to consider why people struggling to "raze out the written troubles of the brain" so often seek CAM "antidotes" for their suffering. Individuals with mental disorders most often reported being drawn to CAM therapies because of congruence between their own beliefs about health and healing and the philosophy of "holism" or "natural care" underlying CAM approaches (5,6). While the orientation toward more "natural" or "holistic" healing is also the most frequently cited reason for CAM use among the general population (7,8), the desire to be seen as a "whole person" may have special salience in understanding the disproportionately high use of CAM among the psychologically distressed. Individuals with psychological problems are likely to have heightened awareness of the mind-body dualism that still pervades conventional biomedicine and psychiatry and that influences western cultural constructs of increased personal blame, responsibility or causation for symptoms perceived to be psychologically based rather than biologically based (9). In such a dualist context, emotionally distressed individuals may be drawn to CAM practitioners and treatments out of a desire to augment routine mental health care with a complementary healing approach that bridges the conventional mind-body divide and perhaps lessens an internalized sense of stigma for experiencing psychological symptoms.

The quality of caregiver time and presence may also have a special impact on the rates of CAM use by individuals with emotional distress. With dramatic changes in the structure and economics of healthcare delivery, and with recent advances in neuroscience leading to more insights regarding the physiology of emotion and cognition, there may be considerable pressure for physicians across all specialties to focus on treating the biological aspects of mind (10,11) while reducing time spent on developing interpersonal bonds with their patients. In contrast, the structure of most practitioner-based CAM encourages empathic discussion of emotional distress and an unhurried exploration of lifestyle and psychospiritual factors that impact wellness (8,12). Thus, while people with psychological problems may obtain conventional mental health care and report satisfaction with that care, they may still turn to CAM practitioners for additional empathy and humanistic elements of care that faciliate adaptive coping with emotional distress.

Limitations in the efficacy and tolerability of conventional mental health treatments may also contribute to high rates of CAM use among psychologically distressed individuals. For example, the first trial of antidepressant medication typically yields remission in only about a third of patients with major depression (13). Moreover, 30%-50% of patients may discontinue antidepressant medication prematurely (14-17), influenced by (18-22) social stigma, expense, delay in the medication's onset of action, and a plethora of side effects. Cognitive-behavioral therapy or interpersonal therapy may be less effective than medication in severe forms of major depression (23), and in mild-to-moderate major depression, these psychotherapies typically yield the same relatively low remission rates obtained with pharmacotherapy (24,25). Like pharmacotherapy, psychotherapy is also limited by high dropout rates; in one large meta-analysis, dropout rates across different forms of psychotherapy averaged about 47% (26). Premature discontinuation of psychotherapy may be due to several factors (27-32), including problematic alliance with the therapist, skill level of the therapist, unfamiliarity with the psychotherapeutic process, duration and expense of office visits, or incongruity with cultural beliefs of the patient.

## Prevalence of CAM Use
## Among Depressed Individuals

Several national surveys have assessed the proportion of individuals with depression who use at least one CAM modality (other than prayer) in any given year. In surveys that employed formal screening criteria to establish a likely diagnosis of major depression, CAM usage rates among depressed respondents ranged from 13% to 22% (1,33). In surveys that relied on self-report of "severe depression," CAM usage rates among depressed respondents were much higher and ranged from 41% to 54% (3,4). As in the general population, people with psychological distress who use CAM are likely to be female, middle-aged, and better-educated (1,2).

It is important to note that CAM use by depressed individuals may not always be for the alleviation of psychological symptoms. In a large regional survey (5), psychiatric outpatients who used CAM therapies primarily did so for improvement of psychiatric symptoms, but also targeted somatic symptoms nearly as often. In a national survey (2), investigators found that among people with mental disorders who made visits to CAM practitioners, only about half of the total visits were for the purpose of treating the mental disorder. Moreover, CAM users with transient stress or adjustment disorders were most likely to visit CAM practitioners for the alleviation of psychological symptoms, while respondents with more serious or persistent mental disorders were most likely to use CAM for non-psychiatric indications.

## CAM Therapies for Depression

Few surveys have attempted to ascertain the specific CAM modalities used most often for depression. Among existing surveys, population samples and methods have differed widely, rendering it difficult to generalize findings. In two large national surveys involving community samples of individuals with self-reported depression (3,4), the two most commonly used CAM modalities for addressing depressive symptoms were "relaxation techniques" (including meditation) and "spiritual healing" (excluding prayer); herbal remedies constituted only a small percentage of total CAM use. In a third national community survey examining use of practitioner-based CAM treatments among individuals with a likely mental disorder, acupuncture and herbal remedies were the most popular CAM remedies (2). In practice, the choice of a specific CAM modality for treating depression is likely influenced by many factors, including symptom severity, familiarity with a given modality, access to that modality, recommendations from trusted others, and trends in the general population.

In the sections below, select CAM modalities for treating major depressive disorder (major depression) will be discussed. Major depression occurs along a spectrum of symptom intensity ranging from mild to moderate to severe. Of note, mild major depression is not synonymous with "minor depression." Minor depression refers to dysthymia, which is a distinct mood disorder not meeting full diagnostic criteria for major depression.

## Yoga Therapy

In western countries, yoga practice typically consists of specific body postures (asanas) and breathing exercises (pranayama). (See p. 426 for more details.) The use of yoga as a CAM therapy is growing in the United States (34), and depression is among the most common health conditions treated with yoga (35).

### Dose and Duration of Treatment

In existing RCTs of yoga for depression, sessions ranged from 20 to 60 minutes practiced 2 to 6 times each week over 4 to 5 weeks. Sessions were practiced individually and in a group setting. Further investigation is needed to establish optimal yoga practice for mental health benefits in western settings.

### Mechanism of Action

Mood benefits of yoga practices are hypothesized to occur via regulation of the autonomic and central nervous systems. Pranayama may stimulate vagal afferents and promote parasympathetic calming and relaxation in key cortical regions. Brain levels of gamma aminobutyric acid (GABA) are observed to increase after yoga asanas, so regular practice of yoga may help to reverse central nervous system effects of GABA depletion associated with depressive disorders. However, much research remains to be done to elucidate yoga's potential mechanisms of action in conventional biomedical terms.

### Evidence of Efficacy

In a recent review by Pilkington and colleagues (2005) (36), investigators identified 5 randomized controlled trials that compared yoga to other interventions for achieving symptom remission in major depression. While these RCTs all had significant methodological problems, they consistently suggest superior mood benefits of yoga in comparison to control interventions.

Among the 5 yoga trials, 2 involved Sudarshan Kriya Yoga (SKY). This intervention consists of a daily 30-minute practice of rhythmic yoga breathing exercises performed in a seated position with eyes closed; it concludes with a supine yoga posture called Shavasana for an additional 10 minutes. In one study of SKY (37), 45 medication-free subjects having a DSM-IV diagnosis of major depressive disorder with melancholic features were randomized to receive ECT, imipramine or SKY. At the end of 4 weeks, scores on the Hamilton Rating Scale for Depression (HRSD) revealed that the ECT group had fared best with a depression remission rate of 93%, but the imipramine and SKY groups were comparable to one another with respective remission rates of 73% and 67%. In a second study of SKY that was a double-blinded RCT (38), 30 medication-free subjects having a DSM-IV diagnosis of major depressive disorder were randomized to receive either SKY or "partial" SKY, which replaced the longest segment of rhythmic yoga breathing with normal breathing. At the end of 4 weeks, both groups showed significant reduction in Beck Depression Inventory (BDI) scores, with an 80% response rate in the full SKY group and 58% response rate in the partial SKY group; the difference in response rate narrowly missed statistical significance.

The remaining 3 RCTs in the review used varying yoga interventions for depression. In one trial (39), 30 outpatients with major depression were randomly assigned to daily 20-minute sessions of a yoga-based relaxation technique (involving deep breathing/spine stretching/leg raising), Jacobson's Progressive Relaxation, or a control intervention in which subjects narrated their states of mind. After 3 days, subjects in both relaxation groups reported significant reduction in depressive symptoms as compared to subjects in the control group. In a second RCT (40), 50 outpatients with depression were randomized to daily 30-minute sessions of Shavasana yoga pose with rhythmic breathing or to no intervention. After 30 days, subjects in the yoga group showed significant reduction in scores on the Zung Self Rating Scale for Depression, as compared to subjects in the control group. In a third RCT (41), 28 subjects with BDI scores suggestive of mild depression were randomized to Iyengar yoga practice of back bends/standing poses/inversions for 60 minutes twice weekly, or to a wait-list control. After 5 weeks, subjects in the yoga group showed significant reduction in BDI scores as compared to wait-listed controls.

### Safety, Adverse Effects and Contraindications

With supervision from an experienced teacher, yoga appears to be safe by a wide margin. None of the yoga studies cited above reported any adverse effects other than mild breathlessness or fatigue. Its safety grade is double thumbs up.

### Recommendations

More RCTs of better methodological quality are needed to verify the mood benefits of yoga in depression. However, existing data suggest there is moderate evidence to support a weak recommedation in favor of yoga as a monotherapy in major depression (see Evidence Summary table at end of chapter).

## Meditation Therapy

A simple definition of meditation is the self-regulation of attention. The medical literature has focused on two types of meditation originating in eastern spiritual traditions of yoga and vipassana: concentration meditation and mindfulness meditation.

### Dose and Duration of Treatment

Further investigation is needed to establish optimal practices for mental health benefits in western settings. In most studies of meditation for mental health purposes, meditation was practiced in 20 to 45 minute sessions once or twice daily; however, some studies have also used daylong meditation retreats as part of the intervention. Sessions are usually practiced individually but may also occur in a group setting.

## Mechanism of Action

Mood benefits of meditation are hypothesized to occur via down-regulation of the sympathetic nervous system and activation of the parasympathetic system. Reduction in heart rate and blood pressure are among the strongest and most consistent neurophysiological effects of meditation. However, much research remains to be done to elucidate meditation's potential mechanisms of action in conventional biomedical terms.

## Evidence of Efficacy

A few RCTs suggest that among patients with primary medical conditions who have associated depressive symptoms, mood benefits may result from meditative practices such as Transcendental Meditation (42), the Relaxation Response (43,44) and Mindfulness-Based Stress Reduction (45). However, there is a paucity of data on potential mood benefits of meditation as an intervention specifically for major depression.

A recent single-blind RCT provides preliminary data on potential benefits of concentration meditation as an adjunct to pharmacotherapy in major depression (46). In this study, 30 subjects with major depression were randomized to daily antidepressant medication versus daily antidepressant medication plus practice of Sahaja concentration meditation for 10 minutes twice daily. After 8 weeks, both groups showed reduction in HRSD scores; however, the pharmacotherapy plus meditation group reportedly had significantly greater reduction in HRSD scores and also had a significantly higher remission rate.

Coelho et al (2007) (47) summarized emerging data on the potential of Mindfulness-Based Cognitive Therapy (MBCT) to help prevent relapse in recurrent major depression. MBCT is a complex intervention that integrates elements of mindfulness meditation with cognitive-behavioral therapy. In one RCT (48), 145 subjects with major depression in remission were randomized to 8 weeks of treatment-as-usual versus treatment-as-usual plus 2 hrs/week of manualized MBCT to target the negative cognitions associated with depression. At the end of 1 year, subjects with 3 or more prior episodes of depression had a relapse rate of only 40% in the MBCT group, compared with a relapse rate of 66% in the treatment-as-usual group. MBCT had no effect in reducing depression recurrence among subjects with 2 or fewer prior episodes of depression. Authors speculated that "depressogenic thinking" may become more entrenched in individuals with 3 or more episodes of major depression, allowing MBCT to demonstrate a more benefical effect in this population. The potential role of MBCT in reducing depression relapse was confirmed in another RCT of similar design using 75 subjects (49); in this trial, subjects with 3 or more prior episodes of depression had a relapse rate of only 36% in the

MBCT group, compared with a relapse rate of 78% in the treatment-as-usual group.

### Safety, Adverse Effects and Contraindications

When meditation is undertaken with supervision from an experienced teacher, the margin of safety appears to be wide. However, meditation may lead to a state of heightened self-awareness, which may disturb individuals unaccustomed to paying close attention to internal sensations, perceptions, and images. There have been a few case reports of meditative practices precipitating psychological crisis in vulnerable individuals. Thus, meditation may not be appropriate for individuals who show impaired reality testing, poor ego boundaries, or need for rigid emotional control. Overall, meditation appears to be safe and well tolerated.

### Recommendations

More RCTs of better methodological quality are needed to verify the mood benefits of meditation in major depression. However, existing data suggest there is limited evidence to support a weak recommendation in favor of MBCT as an adjunct therapy in preventing relapse of major depression. There are insufficient data as yet to support or refute the use of any meditation technique to treat active major depression (see Evidence Summary table at end of chapter).

## Tai Chi and Qi Gong Therapy

Tai chi and Qi gong are traditional Chinese health practices involving physical movements and breathing exercises performed in a characteristically slow, graceful, and relaxed manner while maintaining meditative awareness in the present moment. (See pp.425-426 for more details.)

### Dose and Duration of Treatment

In the few published English language studies of qi gong for mental health purposes, qi gong was practiced in 15 to 60 minutes sessions daily for 12 to 16 weeks. Tai chi was practiced in 45 minute sessions 3 times a week for 12 weeks. Qi gong and tai chi were practiced individually as well as in group settings. Needs further investigation to establish optimal practice for mental health benefits.

### Mechanism of Action

Mood benefits of qi gong practice are hypothesized to occur, in part, via modulation of the hypothalamic-pituitary-adrenocortical axis; qigong practice has been associated with a significant drop in the plasma concentrations of ACTH, cortisol, and aldosterone. However, much research remains to be done to elucidate the potential mechanisms of action for tai chi and qi gong in a biomedical context.

## Evidence of Efficacy

Controlled clinical trials of qi gong and tai chi in major depression are scant, at least in English-language publications. One RCT (50) recruited 82 elderly subjects with either a pre-existing diagnosis of depression or "obvious features of depression" as measured by the Geriatric Depression Scale (GDS). Subjects were randomized to individual qi gong for 15 minutes daily plus group qi gong for 30 to 45 minutes 3 times a week versus instructor-led newspaper reading group control for 30 to 45 minutes 3 times a week. At the end of 16 weeks, a drop in GDS scores was significantly greater in the qi gong cohort than in the control cohort; however, when GDS scores were re-assessed 4 weeks and 8 weeks after the intervention, there was no longer a difference between the two cohorts. A second RCT (51) recruited 14 elderly subjects meeting criteria for depression according to the Chinese version of the Center for Epidemiological Studies Depression Scale (CES-D). Subjects were randomized to an instructor-led tai chi group session for 45 minutes 3 times a week versus waitlist control group. At the end of 3 months, CES-D scores had dropped significantly in the tai chi group, while scores increased slightly in the control group.

## Safety, Adverse Effects and Contraindications

When qi gong and tai chi are undertaken with supervision from an experienced teacher, the margin of safety appears to be wide, as evidenced by the lack of reported adverse effects even in elderly subjects with significant co-morbid medical illness. However, there have been a few reports of qi gong practices precipitating psychological crisis in vulnerable individuals. As with meditation, qi gong and tai chi may not be appropriate for individuals who show impaired reality testing, poor ego boundaries, or need for rigid emotional control. Overall, these practices appear safe and well tolerated.

## Recommendations

In view of very limited data from RCTs, there are insufficient data as yet to support or refute the use of qi gong to treat active major depression (see Evidence Summary table at end of chapter).

## Acupuncture Therapy

Acupuncture is a healing art practiced within traditional Chinese medicine. The application of fine needles, low voltage electrical current, or a laser beam along key energy points on the body are said to regulate and rebalance the flow of vital force (chi), thus alleviating physical or emotional distress. (See pp. 417-419, 421 for more details.)

## Dose and Duration of Treatment

The frequency, duration, and sites of acupuncture are determined by a skilled practitioner and adjusted on the basis of the individual's symptoms and clinical course. In RCTs examining acupuncture for depression, acupuncture was conducted in 30 to 60 minute sessions 1 to 6 times per week for a period of 4 to 8 weeks.

## Mechanism of Action

Mood benefits of acupuncture are hypothesized to occur via stimulation of efferent and afferant nerve tracts and neurohormonal mechanisms. For example, evidence from animal experiments suggests that neural stimulation from acupunture may accelerate the production and release of norepinephrine and serotonin in the central nervous system. However, much research remains to be done to elucidate acupunture's potential mechanisms of action in western biomedical terms.

## Evidence of Efficacy

In recent years, 3 systematic reviews have been published that critically assess the RCTs conducted of acupuncture as an intervention in major depression. While inclusion criteria varied somewhat between the 3 reviews, all included RCTs that compared antidepressant effects of acupuncture to wait-list control, to sham acupuncture, or to an established conventional treatment for depression. The first review identified 7 RCTs (52), the second review identified 7 RCTs of a slightly different composition (53), and the third review identified 9 RCTs (54). Authors of all 3 reviews noted that the scientific design of the included studies tended to be quite poor overall. In all 3 reviews, meta-analysis was unable to demonstate consistent differences in depression outcome between subjects in the acupuncture group and those in the wait list, sham acupuncture, or tricyclic antidepressant groups. Because of this inconclusive evidence, authors of all 3 reviews concluded that the role of acupuncture in the treatment of depression remains unclear.

In an effort to address the methodological flaws of earlier studies, a recent double blind RCT was conducted of laser acupuncture for mild to moderate depression (55). Laser acupuncture involves stimulation of a specific body site with a low-energy pulse of light that does not produce a detectable tactile sensation; therefore, it is amenable to sham control and double-blinding in clinical trials via use of a light beam simulating an actual laser pulse. Thirty subjects diagnosed with mild-to-moderate depression were randomized to 12 sessions of either active laser treatment or sham laser treament at 6 to 8 individualized acupuncture points. At the end of the 8-week clinical trial, BDI scores were significantly lower in the active laser group than in the sham laser group; 4 weeks after treatment, the difference in scores was no longer significant, but became significant again 12 weeks after treatment.

## Safety, Adverse Effects and Contraindications

When acupuncture is administered by competent, licensed practitioners, it tends to be a relatively safe procedure with the risk of serious adverse events being significantly lower than many conventional medical procedures. Overall, it appears relatively safe with infrequent, non-serious adverse events.

### Recommendations

Despite several RCTs of acupuncture in depression, findings have been inconclusive. Therefore, there are insufficient data as yet to support or refute the use of acupuncture to treat active major depression (see Evidence Summary table at end of chapter).

## Massage Therapy

Massage therapy involves manipulation of the muscles and other soft tissues of the body with varying pressures and techniques. The intent may be to decrease tension in soft tissues, increase delivery of blood and oxygen to massaged areas, and promote a sense of overall well-being.

### Dose and Duration of Treatment

Further investigation is needed to establish optimal therapy for mental health benefits. In RCTs of massage therapy for emotional distress, single-visit treatments ranged from 5 to 60 minutes, while multiple-visit treatments ranged from sessions of 15 to 40 minutes once or twice weekly over 4 to 6 weeks.

### Mechanism of Action

Several theories have been proposed to explain the mood benefits of massage. These include promotion of parasympathetic activity, as well as release of endorphins or serotonin into the bloodstream through mechanical stimulation of body tissue. However, more investigation remains to be done to elucidate the mechanisms of action underlying the mood benefits of therapeutic massage.

### Evidence for Efficacy

A large meta-analysis of massage therapy research suggests that among adults with primary medical conditions who have associated depressive symptoms, mood benefits from a course of massage therapy may be comparable to a course of psychotherapy (56). However, there is a paucity of data on potential mood benefits of massage as an intervention specifically for major depression in adults.

A recent systematic review (57) describes two RCTs investigating massage therapy in depressed peripartum women. In one small RCT (58), 32 young post-partum mothers with BDI scores suggestive of depression were randomized to 30-minute sessions of massage twice weekly, or to 30-minute sessions of yoga or progressive muscle relaxation twice weekly. At the end of 5 weeks, only the massage group had a significant reduction in BDI scores. A second RCT (59) recruited 84 pregnant women who scored in the depressive range on the Center for Epidemiological Studies Depression Scale (CES-D). Subjects were randomized to 20-minute sessions of massage administered weekly by significant others, 20-minute sessions of progressive muscle relaxation self-administered weekly, or to routine prenatal care alone. At the conclusion of 16 weeks, subjects in the massage group had a significantly greater reduction in CES-D scores than those in the two comparison groups.

### Safety, Adverse Effects and Contraindications

Massage therapy appears to have a wide margin of safety when delivered by professionals. Overall, it appears safe and well tolerated.

### Recommendations

Due to insufficient data from RCTs, there are insufficient data as yet to support or refute the use of massage to treat active major depression (see Evidence Summary table at end of chapter).

## Relaxation Techniques

During the early 20th century, two behavioral techniques were developed by western physicians to promote relaxation via regulation of the autonomic nervous system: progressive muscle relaxation (PMR) and autogenic training (AT). (See p. 425 for more information.)

### Dose and Duration of Treatment

Classical progressive muscle relaxation is practiced in 30 to 60 minute sessions several times a week for up to a year; in most clinical trials, an abbreviated form is used, consisting of 60-minute sessions weekly over 8 to 12 weeks. For autogenic training, sessions in clinical trials have ranged from 15 to 90 minutes 2 to 10 times per week over a period of 1 to 12 weeks.

### Mechanism of Action

One theory views relaxation techniques as methods for de-activating the generalized physiological stress response that accompanies depression, anxiety and many chronic medical conditions. By de-activating a single subsystem of the stress response, such as the voluntary muscle system, the relaxation technique is said to reduce activity in other central and peripheral physiological pathways comprising overall sympathetic arousal. However, this theory has not been consistently supported by physiological research, and more investigation is needed regarding the mechanisms of action underlying relaxation techniques.

### Evidence for Efficacy

Several RCTs suggest that among patients with primary medical conditions who have associated depressive symptoms, mood benefits may result from the practice of relaxation techniques (60-62). However, data are limited regarding potential mood benefits of relaxation therapy specifically for major depression.

Among 4 RCTs of PMR in depressed adults, the results have been intriguing. In one rigorously designed trial involving 121 subjects with unipolar major depression, investigators found antidepressant effects of PMR to be equivalent to pharmacotherapy but inferior to behavior therapy (63); authors speculated that "the relative success of the relaxation therapy indicates not only that drug therapy (is) less powerful than might have been thought, but also that a large number of non-specific variables undoubtedly influence treatment outcome." A second, smaller trial with a total of 37 subjects found antidepressant effects of PMR to be equivalent to cognitive-behavior therapy and superior to pharmacotherapy (64); however, these results must be viewed with caution due to the small sample size, lack of a placebo control, and high rates of non-adherence to the tricyclic antidepressant used in this study. Finally, two small trials with 30 subjects each found that augmentation of pharmacotherapy with PMR resulted in improved depression outcomes compared to pharmacotherapy alone (39,65).

Stetter and Kupper (2002) (60) undertook a comprehensive review of all controlled clinical trials related to autogenic training (AT), performing separate meta-analyses to determine the clinical effectiveness of AT for specific medical conditions. In their meta-analysis of 3 controlled clinical trials of AT involving a total of 67 subjects with depression or dysthymia, AT was found to have a moderate antidepressant effect that was signicantly greater than that obtained with non-psychological control treatments such as self-directed relaxation; however, when AT was compared to cognitive behavioral therapy for the treatment of major depression, the mood benefits of cognitive behavioral therapy were superior. Of note, the use of AT as an augmentation to cognitive behavior therapy yielded better outcomes in depression than cognitive behavioral therapy alone. Thus far, AT has not been compared to pharmacotherapy in the treatment of major depression.

### Safety, Adverse Effects and Contraindications

In the studies cited above, no adverse effects of relaxation techniques were reported. However, relaxation techniques are typically not recommended for patients with psychosis, depersonalization or dissociation because the exercises involved may be disturbing to patients with difficulty in reality-testing. Overall, the practice appears safe and well tolerated.

### Recommendations

More RCTs of high methodological quality are needed to investigate the mood benefits of relaxation techniques in major depression. However, existing data suggest there is moderate evidence to support a weak recommendation in favor of PMR and AT as adjunctive therapies in major depression. Due to inconclusive data, no recommendations can be made at this time about the role of relaxation techniques as monotherapy in major depression (see Evidence Summary table at end of chapter).

## Phototherapy (Bright Light Exposure)

Phototherapy with bright, white light boxes has been used routinely within conventional psychiatry as a highly effective, first-line treatment for seasonal affective disorder (SAD) during the winter months. However, because circadian rhythms are dysregulated in depressive disorders other than SAD, phototherapy will be reviewed here as a possible treatment for non-seasonal major depressive disorder.

### Dose and Duration of Treatment

To achieve antidepressant effects, the minimum effective dose of phototherapy appears to be bright white light of 10,000 lux intensity administered for 30 minutes in the early morning for at least 1 week.

### Mechanism of Action

In susceptible individuals, circadian and seasonal elevations in melatonin levels contribute to dysphoria as the increase in melatonin production depletes brain serotonin. Phototherapy stimulates serotonin production and suppresses melatonin release, making more serotonin available to the brain to help alleviate depression.

### Evidence for Efficacy

Golden and colleagues (2005) (66) conducted a recent review and meta-analysis of RCTs that examined bright, white light therapy for mood disorders in a non-geriatric adult population; the control group in most of these RCTs was exposed to very low intensity white or red "placebo" light therapy. For non-seasonal major depression, meta-analysis of 3 studies with 61 subjects demonstrated that bright light monotherapy was associated with significant reduction of depression symptoms. Effect sizes in these trials of light therapy were comparable to those obtained in most antidepressant medication trials. In their meta-analysis, Golden and colleagues found that bright light as an adjunct to pharmacotherapy for non-seasonal depression proved to be no more efficacious than pharmacotherapy plus placebo light. An earlier meta-analysis by Tuunainen et al (2004) (67) had also reported an overall negative finding related to bright light as an adjunct to pharmacotherapy in non-seasonal depression; however, when Tuunainen et al limited their analysis to data from studies of the highest methodological quality (2 studies with a total of 50 subjects suffering from non-seasonal depression), they found "unequivocal superiority" of pharmacotherapy plus bright light in comparison to pharmacotherapy plus placebo light.

## Safety, Adverse Effects and Contraindications

In the meta-analysis by Tuunainen et al (2004) (67), sleep onset difficulties and hypomania were reported to be more prevalent among subjects receiving bright light therapy; authors estimated that hypomania developed in approximately 1 in 8 subjects exposed to bright light. Agitation, headache and eye irritation also showed a trend toward higher prevalence among subjects exposed to bright light. However, the authors make the point that some of the adverse events reported in RCTs of bright light therapy may be due, in part, to subjects' concomitant use of tricyclic antidepressants which influence pupil size. Overall, phototherapy appears to be a relatively safe and acceptable treatment for unipolar depression. Phototherapy may induce mania in patients with bipolar disorder, so close monitoring and concurrent use of a mood stabilizer are adviseable. Overall, it appears safe and well tolerated for unipolar depression.

## Recommendations

Data from existing RCTs suggest there is moderate evidence to support a weak recommedation in favor of phototherapy as a monotherapy for non-seasonal major depression. Due to inconclusive data, no recommendations can be made at this time about the role of phototherapy as an adjunctive treatment for non-seasonal major depression (see Evidence Summary table at end of chapter).

# Aerobic Exercise Therapy

Aerobic exercise may include walking, jogging, cycling or swimming. While aerobic exercise is often recommended as a component of conventional care for cardiac disease, diabetes and other medical conditions, it is increasingly being investigated for its efficacy in depressive disorders.

## Dose and Duration of Treatment

In RCTs of exercise therapy for depression, exercise sessions ranged from 20 to 60 minutes per day, 2 to 5 times a week, for 4 to 16 wks. To achieve mood benefits, exercise intensity (total caloric expenditure per week) appears to be more important than exercise duration per se (68).

## Mechanism of Action

Several theories have been proposed to explain the mood benefits of exercise. These include exercise-mediated increase in monoamine neurotransmitter levels, release of endorphins, interruption of "depressogenic" thoughts and increase in social interaction if exercise is undertaken within a group setting. However, more investigation remains to be done to elucidate the mechanisms of action underlying the mood benefits of exercise.

## Evidence for Efficacy

In one meta-regression analysis (69), 14 RCTs were identified involving exercise as a monotherapy for depression; in all but one of these trials, the intervention studied was aerobic exercise. Exercise was found to have significant mood benefits in comparison to no exercise, and the effect size was comparable to that seen with cognitive therapy. However, investigators noted several methodological weaknesses among the 14 trials, such as lack of rigor in diagnosing major depression, inadequate blinding, inadequate concealment of randomization, and failure to use an intent-to-treat analysis.

Since this meta-regression analysis was performed, other randomized controlled trials of exercise therapy for depression have been conducted with fewer methodological limitations. In one such recent RCT (70), 202 adults diagnosed with major depression were assigned randomly to one of four conditions: treadmill exercise of 45 minutes duration 3 times a week in a group setting; home-based treadmill exercise of 45 minutes duration 3 times a week; sertraline 50-200 mg daily; or placebo pill daily. After 16 weeks, reduction in scores on the Hamilton Rating Scale for Depression were comparable among subjects in both exercise groups and those in the medication group; active treatment with either exercise or medication was more efficacious than placebo in reducing depressive symptoms.

## Safety, Adverse Effects and Contraindications

None of the exercise studies cited above reported any serious adverse effects. When aerobic exercise is undertaken with supervision from a qualified health professional, the margin of safety is high. Risk of injury may be minimized by selecting an exercise that accommodates for limited mobility or other specific medical problems.

## Recommendations

Existing data suggests moderate evidence to support a strong recommendation for aerobic exercise as a monotherapy for major depression. Exercise tolerance and medical risk factors must be carefully assessed prior to recommending aerobic exercise to any individuals (see Evidence Summary table at end of chapter).

## St. John's Wort Therapy (*Hypericum perforatum*)

St. John's Wort (*Hypericum perforatum*) is a common roadside plant used for centuries in Europe as an herbal remedy for depression and pain symptoms. Many dozens of over-the-counter preparations are available, only some of which are produced in accordance with good manufacturing practices. For medicinal use, the flowering tops of a mature St. John's Wort plant are dried and powdered to prepare teas and tablets; sometimes, the flowers are pressed to produce a concentrated oil extract. Preparations are typically standardized to either hypericin or hyperforin content, considered to be the two active ingredients of St. John's Wort.

### Dose and Duration of Treatment

Further investigation is needed to establish optimal therapy for depression. Most clinical trials have used St. John's Wort preparations of 300 mg po TID; however, these preparations were standardized to hypericin content, rather than to hyperforin, and the latter is now thought to be the more active ingredient for antidepressant effects. Thus, hyperforin preparations at higher doses (up to 1800 mg per day) may prove to be more effective. As with conventional antidepressants, it is recommended that treatment with St. John's Wort be maintained for at least 6 months to achieve full remission of a major depressive episode.

### Mechanism of Action

Hypericin and hyperforin are identified as the two most active ingredients in St. John's Wort. However, hyperforin is now considered to be the more important of the two, as it has been shown to inhibit reuptake of serotonin, norepinephrine, and dopamine, probably accounting for the antidepressant effect of St. John's Wort.

### Evidence for Efficacy

Over the past two decades, numerous RCT trials of St. John's Wort in depression have been conducted, including two large trials in the United States (71,72). All of these trials have been cumulatively reviewed in several meta-analyses, and the findings appear somewhat paradoxical, as described below.

Six meta-analyses examined trials of St. John's Wort versus placebo in depression (73-78). In the earlier of these meta-analyses, St. John's Wort was more effective than placebo. However, in later meta-analyses where larger, more rigorously designed studies were included for review, the effect size of St. John's Wort was reduced. In the latest Cochrane review by Linde and colleagues (2005) (78), the effect size of St. John's Wort and placebo were nearly identical in pooled data from large trials; sub-analysis suggested that any mood benefits of St. John's Wort were limited to mild depression rather than to moderate or severe depression.

Four meta-analyses also examined St. John's Wort versus tricyclics, maprotiline or selective serotonin reuptake inhibitors in depression (73-78). In these meta-analyses, the effect of St. John's Wort in depression was comparable to that of standard antidepressant medication. These findings are consistent with a recent RCT, not included in previous reviews, which demonstrated that hyperforin at 1800 mg per day provided mood benefits equivalent to paroxetine in subjects with moderate or severe depression (79).

Collectively, these meta-analyses are challenging to interpret: on the one hand, they suggest that St. John's Wort may be comparable to placebo in treating depression; on the other hand, they also suggest that mood effects of St. John's Wort may be comparable to standard antidepressant medication. By inference, one may conclude that St. John's Wort, standard antidepressants, and placebo all have comparable mood effects. Indeed, in a large NIH-funded placebo-controlled trial of St. John's Wort versus antidepressant medication (sertraline), neither hypericum nor sertraline was more effective than placebo (Hypericum Study Group, 2002) (72). These meta-analyses underscore the point that while it is important to question the efficacy of herbal remedies for depression, it is equally important to question the evidence base supporting conventional treatments for depression. Further large trials of St. John's Wort in dysthymia are pending.

### Safety, Adverse Effects and Contraindications

In recent years, there has been an increasing focus on the safety of St. John's Wort. St. John's Wort may cause photosensitivity and side effects similar to those seen with SSRIs (e.g., dry mouth, dizziness, diarrhea, nausea, fatigue, risk of serotonin symdrome). However, the main concern has been its capacity to induce the cytochrome P450 enzyme system and P-glycoprotein transplant sytem, thereby altering blood levels of many conventional medications metabolized through the liver. For this reason, St. John's Wort is contraindicated in people taking one of a long list of medications (see p. 392, Box 15-1 for a specific listing). Use of St. John's Wort with MAO antidepressant medications may cause a life-threatening hypertensive crisis. Thus, although St. John's Wort taken alone may have a relatively low incidence of serious adverse events, its use is limited by the many adverse interactions it can have with conventional medicines.

### Recommendations

Data from existing RCTs suggest there is limited evidence to support a weak recommedation in favor of St. John's Wort as a monotherapy for mild forms of major depression. Due to inconclusive data from previous RCTs and the likelihood that they examined the less pharmacologically active hypericum extract of St. John's Wort rather than hyperforin, no recommendation can be made at this time about the role of St. John's Wort as a monotherapy in moderate to severe major depression. In view of the many adverse herb-drug interactions seen with St. John's Wort, it may be prudent to discourage its use in individuals taking hepatically metabolized conventional medications (see Evidence Summary table at end of chapter).

## S-adenosylmethionine (SAMe) Therapy

In the human body, S-adenosylmethionine (SAMe) is a naturally occurring molecule that serves as an important methyl donor in many biochemical pathways, including the synthesis of monoamine neurotransmitters. It has been used as an antidepressant in Europe for more than 25 years, but has been available in the United States only since 1999 as a dietary supplement. SAMe is synthesized from the amino acid L-methionine through a costly manufacturing process. In the United States, SAMe is typically available as an over-the-counter enteric coated tablet, although a prescription parenteral formulation is also available in Europe. The current cost of SAMe is at least $1 per 400 mg dose and is not covered by insurers, rendering this treatment prohibitively expensive for many individuals on a limited income.

### Dose and Duration of Treatment

Most clinical trials demonstrating antidepressant efficacy of SAMe have used oral doses of 1200 to 1600 mg per day over a course of 4 to 6 weeks. As with conventional antidepressants, it is recommended that treatment be maintained for at least 6 months to achieve full remission of a major depressive episode.

### Mechanism of Action

While further investigation is required to establish the exact mechanism of action underlying potential mood benefits of SAMe, it role in methylation reactions may be critical. SAMe is an important methyl donor during the rate-limiting step in biosynthesis of dopamine, serotonin and norepinephrine; moreover, SAMe is also an important methyl donor in the biosynthesis of phosphatidylcholine, which increases cell membrane fluidity and may increase neurotransmission.

### Evidence for Efficacy

With over 3 decades of scientific investigation, SAMe is one of the most extensively researched nutritional supplements in major depression. Two meta-analyses in the 1990s reported the superiority of SAMe over placebo in the treatment of major depression and found SAMe and tricyclics to have comparable antidepressant efficacy (80,81). A third meta-analysis was conducted by the U.S. Agency for Healthcare Research and Quality (AHRQ) in 2002 (82) and involved 28 RCTs of SAMe in major depression. AHRQ investigators found that compared to placebo, treatment with SAMe was associated with an improvement of approximately 6 points in subjects' scores on the Hamilton Rating Scale for Depression measured at 3 weeks; this degree of improvement was noted to be statistically as well as clinically significant. Furthermore, AHRQ investigators found depression outcomes with SAMe treatment were equivalent to outcomes achieved with conventional antidepressant medication.

Finally, there is preliminary data that SAMe may have a more rapid onset of action than conventional antidepressants, and may be useful as an adjunctive therapy in cases of partial response or nonresponse to SSRIs (83).

### Safety, Adverse Effects and Contraindications

SAMe appears to be a safe and well-tolerated intervention for depression, with a side effect profile much more favorable than tricyclics. Common transient side effects are similar to those often seen in SSRIs: heachache, dry mouth, gastrointestinal distress, anxiety, agitation, insomnia, palpitations, dizziness, and sweating. In contrast to SSRIs, however, sexual dysfunction is not a characteristic side effect of SAMe. As with most conventional antidepressant medications, SAMe may induce mania in patients with bipolar disorder, so concurrent use of a mood stablizer may be adviseable.

### Recommendations

There is strong evidence to support a strong recommendation for the use of SAMe as a monotherapy in major depression. There is limited evidence to support a weak recommendation for the use of SAMe as an adjunct to conventional pharmacological treatment of major depression. Caution should be exercised in prescribing SAMe to patients with bipolar disorder, as induction of mania may occur (see Evidence Summary table at end of chapter).

## Folate (Vitamin B9) Augmentation Therapy

Folate is a water-soluble B-vitamin found abundantly in green leafy vegetables and in many fruits and legumes. Epidemiological surveys have consistently found associations between folate deficiency and psychiatric disorders, especially depression. Dietary folate is converted in the body to methylfolate, which serves as an important methyl donor in many biochemical reactions including synthesis of DNA, RNA, red blood cells, and neurotransmitters. Folate supplements are available in three tablet formulations: folic acid, folinic acid or methylfolate. Because folic acid must pass through several biochemical steps in vivo before successful conversion to folinic acid and then to methylfolate, dietary supplementation directly with folinic acid or methyl folate is preferred.

### Dose and Duration of Treatment

Most clinical trials demonstrating mood benefits of folate have used oral doses of 0.4 to 1 mg per day in conjunction with a standard antidepressant medication. Folate supplementation is typically continued for the duration of treatment with antidepressant medication. When using folate supplements, it is prudent to also use vitamin B12 supplements of 1 mg per day to help prevent B12 deficiency.

## Mechanism of Action

Further investigation is required to establish the exact mechanism of action underlying potential mood benefits of folate supplementation. However, folate is required to synthesize methionine from homocysteine. As discussed above, methionine is then converted in vivo to SAMe, which is a key methyl donor in the synthesis of dopamine, serotonin, and norepinephrine. Thus, folate supplementation may help ensure robust production of central nervous system neurotransmitters.

## Evidence for Efficacy

Coppen and Bolander-Gouaille (2005) (84) reviewed two double-blind RCTs in which folate augmentation improved response rates to conventional antidepressant medication. In the first of these studies (85), 24 depressed subjects with folate deficiency were randomized to antidepressant medication plus folic acid versus antidepressant medication plus placebo. After 6 months, subjects receiving folate augmentation group had significantly greater reduction in HRSD scores than did subjects receiving placebo augmentation. One decade later, a larger study of folate augmentation in 127 depressed subjects was conducted (86); in this larger study, all subjects had normal serum folate levels and were randomized to antidepressant medication plus 0.5 mg of methyl folate versus antidepressant medication plus placebo. After 10 weeks, the folate augmentation group had significantly greater reduction in HRSD scores than the placebo augmentation group, but this positive effect was confined to female subjects. The folate augmentation group also had fewer side effects to floxetine therapy than did the placebo augmentation group. In reviewing the results of these two studies, it is possible that higher doses of folate augmentation for longer periods of time (as in the first, smaller study) may be required to achieve mood benefits in depressed men, whereas depressed women may respond at lower doses of shorter duration (as in the second, larger study). It is unclear to what extent initial folate deficiency in the first study may have influenced response of depressed male subjects to folate augmentation. Alternatively, the first study may have been underpowered to detect a gender-specific response to folate augmentation, while the second study was adequately powered to detect this difference.

## Safety, Adverse Effects and Contraindications

As a water soluable vitamin, folate is associated with a wide margin of safety. Mild insomnia, gastrointestinal distress and concentration difficulties are reported as occasional side effects. Folate augmentation of fluoxetine therapy may also be associated with fewer side effects than floxetine therapy alone. It is advisable to limit intake of supplemental folate to 1 mg per day because higher doses may precipitate seizures in patients taking anti-convulsant medications and may also trigger and mask vitamin B12 (cyanocobalamin) deficiency.

Folate supplementation may be paired with vitamin B12 supplemention of 1 mg per day to help prevent B12 deficiency. Overall, it is relatively safe with infrequent, non-serious adverse events.

## Recommendations

Existing data suggest there is moderate evidence to support a weak recommendation for the use of folate as an adjunct to conventional pharmacological treatment of major depression, even when folate deficiency may not be present. Folate augmentation may have the additional benefit of reducing side effects associated with conventional SSRI therapy, but further data are required before a recommendation can be made in this regard. Due to insufficient data from RCTs, no recommendation can be made as yet regarding folate monotherapy in major depession (see Evidence Summary table at end of chapter).

## Omega-3 Fatty Acid Therapy

Omega-3 essential fatty acids are polyunsaturated fat molecules that must be obtained from the diet in order to serve many vital physiological roles including proper maturation and functioning of the human nervous system. Epidemiological studies have suggested a strong inverse relationship between intake of omega-3 fatty acids through fish consumption and the prevalence of depressive disorders. Omega-3 fatty acids include the short chain alpha-linolenic acid (ALA), as well as its long-chain derivatives eicosapentaenoic acid (EPA) and docosahexanoic acid (DHA). Nuts from cold-adapted terrestrial plants such as flax or walnut provide ALA, which must be converted in the body to EPA and DHA. However, marine plants such as chlorella and spirulina algae directly provide DHA and EPA, as do coldwater fish such as salmon and halibut, which feed on marine algae rich in omega-3 fatty acids. Only moderate doses of omega-3 fatty acids are available through the food sources as described above. Higher doses of omega-3 fatty acids such as EPA or DHA may be obtained via dietary supplements in the form of fish oil, fish oil capsules, cold-pressed flaxseed oil, cold-pressed canola oil, or marine algae extracts and tablets.

## Dose and Duration of Treatment

Further investigation is needed to establish optimal therapeutic practice in depression. Clinical trials demonstrating antidepressant efficacy of omega-3 fatty acids have typically used either EPA or an EPA-predominant combination of EPA/DHA. Doses have ranged widely from 1 gram per day to 9 grams per day, and duration of clinical trials have ranged from 4 weeks to 12 weeks. Adjunctive treatment with omega-3 fatty acids should be maintained for at least 6 months to help achieve full remission of a major depressive episode.

## Mechanism of Action

Omega-3 fatty acids are critical structural components in neuronal membranes and may exert antidepressant effects via modulating sensitivity of these membranes to neurotransmitter signaling. Omega-3 fatty acids also may exert antidepressant effects by inhibiting secretion of the pro-inflammatory cytokines, which adversely alter neurotransmitter availability and metabolism in severe depression. Finally, omega-3 fatty acids may confer mood benefits by supporting production of a polypeptide called brain derived neurotrophic factor (BDNF), which supports the survival and growth of neuronal tissue; high BDNF levels have been negatively correlated with severity of depressive symptoms.

## Evidence for Efficacy

In a comprehensive review by Parker et al (2006) (87), RCTs examining potential mood benefits of omega-3 fatty acids are described. It is noteworthy that the positive trials involved either EPA or EPA/DHA combinations with EPA predominance, while the negative trials involved DHA or EPA/DHA combinations with DHA predominance.

Among two positive trials, both examined omega-3 fatty acids as an adjunct to antidepressant medication. In one double-blind RCT (88), 20 subjects with recurrent unipolar major depression all received the same antidepressant medication but were randomly assigned to either 2 grams per day of adjunctive EPA or adjunctive placebo. At the conclusion of 4 weeks, subjects taking EPA had significantly lower scores on the Hamilton Rating Scale for Depression than did their counterparts taking placebo. In a second double-blind RCT (89), 22 subjects with recurrent unipolar major depression all received the same antidepressant medication but were randomly assigned to adjunctive therapy with either 4.4 grams EPA plus 3.4 grams DHA per day or placebo. At the conclusion of 4 weeks, subjects taking EPA had significantly lower scores on the Hamilton Rating Scale for Depression than did their counterparts taking placebo. While these trials indicate mood benefits of omega-3 fatty acids in major depression, there is no clear indication as to the optimal dose in depression, nor how supplementation with only EPA might compare to a EPA/DHA combination.

Among the negative trials, one study examined omega-3 fatty acids as a monotherapy in depression, while the second study considered omega-3 fatty acids as an adjunct to antidepressant medication. In one double-blind RCT (90), 35 subjects with major depression were randomized to receive either 2 grams per day of DHA or placebo. At the conclusion of 6 weeks, subjects in both groups had a similar response to treatment as measured by scores on the Hamilton Rating Scale for Depression. In another double-blind RCT (91), 77 subjects with major depression all received the same antidepressant medication but were randomly assigned to adjunctive therapy with either 0.6 grams EPA plus 2.4 grams DHA per day or placebo. At the conclusion of 12 weeks, subjects in both groups had a similar response to treatment as measured by scores on the Hamilton Rating Scale for Depression.

### Safety, Adverse Effects and Contraindications

Data from the clinical trials above indicate that omega-3 fatty acids are safe and well-tolerated among individuals with depression. Common side effects of fish oil supplementation are gastrointestinal upset and fishy aftertaste, but these can be minimized by using pure preparations with doses below 5 grams per day. In vitro data suggest omega-3 fatty acid supplementation may cause elevations in the INR, especially at doses greater than 3 grams per day, so concurrent use of warfarin, NSAIDs and other anticoagulants should be monitored closely (see pp. 395-6). As with conventional antidepressant medications, omega-3 fatty acids may occasionally induce mania in patients with bipolar disorder, so concurrent use of a mood stablizer is adviseable in this population. Its safety grade is double thumbs up.

### Recommendations

There is moderate evidence to support a weak recommendation for the use of omega-3 fatty acids (EPA or EPA/DHA combinations with EPA predominance) as adjuncts to conventional pharmacological treatment of major depression; however, optimal dosing strategies are unclear. As yet, there are insufficient data to make a recommendation regarding the use of omega-3 fatty acids as a monotherapy in major depression (see Evidence Summary table at end of chapter).

## Therapy with Other Herbs and Nutritional Supplements

A number of other herbs and nutritional supplements have either limited or conflicting data regarding potential mood benefits in major depession. Three of these are briefly discussed below.

### Saffron (Crocus sativus)

For many centuries, the dried stigmas of flowering saffron plants have been used in India and Persia as a key ingredient in many indigeneous herbal medicines, including remedies for depression. It is hypothesized that two active ingredients of saffron—namely, crocin and safranal—exert antidepressant effects via inhibiting reuptake of dopamine, norepinephrine, and serotonin. A research group in Iran has recently produced a series of 5 small, double-blind RCTs examining mood effects of saffron in mild-to-moderate depression; a total of 190 depressed subjects were involved across all 5 trials (92). Two of these studies compared antidepressant efficacy of saffron to placebo and found saffron to be superior to placebo in reducing subjects' scores on the Hamilton Rating Scale for Depression; the remaining three studies compared depressed subjects treated with saffron to those treated with imipramine or fluoxetine and found saffron to be comparable to antidepressant medication in lowering scores on the Hamilton Rating Scale for Depression. Side effects of saffron were similar to those observed with SSRIs. These studies provide sufficient evidence to warrant a weak recommendation in favor of saffron as monotherapy for MDD.

## 5-Hydroxytryptophan (5-HTP)

In the human body, 5-hydroxytryptophan (5-HTP) is an aromatic amino acid that is the immediate precursor to serotonin. It is hypothesized that dietary supplementation with 5-HTP increases serotonin synthesis in depressed individuals. In a recent, comprehensive review (93), investigators identified 11 double-blind, placebo-controlled studies of 5-HTP in depression. However, only 5 of these trials were able to demonstrate that 5-HTP supplementation resulted in statistically significant improvement of depressive symptoms over placebo. Among these 5 positive trials, 3 trials used 5-HTP as an adjuvant to conventional pharmacotherapy; 1 trial tested a combination of 5-HTP plus dopamine agonist versus placebo in depression; 1 trial used 5-HTP monotherapy to help prevent relapse in depression. Based on the existing ratio of negative to positive RCTs, the mood benefits of adjunctive 5-HTP in major depression are uncertain. No data support use of 5-HTP as a monotherapy during acute major depression (see Evidence Summary table at end of chapter).

## Inositol

Inositol is a naturally occurring isomer of glucose and is available in the diet through a range of foods including whole-grain cereals, citrus fruits, nuts, and blackstrap molasses. Within the human body, inositol is used for the production of important secondary messengers that modulate cell surface receptors for serotonin and other neurotransmitters. It is hypothesized that dietary supplementation with inositol optimizes cellular response to serotonin in depressed individuals. A recent review (94) identified 4 small, double-blind, placebo-controlled trials of inositol in depression; a total of 141 depressed subjects were involved across all 4 trials. One trial compared inositol monotherapy to placebo and was favorable toward inositol; the other 3 trials examined inositol versus placebo as adjuncts to conventional pharmacotherapy, and showed no significant difference in outcome between the two interventions. The role of inositol in the treatment of depression remains unclear (see Evidence Summary table at end of chapter).

---

## Case 14-1

Mr. Arnold is a 66-year-old married man who has struggled with low mood for most of his life but has never sought treatment. He believes that "work is the best medicine," and despite his mood problems he successfully developed and managed a small business selling auto parts. After more than 3 decades of operation, his business was recently acquired by a larger company, with Mr. Arnold making a substantial profit and retiring. However, within a few months of retiring, Mr. Arnold developed worsening dysphoria, accompanied by insomnia, loss of appetite, psychomotor slowing and poor concentration. He attempted to resume employment in a new part-time job, but his symptoms were too debilitating. At the urging of his wife, Mr. Arnold consulted his family physician and was diagnosed with major depressive disorder. Mr. Arnold was started on paroxetine (Paxil) and also referred for interpersonal psychotherapy. Mr. Andrews took the paroxetine "like clockwork, along with my blood pressure pill every morning." However, he saw the psychotherapist only a handful of times, saying "I don't see how talking will help." Despite tolerating 8 weeks of paroxetine at the maximum dose, Mr. Arnold noted little improvement in his symptoms, and the paroxetine was discontinued. Mr. Arnold subsequently underwent 2 more antidepressant medication trials, but these too were discontinued after he reported few mood benefits while developing significant side effects including sexual dysfunction.

At the next physician visit, Mr. Arnold's wife inquired about possible complementary medicine approaches to treating her husband's depression. After a review of the literature, the family physician suggested the following to Mr. Arnold:

1. Restart paroxetine, but this time augment with folate and omega-3 fatty acids (EPA)

2. Walk 30 minutes daily and attend a yoga class twice weekly with his wife

3. Use a 10,000 lux light-box for 30 minutes every morning while eating breakfast

Despite some initial concerns that he might be "too stiff to twist into a yoga pretzel," Mr. Arnold agreed to try these interventions. Within 6 weeks, he began to notice improvements in his sleep and appetite, and by 12 weeks he reported a brighter mood with more energy, finally able to accompany his wife to social events. After 20 weeks, Mr. Arnold began volunteer work at a local hospital, and both he and his wife felt that his mental status was better than it had been prior to retirement. Mr. Arnold remained on the above treatment regimen for approximately 1 year and was then successfully tapered off the paroxetine and phototherapy. However, he was encouraged to maintain the dietary supplements as well as the yoga and aerobic exercise. He did so with no evidence of depression relapse over the next year.

# Conclusions

Etymologically speaking, psychiatric care is "healing of the soul." Yet, when confronted with the suffering of depressed individuals, physicians in many treatment settings may experience pressure to constrain their practice to the empirical assessment of mood disorders and to the prescription of appropriate medication. This push toward biological reductionism renders it difficult to practice the classical art of healing embodied in the archetype of the wise and patient "old country doctor." In such a context, it is not surprising that individuals with psychological distress may be drawn to complementary and alternative systems of healing, which articulate the view that body, mind and spirit comprise an integral whole, and that all aspects of this whole must be given proper attention during the treatment of any suffering. Through a responsible and thoughtful collaboration with depressed individuals interested in exploring CAM therapies, physicians have an opportunity to expand their effectiveness as caregivers to the soul.

**Evidence Summary of CAM Treatments for Depression**

| Clinical Indication | Category | Specific Therapy | Dose Studied | Outcome Measures | Confidence of Estimate on Effectiveness | Magnitude of Effect* | Safety† | Recommendation‡ | Comments |
|---|---|---|---|---|---|---|---|---|---|
| Major depressive disorder | Mind-body medicine | Yoga breathing and/or poses | 20-60 min; 2-6x / wk; 4-5 wks | HRSD BDI Zung Scale | Grade B | Moderate | Double thumbs up | Weak in favor | Studied as monotherapy for active MDD (mild-severe). |
| Major depressive disorder | Mind-body medicine | Sahaja conc meditation; MBCT | 20 min/day-2 hr/wk; 8 wks | HRSD | Grade C | Small | Double thumbs up | No recommendation for active MDD. Weak in favor of relapse prevention | Studied as adjunct therapy only. Sahaja meditation for active MDD (unspecified severity); MBCT for relapse prevention in remitted MDD. |
| Major depressive disorder | Mind-body medicine | Tai chi and Qi gong | 15-60 min/d 3-7x/wk; 12-16 wks | CES-D | Grade C | Small | Double thumbs up | No recommendation | Studied as monotherapy for active MDD (mild-moderate). |

(continued)

Evidence Summary of CAM Treatments for Depression (continued)

| Clinical Indication | Category | Specific Therapy | Dose Studied | Outcome Measures | Confidence of Estimate on Effectiveness | Magnitude of Effect* | Safety† | Recommendation‡ | Comments |
|---|---|---|---|---|---|---|---|---|---|
| Major depressive disorder | Whole medical system | Needle, laser, or electro-acupuncture | 30-60 min; 1-6x/wk; 4-8 wks | HRSD BDI, CGI CES-D SCID | Grade B | Inconclusive | Single thumb up | No recommendation | Studied as mono-therapy for active MDD (mild-severe). |
| Major depressive disorder: prenatal and postnatal | Manipulative and body-based therapies | Massage by trained staff or signif other | 20-30 min; 1-2x/wk; 5-16 wks | CES-D POMS | Grade C | Small | Double thumbs up | No recommendation | Studied as mono-therapy for active MDD (mild-moderate). |
| Major depressive disorder | Mind-body medicine | Progressive Muscle Relaxation; Autogenic Training | 15-90 min; 1-10x/wk; 1-12 wks | BDI HRSD | Grade B | Moderate | Double thumbs up | No recommendation re: monotherapy. Weak in favor of adjunct therapy. | Studied as mono-therapy and adjunct therapy for active, MDD (mild-moderate). |
| Major depressive disorder: non-seasonal | Energy medicine | Phototherapy; exposure to bright light | 10,000 lux/ hr 1 hr/day; 1-4 wks | HRSD POMS | Grade B | Moderate | Single thumb up | Weak in favor of mono-therapy. No recommendation re: adjunct therapy | Studied as mono-therapy and adjunctive therapy for active, MDD (mild-severe). |

| Condition | Approach | Intervention | Dosage | Outcome | Grade | Effect | Rating | Recommendation | Notes |
|---|---|---|---|---|---|---|---|---|---|
| Major depressive disorder | Aerobic exercise | Walking, running, swimming | 20-60 min; 2-5x/wk; 4-16 wks | HRSD BDI | Grade B | Moderate | Double thumbs up | Strong in favor | Studied as monotherapy for active MDD (mild-moderate). |
| Major depressive disorder | Biologically based practices | St. John's Wort | 300-600 mg; 3x/day 4-8 wks (standardized to hyperforin or hypericin, now considered more biologically active) | HRSD CGI | Grade B | Inconclusive for moderate-severe MDD; Small for mild MDD | Single thumb down | No recommendation | Studied as monotherapy for active MDD (mild-severe). Activation of cytochrome P450 leads to risk of adverse herb-drug interactions. |
| Major depressive disorder | Biologically based practices | SAMe | 600-800 mg; 2x/day 4-6 wks | HRSD | Grade A | Moderate | Double thumbs up | Strong in favor of monotherapy. Weak in favor of adjunct therapy. | Studied as both monotherapy and adjunct therapy for active MDD (mild-severe) |

(continued)

**Evidence Summary of CAM Treatments for Depression (continued)**

| Clinical Indication | Category | Specific Therapy | Dose Studied | Outcome Measures | Confidence of Estimate on Effectiveness | Magnitude of Effect* | Safety† | Recommendation‡ | Comments |
|---|---|---|---|---|---|---|---|---|---|
| Major depressive disorder | Biologically based therapies | Folate | 0.4-1 mg; 1x/day; 4-12 wks | HRSD | Grade B | Moderate for adjunct therapy; Inconclusive for mono-therapy | Single thumb up | Weak in favor of adjunct therapy. | No recommen-dation for mono therapy. Studied as both mono-therapy and adjunct therapy for active MDD (mild-severe). Women may respond more readily to adjunct therapy. Possible reduction of SSRI side effects with adjunct therapy. |

| Major depressive disorder | Biologically based practices | Omega-3 fatty acids (EPA to DHA predominance) | 0.5-3 gm 3x/day 4-24 wks | HRSD BDI MADRS | Grade B | Small | Double thumbs up | Weak in favor of adjunct therapy. No recommendation for monotherapy. | Studied as both monotherapy and adjunct therapy for active MDD (mild-severe). EPA likely more effective than DHA in MDD. |
|---|---|---|---|---|---|---|---|---|---|
| Major depressive disorder | Biologically based practices | Saffron | 30 mg; 1x/day 6-8 wks | HRSD | Grade B | Moderate | Double thumbs up | Weak in favor | Studied as monotherapy for active MDD (mild-moderate). |
| Major depressive disorder | Biologically based practices | 5-HTP | 25-100 mg; 2-4x/day; 1-10 wks | HRSD CGI | Grade B | Conflicting results | Unclear | No recommendation | Studied as adjunct therapy only for active MDD (mild-severe). |

(continued)

**Evidence Summary of CAM Treatments for Depression (continued)**

| Clinical Indication | Category | Specific Therapy | Dose Studied | Outcome Measures | Confidence of Estimate on Effectiveness | Magnitude of Effect* | Safety† | Recommendation‡ | Comments |
|---|---|---|---|---|---|---|---|---|---|
| Major depressive disorder | Biologically based practices | Inositol | 3-6 g; 2-4x/day; 4-6 wks | HRSD CGI MADRS | Grade B | Conflicting results | Double thumbs up | No recommendation for either adjunct or monotherapy | Studied as both mono-therapy and adjunct therapy for active MDD (unspecified severity). |

* Small, moderate (OR>1.2-2) or large (OR>2)

† 5 categories: Double thumbs up, single thumb up, no recommendation, single thumb down, double thumb down

‡ 5 categories: Strong (in favor), weak (in favor), no recommendation, weak (against), strong (against)

BDI= Beck Depression Inventory; CES-D= Center for Epidemiologic Studies Depression Scale; CGI=Clinical Global Inventory; EPA=Eicosapentaenoic acid; DHA=Docosahexaenoic acid; HRSD= Hamilton Rating Scale for Depression; GDS=Geriatric Depression Scale; MBCT=Mindfulness Based Cognitive Therapy; MDD=Major Depressive Disorder; MDRS=Montgomery-Asberg Depression Rating Scale; POMS=Profile of Mood States; SCID= Structured Clinical Interview for Diagnostic and Statistical Manual of Mental Disorders; SJW=St. John's Wort

## SELECTED REFERENCES*

1. **Unützer J, Klap R, Sturm R, et al.** Mental disorders and the use of alternative medicine: results from a national survey. Am J Psychiatry. 2000;157:1851-7.

2. **Druss BG, Rosenheck RA.** Use of practitioner-based complementary therapies by persons reporting mental conditions in the United States. Arch Gen Psychiatry. 2000;57:708-14.

36. **Pilkington K, Kirkwood G, Rampes H, Richardson J.** Yoga for depression: the research evidence. J Affect Disord. 2005;89:13-24.

46. **Sharma VK, Das S, Mondal S, et al.** Effect of Sahaj Yoga on depressive disorders. Indian J Physiol Pharmacol. 2005;49:462-8.

47. **Coelho HF, Canter PH, Ernst E.** Mindfulness-based cognitive therapy: evaluating current evidence and informing future research. J Consult Clin Psychol. 2007;75:1000-5.

50. **Tsang HW, Fung KM, Chan AS, et al.** Effect of a qigong exercise programme on elderly with depression. Int J Geriat Psychiatry. 2006;21:890-7.

51. **Chou KL, Lee PW, Yu EC, et al.** Effect of Tai Chi on depressive symptoms amongst Chinese older patients with depressive disorders: a randomized clinical trial. Int J Geriatr Psychiatry. 2004;19:1105-7.

54. **Leo RJ, Ligot JS Jr.** A systematic review of randomized controlled trials of acupuncture in the treatment of depression. J Affect Disord. 2007;97:13-22.

55. **Quah-Smith JI, Tang WM, Russell J.** Laser acupuncture for mild to moderate depression in a primary care setting—a randomised controlled trial. Acupunct Med. 2005;23:103-11.

57. **Coelho HF, Boddy K, Ernst E.** Massage therapy for the treatment of depression: a systematic review. International Journal of Clinical Practice 2008;62:325-3.

60. **Stetter F, Kupper S.** Autogenic training: a meta-analysis of clinical outcome studies. Appl Psychophysiol Biofeedback, 2002;27:45-98.

63. **McLean PD, Hakstian AR.** Clinical depression: comparative efficacy of outpatient treatments. J Consult Clin Psychol. 1979;47:818-36.

64. **Murphy GE, Carney RM, Knesevich MA, et al.** Cognitive behavior therapy, relaxation training, and tricyclic antidepressant medication in the treatment of depression. Psychological Reports. 1995;77:403-20.

66. **Golden RN, Gaynes BN, Ekstrom RD, et al.** The efficacy of light therapy in the treatment of mood disorders: a review and meta-analysis of the evidence. Am J Psychiatry. 2005;162:656-62.

67. **Tuunainen A, Kripke DF, Endo T.** Light therapy for non-seasonal depression. Cochrane Database Syst Rev. 2004;(2):CD004050.

69. **Lawlor, Debbie A.** and Stephen W. Hopker. The effectiveness of exercise as an intervention in the management of depression: systematic review and meta-regression analysis of randomised controlled trials. BMJ. 2002;322:1-8.

71. **Shelton RC, Keller MB, Gelenberg A, et al.** Effectiveness of St John's wort in major depression: a randomized controlled trial.

72. **Hypericum Depression Trial Study Group.** Effect of Hypericum perforatum (St John's wort) in major depressive disorder: a randomized controlled trial. JAMA. 2002;287:1807-14.

78. **Linde K, Mulrow CD, Berner M, Egger M.** St John's wort for depression.Cochrane Database Syst Rev. 2005;CD000448. Review.

82. S-Adenosyl-L-Methionine for Treatment of Depression, Osteoarthritis, and Liver Disease. Summary, Evidence Report/Technology Assessment: Number 64. AHRQ Publication No. 02-E033, August 2002. Agency for Healthcare Research and Quality, Rockville MD. www.ahrq.gov/clinic/epcsums/samesum.htm.

84. **Coppen A, Bolander-Gouaille C.** Treatment of depression: time to consider folic acid and vitamin B12. J Psychopharmacol. 2005;19:59-65.

---

* The complete reference list is to be found on the book's Web site.

87. **Parker G, Gibson NA, Brotchie H, et al.** Omega-3 fatty acids and mood disorders. Am J Psychiatry. 2006;163:969-78. Review.

92. **Basti A, Moshiri E, Noorbala AA, et al.** Comparison of petal of Crocus sativus L and fluoxetine in the treatment of depressed outpatients: a pilot double-blind randomized trial. Prog Neuropsychopharmacol Biol Psychiatry. 2006; Dec 14.

93. **Turner EH, Loftis JM, Blackwell AD.** Serotonin a la carte: supplementation with the serotoninprecursor 5-hydroxytryptophan. Pharmacol Ther. 2006;109:325-38.

94. **Taylor MJ, Wilder H, Bhagwagar Z, Geddes J.** Inositol for depressive disorders. Cochrane Database Syst Rev. 2004;(2): CD004049.

# Chapter 15

# Drug-Supplement Interactions: The Good, The Bad and The Undetermined

Leo Galland, MD

Concomitant use of dietary supplements with medication may produce adverse or beneficial effects, which are determined by the specific substances and circumstances of use. In conducting a detailed analysis of the available literature during 2004 (1), the author made the following general observations, the details of which will form the basis for this chapter:

1. The number of documented adverse interactions is matched by the number of documented beneficial interactions.
2. Most adverse interactions are pharmacokinetic, i.e., the supplement alters the solubility, absorption, excretion, protein binding or metabolism of the drug, resulting in subtherapeutic or toxic plasma concentrations.
3. Many potential interactions mentioned in reviews or compendia fail to be confirmed when tested in controlled human studies.
4. Beneficial interactions between drugs and supplements are of 3 major types: a) Drugs may deplete or inhibit the actions of individual nutrients or metabolic intermediates like coenzyme Q10; dietary supplements may compensate; b) Specific supplements may decrease toxicity or side effects of individual drugs or drug classes, through diverse mechanisms; c) A supplement may actually enhance the pharmacodynamic action of a drug.

The goal of this chapter is twofold: to help clinicians guide their patients in avoiding hazardous drug-supplement interactions and to help them identify supplements that may improve the performance of medications they are prescribing. Because of the diversity of substances and interactions, the information will be presented according to categories of clinical use specific to the practice of internal medicine. Space limitation precludes discussion of medications primarily used in psychiatry, neurology, and gynecology.

In the medical literature, the Naranjo nomogram is often used to describe the certainty of adverse drug reactions. This scale, however, was intended to evaluate single drug adverse events. More recently a Drug Interaction Probability Scale (DIPS) was proposed. This scale was designed to better assess drug interaction causation in adverse events (1a). There is unfortunately no scale that is designed well to assess the interactions, positive and negative, of dietary supplements with prescription and conventional over-the-counter medicines. Many incident reports contain a paucity of detail, and the poor quality control of some supplements increases the likelihood that a reported interaction had nothing to do with the labeled active ingredients. In this chapter only the results of clinical trials, controlled human experiments and significant case reports will be included, but it is important to realize the limitations of the evidence, and clinicians are encouraged to scrutinize the individual references.

## Analgesic/Anti-Inflammatory

### Aspirin and NSAIDs

Three areas of potential interaction between aspirin or non-steroidal anti-inflammatory drugs (NSAIDs) and dietary supplements have been reported: gastrointestinal toxicity, antiplatelet effects and relief of pain and inflammation. Table 15-1 lists six supplements that may diminish gastrointestinal side effects of aspirin or NSAIDs, based upon controlled experiments with healthy humans. The protective effect of vitamin C is noteworthy because regular use of aspirin depletes intragastric vitamin C and suppresses gastric blood flow in humans (2).

| Table 15-1 | Supplements That Decrease Gastrointestinal Toxicity of Aspirin or NSAIDs | |
|---|---|---|
| **Drug** | **Supplement** | **Effects** |
| Aspirin | Vitamin C | Prevents duodenal injury (140) and gastric lesions (141) |
| Aspirin | Deglycyrrhizinated licorice (DGL) | Reduces fecal blood loss (142) |
| Aspirin | Cayenne | Pretreatment reduces gastric mucosal damage (143) |
| Aspirin | S-adenosylmethionine | Co-administration reduces erosive gastritis (144) |
| Indomethacin | L-glutamine | Prevents increased small bowel permeability (145) |
| Indomethacin | Bovine colostrum | Prevents increased small bowel permeability (146) |

Numerous food components and herbs have anti-inflammatory effects when studied in vitro. Degradation by intestinal flora, poor absorption and rapid inactivation by conjugation render most of these ineffective in vivo. The only supplements shown to affect the anti-inflammatory activity of NSAIDs in controlled clinical trials are fish oil and evening primrose oil. Of all dietary supplements, omega-3 fatty acids derived from fish oil have demonstrated the greatest range of therapeutic drug enhancement (Table 15-2). In patients with active rheumatoid arthritis, fish oil supplying 1710 mg of eicosapentaenoic acid (EPA) and 1140 mg of docosahexaenoic acid (DHA) per day (3) or evening primrose oil supplying 540 mg of gamma-linolenic acid (GLA) per day appear to allow a significant reduction in NSAID use without increasing indices of disease activity. A combination of evening primrose oil and fish oil supplying 450 mg of GLA and 240 mg of EPA per day may have a similar effect (4). The effect

**Table 15-2    Omega-3 Fatty Acid Enhancement of Clinical Response to Medication in Controlled Clinical Trials**

| Drug/Class | Diagnosis | Omega-3 Dose | Effect |
|---|---|---|---|
| 5-ASA inhibitor | Ulcerative colitis | 4.2 to 5.1 g/day | Prevent early relapse (147), Permit reduced drug dose (148) |
| Antidepressant | Unipolar depression | 6.6 g/day | Improved mood (149) |
| Beta-blocker | Mild hypertension | 2.9-3.4 g/day | Reduced blood pressure (150,151) |
| Bronchodilator | Exercise-induced bronchospasm | 5.2 g/day | Improved pulmonary function reduced bronchodilator use (152) |
| Cyclosporine | Liver transplant | 4 g/day | Improved renal function (153) |
| | Renal transplant | 3 g/day | Improved renal function (154) |
| | Heart transplant | 3.4 g/day | Reduced blood pressure (155) |
| Lithium | Bipolar disorder | 9.6 g/day | Global clinical improvement (156) |
| Neuroleptic | Schizophrenia | 2 g/day of EPA | Improved symptom control (157) |
| NSAID | Rheumatoid arthritis | 2.85 g/day | Reduction of NSAID dose (158) |
| Statin | Combined hyperlipidemia | 1400-2800 mg/day as ethyl esters | Increased HDL-C and decreased postprandial hypertriglyceridemia (159) and hyper-coagulability (101,160) |

of fish oils in reducing NSAID requirements of patients with rheumatoid arthritis is measurable by 12 weeks and persists for at least 12 months.

## 5-ASA Derivatives

5-ASA derivatives are primarily used to treat colonic inflammation. Drugs of this class, sulfasalazine in particular, can impair folic acid transport (5), creating hyperhomocysteinemia (6), a risk factor for deep vein thrombosis (7), which is an extra-intestinal complication of inflammatory bowel disease. Co-administration of folic acid with 5-ASA derivatives is effective in preventing hyperhomocysteinemia; folic acid may also reduce the incidence of colon cancer in patients with ulcerative colitis (8,9). One study found that a high dose of folic acid (15 mg/day) reversed sulfasalazine-induced pancytopenia in two patients (10).

Fish oil capsules may reduce requirements for 5-ASA derivatives and improve maintenance of remission for patients with ulcerative colitis receiving 5-ASA therapy (see Table 15-2).

Two specific probiotic supplements appear to enhance the therapeutic efficacy of 5-ASA derivatives for induction or maintenance of remission in patients with inflammatory bowel disease. VSL-3, a proprietary mixture of *Lactobacillus acidophilus, L. bulgaricus, L. casei, L. plantarum, Bifidobacteriium brevis, B. infantis, B. longum* and *Streptococcus salivarius ssp thermophilus*, at a dose of 900 billion CFU twice a day added to therapy with balsalazide, induced faster remission of active ulcerative colitis than balsalazide or mesalazine alone (11). *Saccharomyces boulardii*, a yeast with anti-inflammatory and immune stimulating effects, appears to potentiate the effects of mesalamine in inducing remission in patients with active ulcerative colitis (12).

## Glucocorticoids

Chromium picolinate, 600 mcg/day, may reverse steroid-induced diabetes in humans; one study demonstrated a decrease in mean blood glucose from 250 mg/dL to 150 mg/dL and a 50% reduction in dose requirement for oral hypoglycemics (14). Similar effects have been described in rats treated with dexamethasone (15).

Calcium plus vitamin D is effective at preventing steroid-induced reduction of lumbar spine density in patients receiving steroids for less than 3 years (16,17). Two reasons for adding calcium and vitamin D supplementation to a glucocorticoid regimen are: 1) glucocorticoids increase calcium excretion, and 2) glucocorticoids induce resistance to the enhancement of intestinal calcium absorption by calcitriol (1,25-dihydroxyvitamin D) (18).

DHEA (dehydroepiandrosterone) may augment the effects of therapy with corticosteroids and diminish side effects. In corticosteroid-treated patients with severe systemic lupus erythematosus (SLE), DHEA, 200 mg/day for 6 months, improved the SLE-disease activity index and prevented steroid-induced bone loss, when compared to placebo (19). DHEA also allowed reduction of prednisone dose to less than 7.5 mg/day in a larger proportion of patients than did placebo (20). In patients with Addison's disease, addition of DHEA, 50 mg/day, to usual steroid replacement therapy, improved energy and mood, compared to placebo (21).

Herbal preparations can alter metabolism of endogenous and exogenous glucocorticoids. Glycyrrhetinic acid (the aglycone of glycyrrhizin), a component of licorice, increases the half-life and area under the curve (AUC) of orally administered prednisolone, presumably by inhibiting renal 11 beta-hydroxysteroid dehydrogenase and hepatic enzymes involved in beta-hydroxysteroid metabolism (22). Despite equal content of glycyrrhizin, however, three separate formulas used in traditional Chinese and Japanese kampo medicine had qualitatively different effects on 11 beta-hydroxysteroid dehydrogenase. Sho-saiko-to (xiao chai hu tang), used in Asia for treatment of chronic hepatitis and now available in the United States, was found to reduce prednisolone AUC by 17%, through an unknown mechanism (23).

## Acetaminophen

Acetaminophen toxicity results from production of N-acetyl-p-benzoquinone imine (NAPQI) by hepatic cytochrome P450 2E1. NAPQI is usually detoxified by conjugation with glutathione (GSH). The amino acid N-acetylcysteine (NAC), a glutathione precursor, protects against this toxicity (24) and, orally or intravenously, is the treatment of choice for acetaminophen overdose (25). Several supplements prevent acetaminophen toxicity in laboratory animals; no human studies of these have been reported.

## Narcotics

Administration of St. John's wort (*Hypericum perforatum*) to four patients on maintenance methadone reduced methadone bioavailability by 47%, producing symptoms of methadone withdrawal in two (26). St. John's wort has shown clinically significant adverse interactions with more medications than any other dietary supplement (Box 15-1). What makes St. John's wort so problematic is its ability with chronic use to induce enzymes of drug metabolism and detoxification, especially the cytochrome P450 isozyme CYP3A4, which metabolizes about 50% of all drugs commonly used in the United States, and the P-glycoprotein (P-gp) transport protein (27). P-gp ejects a variety of xenobiotics from cells. Drugs that are slowly absorbed and also are substrates for intestinal P-gp may have their plasma levels significantly reduced by St. John's wort. Variability of pharmacokinetic interactions with St. John's wort may reflect the variability of hyperforin content in St. John's wort preparations. Hyperforin appears to be the component of St. John's wort responsible for CYP induction (28).

Yohimbine, an alkaloid derived from yohimbe bark, which is used to enhance sexual function, elicited signs and symptoms of opioid withdrawal in patients receiving methadone maintenance therapy (29). Yohimbine inhibits central alpha 2-adrenergic receptors that enhance narcotic effects (30).

## Antiarrhythmic/ Antihypertensive

---

**Box 15-1 Drugs with Significant Reduction in Plasma Levels When Co-Administered with St. John's Wort in Human Studies**

Alprazolam* (103)
Amprenavir (104)
Amitriptyline (105)
Benzodiazepines (162)
Cyclosporine (106)
Dextromethorphan (107)
Digoxin*(108)
Fexofenadine (109)
Imatinib (110)
Indinavir (111)
Irinotecan (112)
Lopinavir (162)
Methadone (see text)
Midazolam (113)
Nevirapine (114)
Omeprazole (varies with genetic polymorphism in CYP3A4 and CYP2C19 activity)(115)
Oral contraceptives (116)
Ritonavir (162)
Simvastain (but not pravastatin) (117)
Tacrolimus (but not mycophenalate) (118)
Theophylline (165)
Verapamil (119)
Warfarin (120)

*Interaction occurs only in St. John's wort that has a high hyperforin content.

---

## Digoxin

The earliest antiarrhythmic drug, digitalis, and the earliest antihypertensive agent, reserpine, were derived from herbal extracts. Numerous herbs contain cardiac glycosides with structural similarity to digitalis (31), but published interactions in humans are limited to alterations in the measurement of digoxin concentration in serum, without clinical effect, caused by ginseng preparations (32,33). Licorice may cause pseudoaldosteronism and hypokalemia (34), which can promote digoxin toxicity.

Magnesium supplementation enhances the anti-arrhythmic effect of digoxin and helps to protect against digitalis toxicity (35); digoxin increases renal magnesium losses, contributing to hypomagnesemia, which lowers the threshold for the development of digitalis toxicity (36). Magnesium supplementation may be beneficial for patients with normal renal function receiving digoxin therapy.

Gum guar, wheat bran and St. John's wort may decrease plasma digoxin concentration by decreasing intestinal absorption (37).

## Beta-Blockers

Adverse clinical interactions between beta-blockers and dietary supplements have not been published, although herbal preparations containing caffeine or ephedra would be expected to counteract the pharmacodynamic properties of beta-blockers.

Fish oils may enhance the antihypertensive effects of beta-blockers (see Table 15-2). Although fish oils show antiarrhythmic effects, they do not appear to have antiarrhythmic synergy with beta-blockers (38).

In patients receiving propranolol, coenzyme Q10 60 mg twice daily may reduce the incidence of cardiac arrhythmia, angina and heart failure during the first 28 days post-myocardial infarction (39) and of cardiac events over the subsequent year (40). At 90 mg twice daily, coenzyme Q10 appears to diminish the negative chronotropic and inotropic effects of ocular timolol, used for treatment of glaucoma, without impairment of therapeutic response (41).

Chromium picolinate 600 mcg/day may raise serum HDL-cholesterol in men taking beta-blockers, without affecting total cholesterol (42).

## Calcium Channel Blockers

The dihydropyridine calcium channel blockers are substrates for CYP3A and are potentially subject to pharmacokinetic interactions with numerous herbs that inhibit or induce CYP3A isozymes (43). This interaction was demonstrated in human volunteers when nifedipine and felodipine were taken with peppermint oil, a CYP3A inhibitor (44). Although garlic extracts may induce CYP3A (and were shown to reduce bioavailability of saquinavir in human volunteers [45]), no interaction between garlic and calcium channel blockers has yet been reported.

Pycnogenol (an extract of bark of the French maritime pine), 100 mg/day for 12 weeks, reduced blood pressure in hypertensive patients taking nifedipine, allowing reduction in drug dosage in a double-blind, placebo-controlled trial (46). In vitro, pycnogenol stimulates endothelial nitric oxide synthesis, an effect that appears to rest with the oligomeric proanthocyanidin fraction (47).

## ACE Inhibitors

ACE inhibitors, captopril in particular, have metal-binding sites. Co-administration of iron (and possibly other metals) with ACE inhibitors may significantly reduce drug absorption, impairing the antihypertensive response (48).

ACE inhibitors decrease potassium excretion, so that administration of potassium to patients taking ACE inhibitors may cause severe hyperkalemia (49).

The addition of NAC 600 mg three times daily to captopril or enalapril treatment of hypertensive male smokers enhanced the antihypertensive effect of the drug, presumably by protecting vascular nitric oxide from oxidation (50).

# Antibiotic

## Tetracyclines and Quinolones

Chelation of minerals by tetracycline and quinolone antibiotics significantly reduces antibiotic intestinal absorption and may lead to therapeutic failure. Studies in rats have demonstrated that common herbs like dandelion (51) and fennel (52) can be so rich in minerals that they inhibit absorption of these antibiotics.

## Metronidazole

Silymarin, a group of flavonoids found in milk thistle, was shown to reduce the bioavailability and blood levels of metronidazole by 30% among healthy volunteers (53), an effect that may lead to therapeutic failure. None of the suspected mechanisms for this interaction are consistent with other known effects of milk thistle.

Vitamin C (250 mg twice daily) plus vitamin E (200 IU twice daily), impaired the effectiveness of metronidazole in the treatment of H. pylori infection (54), again through an unidentified mechanism.

Saccharomyces boulardii 250 mg administered three times daily enhanced therapeutic efficacy of metronidazole and diiodoquinol in treatment of acute amebic colitis, reducing the duration of diarrhea by 75% and of fever and abdominal pain by 50% and reducing the prevalence of post-treatment amebic cystosis from 18% to 0% (55). S. boulardii (1000 mg/day) appears to enhance therapeutic efficacy of metronidazole (56) and vancomycin (57) in the treatment of recurrent Clostridium difficile colitis but may not be beneficial for a first attack of C. difficile colitis.

## Nitrofurantoin

Deglycyrrhizinated licorice (DGL) administered along with nitrofurantoin to patients with urinary tract infection may increase the urinary concentration of nitrofurantoin, possibly enhancing efficacy (58). One early controlled study found that combining DGL with nitrofurantoin improved outcome of patients being treated for pyelonephritis (59).

## Trimethoprim

Although used as an antibiotic, trimethoprim is also a potassium-sparing diuretic, similar in action to amiloride. Concomitant use of trimethoprim with potassium salts may contribute to hyperkalemia (60).

## Antibiotic-Associated Diarrhea

Probiotic supplements are effective in reducing the incidence of antibiotic-associated diarrhea in children (61,62) and adults (63), although the magnitude of the effect varies considerably. The majority of positive studies has been done with *Lactobacillus rhamnosus* GG and *S. boulardii.*

# Antithrombotic

## Aspirin and Other Inhibitors of Platelet Function

Numerous dietary supplements inhibit platelet function in laboratory experiments (31). Many of these, however, do not manifest antiplatelet effects when taken orally by human volunteers. Turmeric (64), flaxseed oil (65), borage oil (a source of GLA) (66) and primrose oil (67) are notable examples of substances identified as antithrombotic that have no demonstrable effect on hemostatic parameters in controlled human experiments. Others, like resveratrol, only inhibit the function of platelets that are washed ex vivo and have no effect on platelets suspended in whole blood, rendering any clinical effect unlikely (68). Dietary supplements that inhibit human platelet function after oral administration are listed in Table 15-3. These might act in an additive fashion with antiplatelet drugs, but few actual interactions have been reported. Vitamin E (alpha-tocopherol) is an exception.

Vitamin E and aspirin have synergistic antiplatelet effects. Aspirin inhibits platelet aggregation; alpha-tocopherol inhibits platelet adhesion to the vascular endothelium. The interaction may be adverse or beneficial, depending upon the clinical circumstances. Use of low doses of alpha-tocopherol (50 IU/day) increased the risk of gingival bleeding by 25% among men taking aspirin, according to an often-cited study (69). The addition of 400 IU/day of alpha-tocopherol to 325 mg aspirin/day significantly reduced the incidence of transient ischemic attacks (TIAs) in patients with previous TIAs, when compared to aspirin alone (70).

Fish oils do not show an additive or synergistic antiplatelet interaction with aspirin (71) but may act synergistically to prolong bleeding time (72). A prospective long-term study, however, found no increase in bleeding episodes or abnormalities of hemostasis attributable to the combination of 300 mg aspirin with 4000 mg fish oil/day (73).

Policosanol, a mixture of primary aliphatic alcohols isolated from sugar cane wax, exerts dose-dependent inhibition of platelet aggregation, with 20 mg of policosanol/day producing an effect similar to 100 mg of aspirin/day. Combination of aspirin and policosanol produces a mild additive effect in healthy volunteers (74).

A single case report describes spontaneous intraocular bleeding associated with the combined use of aspirin and Ginkgo biloba extract (43).

Table 15-3   Dietary Supplements That Inhibit Platelet Function After Oral Administration to Humans

| Supplement | Comments |
| --- | --- |
| Dong qua | Inhibits pathological platelet activation in ulcerative colitis (121) |
| Fish oil | Reduced PAF- and collagen-activated aggregation (122) |
| Garlic | Inhibits thromboxane synthesis (123) |
| Ginger | May decrease thromboxane synthesis (124) |
| Gingko biloba | Inhibits collagen-activated aggregation (125), effect inconsistent (126) |
| Licorice | Glycyrrhizin exerts in vivo effect (127) |
| Policosanol | Decreases thromboxane synthesis (128) |
| Pycnogenol | Only inhibits cigarette-induced aggregation in smokers (129) |
| Reishi | Effect requires high-dose extracts (130) |
| Resveratrol | Inhibits ADP (131) and thrombin-induced (132) aggregation |
| Saw palmetto | Case report of increased bleeding time and hemorrhage (133) |
| Tocopherols, mixed | Mild inhibition of ADP-induced aggregation (134) |
| Tocotrienols | Decrease thromboxane synthesis (135) but not hemostasis (136) |
| Vitamin E | Inhibits platelet adhesion, not aggregation (137) |

## Warfarin

Although many reviews warn of potential interactions between dietary supplements and warfarin, few have actually been reported (Table 15-4), and some highly publicized case reports have failed confirmation in controlled studies.

Coenzyme Q10 is structurally similar to vitamin K and has been reported to interfere with response to warfarin, based upon uncontrolled case reports (75,76); however, no effect of coenzyme Q10, 100 mg/day for 4 weeks, on warfarin effect was seen in a placebo-controlled trial (77). Similarly, early reports indicated increased bleeding in patients receiving warfarin along with vitamin E (78), but a controlled study showed no effect of vitamin E on the anticoagulant response to warfarin, as measured by INR, at doses up to 1200 IU/day (79). Case reports of vitamin C and fish oil (80) increasing warfarin effect have also not been validated in controlled experimental studies (81). Although two case reports suggest a decreased warfarin effect in patients taking ginseng (82,83), a controlled study showed no interaction (84). Variations in the ginseng preparations used may account for the differences.

Because of its narrow therapeutic range, extensive binding to plasma protein and extensive hepatic metabolism, warfarin is likely to be sensitive to interactions with numerous drugs and herbs, so that extreme caution should always be used by patients taking warfarin when adding any dietary supplement.

Table 15-4 Dietary Supplements with Documented Interactions with Wafarin

| Supplement | Comments |
|---|---|
| Boldo | Hemorrhage, single case report (138) |
| Chlorella | Vitamin K content may inhibit warfarin effect (139) |
| Danshen | Increases INR (140) |
| Devil's claw | Purpura, single case report (141) |
| Dong quai | Increased INR, single case report (142) |
| Fenugreek | Hemorrhage, single case report |
| Garlic | Two case reports of increased INR (143) |
| Ginkgo biloba | Intracerebral hemorrhage, case report (144) |
| Lyceum barbarum | Case report of increase INR (145) |
| Panax ginseng | Increased clearance without effect on hemostasis (146) |
| Red yeast rice | Monacolin K, identical with lovastatin, augments the anticoagulant effect of warfarin (147) |
| St John's wort | Decreased INR in multiple case reports (148) |
| Vinpocetin | Mild reduction in warfarin effect, unknown mechanism (149) |

## Antilipemic

Most HMG coA reductase inhibitors (statins) are substrates for P-gp and CYP3A, making them candidates for pharmacokinetic interactions with herbs that alter activity of these enzymes (43). St. John's wort decreases the serum concentration of simvastatin (see Box 15-1), but does not affect pravastatin pharmacokinetics, because pravastatin metabolism is less subject to the activity of CYP and P-gp.

Red yeast rice contains monacolin K, which is identical with lovastatin, and yields similar clinical and toxicological effects (85). Presumably, red yeast rice would have added therapeutic and toxic effects with any statin, although commercial preparations of red yeast rice extract vary considerably in their monacolin content (86).

An antioxidant cocktail consisting of beta-carotene 25 mg, vitamin C 1000 mg, vitamin E 800 mg, and selenium 100 mcg adversely affected the reduction in cardiovascular events of simvastatin-niacin therapy among 160 patients with coronary artery disease, low HDL-cholesterol (HDL-C <35) levels and normal LDL-cholesterol (mean LDL-C,140) (87). Further analysis found that the antioxidant cocktail prevented the increase in protective HDL2-C produced by simvastatin-niacin (88) and blunted the protective increase in HDL-C particle size associated with simvastatin-niacin therapy (89). These adverse effects were reproduced using vitamin E and vitamin C alone (90). Selenium by itself actually enhanced the simvastatin-niacin increase in HDL-C2 (91). In contrast, a large prospective study of 20,563 hyperlipidemic individuals receiving simvastatin without niacin found that a similar antioxidant cocktail (650 IU vitamin

E, 250 mg vitamin C and 20 mg beta-carotene) produced no alteration, positive or negative, in any therapeutic parameter (92). The adverse effect of vitamins E and C on antilipemic therapy may be specific to patients with low HDL-C.

All statins reduce synthesis of the endogenous antioxidant, coenzyme Q10 (93). Statin-induced coenzyme Q10 depletion may impair mitochondrial function, raising the serum lactate/pyruvate ratio (94). Supplemental coenzyme-Q10, 100 mg/day, prevents the decline in serum coenzyme Q10 levels without impairment of the hypolipidemic effect of the statin (95) and may reduce symptoms of statin myopathy, according to a small controlled study (96). Statin-induced coenzyme Q10 depletion may actually be increased by vitamin E (700 IU/day) (97), possibly because coenzyme Q10 is consumed in the recycling of the oxidative metabolites of vitamin E (tocopheryl quinones) to tocopherols (98). Co-enzyme Q10 depletion might possibly explain the reversal by vitamin E of the vascular benefits of atorvastatin in patients with heart failure (99).

## Antineoplastic

Because most antineoplastic agents are highly toxic and have a narrow therapeutic range, the use of dietary supplements by cancer patients has generated considerable concern. St. John's wort is a particular problem, not only because of adverse pharmacokinetic interactions due to enzyme induction by one of its components, hyperformin (see Box 15-1), but also because another component, hypericin, may interfere with a pharmacodynamic mechanism shared by many antineoplastic agents, topoisomerase inhibition (100).

Natural substances other than St. John's wort that induce P-gp or other transport proteins have the potential to diminish effectiveness of cancer chemotherapy. Although studies in vivo are lacking, in vitro studies indicate that the chronic exposure to the flavonoids quercetin, kaempferol, and silibinin (derived from milk thistle) induce P-gp (101). Other herbal derivatives are being tested for P-gp inhibition in an effort to find substances that can overcome multi-drug resistance to cancer chemotherapy (102). Green tea catechins may either inhibit or induce P-gp, depending upon their structure (101). The use of herbal therapies in conjunction with chemotherapy creates a serious potential risk for adverse interaction. During the course of a clinical trial, self-administration of essiac tea, a polyherbal product specifically marketed for cancer treatment, was associated with markedly elevated levels of exatecan mesylate and significant clinical toxicity, although the mechanism of the interaction has not been established (103).

Other dietary supplements contraindicated with chemotherapy include zinc and high-dose vitamin B6 for patients receiving platins. Zinc supplementation induces synthesis of metallothionein, a metal efflux enzyme that can reduce cellular concentration of platinum-derived antineoplastic drugs, inhibiting effectiveness of cisplatin in rodents (104). An interaction in humans has not been reported, but it seems prudent to avoid zinc supplementation in patients receiving platins. Many commonly used multivitamin preparations contain zinc. Although high-dose pyridoxine (300 mg/square meter/day for 3 weeks) decreased toxicity of cisplatin/hexamethylmelamine therapy of patients with advanced ovarian cancer, its use was associated with decreased duration of the treatment response (105).

In contrast, there are several dietary supplements that have been shown to decrease the side effects of chemotherapy without adversely effecting therapeutic outcome, according to small clinical trials (Table 15-5). Some of these substances are classified as antioxidants.

A detailed discussion of the controversy concerning co-administration of antioxidants with cancer chemotherapy is outside the scope of this chapter. The controversy itself is based upon a misunderstanding of the concept of "antioxidant," which is a conditional term, not an absolute one. Almost all antioxidants exist in at least two redox states and function as pro-oxidants under appropriate conditions. The notion that antioxidants protect cancer cells from the effects of chemotherapy is not supported by empirical data; on the other hand, the notion that antioxidants protect normal tissue from the toxicity of antineoplastic agents needs to be established with specific doses of specific supplements used in conjunction with defined chemotherapeutic agents.

Table 15-5 Dietary Supplements That May Prevent Toxicity of Antineoplastic Chemotherapy: Clinical Trials

| Supplement | Antineoplastic | Interaction |
|---|---|---|
| Coenzyme Q10* | Adriamycin | Decreased cardiotoxicity (150) |
| Glutamine | Various | Decreased mucositis (151), anthracycline cardiotoxicity, irinotecan diarrhea, paclitaxel neuropathy (152) |
| Magnesium** | Cisplatin | Decreased renal tubular damage (153) |
| Melatonin | Cisplatin, etoposide | Decreased myelosuppression and neuropathy (154) |
| | Interleukin-2 | Decreased hypotension (155) |
| N-acetyl cysteine | Ifosfamide | Decreased hemorrhagic cystitis (156) |
| Selenium | Cisplatin | Reduced myelosuppression and nephrotoxicity (157) |
| Vitamin B6 | 5-fluorouracil | Reverse palmar-plantar dysesthesia (158) |
| Vitamin E | Cisplatin | Decreased neurotoxicity (159) |

* Adriamycin inhibits coenzyme Q10 synthesis (160)
** Cisplatin induces severe intracellular magnesium depletion (161)

## Diuretic

Numerous case reports of severe hypokalemia resulting from the combination of various diuretic agents with licorice have appeared (106). Licorice may also reverse the antihypertensive effects of diuretics. The presumed mechanism for both effects is pseudoaldosteronism, produced by a metabolite of glycyrrhizin that inhibits 11-beta hydroxysteroid dehydrogenase.

A single case report describes hypertension in a patient taking Ginkgo biloba along with a thiazide diuretic (107). The presence of an interaction was not established.

Several case reports describe symptomatic hypercalcemia resulting from the combination of thiazide diuretics, which inhibit renal calcium excretion, and vitamin D (108-110) or calcium supplements (111).

Potassium-sparing diuretics decrease magnesium excretion. Severe hypermagnesemia has occurred when magnesium-containing products were taken by patients using amiloride (112). The interaction has not yet been reported for triamterene; and may not occur with spironolactone; in healthy unsupplemented subjects, spironolactone, in contrast to amiloride, does not elevate serum magnesium concentration (113).

Numerous herbs are alleged to have diuretic or cathartic effects. Herbs with diuretic action traditionally ascribed to them include buchu, burdock, butcher's broom, celery seed, cornsilk, couch grass, dandelion, elder broom, goldenrod, gravel root, horsetail, parsley, juniper, stinging nettle, uva-ursi and wild carrot. Potentiation of diuretic medication by these herbs is possible, but not demonstrated. Abuse of Cascara segrada has been associated with hypokalemia (114); concomitant use of an herbal laxative with a diuretic might produce additive depletion of potassium.

## Hypoglycemic

Almost all reported interactions between dietary supplements and anti-diabetic agents are pharmacodynamic and result from potentiation of hypoglycemia. In a systematic review of interactions between drugs and herbs in a hospital clinic population, two-thirds of the observed interactions was potentiation of oral hypoglycemics by nopal (prickly pear cactus)[115]. The most frequently prescribed oral hypoglycemic, the biguanide metformin, is itself an herbal derivative, originally found in French lilac (Galega officinalis), used traditionally for treatment of diabetes.

A review of clinical research on the hypoglycemic effect of natural products concluded that the best evidence for efficacy from adequately designed randomized controlled trials is available for Coccinia indica and American ginseng (116). Table 15-6 lists supplements demonstrated to reduce blood sugar or improve insulin sensitivity in small clinical trials of diabetic patients. None of these agents appears adequate as stand alone therapy (117), but many of them

Table 15-6    Dietary Supplements with Hypoglycemic or Insulin-Sensitizing
Effects Demonstrated in Diabetic Humans

| Supplement | Effect |
|---|---|
| Aloe vera, dried sap, .5 tsp/day | Reduces fasting blood sugar in NIDDM (162) |
| Aloe vera, juice, 1 tbsp twice daily | Potentiates action of glyburide (163) |
| Alpha lipoic acid (600 mg/day) | Improves insulin sensitivity (164) Improves diabetic control and neuropathy (165) |
| Bitter melon (Momordica charantia) | Weak hypoglycemic action in NIDDM (166) |
| Chromium | Most extensively studied with inconclusive and conflicting results in NIDDM (167-171) |
| Coccinia indica | Reduces blood sugar (172) |
| Fenugreek (25 g/day) | Reduces blood sugar in NIDDM (173) |
| Ginseng, American (3000 mg) | Reduces glycemic response to glucose challenge (174,175) |
| Ginseng, Asian (200 mg/day) | Reduces blood sugar and glycohemoglobin (176) |
| Gymnema silvestre (400 mg/day) | Reduces insulin requirements (177) Reduces need for oral hypoglycemics (178) |
| Nopal (Opuntia spp.) | Broiled stems (500 g) reduce blood sugar (179,180) Capsules are ineffective (181,182) |
| Pycnogenol (100 mg/day) | Reduces glucose, improves endothelial function (183) Improves diabetic retinopathy (184) |
| Saltbush (Atriplex halimus) | Hypoglycemic, insulin potentiating (185) |
| Vanadyl sulfate (100-150 mg/day) | Small reduction in insulin requirement (190) |
| Vijayasar (Pterocarpus marsupium) | Reduces blood sugar in mild NIDDM (191) |
| Vitamin D | Increases insulin sensitivity in vitamin D deficiency (192) |
| Vitamin E (600-900 IU/day) | Improves glycemic control (193) and insulin action (194) Reduces glycohemoglobin and plasma insulin (195) |

are in common use among different ethnic groups, creating the potential for clinically significant drug interactions among diabetics who use them. Nopal is the most widely used herbal hypoglycemic among persons of Mexican descent and bitter melon (karela) is more commonly used by persons from Asia (118).

Concerns that glucosamine (119) or fish oil (120) supplementation might impair glycemic control have not been supported in controlled studies.

## Immune Modulation

Cyclosporine blood levels are subject to control by P-gp and CYP3A activity, creating great potential for pharmacokinetic interactions with natural products. The increase in cyclosporine trough concentration by grapefruit juice is well-known and has been used therapeutically (121). St. John's wort, conversely, reduces cyclosporine levels (see Box 15-1). Cyclosporine in its turn inhibits metabolism of statins, increasing blood levels and the potential for toxicity. Rhabdomylosis, a manifestation of statin toxicity, occurred in a renal transplant patient taking cyclosporine and red yeast rice, which contains the natural lovastatin analogue, monacolin K (122).

Cyclosporine nephrotoxicity in transplant patients has been mitigated by fish oils (see Table 15-2) and in one study by vitamin E (alpha-tocopherol acetate 500 mg/day) (123).

Folic acid, 1 to 5 mg/day, decreases the toxicity of low-dose methotrexate in patients with rheumatoid arthritis (124) or psoriasis (125) without affecting the therapeutic efficacy of methotrexate. At 5 mg/day, folic acid may prevent methotrexate-induced nausea (124) and the rise in homocysteine associated with methotrexate therapy (126). It also may increase the cellular uptake of methotrexate (127) and perhaps should not be taken on the day methotrexate is injected.

Interferon-alpha, used in the treatment of chronic hepatitis C infection, may have its therapeutic and toxic effects enhanced by dietary supplements. The polyherbal medicine sho-saiko-to, used in Japan to treat chronic hepatitis C, is now available in the United States. Allergic pneumonitis, an uncommon side effect of both sho-saiko-to and interferon alpha, is several times more likely to occur when the medications are administered together (128) Sho-saiko-to's principal ingredient, bupleurum, is thought to owe its anti-fibrotic effects to the flavonoids baicalin and baicalein, which are structurally similar to the antifibrotic flavonoid silibinin, found in milk thistle (129), an herb frequently taken by patients with chronic liver disease. Until more information is available, it seems prudent to advise patients receiving interferon to avoid concomitant use of milk thistle and bupleurum-containing herbs.

On the other hand, the addition of zinc (150 mg/day as zinc carnisonate [130] or 300 mg/day as zinc sulphate [131]) may enhance the response to interferon therapy without increasing toxicity.

## Nitrates

Three supplements appear to prevent or reverse nitrate tolerance, according to small human studies. NAC, 2400 mg orally, bid for 2 days, increased the exercise tolerance of patients receiving isosorbide mononitrate (ISMN), when compared to ISMN plus placebo (132). High-dose NAC helps to prevent nitrate tolerance in patients with normal left ventricular function, but results are variable in patients with congestive heart failure (101,102,135). Oral NAC at a dose of 400 mg tid did not prevent nitrate tolerance in patients with normal cardiac function and stable angina pectoris (136). Organic nitrates release nitric oxide (NO), a step that requires the presence of thiol groups; depletion of thiols by oxidation is thought to be responsible for nitrate tolerance and NAC is used as a source of replacement sulfhydryl groups. NAC not only potentiates the cardioprotective effects of nitrates, but also aggravates nitrate-induced headache (137).

L-arginine, the amino acid precursor of nitric oxide, at a dose of 700 mg q.i.d. by mouth, attenuated the development of tolerance to transdermal nitroglycerine over a 2 week period in patients with stable angina pectoris, but had no effect on initial response to nitrate (138).

Folic acid 10 mg/day prevented both nitrate tolerance and nitric oxide synthase dysfunction induced by continuous nitroglycerine in the arterial circulation of healthy volunteers (139). Continuous treatment with nitroglycerin may reduce bioavailability of tetrahydrobiopterin, an essential cofactor for nitric acid synthase. Folate is involved in regeneration of tetrahydrobiopterin.

# Conclusion

Because clinically significant interactions between dietary supplements and medication exist, physicians must know all the supplements their patients are taking. Extreme caution should be taken by patients using high-risk medications like warfarin, cytotoxic agents and anti-retroviral protease inhibitors. The literature on drug-supplement interactions is dominated by reviews that stress potential adverse interactions due to CYP or P-gp induction/inhibition or to additive pharmacodynamic effects. Many of these are not substantiated when tested in controlled human experiments. A number of small clinical trials demonstrate benefits of dietary supplements in augmenting drug effects or decreasing toxicity. Familiarity with these will allow physicians to direct their patients in the use of dietary supplements to enhance the effectiveness of conventional care. Prescribed in this fashion, it may be possible to apply precision to the use of dietary supplements.

SELECTED REFERENCES*
1. **Galland, L.** Drug-Nutrient Workshop. New York. Applied Nutrition, Inc., 2004.
1a.**Horn J, Hansten P, Chan L.** Proposal for a new tool to evaluate drug interaction cases. Annals Pharmacother. 2007;41:674-80.
27. **Hennessey et al.** St Johns wort increases expression of P-glycoprotein: implications for drug interactions. Br J Clin Pharmacol. 2002;53:75-82.

* The complete reference list is to be found on the book's Web site.

31. **Ulbrect C, Basch E, Weissner W, Hackman D.** An evidence-based systematic review of herb and supplement interactions by the Natural Standard Research Collaboration. Expert Opin Drug Saf. 2006;5:719-28.

36. **Young et al.** Magnesium status and digoxin toxicity. Br J Clin Pharmacol. 1991;32:717-21.

37. **Izzo AA, Di Carlo G, Borrelli F, Ernst E.** Cardiovascular pharmacotherapy and herbal medicines: the risk of drug interaction. Int J Cardiol. 2005;98:1-14.

43. **Izzo AA, Di Carlo G, Borrelli F, Ernst E.** Cardiovascular pharmacotherapy and herbal medicines: the risk of drug interaction. Int J Cardiol. 2005; 98:1-14.

45. **Brazier MC, Levine MAH.** Drug-Herb Interactions Among Commonly Used Conventional Medicines: a Compendium for Health Care Professionals. Am J Therapeutics. 2003;10:163-9.

56. **McFarland et al.** A randomized, placebo-controlled trial of Saccharomyces boulardii in combination with standard antibiotics for Clostridium difficile disease. JAMA. 1994;271:1913-8.

61. **Johnston BC, Supina AL, Ospina M, Vohra S.** Probiotics for the prevention of pediatric antibiotic-associated diarrhea. Cochrane Database Syst Rev. 2007;:CD004827.

63. **McFarland LV.** Meta-analysis of probiotics for the prevention of antibiotic associated diarrhea and the treatment of Clostridium difficile disease. Am J Gastroenterol. 2006;101:812-22.

77. **Engelsen et al.** Effect of Coenzyme Q10 and Ginkgo biloba on warfarin dosage in patients on long-term warfarin treatment. A randomized, double-blind, placebo-controlled cross-over trial. Ugeskr Laeger. 2003;165:1868-71.

87. **Brown et al.** Simvastatin and niacin, antioxidant vitamins, or the combination for the prevention of coronary disease. N Engl J Med. 2001;345:1583-92.

96. **Caso G, Kelly P, McNurlan MA, Lawson WE.** Effect of coenzyme q10 on myopathic symptoms in patients treated with statins. Am J Cardiol. 2007;99:1409-12.

97. **Kaikkonen et al.** Antioxidative efficacy of parallel and combined supplementation with coenzyme Q10 and d-alpha-tocopherol in mildly hypercholesterolemic subjects: a randomized placebo-controlled clinical study. Free Radic Res. 2000;33:329-40.

# Appendix 1: Systems of Practice

BRADLY JACOBS, MD, MPH
KATHERINE GUNDLING, MD

This section familiarizes readers with some of the more common systems of practice. Helpful resources are provided for those who desire more information. As seen in the preceding pages, the range of complementary and alternative therapies is extraordinarily broad. Many techniques are derived from systems of practice that have been used historically in a more comprehensive fashion. Traditional Chinese medicine (TCM) is an example of a system of practice that, in its purest form, coordinates a variety of therapeutic techniques, such as herbal medicine, acupuncture, massage, nutrition, and programs of physical activity. Ayurvedic medicine, of which yoga is one of several components, also utilizes multiple techniques simultaneously. It is recognized and practiced within the federal health system of India, and its early influences can be seen in traditions of medical care around the world.

Do such systems of practice translate well to western cultural conventions? Westerners are more likely to sample components of comprehensive systems (almost a smorgaasbord type of approach) than they are to receive all treatments at once under the guidance of a single practitioner. Acupuncture administered by medical doctors, for example, is often used exclusive of the medicinal herbs, physical activity and diet that would accompany it with traditional Chinese medicine, and most people who practice yoga do so independent of a comprehensive Ayurvedic program.

## Ayurvedic Medicine

### Definition

The term "Ayurveda" is derived from two Sanskrit words, *ayur* (life), and *veda* (knowledge or science). Hence, Ayurveda is the knowledge or science of life. Many of its origins are in Hinduism as well as Persian thought, and it is still actively practiced and researched alongside Western medicine in India. Its comprehensive approach to health includes not only assessment of the internal and external health of the patient, but also the patient's health within the family and community. Early documents of Ayurveda set forth guidelines for general hygiene, including rules about how to bathe or wash cooking utensils. A single Ayurvedic physician, in a role more reflective of a combination of doctor/ public health officer or perhaps home visiting nurse specialist in the West, might provide care to an entire village in India.

Health is considered to be a state of balanced forces. The five categories of elements (air, fire, water, earth and ether) combine in different ways to produce three principal forms of energy (doshas) that control the body. Vata is a combination of air and ether, and concerns bodily functions of movement such as breathing, circulation, childbirth, elimination, etc. Kapha is a combination of water and earth, and is associated with fluid balance, immunity, and processes such as mucus production, long-term memory and sleep. Pitta, a combination of fire and water, is related to energy production, heat, digestion and metabolism. Each of the doshas is associated with certain seasons, and individuals usually are thought to have a normal predominance of one or two doshas, although more complex relationships between the three doshas in a given individual are possible. Optimal balance of the individual combination of doshas for each individual supports health and prevention of illness. Ayurveda also recognizes causes of illness including genetics, karma, accidents, and infectious agents, although it is generally believed that one's doshas are out of balance first, which creates the environment that permits disease to manifest.

Principles of Ayurvedic medicine greatly influenced the origins of other eastern medical traditions as well as western medicine. One can easily find remnants of Ayurveda in the West. The concept of toxins and detoxification is central to Ayurveda, and many modern supplements are claimed to be "detoxifiers." The practice of yoga, an Ayurvedic form of meditation and physical discipline, has enjoyed renewed popularity in the West.

## Modalities Used

An Ayurvedic practitioner determines a person's constitutional type by the examination of multiple physical factors. Major components of the physical examination include pulse diagnosis, tongue examination, and assessment of urine and stool. Pulse and tongue diagnosis are primary methods used to determine the state of balance between the doshas. After the physical examination, the practitioner might recommend a range of therapies as part of a treatment program that might include herbal medicine, topical applications, massage, meditation, yoga, and psychotherapy, including herbal medicines, non-herbal supplements, other dietary modifications, yoga or other directed meditation.

## Licensure

The status of Ayurvedic medicine in the United States has been compared to the practice of naturopathy in the states that do not officially sanction its practice (1). In other words, Ayurvedic practitioners have extremely variable levels of training and experience. There is no federal or state licensing system in the United States, and patients must take it upon themselves to investigate an individual practitioner's credentials (individual schools, however, may have state licensure for teaching purposes).

Some Ayurvedic practitioners in the United States carry the title, "CAS," which stands for "Clinical Ayurvedic Specialist." This term was established at the California College of Ayurveda (CCA) in 1995, and is used by individuals who have completed their training program. According to the CCA website, this title is reflective of the highest current standard of training in the United States. Training programs vary from weekend classes to full-time programs. At CCA, for example, a high school education is required to enroll, and a community college course in anatomy/physiology is required if one has not already been completed (2).

With the current lack of a licensing system in the United States, it is difficult for Ayurvedic practitioners trained in the traditional schools in India to distinguish themselves from their less-trained counterparts. Some of the states that have Ayurvedic research and training centers include California, Iowa, Massachusetts, New Mexico and New York.

The National Ayurvedic Medical Association is currently working toward developing guidelines for qualified practitioners. This is part of an attempt to unify the Ayurvedic community, to provide educational standards to meet the needs of the general public, and to lay the foundation for Ayurvedic licensure requirements.

## Efficacy

Although many of the medical traditions of Ayurveda have been applied for a long time, their efficacy has not been evaluated in a rigorous manner until recent years. Areas of intense study include therapies for Type 2 diabetes mellitus, herbal agents that have in-vitro anti-inflammatory activity, and effects of physical modalities, such as yoga, on cardiovascular function and other organ systems.

## Safety

The main safety issue has pertained to the content of over-the-counter Ayurvedic medicines. A particular concern is the recurrent finding of excessive lead and other heavy metals that can lead to significant morbidity (3). Because Ayurvedic medicines are not regulated as drugs in the United States (and can be obtained over the internet), buyers are dependent upon the good faith of the manufacturer to sell products that are safe and efficacious.

## Additional Information

National Ayurvedic Medical Association (NAMA) www.ayurvedic-association .org, 620 Cabillo Ave., Santa Cruz, CA 95030.

# Homeopathy

## Definition

Contrary to the assumptions of many medical doctors and lay people, homeopathy is not synonymous with "herbal" or "natural" medicine. Homeopathy is a system of practice developed by German physician Samuel Hahnemann at the turn of the 19th century. Dr. Hahnemann viewed the common medical practice of bloodletting, purging, and induced emesis as harsh and unnecessary. Hahnemann called these harsh therapies "allopathic" because he felt they were "other than" the symptoms they purported to treat. In contrast, he called his own system "homeopathic."

Homeopathy is based on the premise that "like treats like," sometimes referred to as the Law of Similars. Substances that cause symptoms or disease in healthy people are thought to treat those same problems when administered in very dilute quantities to sick people. For example, whereas coffee (the hot beverage) has stimulant properties in large doses, the homeopathic preparation, "coffea" is used to induce restfulness and sleep in people who suffer from insomnia. To be effective, a remedy must match the patient's individual symptoms; correctly prescribed, it is theorized to catalyze a healing response in the patient's self-regulatory systems.

Another key concept is that more dilute solutions are thought to have greater potency. The most potent medicines are those diluted beyond Avogadro's number, which means there may be no molecules of the "active" ingredient left in the administered product. Some supporters of homeopathy believe that an imprinted memory of the molecules is left in the solution, and that this memory solution has potent effect. There is preliminary research in the material sciences literature documenting transfer of information from solid to liquid (4). These findings are quite controversial. At this time, this concept is generally not accepted by the scientific community.

Homeopathy has been practiced consistently in some European countries, and India has many homeopathic colleges and practitioners. Homeopathic practice and education fell out of favor in the United States in the early 1900s once greater standardization of American medical schools occurred following release of the Flexner Report. However, recent years have seen revived interest in and practice of homeopathic medicine in the United States. Unlike dietary supplements, the manufacturing process for homeopathic remedies is standardized and regulated by the FDA through the Homeopathic Pharmacopoeia of the United States (HPUS.com): "Homeopathic drugs are drugs under the law. The initial 'HPUS' on the label of a drug product assures the legal standards of strength, quality, purity, and packaging exist for the drug product in the package."

## Modalities Used

Practitioners of homeopathy gather much information about their patients and prescribe one or more homeopathic remedies, which may be prepared from botanical products, minerals such as iron phosphate or arsenic oxide, animal products, or drugs such as penicillin. These substances are diluted significantly prior to administration. Homeopaths will prescribe treatments for chronic conditions based on the unique presentation and symptoms of the patients. These remedies are usually more potent (i.e., greater than 200C dilution). Acute self-limiting conditions such as poison ivy, colds, coughs, flus, and ear infections usually require lower-potency remedies, which can be purchased over the counter. There are useful lay texts describing symptoms often characteristic of commonly used over-the-counter remedies.

With respect to the labeling nomenclature of homeopathic preparations, most prescriptions use the Latin name of the base substance. The degree of dilution is indicated by a number and lettering system. For example, "Nux Vomica 5 CH" means that the base substance is Nux Vomica (Mother Tincture of Nux Vomica). The original preparation is diluted 5 times at 1/100 (centesimal dilution) with succussions (vigorous shaking) between each dilution step. The "H" indicates a preparation made according to the Hahnemann method. If the solution is diluted at 1/10, the label "X" is attached.

Homeopathic products on the market come in a variety of vehicles, including creams, ointments, lotions, or tinctures. Some are globules, pellets, tablets, capsules, lozenges, gum, or nasal sprays. They are even produced as eye drops, suppositories and injectables. Products can contain several remedies and have potency ranging from 3X to 30C (5). However, the classical homeopathy developed by Dr. Hahnemann uses only one remedy at a time. This is distinct from "complex" (multiple remedy) homeopathy and from injectable forms.

## Licensure

Arizona, Connecticut and Nevada allow licensed physicians to obtain an additional license in homeopathic medicine. Nevada and Arizona allow "Advanced practitioners of homeopathy" to practice alongside physicians who are trained in homeopathy (6).

Because of the varied licensing laws in the United States, there is confusion about experience and certification. The National Center for Homeopathy states that a practitioner's level of competence in homeopathy often has little to do with the type of licensure. Several titles that seem to indicate greater competence include:

- CCH: Certified Classical Homeopath
- DHt: Diplomate in Homeotherapeutics (available for MDs and DOs)
- DHANP: Diplomate of the Homeopathic Academy of Naturopathic Physicians (available for naturopathic physicians)

One needs to ask about specific training and experience when seeking homeopathic care.

## Safety

In general, homeopathic medications are unlikely to be dangerous because the preparations have so little active ingredient. There have been case reports, however, of adverse reactions related to homeopathic preparations, and this is particularly true with topical agents (7-9). Some argue that the greater danger of homeopathy lies in the potential for indirect adverse effects, such as the failure to recognize and treat significant disease in a timely manner, or the recommendation that vaccinations should be avoided (10).

## Efficacy

Much has been written in recent years about the efficacy (or lack thereof) of homeopathic "remedies." Because the claims of mechanism for homeopathy seem to contradict current concepts of science, some believe that extraordinary proof of efficacy is required. One challenge pertains to the question of how homeopathy should be investigated. Can single-agent remedies be evaluated in a manner similar to modern drug trials? Can individualized treatments be incorporated into well-designed clinical trials? When does a trial test a particular remedy, and when does it speak to the legitimacy of homeopathic principles?

Several major analyses of clinical trials of homeopathy have been conducted. A large meta-analysis concluded that there appeared to be an effect beyond placebo but that the evidence did not support use of homeopathy for any specific problem (see the text for additional discussion).

## Additional Information

National Center for Homeopathy, www.nationalcenterforhomeopathy.org. This website is "the leading open-membership organization supporting and promoting homeopathy in the United States." Homeopathic pharmacopoeia of the United States, www.HPUAS.com, considered the official compendium of homeopathic drugs in the U.S.

# Spinal Manipulation

Spinal manipulation is a form of manual therapy and is one of the most commonly used complementary and alternative methods. Used throughout recorded history, there are many systems of manual therapy, and differing schools within each system using joint mobilization (low-velocity), joint manipulation (high-velocity), soft-tissue techniques including massage, muscle energy techniques, movement, neuro-muscular techniques, myofascial techniques, and cranio-sacral techniques among others. Some techniques are controversial among practitioners.

The terms 'manual therapy' and 'manipulation' or 'manipulative therapy' are often used interchangeably. Manipulation is a form of joint mobilization that involves a forceful, low-amplitude thrust directed to a specific joint. Three professions provide manual therapy in the US: 65,000 chiropractors (192 million visits per year seeing 3%-16% of US adults each year); 53,000 osteopaths (only 5%-10% dedicated to manipulative therapy exclusively); and physical therapists. By comparison, in Germany, where spinal manipulation is considered part of conventional medicine, 15,000 MDs (5% of all MDs) are trained and state board certified in spinal manipulation. Whether physical therapists are trained in and practice spinal manipulation depends on state and national regulations. Currently physical therapists may provide spinal manipulation in Texas and Florida but not in California; outside of the US they may provide it in Sweden, Norway and the Netherlands but not in Germany. Where physical therapists provide spinal manipulation, it is seen as a conventional therapy.

## Safety

Spinal manipulation for uncomplicated low back pain is generally safe if medical causes of back pain such as trauma, infection, inflammatory or malignant disorders and progressive neurologic deficits (radiculopathy or sciatica) are ruled out by careful history and physical examination (10). Laboratory tests (i.e., erythrocyte sedimentation rate) and imaging may be appropriate when there are "red flags," such as in the elderly or in high-risk populations. A review of 31 trials of spinal manipulation for low back pain included over 5000 participants without any complications (11). A systematic compilation of complications from spinal manipulation to the lumbar spine primarily from case reports estimated the risk for cauda equine syndrome at less than 1 in a million spinal manipulations (12).

## Quality Control

Doctors of chiropractic (DC) are trained in 16 chiropractic colleges (since 1897) requiring a 4200-hour curriculum over 4 years, have no MD-equivalent training, and learn 555 hours of manual techniques (see the ACA website). Doctors of chiropractic also receive extensive training in the manual manipulation of the other joints of the body. Doctors of osteopathy (DO) are trained in 23 osteopathic schools (since 1892) equivalent to medical school training, with additional mandatory 210 hours of osteopathic manipulative therapy course training (AOA website). In 75% of physical therapy schools, students are exposed to some manual therapy, and only 22% offer any elective training in joint manipulation (13,14). After graduation, mechanisms of quality control for practitioners are non-existent for each of the professions. The National Institute of Health supports research in manual therapies for which, generally, the mechanisms of action are unclear (15).

# Chiropractic

## Definition

According to the American Chiropractic Association (ACA), chiropractic doctors "devote careful attention to the biomechanics, structure and function of the spine, its effects on the musculoskeletal and neurological systems, and the role played by the proper function of these systems in the preservation and restoration of health." Chiropractic treatments include spinal manipulation, dietary prescriptions, dietary supplements, exercise and rehabilitation, posture and biomechanical training and other modalities depending upon the scope of practice allowed by individual states and the practitioner's training.

The Council on Chiropractic Education considers chiropractors to be "primary care providers" and many chiropractic doctors diagnose and treat "non-neuromusculoskeletal disorders such as allergies, asthma, digestive disorders, otitis media (non-suppurative) and other disorders" (16). Core patients, however, are those who suffer from neuromusculoskeletal complaints, such as headaches, joint pain, neck pain, low back pain and sciatica, as well as osteoarthritis, spinal disk conditions, carpal tunnel syndrome, tendonitis, sprains, and strains. Chiropractors believe the body has a strong ability to heal itself without surgery or medication.

Chiropractic was developed at the end of the 19th century by an American, Daniel David Palmer, who founded the Palmer School of Chiropractic in Iowa. During the 20th century chiropractic achieved licensure in all 50 states and is practiced in a number of other countries as well. To attend chiropractic schools, students must have 90 hours of undergraduate courses. As mentioned above, students undergo 4200 hours of classroom, laboratory and clinical experience, about 555 hours of which are devoted to learning about spinal analysis and spinal manipulation techniques. Once students pass their board examinations, they are considered capable of diagnosing and treating patients.

## Modalities Used

Radiology is used to evaluate initial musculoskeletal complaints and as part of the patient's evaluation to rule out contraindications to spinal manipulation. A program of spinal manipulation is usually recommended, based upon the history, physical examination and x-ray findings. The program often entails at least weekly visits, particularly at the onset of care. In addition to spinal manipulation, patients may be advised to work on posture, start an exercise program, perform stress management, alter work or domestic-related ergonomic issues, use supplements, or change dietary habits and lifestyle.

## Licensure

Chiropractors are licensed in all 50 United States. Schools located in the United States are listed in Box A-1. There are also two chiropractic schools in England, two in Canada, three in Australia, two in South Africa, two in Japan, two in Brazil, and one each in France, Denmark, Sweden, Korea, and Mexico.

## Safety

Concern about the safety of chiropractic has centered on the potential for harm created by the thrusting movements that characterize chiropractic treatment. The incidence of adverse outcomes is not well known or described. A number of case reports of damage to the spinal column and arterial system have raised concerns, particularly about some of the high-velocity techniques (17-19). Estimates of serious adverse events from cervical manipulation range from 1 in 200,000 to 1 in a few million. A 2007 national prospective survey followed 19,722 patients who underwent 28,807 treatment consultations and 50,276 cervical manipulations (20). These manipulations were described as high-velocity/low-amplitude or mechanically assisted thrust to the cervical spine. They reported that minor adverse events were relatively common but identified no serious adverse events (defined as a severe onset or worsening of symptoms immediately after treatment, persistent or significant disability/incapacity, or referral to hospital for immediate evaluation). Based on conservative estimates, they suggest the serious adverse event rate would be 1 per

> **Box A-1  Schools of Chiropractic in the United States (All Private)**
>
> Cleveland Chiropractic College, Los Angeles, CA
> Cleveland Chiropractic College, Kansas City, MO
> D'Youville College, Buffalo, NY
> Life Chiropractic College West, Hayward, CA
> Life University, Marietta, GA
> Logan College of Chiropractic, Chesterfield, MO
> National University of Health Sciences, Lombard, IL
> New York Chiropractic College, Seneca Falls, NY
> Northwestern Health Sciences University, Bloomington, MN
> Palmer Chiropractic University, Davenport, IA
> Palmer College of Chiropractic Florida, Port Orange, FL
> Parker College of Chiropractic, San Jose, CA
> Parker College of Chiropractic, Dallas, TX
> Sherman College of Straight Chiropractic, Spartanburg, SC
> Southern California University of Health Sciences, Whittier, CA
> Texas Chiropractic College, Pasadena, TX
> University of Bridgeport, Bridgeport, CT
> Western States Chiropractic College, Portland, OR

10,000 treatment consultations immediately after cervical spine manipulation, 2 per 10,000 treatment consultations up to 7 days after treatment, and approximately 6 per 100,000 cervical spine manipulations. Minor adverse events such as fainting/dizziness/light-headedness/numbness/tingling were, at worse, approximately 13-16 per 1000 treatment consultations, and 4 per 100 for headache for up to 7 days after treatment. Of significant concern was the finding of rare incidents of vertebrobasilar stroke occurring after patients underwent cervical manipulation. However, a recent review of the literature by The Bone and Joint Decade 2000-2010 Task Force on Neck Pain and Its Associated Disorders, reported in the journal *Spine*, found a similar association among people presenting to their general practitioners with neck complaints. The authors concluded that these associations are explained by patients with vertebrobasilary artery dissection-related neck pain or headache seeking care before having their stroke (21). Notwithstanding, the contralateral vertebral artery undergoes maximal stretch and compression as it exits the C1 transverse foramen (22). Consequently, given the unique anatomy of the vertebral artery, the difficulty of calculating risk for rare events, and the reality that vertebral artery dissection is a serious adverse event, we recommend practitioners performing spinal manipulation avoid high-velocity rotation of C1-C2 whenever possible.

## Additional Information

American Chiropractic Association, 1701 Clarendon Blvd., Arlington, VA 22209, www.americhiro.org/.

# Naturopathic Medicine

## Definition

Naturopathic medicine is based upon the premise that the body has a strong ability to heal itself and naturopathic physicians should apply interventions to facilitate the capacity for self-healing. Licensed naturopathic doctors (NDs) consider themselves to be physicians, and the website for The American Association of Naturopathic Physicians (AANP) states that "Naturopathic physicians are the highest trained practitioners in the broadest scope of naturopathic medical modalities. In addition to the basic medical sciences and conventional diagnostics, naturopathic education includes therapeutic nutrition, botanical medicine, homeopathy, natural childbirth, classical Chinese medicine" (23). Training is completed in a 4-year program and requires undergraduate education.

In the primary care setting, naturopathic physicians devote significant attention to disease prevention and health promotion. According to naturopathic medical theory, when patients present with symptoms or an illness, the practitioners focus on identifying triggers and physiological imbalances that may suggest underlying causes or antecedents of the presenting health issue. They then utilize lifestyle modification (diet, exercise, stress management) as well as mind-body medicine, psychological counseling, dietary supplements, and other CAM modalities as their first-line interventions, and reserve adding medications, referral for procedures, or medical devices as second-line therapy.

There are currently five schools in the US with 4-year curricula, and two in Canada (Box A-2). These schools require a bachelor's degree or higher from a regionally accredited college or university for admission. They include extensive clinical training in the outpatient setting, do not routinely have inpatient training, and have variable residency opportunities following graduation.

The accrediting body, the Council on Naturopathic Medical Education (CNME), lost approval from the Department of Education in 2001, but the National Advisory Committee to the U.S. Secretary of Education recommended restoration of approval in 2003. Of the schools noted in Box A-2 the newest program is the National University of Health Sciences, which is currently a candidate for accreditation with CNME, but does have institutional accreditation with the Higher Learning Commission.

---

**Box A-2  North American Schools with Four-Year Naturopathy Curricula**

Bastyr University, Seattle, WA (Baccalaureate, Master's and Doctorate)
  Accredited by Council on Naturopathic Medical Education since 1987,
  Northwest Commission on Colleges and Universities since 1989, and
  Accreditation Commission for Acupuncture and Oriental Medicine
Boucher Institute of Naturopathic Medicine, New Westminster, British Columbia
  Accredation candidate with Council on Naturopathic Medical Educaion since
    December 2003
Canadian College of Naturopathic Medicine, Toronto, Ontario
  Accredited by Council on Naturopathic Medical Education since September 2000
National College of Natural Medicine, Portland, OR (Master's and Doctorate)
  Accredited by Council on Naturopathic Medical Education since September 2000,
  Northwest Commission on Colleges and Universities since 2004, and
  Accreditation Commission for Acupuncture and Oriental Medicine
National University of Health Sciences, Lombard, IL
  Accreditation candidate with Council on Naturopathic Medical Education since
    March 2008
Southwest College of Naturopathic Medicine, Tempe, AZ
  Accredited by Council on Naturopathic Medical Education since 1999 and North
    Central Association of Colleges and Schools since 2004
University of Bridgeport College of Naturopathic Medicine, Bridgeport, CT
  Accredited by New England Association of Schools and Colleges since 1951

## Licensure

Naturopathic physicians who have graduated from a CNME-accredited school are eligible for licensure in 14 states (Box A-3). Additional states with active campaigns for licensure include Florida, Massachusetts, Missouri, North Carolina, New York, Colorado, Minnesota, Virginia, Pennsylvania and Illinois.

There is a large community of unlicensed naturopaths, many of whom trained through correspondence courses and believe that naturopathy should avoid the formality of structured curricula, state licensure, and standardization of education and testing.

The important point for medical doctors is that this group of practitioners has no formal clinical training, and they should be distinguished from licensed NDs who are graduates of accredited 4-year naturopathic medical schools. In general, states that have licensure allow only those who are licensed to call themselves naturopaths or naturopathic physicians and use the terms, "ND" (Doctor of Naturopathy) or "NMD" (Doctor of Naturopathic Medicine).

## Modalities Used

As noted above, the curriculum in naturopathic schools encompasses a variety of techniques and systems of practice, and includes such topics as nutrition, botanical medicine, classical Chinese medicine, homeopathy, spinal manipulation, etc. The scope of practice varies by state, with some states allowing minor surgery, intravenous administration, or prescription of medications such as antibiotics.

## Safety and Efficacy

Licensed naturopathic physicians have a good track record for safety. NCMIC Insurance Company, which insures NDs in all of the licensing states and also insures naturopathic medical schools, has "never opened a claim against a naturopathic physician involving prescription medications." In contrast, there are numerous jury verdicts, including cases of manslaughter, involving unlicensed practitioners of naturopathy.

As a system of practice, naturopathic medicine has not undergone rigorous testing, perhaps because of the evolution of the profession itself, or because of the variety of techniques used. Many of the individual techniques, such as therapeutic nutrition, spinal manipulation, homeopathy and use of botanical agents, have undergone more rigorous testing (in terms of

---

**Box A-3  States and Provinces in North America That License Naturopathic Physicians**

United States: Alaska, Arizona, California, Connecticut, Hawaii, Idaho, Kansas, Maine, Montana, New Hampshire, Oregon, Utah, Vermont, and Washington.

Canada: British Columbia, Manitoba, Ontario, Saskatchewan

safety and efficacy) in the past 15 years, and examples are found throughout this book.

## Acupuncture and Oriental Medicine

### Definition

For thousands of years acupuncture and oriental medicine (AOM) has acknowledged that there is a vital life force that flows through all things which is called "*qi*" (pronounced "chee"). In Western culture, it is often referred to as "energy." Energy (*qi*) flows along pathways in the human body that are related to the organs, the muscular system, and nervous system. When the balance of this energy is disturbed due to trauma, poor diet, medications, stress, hereditary conditions, environmental factors, or excessive emotional issues, then pain or illness results. Oriental medicine focuses on correcting these imbalances, which stimulates the body's natural ability to heal itself. In other words, oriental medicine focuses on treating the factors that cause disease (24). Acupuncture needling is one of several methods of treatment that may also include Chinese herbal medicine, moxibustion, cupping, acupressure, Qigong, Tai ji quan, Oriental therapeutic massage, nutritional counseling, or other modalities.

### Education

While AOM is 3000 years old, the first school in the United States was established in 1975. Currently, there are 64 accredited schools of AOM in the United States (Table A-1).

The entry-level standard for AOM is the master's degree. In most states, practitioners are designated "licensed acupuncturists"; however, they are called "acupuncture physicians" or "doctors of Oriental medicine" in a few other states. This can be confusing because these titles do not reflect an earned academic degree at the doctoral level. Instead, they reflect a licensure title designated by the state only (25).

There are currently two types of master's degrees accredited by the Accreditation Commission for Acupuncture and Oriental Medicine (ACAOM):

1. Master's in acupuncture, which is a 3-year program requiring a minimum of 1905 hours; and
2. Master's in Oriental medicine, which is a 4-year program requiring a minimum of 2625 hours and includes acupuncture and Chinese herbology.

While these are the minimum academic hours required, the vast majority of schools require a much higher number of hours to graduate. The national average is 2700 hours, with many schools requiring more than 3000 hours. Eighteen college programs offer a separate acupuncture-only program (25).

## Doctorate in Acupuncture and Oriental Medicine

The doctorate in acupuncture and oriental medicine (DAOM) is a new degree established in 2002 and is offered by 8 of the 64 colleges. A minimum of 4000 hours is required to earn this academic degree, which confers a master's degree in addition to the doctorate degree. A minimum of 1200 hours is required at the doctoral level (25).

## Professional Organizations, Certification and Licensure

The national professional association for AOM is the American Association of Acupuncture and Oriental Medicine (AAAOM) (26).

The National Certification Commission for Acupuncture and Oriental Medicine (NCCAOM) is the national certifying body for the AOM profession. NCCAOM has set voluntary certification standards and certified over 20,000 diplomates. NCCAOM offers national certification exams in acupuncture, Oriental medicine, Chinese herbology, and Asian bodywork therapy. The national accrediting body for programs of AOM in the US is the Accreditation Commission for Acupuncture and Oriental Medicine (ACAOM), which is the only organization recognized by the US Department of Education for this purpose. Currently, there are 64 AOM educational institutions or programs that have received accreditation candidacy or full accreditation status from ACAOM.

Forty-two of 50 states in the US, in addition to the District of Columbia, have adopted formal acupuncture practice acts that typically establish a licensing system for acupuncture practice and confer the licensing title "licensed acupuncturist" (LAc). You can see a complete listing of state licensing information on the NCCAOM website (27). Most states use NCCAOM examination modules as a qualification for licensure, excluding California, for example, which has its own state licensing exam. There are approximately 20,000-25,000 acupuncture licensees in the US, and about one-third of these practitioners reside in California (25). There are multiple credentialing titles for acupuncturists that reflect varying state regulatory, academic, or national certification titles, as listed in the following section.

## Types of Credentials for Acupuncturists

State regulatory titles:

- AP: Acupuncture Physician
- CA: Certified Acupuncturist
- DOM: Doctor of Oriental Medicine
- LAc: Licensed Acupuncturist
- RAc: Registered Acupuncturist

Academic titles:

- DAOM: Doctorate of Acupuncture and Oriental Medicine
- MA: Master of Acupuncture
- MOM: Master of Oriental Medicine

National certification titles (NCCAOM):

- Dipl Ac: Diplomate of Acupuncture
- Dipl CH: Diplomate of Chinese Herbology
- Dipl OM: Diplomate of Oriental Medicine

## Modalities Used

The diagnosis and treatment varies according to the training and skills of the individual practitioner, including the specific tradition used by the practitioner, such as the traditional Chinese medicine, Japanese, Korean, Vietnamese, and Five Element traditions. Recommended treatments might include herbal medicines, acupuncture, dietary recommendations, mind-body exercises, Tui Na (Chinese massage and manipulation), or other modalities. Some practitioners are trained in just one area, such as acupuncture.

## Safety

In general, acupuncture is considered safe when performed by skilled hands. One review that evaluated more than a million treatments estimated the risk of significant adverse events to be 0.05 per 10,000 treatments and 0.55 per 10,000 patients (28). Another review reported the most common minor adverse events were needle pain (1%-45%), tiredness (2%-41%), and minor bleeding (0.03%-38%). Feeling of faintness and syncope were relatively uncommon (0%-0.3%) and pneumothorax occurred twice in almost 250,000 treatments. Feelings of relaxation were quite common (86% of patients), and several reviews of safety issues have been performed (29-31). All persons who seek national certification from the NCCAOM are required to demonstrate competency in needle safety through formal certification in the clean needle technique course offered by the Council of Colleges of Acupuncture and Oriental Medicine.

SELECTED REFERENCES

2. www.Ayurvedacollege.com/services/index.htm.
3. **Lead Poisoning Associated with Ayurvedic Medications: Five States, 2000-2003.** 53(26);582 (07/09/2004). www.cdc.gov/mmwr/PDF/wk/mm5326.pdf. www.fammed.washington.edu/predoctoral/CAM/images/aom.pdf.
5. USPharm: www.uspharmacist.com.

* The complete reference list is to be found on the book's Web site.

6. www.homeopathy.org.
8. **Cardinali C, Francalanci S, Giomi B, et al.** Contact dermatitis from Rhus toxicodendronin a homeopathic remedy. J Am Acad Dermatol 2004;50:150-1.
10. **Schmidt K, Ernst E.** MMR vaccination advice over the Internet. Vaccine 2003;21:1044-7.
11. **Bronfort G, Haas M, Evans RL, Bouter LM.** Efficacy of spinal manipulation and mobilization for low back pain and neck pain: a systematic review and best evidence synthesis. Spine. 2004;4:335-56.
12. **Assendelft WJ, Bouter LM, Knipschild PG.** Complications of spinal manipulation: a comprehensive review of the literature. J Fam Pract. 1996;42:475-80.
16. www.amerchiro.org/media/whatis/history_chiro.shtml.
17. **Jeret JS, Bluth M.** Stroke following chiropractic manipulation. Report of 3 cases and review of the lierature. Cerebrovasc Dis. 2002;12:210-3.
18. **Smith WS, Johnston SC, Skalabrin EJ, et al.** Spinal manipulative therapy is an independent risk factor for vertebral artery dissection. Neurology. 2003;13;60:1424-8.
20. **Thiel HW, Bolton JE, Docherty S, Portlock JC.** Safety of chiropractic manipulation of the cervical spine: a prospective national survey. Spine. 2007;32:2375-8.
21. **Haldeman S, Carroll L, Cassidy JD, et al.** Bone and Joint Decade 2000-2010 Task Force on Neck Pain and Its Associated Disorders. The Bone and Joint Decade 2000-2010 Task Force on Neck Pain and Its Associated Disorders: executive summary. Spine. 2008;33(4 Suppl): S5-7.
22. **Sheth TN, Winslow JL, Mikulis DJ.** Rotational changes in the morphology of the vertebral artery at a common site of artery dissection. Can Assoc Radiol J. 2001;52:236-41.
23. www.naturopathic.org/viewbulletin.php?id=29.
24. American Association of Acupuncture and Oriental Medicine website: www .aaaomonline.org/default.asp?pagenumber=40#om.
25. **Lixing Huang.** Acupuncture and Oriental Medicine in the United States. Second International Congress of Chinese Medicine. Paris, France. Sept 30-Oct 2, 2005. www .ccaom.org/downloads/PaperOfLixinHuang.pdf
26. www.aaaomonline.org.
27. www.nccaom.org/applicants/state_data/State_sheet.htm.
28. **White A.** A cumulative review of the range and incidence of significant adverse events associated with acupuncture. Acupunct Med. 2004;22:122-33.
29. **Yamashita H, Tsukayama H, White AR, et al.** Systematic review of adverse events following acupuncture: the Japanese literature. Complement Ther Med. 2001;9:98-104.
30. **Ernst E, White AR.** Prospective studies of the safety of acupuncture: a systematic review. Am J Med. 2001;110:481-5.
31. **Ernst E, White AR.** Life-threatening adverse reactions after acupuncture? A systematic review. Pain 1997;71:123-6.

# Appendix 2: Complementary and Alternative Medicine Terms*

*Acupuncture*—Acupuncture is based on the theory that health is determined by a balanced flow of energy (*chi* or *qi*), which is thought to be present in all living organisms. This life energy circulates throughout the body along a series of energy pathways (meridians). Each of these meridians is linked to specific internal organs and organ systems. Within this system of energy pathways, there are over 1000 acupoints that can be stimulated through the insertion of needles. This is thought to help correct and rebalance the flow of life energy and restore health. Acupuncture has been used to treat health problems and conditions ranging from the common cold to addiction and chronic fatigue syndrome.

*Alternative provider or practitioner*—Someone who is knowledgeable about a specific alternative health therapy provides care or gives advice about its use and usually receives payment for his or her services. For some therapies, the provider may have received formal training and may be certified by a licensing board or related professional association. For example, a practitioner of biofeedback (biofeedback therapist) has usually received training in psychology and physiology and may be certified by the Biofeedback Certification Institute of America.

*Atkins diet*—A diet emphasizing a drastic reduction in the daily intake of carbohydrates (to 40 grams or less), it is countered by an increase in protein and fat. According to proponents of this diet, obesity results from the over-consumption of carbohydrates, and reducing the intake of carbohydrates typically consumed for energy causes the body to lose weight by burning stored fat.

---

* Modified from Barnes P, Powell-Griner E, McFann K, Nahin R. CDC Advance Data Report #343. *Complementary and Alternative Medicine Use Among Adults: United States, 2002.* May 27, 2004 (page 17 technical notes: Complementary and Alternative Medicine terms).

*Ayurveda*—This comprehensive system of medicine, developed in India over 5000 years ago, places equal emphasis on body, mind, and spirit. The goal is to restore the natural harmony of the individual. An Ayurvedic doctor identifies an individual's "constitution" or overall health profile by ascertaining the patient's metabolic body type (Vata, Pitta, or Kapha) through a series of personal history questions. Then the patient's constitution becomes the foundation for a specific treatment plan designed to guide the individual back into harmony with his or her environment. This plan may include dietary changes, exercise, yoga, meditation, massage, herbal tonics, and other remedies.

*Biofeedback*—This method teaches clients, through the use of simple electronic devices, how to consciously regulate normally unconscious bodily functions (e.g., breathing, heart rate, blood pressure) to improve overall health. Biofeedback has been used to reduce stress, eliminate headaches, recondition injured muscles, control asthmatic attacks, and relieve pain.

*Chelation therapy*—This therapy involves a series of intravenous injections of a binding (chelating) agent, such as the amino acid EDTA, to remove toxic metals and wastes from the bloodstream. Following injection, the binding agent travels through the bloodstream attaching itself to toxic metals and wastes, which are subsequently excreted through the patient's urine. Used initially to treat lead poisoning, chelation therapy is used by a growing number of practitioners to treat and reverse the process of arteriosclerosis (hardening of the arteries).

*Chiropractic care*—This care involves the adjustment of the spine and joints to influence the body's nervous system and natural defense mechanisms to alleviate pain and improve general health. It is primarily used to treat back problems, headaches, nerve inflammation, muscle spasms, and other injuries and traumas.

*Complementary and alternative medicine*—Therapies not usually taught in US medical schools or generally available in US hospitals, it includes a broad range of therapies and beliefs such as acupuncture, chiropractic care, relaxation techniques, massage therapy, and herbal remedies.

*Deep breathing*—Deep breathing involves slow, deep inhalation through the nose, usually for a count of 10, followed by slow and complete exhalation for a similar count. To help quiet the mind, one generally concentrates fully on breathing and counting through each cycle. The process may be repeated 5 to 10 times, several times a day.

*Energy healing therapy/Reiki*—This method helps the body's ability to heal itself through the flow and focusing of healing energy (Reiki means universal healing energy). During treatment, this healing energy is channeled through the hands of a practitioner into the client's body to restore a normal energy balance and health. Energy healing therapy has been used to treat a wide variety of ailments and health problems and is often used in conjunction with other alternative and conventional medical treatments.

*Folk medicine*—These systems of healing (such as Curanderismo and Native American healing) have persisted since the beginning of culture and flourished long before the development of conventional medicine. Folk healers usually participate in a training regimen of observation and imitation, with healing often considered a gift passed down through several generations of a family. Folk healers may employ a range of remedies including prayer, healing touch or laying on of hands, charms, herbal teas or tinctures, magic rituals, and others. Folk healers are found in all cultures and operate under a variety of names and labels.

*Guided imagery* —This method involves a series of relaxation techniques followed by the visualization of detailed images, usually calm and peaceful in nature. If used for treatment, the client may visualize his/her body as healthy, strong, and free of the specific problem or condition. Sessions, conducted in groups or one-on-one, are typically 20-30 minutes and may be practiced several times a week. Guided imagery has been advocated for a number of chronic conditions, including headaches, stress, high blood pressure, and anxiety.

*Healing circles*—These spiritual gatherings usually occur in informal settings, may involve invocations (calling upon a higher power or authority), and may use other healing approaches such as prayer, energy healing therapy/Reiki, and natural herbs.

*High-dose or megavitamin therapy*—This therapy refers to the use of vitamins in excess of the Recommended Daily Allowances (RDA) established by the National Academy of Sciences, Food and Nutrition Board. Although these therapies have been used for the prevention and treatment of diseases and illnesses such as cancer, heart disease, schizophrenia, and the common cold, some high-dose or megavitamin regimens can produce adverse or toxic effects.

*Homeopathic treatment*—This system of medical practice is based on the theory that any substance that can produce symptoms of disease or illness in a healthy person can cure those symptoms in a sick person. For example, someone suffering from insomnia may be given a homeopathic dose of coffee. Administered in diluted form, homeopathic remedies are derived from many natural sources, including plants, metals, and minerals. Numbering in the thousands, these remedies have been used to treat a wide variety of ailments including seasonal allergies, asthma, influenza, headaches, and indigestion.

*Hypnosis*—An altered state of consciousness that is characterized by increased responsiveness to suggestion. The hypnotic state is attained by first relaxing the body, then shifting the client's attention toward a narrow range of objects or ideas as suggested by the hypnotist or hypnotherapist. The procedure is used to access various levels of the mind to effect positive changes in a person's behavior and to treat numerous health conditions. For example, hypnosis has been used to lose weight, improve sleep, and reduce pain and stress.

*Laying on of hands*—This religious ceremony involves the placement of hands, by one or more persons (lay or clergy), on the body of the recipient. Usually including prayer, the ceremony may occur in a church or less formal setting and may be used for minor as well as more serious ailments and illnesses.

*Macrobiotic diet*—This low fat diet emphasizes whole grains and vegetables and restricts the intake of fluids. Consumption of fresh, unprocessed foods is especially important. Daily intakes break out as follows: 50%-60% whole grains; 25%-30% fresh vegetables; 5%-10% beans, soy-based products, and sea vegetables; and 5%-10% soups. Meat, poultry, dairy products, eggs, alcohol, coffee, caffeinated tea, sweets and sugar, and strong spices are to be avoided.

*Massage*—This therapy involves pressing, rubbing, and otherwise manipulating muscles and other soft tissues of the body, causing them to relax and lengthen and allowing pain-relieving oxygen and blood to flow to the affected area. Using their hands and sometimes feet, elbows, and forearms, massage therapists may use over 75 different methods, such as Swedish massage, deep-tissue massage, neuromuscular massage, and manual lymph drainage. Massage is considered effective for relieving any type of pain in the body's soft tissue, including back, neck, and shoulder pain, headaches, bursitis, and tendonitis.

*Meditation*—Mental calmness and physical relaxation is achieved by suspending the stream of thoughts that normally occupy the mind. Generally performed once or twice a day for approximately 20 minutes at a time, meditation is used to reduce stress, alter hormone levels, and elevate one's mood. In addition, a person experienced in meditation can achieve a reduction in blood pressure, adrenaline levels, heart rate, and skin temperature.

*Natural products*—See Nonvitamin, nonmineral, natural products.

*Naturopathy*—This broad system of medicine is based on the theory that the body is a self-regulating mechanism with the natural ability to maintain a state of health and wellness. Naturopathic doctors, who generally reject invasive techniques and the use of synthetic drugs, try to cure illness and disease by harnessing the body's natural healing powers. This is done with the use of various alternative and traditional techniques, including herbal medicine, homeopathic treatment, massage, dietary supplements, and other physical therapies.

*Nonvitamin, nonmineral, natural products*—These products are taken by mouth and contain a dietary ingredient other than vitamins and minerals that is intended to supplement the diet. They include herbs or herbal medicine (as single herbs or mixtures), other botanical products such as soy or flax products, and dietary substances such as enzymes and glandulars. Among the most popular are echinacea, ginkgo biloba, ginseng, feverfew, garlic, kava kava, and saw palmetto. Garlic, for example, has been used to treat fevers, sore throats, digestive ailments, hardening of the arteries, and other health problems and conditions. The text in this report uses a shorter version of the CAM therapy term "nonvitamin, nonmineral, natural products" for conciseness, but the tables use the complete term. The therapy "nonvitamin, nonmineral, natural products" is referred to as "natural products" in the text.

*Ornish diet*—This is a high-fiber, low-fat vegetarian diet that promotes weight loss and health by controlling what one eats, not by restricting the intake of calories. Fruits, beans, grains, and vegetables can be eaten at all meals, and nonfat dairy products such as skim milk, nonfat cheeses, and egg whites are consumed in moderation. Products such as oils, avocados, nuts and seeds, and meats of all kinds are avoided.

*Pritikin diet*—This diet (or Pritikin Principle) is a low-fat diet (10% fat or less) that emphasizes the consumption of foods with a large volume of fiber and water (low in caloric density), including many vegetables, fruits, beans, and natural, unprocessed grains. According to this diet, weight loss will occur if the average caloric density of a meal is kept below 400 calories per pound.

*Progressive relaxation*—This therapy involves the successive tensing and relaxing of each of the 15 major muscle groups. Performed lying down, one generally begins with the head and progresses downward, tensing each muscle as tightly as possible for a count of 5 to 10 and then releasing it completely. Often combined with deep breathing, progressive relaxation is particularly useful for reducing stress, relieving tension, and inducing sleep.

*Qi gong*—This ancient Chinese discipline combines the use of gentle physical movements, mental focus, and deep breathing designed to integrate the mind, body, and spirit, and to stimulate the flow of vital life energy (*qi*). Directed toward specific parts of the body, qi gong exercises are normally performed two or more times a week for 30 minutes at a time and have been used to treat a variety of ailments including asthma, arthritis, stress, lower back pain, allergies, diabetes, headaches, heart disease, hypertension, and chronic pain.

*Reiki*—See Energy healing therapy/Reiki.

*Tai chi*—This Chinese self-defense discipline and low-intensity, low-impact exercise regimen is used for health, relaxation, and self-exploration. Usually performed daily, tai chi exercises include a set of forms, with each form comprising a series of body positions connected into one continuous movement. A single form may include up to 100 positions and may take as long as 20 minutes to complete. Some of the proposed benefits of tai chi include improved concentration, circulation, and posture, reduction of stress, and prevention of osteoporosis.

*Vegetarian diets*—These diets are devoid of meat. There are, however, numerous variations on the nonmeat theme. For example, some vegetarian diets are restricted to plant products only, and others may include eggs and dairy products. Another variation limits food consumption to raw fruit, sometimes supplemented with nuts and vegetables. Some vegetarian diets prohibit alcohol, sugar, caffeine, and processed foods.

*Yoga*—This combination of breathing exercises, physical postures, and meditation, practiced for over 5000 years, calms the nervous system and balances body, mind, and spirit. It is thought to prevent specific diseases and maladies by keeping the energy meridians (see acupuncture) open and life energy (qi) flowing. Usually performed in classes, sessions are conducted at least once a week and for approximately 45 minutes. Yoga has been used to lower blood pressure, reduce stress, and improve coordination, flexibility, concentration, sleep, and digestion. It has also been used as supplementary therapy for such diverse conditions as cancer, diabetes, asthma, and AIDS.

*Zone diet*—Each meal in this diet consists of a small amount of low-fat protein (30%), fats (30%), and carbohydrates in the form of fiber-rich fruits and vegetables (40%). The basic goal is to alter the body's metabolism by controlling the production of key hormones. According to proponents, this will aid in weight loss, help prevent heart disease, high blood pressure, diabetes, and enhance athletic performance.

# Index

*Acanthopanacis senticosi*, 138
Accreditation Commission for Acupuncture and Oriental Medicine (ACAOM), 417, 418
Acetaminophen, 391
Acetyl cysteine, 215t, 220t, 399t
Acid-base balance, effect on bone health, 263-264
Acquired immunodeficiency syndrome (AIDS), 213. *See also* Human immunodeficiency virus (HIV) infection
Acupressure, 417
  as allergic rhinitis treatment, 51-52
  as asthma treatment, 65, 72t
  as motion sickness treatment, 141, 155
Acupuncture, 417-419
  action mechanism of, 361
  adverse effects of, 361-362
  for alcohol abuse control, 144, 157t
  as allergic rhinitis treatment, 48, 51-52, 56t
  as anxiety treatment, 103-104, 123
  as asthma treatment, 60, 61, 65-66, 72t, 73-74, 75

  as atopic dermatitis treatment, 53
  in cancer patients, 83, 84, 85, 89, 92, 96t, 97t, 98t
  contraindications to, 84
  as cardiovascular disease preventive, 163t
  Chinese forms of, 19
  clinical trials in, 15
  as Crohn's disease treatment, 136, 152t
  definition of, 360, 421
  as depression treatment, 355, 360-362, 380t
  as diabetic neuropathy treatment, 127t
  as dysmenorrhea treatment, 255, 279t
  as dyspepsia treatment, 136, 152t
  electro, 19, 307-308, 380t
  as fibromyalgia treatment, 307-308, 321
  as gastrointestinal pain treatment, 143, 156t
  as headache treatment, 119
  health insurance coverage of, 39, 40
  as hot flashes treatment, 275
  as human immunodeficiency virus (HIV) infection treatment, 202, 210-211, 220t

  as infertility treatment, 260-261, 281t
  as irritable bowel syndrome treatment, 138-139, 153t
  Japanese forms of, 19
  laser, 301, 320, 380t
  as menopausal symptoms treatment, 242, 245
  as migraine headache preventive, 119, 120, 128
  as musculoskeletal disorders treatment
    for acute low back pain, 310t
    for carpal tunnel syndrome, 306, 320t
    for chronic low back pain, 293-294, 298, 311t, 315t
    for lateral epicondyle pain, 304-305, 319t
    for neck pain, 298, 315
    for osteoarthritis of the knee, 17, 300-301, 304, 317t
  for nausea and vomiting control, 140-141, 154t, 155t
  needle size in, 19
  neurophysiologic and biochemical effects of, 103
  for osteoporosis preventive or treatment, 268, 285

as perioperative pain
treatment, 144, 157
as premenopausal
syndrome (PMS)
treatment, 250
safety and efficacy of, 419
as urinary incontinence
treatment, 286
Acupuncture and oriental
medicine (AOM), 417-
419
Acupuncturists, 417-419
Acyclovir, 114
Adjustment disorders, 355
Adrenocorticotropic
hormone, 359
Adulterants, in dietary
supplements, 26
Aerobic exercise therapy,
for depression, 366-367,
381t
*Agastache seu pogostemi*,
137
Agency for Healthcare
Research and Quality
(AHRQ), 111, 113, 370
Aging
healthy, 3
premature, 232
ALA. *See* Alpha-linolenic
acid
Alcohol abuse
acupuncture-related
control of, 144, 157t
as liver disease cause, 144,
145, 146, 158t
Alcohol use
cardioprotective effects of,
184-185
as migraine headache
trigger, 116
Aldosterone, 359
Alexander Technique, 295-
296, 298, 312t
Allergic disorders, 43-58
CAM diagnostic tests for,
43, 44-48
cytotoxicity assays or
cell-volume change
assays, 45-46
electrodermal testing,
47-48

muscle-response testing,
47
provocation/neutralizati
on test, 46
pulse test, 46
specific immunoglobulin
G assays, 44-45
unproven or disproved
tests, 45, 46, 47-48
CAM therapies for, 48-57
for allergic rhinitis, 48-
52
for atopic dermatitis, 52-
53
Evidence Summary of,
56-57t
for food allergies or
intolerance, 53-54
as contraindication to
*Echinacea* use, 108
conventional diagnostic
tests for, 44
definition of, 43
Allicin, 173
Allopathy/allopathic
medicine, 7-8, 408
Aloe, 203
Aloe saponins, 330t
Aloe vera, 112, 401t
Aloe vera gel, 143
Alpha-linolenic acid, 171-
172
dietary sources of, 177,
373
as Mediterranean diet
component, 183
Alpha-Tocopherol, Beta-
Carotene (ATBC) study,
176
Alternative medicine,
definition of, 6
Alternative Medicine Care
Outcomes in AIDS
(AMOCA) study, 202,
213
Amalaki, 136
American Association of
Acupuncture and Oriental
Medicine, 418
American Association of
Naturopathic Physicians,
414

American Cancer Society
Guidelines for Using
Complementary and
Alternative Medicine,
83
website, 93, 94
American Chiropractic
Association, 412, 414
American College of Chest
Physicians, 87
American College of
Physicians
Clinical Efficacy
Assessment
Subcommittee, 298
position on physicians'
sale of CAM products,
41
American College of
Rheumatology, 307
American Heart
Association Guidelines for
Primary Prevention of
Cardiovascular Disease
and Stroke: 2002, 179
Nutrition Committee, 175
recommendations for fish
oil supplement use, 170-
171, 206
American Medical
Association
ICD-9 codes of, 38-39
position on physicians'
sale of CAM products,
40-41
American Medical Students
Association, 4
American Pain Society,
Low Back Pain Guidelines
Panel, 298
Amiloride, 400
Amino acids, as
cardiovascular disease
preventive, 177-179
Amitriptyline, 103, 120,
211
Anabolic steroids, 224-225
Anaphylaxis, food allergy-
related, 53-54
Androgen deficiency, 234t
Androgens, 224
Andropause, 224
Androstenediol, 225, 234t

Androstenedione, 225, 234t
Androstenetrione, 234t
Androstrione, 224, 225
Angiotensin-converting
    enzyme inhibitors
    (ACEIs), interaction with
    dietary supplements, 393
*Annals of Internal
    Medicine*, 41
Anorexia, as weight loss
    cause, 208-210
Antiarrhythmic drugs,
    interaction with dietary
    supplements, 392-393
Antibiotic resistance, 106
Antibiotics
    as common cold
        treatment, 106
    interaction with dietary
        supplements, 243, 394-
        395
    as urinary tract infection
        risk factor, 120
    as urinary tract infection
        treatment, 121
Anticoagulants. *See also*
    Warfarin
    interactions with dietary
        supplements, 247, 266,
        375
Antidepressant drugs
    clinical trials of, 354
    comparison with
        S-adenosylmeth-ionine
        (SAMe), 370-371
    St. John's wort, 368-369
    interaction with omega-3
        fatty acids, 389
    lack of efficacy of, 354
Antidiabetic agents,
    interaction with dietary
    supplements, 400-401,
    401t
Antihypertensive drugs,
    interaction with dietary
    supplements, 243, 393
Anti-inflammatory agents,
    herbal, 61, 62t
Antilipemic therapy, 165.
    *See also* 3-Hydroxy-3-
    methylglutaryl coenzyme
    A inhibitors (statins)
    cinnamon, 109, 110

in human
    immunodeficiency virus
    (HIV) infection, 205-
    207
    interaction with dietary
        supplements, 397-398
Antineoplastic agents
    interaction with dietary
        supplements, 81, 398-
        399, 399t, 402
    from plant sources, 80
    side effects of, 83-84, 399,
        399t
"Antioxidant cocktail," 165,
    397-398
Antioxidants
    as cardiovascular disease
        preventive, 163t, 164-
        167
    co-administration with
        cancer chemotherapy,
        399
    as gastric cancer
        preventive, 147, 158
    as infertility treatment,
        257
    interaction with cancer
        treatments, 81
Antipsychotic drugs,
    interaction with chaste
    tree berry, 246
Antiretroviral activity, of
    dietary supplements, 203-
    205
Antiretroviral therapy
    adverse effects of, 205-
        207, 216-218t
    in combination with
        CAM therapies, 201-
        202, 203, 205
    interaction with St. John's
        wort, 369
Antithrombotic drugs,
    interaction with dietary
    supplements, 395-397,
    396t, 397t
Anti-tussive agents, herbal,
    61, 62t
Anxiety
    CAM therapies for, 101-
        106, 123-214t
    acupuncture, 103-104
    aromatherapy, 104

behavioral therapy, 258-
    259
    for cancer patients, 86-
        88, 90, 98
    dietary supplements,
        101-103, 247, 248
    in infertility, 258, 259
    meditation, 105
    in premenstrual
        syndrome, 247, 248
    prevalence of use of, 353
    relaxation therapies,
        105-106
    economic costs of, 101
    as motivation for CAM
        utilization, 241
    preoperative, 103, 104,
        144, 157
    prevalence of, 101
Apple pectin-chamomile
    extract, 139, 153
Arachidonic acid, as
    dysmenorrhea cause, 251,
    252
Arginine, 115
L-Arginine
    as cardiovascular disease
        preventive, 163t, 177-
        178, 196
    as erectile dysfunction
        treatment, 227, 228,
        235t
    as fertility blend
        component, 258
    interaction with
        nitroglycerine, 403
    as weight loss supplement,
        328
Aromatherapy
    for anxiety, 104, 123, 124
    for cancer patients, 90-91,
        98t
    definition of, 104
*Artemesiae capillaris*, 137
Artichoke leaf extract
    (ALE), 136, 151t
5-ASA
    derivatives/inhibitors,
        interaction with omega-3
        fatty acids, 389t, 390
Asparagus, as weight loss
    supplement, 335t, 345
Aspartame, 116, 269-270

Aspirin
  antiplatelet effects of, 395
  gastrointestinal effects of,
    388, 388t
  as herbal remedy
    adulterant, 63
  interaction with dietary
    supplements, 171, 388,
    395
Asthma, 59-76
  CAM therapies for, 59-75
    acupuncture, 60, 61, 65-
      66, 72t, 73-74, 75
    case studies, 71-74
    chiropractic
      manipulation, 66-67,
      69t, 72t, 75
    Evidence Summary of,
      75t
    herbal remedies, 60-64,
      61t, 71t, 75
    homeopathy, 61, 64-65,
      72t, 75
    information resources
      regarding, 71
    manual therapies, 68-69t
    mind-body therapies,
      67-70, 72t, 75
    prevalence of use of, 59-
      60
    safety and efficacy
      evaluation of, 72t, 75t
  conventional treatment
    for, 59
  definition of, 59
  preventive approach to,
    59
Astragulus (Astralagus), 146
  as weight reduction
    supplement, 336t, 337t,
    347
Atkins diet, 163t, 421
Atorvastatin, 398
Autogenic training, 97t,
  363, 364-365, 380t
Avocado soybean
  unsaponifiables (ASU),
  303, 304, 317
Avogadro's number, 17, 408
Ayurvedic medicine, 5, 135,
  137, 146, 158, 405-407
  as cardiovascular disease
    preventive, 163t

clinical trials of, 14-15,
  16, 18
  definition of, 405-406,
    422
  detoxification concept of,
    7
  as diabetes mellitus type 2
    treatment, 113-114,
    127t
  as food allergy and
    intolerance treatment,
    54
  as gastrointestinal
    disorders treatment, 135,
    137, 146, 158t
  influence on western
    medical practices, 408
  licensure in, 406-407
  safety and efficacy of, 407
  for weight loss, 328, 341,
    348, 349t
Ayurvedic practitioners,
  406-407

Bach Flower remedy, for
  anxiety, 102-103, 123
Back pain, 289
  acute low back pain, 289-
    292, 310-311t
  chronic low back pain,
    293-298, 311-315t
Baile Ercha, 138
Baldness, male pattern, 231
Balsalazide, 390
Banana powder, 136
Banting, William, 185
Ban Zhi Lian (Scutallaria
  barbata), 256, 280t
Basophil degranulation, 17
Bean peel, as weight loss
  supplement, 345
Bean pods, as weight loss
  supplement, 335t
Beans, as weight loss
  supplements, 330t, 331t,
  335t, 342, 345, 348, 349t
Beck Depression Inventory,
  356-357, 361
Bee pollen, as allergic
  rhinitis treatment, 51
Behavioral therapies/training
  for cancer patients, 96t

as infertility treatment,
  258-259, 281t
  as migraine headache
    prevention, 120, 129
  as urinary incontinence
    treatment, 270-271,
    285t
Belladonna 30C, 17
Benign prostatic
  hypertrophy (BPH), 229-
  230, 236-237, 269
Benson, Herbert, 105-106
Berberine, 134
Beta-blockers, 393
Beta-carotene
  as cardiovascular disease
    preventive, 163t, 165,
    166, 193t
  as gastrointestinal cancer
    preventive, 147, 158t
  interaction with
    antilipemic drugs, 397
  as uterine fibroid
    (leiomyoma) treatment,
    256, 279
Beta-glucan, as weight loss
  supplement, 330t
Betaine, as weight loss
  supplement, 330t
Bias, in clinical trials, 14
Bifidobacterium spp., 136
Bimminne (bimin), 49
Biofeedback
  as asthma treatment, 67,
    70, 72t
  definition of, 422
  as fibromyalgia treatment,
    309, 322t
  as menopausal symptoms
    treatment, 244
  as migraine headache
    preventive, 120, 129
  as urinary incontinence
    treatment, 271, 285t
Biologically-based therapies,
  5. See also Dietary
  supplements; Herbal
  medicine; specific
  vitamins and minerals
  cancer patients' use of, 79-
    80
  definition of, 6

for human immunodeficiency virus (HIV) infection, 203-210, 215-217t

for musculoskeletal disorders

carpal tunnel syndrome, 321

chronic low back pain, 312, 314

fibromyalgia, 322, 323

lateral epicondyle pain, 320

neck pain, 316

osteoarthritis of the knee, 317, 318-319

Bioresonance, as allergic rhinitis treatment, 48

Bitter melon *(Momordica charantia)*, hypoglycemic effect of, 401, 401t

Bitter orange *(Citrus aurantium)*, as weight loss supplement, 329t, 339t, 341, 348, 349t

Black cohosh *(Cimiciguga racemosa)*, 149, 243, 247, 275

Black haw *(Viburnum prunifolium)*, 252

Blood injection, autologous, as allergic rhinitis treatment, 48

BN 52021, 61

Body awareness therapy, 295-296, 298, 312t

Body-based therapies, 5

definition of, 6

as dysmenorrhea or endometriosis treatment, 254, 278

for human immunodeficiency virus (HIV)-infected patients, 213-214

for infertility, 259-260

for menopausal symptoms, 244-245

for musculoskeletal disorders

acute low back pain, 310-311

carpal tunnel syndrome, 320-321

chronic low back pain, 312, 313

fibromyalgia, 322, 323

lateral epicondyle pain, 320

neck pain, 316-317

osteoarthritis of the knee, 319

as uterine fibroid (leiomyoma) treatment, 256

Body movement therapies

for cardiovascular disease prevention, 190-192

as neck pain treatment, 299

Bofu-tshusho-san, 331t

Boldo, 397t

Bone and Joint Decade 2000-2010 Task Force on Neck Pain and Its Associated Disorders, 414

Bone mineral density (BMD)

effect of acupuncture on, 268

osteoporosis-related decrease in, 261-262, 263, 264, 267

Borage oil, 53, 57t, 395

*Boswellia*

anti-inflammatory effects of, 255, 279

as asthma treatment, 62t, 63, 64, 72t

as uterine fibroid (leiomyoma) treatment, 255, 279

Bovine colostrum, 388t

Bovine colostrum enemas, 143

Brain derived neurotrophic factor, 374

Breast cancer

CAM therapies for

acupuncture, 84

adverse effects of, 81

mind-body techniques, 83, 90

prevalence of use of, 78

as primary treatment, 81

dehydroepiandrosterone (DHEA) as risk factor for, 233

Breathing techniques

as asthma treatment, 67, 70, 72t, 75

as chronic low back pain treatment, 295-296, 312t

as hot flashes treatment, 275

as menopausal symptoms treatment, 244

in yoga, 356

Bromelain, 51, 328

Bronchodilators, herbal, 61, 62t

Buchu, diuretic effects of, 400

Bupleurum, 402

*Bupleurum chinese*, 137

Burdock, diuretic effects of, 400

Butcher's broom, diuretic effects of, 400

Butterbur *(Petasites hybridus)*, 116-117, 127

as allergic rhinitis treatment, 50-51, 56t

as asthma treatment, 64, 72t

Buzhong Yiqi Tang, 138

Cachexia, human immunodeficiency virus (HIV) infection-related, 208-210, 220t

Caffeine

as bladder irritant, 269-270

as migraine headache trigger, 116

premenstrual syndrome-exacerbating effect of, 248

as weight loss supplement, 331t, 332t, 333t, 339t, 343

Calanolide A, 203, 215t

Calcium

as cardiovascular disease preventive, 162

interaction with glucocorticoids, 390

as osteoporosis preventive or treatment, 264-265, 282t

as premenstrual syndrome treatment, 249

side effects of, 265

use with glucocorticoid therapy, 390

Calcium channel blockers, 393

Calcium chelation therapy, 187

Calcium phosphate, as weight loss supplement, 334t

California College of Ayurvedic (CCA), 407

Calorie restriction, for longevity enhancement, 232, 238t

CAM. *See* Comp-lementary and alternative medicine

Cambridge Heart Antioxidant Study, 165

Camptothecin, 80

Cancer, CAM therapies for, 77-100. *See also specific types of cancer*
as adjunctive therapy, 77-78
case study of, 92-95
effectiveness and safety of, 82
Evidence Summary of, 96-99t
health insurance coverage of, 40
for improving the quality of life, 82-91, 98
for fatigue, 84, 97
for hot flashes, 84, 96
for insomnia treatment, 88-89, 98
for nausea and vomiting control, 83-84, 96
for stress reduction, 86-88, 97
for pediatric patients, 78, 79, 88
physician-patient communication about, 93

prevalence of use of, 77-79

Cancer pain, 85, 88, 89, 96, 97

Candy tuft, 135

Cannabis, 297. *See also* Marijuana

Capsaicin, 135

Captopril, 393

Caraway oil, 134-135, 137, 152

Cardiovascular disease, CAM therapies for
biologically-based, 162-179, 193-196
case study of, 162-164
chelation therapy, 187-188, 197
Evidence Summary of, 193-198t
mind-body therapies, 162, 163t, 189-192, 190t, 197-198
movement therapies, 190-192
prevalence of use of, 161
special diets, 179-187, 180-181t, 188, 197

L-Carnitine
acetyl, 210
as cardiovascular disease preventive, 163t, 178-179, 196t
as human immunodeficiency (HIV) infection treatment, 210, 215, 215t
as weight loss supplement, 334t

Carnitine, as erectile dysfunction treatment, 227-228, 235t

Carob bean juice, 139, 153

Carpal tunnel syndrome, 305-307, 320-321t

Carrot, wild, diuretic effects of, 400

Cascara, hepatotoxicity of, 149

*Cascara segrada*, 400

Cassia powder, 109-110

Cat allergens, 47

Catechins, 335t

Cauda equina syndrome, 411

Cayenne, gastroprotective effects of, 388t

CEDIM trial, 178-179

Celandine, greater, 136, 148

Celery seed, 400

Cell-volume change assays, for food allergies, 45-46

Center for Epidemiological Studies Depression Scale (CES-D), 360, 362, 363

Centers for Disease Control and Prevention (CDC), 24
National Center for Health Statistics, 11

*Ceratonia siliqua*, as weight loss supplement, 330t

Cetyl myristoleate, 304

CH-100, 146

Chaicang Yuxiang Tang, 138

Chaihu Shugan Yin, 138

Chamomile, German, 137

Chamomile extract-apple pectin, 139, 153t

Chaparral, hepatotoxicity of, 148

Chaso, hepatotoxicity of, 148

Chaste tree berry *(Vitex agnus-castus)*
as infertility treatment, 257-258, 280
as premenstrual syndrome treatment, 246, 276t
as uterine fibroid (leiomyoma) treatment, 255, 279t

Chelation therapy
for cardiovascular disease, 163t, 187-188, 197t, 422
definition of, 422

Chemotherapy. *See* Antineoplastic agents

Chi (qi), 16-17, 360, 417, 425

Chicago Western Electric Company, 172

Children, CAM therapies for during cancer treatment, 88
for diarrhea prevention and treatment, 139, 140, 149, 153, 154, 395
prevalence of use of, 78, 79
Chili peppers, 135, 151t
Chinese herbal medicine. *See also specific herbs*
adverse effects of, 52
as allergic rhinitis treatment, 49-50, 56t
as atopic dermatitis treatment, 52-53, 56
as diabetes mellitus type 2 treatment, 112, 126
as dysmenorrhea or endometriosis treatment, 254, 278t
as hepatitis treatment, 157t
as human immunodeficiency virus (HIV) infection treatment, 203
hypoglycemic effect of, 112
as irritable bowel syndrome treatment, 137, 138, 152
as liver disease treatment, 144, 145, 146, 157
as menopausal symptoms treatment, 245, 276t
as premenopausal syndrome (PMS) treatment, 250
as uterine fibroid (leiomyoma) treatment, 256-257, 280
Chiropractic care, 5. *See also* Spinal manipulation
adverse effects of, 67
for asthma, 66-67, 69t, 72t, 75
clinical trials of, 16
contraindications to, 67
definition of, 422
for dysmenorrhea or endometriosis, 254, 278

health insurance coverage of, 39, 40
for menopausal symptoms, 242
for migraine headache prevention, 120, 129
for musculoskeletal disorders
acute low back pain, 310-311
chronic low back pain, 295, 298, 314
fibromyalgia, 308, 323
neck pain, 299, 316-317
safety of, 413-414
schools of, 412, 413b
Chiropractors (doctors of chiropractic), 13, 412, 413
Chitosan, as weight loss supplement, 330t, 334t, 341-343, 348, 349t
Chlorella, 397t
Chocolate, 116, 269-270
Cholestin, 206, 207, 216-217t
Choline, 215t
Chromium, 111-112, 126, 401t
Chromium picolinate
effect on high-density lipoprotein levels, 393
as hyperglycemia treatment, 390
as weight loss supplement, 330t, 334t, 339t, 342, 348, 349t
Chromium polynicotinate, 333t
Chronic diseases, health care expenditures on, 11
Chronic fatigue syndrome, 54
Chronic low back pain, 293-298, 311-315t
Chrysanthemum allergy, 108
Cinnamon, 109-110, 125
Cirrhosis, alcoholic, 145
Cisapride, 134-135, 138
Cisplatin, 398-399, 399t
Citrus fruits, as bladder irritants, 269-270
Cleansing, 7

*Clematius mandshurica*, 304
Cleveland Clinic Foundation, 88
Cleveland Music School, 88
Clinical Ayurvedic Specialist (CAS), 407
Clinical encounters, CAM therapy-related issues in, 23-42
coordination of therapies, 25-27
office practice basics, 28-37
CAM questionnaire, 28-31b
information resources, 32-33b, 34-37b
physician-patient relationship, 25
physician's knowledge of CAM therapies, 23-24, 23-28
Clinical Global Impression Scale, 103
Clinical trials, of CAM therapies, 13-20
*Coccinia indica*, 113, 127t, 400
hypoglycemic effect of, 401t
Cochrane Collaboration, 4
Cochrane Library, 134
Cochrane Central Register of Controlled Trials (CENTRAL), 14
*Codonopsis pilosulae*, 137
Coenzyme Q10 (ubiquinone)
cardioprotective effects of, 162, 163t, 166-167, 188, 193t, 393
co-administration with cancer chemotherapy, 399t
drug interactions of, 393, 396, 398
as migraine headache preventive and treatment, 118, 128
as uterine fibroid (leiomyoma) treatment, 256, 279

as weight loss supplement, 328

Coffea (homeopathic preparation), 408

Coffee enemas, 92

Cognitive-behavioral therapy
for back pain, 300
with breast cancer patients, 90
for depression, 354
as migraine headache preventive, 120, 129
for neck pain, 300

Cognitive therapy, mindfulness-based, 105, 358-359, 379t

*Coicis lachryma-jobi*, 137

Colchicine, 80

*Coleus forskii*, as asthma treatment, 61, 62t

Colic, 137, 143, 153

Colitis
*Clostridium difficile*, 394
ulcerative, 142, 155, 156, 389t, 390

Colon cancer, 26, 79, 390

Coltsfoot, as asthma treatment, 61

Common cold, 106-107, 124-125

Community Programs for Clinical Research on AIDS (CPCRA), 211

Complementary and alternative medicine practitioners
definition of, 421
licensing of, 13
physicians' consultations with, 27-28
qualifications of, 82
training programs for, 82

Complementary and alternative medicine products, physicians' sale of, 39, 40-41

Complementary and alternative medicine therapies
as adjunct to conventional therapies, 24

adverse effects of, 26
categories of, 5, 6, 241
definition of, 5-6, 7, 422
information resources about, 32-33b, 34-37b
PubMed database, 32-33b 33
reference books, 36-37b
web sites, 34-35b
medical-legal aspects of, 37-40
most commonly used, 11, 12
motivations for use of, 11-13, 24, 289
prevalence of use of, 3-4, 24
among overweight and obese individuals, 327-328
risks and benefits of, 27, 27b
terminology of, 6-8, 421-426

Complementary medicine, definition of, 6-7

Complete German Commission E Monographs, 109

"Complete Thymic Formula," 146

Consortium of Academic Health Centers in Integrative Medicine, 4

Constipation, dietary fiber treatment of, 137

Contaminants, in dietary supplements, 26

Copaltra, hepatotoxicity of, 149

Corn oil, 172

Cornsilk, diuretic effects of, 400

Coronary heart disease. *See* Cardiovascular disease

Corticotropin-releasing factor-like immunoreactivity (CRF-LI), 308

Cortisol, 359

Couch grass, diuretic effects of, 400

Council on Chiropractic Education, 412

Council on Naturopathic Medical Education (CNME), 415, 416

Cramp bark *(Viburnum opulus)*, as dysmenorrhea and endometriosis treatment, 252, 276t

Cranberry *(Vaccinium macrocarpon)*, as urinary tract infection preventive or treatment, 121-122, 269, 285t

Creatine, 224, 225-226, 234t
as HIV infection-related cachexia treatment, 209-211, 220t
renotoxicity of, 210

Crohn's disease, 133, 136, 142-143, 152, 155, 156, 390

*Curcuma xanthorrhiza* (turmeric, Japanese), 137

Curcumin, 143

Cyclosporine, interaction with dietary supplements, 360, 389, 392t, 402

Cystitis, interstitial, 270

Cytochrome P450 enzyme system, 369, 393, 402

Cytotoxicity assays, for food allergies, 45-46

Daidzein, 174

Daisy allergy, 108

Damiana *(Turnera diffusa)*, 347

Dandelion, 394, 400

Danshen, 163t, 397t

Dapoxetine, 227

*Datura stramonium*, 61, 62t

Deep breathing, 79, 422

Dehydroepiandrosterone (DHEA), 256
"anti-aging" properties of, 232-233, 238t
as cancer risk factor, 233
as osteoporosis preventive or treatment, 267, 284t

use in human
immunodeficiency virus
(HIV) infection
as cachexia treatment,
209, 210, 220t
as depression treatment,
208, 219t
Delta-9-tetrahydrocannibol
(dronabinol), 208-209
Depression, 353-386
CAM therapies for
as adjunct to
conventional
treatment, 353, 354
in cancer patients, 86
case study of, 376-377
Evidence Summary of,
379-384t
in HIV-positive
individuals, 207-208
motivations for use of,
353-354
during postpartum
period, 3620363
in premenstrual
syndrome, 247, 248
prevalence of use of,
353, 354-355
minor, 355
premenstrual syndrome-
related, 247, 248
Dermatitis, atopic, 48, 52-
53, 56-57
Detoxification, 7, 406
Devils' Claw
*(Harpagophytum)*, 297,
304, 312t, 397t
Dexamethasone, 390
Diabetes mellitus, type 2.
*See also* Hyperglycemia;
Hypoglycemia
CAM therapies for, 109-
113
as adjunctive therapies,
109
Ayurvedic interventions,
113-114
chromium, 111-112
dietary supplements,
109-113, 125-126t
omega-3 fatty acids, 111
prevalence of, 109
vitamin E dosage in, 231

Diarrhea, 139-140, 395
Didanosine, 210
Diet(s)
for cardiovascular disease
prevention, 163t, 172,
179-187, 180t, 197t
Andrew Weil, 181t
Atkins, 180t, 185, 186
case study of, 179
Jenny Craig, 180t
LEARN, 186
low carbohydrate, 180t,
181t, 185-187, 197t
Mediterranean, 163t,
172, 180t, 182-185,
188, 197t
National Cholesterol
Education Program
(NCEP), 183
Ornish, 180t, 181-182,
186, 187, 197t, 425
Pritikin, 180t, 425
Protein Power, 180t
Schwarzbein, 180t
Sugar Busters, 180t
Suzanne Somers, 180t
Therapeutic Lifestyle
Changes, 181t
very-low-fat, 180t, 181-
182, 187, 188
Weight Watchers, 181t
Zone, 181t, 186
Dietary Approaches to
Stopping Hypertension
(DASH), 264
"fertility," 259
four-day rotation, as food
allergy treatment, 54,
57t
high-fiber, 256, 279
macrobiotic, 424
for osteoporosis
prevention or treatment,
263-264, 282
as premenstrual syndrome
treatment, 248-249
for urinary incontinence
prevention or treatment,
269-270, 285
as uterine fibroid
(leiomyoma) treatment,
256, 279
vegetarian, 252, 277, 426

Zone, 426
Diet and Reinfarction Trial
(DART), 170
Dietary Approaches to
Stopping Hypertension
(DASH) diet, 264
Dietary Guidelines for
Americans 20005, 170
Dietary Supplement Health
and Education Act
(DSHEA) of 1994, 8-10,
80, 81, 149, 164
Dietary supplements. *See
also specific dietary
supplements*
adverse effects of, 10-11,
80
as anxiety treatment, 101-
103, 123
for body weight reduction,
327-352
cancer patients' use of, 79-
81
as cardiovascular disease
preventive, 163t, 164-
179, 188
as chronic low back pain
treatment, 297-298, 312
as common cold
preventive and
treatment, 106-107, 109-
113
contaminants and
adulterants in, 26
definition of, 8-9, 164, 425
drug interactions of, 26
effectiveness claims for, 9
for fitness and muscle bulk
improvement, 224-226
governmental regulation
of, 80, 81
as herpes virus infection
preventive and
treatment, 114-115
as human
immunodeficiency virus
(HIV) infection
treatment, 203, 204-210
hypoglycemic effect of,
400-401, 401t
interaction with
anti-diabetic agents,
400-401, 401t

antithrombotic drugs, 395-397, 396t, 397t
as knee osteoarthritis treatment, 301-304
labeling requirements for, 164
as lateral epicondyle pain treatment, 305
as migraine headache preventive and treatment, 116-118
as neck pain treatment, 300
prevalence of use of, 24
quality assurance for, 9-10
quality-assurance testing of, 9-10, 81
safety requirements for, 10
as urinary tract infection treatment, 121-122
Diethylstilbestrol, 231
Digitalis, 392
Digoxin, 369, 392
Diiodoquinol, 394
Distant healing, 213, 216t
Diuretics, 400
Docosahexaenoic acid (DHA)
  cardioprotective effects of, 169-171, 206-207
  as depression treatment, 373, 374-375
  interaction with nonsteroidal anti-inflammatory drugs, 389
Dong quai, 80, 243, 396t, 397t
Dopamine agonists, interaction with chaste tree berry, 246
Drug allergy reactions, 43
Drug interactions, with dietary supplements, 10-11, 26, 387-404
  of analgesics/anti-inflammatory agents, 388-392
  of antiarrhythmic/antihypertensive agents, 392-393
  of antibiotics, 394-395

of antilipemic agents, 397-398
of antineoplastic agents (chemotherapy), 398-399, 399t
of antithrombotic agents, 395-397, 396t, 397t
beneficial effects of, 387
of diuretics, 400
Drug Interaction Probability Scale (DIPS) for, 388
of immune modulating agents, 402
Naranjo nomogram for, 388
of nitrates, 402-403
Duhuo Jisheng Wan, 304
Duodenal ulcers, 135
Dust mite allergens, 47
Dysmenorrhea
  CAM therapies for, 252-255, 276-279t
  definition of, 251
Dyspepsia, 134-136, 149
Dysthymia, 355

Ear acupuncture, 103, 144, 157
*Echinacea*
  cancer patients' use of, 79-80
  clinical trials of, 19
  as common cold treatment, 107-108, 124
  contraindications to, 108
  as human immunodeficiency virus (HIV) infection treatment, 203
  variations in potency of, 19
Eicosapentaenoic acid (EPA), 206-207
  cardioprotective effects of, 169-172
  as depression treatment, 373, 374-375
  interaction with nonsteroidal anti-inflammatory drugs, 389
  of marine origin, 169-171
  of plant origin, 171-172

Elder broom, 400
Electrodermal testing, 47-48
Electrotherapy, 299, 315t, 318t
Enalapril, 393
Endocrine Society, 224
Endometriosis
  CAM therapies for, 252-255, 277t
  definition of, 251
  as infertility cause, 257
Energy medicine, 5
  as carpal tunnel syndrome treatment, 320
  definition of, 6, 422-423
  as menopausal symptoms treatment, 245
  as neck pain treatment, 315t, 316t
  as uterine fibroid (leiomyomas) treatment, 256
Enterolactone, 176
Environmental hypersensitivity disorder, 54
Ephedra (Ma Huang)
  adverse effects of, 63, 148, 343-344
  as asthma treatment, 61, 62t, 63, 64, 72t
  drug interactions of, 63-64
  hepatotoxicity of, 148
  as weight loss supplement, 340t, 343-344, 348, 350t
Ephedrine
  adverse effects off, 343-344
  as asthma treatment, 61
  as weight loss supplement, 331t, 340t, 343-344, 350t
Epicondylitis, lateral, 304-305, 319-320
Erectile dysfunction, 226-228
Essiac tea, 398
Estrogen-containing compounds, interaction with chaste tree berry, 246
Estrogens
  in men, 224

as premenstrual syndrome
cause, 248
Ethylenediamine tetraacetic
acid (EDTA) chelation
therapy, 187-188
Evening primrose oil
(Oenothera biennis)
adverse effects of, 247
antithrombotic effects of,
395
as atopic dermatitis
treatment, 53
contraindications to, 247
interaction with
nonsteroidal anti-
inflammatory drugs, 389
as menopausal symptoms
treatment, 243
as premenstrual syndrome
treatment, 247-248
as weight loss supplement,
328
Evidence-based medicine,
applied to CAM therapies,
13-20. See also Evidence
Summary under specific
medical conditions
research challenges in, 15-
20
Exatecan mesylate, 398
Exercise
aerobic, as depression
treatment, 366-367, 381t
as menopausal symptoms
treatment, 244, 275t
as osteoporosis preventive
or treatment, 262, 282t
as premenstrual syndrome
treatment, 248
Expectorants, herbal, 61,
62t

Fatigue, in cancer patients,
84, 88-89
Federation of State Medical
Boards (FSMB), 37-38
Feldenkrais Method, 295-
296
Felodipine, 393
Fennel, antibiotic
absorption-blocking
effects of, 394

Fenugreek
hypoglycemic effect of,
113, 127t, 401t
interaction with warfarin,
397t
as weight loss supplement,
334t
Fertility blend, 258, 280t
Feverfew, 117, 128
Fexofenadine, 50
Fiber, dietary, 137, 152t
Fibromyalgia, 307-308, 321-
323
Finasteride (Propecia), 231
Fish oil supplements, 142,
155. See also Omega-3
fatty acids
adverse effects of, 171
antiarrhythmic effects of,
393
antiplatelet effects of, 396t
as cardiovascular disease
preventive, 162, 206-
207, 393, 396t
as cyclosporine toxicity
preventive, 389t, 402
drug interactions of, 395,
396
as hypertriglyceri-demia
treatment, 206-207
mercury and PCB
contamination
of, 171
Fitness, athletic, 224-226,
234
Flavonoids, as prostate
cancer preventive, 230
Flaxseed/flaxseed oil, 172,
176-177, 196, 395
Flexner Report, 408
Fluoxetine, 372
Flutamine, 210
Folate/folic acid
as cardiovascular disease
preventive, 163t, 168,
169
as depression treatment,
371-373, 383t
as fertility blend
component, 258

as human
immunodeficiency virus
(HIV) infection
treatment, 215t
interaction with
methotrexare, 402
as nitrate tolerance
preventive, 403
Folk medicine, 423
Food, as bladder irritants,
269-270
Food, Drug and Cosmetic
Act of 1938, 9
Food allergy, 43
CAM therapies for, 53-54,
57
diagnostic tests for, 44-47
false diagnosis of, 55
Food Allergy and
Anaphylaxis Network, 53-
54
Food and Drug
Administration (FDA)
Consumer Advisories, 102
Good Manufacturing
Practices and, 9-10, 111
Homeopathic
Pharmacopoeia of the
United States, 408
regulatory authority, 80,
164
Food intolerance, 53-54, 55
Fractures, osteoporosis-
related, 261-262, 263,
264-265, 266
Fumaria officinalis
(fumatory), 137
Functional foods, 8, 303-304
Functional medicine, 8

Gaitianli, 268
Gallic acid, as weight
reduction supplement,
337t
Galphimia glauca, 49
Galvanometers, 47
Gamma aminobutyric acid
(GABA), 356
Gamma linolenic acid, 24-
25
Ganpi Lunzhi, 138

*Garcinia cambogia*, as weight loss supplement, 331t, 332t, 333t, 334t, 335t, 344, 345, 348, 350t

Garlic *(Allium sativum)* adverse effects of, 173-174 antiplatelet effects of, 396t as cardiovascular disease preventive, 163t, 172-174, 195t as common cold prophylaxis and treatment, 108, 125 CYP3A-inducing activity of, 393 as HIV infection treatment, 216t as human immunodeficiency (HIV) infection treatment, 202, 203, 205-206, 207 interaction with warfarin, 397t as weight loss supplement, 328

Gastric ulcers, 135

Gastrointestinal cancer, prevention of, 147, 158

Gastrointestinal disorders, CAM therapies for, 133-160 for alcohol abuse, 144, 157 for Crohn's disease, 155t, 156t for diarrhea, 139-140, 153t Evidence Summary of, 151-158t for gastric cancer prevention, 147, 158t for inflammatory bowel disease, 142-143, 149t for irritable bowel syndrome/colic, 137-139, 152t, 153-154t for liver disease, 144-147, 157t, 158t for nausea and vomiting, 140-142, 154-155t for pain, 143, 152t, 156t

for peptic ulcer disease/dyspepsia, 134-136, 151t, 152t in perioperative care, 144 recommendations regarding, 147, 149-150 for ulcerative colitis, 142, 155-156, 389t, 390

Generalized anxiety disorder CAM therapies for, 103, 104, 105, 106, 124 prevalence of, 101

Genistein, 174

Geriatric Depression Scale, 360

Germander, hepatotoxicity of, 148

Ginger antiemetic effects of, 140, 149, 154t anti-inflammatory effects of, 255, 279 antiplatelet effects of, 396t as uterine fibroid (leiomyoma) treatment, 255, 279 as weight loss supplement, 329t, 337t, 347

*Ginkgo biloba*, 247 adverse effects of, 63 antiplatelet effects of, 396t as asthma treatment, 61, 62t, 63, 64, 72t as cardiovascular disease preventive, 163t drug interactions of, 64, 395

Ginkolic acid, 62

Ginseng American, hypoglycemic effect of, 400 as diabetes mellitus type 2 treatment, 112 as erectile dysfunction treatment, 227, 228, 235t estrogenic effect of, 80

as human immunodeficiency virus (HIV) infection treatment, 203 hypoglycemic effect of, 401t interaction with warfarin, 396, 397t as menopausal symptoms treatment, 243, 245 as weight loss supplement, 335t, 345

GISSI Prevention Study, 170

Global Severity Index, 105

Glucocorticoids, adverse effects of, 390-391

Glucomannan, as weight loss supplement, 334t, 344-345, 348, 350t

Glucosamine, 9

Glucosamine/chondroitin, 301-303t, 318-319t

Glutamine, 210, 220t, 399t

L-Glutamine, gastroprotective effects of, 388t

Glycemic control, in diabetes mellitus, 109-110, 111, 112, 113

Glycitein, 174

Glycosides, cardiac, 392

Glycyrrhetinic acid, 391

Glycyrrhizin, 146, 391, 400

Glycyrrhizinic acid, 135

Goldenseal/golden rod *(Hydrastis canadensis)*, 134, 328, 400

Golfers, magnet therapy use by, 91

Gonadotropin-releasing hormone, 260

Gonadotropin-releasing hormone agonists (GnRHa), 252

Good Manufacturing Practices, 9-10, 111

Grapefruit juice, 402

Grapeseed extract, 50, 79-80

Gravel root, diuretic effects of, 400

Greater celandine, 136

Green coffee extract, as weight loss supplement, 335t, 345, 348, 350t

Greene Menopause Index, 84

Green tea, 79-80
catechins of, 398
as fertility blend component, 258
as fibromyalgia treatment, 309, 322t
P-glycoprotein-inducing activity of, 398
as prostate cancer preventive, 230
as weight loss supplement, 329t, 332t, 335t, 345, 348, 350t

G sylvestre, as weight loss supplement, 334t

Guarana (Paullinia cupana), as weight loss supplement, 329t, 332t, 335t, 338t, 347

Guar gum
interaction with digoxin, 392
as weight loss supplement, 340t, 346, 348, 350t

Guava leaf extract, 139

Guggul (Commifora mukul), as weight loss supplement, 328, 329t, 334t

Guggulipid, 163t

Guided imagery
cancer patients' use of, 86, 88, 98
definition of, 423
as uterine fibroid (leiomyoma) treatment, 256

Guidelines for the Evaluation and Management of Dyslipidemia in Human Immunodeficiency Virus (HIV)-Infected Adults Receiving Antiretroviral Therapy, 207

Guizhi Fuling, as uterine fibroid (leiomyoma) treatment, 257-258

Gymnema sylvestra, 113, 127, 401t

Gynecological cancers, 79, 86

Hadassah University Hospital, Israel, 86

Hahnemann, Samuel, 8, 17, 408, 409

Hamilton Rating Scale for Depression, 103, 356, 358, 367, 372, 374, 375-376

Hawthorn, 163t

Headaches
acupuncture treatment for, 119
as "allergy," 44
migraine
CAM therapies for, 116-120, 127-128t
definition of, 115
triggers of, 116
phototherapy (bright light exposure)-related, 366

Headache Society, 116

Healing circles, 423

Health insurance coverage, for CAM therapies, 38-40

Health Research and Educational Trust, 39

Heart and Estrogen/ Progestin Replacement Study (HERS), 270

Heart Outcomes Prevention Evaluation (HOPE), 168

Heart Outcomes Prevention Evaluation-The Ongoing Outcomes (HOPE-TOO) trial, 165

Heart Protection Study, 165

Heavy metals, as herbal product contaminants, 80

Helicobacter pylori infections, 394

Helicobacter pyrlori infections, 136, 149

Hemoglobin A1c, 110, 111, 112

Hemosiderosis, food-induced pulmonary, 45

Hepatitis, human immunodeficiency virus (HIV) infection-related, 206

Hepatitis B, 144, 145, 146, 157

Hepatitis C, 144, 145, 146, 157, 402

Hepatotoxins, herbal, 146-147, 148-149

Herbal remedies. See also names of specific herbs
as allergic rhinitis treatment, 49-51
"anti-estrogenic" effects of, 279
as asthma treatment, 60-64, 61t, 62t, 71t, 72t, 75
cancer patients' use of, 79-80
for cardiovascular disease prevention, 162, 163t, 172-174
as chronic low back pain treatment, 297-298
clinical trials of, 14-15, 16
as Crohn's disease treatment, 133
as depression treatment, 355, 381t, 382t
as diarrhea treatment, 139-140
diuretic or cathartic effects of, 400
drug interactions with, 80-81
as dysmenorrhea and endometriosis treatment, 252t, 276-277t
as dyspepsia treatment, 134-136
effect on absorption of antibiotics, 394
effect on glucocorticoid metabolism, 391
federal regulations regarding, 80
as gastrointestinal disorders treatment, 152t, 153t, 154t, 157t
gastrotoxicity of, 134

hepatotoxicity of, 80, 146-
147, 148-149
as human
immunodeficiency virus
(HIV) infection
treatment, 203-204
as infertility treatment,
257-258, 280
as inflammatory bowel
disease treatment, 142-
143
information sources
regarding, 94-95
as irritable bowel
syndrome treatment,
137-138
as lateral epicondyle pain
treatment, 305, 320
as liver disease treatment,
144-147
as menopausal symptoms
treatment, 242-243, 243
as neck pain treatment,
300, 316
as peptic ulcer disease
treatment, 135
as premenstrual syndrome
treatment, 246-248
prescriptions for, 149-150
"standardized," 10
as uterine fibroid
(leiomyoma) treatment,
255, 279
variations in potency of,
19
for weight loss, 327, 329-
340t, 341, 342, 343-348
Herbs. See also names of
specific herbs
definition of, 9
Herpes virus infections, oral
and genital, 114-115, 127t
High-density lipoprotein
levels, chromium
picolinate-induced
increase in, 393
Holy basil, 112, 113, 127t
Homeopathic
Pharmacopoeia of the
United States, 408
Homeopathic remedies,
classification as drugs, 9
Homeopathy, 408-410

adverse effects of, 65
as allergic rhinitis
treatment, 48-49, 56t
as asthma treatment, 61,
64-65, 72t, 75
cancer patients' use of, 90,
98t
clinical trials of, 17-18
as Crohn's disease
treatment, 133
definition of, 408, 423-
424
as diarrhea treatment,
140, 149, 154
as dyspepsia treatment,
136, 152t
electrodermal testing use
in, 47-48
first double-blind
experiment on, 13
founder of, 8
licensure in, 409-410
as menopausal symptoms
treatment, 242
as postoperative ileus
treatment, 144, 157
as premenopausal
syndrome (PMS)
treatment, 250
safety and efficacy of, 410
Home remedies, cancer
patients' use of, 79
Homocysteine, elevated
levels of, 167-168, 169,
184, 390, 402
Honey, as allergic rhinitis
treatment, 51
Hops (Humulus lupulus),
102
Hormone therapy, for
menopausal symptoms,
242, 244
Horse chestnut, as
cardiovascular disease
preventive, 163t
Horsetail, diuretic effects of,
400
Hospital Anxiety and
Depression Scale, 86
Hot flashes
CAM therapy for, 242-
245, 275-276t

in cancer patients, 84, 89,
91, 96t
definition of, 242
House dust mite allergens,
64-65
Human immunodeficiency
virus (HIV) infection,
CAM therapies for, 114,
201-222
with antiretroviral and/or
immunostimulatory
activity, 203-205
case study of, 201-202
in combination with
antiretroviral therapy,
201-202, 203, 205
Evidence Summary of,
215-220t
for HIV-related
comorbidities, 205-210
implication for
antietroviral therapy,
201-202
interaction with
antiretroviral agents,
201-202
motivations for use of, 202
prevalence of use, 201,
202
Huoxue Jiangtang Pingzhi,
112
3-Hydroxy-3-methylglutaryl
coenzyme A inhibitors
(statins)
co-administration with
coenzyme Q10, 166-167
as coenzyme Q10
deficiency cause, 193
interaction with
cyclosporine, 402
interaction with dietary
supplements, 389, 392b,
397-398
naturally occurring, 206
as rhabdomyolysis cause,
402
use in human
immunodeficiency virus
(HIV)-infected patients,
205-207
5-Hydroxytryptophan (5-
HTP), as depression
treatment, 376, 383t

Hypercalcemia, 400
Hypercholesterolemia, antiretroviral therapy-related, 205-206
Hyperforin, 10, 368, 369, 392
Hyperglycemia. *See also* Diabetes mellitus, type 2
dietary supplement treatment for, 390
Hypericin, 368
Hypericum, 369
Hyperkalemia, 393, 394
Hyperlipidemia. *See also* Lipid-lowering therapies
conjugated linolenic acid-related, 343
human immunodeficiency virus (HIV) infection-related, 205-207
Hypermagnesemia, 400
Hypersensitivity, 43-44. *See also* Allergic disorders
Hypertension
CAM therapies for, 189-192
*Ginkgo biloba*-related, 400
Hypertriglyceridemia, antiretroviral therapy-related, 206-207
Hypnotherapy
for asthma, 67, 70, 72t
cancer patients' use of, 83-84
for chemotherapy-related nausea and vomiting, 142
definition of, 424
for dyspepsia, 136, 152t
for gastrointestinal pain, 143
for infertility, 259, 281
for irritable bowel syndrome, 139, 153t
for urinary incontinence, 271-272, 285t
Hypnotics, interaction with black cohosh, 243
Hypoglycemia

Hypoglycemia, dietary supplement-related potentiation of, 400-401, 401t
Hypokalemia, 392, 400
Hypomagnesemia, 392

Ileus, postoperative, 144, 157t
Immune-compromised patients. *See also* Human immunodeficiency virus (HIV) infection
*Echinacea* use by, 107
Immune modulation, 402
Immunoglobulin A, food-specific, 45
Immunoglobulin G assays, food-specific, 44-45
Immunotherapy
allergen, 64
homeopathic (isopathy), as asthma treatment, 64-65
for inhalant allergies, 49
Indian Experiment of Infarct Survival trial, 172
Indinavir, 207-208
Indomethacin, as PC-SPES component, 231
Indomethacin, gastrointestinal effects of, 388t
Infertility
CAM therapies for, 257-261, 280-281t
definition of, 257
Inflammatory bowel disease, 142-143, 149
Inolter, 112
Inositol, as depression treatment, 376, 384t
Insomnia, in cancer patients, 88, 89
Institute of Functional Medicine, 8
Institute of Medicine, From Cancer Patient to Cancer Survivor: Lost in Transition, 82
Insulin sensitivity, 400-401, 401t

Integrative medicine, definition of, 7
Interferon-alpha, 402
International Classification of Diseases (ICD-9) codes, 33, 38-39
International Headache Society, 117
International Incontinence Society, 268
Ipriflavone, 267, 283t
Iridology, 8
Irinotecan, interaction with St. John's wort *(Hypericum perforatum)*, 369
Iron, as fertility blend component, 258
Irritable bowel syndrome, 133, 134, 137-139
Isoflavones
definition of, 174
in red clover, 243
in soy, 174-176, 196, 242, 262, 275, 281
"Isopathic" solutions, 49
Isosorbide mononitrate, 402
Ivy leaf extract, as asthma treatment, 64, 72t

Jacobson's Progressive Relaxation, 357
Japanese herbal medicine, as dysmenorrhea treatment, 254-255
Japanese kampo medicine, 391
Jiechang Kang, 138
Jin-bu-huan, hepatotoxicity of, 148
Johns Hopkins, 230
*Journal of the American Medical Association*, 13
Juniper, diuretic effects of, 400

Kaiser Family Foundation, 39
Kampo medicine, 50, 391
Kangdu Wan, 145

Kangfu Xiaozheng, as uterine fibroid (leiomyoma) treatment, 256-257, 280t
Kavalactones, 101-102
Kava *(Piper methysticum)*
  as anxiety treatment, 101-102, 123
  hepatotoxicity of, 102, 148
  as premenstrual syndrome treatment, 248
  as weight loss supplement, 328
Kinesiology, applied, 8
Knee, osteoarthritis of, 300-304, 317-319t
Kola nut, as weight loss supplement, 343
Kombucha, hepatotoxicity of, 149
Krill oil, as premenstrual syndrome treatment, 249

*Lactobacillus*, 136
*Lactobacillus rhamnosus*, 395
Lady's mantle, as uterine fibroid (leiomyoma) treatment, 255, 279
Laser therapy, low-level (LLLT), 306-307, 320t
Lateral epicondyle pain (epicondylitis), 304-305, 319-320t
Lavender oil, 298-299
Law of Similars, 408
Laxatives, herbal, hepatotoxicity of, 149
"Laying on of hands," 424
*Ledebouriellae sesloidis*, 137
Legal aspects, of CAM therapies, 37-40
Lemon balm *(Melissa officinalis)*, 115, 217
*Letter on Corpulence* (Banting), 185
Leukotrienes, s dysmenorrhea cause, 251

Lian *(Scutellaria barbata)*, as uterine fibroid (leiomyoma) treatment, 280
Lichang Tang, 138
Licorice *(Glycyrrhiza glabra)*
  adverse effects of, 392
  antiplatelet effects of, 396t
  as asthma treatment, 61, 62t, 63
  deglycyrrhizinated (DGL), 388t, 394
  gastroprotective effects of, 135, 151t
  interaction with diuretics, 400
  as osteoporosis preventive, 282t
  as weight loss supplement, 328
Licorice root formulation, 145
Lifestyle therapies
  for cardiovascular disease prevention, 197-198t
  for urinary incontinence prevention or treatment, 269-272, 285t
Lignans, as cardiovascular disease preventive, 176-177, 196
Lind, James, 13
Lingonberry juice, 121
α-Linolenic acid, 171-172
γ-Linolenic acid, 24-25
Linolenic acid, conjugated, as weight loss supplement, 339t, 343, 348, 349t
Lipid-lowering therapy. *See* Antilipemic therapy
α-Lipoic acid, hypoglycemic effect of, 401t
Lipokinetix, hepatotoxicity of, 148t
Lithium, interaction with omega-3 fatty acids, 389
Liu-Jun-Zi-Tang, 136
Liv-52, 146, 158t
Liver cleansers, 7

Liver diseases, 144-147, 157t, 158t
  alcoholic, 158
Liver failure, 102, 243
Lomatol, 136
Longevity, 232-233
Lotus rhizomes, as weight loss supplement, 335t, 345
Lovastatin, 397
Lovaza, 171
Low density lipoprotein cholesterol levels, omega-3 fatty acid-related reduction in, 111
Lung cancer patients, CAM therapies for, 85, 87, 92
*Lyceum barbarum*, 397t
Lycopene, 8
  as prostate cancer preventive, 230, 231, 237t
Lyon Heart Trial, 183
L-Lysine, 114-115, 127

*Macbeth* (Shakespeare), 353
Magnesium
  as cardiovascular disease preventive, 163t
  co-administration with cancer chemotherapy, 399t
  as dysmenorrhea or endometriosis treatment, 253-254
  as fertility blend component, 258
  as fibromyalgia treatment, 309, 322t
  interaction with
    digoxin, 392
    diuretics, 400
  as migraine headache preventive or treatment, 118, 128t
  as osteoporosis preventive or treatment, 264, 282t
  as premenstrual syndrome treatment, 249
Magnetic devices, 91, 99t, 245, 275
Maguire, Mark, 225

Maharishi Vedic Medicine (MVM), 189-190

Ma Huang. *See* Ephedra

Malpractice liability, CAM-related, 37-38

Mania, 371, 375

Manipulative therapies, 5
  adverse effects of, 26
  for asthma, 68-69t, 68t-69t
  definition of, 6, 411
  for dysmenorrhea or endometriosis, 254, 278
  for human immunodeficency virus (HIV)-infected patients, 213-214
  for infertility, 259-260, 281, 282t
  for menopausal symptoms, 244-245
  as migraine headache prophylaxis, 120, 129t
  for musculoskeletal disorders
    acute low back pain, 310-311
    carpal tunnel syndrome, 306, 320-321t
    chronic low back pain, 312t, 313t, 314t
    fibromyalgia, 322t, 323t
    lateral epicondyle pain, 305, 320t
    neck pain, 316-317t
    osteoarthritis of the knee, 319
  for osteoporosis prevention or treatment, 267-268, 284t
  for urinary incontinence, 272-273, 286t
  for uterine fibroids (leiomyomas), 256, 280t

Manual soft-tissue therapies, for infertility, 281

Manual therapies. *See also* Chiropractic care; Manipulative therapies; Spinal manipulation
  systems of, 411-412

Maprotiline, 368

Marigold allergy, 108

Marijuana, 209, 210, 220t

*Marmelos correa*, 137

Massage therapists, qualifications of, 82

Massage therapy
  action mechanism of, 362, 363
  for anxiety, 104
  for asthma, 68t, 72t
  for cancer patients, 79, 81-82, 84, 85, 87, 90, 97t
  for carpal tunnel syndrome, 306
  definition of, 424
  for depression, 362-363, 380t
  health insurance coverage of, 39, 40
  for human immunodeficency virus (HIV)-positive patients, 202, 213-214, 216t
  for menopausal symptoms, 242, 245
  for musculoskeletal disorders
    acute low back pain, 310
    chronic low back pain, 294-295, 298, 313t, 314t
    fibromyalgia, 308, 309, 322t
    lateral epicondyle pain, 305, 320t
    neck pain, 298-299, 316t
    osteoarthritis of the knee, 301, 319t
  for premenopausal syndrome (PMS), 250
  for uterine fibroids (leiomyomas), 256, 257, 280, 280t

Mastic, 136

Mayo Clinic, 307

M.D. Anderson Cancer Center, 89
  website, 93-94

Medical schools, CAM curricula in, 4

Medical University of South Carolina, 109

Meditation
  action mechanism of, 358

adverse effects of, 359
  as anxiety treatment, 105
  as asthma treatment, 67, 70
  cancer patients' use of, 79, 80, 98t
  as cardiovascular disease preventive, 163t, 189-190, 197t
  as chronic low back pain treatment, 297, 314t
  concentration, 105, 357
  contraindications to, 359
  definition of, 357, 424
  as depression treatment, 355, 357-359, 379t
  as human immunodeficiency virus (HIV) infection therapy, 202
  mindfulness, 105, 357
  Transcendental, 105, 189-190, 197t, 358

Megavitamin therapy, 12, 204, 423

Melatonin, co-administration with cancer chemotherapy, 399t

Memorial Sloan-Kettering Cancer Center, 94-95
  Integrative Medicine website, 25

Menaquinone, 266

Menopausal symptoms, 241-245, 275-276t
  in cancer patients, 84

Menopause, average age of, 241

Men's health, CAM therapies for, 223-229
  for androgen deficiency, 224
  Evidence Summary of, 234-238t
  for improved sexual function, 226-228, 235-236t
  for longevity enhancement, 232-233, 238t
  for male pattern baldness, 231

for prostate cancer prevention, 237t
for prostate disorders, 229-231
Mercer Human Resource Consulting, 39
Mercury, as fish oil supplement contaminant, 111, 171
Mesalamine, 142, 390
Metabolic syndrome, 189-190
Methadone, interactions with dietary supplements, 392, 392b
Methotrexate, 402
Methylfolate, 371
Methylsulfonylmenthane (MSM), 303-304, 319t
Metronidazole, 394
Micronutrients, as human immunodeficiency virus infection (HIV) treatment, 204
Milk allergy, 45
Milk thistle *(Silybum marianum)*, 7, 207
cancer patients' use of, 79-80
as human immunodeficiency virus (HIV) infection treatment, 218t
interaction with interferon, 402
metronidazole, 394
as liver disease treatment, 144-145, 157t
silibinin content of, 402
as uterine fibroids (leiomyomas) treatment, 255
Mind-body dualism, 353-354
Mind-body therapies, 5
for asthma, 67-70, 72t, 75
for cancer patients, 80, 83-84, 85, 88-89, 96t, 97t, 98t
for cardiovascular disease prevention, 189-192, 190t, 197-198
definition of, 6

for human immunodeficiency virus (HIV) infection, 211-213
for infertility, 259, 281t
for menopausal symptoms, 244
for migraine headaches, 120, 129
for musculoskeletal disorders
carpal tunnel syndrome, 321t
chronic low back pain, 314t, 315t
fibromyalgia, 322t
lateral epicondyle pain, 320t
neck pain, 317t
for osteoporosis prevention or treatment, 282t
for urinary incontinence prevention or treatment, 269-272, 285t
Mineral supplements
cancer patients' use of, 79-80
as human immunodeficiency virus (HIV) infection treatment, 204
Minoxidil, 231
Mistletoe, hepatotoxicity of, 148
Monniere Linn, 137
Monosodium glutamate, as migraine headache trigger, 116
Monoxidase amine inhibitors, interaction with St. John's wort, 369
Morning sickness, pregnancy-related, 140
Morphine, 85
Motion sickness, 140, 141, 149t
Movement therapies
for cardiovascular disease prevention, 190-192
for neck pain, 299
Moxibustion, 417

Multicenter Lifestyle Demonstration Project (MLDP), 182
Multisite Cardiac Lifestyle Intervention Program, 182
Multivitamins
as cardiovascular disease preventive, 162
as human immunodeficiency virus (HIV) infection treatment, 205, 215t
Muscle bulk, dietary supplements for, 224-226
Muscle-response testing, 47, 48
Musculoskeletal disorders, CAM therapies for, 289-325
acute low back pain, 289-292, 310-311t
carpal tunnel syndrome, 305-307, 320-321t
chronic low back pain, 293-298, 311-315t
Evidence Summary of, 310-322t
fibromyalgia, 307-308, 321-323t
lateral epicondyle pain, 304-305, 319-320t
neck pain, 298-300, 315-317t
osteoarthritis of the knee, 300-304, 317-319t
Mushrooms
maitake, 256, 279
oyster, 206
Music therapy, for cancer patients, 80, 87-88, 97t
Mussels, green-lipped, 304
Myofascial release, as uterine fibroids (leiomyomas) treatment, 256, 257, 280t

NAC, 393, 402-403
National Academy of Sciences, Food and Nutrition Board, 423
National Ayurvedic Medical Association, 407

National Cancer Institute, 230
  website, 93, 94
National Center for Complementary and Alternative Medicine (NCCAM), 4, 114, 230, 241
  website, 93, 94
National Center for Health Statistics, 327
National Center for Homeopathy, 409, 410
National Cholesterol Education Program (NCEP) diet, 183
National Death Index, 212
National Health Interview Survey, 11, 161
National Institutes of Health, 5, 6-7
  CAM medical education projects of, 4
  Office of Alternative Aging, 4
  PubMed database on CAM, 32-33b
  State-of-the-Science Conference, 271
  support for manual therapy research, 412
  website, 25
National Institutes of Medicine, CAM research funding by, 14
National Library of Medicine, PubMed database on CAM, 32-33b, 33
National Overactive Bladder Evaluation (NOBLE) study, 270
National Science Foundation, 111
National Science Foundation International, 81
Natural Database, 109
Natural Standard, 109
Naturopathic physicians, 414-415
  licensure of, 416, 416b
Naturopathy, 7-8, 414-417

definition of, 414-415, 424-425
  health insurance coverage of, 39, 40
  safety and efficacy of, 416-417
  schools of, 415, 415b, 416
Nausea and vomiting, 140-142
  cancer treatment-related, 83-84, 96t
  chemotherapy-related, 141, 142, 155
  motion sickness-related, 140, 141, 154t
  postoperative, 140, 141, 154t
  pregnancy-related, 140, 141, 149, 154t, 155t
Neck pain, acute and chronic, 298-300, 315-317t
Nettle root, as benign prostatic hypertrophy treatment, 229, 236t, 237t
Neuroleptics, interaction with omega-3 fatty acids, 389
Neuropathy
  diabetic, 113, 127
  human immunodeficiency virus (HIV)-related, 210, 211
Nevirapine, 208
New York Times, 41
Niacin, 397
Nifedipine, 393
Nitrates, interaction with dietary supplements, 402-403
Nitrofurantoin, 394
Nitroglycerine, 403
Nonnucleoside analogues, 208
Nonsteroidal anti-inflammatory drugs
  in combination with glucosamine, 302
  interaction with dietary supplements, 375, 388-390, 389t
Nopal (Opuntia spp.), 401
Norepinephrine, 361

Nova Scotia Environmental Health Centre, 46
Nurses' Health Study, 172, 179, 266
Nutraceuticals, 8, 303-304
Nutrifen, 345
Nuts, as migraine headache trigger, 116

Oat fiber, as weight loss supplement, 330t
Obesity, 327. See also Weight loss
Omacor, 171
Omega-3 fatty acids, 142, 155
  action mechanism of, 374
  adverse effects of, 375
  as cardiovascular disease preventive, 169-172, 188, 194t, 195t
  as Crohn's disease treatment, 155t
  as depression treatment, 373-375, 382t
  as diabetes mellitus type 2 treatment, 111, 126
  as dysmenorrhea or endometriosis treatment, 253, 277t
  effect on bone density, 267
  as human immunodeficiency virus (HIV) infection treatment, 217t
  nonsteroidal anti-inflammatory drug-enhancing effects of, 389, 389t
  as osteoporosis preventive or treatment, 284t
  sources of, 169-171, 373
Onshido, hepatotoxicity of, 148
Opiates, as chronic low back pain treatment, 297-298
Oral contraceptives, interaction with dietary supplements, 243, 369
Oregon Health and Sciences University, 52

Oriental medicine, 417-419. *See also* Acupuncture; Traditional Chinese medicine

Ornish Diet, 163t

Osteoarthritis, of the knee, 300-304, 317-319t

Osteopaths (doctors of osteopathy), 411

Osteopathy, 7-8, 254, 275, 278

Osteoporosis
CAM therapies for, 262-268, 281-285t
definition of, 261

Ovarian cancer, dehydroepiandrosterone (DHEA) as risk factor for, 233

Over-the-counter products, recall of, 26

Overweight, 327. *See also* Weight loss

Padma-Lax, 137, 153t

Pain
chronic, 289
gastrointestinal, 137, 143, 144, 152, 156t
as motivation for CAM utilization, 241

Pain visual analog scale (VAS), 300, 302

Palmer, Daniel David, 412

Palmer School of Chiropractic, 412

Pancreatitis, 143

Pantothenic acid, as weight loss supplement, 329t

Paroxetine, 368

Parsley, diuretic effects of, 400

Passionflower, 102, 123

Patient-controlled analgesia, 85

PC-SPES, 230, 231, 237t

Peanuts, as migraine headache trigger, 116

Pelvic floor electrical stimulation, 272-273, 286t

Pelvic floor muscle exercises, 270-271, 272, 286t

Pennyroyal, hepatotoxicity of, 148

Peppermint, 149, 152t

Peppermint oil, 134-135, 137, 151t

Peptic ulcer disease, 135, 136

Perioperative care, 144

Pessaries, as urinary incontinence treatment, 285t

Petadolex, 116, 117

P-glycoprotein transport protein (P-gp), 391-392, 398, 402

Phenothiazines, interaction with evening primrose oil, 247

Phosphodiesterase-5 inhibitors, 227, 228

Phototherapy (bright light exposure)
adverse effects of, 366
for depression, 365-366, 380t
for premenstrual syndrome, 248

*Phyllanthus*, 145, 146

Phylloquinone, 266

Physical therapists, as spinal manipulation providers, 411

Physical therapy
for infertility, 259-260
for migraine headache prevention, 120, 129
for osteoporosis prevention or treatment, 267-268, 284t

Physician-patient relationship, 25, 354

Physicians
education in CAM therapies, 37-38
as information sources about CAM therapies, 24-25
knowledge of CAM therapies, 23-28

Phytoestrogens, 242-243. *See also* Coumestans; Isoflavones; Lignans

anti-estrogenic effects of, 174
as cardiovascular disease preventive, 174-177
definition of, 174
proestrogenic effects of, 174
as prostate cancer preventive, 230

Phytomedicine, 8

Phytonadione, 266

Pickled foods, as migraine headache trigger, 116

*Picrorrhiza kurroa*, as asthma treatment, 62t, 72t

Pine bark *(Pinus maritime)*, as dysmenorrhea and endometriosis treatment, 252, 277t

*Pinellia*, as asthma treatment, 61, 62t

Pingheng Zhixie Jianpi, 138

Placebo controls, in CAM clinical trials, 20

Platelet function, effect of dietary supplements on, 395, 396t

Podophyllotoxin, 80

Policosanol, 163t, 395, 396t

Polychlorinated biphenyls (PCBs), as fish oil supplement contaminants, 171

Polyphenols, antioxidant, 49

*Polyporus umbellatus*, 145

Postmenopausal Estrogen Interventions (PEI), 266

Potassium
interaction with angiotensin-converting enzyme inhibitors, 393
as premenstrual syndrome treatment, 249

Potassium salts, interaction with trimethoprim, 394

Pravastatin, 397

Prayer, 11, 12, 24, 202, 212, 424

Prednisolone, 391

Pregnancy

as contraindication to black cohosh, 243
human immunodeficiency virus (HIV) infection during, 205
nausea and vomiting during, 140, 141, 149, 154t, 155t
Premature ejaculation, 227, 235t
Premenstrual dysphoric disorder (PMDD), 246, 248
Premenstrual syndrome (PMS)
CAM therapies for, 246-250, 276t
definition of, 245-246
Prescriptions, for herbal and natural products, 149-150
Preserved foods, as migraine headache trigger, 116
Primrose oil. *See* Evening primrose oil
Probiotics
as antibiotic-associated diarrhea preventive, 395
as Crohn's disease treatment, 156t
as diarrhea prophylaxis and treatment, 139-140, 154t
as *Helicobacter pyrlori* infection treatment, 136, 151t
as inflammatory bowel disease treatment, 142-143
as irritable bowel syndrome treatment, 137-138, 153t
as pouchitis treatment, 156t
as ulcerative colitis treatment, 155t, 156t
Product recall advisories, 26b
Profile of Mood States (POMS), 86
Progressive muscle relaxation (PMR), 105-106

as anxiety treatment, 105-106
definition of, 425
as depression treatment, 363, 364-365, 380t
as menopausal symptoms treatment, 244
Propranolol, 393
Prostaglandins, as dysmenorrhea cause, 251
Prostate cancer, 78-79, 230-231, 237
Prostate disorders, 229-231
Protease inhibitors, interactions with dietary supplements, 205-206, 207-208
Protein, dietary, effect on urinary calcium excretion, 263-264
Provocation/neutralization method, 46, 48
*Prunella vulgaris*, 304
Psychotherapy, 80, 212
Psyllium *(Plantago)*
as constipation treatment, 137
hepatotoxicity of, 149
as irritable bowel syndrome treatment, 137
as weight reduction supplement, 336t, 346t, 348t, 350t
PubMed database, 32-33b, 33
Pulse test, 46
Pumpkin seed extract, as benign prostatic hypertrophy treatment, 229-230, 237t
Pycnogenol, 393, 396t, 401t
Pyelonephritis, 394
Pygeum, as benign prostatic hypertrophy treatment, 229, 230, 237t
Pyroxidine, interaction with antineoplastic agents, 399
Pyrrolizidine alkaloids, hepatotoxicity of, 116, 148
Pyruvate, as weight reduction supplement, 336t, 346t, 348t, 350t

Qi (chi), 16-17, 360, 417, 425
Qidan Tongmai, 112
Qi gong, 417
adverse effects of, 360
as cardiovascular disease preventive, 163t, 198t
contraindications to, 360
definition of, 425-426
as depression treatment, 359-360, 379t
Quality of life
of cancer patients, 80, 82-91
of cancer patients' caregivers, 91
of human immunodeficiency virus (HIV)-infected patients, 211
Quercetin, as allergic rhinitis treatment, 51
Quinolone antibiotics, 394

Radiation therapy, interaction with antioxidants, 81
Radioallergosorbent tests, immunoglobulin G, 44
Ragweed allergy, 108
Randomized controlled trials (RCTs), 13-14
Red clover *(Trifolium pratense)*, 275, 328t
Red wine, as cardiovascular disease preventive, 184
Red yeast rice *(Monascus purpureus)*, 8
as cardiovascular disease preventive, 163t
interaction with statins, 397
warfarin, 397t
as weight loss supplement, 328
Referrals, from CAM practitioners, 27
Reflexology
as asthma treatment, 68t, 69t, 72t
cancer patients' use of, 91, 99t

as menopausal symptoms treatment, 245, 275t

as premenopausal syndrome (PMS) treatment, 250

Reiki, 422-423

Reishi, 396t

"Relaxation response," 105-106, 358

Relaxation techniques
acupuncture-related, 103
as anxiety treatment, 105-106
as asthma treatment, 67, 68t, 70, 72t, 75
cancer patients' use of, 79, 83-84, 86, 96t, 97t
as depression treatment, 355, 357, 363-365, 380t
as infertility treatment, 258-259
as menopausal symptoms treatment, 242
as migraine headache preventive, 120, 129t

Reserpine, 392

Resveratrol, 395, 396t

*Retardation of Aging and Disease, The* (Walford and Weindruch), 232

Rhabdomyolysis, 402

Rhinitis, allergic, 24-25, 43, 48-52, 56

Rhubarb *(Rheum)*, as weight reduction supplement, 336t, 337t, 347, 348, 351t

Ritonavir, interaction with St. John's wort, 369

RMIT Chinese Medicine Research Group, 49-50

*Saccharomyces boulardii*, 136, 394, 395

S-adenosyl-methionine (SAMe), 303, 304
action mechanism of, 370
definition of, 370
as depression treatment, 208, 219t, 370-371, 382t
as fibromyalgia treatment, 309, 323t

gastroprotective effects of, 144, 145, 157t, 388t
as osteoarthritis of the knee treatment, 319t
synthesis of, 370, 372

Saffron *(Crocus sativus)*, as depression treatment, 375-376, 382t

Sage, red *(Salvia miltiorrhiza)*, as weight reduction supplement, 336t, 337t, 347

*Saibuko-to* (TJ96), as asthma treatment, 61, 63, 64, 72t

St. John's wort *(Hypericum perforatum)*
adverse effects of, 369
CYP3A4-inducing activity of, 391, 392
as depression treatment, 367-369, 381t
as "detoxifier," 11
drug interactions of, 11, 80-81, 207-208, 369, 391-392, 392b, 392t, 397t, 398, 402
as human immunodeficiency virus (HIV) infection treatment, 218-219t
as premenstrual syndrome treatment, 248
"standardized," 10, 368
as weight loss supplement, 339t

Saltbush *(Atriplex halimus)*, hypoglycemic effect of, 401t

Sanbai San, 138

Saquinavir, 174, 393
interaction with garlic, 206

Saw palmetto *(Serenoa repens)*, 134
antiplatelet effects of, 396t
as benign prostatic hypertrophy treatment, 229, 236, 236t, 269
hepatotoxicity of, 148
as urinary incontinence treatment, 269

as uterine fibroids (leiomyomas) treatment, 255, 279t

Scalp massage, 116

Scullcap, hepatotoxicity of, 148

Scurvy, 13, 266

Seasonal affective disorder (SAD), 365

Seaweed/kelp *(Fucus vesiculosus)*, as weight loss supplement, 328

Secoisolariciresinol, 176

Sedatives, interaction with black cohosh, 243

Selective serotonin reuptake inhibitors, 370-371, 373

Selenium, 158
as fertility blend component, 258
as human immunodeficiency virus (HIV) infection treatment, 204-205, 215t
interaction with statins, 397
as prostate cancer preventive, 230
as uterine fibroids (leiomyomas) treatment, 256, 279t

Self-hypnosis, 86, 257

Senna, hepatotoxicity of, 149

Senna leaf, 138

Sennomoto-kouno, hepatotoxicity of, 148

Serotonin, 361

Sertraline, 367, 369

Sex-hormone-binding globulin, 252

Shakespeare, William, 353

Shark cartilage, 79-80, 92t

Shenxiahewining, 136

Sho-saiko-to (xiao chai hu tang), 61, 63, 391, 402
hepatotoxicity of, 148

Shugan Jianpi Tang, 138

Silibinin, 402

Silymarin, 394

Simvastatin, 165, 397

SKI306X, 304
Sleep therapy, 88-89
Smoking, 11, 241
Smoking cessation, 270, 285
Somers, Suzanne, 226
*Sophorae flavescentis*, 146
Soy
  as cardiovascular disease
    preventive, 174-176,
    195t, 196t
  as hot flashes treatment,
    275t
  as menopausal symptoms
    treatment, 242-243, 275t
  as osteoporosis preventive
    or treatment, 262, 281t
  as premenstrual syndrome
    treatment, 249
  as vitamin K source, 266
Soy sauce, as migraine
  headache trigger, 116
Spiced foods, as bladder
  irritants, 269-270
*Spie*, 414
Spinal manipulation, 120,
  129, 410-413. *See also*
  Chiropractic care
  adverse effects of, 413-414
  definition of, 410
  as dysmenorrhea or
    endometriosis treatment,
    254
  as low back pain
    treatment, 310t
  as neck pain treatment,
    316t
Spiritual healing, 80, 355
Spirituality, 211-213
Spironolactone, 400
*Spirulina*, as allergic
  rhinitis treatment, 51
Squeeze Technique, 227,
  235t
Statins. *See* 3-Hydroxy-3-
  methylglutaryl coenzyme
  A inhibitors (statins)
Stavudine, 210
Stinging nettle, 51, 400
*Streptococcus thermophilus*,
  136
Stress
  as cardiovascular disease
    risk factor, 189

transient, 355
Stress reduction therapies
  for cancer patients, 86-88
  for cardiovascular disease
    patients, 189-190
  dietary supplements as,
    102
  for human
    immunodeficiency virus
    (HIV)-infected
    individuals, 214
  for menopausal symptoms
    management, 242, 244
  for migraine headache
    management, 116, 120,
    129
  mindfulness-based
    (MBSR), 105
    as chronic low back pain
      treatment, 297, 314t
    as depression treatment,
      308, 358
    as fibromyalgia
      treatment, 308-309,
      323t
    as uterine fibroids
      (leiomyomas) treatment,
      256, 280t
Stroke, prevention of, 167-
  168
Study of Osteoporotic
  Fractures, 264
STW5, 137, 153
STW5-I, 151t
STW5-II, 135, 137, 151t,
  152t, 153
Sulfasalazine, 390
Support groups, for cancer
  patients, 80
Surgical procedures, anxiety
  associated with, 103-104
Symptom Checklist (SCL-
  90-R), 105
Symptoms of Stress
  Inventory (SOSI), 86

Tai Chi
  as cardiovascular disease
    preventive, 163t, 191-
    192, 198t
  contraindications to, 360
  definitions of, 426

as depression treatment,
  359-360, 379t
as fibromyalgia treatment,
  308, 323t
as lateral epicondyle pain
  treatment, 305, 320t
as neck pain treatment,
  299, 317t
as osteoporosis preventive
  or treatment, 263, 282t
Tamoxifen, 84
Tamsulosin, 229
Tart cherries, as chronic low
  back pain treatment, 297,
  314t
Taxol, 80
Tea. *See also* Green tea
  premenstrual syndrome-
    exacerbating effect of,
    248
Testosterone deficiency, 224
Testosterone replacement
  therapy, 224
  adverse effects of, 226-227
  for androgen deficiency,
    234t
  for improved male sexual
    function, 235
  for testosterone deficiency,
    226-227
Tetracyclines, 394
Thiamine. *See* Vitamin B1
Thrombosis, deep venous,
  390
Tiaogan Yichang Tang, 138
Tibetan herbal medicine,
  137, 153t
TJ-43, 136
Tocotrienols, antiplatelet
  effects of, 396t
Toki-shakuyaku-san, 254-
  255, 278t
Tongxie Yaofang, 137, 138,
  152t
Tormentil root extract, 139,
  153t
Toxins, 7, 406
Traditional Chinese
  medicine (TCM), 5. *See
  also* Chinese herbal
  medicine
  as asthma treatment, 60

as cardiovascular disease preventive, 163t
clinical trials of, 14-15, 16
as menopausal symptoms treatment, 245, 276t
Qi concept in, 16-17
Transcutaneous electrical nerve stimulation (TENS), 254, 278t, 306-307
*Trichosantes kirilowii*, 304
Tricyclic antidepressants, 368, 370
Triglyceride levels, omega-3 fatty acid-related reduction in, 111
Trimagnesium dicitrate, 128
Trimethoprim, 394
Tryptophan, 248-249
Turmeric *(Curcuma longa)*
anti-inflammatory effects of, 255, 279
antithrombotic effects of, 395
gastroprotective effects of, 135, 151t
Japanese *(Curcuma xanthorrhiza)*, 137
as uterine fibroids (leiomyomas) treatment, 255, 279
as weight reduction supplement, 337t, 347t
*Tylophora indica*, as asthma treatment, 62t, 63, 64, 72t
L-Tyrosine, as weight loss supplement, 334t

United Stated Department of Health and Human Services, Guidelines for the Use of Antiretroviral Agents in HIV-1-Infected Adults and Adolescents, 206, 208
United States Pharmacopeia, 81
United States Preventive Services Task Force, 223
University of Exeter, 4
University of Maryland, 24-25
Urinary incontinence

CAM therapies for, 269-274, 285-286t
definition of, 268
Urinary tract infections
CAM therapies for, 269, 285t
combination therapy for, 394
recurrent, 120-122
Uterine fibroids (leiomyomas), 255-257, 279-280t
Uva-ursi, diuretic effects of, 400

Vaccinations, 26
Vaginal cones, weighted, 273, 286t
Valcyclovir, 114
Valerian *(Valerian officialis)*
hepatotoxicity of, 149
as premenstrual syndrome treatment, 248
Vancomycin, 394
Vandadyl sulfate, hypoglycemic effect of, 401t
Vascular Interaction with Age in Myocardial Infarction (VANTAGE MI) study, 177
Vegatest, 47
Venlafaxine (Effexor), 227
Very-low density lipoprotein cholesterol levels, omega-3 fatty acid-related reduction in, 111
Viagra, 227, 228
Vijayasar *(Pterocarpus marsupium)*, hypoglycemic effect of, 401t
Vinblastine, 80
Vincristine, 80
Vinpocetin, 397t
Visualization training. *See also* Guided imagery
as uterine fibroids (leiomyomas) treatment, 257
Vitamin A

gastroprotective effects of, 147, 158t
as human immunodeficiency virus (HIV) infection treatment, 205, 215, 215t
as infertility treatment, 258
Vitamin B
as cardiovascular disease preventive, 163t
as carpal tunnel syndrome treatment, 306
as human immunodeficiency virus (HIV) infection treatment, 204, 215t
Vitamin B1, as dysmenorrhea or endometriosis treatment, 253, 278t
Vitamin B6
as cardiovascular disease preventive, 163t, 168
as carpal tunnel syndrome treatment, 307, 321t
co-administration with cancer chemotherapy, 399t
as dysmenorrhea or endometriosis treatment, 253, 278t
as fertility blend component, 258
interaction with antineoplastic agents, 398
as premenstrual syndrome treatment, 249
Vitamin B12
as cardiovascular disease preventive, 163t, 168
deficiency of, 372, 373
as fertility blend component, 258
Vitamin B complex
as cardiovascular disease preventive, 162, 167-169, 194t
as infertility treatment, 258

as uterine fibroids (leiomyomas) treatment, 256, 279t
Vitamin C, 147, 158
as allergic rhinitis treatment, 51
cancer patients' use of, 79, 92
as cardiovascular disease preventive, 162, 163t
as common cold preventive and treatment, 108, 125
drurg interactions of, 394, 396, 397-398
gastroprotective effects of, 388, 388t
as human immunodeficiency virus (HIV) infection treatment, 204, 205, 215t
as infertility treatment, 258, 280
as osteoporosis preventive or treatment, 266, 283t
as uterine fibroids (leiomyomas) treatment, 256, 279t
as weight loss supplement, 334t
Vitamin D
adverse effects of, 265
as cardiovascular disease preventive, 162
as human immunodeficiency virus (HIV) infection treatment, 205
hypoglycemic effect of, 401t
interaction with thiazide diuretics, 400
as osteoporosis preventive or treatment, 283t
as osteoporotic fracture preventive, 264-265
as prostate cancer preventive, 230
use with glucocorticoid therapy, 390
Vitamin E (tocopherol), 147, 158

antiplatelet effects of, 395, 396t
cancer patients' use of, 79, 399t
as cardiovascular disease preventive, 162, 163t, 164-165, 193t
co-administration with cancer chemotherapy, 399t
coenzyme Q10-related increase in, 167
contraindication to, 231
as cyclosporine toxicity preventive, 402
drug interactions of, 386, 394, 395, 397-398
as dysmenorrhea or endometriosis treatment, 253, 277t
as human immunodeficiency virus (HIV) infection treatment, 205, 215t
hypoglycemic effect of, 401t
as infertility treatment, 258
as premenstrual syndrome treatment, 249
as prostate cancer preventive, 230-231, 237t
as uterine fibroid (leiomyoma) treatment, 256, 279t
Vitamin Intervention for Stroke Prevention (VISP), 167-168
Vitamin K, as osteoporosis preventive or treatment, 266, 283t
VSL#3, 143, 149, 390

Walking, as osteoporosis preventive or treatment, 262
Warfarin
interactions with dietary supplements, 11, 171, 266, 369, 375, 396, 397t
as PC-SPES component, 231

Websites, CAM-related, 93, 94
Weight gain aids, for human immunodeficiency virus (HIV)-positive individuals, 220t
Weight loss
anorexia-related, in human immunodeficiency virus (HIV)-positive individuals, 208-210
dietary supplements for, 327-352
Evidence Summary of, 349-351t
hepatotoxicity of, 148
herbal remedies, 327, 329-340t, 341, 342, 343-348
randomized, double-blind trials of, 329-338t
systemic reviews and meta-analyses of, 339-340t
as urinary incontinence preventive or treatment, 285t
Western medicine, 5
Western Ontario and McMaster Universities Osteoarthritis Index (WOMAC), 300, 301, 302
Wheat bran, interaction with digoxin, 392
Wheat grass juice, 143
White willow bark, as weight loss supplement, 329t, 332t
Whole medical systems, 5. See also Ayurvedic medicine; Chiropractic care; Homeopathy; Naturopathy; Traditional Chinese medicine
definition of, 6
for human immunodeficiency virus (HIV) infection treatment, 210-213

Wild carrot, diuretic effects of, 400
Wild yam, as menopausal symptoms treatment, 243
Willow bark, as weight loss supplement, 329t, 343
Wine, as migraine headache trigger, 116
Women's health, 241-288
Women's health, CAM therapies for
  dysmenorrhea and endometriosis, 251-255, 276-279t
  Evidence Summary of, 275-286t
  infertility, 257-261, 280-281t
  menopausal symptoms, 241-245
  osteoporosis, 262-268, 281-285t
  premenstrual syndrome (PMS), 245-250, 276t
  urinary incontinence, 268-274, 285-286t
  uterine fibroids (leiomyomas), 255-257, 279-280t
Women's Health Initiative (WHI), 242
Wrist joint manipulation, as carpal tunnel syndrome treatment, 320t

Xerostomia, in cancer patients, 89
Xianzhen Pian, 112
Xiaoyao San, 138

Xin wei decoction, 136
Xuefu Zhuyu Tang, 138
Yarrow flowers, as uterine fibroids (leiomyomas) tpreatment, 255, 279t
Yeast, 136
  chromium, as weight loss supplement, 335t, 345

Yerbe maté (Ilex paraguayensis), as weight loss supplement, 338t, 347, 348, 351t
Yichang San, 138
Yigan Fupi Huatan Quyu, 138
Yiji Tiaochang Tang, 138
Yoga
  action mechanisms of, 356
  as asthma treatment, 67, 70, 72t, 73, 75
  cancer patients' use of, 80, 89, 90
  as cardiovascular disease preventive, 163t, 191, 198t
  as carpal tunnel syndrome treatment, 306, 307, 321t
  as chronic low back pain treatment, 296-297, 298, 315t
  definition of, 426
  as depression treatment, 356-357, 379t
  efficacy evaluation of, 19-20
  as fibromyalgia treatment, 308, 323t

  as lateral epicondyle pain treatment, 305, 320t
  as menopausal symptoms treatment, 244, 245
  as neck pain treatment, 299, 317t
  as sleep disorder treatment, 89, 98t
  styles of, 19-20, 191, 356-357
  use by cancer patients, 89, 98
Yohimbe (Pausinystalia yohimbe)
  adverse effects of, 228
  as erectile dysfunction treatment, 228, 236, 237t
  interaction with methadone maintenance therapy, 392
  as weight loss supplement, 338t, 347-348, 351t

Zalcitabine, 203
Ze 339, 50-51
Zen meditation, 105
Zidouvidine, 203
Zinc, 106-107, 124
  as fertility blend component, 258
  interaction with antineoplastic agents, 398-399
  as uterine fibroids (leiomyomas) treatment, 256, 279t
Zung Self Rating Scale for Depression, 357